21.95/mc

WITHDRAWN

port engineering

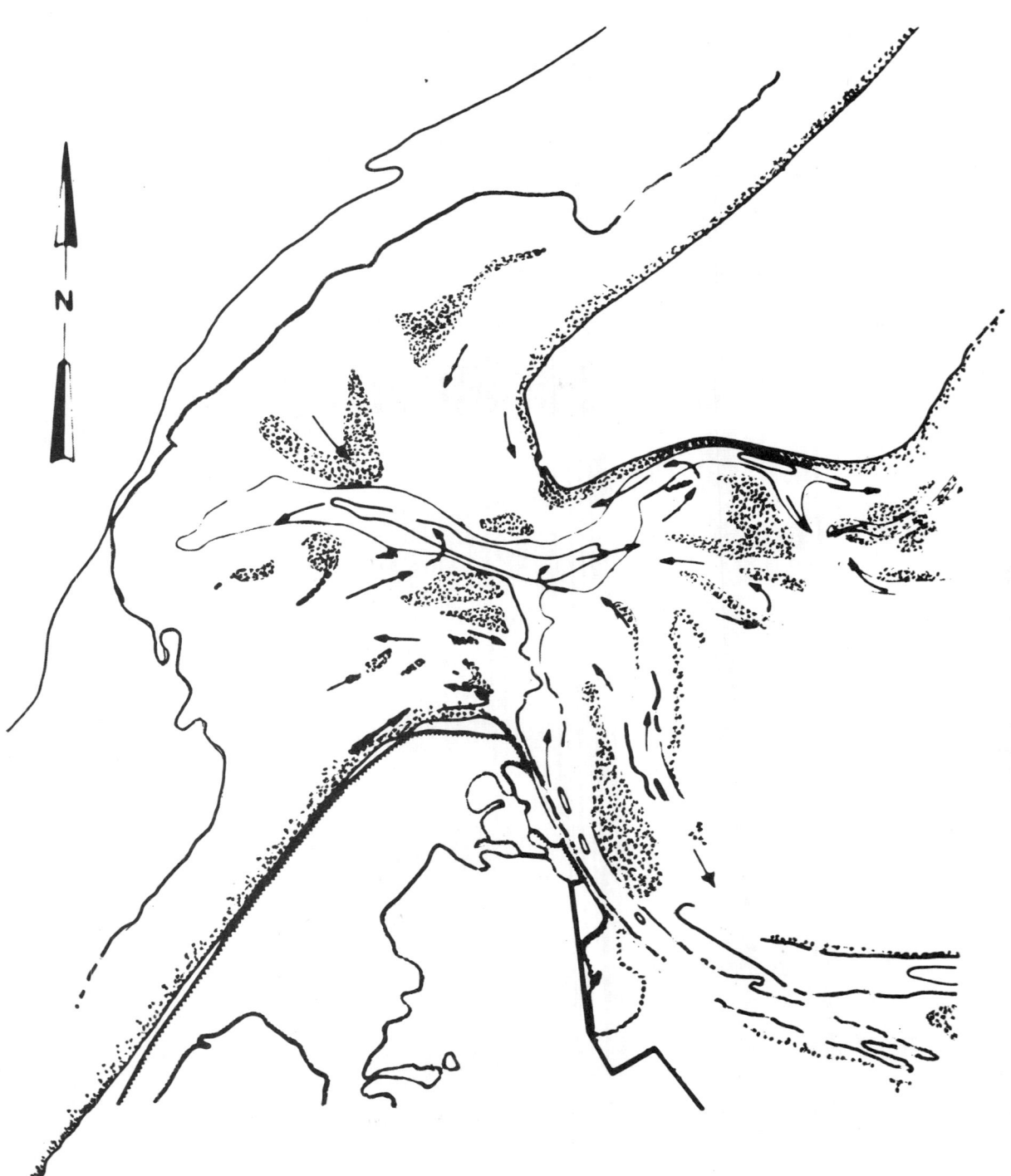

port engineering
per bruun

Gulf Publishing Company
Houston, Texas

259351

TC
205
B78

PORT ENGINEERING

Copyright © 1973 by Gulf Publishing Company, Houston, Texas. All rights reserved. Printed in the United States of America. This book, or parts thereof, may not be reproduced in any form without permission of the publisher.

Library of Congress Catalog Card Number: 76-184682

ISBN 87201-738-9

contents

preface   ix

1 modern trends in port engineering   1
Development of Facilities for Deep-Draft Vessels
Transport of Ore
Unitized Transport
Marinas

2 planning and layout of ports   9
port navigation and hydraulics
Harbor Entrances and Channels
Harbor Hydraulics

3 planning and layout of ports   49
breakwaters, jetties and piers
Breakwaters and Jetties
Rubble-Mound Breakwaters
Design Wave Height
Recent Development
Economic Feasibility; Optimum Design
Open-sea and Pier Facilities

4 planning and layout of ports   102
wharves, quays, fenders dolphins and mooring devices
Berthing and Berthing Forces on Structures
Moorings
Pontoon-Wharves and Piers
Transport Equipment

5 planning and layout of ports
transportation systems
155

Conventional Transport
Unitization of Container Systems
Future Development
Special Vessels
Pallet System
Dimensions of Unit Loads
Comparative Cost Figures for Various Systems
Port Transportation Studies

6 littoral drift and sedimentation problems
200

Littoral drift
Littoral drift and Coastal Structures
Tracing
Sediment Problems in Estuaries
Shoaling of Estuaries

7 coastal geomorphology vs. port engineering
255

Static and Evolutionary Descriptions
Dynamic Approach
Erosion and Accretion
Influence of Rise in Sea Level
Shore Geometry
Development of Beach Proficles
Uprush/Downrush and Profile Development
Influence of Port Installations on Coastal Morphological Development

8 tidal inlets on alluvial shores
319

Tidal Hydraulics
Tidal Inlets on Alluvial Shores
Cross-Sectional Stability
Importance of the Ω/M or A/M Ratio
Design Procedures

9 dredging technology — 350
Types of Dredges
Dredge Specifications
Dredging Methods

10 fishing ports
small craft harbors — 364
Establishment of Fisheries
Requirements of Harbor Facilities
Marinas

appendix 1
pile foundations — 382
Piles in Clay
Piles in Sand
Piles to Rock
Load Tests on Piles

appendix 2
anchored bulkheads — 388
Basis for Design
Bulkheads in Sand
Bulkheads in Clay

appendix 3
berthing maneuvers — 401
Motion of a Ship
Choice between Translation and Rotation
Combined Translation and Rotation
Impact on Berthing Structure
Impact on Quay Wall
Berthing to Dolphins

Berthing to Berthing Beams
Berthing to Wharves and Piers
Choice of First Impact
Improvement of Impact Conditions
Use of Tugboats

appendix 4   418
use of tracers in harbor, coastal and ocean engineering

Various Methods of Tracing
Practical Use of Tracers

index   431

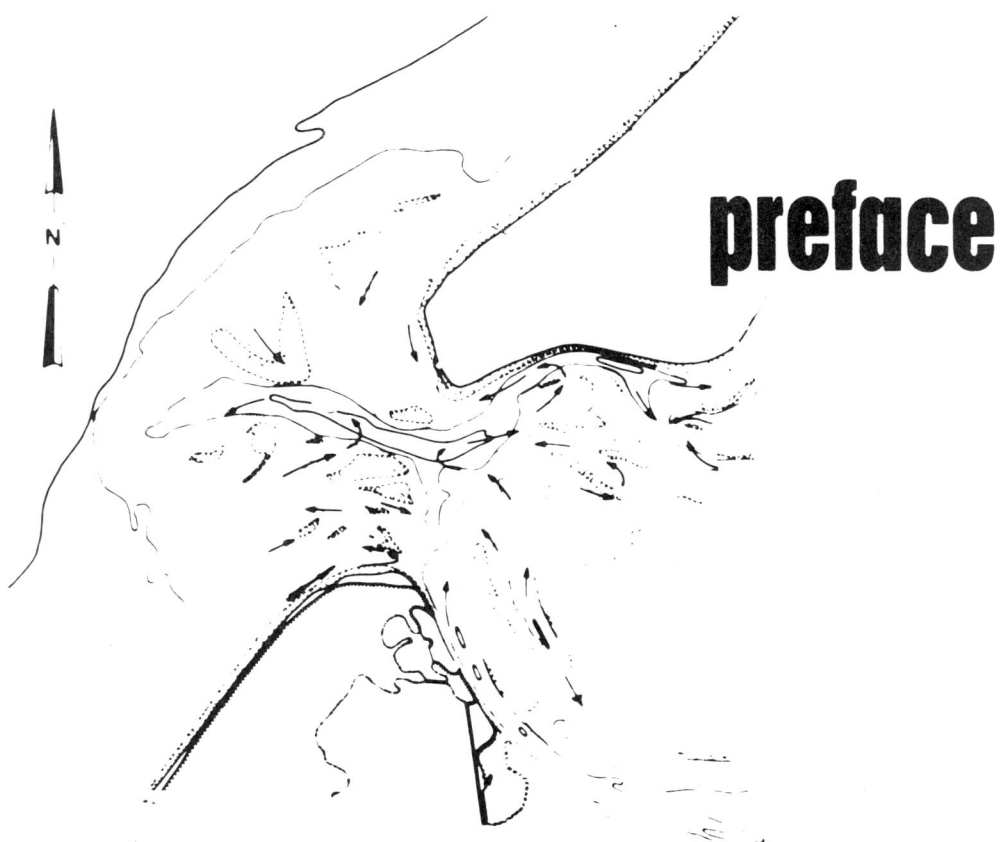

preface

This book emphasizes fields of port engineering which are covered to a lesser degree by other books on the subject. Sediment transport and hydraulic problems have received relatively more attention than structural problems. Geotechnical problems related to problems in port design and hydrodynamic problems related to the berthing of vessels have been treated by prominent authors in three appendixes.

The author wishes to express his appreciation to the National Science Foundation and to the University of Hawaii Department of Port and Ocean Engineering, under whose sponsorships these lectures in port engineering were held at the University of Hawaii in 1969.

He is indebted to Drs. L. Bjerrum and N. Janbu, Associate Professors B. Kaernsli and E.I. Hjeldness, Norway, for authoring or translating Appendixes 1 and 2, and to Professor Vasco Costa, Portugal, for permission to reprint his articles in Appendix 3.

Gratitude is expressed to Duncan Hays, Vancouver, British Columbia, A.L. McKnight, Jacksonville, Florida, and J.D. Mettam, Bertlin and Partners, London, for permission to use comprehensive material and figures from their articles.

Material including figures was also used from a number of publications including those written by Drs. F.M. Abecasis, C. Bretschneider, A. Brandtzaeg, R.E. Dean, P. Eagleson, H. Fugl-Meyer, William Gaither, I. Getz, A. Ippen, J. Larras, H. Lundgren, B. LeMéhauté, A. Price, A. de Quinn, J.A. Steers, I.A. Svendsen, B. Wilson, V.P. *Zenkovich and several others acknowledged in the references. The author also wishes to express his appreciation to the Dock and Harbour Authority, London, and to the American Society of Civil Engineers for permission to use reference articles.

port engineering

1 modern trends in port engineering

Recent development trends in port engineering are characterized by the need to accommodate vessels with greater drafts. Tankers for crude-oil, continuously increasing in size, are expected to reach 0.5 million dwt (dead weight tons) in the near future. Ore carriers presently range up to 0.08 million dwt and are expected to increase to 0.15 million dwt in the near future. [The largest vessel in existence in 1969 was the tanker *Universe Ireland* 312,000 dwt and 1,000 feet long with 175-foot beam and 80-foot draft (Figure 1.1) but vessels approaching 400,000 dwt were launched from Japanese shipyards in 1970.] Unitized transport by containers and pallets including roll-on roll-off transport is expanding very rapidly. This has required the development of special port installations and transportation systems. One of the following chapters will deal with container transport. Another interesting feature in the present trend is the increasing need for marinas for small craft.

Development of Facilities for Deep-Draft Vessels

Port development for bulk carriers includes facilities for mooring of tankers in the open sea either at buoys or at platforms with no connection to land other than a pipeline for loading and unloading oil. Open sea loading terminals for ore carriers are usually connected to land by a bridge structure carrying conveyors and other necessary installations.

Figure 1.2 shows an open-sea free-mooring arrangement at Sidon, Lebanon. It may be operated under low to medium wave conditions. The ESSO bow-mooring facility, an example of a platform mooring for tankers, is located on the north coast of Libya at Marsa el Brega. This facility is explained in Reference 6 by L.E. van Houten and G.A. McCamenon. Tankers with 97,000 dwt capacity have been loaded during winds of over 50 knots and waves of over 17 feet. It is located 6,000 feet offshore in 100 feet of water. The platform is connected to shore by a 42-inch submarine pipeline. It consists of a tower fixed to the floor. A rotating mooring boom is mounted on the tower, and a submerged loading arm is suspended from it by a ball joint. When no ship is at the mooring, the loading arm is free to swing and assume a position so that the resulting wave and current forces are parallel to the longitudinal axis of the arm. Ships make their approach heading into weather or waves. When the ship has approached within 300 to 500 feet from the platform, a launch runs a temporary mooring to it from a bollard on the fendering. After the ship has fallen back on the temporary mooring line and assumed its natural position, the loading arm is swung alongside. The permanent mooring lines are made fast between the mooring boom and the

Figure 1.1 The Universe Ireland, *Gulf Oil, 312,000 dwt, 1,000 feet long, 175 feet wide, 80-foot draft.* (The Dock and Harbour Authority, *November, 1968.)*

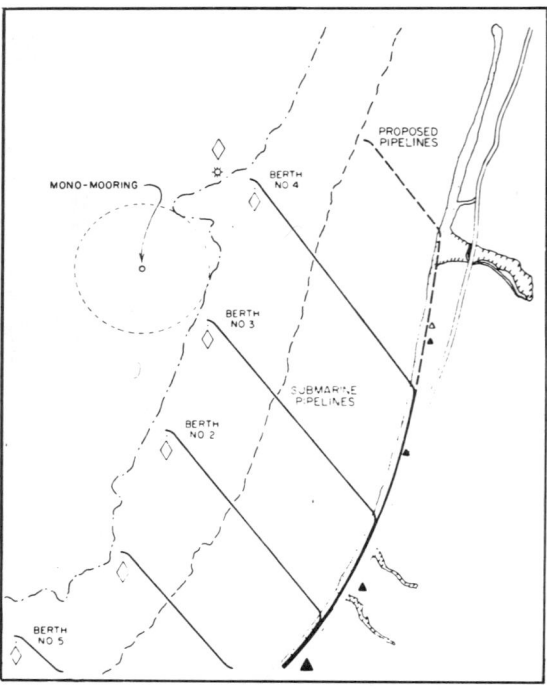

Figure 1.2 Open sea terminal at Sidon, Lebanon.

ship. A spring line is run between the loading platform and the ship after which the ship is ready to connect the loading hoses (see Figure 1.3).

When loading has been completed, this system allows a reliable and quick disconnection and ships may stay in berth longer under much more adverse conditions than they are able to do with any other mooring arrangement. It also permits a short head space between ships with increased utilization and makes it possible to bring pipes of large diameter close to ship's side.

The prime reason for selecting the bow mooring at Marsa el Brega was that it does provide the most reliable tanker berthing and loading device possible without the construction of a very costly deep-water harbor.

After installation, the loading arm was damaged during a heavy storm causing excessive torsion forces on the arm so that it broke free of the platform. A new arm, a hammer-head type of rotating boom with the submerged loading arm in suspension and supported on a ball joint, was constructed. The end of the boom was also used as the mooring point for the tankers.

It is interesting to note that the entire design was based on hindcasted waves. Waves of a maximum 12 feet were hindcast to occur 90% of the time. Maximum waves of 30 feet with an occasional storm causing 40-foot waves were assumed. The mooring was designed for full operation in waves of 12 feet and for fatigue stresses for a 30-foot wave without a ship at the platform.

The largest mooring buoy for arctic conditions, suitable for tankers of up to 350,000 dwt, was installed in Canada off St. John, New Brunswick, in 1970. In addition to being the largest in existence, this buoy is unique in that it is equipped with a heated cap, enabling it to be used in the most extreme weather conditions (see Figure 1.4).

Heated oil circulating through the buoy prevents the formation of ice. Without special precautions, a buoy of this type operating in such

Figure 1.3 Platform mooring for tanks at Mars el Brega, Libya. (ASCE Journal of the Waterways and Harbors Division, *WW 3, 1971.*)

conditions would capsize or sink under the weight of ice. The buoy is positioned some distance from the shore and is operated automatically.

As it will frequently be impossible to carry out routine inspection during the winter, a highly sophisticated scanning and alarm system has been incorporated. Inside the cap is an engine room housing two diesel-driven generators, two oil heating vessels with associated circulating pumps, an air replenishment system, a fire extinguishing installation and a control panel. The control panel contains an automatic oil temperature control, starting and alarm systems and a comprehensive safety system.

All main systems are duplicated, and in the event of a fault developing, the reserve unit is immediately brought into use. Coded signals indicating the nature and extent of all possible failures have been devised, and should one occur the appropriate signal is automatically radioed to the shore. A week's supply of fuel is carried on the buoy.

In order to keep the temperature of the cap within the required cap range of 0-2° C, oil at a temperature of up to 250° C is circulated through a system of pipes totaling some 2,200 meters in length. The heating system is controlled by thermostats which, in turn, are controlled by sensors mounted on the outside of the buoy.

The temperature control system was specially designed to eliminate the so-called igloo effect, i.e., heating insulation resulting from the formation of a thin layer of ice on the sensors, the result of which would be to shut down the heating installation, allowing dangerous ice formation on the cap.

The buoy is claimed to be unsinkable, the compartments are filled with expanded polyurethane, a hard plastic material with a weight of 35-37 kilograms per cubic meter. In all, the buoy contains 700,000 liters of this material.

As explained above, tanker size most likely will continue to increase. Offshore mooring will become more common, replacing uneconomical fixed deepwater port installations, basins or lagoons connected to deep water by deep, and often long, navigation channels that are expensive to construct and maintain.

Figure 1.4 Mooring buoy for tankers up to 350,000 Dwt installed off St. Johns, New Brunswick, Canada. (The Dock and Harbour Authority, November 1969.)

Transport of Ore

It should be noted that in any industry the cost of a manufactured article depends upon the price of the raw material delivered to the manufacturer, i.e., the cost of the material itself at source plus transport charges. With steel, it has been estimated that about half the cost is accounted for by the delivery cost of the materials. Thus, the lower the delivery cost for raw materials from source to works, the more competitive will be the price of the finished article.

In many cases, large bulk carriers were built to fit the terminal ports between which the charter operated. However, most ships were still built for less than life-time charters with a view of retaining as wide a trading pattern as possible and combining a high deadweight with the least possible draft to ensure good port availability. This led to significant changes in the ratios of a ship's main dimensions. For example, a maximum draft of 42 feet when loaded would have implied a deadweight of about 65,000 dwt. Recent construction practices developed vessels with relatively wider beams, some increase in length and deadweights up to 80,000 dwt, but with the same draft of 42 feet.

Throughout the world, iron ore is now being carried in ships with drafts up to 43 feet corresponding to about 80,000 to 90,000 dwt. It is likely that in the near future some of the Japanese ore ports will be receiving ships of 100,000 dwt, with a draft of about 47 feet. The trend undoubtedly will be toward a steady increase in ship size. Ore-loading ports will be improved to make ore

Modern Trends 5

*Figure 1.5 Ore unloading at Port Talbot, South Wales. (*The Dock and Harbour Authority, *June, 1968.)*

*Figure 1.6 Shiploading facility at Port Latta, Tasmania. (*Civil Engineering, *January, 1969.)*

more competitive on world markets, and unloading ports will follow suit to obtain the lowest freights or to give the greatest possible commercial freedom.

Figure 1.5 is an artist's impression of an ore carrier unloading at Port Talbot, South Wales, a new large ore port installation completed and put in operation in 1969 (2). The British Transport Docks Board carried out a comprehensive study to develop this ultramodern ore terminal facility. Initially, the terminal will receive vessels of 100,000 dwt, maximum, but it can be deepened for ore carriers of 150,000 dwt.

Port Latta, an open-sea loading terminal in Tasmania, Australia, is an example of a modern ore-loading facility (3). Development of the Savage River magnetite iron ore body in northwestern Tasmania required a suitable port site for a pelletizing plant and for loading the iron ore pellets into large ore carriers for export to Japan. A 53-mile long ore slurry pipeline, the longest in existence, was built to connect the site with the Savage River mine. In concept, the shiploading facility creates an offshore buoy-type anchoring system that vessels can approach and depart from with or without tug assistance. During berthing, vessels can maintain a breast-off position or moor alongside as conditions dictate (see Figure 1.6).

The loading is accomplished by two novel slewing-bridge type shiploaders. Each loader incorporates a 100-foot long conveyor loading boom that can be raised or lowered, and a 100-foot horizontal shuttle movement. The two units cover

540-feet or the full length of the ship while the ship remains stationary. The loaders were developed as part of an integrated design concept that resulted in great overall savings compared to conventional shiploaders which travel on a full-length pier. This arrangement made it possible to protect the entire facility with only two dolphins.

Ships can be loaded without interruption by switching material flow from one loader to the other at a stipulated rate of 48,000 tons per day. The iron ore pellets are reclaimed from stockpiles on shore by two bucket-wheel excavators feeding a reclaiming conveyor between the stockpiles and in turn discharging through a sampling station to the 5,860-foot bridge conveyor. The terminal also provides for unloading fuel oil from tankers.

Surveys of the site indicated a sloping ocean bottom of continental shelf rock with negligible sand cover. Sonar and sweep surveys demonstrated that a berth suitable for ore carriers of 100,000 dwt would have to be located 6,000 feet from shore. Rock dredging was economically infeasible. Driving of steel piles would give insufficient penetration.

Steel box trusses 200 feet long and supported on bents with 200 feet spacing were selected as an economical gallery for the mile-long approach conveyor. Individual 103-foot and 280-foot box trusses were used for each of the cross conveyors and slewing bridges. Support platforms for the truss bents were placed 25 feet above mean low water to avoid the impact of storm waves on the platforms. In addition, the bents were designed to resist wave forces on the piles, wind forces on the superstructure acting from varying directions and conveyor belt reactions.

The rock bottom required the use of steel piles. The unusual design is described in Chapter 3 and in greater detail in Reference 3.

Another very important trend in port engineering is the construction of deep-water navigation channels (4). Large ports having sufficient depth to accomodate vessels of considerable draft had developed in rivers and estuaries. Examples are the ports of London, Antwerp and New York. The draft increase particularly after World War II, necessitated dredging deeper channels. The natural tide and river flow was able to maintain certain cross-sections and depths; but the development of port installations, often decreased tidal flow capacity, the corresponding land-based facilities including sewage systems, often caused additional siltation problems and dredging of channels increased saltwater intrusions. As explained in Chapter 6, this is the general experience today at many places where maintenance dredging has increased at many river and estuary ports.

The examples mentioned above are characteristic in this respect. In Antwerp, comprehensive model studies have been made to determine a better geometry including the location and cross-sectional shape of a 40-foot navigation channel. London, where there is a problem of finding safe dumping places for the dredged material, gave rise to use of comprehensive tracer experiments. Now, it is generally recognized that dumping dredged silt into an estuary where strong tidal currents prevail may be a very dangerous practice. Silt can be carried back into the channel as proven by the above-mentioned (radioactive) tracer experiments in the Thames, mentioned in Chapter 6. For reasons of conservation of biological life, the U.S. Department of the Interior has in recent years introduced regulations prohibiting dredged material from being dumped where it may pollute waters and adversely effect biological life. The material must be spoiled behind dikes that will at the same time minimize possibilities of scouring that in turn could result in redredging the dumped material.

In some places hauls of large bulk quantities made it necessary to adjust channel depth to the ship's draft. The best examples are probably the channel at Lake Maracaibo, requiring depths of 45 to 50 feet, and at the Orinoco River entrance in Venezuela which is all-important for transportation of iron ore. These cases were responsible for the development of the sidecasting dredging technique. This is also explained in Chapter 9. The most remarkable thing is not only that a very effective new technique resulted, but it was proven that sand sidecasted 300 to 400 feet away from the dredger built up a kind of submerged jetty that contributed protection of the dredged channel against drift from the sides—regardless that some of the dumped material came back into the channel. This situation convinced the U.S. Army Corps of Engineers that sidecast dredging offered some distinct advantages under proper circumstances. Essentially, it is an improved method of "agitation dredging" which is performed, to some extent, by all hopper dredges. The term *agitation dredging* denotes the effect of solid particles being disturbed from their *in situ* condition by prevailing currents outside the dredging area where they are later deposited. Although sidecasting, also called "boom dredging," must be limited in application, it has unquestioned applicability in areas where the material is relatively fine and where there is a prevailing current which is able to carry material away from the area. For further information the reader is referred to Chapter 9.

Unitized Transport

Rational handling of cargo is another very important development. The key word to rational cargo handling is *unitizing*. Before any improvement can be obtained, the cargo must be consolidated into larger units suitable for mechanical handling. There are two main systems of unitized cargo (1): the *container system* and the *pallet system*.

General aspects of container transport in units up to 38 tons transported on vessels from about 15,000 to 30,000 dwt (Figures 5.4a and 5.4b) are described in Reference 5. Details of container transport are dealt with in Reference 1 and in Chapter 5.

In the shipping industry, container traffic may be divided conveniently into four categories: roll-on roll-off services, common-user containers in short sea and coastal trading, similar containers in ocean routes and containership operations. Roll-on roll-off has been particularly successful in the short sea trades, where its popularity undoubtedly will increase. Common-user containers, also plentiful in short sea trading, form only a very small proportion of the deep-sea vessel freight.

The carriage of common-user containers in general cargo vessels is often restricted by the structural limitations of the holds. If a compromise is made and the vessel is loaded partly with containers and partly with loose goods, much of the quick turnaround advantage, which is the primary benefit of containerization, is lost and the ship may also suffer intermittently from overmanning. Although for these reasons it is said that efficient transport of large quantities of general cargo in containers involves the construction of special ships or major modifications of existing ones, it must be kept in mind that a general cargo vessel converted for container traffic can suffer a serious loss of underdeck space. In short, if containers are going to be carried in large quantities, most points favor the special ship. Of great importance in ocean trading, however, is the fact that the benefit derived from rapid turnaround decreases in value inversely to the length of the voyage. With a voyage lasting, say, three days, two days in port instead of four represents a saving in cycle time of nearly 30%. With a voyage of six days, the same reduction of turnaround time represents a saving of only 20% (5).

Fifteen years ago, those concerned with freight movement were making preparations to handle and transport palletized loads in large quantities. Although palletization developed rapidly in the short sea trades, it did not become popular in intercontinental trading. It was evident that long hauls of huge quantities of homogeneous goods provided the right economic conditions for systems employing containers. The most effective system has proven to be the *door-to-door system* serving forwarder and receiver equally well. In the door-to-door system, the whole operation—the inland transport of containers, the marshalling at the berth, ship loading and discharging and sea carriage—is usually completed by one firm. This arrangement inevitably reduces difficulties and costs. Some of these systems have been developed by "the trucker going to sea" rather than by the shipping company integrating inland operations.

The more conservative *port-to-port service*, already operating at deep-water berths with common-user containers, has not always proved profitable. Experience has shown that the costs of emptying and filling containers and of moving empties at the berth can prove prohibitive. Furthermore, the goods themselves still create many handling problems. With containerships working, this kind of service postulates the need for big sheds at the berth for emptying imported containers and stowing their freight for quick delivery and for receiving and containerizing exports. Also demanding huge marshalling yards, it often calls for far more space at the berth than is readily available in existing busy ports.

In Japan, the Container Association's disappointing experience was that Yokohama, which handled 60% of the containerized cargo imported in 1966, still worked mostly on the pier-to-pier system, instead of on the more desirable door-to-door basis. It is of interest, too, that in 1964, 70% of Yokohama's incoming containers were empty ones. Containerization can only succeed if the same "packing case" is used over and over again and not only in one direction. The door-to-door system, therefore, undoubtedly will penetrate the container transport system in the future. This is reflected in the development of containership terminals, most of which are built to serve bulk container services using containers of up to 30 tons. Others are built to serve roll-on roll-off transport by trailers which are loaded and unloaded on the ship by tractors. As mentioned above, this system is particularly useful for short hauls in larger quantities of standard goods, e.g., in the trade between England and other countries on the North Sea.

Important containership terminals have now been completed and are in use in Rotterdam, Antwerp and New York. Special containerships are operating between eastern United States ports and ports in England, Belgium, Holland and Sweden. In the Pacific, container transport is developing fast between western United States ports and Japan. Honolulu has a very modern container vessel facility. To make such facilities fully effective, adequate land areas, cranage and land-transport facilities and depots are needed (see chapter 5). A great variety of effective transportation equipment has been developed. One of the most advanced countries in container transport is Australia.

As discussed by Getz et al. in Reference 1, the pallet system so far is more common that the container system on all shorter hauls. It concentrates on much smaller units for transport with weights usually varying between 0.5 and 2.0 tons, making handling of cargo on ship, on quay and in shed much easier and less expensive than in the case of container transport. Because the pallet system, contrary to the container system, is suitable for transport in modest quantities over modest distances, it has become very popular in the coast traffic. It does not require nearly so much expensive equipment as container transport. The most efficient way to load and discharge pallets is by forklift, which handles them through combined side doors and side hatches. By combining the side door with the side hatch, it is possible to handle pallet loads through the opening, independent of the ship's relative height compared to the quay. This is one of the many advantages of the pallet system compared to the conservative common carrier system. While container transport always requires heavy land-based trailer and truck equipment, pallet transport can get by with inexpensive pallets (e.g., $2.50 for 12 square feet) and normal trucks. Containers require a much larger quay and shed area than palletized cargo. When handled by straddle carriers, eight hundred 20-foot containers or four hundred 40-foot containers will need a total parking area of about 10 acres. When the containers are stacked two high, about 60% of this area will be sufficient. A fully door-to-door containerized service will not require any shed on the quay, whereas it will be necessary to have a shed in case any stuffing or unstuffing of container cargo is to take place in the port.

The trend will probably develop into increased container transport on vessels designed for this type of transport and operating over still increasing distances at cruising speeds of 20 knots or more. The use of pallets on special vessels with side doors, side hatches and pallet elevators will increase too, particularly in local coast traffic and transport over shorter distances. In addition, some very special vessels like the LASH ship (lighter aboard ship) will be used on routes particularly suitable for that kind of transport.

Marinas

Another entirely different development has taken place in the area of marinas for small craft. A terrific need has developed for mooring and berthing facilities for small craft. On the Pacific Coast the number of small craft now exceeds 500,000. Even if some of the old fishing ports are converted to marinas, the bulk quantities of small craft will have to be accommodated in new marinas which include all necessary facilities.

The Long Beach Marina at Los Angeles, California, is probably the largest marina in existence. The Long Beach Marina, constructed and operated by the city of Long Beach, provides complete berthing facilities for 1800 boats, ranging from outboard to ocean-going craft over 100 feet long. Built on tidelands that were originally mudflats, the marina covers a total area of 158.2 acres, 66.8 land and 91.4 water. The marina has been in operation since 1960 at a cost of about 14 million dollars.

The possibility for surge problems, which are important for such marinas, was investigated in scale models. Because of tidal changes of approximately 9 feet, floating docks were necessary. They were constructed of timber supported by model fiberglass pontoons. Prestressed and reinforced concrete floating docks are now invading the marina market with increasing success. Structural details and special new designs and trends in harbor structures are mentioned in Chapters 3 and 4. Chapter 10 deals specifically with fishing ports and marinas.

References

1. Getz, J.R., Erichsen, S., and Heirung, E. 1968. *Design of a Cargo Liner in Light of the Development of General Cargo Transportation.* Trondheim: The Ship Research Institute of Norway.
2. Prefement. R., and Radway, E.R. 1968. " Port Talbot, ore terminal of the future." *The Dock and Harbour Authority* 49(June): 45-50.
3. Soros, P. 1969. "Port Latta—open sea loading terminal." *Civil Engineering* (Jan.):62-65.
4. Steenmeyer, A., and Pheu, W.S. 1968. "Influence of ship building tendencies on harbor construction." *Proceedings of the 5th International Harbor Congress* s 2. Antwerp.
5. Tooth, E.S. 1966. "Containerships in the ocean trades." *The Dock and Harbour Authority* 47(July):73-76.
6. van Houten, L.E. 1964. "The bow mooring for berthing tankers." *Civil Engineering* (March):60-62.

2 planning and layout of ports
port navigation and hydraulics

The first ports ever built were located in fjords and rivers, some of the most magnificent of these being built by the Vikings in Scandinavia. Four to five thousand years ago, the Phoenicians attempted and succeeded in establishing a port on the open-sea coast at Tyre. It was built of heavy blocks locked together with cobber dowels. The Romans built the famous naval port on the Tiber River at Ostia. Medieval ports like London, Rotterdam and Hamburg were all located in rivers, estuaries, bays or sounds. The same was true of the first American ports—New York, Boston, Baltimore, Washington (Georgetown) and New Orleans.

Open-sea coast harbors were and are still few because of high costs of construction and maintenance. Examples of port construction in this century are the Port of Rota, Spain, Burns Harbor, Indiana, on Lake Michigan, Hanstholm, Denmark on the North Sea Coast and Abidjan on the African Gold Coast.

Very important for these harbors are their approach channels, entrances, basins, etc. With respect to their design, certain navigational and hydraulic aspects must be considered.

The article by Duncan Hay on harbor entrances, channels and turning basins (11) gives excellent information on this topic and is therefore repeated here in abstract form.

Harbor Entrances and Channels

The design of harbor entrances, channels and turning basins is dictated by the size of the largest vessel anticipated to enter the harbor. Although meteorological and oceanographical factors are important in harbor design, primary importance lies in determining the size of the design vessel which should be realistic, bearing in mind that the recent trend in ship construction is toward larger and faster ships.

Figures 2.1, 2.2 and 2.3 have been constructed from dimensions of ships in service in 1968-1969 to show the draft and beam against deadweight tonnage of typical oil tankers, bulk carriers and general cargo vessels, respectively. The draft shown is the midships mean summer saltwater static draft. Similarly, Figure 2.4 shows a plot of overall length against deadweight tonnage for the three general classes of ships. Their dimensions have grown steadily in the last few years, particularly for tankers and bulk carriers where dimensions have reached 400,000 dwt and 150,000 dwt respectively. See Chapter 1.

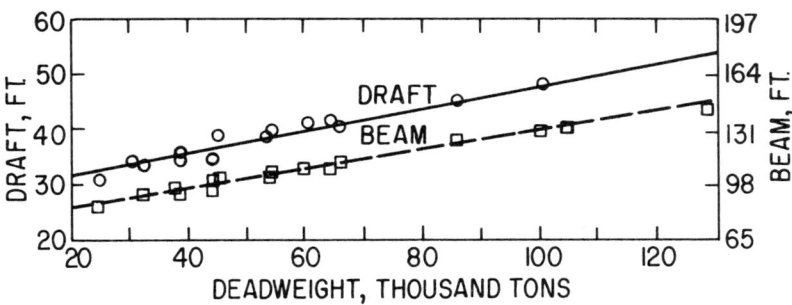

Figure 2.1. Typical oil tanker dimensions (11).

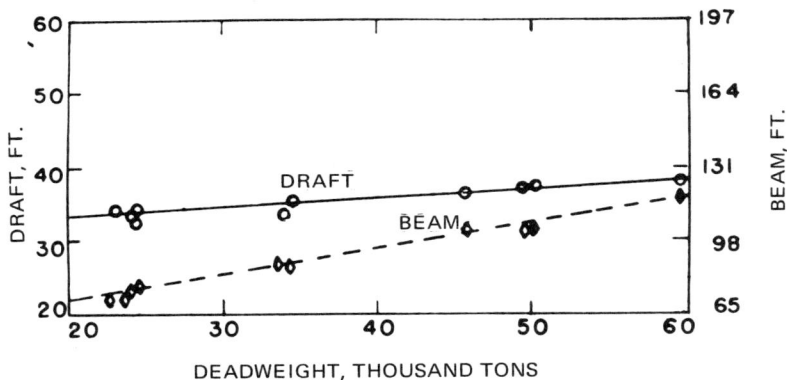

Figure 2.2. Typical ore carrier dimensions (11).

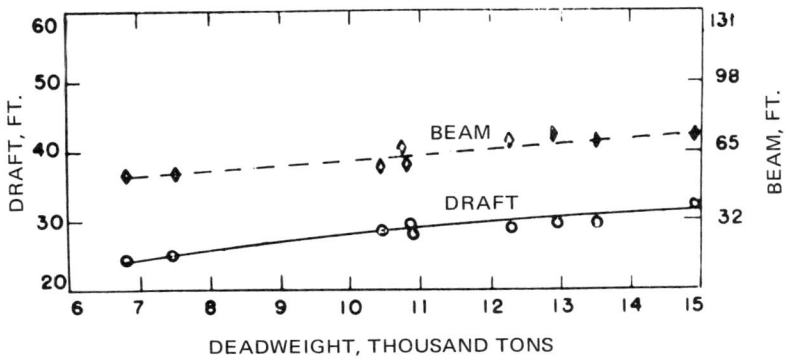

Figure 2.3. Typical general cargo vessel dimensions (11).

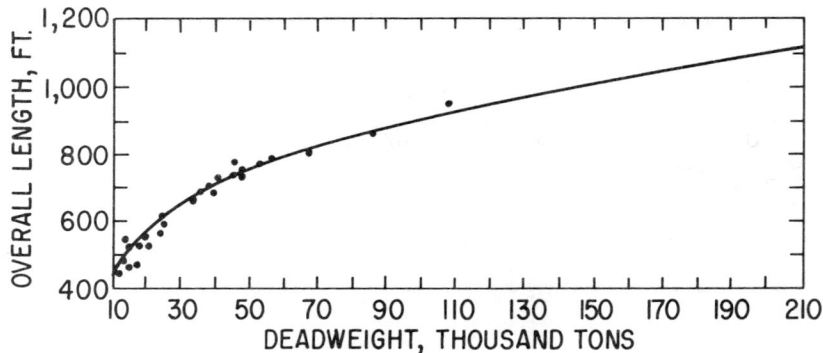

Figure 2.4. Typical lengths for tankers, bulk carriers and general vessel versus deadweight (11).

Entrance and Channel Depths

The differentiation between entrance and channel depths is made to suggest that these depths need not be the same. A harbor entrance is usually exposed to larger waves than those which occur within the harbor. Consequently, the *scend* or pitching of a vessel may be larger at the entrance to a channel than within the channel. The anticipated scend is a factor which is included in the determination of the required depth.

The Permanent International Association of Navigational Congresses recommends that the minimum design depth should be the static summer saltwater draft of the design vessel plus 5 to 8 feet (1.5 to 2.5 meters) (32). While this criterion is useful in estimating the required channel depth, a detailed calculation of the required depth could be based upon a summation of the following factors:

1. Loaded draft
2. Tide
3. Density change
4. Squat
5. Pitching and rolling
6. Trim
7. Empirical factors.

Loaded Draft

The loaded draft is the depth of water the design vessel draws when loaded to the *load line* or *plimsoll mark* at midships while stationary in mean summer salt water. If the design vessel is a hypothetical ship, the loaded draft may be obtained from Figures 2.1, 2.2 or 2.3. It would appear that loaded drafts of 32, 38 and 40 feet (9.75, 11.58 and 12.19 meters) for general cargo, bulk carriers and oil tankers, respectively, would represent with some leeway the maximum draft of most vessels in service today. However, the trend toward increased drafts must be taken into account (see Chapter 1).

Tide

The depth of the channel may be designed to facilitate the entrance of the design vessel at all stages of the tide or at only the higher stages of the tide. The datum to which the design depth is referred should be carefully established on a probability basis, as it is possible to have tides below the local low-water datum.

A harbor entrance or channel that relies upon tides to produce the necessary depths is becoming less attractive to shipowners. The larger and faster modern vessels rely upon a short turnaround time to make their operation economical. If the amplitude of the tide is large at the site and the largest anticipated vessel calls infrequently at the port, it may be economical to utilize a portion of the tidal range to produce the necessary depths. The American policy, at present, is that when the cost-benefit ratio of providing access at all stages of the tide equals unity, the provision of this depth is considered justified (40).

Density Change

A vessel leaving salt water and entering brackish or fresh water will increase its draft due to the density difference of the water: 64.0 to 62.5 pounds per cubic foot (1.025 gram to 1.000 gram per cubic centimeter) from salt to fresh water. The additional draft in fresh water is usually assumed to be 2 or 3% of the saltwater draft, depending slightly upon the hull shape (12, 42). A ship drawing 35 feet (10.7 meters) in salt water would draw approximately 36 feet (11.0 meters) in fresh water. Shoreline harbors are normally not concerned with density change, but estuary, river and off-channel river harbors should take this factor into account.

Squat

When a ship enters shallow water, there is a rapid increase in the height of the waves produced by the ship. Accompanying this increase in the wave height is an average decrease in the water surface along the profile of the ship relative to the still-water level. This surface depression causes the ship to sink or *squat* relative to the channel bottom. Sorensen (37), in his study on ship waves, predicts the condition of shallow water when $V^2/gd > 0.7$, where V is the velocity of ship in feet per second, relative to the water, g is the acceleration due to gravity and d is the water depth in feet.

Other factors affecting the amount of squat are given by Wicker, McAleer and Johnston (41) as (a) the distance between the keel and bottom, (b) the trim of the vessel, (c) the cross-sectional area of the channel and whether the channel is located in a wide or narrow waterway, (d) whether the vessel is passing or overtaking another vessel, (e) the location of the vessel relative to the centerline of the channel and (f) the characteristics of the vessel itself.

There are two methods available for determining the squat of the design vessel as it traverses the centerline of the channel. One method has been developed by the David Taylor Model Basin (43) and Schijf (36) and the other method by the Sogreah Laboratory for the Royal Dutch Shell Group Companies (10).

The basic equation used by Schijf was derived from the Bernoulli equation. The equation is

$$F = \left[\frac{2d(1-d-s)^2}{1-(1-d-s)^2} \right]^{\frac{1}{2}} = \frac{V}{\sqrt{gh_1}} \quad (2.1)$$

where F is the Froude number, h_1 is the undisturbed mean depth of water, d is the dimensionless squat $= (h_1 - h_2)/h_1$, h_2 is the depth of water in the cross-section occupied by the vessel, s is the ratio of the midships cross-section to the channel cross-section, V is the velocity of the ship relative to the water, g is the acceleration due to gravity.

A plot of Equation 2.1 is shown in Figure 2.5 for various values of s. Also shown in Figure 2.5 is Schijf's limiting velocity above which any increase in power theoretically does not increase the ship's speed because of increased resistance and decreased propeller efficiency. The asymptotic lines are similar, if not related to the plots of ship wave heights versus speed (20, 36).

With values of V, h_1 and s for design conditions, it is possible to determine a value of squat from Figure 2.5. If a channel is being designed, a minor reiteration is usually involved as a channel depth has to be assumed and made equal to h_1. The value of the squat is $h_1 - h_2$.

The graphical method of the Sogreah Laboratory is shown in Figure 2.6. The results were obtained from model tests on 18,000 and 33,000 dwt tankers. The channel depth for the tests was between 1.1 and 2.8 times the ships' drafts, the mean width of the channel was between 2.3 and 10.0 times the ships' beams and the channel side slopes were 1:3. Dickson (10) has suggested that the channel width to a ship's beam ratio of 10 could be used for open-water channels, thus providing a factor of safety.

The methods of determining the squat from Figure 2.6 are as follows:

1. Knowing s and h_1 (as defined previously), enter Figure 2.6a and determine the limiting velocity, V_L.
2. Calculate the ratio $V:V_L$ and the ratio of the

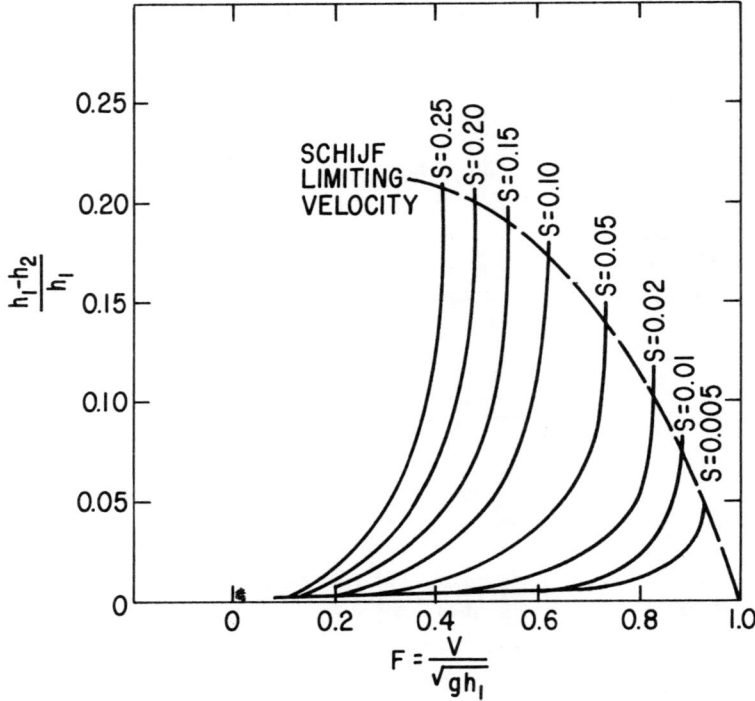

Figure 2.5. Dimensionless squat versus Frode number (11).

undisturbed water depth at the vessel to the draft of the vessel.

3. With these two ratios enter Figure 2.6b and determine Z_{max}, which is the squat for a waterway width to vessel beam of 6.
4. If the waterway width to vessel beam ratio is not equal to 6, enter Figure 2.6c to find the positive or negative percent correction for Z_{max} as determined from Figure 2.6b.

A comparison between the two methods mentioned and actual squat measurements (41) suggests that it is best to use the Sogreah method when s is less than 0.080 and to use Equation 2.1 when s is greater than 0.080. Using this criteria, a plot of observed versus computed squats for a ship in various channels as shown in Figure 2.7 demonstrates that by combining the two methods, with the above criteria, a good approximation of the value of squat may be obtained for a ship traversing the centerline of a channel.

The amount of the squat increases as a ship departs from the centerline of the channel. Data from the David Taylor Model Basin (43) appears to be the only information available for determining this additional squat. A plot of the data from the model basin is shown in Figure 2.8. The data and the plot is for a canal of fixed dimensions as noted in the figure. The figure shows that the additional squat due to being off the centerline of the channel is small for slow speed but is approximately 50% above the centerline value for higher speeds.

The most probable reason for a ship being off the centerline in a channel would be that it is passing another vessel. The effective cross-sectional area of the channel is reduced by the cross-sectional area of the ship being passed. Therefore, if

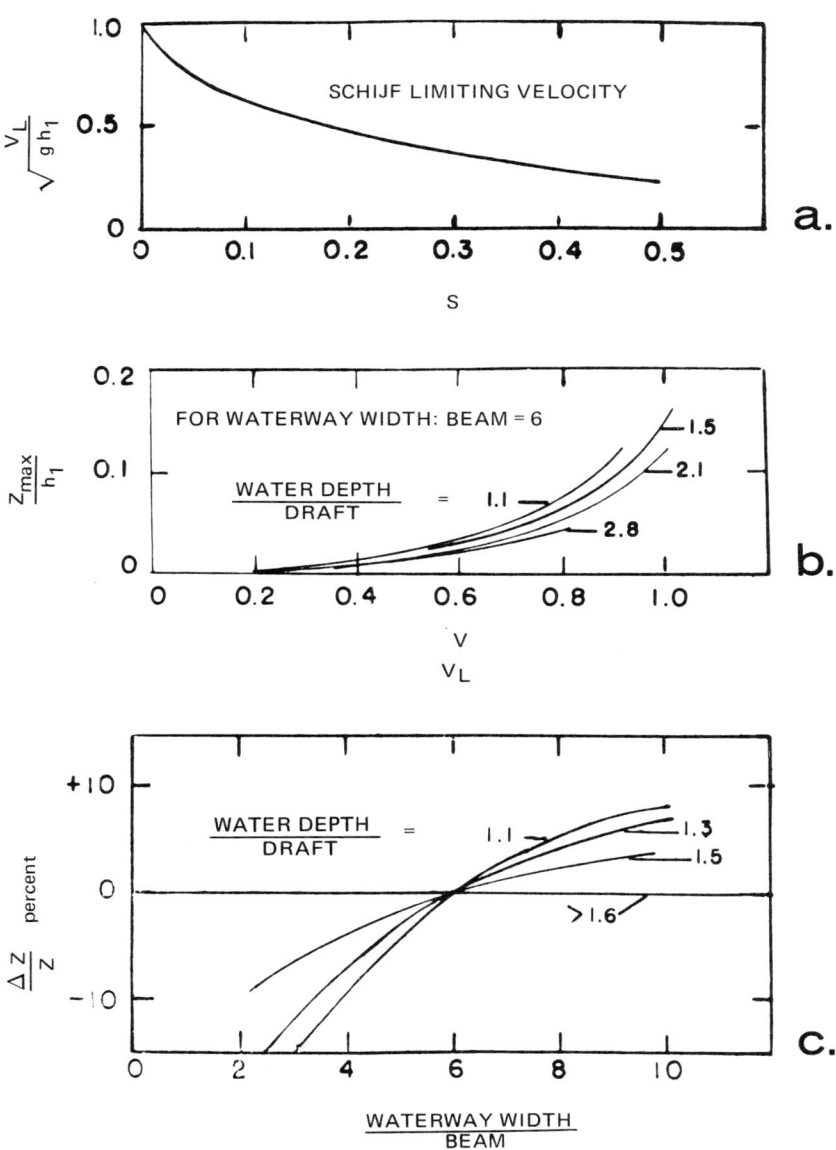

Figure 2.6, a, b, c, Sogreah Laboratory squat curves (11).

the squat of a ship is to be determined in a channel where vessels will be passed, the effective area of the channel must be used in determining the value of centerline squat for the design vessel. Added to the centerline squat will be the additional squat due to being off centerline which will give the total squat for the design vessel in a channel where another ship will be passed.

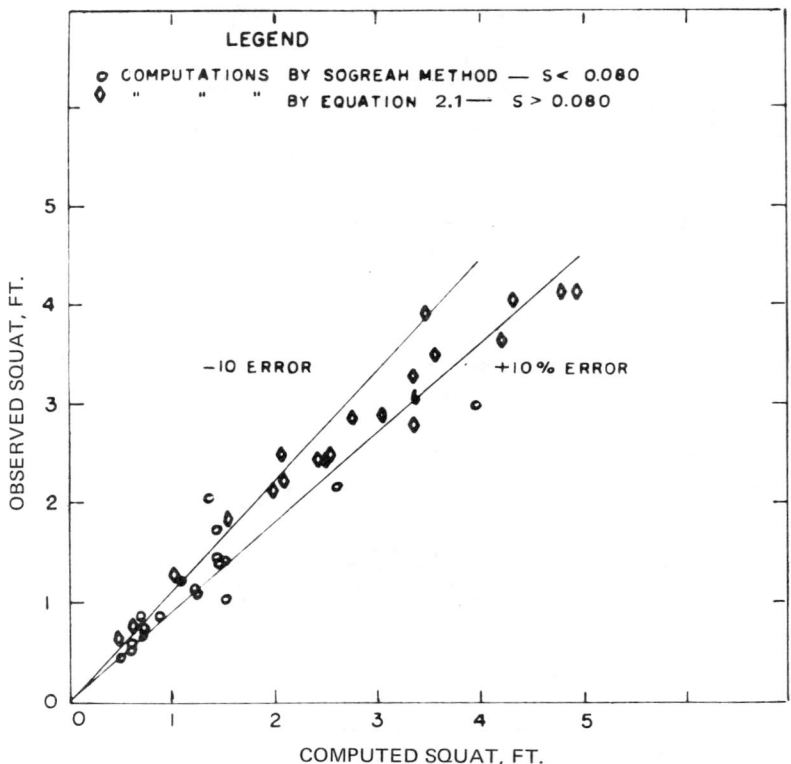

Figure 2.7. Observed squat versus computed (11).

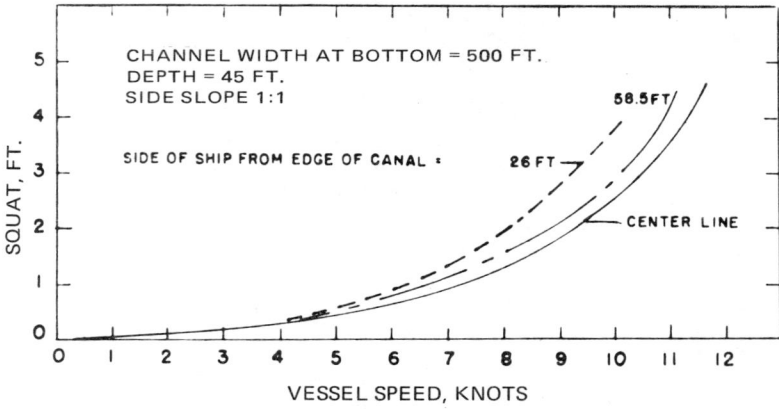

Figure 2.8. Effect of ship's location in channel on squat (11).

Pitching (Scend) and Rolling

The pitching and rolling of a vessel when subject to wave action has to be taken into account when determining the required depth for the design vessel. This factor is important at harbor entrances where the wave action is usually most severe.

There is very little quantitative information on the magnitude of pitching. Quinn (34) suggests that half the wave height to which the ship is subjected should be considered as the amplitude of pitching. If the amount of pitching in degrees is known for the design ship under design conditions, the amplitude of pitching can be determined knowing the ship's length.

A 5° amplitude of roll is not uncommon at harbor entrances (41, 42). Therefore, a ship having a beam of 100 feet (30.48 meters) would increase the midships draft approximately 4 feet (1.22 meters) due to a roll of 5°. Newland (30) states that due to the pitching and rolling of ships, a keel clearance of 10 to 12 feet (3.05 to 3.66 meters) would be desirable for large vessels in the open water prior to reaching the lee of a breakwater or protected channel.

Trim

Often a vessel is not loaded to an even keel in an attempt to improve its steering ability. Eisiminger (12) observes that the vessel is usually set down at the stern approximately 3 inches for every 100 feet (25 millimeters per 10 meters). Others (40) report that the trim at the stern is usually 1 or 2 feet (0.3 to 0.6 meter).

When the vessel is underway, the trim can change, though the amount of change is uncertain. The tests carried out by Sogreah Laboratory indicated that ships in channels at slow speeds trimmed down at the bow and for faster speeds trimmed down at the stern.

Empirical Factor

An empirical factor is required in addition to those factors discussed previously to facilitate maneuverability, economic propeller efficiency and a factor of safety. The empirical factor is usually 2 to 4 feet (0.6 to 1.2 meters), the lesser value being for sand bottoms and slow speeds and the higher value for rock bottoms and fast speeds. The empirical factor reduces the chance of the ship's propeller striking a sunken log or debris and also reduces the possible displacement of material which could be piled up in the path of a following ship.

In a channel which is subject to shoaling by sediment transport or littoral drift, it may be wise to use an empirical factor of 4 feet (1.2 meters) or greater to facilitate channel maintenance.

The total depth required for the design vessel at a harbor entrance or in a channel is the summation of the pertinent factors discussed above, which are applicable to a specific case. It should be emphasized that local experience should be utilized in assigning a value to each factor.

The depth required for the design vessel may require substantial dredging to provide this depth. This has led to the development of harbors for large draft vessels in areas where natural deepwater conditions exist (see Chapter 1).

Channel Widths

The channel width is usually measured at the toe of the side slopes or at the design depth. The channel width depends upon the following factors: (a) the beam, speed and maneuverability of the design vessel, (b) whether the vessel is to pass another vessel, (c) the channel depth, (d) the channel alignment and whether the channel is in a restricted or wide waterway, (e) the stability of the channel banks and (f) the winds, waves, currents and crosscurrents in the channel. There are no formula which explicitly include all these factors, but some criteria have been established based upon the beam of the design vessel which include these factors implicitly. The Permanent International Association of Navigation Congresses recommends that if there is no passing of vessels, the channel width should be three to four times the beam of the design vessel; if vessels pass, the channel width should be six to seven times the beam of the design vessel (32). They suggest these criteria

Table 2.1

Maneuvering Lane Width at Quarter Mile	
Controllability	Width in %
Very good	160
Good	180
Poor	120

*Percent of vessel beam.

would be for ideal conditions and that cross winds and crosscurrents should be considered.

Another method of determining the required channel width is based upon investigations made during studies of the sea level Panama Canal during which model and prototype vessels were observed in motion (40, 41, 42). The opinion of pilots and navigators were included in the criteria presented. This method divides the total channel width into (a) width of the maneuvering lane, (b) width of the ship clearance lane and (c) width of bank clearance.

Width of the maneuvering lane

The maneuvering lane is analogous to a car lane on a highway. Experimentally, a vessel navigating within this lane will not be hindered by the channel banks or another vessel. The width of the maneuvering lane for a vessel depends upon the controllability of the vessel. The controllability of various vessels was defined as follows:

1. *Very Good* for naval fighting vessels and freighters of the Victory ship class,
2. *Good* for naval transports and tenders, T-2 tankers, new ore ships and freighters of the Liberty ship class,
3. *Poor* for old ore ships and damaged vessels.

Based upon this classification, the criteria shown in Table 2.1 were recommended for a ship navigating the quarter point of the channel. A maneuvering lane equal to 140 percent of the vessel's beam was recommended for a ship on the centerline of the channel, regardless of controllability.

The criteria presented for the width of the maneuvering lane are for ideal conditions. They should be considered as minimum requirements. Allowance must be made for the yaw of a ship if crosscurrents or cross winds occur in the channel. A vessel 700 feet (213 meters) long with a beam of 90 feet (27 meters) yawing 5° would require a channel width of approximately 180 feet (55 meters) just for yawing. A yawing of 5° is reasonable for a vessel of this size in a semiprotected waterway subject to cross winds and crosscurrents. It is suggested that the maneuvering lane width be the sum of the yawing width plus 60, 80 or 100% of the vessel's beam for very good, good and poor controllability, respectively.

Width of the ship clearance lane

The width of the ship clearance lane is measured between maneuvering lanes. The hydraulic phenomena associated with ships passing in a channel creates suction and repulsion forces between the ships. The width of the ship clearance lane is established to minimize the hazards of these forces. The minimum width desired by many pilots and navigators is 100 feet (30.5 meters).

Width of bank clearance

When a vessel departs from the centerline of the channel and approaches the banks, the suction and repulsion forces create yawing moments. A rudder angle has to be applied to compensate for these forces in order to maintain a straight course. The rudder angle necessary for a vessel to maintain a straight course at a given speed, water depth and distance from the bank is called the *equilibrium rudder angle*.

Studies by the Panama Canal engineers led them to conclude that the bank clearance should be based upon an equilibrium angle of 5° (22). This criterion would permit an additional rudder deflection of 30° on most ships. Based upon a 5° equilibrium angle and upon the results of the sea

Port Navigation   19

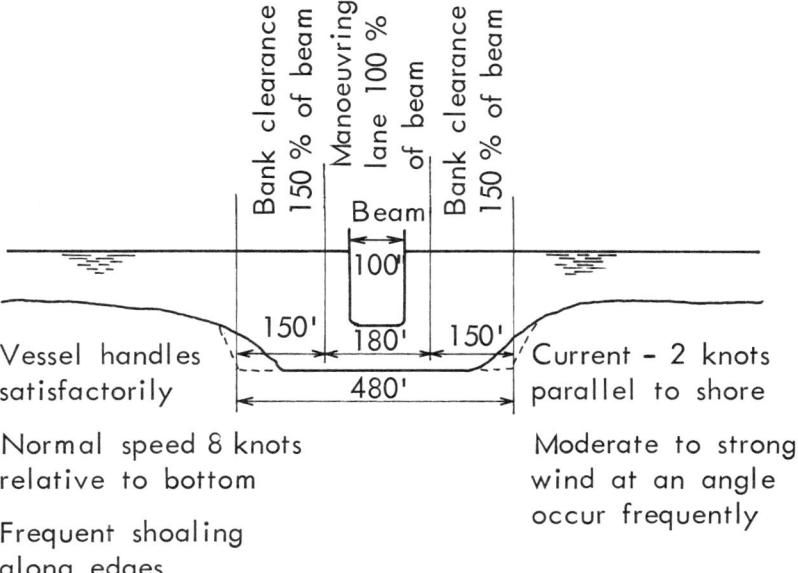

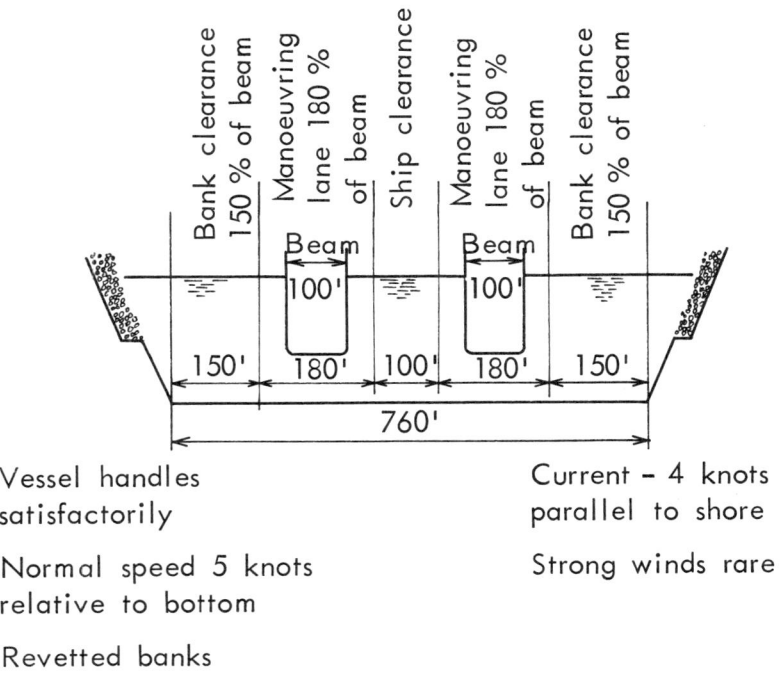

Figure 2.9. Typical width calculations (11).

22   Port Engineering

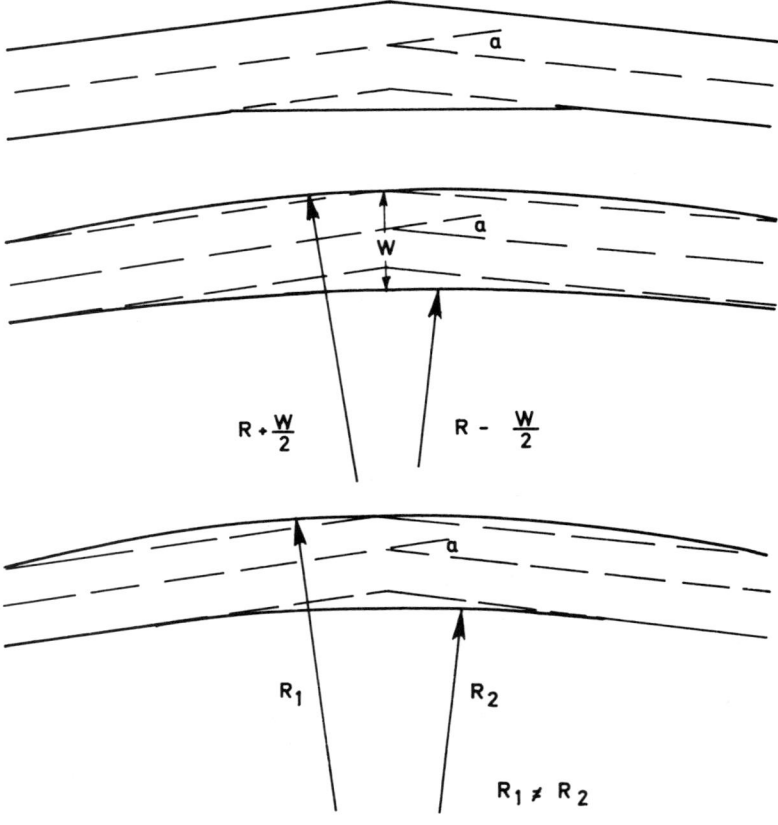

Figure 2.11. Methods of widening channel at bends (11).

ship if it does not approach the entrance at right angles.

The effect the harbor entrance width has upon wave and current conditions within the harbor is best studied by a hydraulic model. The maximum allowable velocity for navigation in confined waters is usually considered to be 2½ to 3½ knots (8, 14, 34). This corresponds to 4 to 6 feet per second. Forces involved in berthing maneuvers are mentioned in Chapter 4 with special reference to Appendix 3.

Harbor Hydraulics

Harbor hydraulics describes the movement of water masses by currents and waves in a harbor. Generally it may be said that any movement of water in a harbor is adverse to navigation, although current action may also include such benefits as flushing of sediments and pollutants. On the other hand, currents may be responsible for sedimentation in navigation channels and harbor basins. This is true in most cases when harbors are built in alluvial rivers, particularly when these rivers are tidal and carry sediments which may flocculate as a result of density currents and the accompanying boundary and mixing processes.

Wave action in navigation channels and harbor basins is always undesirable because it causes navigation difficulties. The degree of wave action which may be considered permissible depends upon the wave height and period (wave length), the size of the vessel and its hydrodynamic characteristics. The wave height is usually of no particular concern to large vessels unless wave length exceeds the vessel length. For large vessels in shallow water this may happen when periods are more than 15 to 20 seconds. For fishing boats and smaller cargo vessels of 1,000 to 2,000 dwt wave heights become a problem when periods exceed 3 to 6 seconds, depending on vessel size, at which time the vessel starts riding on part of a wave only.

The following two sections discuss problems related to current and wave action in harbors.

Current Action

Currents in General

Currents may be fresh-water (river) currents, tidal currents including density currents and wind currents.

The first ports in existence were built in rivers or estuaries. Examples of such ancient river ports are Alexandria in Egypt on the Nile, Ostia in Italy on the Tiber and London on the Thames. Almost all river ports suffered from deposits of sediments; several of them got choked and became completely landlocked. Ostia, the famous Roman Naval port, is probably the best known example. Other ancient or medieval ports were gradually moved oceanward, thereby putting off the problem without solving it. Alexandria is one example. Others like London, Hamburg and Liverpool benefited from tidal currents which helped by keeping a channel of rather fixed cross-sectional area open, but their problems worsened with growing vessel size. Gradually they had to be provided with "satellite ports" closer to the ocean at deeper natural waters. Only a few were stubborn enough to continue their fight against the still increasing deposits. All kinds of means, including extensive dredging operations combined with river regulations, were used. The best known example is probably Antwerp, where recent efforts concentrate on keeping a 40-foot navigation depth by comprehensive regulation works. New Orleans, Charleston and Savannah are good American examples. Chapter 6 gives many examples on sedimentation problems related to port engineering. One of the most recent publications on the subject by the PIANC (33) is mainly concerned about navigability in relation to the problem of bedload in canalized rivers and waterways, particularly at the mouth of tributaries.

Current mechanics problems in harbors are usually related to problems of navigation that affect the ship's ability to proceed safely regardless of cross, head or tail currents. A ship's maneuvering ability depends upon its hull, rudder, propeller and machine power characteristics. There is, therefore, no exact rule for "allowable current velocity," etc. Tidal current velocities in channels with bottoms in alluvial material usually do not exceed 3 to 5 feet per second, which is acceptable to most navigation. Five feet per second, or about 3 knots, is usually considered maximum velocity for safety in navigation channels like the intracoastal waterway along part of the Atlantic and the Gulf of Mexico Coast.

Currents and Navigation

When a vessel approaches a harbor or basin entrance or has to turn in a natural or dredged basin, special problems arise because the ship's speed is low and its maneuvering ability consequently less. The port designer has to consider this situation very seriously, for reasons of safety as well as economy, with respect to proper utilization of the area available for harbor basins. Determination of a ship's movement in a port is a question of the hydrodynamic forces acting on the ship. The equations which govern a ship's movement are, however, very complicated and can hardly handle a rapidly varying situation of current and wind actions. Furthermore, the human factor is greatly

Table 2.2. Maneuvering Forces*

Force	Calculation	Example 120,000 dwt tanker
Inertia	$\rho(m + m')\,dv/dt$ m = ships mass m' = "added mass" v = resulting speeds caused by forces or combination of forces by wind, current, waves, propellers, rudder, rudder's position (change of direction); furthermore by moorings, anchor chains, tugboats, etc.	
Resulting pressure forces caused by changes in ship's course	$m\,w^2\,r$ when w = angular velocity r = radius of curvature	225 (for 6 knots and r = 600 meters = 2,000 feet)
Propeller	Ship's particular design date	20-30 (for 6 knots)
Rudder	Ship's particular design date	$\cong 15$ (for 6 knots)
Force by propellers perpendicular to the vessel	Ship's particular design date may be 10% of force by propellers when in reverse	
Force in anchor chain or cable	Varies greatly. For sand bottom and ample length of chain, it is of the order of magnitude five times the weight of anchor	$\cong 100$
Tugboats	Depends upon tug design. Towing or push force by 4,000 hp at zero speed = 40 t	40
Thrusters	Depends upon design. A normal propeller-thruster at 500 hp has a push-force of 6 t when ships movement is zero	6
Moorings	Depends upon character of mooring. For 120,000 dwt vessel according to Lloyds min. 48 t for one mooring line.	40 per line
Wind	Wind velocity 20 m/sec. or 70 ft/sec. (50 mph)	80 (loaded) 125 (not loaded)
Crosscurrents	Depends upon current velocity and direction and ship's hull characteristics. At 1 kts $\cong$ 140 t.	140

*I.A. Svendsen, 1968, Danish text.

involved in all maneuvers, as is the engine's ability to respond to its "orders." An exact theoretical solution is therefore too "academic" to solve any practical problem. Model experiments have been used in cases of oil tanker maneuvering in ports using pilots as "consultants" on the test program, e.g., at the harbor of Curacao in the Netherland Antilles. This method has certain advantages, but it cannot reproduce prototype conditions adequately. An analog computer model may be possible but has so far not been used. The most applicable method today is probably the "graphical" or "experience method" by which all acting forces are taken into account. The vessel is moved accordingly step by step with the captain on the bridge and the engineer in the engine room, but their knowledge and experience are combined with that of the naval architect and harbor engineer.

The forces acting on a vessel are summarized by I.A. Svendsen in a publication, *Ships and ships maneuvers*, from the Department of Coastal Engineering, Technical University of Denmark (1968, Danish text). These forces are listed in Table 2.2 using his example, a 120,000 dwt tanker, for computation of actual forces in tons. The figures of Table 2.2 are of approximate nature only.

When a ship approaches a harbor entrance or any type of berthing place, it may perform the following general maneuvers: (a) entrance maneuvers to bring the ship into position to enter and next the entering itself, (b) maneuvers to bring the vessel into position to berth and (c) the actual berthing maneuver.

A ship must enter a harbor with enough speed to maintain its maneuverability. The passage becomes more difficult in the case of crosscurrents and cross winds. When the vessel is well inside the protective jetties, it has to stop and usually also has to turn in order to bring it into a proper berthing position. In the most simple case, this may involve a number of forward and reverse maneuvers with maximum changes in the rudder position. However, anchors or even tugboats may also be used. Following approach maneuvers to berth, the vessel may finally winch itself to the berth or tugboats may push it to the berth. Some of the large oil tankers have bow and stern thrusters which make tugboat use unnecessary. When the ship leaves the berth, maneuvers take place in the opposite sequence. It is common practice to make arrival maneuvers the more difficult compared to departure maneuvers. This has the advantage that the ship can leave more easily at any time of the day and with minimum assistance.

The influence of currents and winds on a vessel principally follows the same laws, but currents are usually more steady and their influence is easier to predict than the influence of winds. Gustiness (squalls) plays an important role and often makes prediction of ship movements difficult. It is good practice to place piers or quay walls as parallel as possible to predominant currents or winds to avoid strong cross forces. While the former has particular reference to piers and quay walls in river ports and tidal channels, the latter is most important when relatively high winds tend to blow almost steadily in one direction, as they do in trade winds and monsoon belts. The concern is the force of the wind itself. The currents set up by the shear stress acting on the water surface may be of the order 1/20 to 1/40 of the wind velocity and are therefore of less importance.

Figures 2.12 to 2.16 are examples of approach and berthing maneuvers given in the paper by Svendsen. Figure 2.12 shows arrival maneuvers in an open-ocean port of a 8,000 dwt vessel with a 17 meters per second $\cong$ 55 feet per second tail cross wind as indicated in the figure. Figure 2.13 demonstrates similar maneuvers when the wind has turned 90° and blows as cross wind at 12 meters per second $\cong$ 40 feet per second. Figure 2.14 shows arrival maneuvers of a large tanker with a strong current parallel to the berth. Berthing always takes place up against the current. Figure 2.15 demonstrates the departure maneuvers by the same vessel, which also takes place up against the current. Figure 2.16 indicates how a vessel turns around a pierhead after having berthed temporarily by means of a dolphin at the pierhead. The vessels shown in Figures 2.12 to 2.16 all undertake maneuvers without assistance of tugboats (which is usually an expensive proposition).

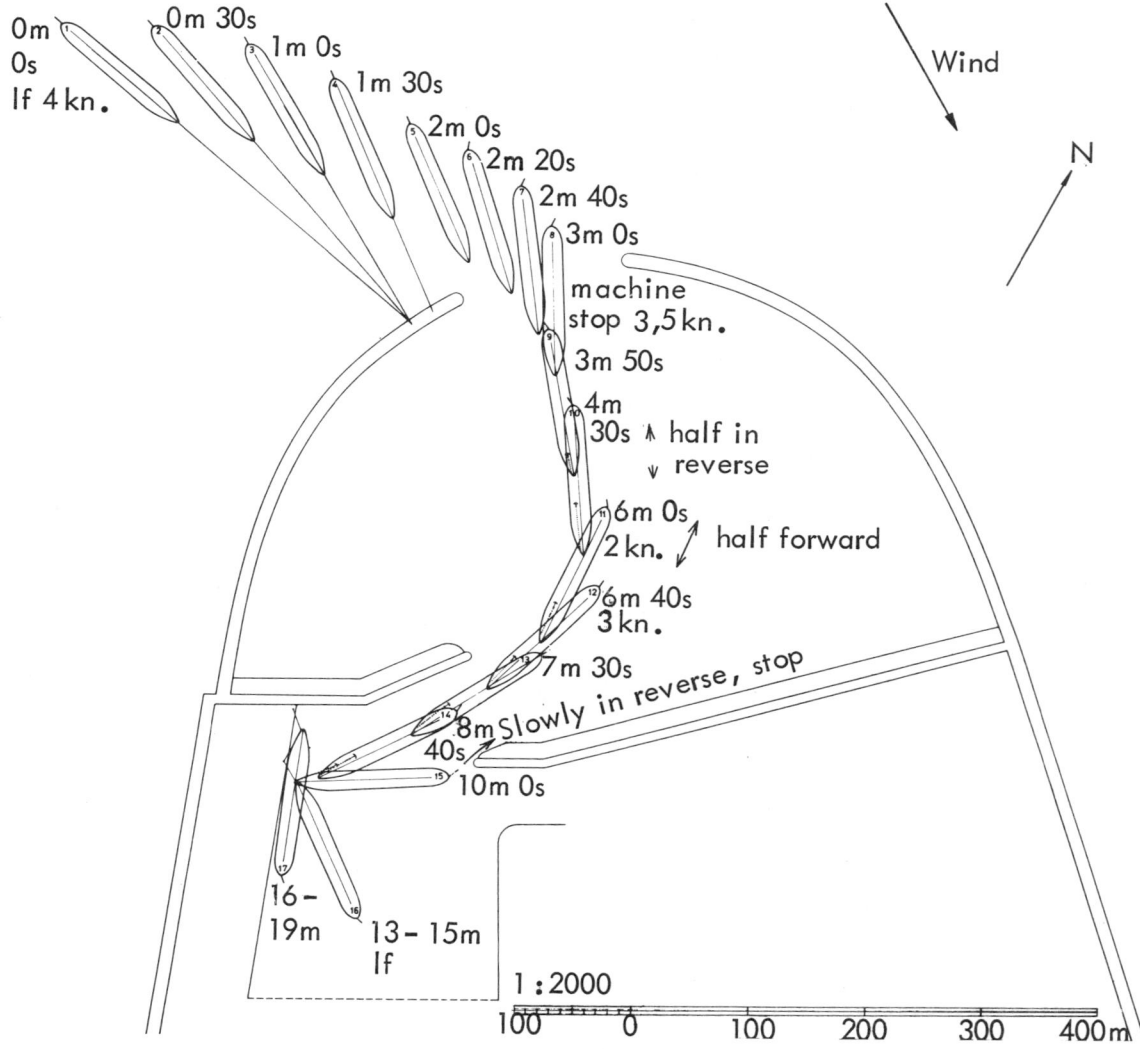

Figure 2.12. Approach and berthing maneuvers for 8.000 DWT vessel in tail wind of 55 feet per second (I.A. Svendsen, 1968).

With respect to the forces acting during the berthing maneuver, the article published by Prof. Vasco Costa in *The Dock and Harbour Authority*, (vol. 48, no. 569, pp. 351-58) gives a very exhaustive review of the mechanics of maneuvering procedures and is therefore included as Appendix 3.

Wave Action in Ports

Wave action is important for any harbor during its construction and for its performance after construction has been completed. Forecasting wave action during construction work has in-

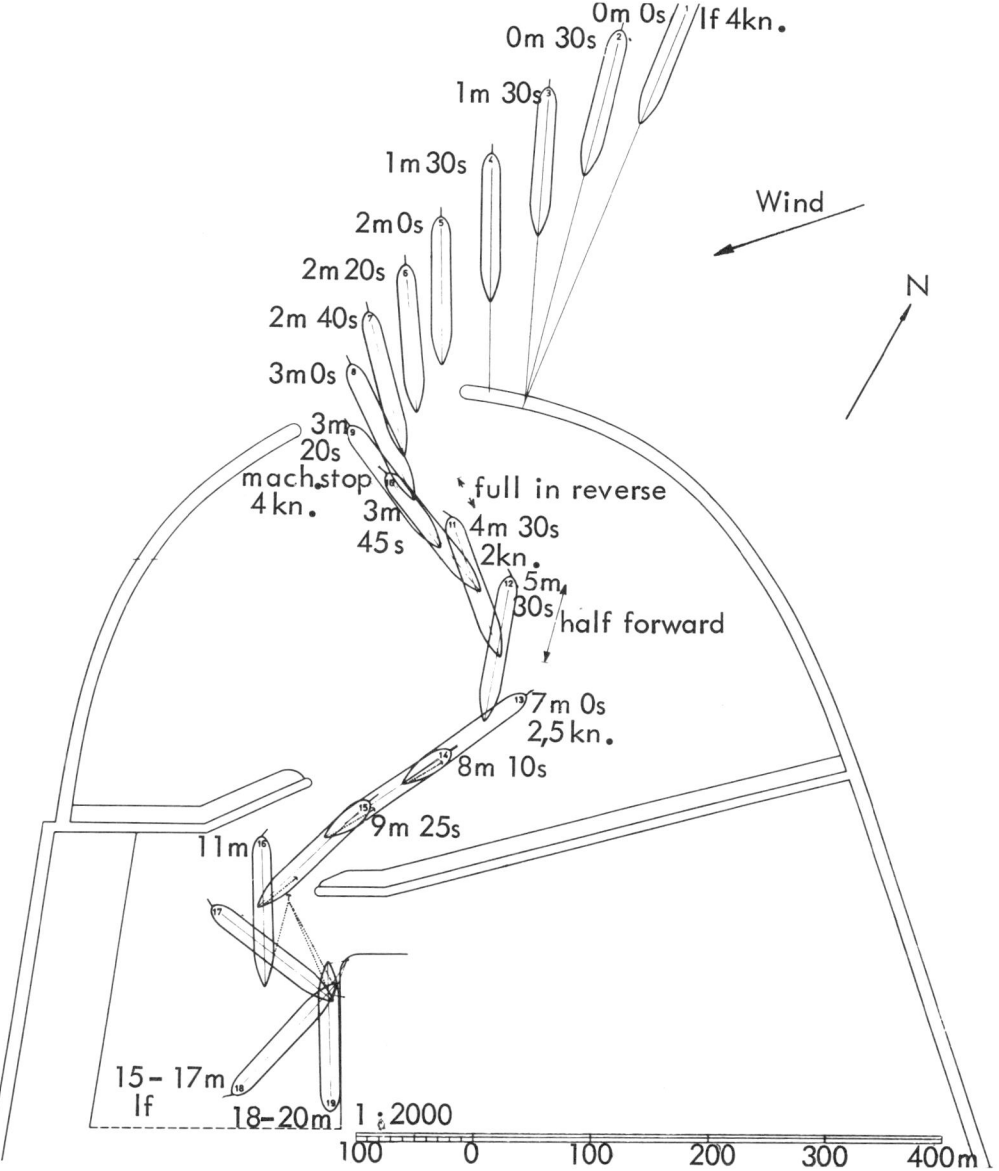

Figure 2.13. Approach and berthing maneuvers for 8.000 DWT vessel in cross wind of 40 feet per second (I.A. Svendsen, 1968).

creased the execution rate of jetty work, in some cases no less than three to four times (49).

Wave action in port basins occurs as normal wind waves penetrating through the entrance and as long waves including harbor seiches of incidental nature and surges of meteorological nature. The tsunami wave is a special and rare phenomenon related to earthquakes and occurs in only a

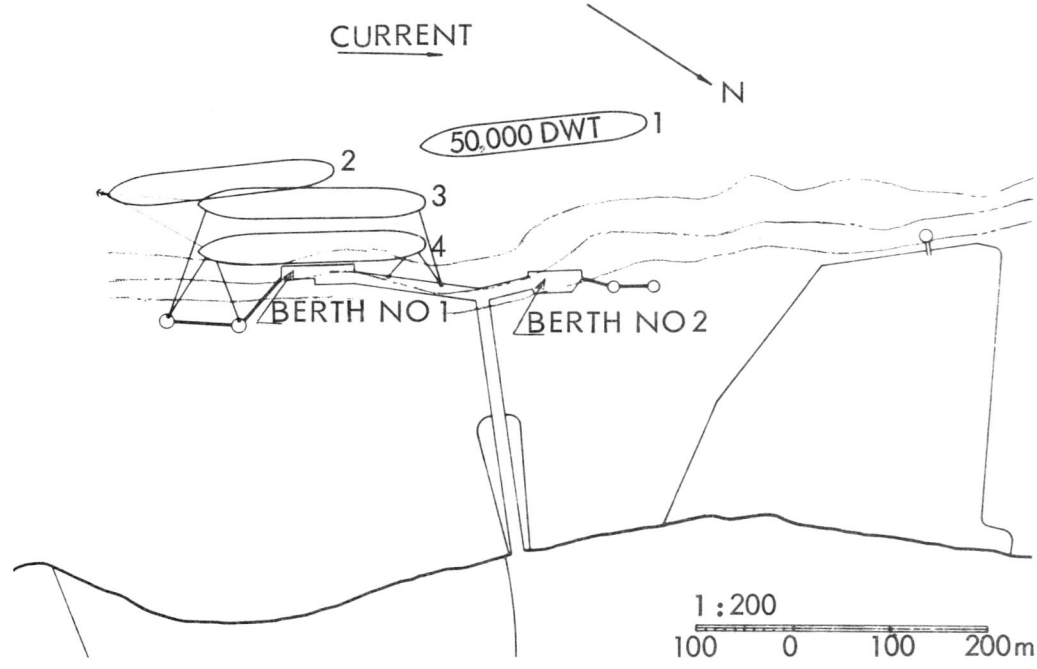

Figure 2.14. Berthing maneuvers for 50.000 DWT tanker with strong current action (I.A. Svendsen, 1968).

few places, mainly in the South Atlantic and in the Pacific, including Hawaii and Japan (47, 49).
ultimately by an energy absorbing beach. The ocean represent a spectrum of frequencies ranging from 3 to 4 seconds to 15 to 20 seconds, the latter associated with very long (Atlantic and Pacific) fetches. *Swells* is the term used to distinguish waves caused by local storms from waves caused by distant storms. Consequently, they only occur in the large oceans and in seas connected with those oceans. Waves beyond approximately 20 seconds are relatively rare and occur as a result of surf beat (nearshore oscillations caused by irregularities in wave breaking) and atmospheric disturbances. This includes wind gustiness that operates in most open-sea territories and steep barometric pressure gradients which are typical for the Great Lakes area. Generally all wind waves and swells with periods less than 20 seconds are predictable by forecasting procedures while waves with periods more than 20 seconds are difficult to predict, and their behavior as a whole is not well known. The experience is that the incident deep-water wave energy spectrum is fairly flat between 30 and 200 seconds, the range of periods characteristic for seiches and surges in harbors, which are often of concern to large moored ships.

Ports on open-sea coasts must be protected against wave action. Of course, design considerations are not the same for short and long period wave action because the behavior of the two types of waves is very different.

Regardless of whether short period or long period waves is the subject, the problem of resonance is very important. Wind waves or swells of 10 to 20 seconds may cause a resonance effect in shorter harbor basins, e.g., when the period, T, of a free oscillation having its mode at the entrance and its loop at the end equals $4L/\sqrt{(gD)}$ where L is length of basin and D is depth of basin, or

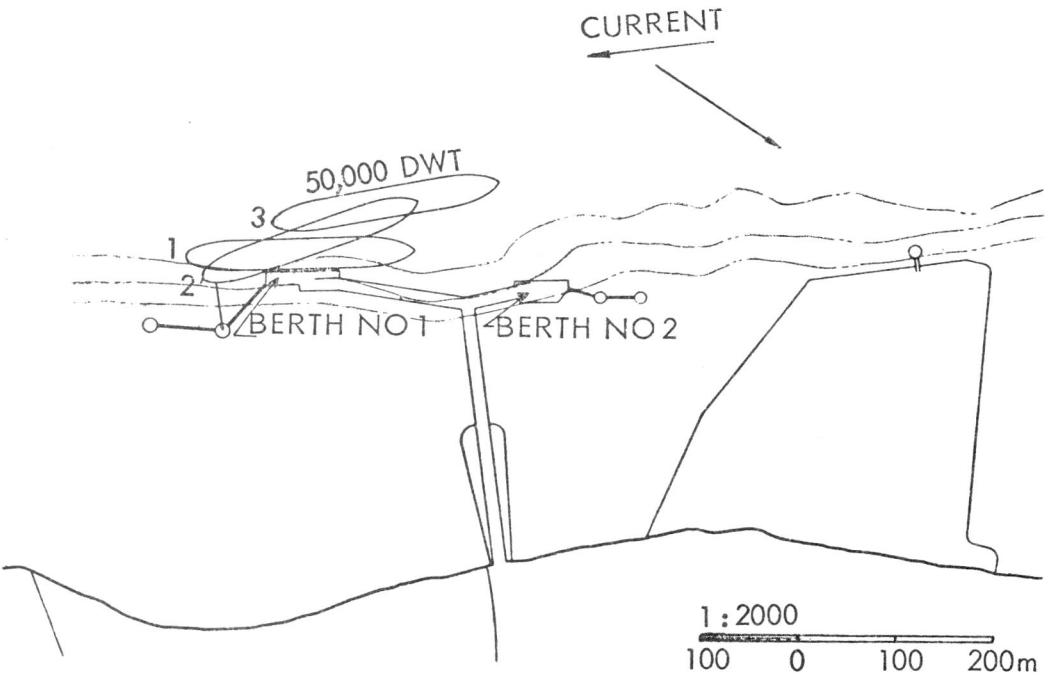

Figure 2.15. Departure from berth by 50.000 DWT tanker with strong current action (I.A. Svendsen, 1968).

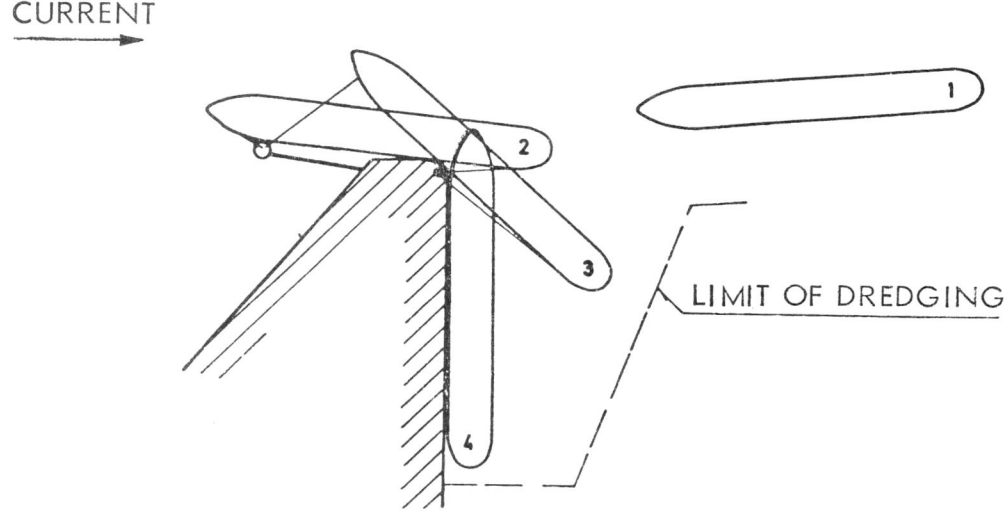

Figure 2.16. Berthing maneuver around pier head (I.A. Svendsen 1968).

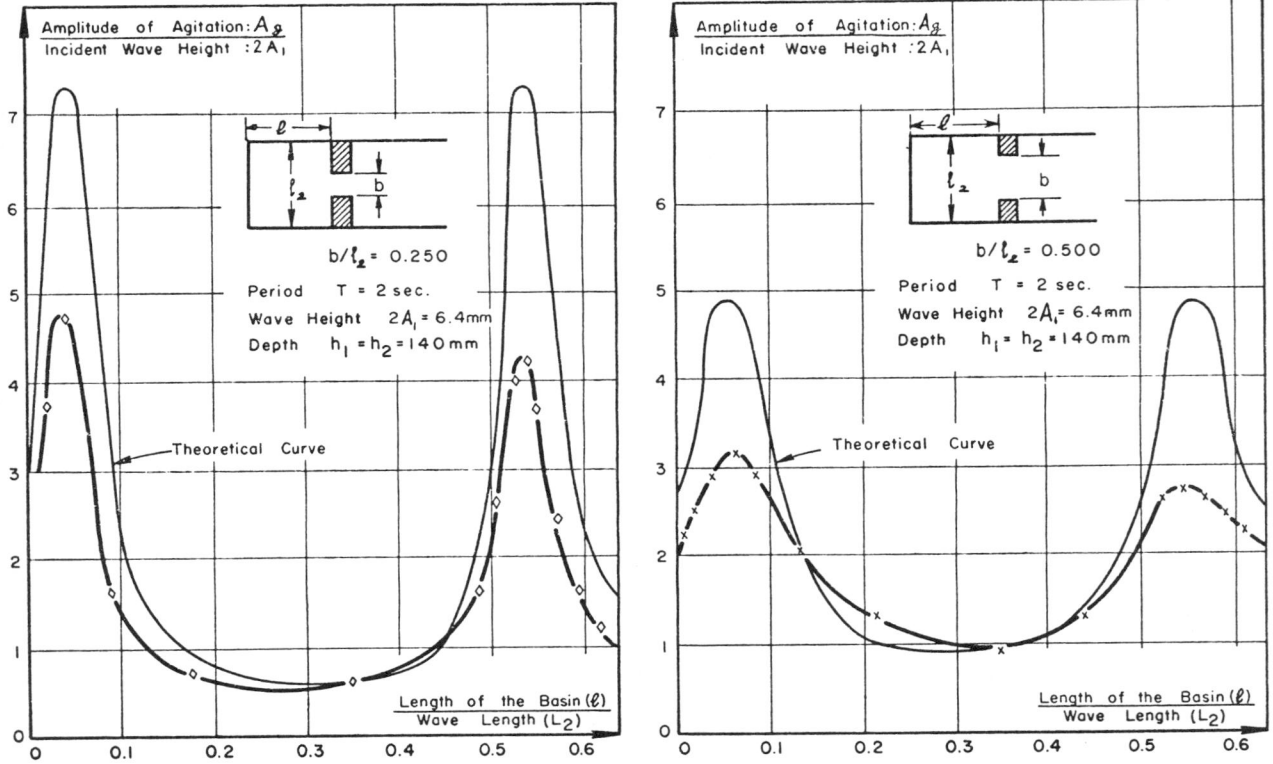

Figure 2.17. Agitation is a basin with an obstruction (24).

$2L/\sqrt{gD}$ for a partly closed entrance. $\sqrt{gD}$ is the propagation velocity of a translatory wave. This is a relatively frequent phenomenon in small Norwegian side fjords and in some oblong harbor basins. Iribarren and Nogales give a number of examples of such resonance in harbor basins of varying geometry (18).

In a comprehensive paper Bernard Le Méhauté's (24) uses a first order theory for the value of the wave agitation in a simple basin caused by an incident periodical gravity wave and gives results of theoretical and experimental studies. He considers the harbor as a combination of discontinuities separated by a definite distance and ultimately by an energy absorbing beach. The value of the agitation is computed assuming that motion is predominantly two-dimensional as a function of the amplitude and period of the incident wave. The influence of the entrance shape and basin geometry is analysed. Figures 2.17 to 2.19 are examples of results indicating the agitation in a basin with an obstruction (Figure 2.17) and agitation in a basin with change of depth (Figure 2.19). Using the notations of Figure 2.20, one has that resonance for wave length L_2 occurs when

$$(n) L_2/2 < l < (n + \tfrac{1}{2}) L_2/2$$

for all cases, and for $l = (n)L_2/2$ in the case of a complete obstruction and for $l = (n + \tfrac{1}{2}) L_2/2$ in the case of a change of depth without obstruction. Minimum agitation occurs when

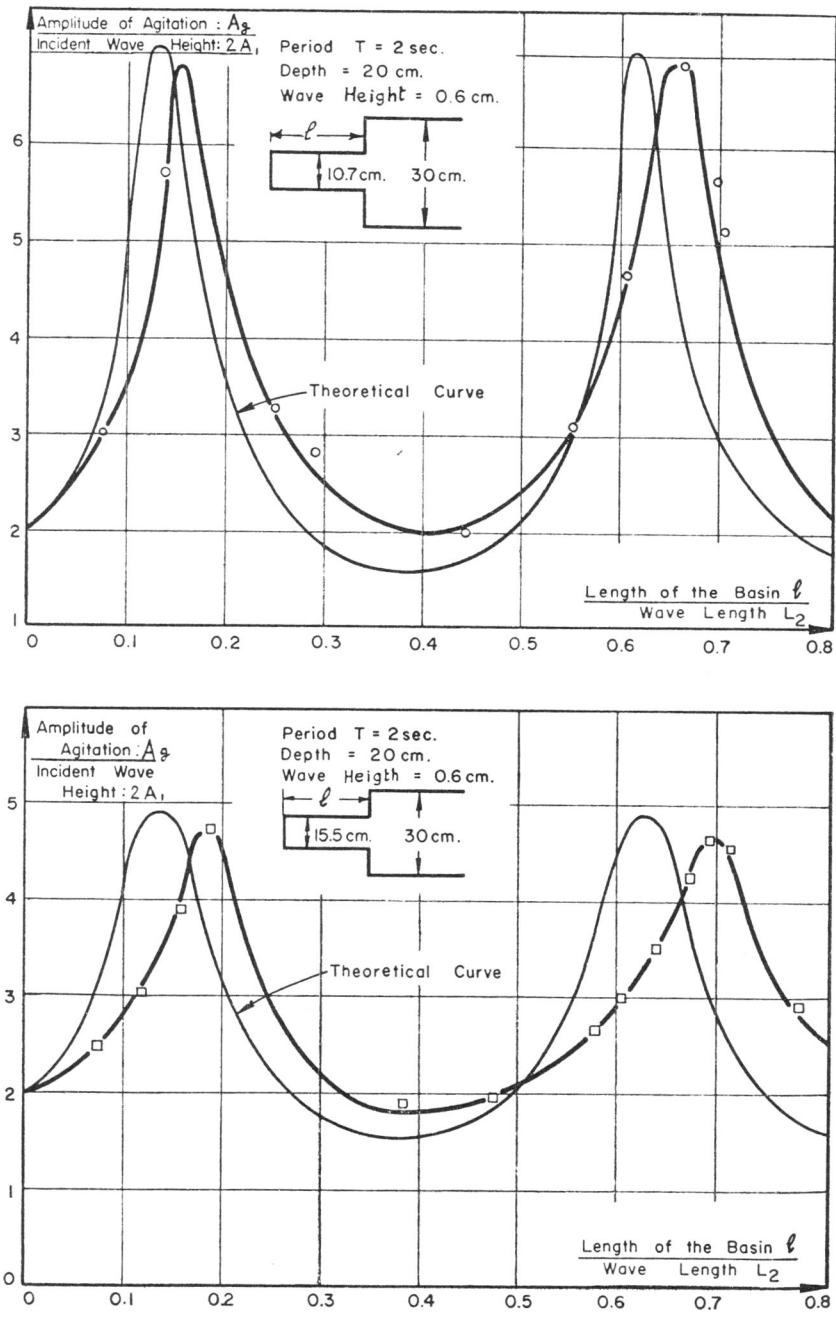

Figure 2.18. Agitation in a basin with change of width (24).

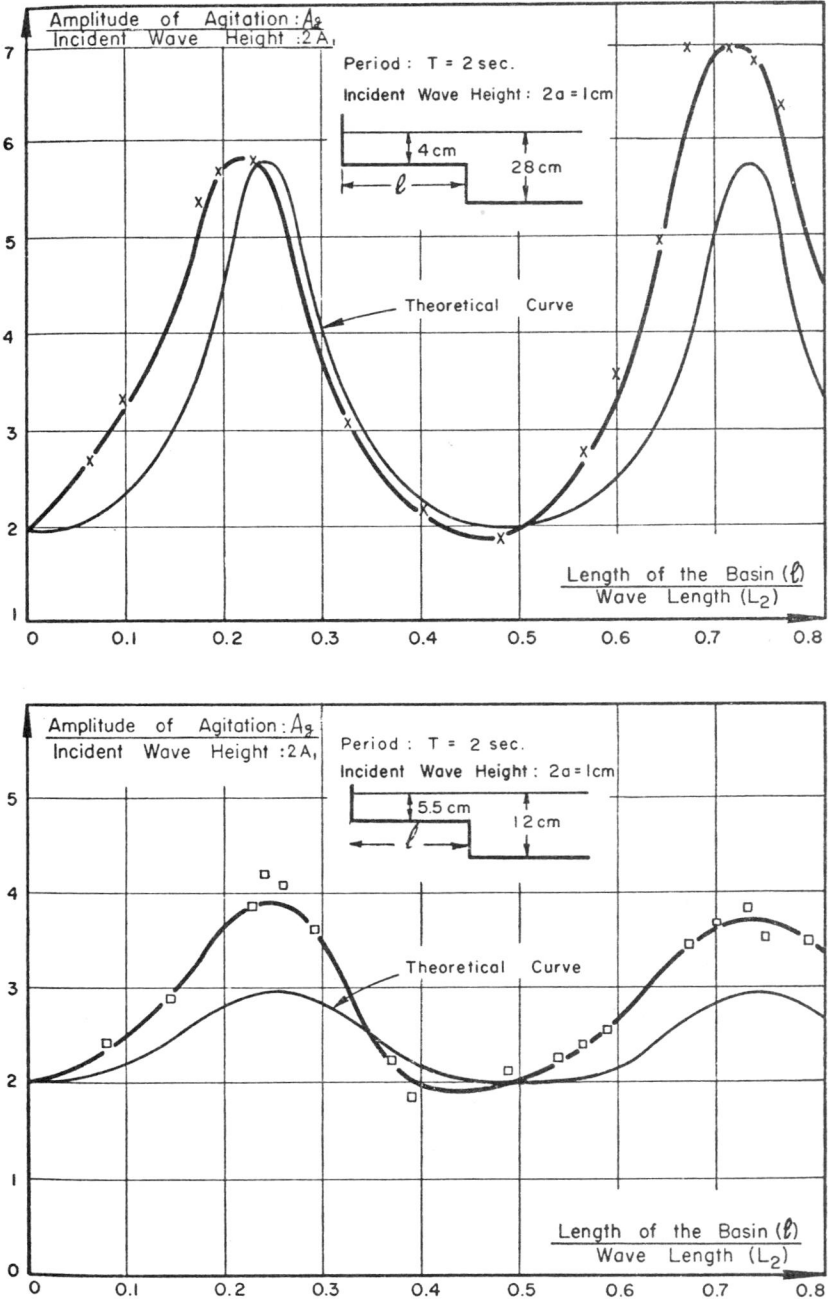

Figure 2.19. Agitation in a basin with change of depth (24).

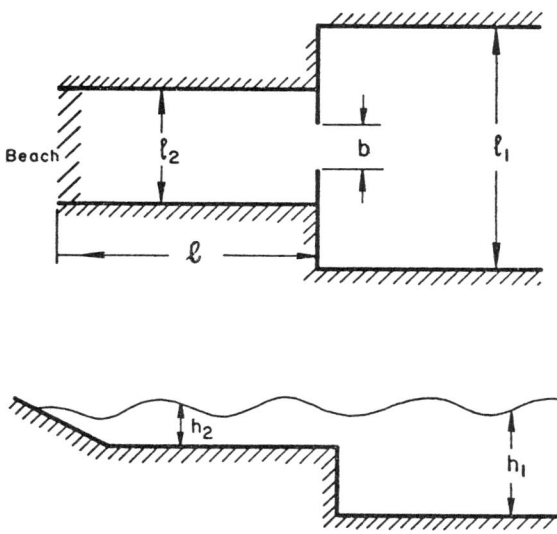

Figure 2.20. Layout of basin, notations (24).

$(n + ½) L_2/2 < l < (n + 1)L_2/2.$

Furthermore, Le Méhauté notes that agitation is proportional to the amplitude of the incident wave, even in the case of viscous friction, as long as the quadratic (V^2) contribution to friction is considered negligible.

Miles and Munk (28) and Raichlen (35) show that at resonance, a fully open harbor of length, l, will act as a quarter-wave length resonator having an effective length:

$$l_{eff} = l + \triangle l = L_R/4 \, ,$$

where
L_R = the wave length of the fundamental mode
and

$$\Delta l = 2d/\pi [1{,}051 + ln(l/2d)] + 2dF$$

and

$$F = (1/\pi)ln \left\{ (2d/c) \csc [(\pi/2)(c/2d)] \right\}$$

This parameter is presented by Figure 2.21 (35).

For a square harbor ($l/2d$ = one) fully open: l_{eff} = 1,34 l, and for a harbor of ratio $l/2d$ = 10 (Figure 2.21), l_{eff} = 1,11 l.

The amplification factor at resonance may be calculated as shown in Reference 35 when the friction and reflection factors of the basin and its geometrical characteristics are known. For further information on forced oscillations in basins of simple platform, the reader is referred to Reference 35.

The input waves for such analyses are deep-water waves carried to the shallow-water entrance by refraction analysis or by model experiments. During this passage over decreasing depths, waves—and particularly long period waves—may be subject to crossing orthogonals, reflection and resonance which may change the input wave spectrum considerably from that occurring in the open deep sea. The very long waves are influenced by bottom topography in even very deep water because the wave length of a 100-second wave is about 5 $(10)^4$ feet. Moreover, the long waves do not break but are always reflected. Figure 2.22 by Thijsse (27, 38) shows the reflection from a smooth impermeable slope as a function of wave length, depth and

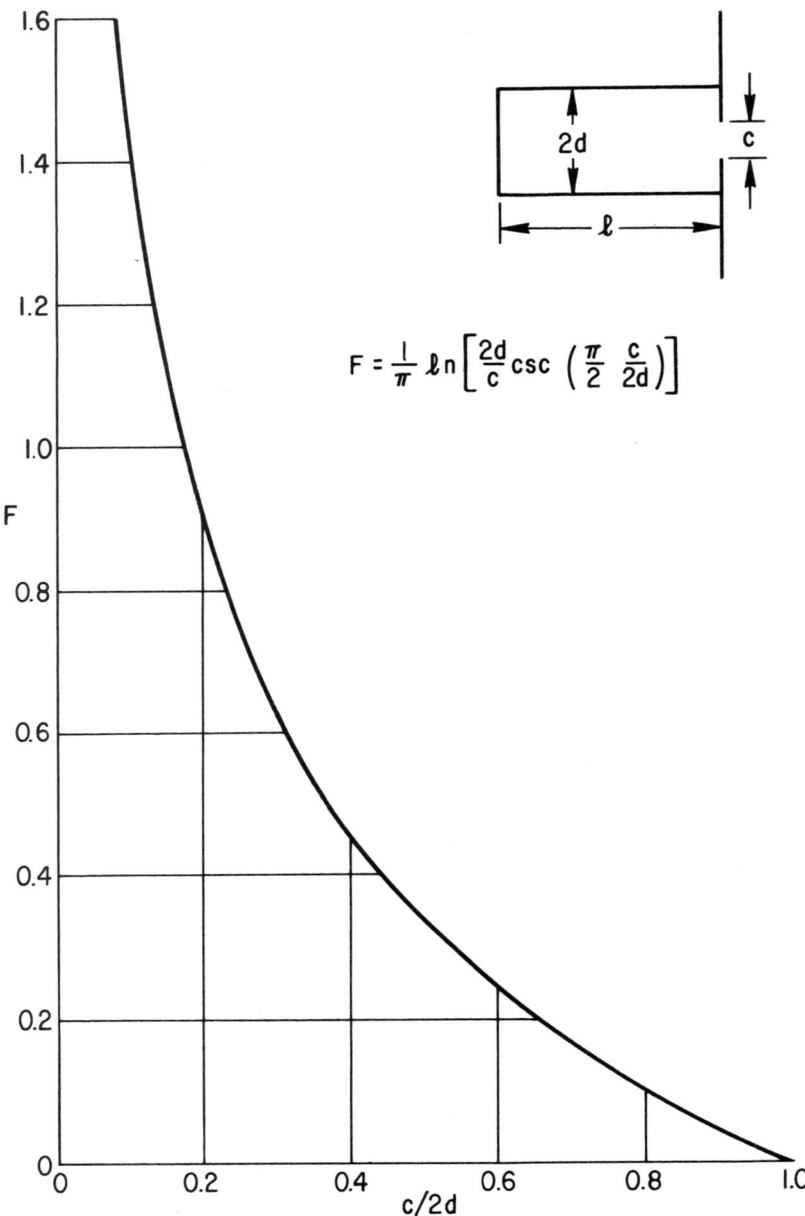

Figure 2.21. Function F versus c/2d (35).

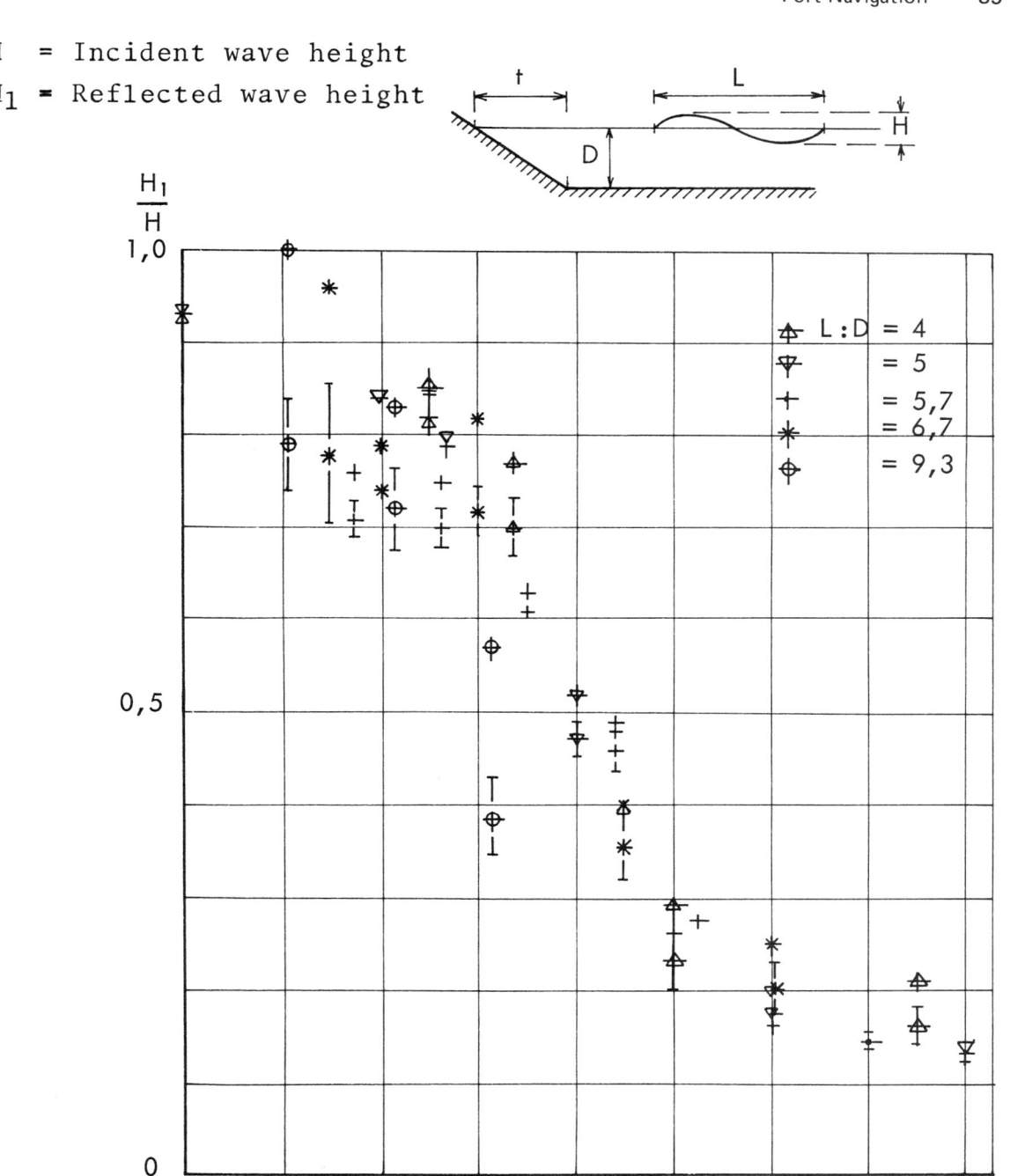

Figure 2.22. Reflection from smooth slope (29).

slope characteristics. With reference to Figure 2.22, the following inequality exists.

$$0.35\,(L/D) < t/D < 0.6\,(L/D)$$

| strong | weak |
| reflection | reflection |

Wave action on a slope and the reflection from it is dealt with by many other authors (4, 26, 27). Miche (27) writes the reflection, $R = H_1/H = R'\rho$, where H_1 is the reflected wave height, and H is the height of the incoming wave. $R' = \gamma_{max}/\gamma_0$ when $\gamma_0 = H_0/L_0$ and γ max = $[\sqrt{(2\alpha/\pi)}]$ $[\sin^2\alpha/\pi]$, where α = slope angle, and ρ is a measure for the roughness of the slope which is 0.8 - 0.9 for smooth slopes. γ_{max} is the steepness ratio for wave breaking.

For long period waves it is of no importance for reflection whether a shore or breakwater slope is smooth or irregular. Irregularities in the horizontal geometry must be very large in order to confuse the reflection. Long waves do, in fact, reflect back from one continent to another. For that reason, continental shelf and bay areas often have a relatively high energy level in the long wave frequency band caused by reflection and refraction of the continental slope and of the bay shores. If modes of oscillation of the shelf and of the bay shores match some dominant natural oscillations of a harbor basin, large seiche amplitudes may result. It is therefore very important to determine the probability distribution of the incident long wave spectrum. An example of such attempt is given in Reference 48, which mentions the surge action in Monterey Harbor, California.

Long period waves, particularly those of 2- to 4-minute periods, may be responsible for considerable surge action in ports, which is of great nuisance to vessels at berth. They occur during storms as well as during calm weather conditions but do not need to be kept up by external effects, although they are always started by oscillations coming from the sea. They are nearly always found in small scale models as a result of irregularities in the wave generating mechanism. Most harbor seiches do not exceed a few centimeters, but they may rise above 1 foot when resonance occurs because of the geometry of the harbor basins. The article by Wemelsfelder, "Origin and effects of long period waves in ports along the Dutch Coast" (16), gives a very thorough description of long period wave and resonance phenomena occurring almost everywhere on the Dutch Coast. Other examples, including Cape Town, South Africa, Terminal Harbor at Los Angeles, Long Beach, California, and Port of Madras, India, are mentioned in Reference 16.

Deepening of a harbor usually increases surge height, which increases with the square root of the increase in depth, provided that the oscillation system and the amount of incident wave energy do not change.

Measures Against Wave Action in Ports

Wind waves of short period (< 20 seconds)

Penetration of wind waves in harbors may be eliminated by (a) restricting possibilities for input of wave energy by breakwaters and other means, (b) energy absorption before waves reach berthing areas, (c) proper geometry of basins and (d) other special means like pneumatic and hydraulic breakwaters, etc. Some of these measures have been in use since Tyre and Sidon and Cleopatra's days and have proved their ability, thanks to simplicity. Nature had already shown how to handle the situation by providing the necessary protection. Others are of a more involved type, requiring knowledge of wave mechanics and of engineering mechanical technology. Figure 2.23 from Reference 5 gives examples on such measures which range from breakwater protection and the selection of proper entrance and basin geometry to energy absorbing (minimum reflecting) structures including beaches (15), jetties, breakwaters, quays, sea walls (3, 4, 13, 39), resonance chambers (45 and Figure 2.23e), density (air-water) currents (Figure 2.23i), submerged and floating breakwaters or mattresses, permeable bottom, etc.

The paragraph of Reference 5 on destruction of wave energy by dividing a reflected wave into

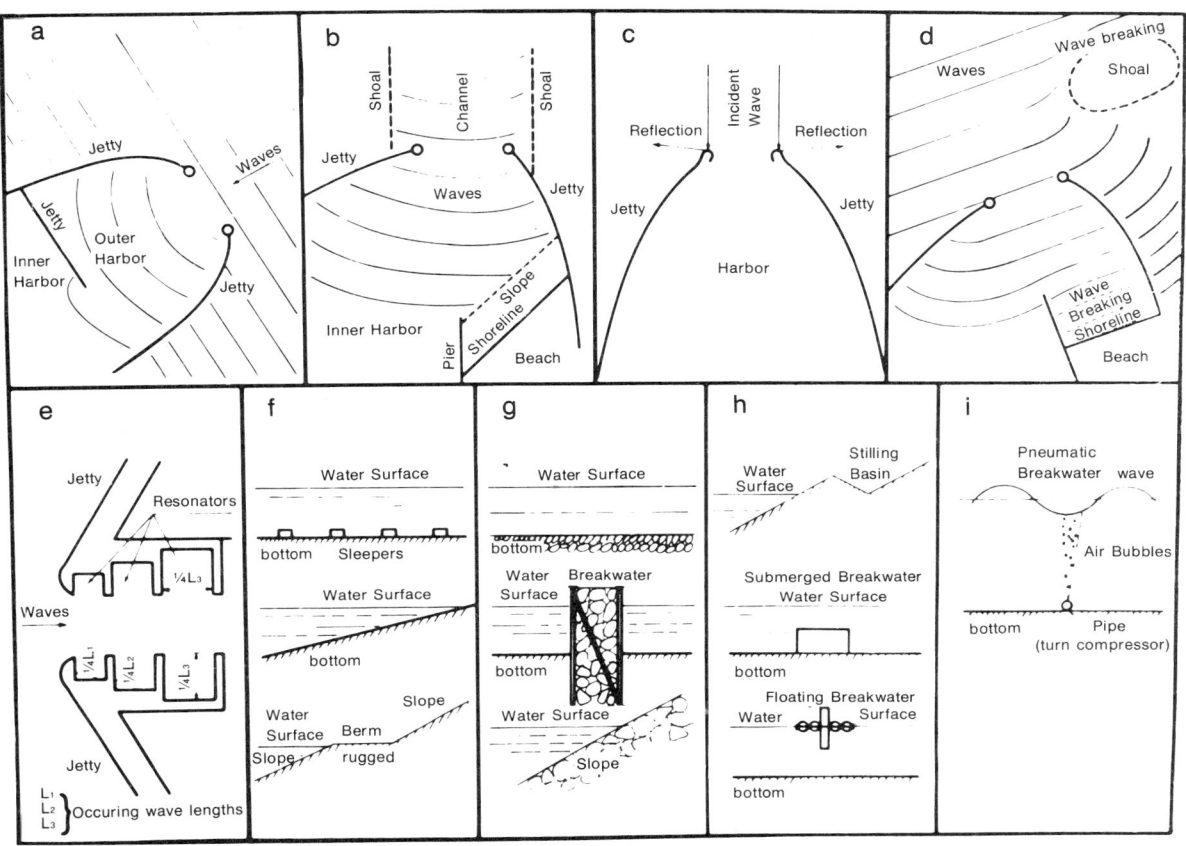

Figure 2.23. Destruction of wave energy as practiced in Harbor Engineering (5).

separate parts of different phases explains how the incident wave is divided into two parts which are reflected with a phase difference, e.g., 180°, that means basin length is $L/4$ in Figure 2.20. One part of the reflected wave, therefore, has a crest when the other part has a trough (Figure 2.24). Consequently, strong transversal currents creating much loss of energy will come into existence. Meanwhile there is the problem of how such conditions can be created. Figure 2.25 shows two walls, the front wall permeable and the back wall impermeable. The space between the two walls (front sides) is shown by a. Thickness of the wall is small compared to the other dimensions.

It is now assumed that the reflection coefficient for the permeable wall is β, and the transmission coefficient is α. With an incident wave height of H, the phase θ, wave length L, height of the reflected wave

$$H_R = \beta\cos\theta + \alpha^2 \cos[\theta + (4\pi a)/L] + \alpha^2\beta\cos[\theta + (8\pi a)/L] + \alpha^2\beta^2 \cos[\theta + (12\pi a)/L] + \ldots$$

When $\theta = 0$,

$$H_R = \beta + \alpha^2 \cos[(4\pi a)/L] + \alpha^2\beta\cos[(8\pi a)/L] + \alpha^2\beta^2 \cos[(12\pi a)/L] + \ldots$$

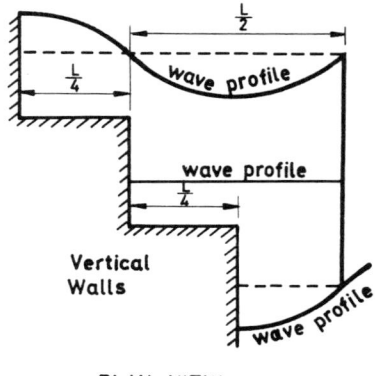

PLAN VIEW

Figure 2.24. Reflection of wave dividing it into several ports (5).

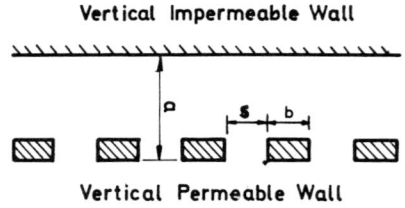

Figure 2.25. Permeable wall (5).

$$2\alpha/(1 + \beta) \qquad (2.4)$$

Meanwhile the energy loss has not been taken into account.

As explained in Reference 5, the coefficient of reflection and the coefficient transmission may be calculated for a shallow-water wave of small amplitude passing through a permeable wall of spaced piles or obstructions using the equation of continuity and the energy equation. This gives:

$$\beta = \frac{kH}{3\pi d}(1-\beta)^2$$

when β is the coefficient of reflection, H is wave height, d is water depth and k is the energy loss coefficient in the equation, $\Delta h = kv^2/2g$, when Δh is the loss in head, v is the velocity in front of the structure and g is the acceleration of gravity. Concerning k, no data seems to be available for experiments with waves in this case.

If an unidirectional flow is considered, the loss of head, Δh, according to investigations carried out in Germany by Kirschener (5), equals

$$\Delta h = k^1 (s/b)^{4/3}(v^2/2g) \qquad (2.5)$$

when s is the width of the single obstruction, b is the space between the obstructions, v is the velocity in front of the obstruction and k' is a form factor, which varies from about 0.8 with streamlined (fish-shaped) obstructions to about 2.5 with rectangular obstructions.

If Lundgren's formula (Equation 2.5) is used with $s = b$, $k = 2.5$ and $H/d = 0.2$, one has $\beta \sim 0.05$.

H_R is minimum for $a = L/4$.

$$H_{R_{min}} = \beta - \alpha^2 + \alpha^2\beta - \alpha^2\beta^2 + \ldots = \beta - \alpha^2/(1+\beta)$$

If the height of the reflected wave shall be zero,

$$\beta \text{ must be equal to } \alpha^2/(1+\beta) \qquad (2.2)$$

According to the equations of continuity

$$\alpha + \beta = 1 \qquad (2.3)$$

Equations 2.2 and 2.3 give $\alpha = 2/3$ and $\beta = 1/3$.

In the space between the two walls, the wave amplitude in distance x from the impermeable wall is

$\alpha \cos \theta + \alpha \cos (\theta + 4\pi x)/L +$
$\alpha\beta \cos (\theta + 4\pi a)/L +$
$\alpha\beta \cos (\theta + 2\pi(2a + 2x)/L +$
$\alpha\beta^2 \cos (\theta + 8\pi a)/L + \ldots$

When $a/L = 1/4$, the maximum agitation in the basin ($\theta = 0, x = 0$) is

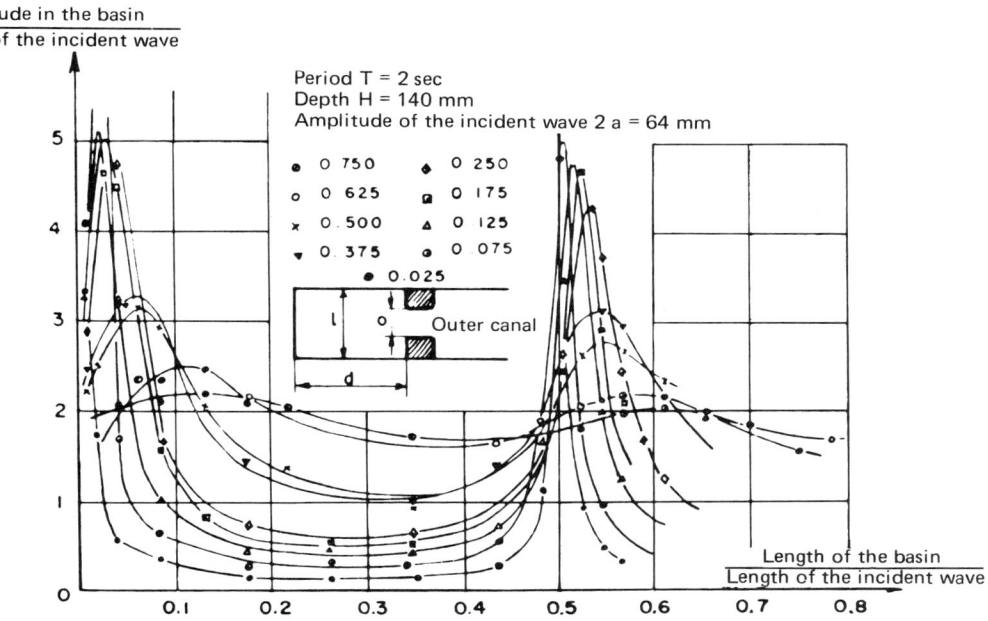

Figure 2.26. Wave agitation in a basin conditioned by an opening (23).

Preliminary experiments with reflection from permeable vertical walls carried out at the Hydraulic Laboratories, Copenhagen (5), showed that k for wave motion must be much greater. This is not surprising because the oscillating motion of water in the waves is entirely different from unidirectional motion.

When $\beta = 1/3$ and $H/d = 0.2$, one has

$$k' (s/b)^{4/3} = 35$$

The earlier mentioned preliminary experiments indicate least reflection for $s = b$ which gives $k' = 35$.

If $\alpha = 2/3$ and $\beta = 1/3$ and comparison is made with expression 2.4, one finds that the maximum agitation between the two walls is the same as the height of the incident wave.

Reference 23 mentions experiments carried out in France. Results are indicated in Figure 2.26. Even though the conditions in Figure 2.25 cannot be compared directly to those in Figure 2.26, it is interesting that the permeability, when the maximum agitation in the space between the two walls equals the height of the incident wave and $a = L/4$, is 30 to 50%. This confirms the results in Denmark and shows that the loss coefficient $k'(s/b)^{4/3} = k$ must be much greater in this special case of wave motion than with unidirectional flow.

As explained in Reference 5, this principle was used in the design and construction of a NATO naval port at Korsor, located in the Great Belt in the Baltic in Denmark. The most exposed jetty was provided with traps arranged in a sawtooth shape in the rubble-mound jetty (see Figure 2.27). A special "trap" in the form of a caisson with a permeable front wall is mentioned in Reference 19 and in Chapter 3. This jetty was built at Comeau in Canada and has proven successful even under freezing conditions. Another device consisting of clusters of pipes of unequal length placed in the direction of wave propagation is mentioned in

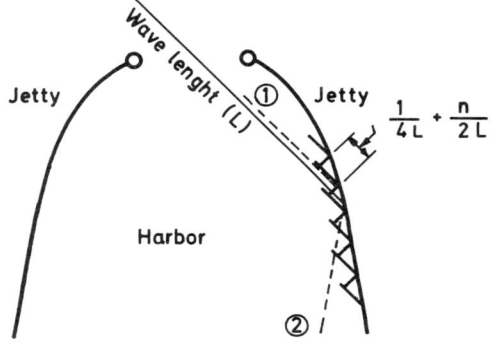

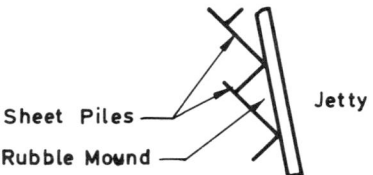

① Reflected with wave traps.
② Reflected without wave traps.

Figure 2.27. Schematic diagram of wave traps (5).

Reference 17. It confuses movement of water in the oscillating wave motion by phase displacement and causes loss of wave energy by friction and turbulence.

It is well known that long parallel jetties bordering an entrance channel to a port or bay have a pronounced energy absorbing effect by energy flux from the middle of the channel toward the sides. Figure 2.28 shows a photograph of model experiments of a tidal entrance in Massachusetts. Wave action is calmed partly by a front port and partly by the energy absorption of the two parallel rubble-mound jetties and revetments which lead to the inner port. Energy absorption in a trapezoidal channel is discussed in Reference 9. Of particular interest in this respect is the wave reflection which occurs when waves are hitting a vertical or sloping wall under an angle. Experiemnts on reflection of solitary waves are mentioned in Reference 7. The conclusion of this report may be summarized as follows:

For vertical walls three types of reflection occurred (Figure 2.29):

1. angle between wave crest and perpendicular to wall, $i < 20°$, no reflection but a wave bent at right angle at the wall,
2. $20° < i < 45°$, Mach type reflection with a bent stem at the wall and some reflection,
3. $i > 45°$, no stem at the wall and normal reflection develops.

When a sloping wall is introduced, the situation becomes more complex. If β is the angle between vertical and horizontal, the situation described in Figure 2.30 develops. It may be noted that β had to be about $65°$ or steeper to obtain a regular reflected wave. For walls of slope between approximately $20°$ and $65°$, the incident wave caused a series of ship-wave type curved ripples when the angle of incidence was less than approximately $10°$ to $25°$. These ripples were caused by backflow of water. When the angle of incidence was above $25°$, the curved envelope of ripples became higher; but if β was less than $65°$, the envelope still remained curved, thus differing from the straight reflected wave observed in the case of steep walls with $\beta \geq 65°$

From the above it follows that in a relatively narrow and long protected navigation channel like most American tidal navigation inlets, there is very little reflection from the sides because waves usually enter the inlet entrance with a direction of propagation which is not very different from the direction of the inlet channel. The energy absorption is therefore rather extensive. However, the question may be raised of whether it may be a more economic and less space-consuming way of absorbing energy than by a rubble mound.

Investigations by Battjes (2) describe a study on the attenuation of water waves in a rectangular (vertical wall) channel, the side walls of which have been provided with regularly spaced vertical roughness strips (Figure 2.31). Such strips were found to be highly effective as wave energy

Figure 2.28. Model experiments on absorption of wave energy in tidal inlet (Horseneck Beach, Mass., University of Florida).

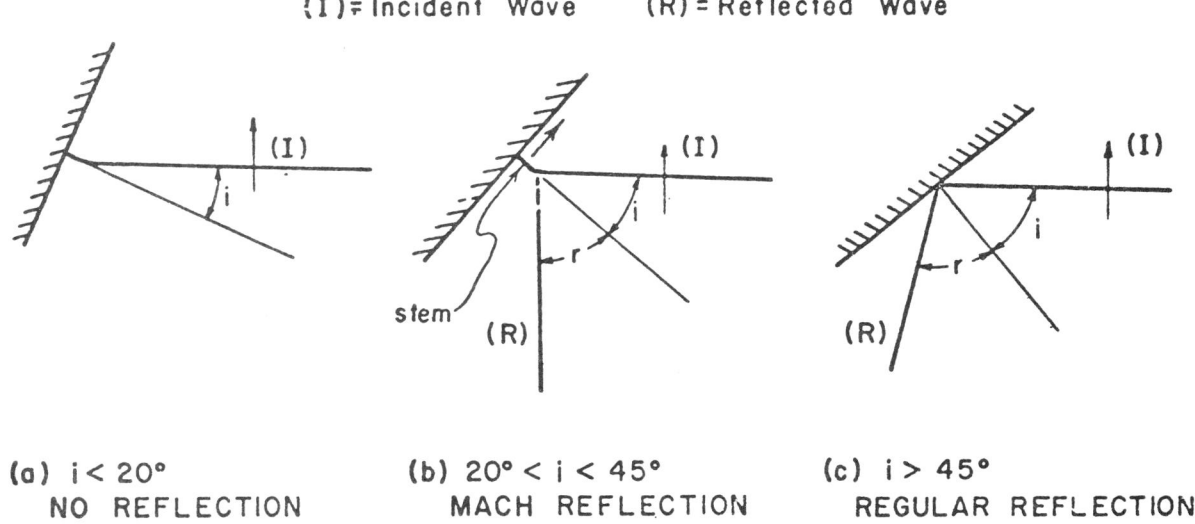

Figure 2.29. Reflection of a solitary wave with vertical wall (7).

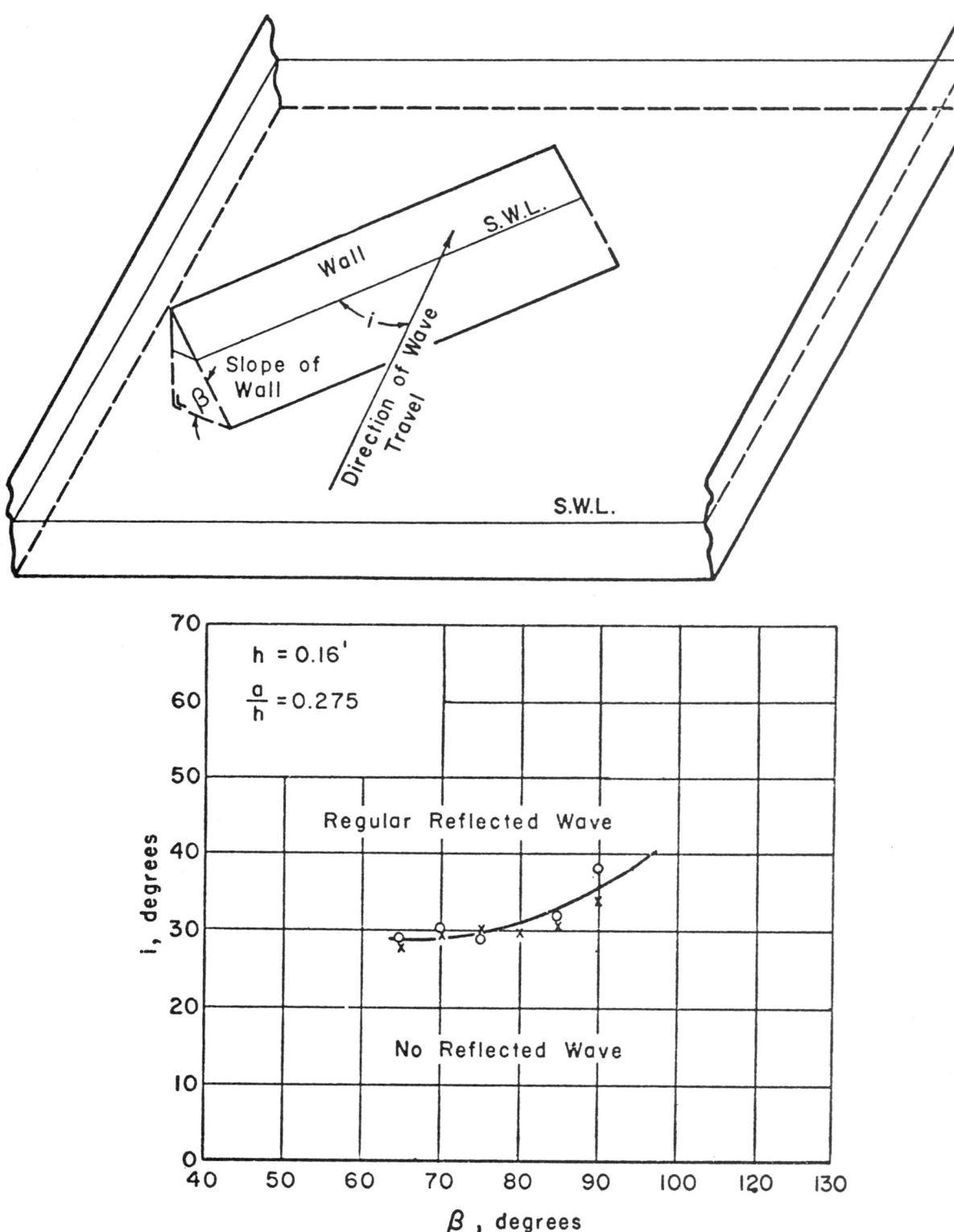

Figure 2.30. Reflection of solitary wave at sloping wall (7).

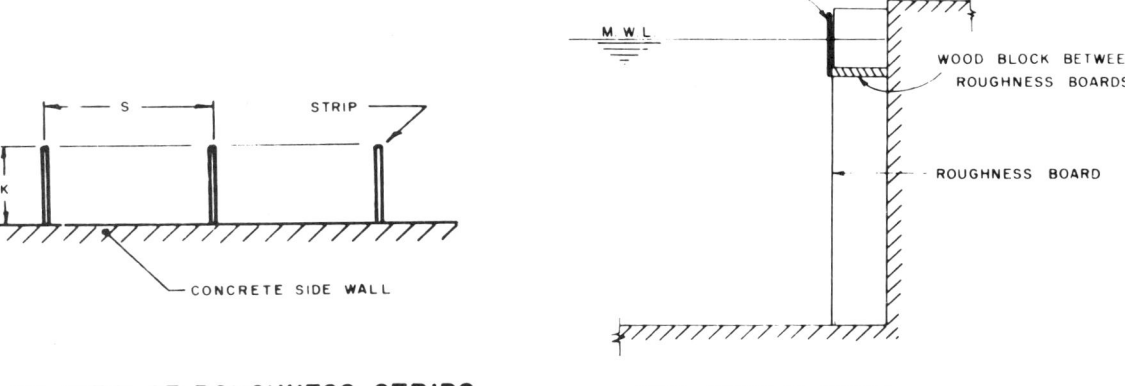

Figure 2.31. Roughness strips in a wave channel (2).

absorbers. A dimensionless resistance coefficient could be deduced from attenuation data. This coefficient is mainly a function of the ratio of horizontal orbit diameter to roughness height. The roughness strips, when compared to wave dampers using the resonance principle, appeared to cover a great portion of the wave frequency spectrum.

The conclusion of Battjes' paper reads as follows:

1. The flux of energy perpendicular to the direction of wave propagation takes place mainly by a large-scale momentum exchange caused by transversal currents which, in turn, are caused by friction elements, e.g., strips at the side walls, which deflect the flow from a direction parallel to the wall to a direction nearly perpendicular to it.
2. Vertical strips at the side walls as used in this study proved to be very effective as wave damping devices.
3. The drag coefficient, C_D, of the strips (drag force = $C_D \frac{1}{2} \rho u^2$, u = water velocity) was found to be a function of amplitude and roughness spacing, both in relation to the roughness height, or $C_D = f(a/k, s/k)$.
4. The unsteady-state drag coefficient may be considerably more than the steady-state value for the same Reynolds number, the ratio depending upon a/k.
5. The effectiveness of strips as wave dampers decreases sharply when resonance occurs in the space between the strips.
6. Strips may provide a good alternative for resonators as wave dampers inasmuch as they are effective over the whole width of the spectrum except near resonance, while just the reverse in the case for resonators.

Figure 2.32 shows the effect of roughness strips in Battjes' experiments. To establish the relationship $C_D = f(a/k, s/k)$ more fully and accurately, further investigations are desirable and each practical case should be investigated separately.

Long period waves

It is impossible to avoid the penetration of long period waves (from 30 seconds and up) into a harbor—unless the entrance is closed! These waves include incidental seiche waves and surge waves caused by wind gustiness or steep barometric gradients. Also included are seismic disturbances of tsunami-type and "surf beats" caused by irregular wave breaking and return of energy from the shore. Long period waves from the ocean may be trapped on the continental shelf and may then continue operating long after the actual input of

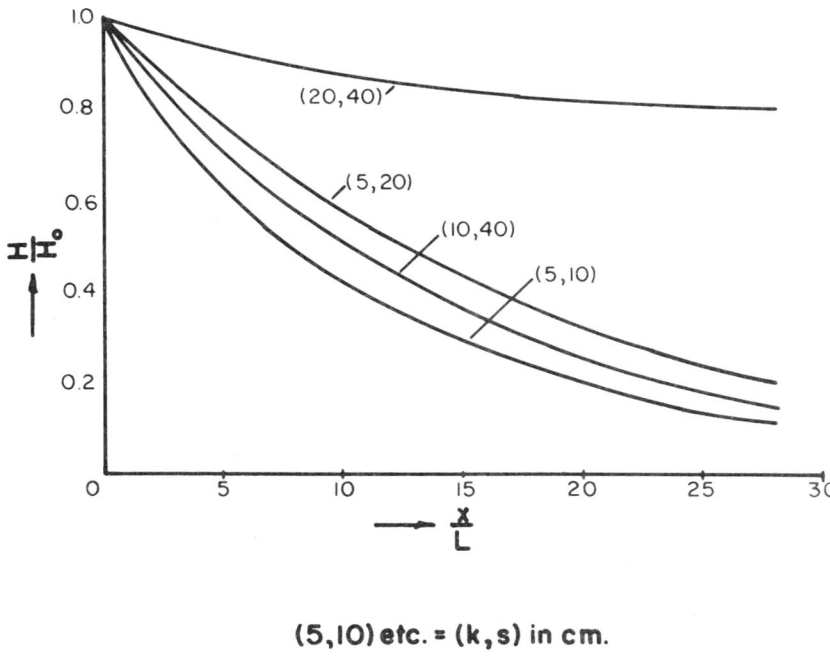

(5,10) etc. = (k,s) in cm.

T = 0.80 sec.

Figure 2.32. The effect of roughness strips as function of K and s in Figure 3.22 (2).

wave energy from the open ocean has ceased. However, long waves in harbors may also come into existence because currents of varying intensity pass the harbor entrance, thereby setting up pressure variations at the entrance and generating alternating Karman vortices. A large ship often causes seiches when leaving or entering the port.

Problems of long wave activity are usually much tougher to handle than short wave problems. Adverse effects by long period waves in port basins may be eliminated to a considerable extent by avoiding natural conditions and basin geometry which will encourage resonance phenomena. This question may be solved by computations and/or experiments as discussed by Dr. Le Méhauté in the Proceedings of Seminars in Ocean Engineering, University of Hawaii, 1970. His conclusion is that theoretical and numerical methods tend to be more suitable for investigating long waves, while scale models are more reliable tools for studying the action by wind waves.

Figure 2.33 was taken from Basil Wilson's article (46) and gives a striking example of surge wave action in the Table Bay Harbor. Note that the amplification factor (actual wave height in harbor divided by height of incident wave) is as high as almost 10 in the innermost basin.

If breakwaters are built in areas subjected to long waves, they should be as impermeable for water as possible. Many rubble-mound breakwaters are too transparent to the very long waves. As mentioned by Le Méhauté (25) in "Harbor design: Scale model or computer" of the Proceedings from the University of Hawaii Seminars (1970), more wave energy of importance actually arrives within the Los Angeles Harbor through the breakwater than through the harbor entrance. Needless to say, such breakwaters are transparent in both direc-

Port Navigation 45

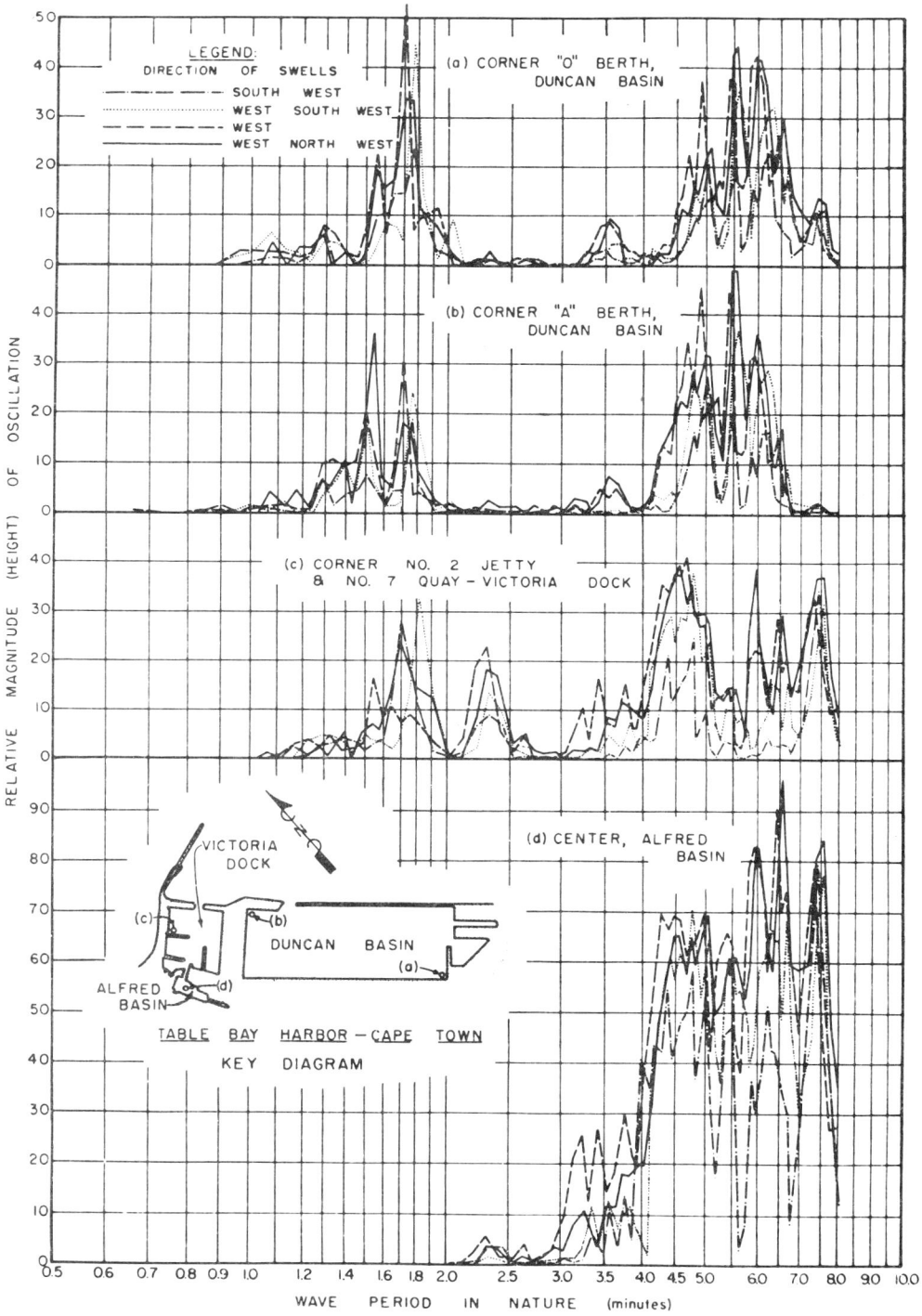

Figure 2.33. Experimental spectra of wave heights, Table Bay Harbor, Cape Town (46).

tions, and basins in the immediate vicinity of the breakwaters are not able to trap large amounts of wave energy. Consequently the problem of resonance only exists in inner basins. It is therefore still important to limit the input of wave energy and to do that, breakwaters must be impermeable even though this may result in more seiche action in the outer port. On the other hand, essentially impervious breakwaters may allow internal basins, berths and quays to be built transparent to avoid local complications of the magnitude demonstrated in Figure 2.33. Rubble-mount walls and even gently sloping beaches are ineffective for energy absorption with long waves. They simply reflect most, if not all, of the energy untouched. As pointed out by Le Méhauté, the solutions to the problem are (a) mismatching the natural frequency of harbor oscillation with the largest spectral components of the incident waves, (b) mismatching the characteristics of successive harbor basins and (c) leaking of trapped energy out of a basin subject to resonance phenomena by means of a large pipe or channel through which the crest of the long waves "flow out" and through which the trough of the long wave provides the "refill."

Transportable breakwaters

P.S. Bulson (6) reviewed this subject rather thoroughly and included floating breakwaters of various design—hydraulic as well as pneumatic breakwaters, etc.—in his study. His conclusion is that none of the present floating breakwater designs are very promising and that research has produced no obvious breakthrough in the field of transportable breakwaters. The best type seems to be the pontoon. However, it is apparent that a floating breakwater of practical dimensions is of little actual value when wave periods exceed about 6 to 7 seconds. They are best for periods less than 5 seconds and for the steep waves. The geometry of a normal pontoon type breakwater is important for its function. As explained in Reference 21, the trapezoidal cross-section with the longest side down is best. Certain devices such as horizontal antiheave plates and vertical antiroll plates will be able to increase efficiency. So will special geometrical shapes like double module pontoons, twin cylinders, A-frames, etc., as reported in a comprehensive study on floating breakwaters carried out in Canada (31). Economy still does not speak loudly in favor of transportable breakwaters for damping of ocean waves. For shorter waves as they occur in fjords and closed bays, however, they may be effective if periods are < about 6 seconds. Old tankers and other wide-beam vessels may find limited use as floating breakwaters.

Conclusion

In conclusion it may be stated that harbor wave hydraulics is a growing field. Further development will probably concentrate mainly on predicting any type of wave action by computation using modern computer equipment. In addition, increased application of various energy absorbing devices to avoid reflection and storage of wave energy in basins is likely.

References

1. Bailey, S.C. 1949. "The construction of harbours." *The Dock and Harbour Authority* 30 (Aug.).
2. Battjes, J.A. 1965. "Wave attenuation in a channel with roughened sides." *Engineering Progress at the University of Florida* 19(7).
3. Beach Erosion Board. 1952. *Reflection of Solitary Waves*. Tech Memo 11. U.S. Army Corp. of Engineers.
4. Bruun, P. 1953. "Breakwaters for coastal protection." *Proceedings of 18th Congress of PIANC* s II – c 1. Brussels.
5. ____. 1956. "Destruction of wave energy by vertical walls." *ASCE Journal of the Waterways and Harbors Division* 82(WW1-912):1-13.
6. Bulson, P.S. 1967. "Transportable breakwaters." *The Dock and Harbour Authority* 48(June):41-45.
7. Chen, T.C. 1961. *Experimental Study on the Solitary Wave Reflection along a Straight Sloped Wall of Oblique Angle of Incidence.* Tech Memo 124. Beach Erosion Board, U.S. Army Corps of Engineers.
8. Cornick, H.F. 1958. *Dock and Harbour Engi-*

neering, vol. 1. London: Charles Griffin and Co. Ltd.
9. Dai Yin-Ben. 1963. *Attenuation of Waves in Trapezoidal Channels*. University of California, Berkeley: Hydraulic Engineering Laboratory.
10. Dickson, Capt. A.F. 1960. "Navigation of tankers through channels." *PIANC Bulletin* 1:85-99.
11. Duncan Hay. 1968. "Harbour entrances, channels and turning basins." *The Dock and Harbour Authority* 4 (Jan.): 269-76.
12. Eisiminger, S.K. 1953. "Widening and deepening the Columbia and Willamette Rivers." *The Dock and Harbour Authority* 34(Feb.): 327-30.
13. Greslau et Mahe. 1955. "Etude du coefficient de reflexion d'une houle sur un obstacle constitué par un plan incliné." *Coastal Engineering* (5):68-84.
14. Grothaus, W., and Ripley, D.M. 1958. "St. Lawrence Seaway, 1958, '27 ft. canals and channels'." *ASCE Journal of the Waterways and Harbors Division* 84(WW1):1:22.
15. Healy, John J. 1953. "Wave damping effect of beaches." *Proceedings of Minnesota International Hydraulic Convention*. pp. 213-20.
16. International Navigation Congress. 1957. "Origin and effects of long period waves in port." *Proceedings of the 19th Congress* s II – c 1. London.
17. Ippen, A.T., and Bourodimos, E.C. 1964. *Breakwater Characteristics of Open-Tube System*. Report 73. MIT: Hydrodynamics Laboratory.
18. Irribarren and Nogales Y Olano. 1949. "Penetration de l'agitation dans les ports, moyens de la prévoir et de la combattre." *Essais de Laboratoire* 17e, s II – c 4:31-81. Losbonne: Congres International de Navigation.
19. Jarlan, G.E. 1961. "A perforated vertical wall breakwater." *The Dock and Harbour Authority* 42(Apr.):394-98.
20. Johnson, J.W. 1957. "Ship waves in navigation channels." *Proceedings of 6th Conference on Coastal Engineering* (Dec.). Miami.
21. Kato, J., et al. 1969. "Damping effect of floating breakwater." *ASCE Journal of the Waterways and Harbors Division* 95(WW3):337-44.
22. Lee, C.A., and Bowers, C.E.; Reeves, J.E., and Bourquard, E.H. 1949. "Panama Canal–the sea level project." *ASCE Transactions* 114(5 and 6).
23. Le Méhauté, B. 1955. "Two-dimensional seiche in a basin subjected to incident waves." *Coastal Engineering* (5):119-50.
24. ____. 1962. "Theory of wave agitation in a harbor." *ASCE Transactions* 127(3313):364-83.
25. ____. 1970. "Harbor design: scale model or computer." *Proceedings of Seminar in Ocean Engineering*. Honolulu: University of Hawaii.
26. Miche, M. 1944. Mouvement ondulatoires de la mer en profondeur constante ou decroissante." *Annales des Ponts et Chaussées*. pp. 25-78, 270-92, 369-406.
27. ____. 1951. "Le pouvoir réfléchissant des ouvrages maritimes." *Annales des Ponts et Chaussées* 121e(3):285-319.
28. Miles, J., and Munk, W. 1961. "Harbor paradox." *ASCE Journal of the Waterways and Harbors Division* 87 (WW3):111-130.
29. Minikin, R.R. 1963. *Winds, Waves and Maritime Structures*. 2nd ed. London: Charles Griffin and Co. Ltd.
30. Newland, C.A. 1959. "Large tankers and port facilities." *The Port Engineer* 8(4):14-15.
31. Ofuya, A.O. *On Floating Breakwaters*. Report 60. Queens University, Kingston, Ontario: Department of Civil Engineering.
32. Permanent International Association of Navigation Congresses. 1961. *Proceedings of 20th Congress of PIANC*. General Report s II – s 2. Baltimore.
33. ____. 1969. *The Problem of Bedload in Canalized Rivers and in Sections of a Partially canalized Waterway, in Particular at the Mouth of River* s I – s 5.
34. Quinn, A. De F. 1961. *Design and Construction of Ports and Marine Structures*. New York: McGraw-Hill Book Company, Inc.

35. Raichlen, F. 1966. *Estuary and Coastline Hydrodynamics.* Edited by A. Ippen. New York: McGraw-Hill Book Company, Inc.
36. Schijf, M.J.B. 1949. *Proceedings of 17th Congress of PIANC* s I – c 2. See also, *Proceedings of 18th congress of PIANC* s I – c 1:61-79.
37. Sorensen, R.M. 1966. *Ship Waves.* Tech Report HEL-12-2. University of California, Berkeley: Hydraulics Engineering Laboratory.
38. Thijsse, J.T., and Schumaker, H. 1951. Figure 3.10. Bulletin 2. Beach Erosion Board, U.S. Army Corps of Engineers.
39. Thorn, R.B. 1960. *The Design of Sea Defence Work.* London: Butterworth and Co. Ltd.
40. "Trends in channel improvement and vessel construction." *The Dock and Harbour Authority* 39(Dec.):248-51.
41. U.S. Army Corps of Engineers. 1959. *Bibliography on Tidal Hydraulics.* Supplement 3, Report 2(May). Vicksburg.
42. ___. 1965. "Tidal hydraulics." *Engineering Manual* (Aug):1110-607.
43. U.S. Navy. 1948. *The Performance of Model Ships in Restricted Channels in Relation to the Design of a Ship Canal.* Report 601 on David Taylor Model Basin.
44. ___. 1954. *Waterfront and Harbor Facilities.* TP-pw-8.
45. Valembois, Jr. 1954. "Etude de l'action d'ouvrages resonants sur la propagation de la houle." *Proceedings of Minnesota International Hydraulic Convention.* pp. 193-99.
46. Wilson, B. 1957. "Origin and effects of long period waves in ports." *Proceedings of 19th Congress of PIANC.* sII – c1.
47. Wilson, B., and Torum, A. 1968. *The Tsunami of the Alaska Earthquake, Engineering Evaluation.* Tech Memo 25. Coastal Engineering Research Center, U.S. Army Corps of Engineers.
48. Wilson, B.W., Hendrickson, J.A., and Kilmer, R.E. 1965. *Feasibility Study for a Surge-Action Model of Monterey Harbor, Cal.* Waterways Experiment Station, U.S. Army Corps of Engineers.
49. Yoshimura, Yoshio. 1968. "Wave forecast for harbor construction." *Proceedings of the 5th International Harbor Congress.* Antwerp.

3 planning and layout of ports breakwaters, jetties and piers

Port structures include breakwaters, jetties, open-sea piers, quays, wharves, harbor piers and special installations like container and roll-on roll-off berths, ferry berths and terminals for oil and ore. Development of structures in port engineering is closely related to the overall development of navigational and transport technological aspects. Deeper drafts require deeper approach channels which do not necessarily need to be protected, but their location and geometry must be related to actual conditions of exposure by winds, waves, currents and sedimentation. Chapter 2 mentions navigation and hydraulic aspects; Chapters 6, 7 and 8, sediment transport problems. Berths must be located in protected areas whether protection is provided by nature or has to be provided by man. Open-sea loading or unloading facilities associated with buoys, fixed or floating platforms are usually placed in areas which are not too exposed; e.g., in a bay (St. Johns, New Brunswick, Canada) or in a sound (Inland Sea, Japan). The same is true for open-sea pier facilities like hammerhead oil piers. Such piers are usually provided with heavy dolphins and fenders to absorb impacts by the vessel during berthing maneuvers as well as under action by winds, currents and waves. But only relatively mild conditions by natural forces can be tolerated if the design shall be economical (see Chapter 4.)

Apart from oil transport, all bulk and general cargo transport must rely upon some protection to make loading and unloading vessels possible without risks of damage to vessel or berthing facility resulting from wave and/or current action during the loading or unloading process. And the only way in which current and wave action can be disclosed is by protective works like jetties, breakwaters, training walls and sea walls.

The following section reviews protective measures of various kinds using recent designs as examples. A few open-sea terminal facilities were mentioned in Chapter 1.

Breakwaters and Jetties

Breakwater and jetty are not entirely synonymous, and there is a difference in American and British definition of *jetty*. In the United States as well as in the United Kingdom, a *breakwater* is a structure protecting a harbor, anchorage or basin from waves, thereby preventing these from exerting their destructive influence upon the area enclosed for shipping reception. A *jetty* in the United States is a structure extending into a body of water to direct and confine the stream or tidal flow to a selected channel or to prevent shoaling. Jetties are built at the river mouth or bay entrance to help deepen and stabilize a channel and thus facilitate navigation. In the United Kingdom, *jetty* is synonymous with *wharf* and *pier*.

In order to avoid any confusion caused by the two terminologies, the term *breakwater* will be used.

Breakwaters

Basically, there are two main types of breakwaters: the *vertical* (or almost vertical) *wall type* which may be built of natural rock, masonry, wood, steel or concrete and the *sloping mound type* which may be built of rock, concrete or of rock/concrete/asphalt mixtures.

Most vertical walls are impermeable. Exceptions are the rock crib, which consists of a box of scattered pile sheets or boards filled with rock and the perforated vertical wall breakwater mentioned later.

Vertical Type Breakwaters

With a single breakwater, the Phoenicians built their famous open coast port at Tyre 4,000 to 5,000 years ago, using rectangular blocks tied together with cobber dowels to a vertical wall. Similar vertical designs were common in the nineteenth and in the beginning of the twentieth century.

Many mishaps proved the big weakness in this design. Collapses were caused partly by waves breaking directly onto the structure and partly by bottom scour in front of the jetty, causing it to overturn. Four hundred meters of the breakwater at the port of Algiers failed in 1934, and 700 meters of the breakwater at Catania failed in 1933. Both breakwaters consisted of a vertical wall of superimposed blocks based on a rubble stone foundation.

Although the two breakwaters were of similar design and caliber, the failures were brought about in entirely different ways due to essential differences in construction. Both breakwaters were built of massive concrete blocks of cyclopean proportions—in the case of Catania, 12 by 4 by 3.25 meters, and in the case of Algiers, 11 by about 4 meters square. These blocks, weighing 320 and 400 tons respectively, were set as headers transversely in the breakwaters, their ends forming the inner and outer faces of the wall. However, where the blocks at Catania were simply superimposed without bedding or bonding, those at Algiers were provided with internal hollow shafts or wells which, on completion of the wall to full height, were filled with concrete reinforced by steel bars so as to form a coherent structure from base to coping. As might be expected under such conditions, the breakwater at Catania failed by the blocks sliding over one another in successive courses; the breakwater at Algiers collapsed as a whole—in intact vertical sections before fracturing and disintegrating, the rubble mound being undermined through wave action and the erosion of a deep trench in the soft sea bed of sand and mud at the foot of the wall. The failure at Catania was very similar to the failure at Genova, mentioned later.

In order to avoid such failures, the great force involved in a breaking wave must be absorbed—or better, be avoided—and adequate scour protection should be provided at the foot or toe. The latter calls for careful planning including hydraulic model experiments and experience.

Wave Forces on a Vertical Wall Breakwater

The main drawback with many similar walls is the high pressure of waves breaking on the wall. Numerous publications have been written about wave forces on vertical walls. Sainflou presented a general formula for the pressure of a standing wave on a vertical wall (see References 35, pp. 49-56, and 8, vol. 2, pp. 77-82).

Figure 3.1 depicts Sainflou's method of computing forces caused by nonbreaking waves. This method has been in general use for many years. The forces acting on the wall are used for calculating the stability against turnover or sliding. Forces acting on the foundation must not exceed certain allowable pressures or shear forces; settlings of the breakwater must not be excessive either. The sin-

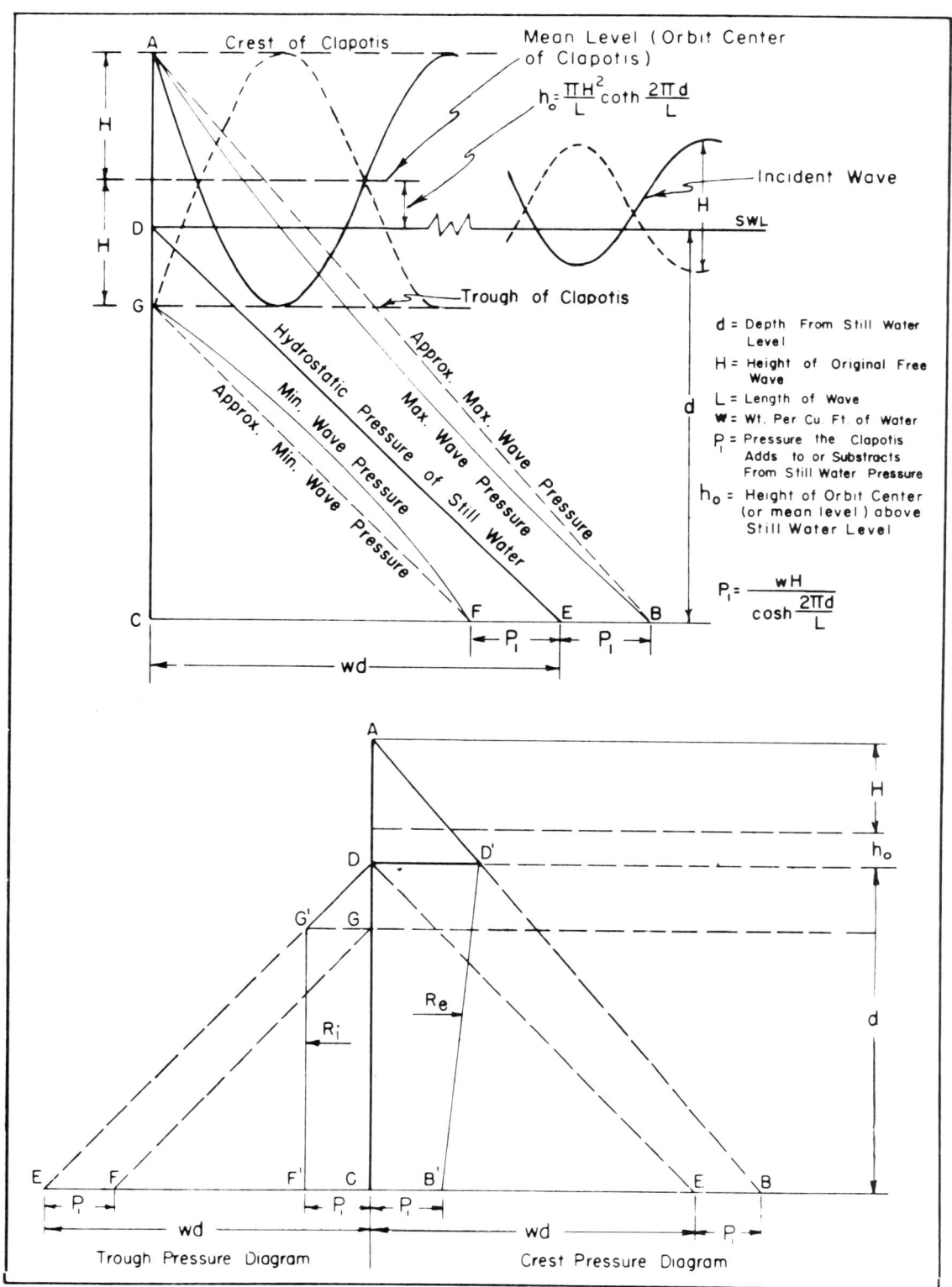

Figure 3.1. Clapotis on vertical wall; Sainflou's pressure diagram (35, 40).

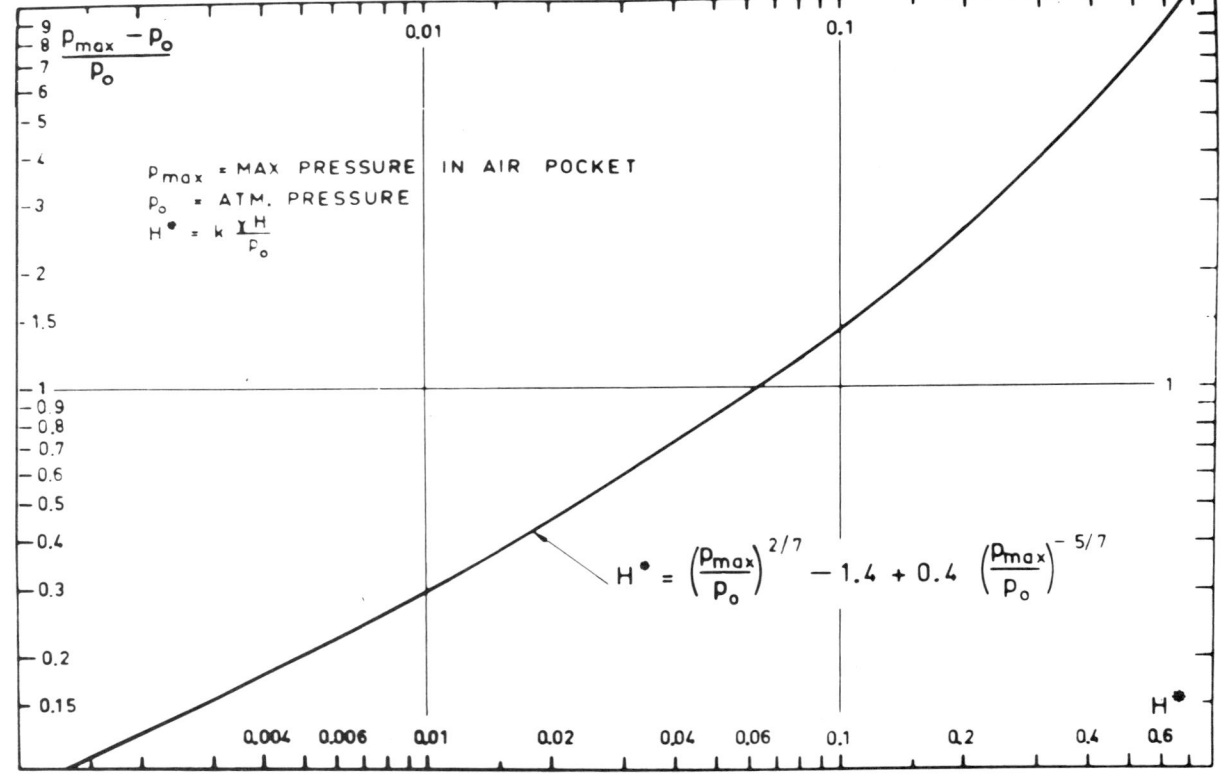

Figure 3.4. Compression model law (28).

the wall first, entrapping an air pocket and producing a compression shock.

The air pocket acts as a spring, the compression of which stops the horizontal movement of water. If the water velocities before "closure" are called C, the total impulse acting on the air pocket from $t = 0$ to $t = t_{rising}$ (maximum pressure in the air pocket) will equal the reduction $C M_{hy}$ of horizontal momentum of the water. M_{hy} is again the equivalent hydrodynamic mass.

In halting the forward motion, some of the kinetic energy of M_{hy} is transformed into pneumatic energy of the air pocket, while the rest is transferred to *vertical motion* of the water. This vertical motion is maximum at the wall and is quite small at a distance of approximately the water depth. A continued vertical motion, also resulting in a gradual rise of the water surface in front of the wall, is due to the nearly horizontal flow of water following behind the decelerated mass M_{hy}.

In addition to these vertical motions that have their analogies in the ventilated shock, the air that escapes through the thin wave crest may give an "explosive" water splash along the wall. The whole process is "an entanglement of velocity fields, acceleration fields, compressibilities, bubble rising and capillary forces, making an exact translation from model to prototype impossible" (28).

In order to obtain an approximate idea of the model law that should be applied, Lundgren considers the water piston model in Figure 3.3, comparing the values of p_{max} in the model and in the prototype. At the instant of closure ($t = 0$), geometric similarity between model and prototype can be assumed to exist. When p_{max} is reached,

Table 3.1. Pressure Scale as a Function of Linear Scale (28).

Linear scale	Pressure scale for a model peak pressure	
	1 t/m²	5 t/m²
10	3.5	6.0
20	5.4	12.4
50	10.0	48.0

the relative compression of the two air pockets is somewhat different, but, since the volume of the air pocket is only a fraction of the total mass of water involved, the different compressions induce only a minor distortion in the geometric similarity at p_{max}.

By expressing the assumption that the ratio of $E_{kinetic} = \rho g H^3$ and

$$E_{pneumatic} = \int_{p_o}^{p_{max}} (p - p_o) dA$$

is the same for model and prototype, Lundgren arrives at the expression:

$$r^{2/7} - 1.4 + 0.4(r^{-5/7}) = k(\gamma H/p_o) = H^*$$

where $r = p_{max}/p_o$, k is a dimensionless constant, and H^* is a dimensionless wave height.

This equation is called the "compression model law." Figure 3.4 shows H^* as a function of $(p_{max} - p_o)/p_o$. Figure 3.4 is entered with the value $p_{max, model}$ (in the model), giving the dimensionless height H^*_{model} in the model. The corresponding value H^*_{prot} for the prototype is obtained from H^*_{model} by multiplication with the linear scale ratio H_{prot}/H_{model}. Finally, the diagram is entered with the value H^*_{prot} which gives the value $p_{max, prot}$ in the prototype.

From Figure 3.4 it appears that around $H^* = 0.2$ the slope of the curve is 45°, and hence the maximum shock pressure (in excess of the atmospheric pressure) is proportional to the wave height. Therefore, in a region around $H^* = 0.2$, the compression model law gives the same result as the Froude law. For small values of H^*, the maximum shock pressure is proportional to $H^{1/2}$, and for the highest values of H^* it is proportional to $H^{7/2}$.

Table 3.1 gives two examples of the application of Figure 3.4. The model peak pressure is measured to be 1 t/m² (= 205 pounds per square feet). In the other, the model peak pressure is 5 t/m² (= 1,025 pounds per square feet). The values in the table are the ratios of the peak pressures in the prototype to the peak pressures in the model. Most of the values in the table are considerably smaller than those produced by Froude's law (= linear scale).

After the maximum has been reached, the pressure in the air pocket drops off again because some air escapes through the covering water and the air pocket expands. The expansion may go so far as to create a negative pressure in the pocket—a pressure less than corresponding to still water level. Some model tests with compression shocks have shown several (strongly damped) oscillations of the pressure in the pocket.

To interpret model tests, the following conclusion on compression shocks is offered. Unless a more detailed analysis is carried out, the values of impulses can be transferred from model to prototype by means of Froude's law, whereas the compression model law applies approximately to the maximum pressures. This will give pressures a little on the conservative side if the concentration of bubbles entrained in the water is higher in the prototype than in the model.

The paper by Führböter et al. in Reference 32 deals, among other things, with destruction of a structure in relation to the duration and direction of swells and waves. The problem was considered statistically. Tests using a water jet which was suddenly directed toward a plate revealed that even under otherwise entirely equal experimental conditions there occurred pronounced differences for p_{max} caused not only by the air retention or

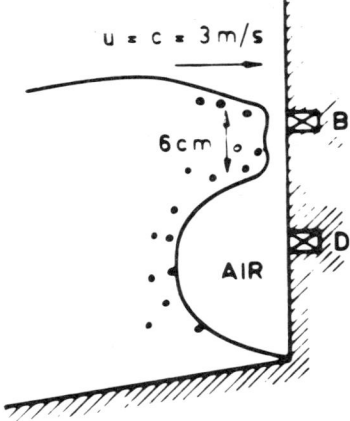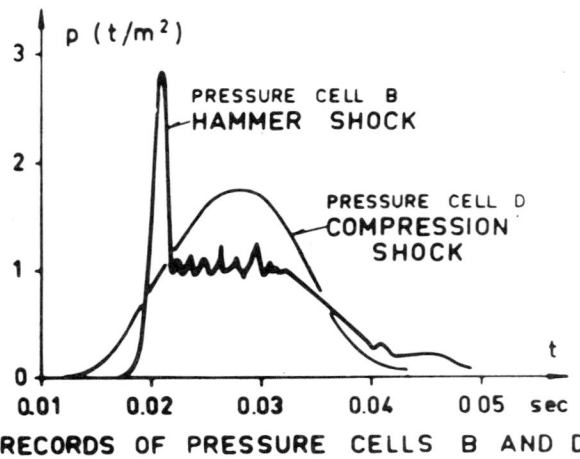

Figure 3.5. Hammer shock (28).

pocket (mentioned above) but also by the area of impact being continually subjected to incidental variations. It was further demonstrated that the frequency distribution could be approximated to Gauss's normal distribution by virtue of $\log p_{max}$. The measured p_{max} in the test described in Reference 32 exceeded by 10 times the magnitude of the pressure of the stationary jet condition.

When the forward pointing crest of a plunging breaker hits the wall as the introduction to a compression shock, it looks as if the wall is struck by a hammer (Figure 3.5). Hence this type of shock will be called a *hammer shock*. As an example Reference 28 mentions that the record of "pressure cell 8" gave $p_{max} = 2.8\ t/m^2$ and $t_{rising} \sim 0.001$ second. Hence the total impulse, per unit area, delivered by the sharp pointed hammer shock is about $i = 0.003\ ts/m^2$.

The water velocity was measured to be $u = c = 3\ m/s$. Thus, the impulse has been able to stop a hydrodynamic mass, per unit area, of

$$M_{hy} = i/u = 0.001\ t\ s^2/m^3.$$

With $\rho = 0.1\ t\ s^2/m^4$, the "thickness" of the hydrodynamic mass is

$b = M_{hy}/\rho = 0.01$ meter = 1 centimeter.

It follows from the rising time that the irregularity of the front face of the hammer has been of the order of magnitude of 1 centimeter. In extremely rare cases it is imaginable that the front face of the wave crest is so plane that a real *water hammer* occurs, that is, an elastic wave in the bubble-containing water. According to von Kármán's formula (46), the maximum pressure in a water hammer corresponding to the water velocity u is

$$p_{max} = \rho u c_e$$

where c_e is the sound velocity. If, for the case in Figure 3.5, we assume that $c_e = 100$ millimeters per second, the water hammer pressure would be found to be

$$p_{max} = 0.1(3)100 = 30\ t/m^2$$

which is an order of magnitude higher than that recorded on pressure cell 8.

Other results of research on shock pressures are mentioned in Reference 44 by the U.S. Waterways Experiment Station. The conclusion of the tests is that "shock pressures resulting from the impact between a solid and a liquid, as is the case of waves breaking against coastal structures, can best be described as a water hammer phenomenon where the compressibility of the liquid and the elasticity of the solid are the governing factors." The water hammer theory predicts the extreme magnitude of shock pressures mainly because it neglects the effect of air that might be entrapped between the solid and the liquid at the moment of impact. In practice, however, in most cases some air is present, and the compression of this air will result in shock pressures that are smaller in magnitude and possibly longer in duration than those predicted by the water hammer theory.

Shock pressures have a short duration and occur only at some spots on the solid surface. Therefore, they should not be considered for checking the stability of a coastal structure as a whole, and they may be absorbed by nonrigid structures. However, shock pressures are a governing factor in the selection of the material and thickness of the casing of rigid structures, such as steel caissons filled with concrete or with rock, since the pressures may cause cracks in the casing. Shock pressures may also affect the stability of structures that have natural frequencies within the range of duration of shock pressures.

The probability of satisfying the condition of a water hammer phenomenon is rather small. Therefore, the probable occurrence of shock pressures equal to different fractions of the pressures predicted by the water hammer theory should be considered in designing coastal structures.

Structures should be designed in such a manner that conditions leading to the occurrence of a water hammer phenomenon are decreased. For example, construction of coastal structures with a continuous vertical face is unfavorable; a structure with a sloping face is more desirable.

Another study by the Waterways Experiment Station (41) considered the ideal case of a smooth, rigid wall which was high enough to preclude overtopping. The most important finding of this study was that the maximum shock pressure was to be proportional to the one-third power of the deep-water wave energy in the first approximation over the entire range of data available from laboratory and prototype tests. However, the shock pressure exhibited wide scatter for seemingly identical conditions. In addition, relations were developed for the distribution of the shock pressure on the test wall. In Reference 41 it is concluded that, although the shock impulse is an important parameter in breakwater design, not enough data are available to make any conclusions other than that the shock impulse also tends to increase with increasing wave energy and is about 10% of the total impulse transferred to the wall. The shock impulse was also found to be fairly constant for given conditions; the higher pressures are associated with the shorter durations and vice versa.

The secondary pressure occurring after the shock pressure was also studied, and it was found that the secondary pressure is nearly equal to the clapotis pressure. The secondary pressure seemed to be fairly constant for similar wave conditions and did not exhibit the degree of scatter that was observed for shock pressures.

An important problem associated with the function of a breakwater under the action of a train of irregular waves is the movement or rocking of the breakwater. This problem was dealt with by Hayashi and Hattori (18) and may be summarized as follows.

The stability of breakwaters against sliding due to wave forces was examined using the expression $\mu W > p_{max}$, where μ is the coefficient of static friction; W, the submerged weight of the structures and p_{max}, the maximum resultant horizontal force of the wave exerted upon the structure. Theoretically, the criterion for wall stability should be $F < \mu W$, F being the shearing resistance which is equal to p minus (or plus) the inertia resistance of the wall. Calculations were made to obtain the time history of this shearing force by accounting for the slight sway or rocking of the wall caused by the initial shock of the breaking wave.

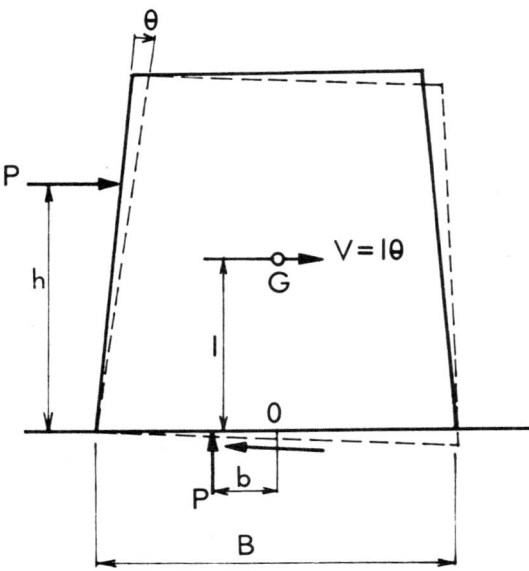

Figure 3.6. Sway of the wall (18).

The calculations show that the behavior of the shearing force depends on two parameters, λ and $\omega\tau$ when λ equals $h1/R^2$ (Figure 3.6), ω is the angular velocity of the rocking of the wall and τ equals half of the duration of the shock pressure. The shearing force caused by the shock pressure (*gifle*) exists even after the shock pressure is gone and is replaced by *bourrage* (sustained) pressure. When the bourrage pressure follows the gifle, the shearing force caused by the gifle is superimposed on that caused by the bourrage pressure.

In many practical cases, the value of λ is as large as or larger than 0.8. In such cases, the maximum shearing force caused by the gifle occurs after the gifle is gone—in the stage of the bourrage. The magnitude of this maximum is given by $2\pi I_s \lambda / T$, where I_s represents the impulse of the breaking wave and T, the period of rocking of the wall. When $\lambda < 0.6$, the maximum shearing force in most cases occurs at the peak of the gifle, its magnitude being given by $p_m [1 - \lambda (\sin \omega\tau / \omega\tau)]$, where p_m is the peak pressure of the gifle.

The angular velocity ω of the rocking of the wall is given by $\omega = M\sqrt{J/k}$ where J is the moment of wall inertia around Point 0 (Figure 3.6). In case of a rectangular wall section

$$\omega = \sqrt{[g\beta^2 (1 + \beta^2)/(18w)]} \, [\sqrt{(k/1)}]$$

where w is the weight of the wall per unit volume and β equals $B/2h_o$. According to Reference 16, the magnitudes of β, $2h_o$ and k may be assumed to be

$$\beta = 0.7 \text{ to } 1.3 \, ; \, 2h_0 = 5 \text{ to } 15 \text{ m}$$

$$k = 2 \text{ to } 20 \text{ (kg/cm}^2) \text{ /cm.}$$

With these magnitudes, the rocking period T, or $2\pi/\omega$, is estimated as follows: for a 5-meter high wall, $T = 0.07$ to 0.5 seconds; for a 10-meter high wall, $T = 0.1$ to 0.8 seconds; for a 15-meter high wall, $T = 0.1$ to 0.9 seconds.

The durations of the shock pressure recorded either at full scale experiments or at laboratories are given in Table 3.2 (18).

Assuming that the wave height to be used for the design of the breakwater is $H = 2$ to 6 meters, and if the Froude similarity is valid, the duration of shock pressure in prototype dimensions based on these laboratory experiments is $2T = 0.50$ to 0.90 seconds. This range agrees with the data on full scale experiments in Table 3.2.

Hayashi (18) shows how the above mentioned shearing forces by the gifle and by the bourrage or by combination of both are calculated.

One consequence of the results mentioned above is that vertical plane and impermeable walls are not very practical if subjected to high wave forces including shocks. Perforated permeable or irregular (nonplane) walls are preferred. An uneven surface of a vertical wall may be provided by steel sheet piling.

Where water is relatively shallow and waves not too high, the breakwater may consist of two parallel lines of sheet piling (irregular surface) with

Breakwaters and Jetties 59

Table 3.2. Duration of Shock Pressures.

Experiment	Place or Author	Duration (sec)	Wave height (m)
Full scale experiments	Port Dieppe	0.05	
	Port Haboro	0.07	
Laboratory experiments	Larras	0.01-0.02	0.095-0.14
	Denny	0.002	0.18-0.36
	Hayashi (18)	0.007-0.02	0.15-0.20
	Lundgren	0.002-0.007	0.05-0.10
	Nagai	0.015-0.03	0.10-0.25
	Mitsuyasy	0.02	0.10

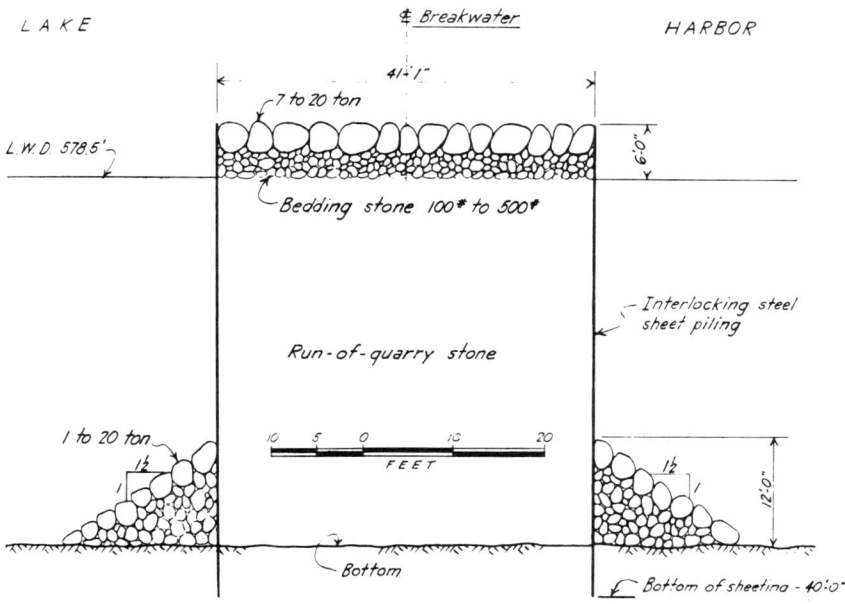

Figure 3.7. Cross-section of cellular sheet pile breakwater at Calumet, Lake Michigan (35).

a rock or granular fill in between with the sheet piling supported by steel walers and tie rods placed at or just above low-water level. Parallel lines of steel or concrete sheet piling are placed a distance apart equal to the water depth plus twice the wave height. The sheet piling in this type of construction is selected for its bending strength and usually with heavy rock or poured-in-place concrete, depending upon whether the structure is also to be used as a quay for docking ships.

Sheet pile cells have been used for temporary installations where they serve not only as a cofferdam to permit unwatering of the harbor but also to protect the construction of the harbor facilities

Figure 3.8. Circular reinforced concrete caissons, 12.5 meter diameter at Hanstholm, Denmark (27).

from the waves. Such an installation was used at Taconite Harbor on the north shore of Lake Superior. The cells, which were filled with sand to within 3 feet of the top, were extended to a height of 12 feet above lake level and were capped with a layer of heavy rock (35).

Sheet pile cells for breakwaters are generally the self-supporting type; each cell is stable by itself when filled with rock or other suitable material. The sheeting must extend to a sufficient depth below the bottom to prevent undermining of the cell by erosion of the bottom. The minimum depth of penetration is usually not less than 10 feet, unless the bottom is rock or other very hard material. It is customary to place riprap against the toe of the sheeting to protect the bottom against erosion. The top of the sheeting may extend to approximately twice the height of the maximum wave above high water, although it may terminate at or just above mean high water to be built up as a sea wall of poured-in-place concrete constructed to the full height. It may be capped with heavy rock, concrete blocks or a poured-in-place concrete slab.

Figure 3.7 (35) shows a cross-section through the cellular sheet pile breakwater at Calumet on Lake Michigan which is 5,000 feet long, and was constructed in 1935 as an extension of the existing timber-crib breakwater. The cells are 41 feet wide and the arcs have a radius of 38 feet 9 inches, which makes a rise of 5 feet. The end walls of each cell are circular arcs with a radius of 35 feet 6 inches and a 3-foot 6-inch rise. The sheeting is 46 feet long, driven through 2 feet of sand and 6 feet of hard clay. The cells are in 32 feet of water and their top is 6 feet above lake level, and are filled with crushed rock and capped with large armor stone.

A remarkable new caisson design (Figure 3.8) was used at the port of Hanstholm, recently completed on the very exposed Danish North Sea Coast (27). Round, reinforced 600-ton concrete caissons, 12.5 meters in diameter, were placed by a 1,200-ton gantry crane. The upper part of the breakwater is a 8.5-meter wave screen built of prefabricated concrete blocks. The advantage of having an uneven wall instead of a plane wall is obvious. Wave pressures will hardly ever occur over a longer section of the wall simultaneously, and the possibility of compression shocks and hammer effects by breaking waves is greatly reduced. A similar design—although not quite as sophisticated—has been used for the breakwaters for the new ore port, Burns Harbor, at Gary, Indiana, (completed 1970).

A very special design was used in Canada when a caisson breakwater having a vertical wall penetrated by holes was built in Comeau Bay in Canada (see Figure 3.29). The salient feature with this design (9, 21) is that the vertical wall facing the impact of the incident wave has circular holes amounting to 25% of the total surface. The diameter of each hole is 1/100th of the length of the striking wave. The interior chambers then function as a sponge absorbing part of the wave impact and

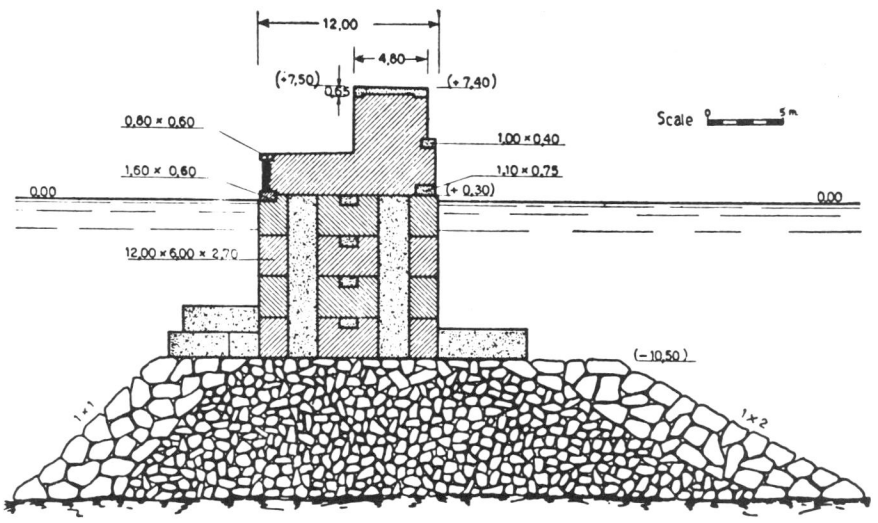

Figure 3.9. Section of outer breakwater, Genoa (8, volume 2).

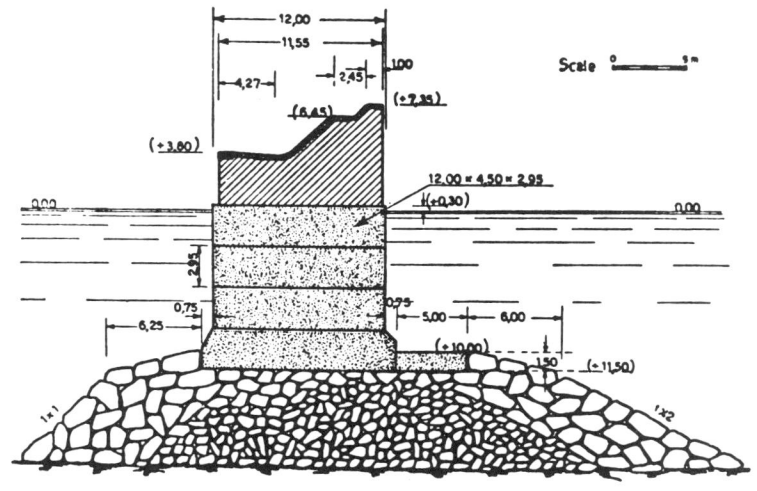

Figure 3.10. Section of western extension of outer breakwater, Genoa (8, volume 2).

water in the wave crest and releasing it through the holes at the wave troughs. The theory of this design by Jarlan, based on model experiments in Canada (21), does not differ much from the basic philosophy on wave traps mentioned in Chapter 2 (section on harbor hydraulics). The breakwater at Comeau has been very effective, and the holes are apparently not blocked by ice during the winter time which would decrease its efficiency as an energy absorber.

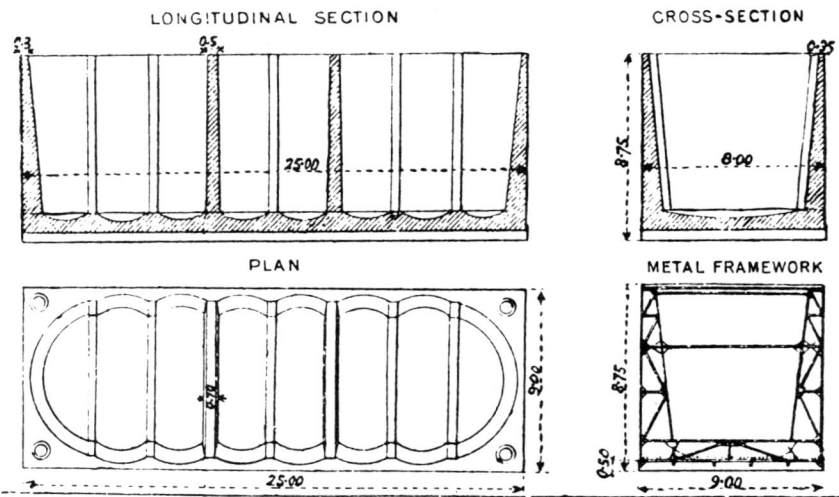

Figure 3.11. Caissons for jetty at Zeebrugge, Belgium (8, volume 2).

Composite Designs

The drawback clinging to vertical designs also gave rise to the development of the so-called *composite designs*. Figures 3.9 and 3.10 show two designs from Genoa, Italy. These breakwaters are examples of learning by very difficult experience for they have probably suffered more damage than any other breakwaters in the world. One major cause for the damage was their design and construction (before the year 1900) which seemed to invite damage. They were built so that under severe conditions breaking waves tended to hit the upper vertical wall directly.

The two designs (Figures 3.9 and 3.10, (8, vol. 2) are examples of improved but not fully satisfactory designs. Maximum wave heights may be 5 to 6 meters. In Figure 3.9, the base of the vertical wall is at −10.5 meters, where the rubble berm is protected along the foot of the wall by a row of blocks. However, immediately after the construction of the breakwater, it was found that even when storms were not excessively violent, very large columns of water rose high above the parapet. Consequently, the design of the breakwater was amended as shown in Figure 3.10. The wall at a level of −11.50 meters was constructed of 420-ton concrete blocks 12 by 4.5 by 2.95 meters, with the base protected by blocks forming a berm 5 meters wide. The depth of water at the berm was 9.5 meters.

However, waves breaking on the breakwater were apparent during most violent storms. During a great storm on February 19, 1955, 150 meters of wall-section was overtopped and sheared off (Figure 3.10). Later the gap opened to 450 meters. Examinations by divers showed that the top blocks and mass-concrete superstructure had cleanly slid into the harbor with the lower three courses of solid blocks and the apron block at the toe remaining in place, for the most part, undisturbed. Also damaged was the design (Figure 3.9) and a cellular-type block jetty which was broken gradually at many points under the heavy blows of the waves.

The unfortunate experience almost resulted in abandoning the composite type breakwater which was replaced by either fully vertical breakwaters like Figure 3.11 from Zeebrugge, Belgium (concrete-filled iron caisson), or mound type breakwaters like Figure 3.12 and those described in the following section. A few very special designs ap-

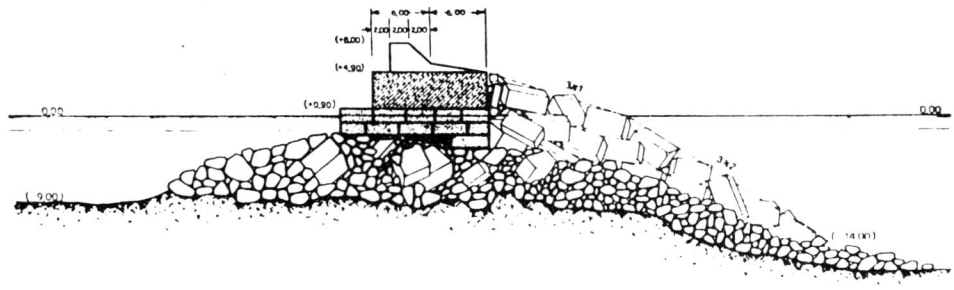

Figure 3.12. Composite mound type breakwater at Crotone, Calabria, Italy (8, volume 2).

peared on the breakwater arena. The double wall breakwater is an Italian design (14). Two parallel vertical wall breakwaters with space in between are built on very exposed shores. Reference 14 also mentions permeable breakwaters where wave reflection is split up in parts by permeable walls, stilling basins, weirs, etc., incorporated in the breakwater design.

Rubble-Mound Breakwaters

Some early breakwaters were formed by dumping stones in sizes that could be handled with available equipment. While this simple method still suffices where wave conditions are relatively mild, experience proved that in most situations great care must be taken in breakwater design. Stone sizes of the material available must be great enough to resist the wave forces so that the mound is not flattened during storms. There may also be considerable settlement of the sea bed under the load of the structure. In certain cases, this may be increased by the addition of the stone intended to make the sinkage. Therefore, stability may have to be secured by replacing poor bottom material with better material before rock material for the jetty is dumped.

The large volume of heavy rock involved in a rubble-mound jetty with stable slopes and the lack of proper equipment for placement of such rock initially made this design improbable and later less practical. Development of heavy construction equipment made it easier to overcome these difficulties. By the end of the nineteenth century an increasing number of rubble-mound jetties were built and considerable research work on rubble-mound structure has been done.

European practice may deviate from American practice in several respects, but it may carry results as good or better than American results under the circumstances given. Figure 3.13 shows a Danish rock-mound breakwater built of material left by glaciers about 20,000 years ago. This rock had been rounded by rough treatment and wear by ice. Used widely in Denmark for breakwater construction, the rounded, all-streamlined rock is more stable than quarried rock with its many edges and a geometry which increases the possibility for exertion by destructive forces. The rock, *sea stone*, is now mainly picked up on the sea bottom; sources of larger rock (> 2,000 pounds) are gradually running out causing Denmark to import quarried rock from Sweden.

Figure 3.14 shows a cross-section of a typical Norwegian rock jetty of quarried rock. In the case of a jetty at Arviksand, Norway, using 10 to 20-ton blocks, wave heights up to 8 meters (25 feet) could be expected. Blocks of up to almost 30 tons were dumped from trollies. The planned slope was 1:1.25, but as a result of wave action, the actual slope is approximately 1:1.5. Many breakwaters in Norway are exposed to considerable wave action although most ports are located in protected fjords. Heavy rock is therefore necessary for stability, but heavy equipment—like the 25-ton cranes now in use—was not available earlier. Breakwaters

64   Port Engineering

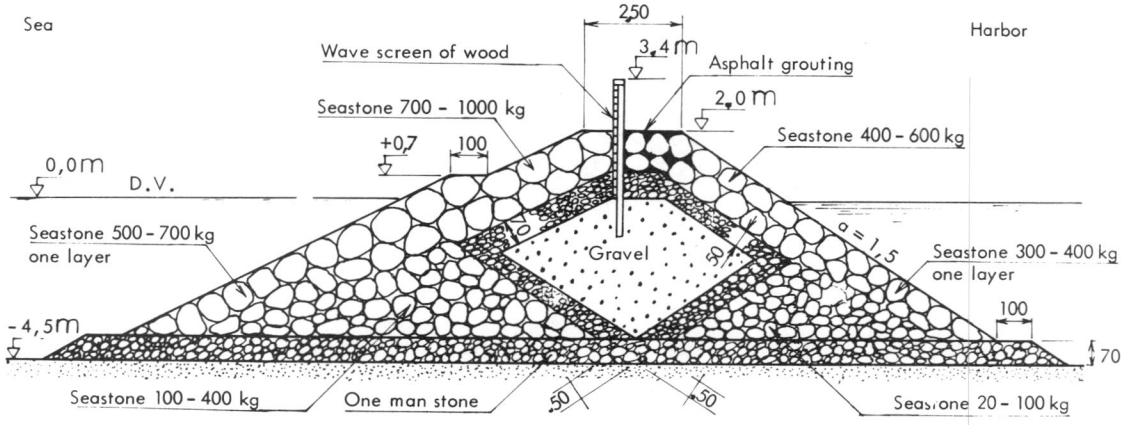

Figure 3.13. Typical Danish rock breakwater built of "seastones" (rock from the bottom of the sea of glacial origin).

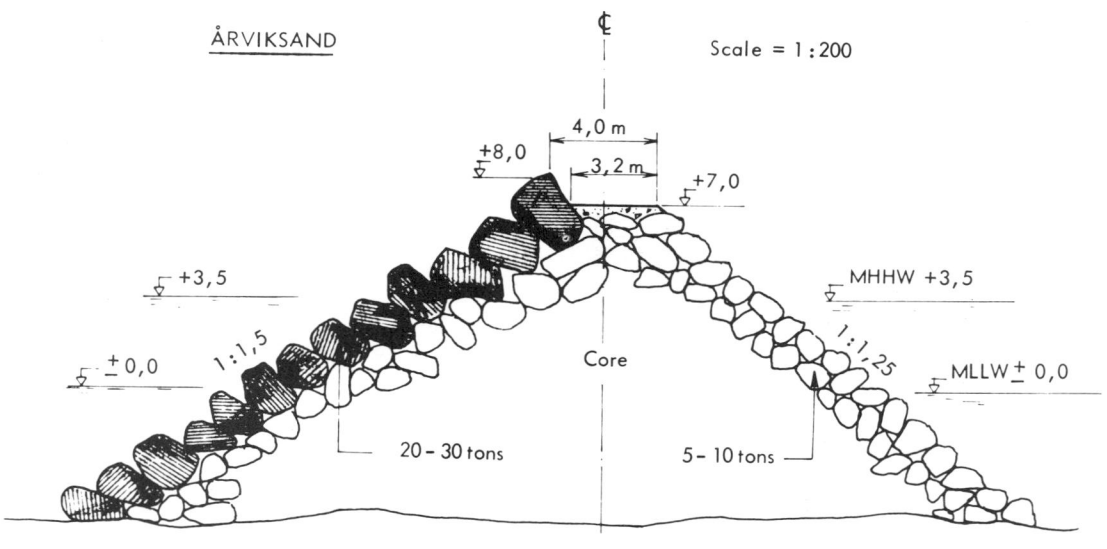

Figure 3.14. Cross-section of typical Norwegian breakwater.

were therefore (and some still are) built so that the core was first tipped from a dumping wagon on rails (now from dump trucks), and next heavy rock was tipped from trolleys. Great skill was developed to dump rock so that it came to rest exactly where it was wanted. Winching might be used to correct a "misfire." This procedure resulted in the initial slope being steeper than the final stable slope which gradually develops as a result of wave action. Surplus armor was therefore placed on the upper slope to supplement the lower slope. Blocksize usually varies from 5 to 10 tons. Because heavier blocks are difficult to handle, artificial concrete blocks like tetrapodes (see later) have been used at extreme locations in Norway (Berlevåg on the Arctic Sea).

Breakwaters and Jetties   65

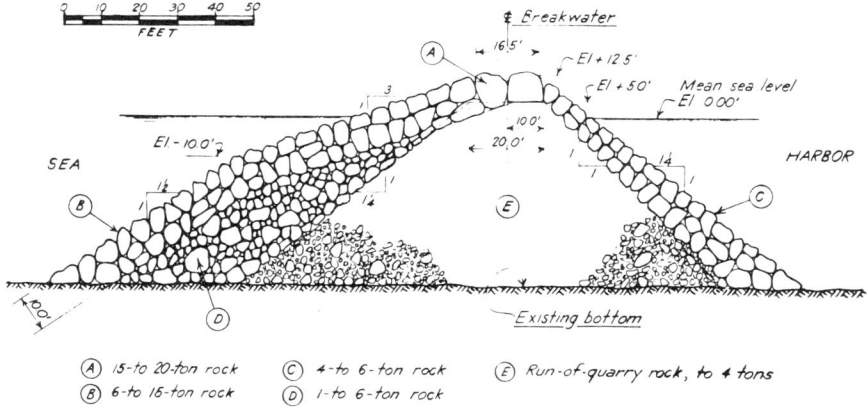

Figure 3.15. West breakwater, La Guaira (35).

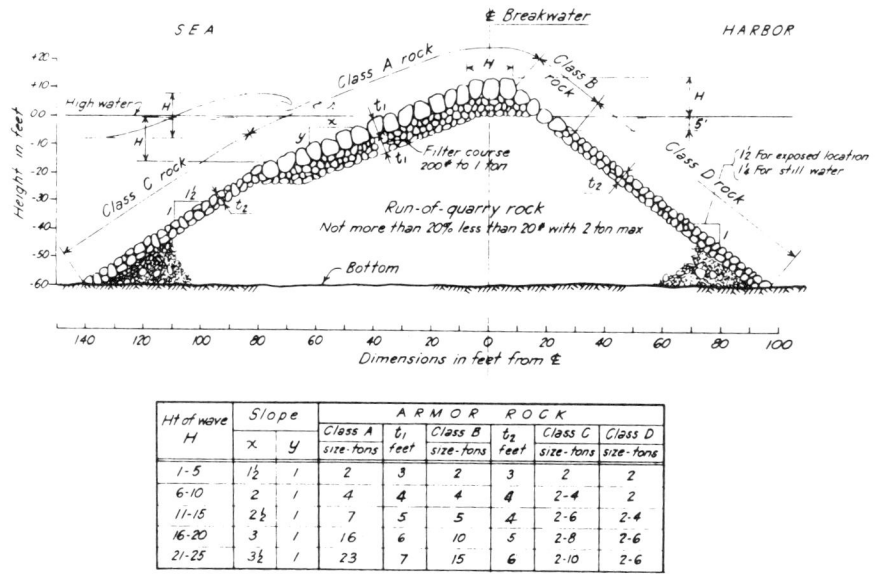

Ht of wave H	Slope x	Slope y	Class A size-tons	t_1 feet	Class B size-tons	t_2 feet	Class C size-tons	Class D size-tons
1-5	1½	1	2	3	2	3	2	2
6-10	2	1	4	4	4	4	2-4	2
11-15	2½	1	7	5	5	4	2-6	2-4
16-20	3	1	16	6	10	5	2-8	2-6
21-25	3½	1	23	7	15	6	2-10	2-6

Figure 3.16. Rock breakwater, layer type (35).

Figure 3.15 (35) shows a typical cross-section of the west breakwater of the Port of La Guaira, Venezuela, constructed in 1950 with equipment operating on the top of the core. Designed to withstand waves up to 20 feet, it has armor rock of basalt up to 20 tons. The core material, which was placed on a firm bottom, is run-of-quarry rock varying from 100 pounds to 4 tons. In order to provide adequate width at the core top for operating 20-ton Euclid trucks which transported rock from the quarry to the breakwater, the corner of the core material on the seaside was removed at the time of setting the armor rock to the required slope.

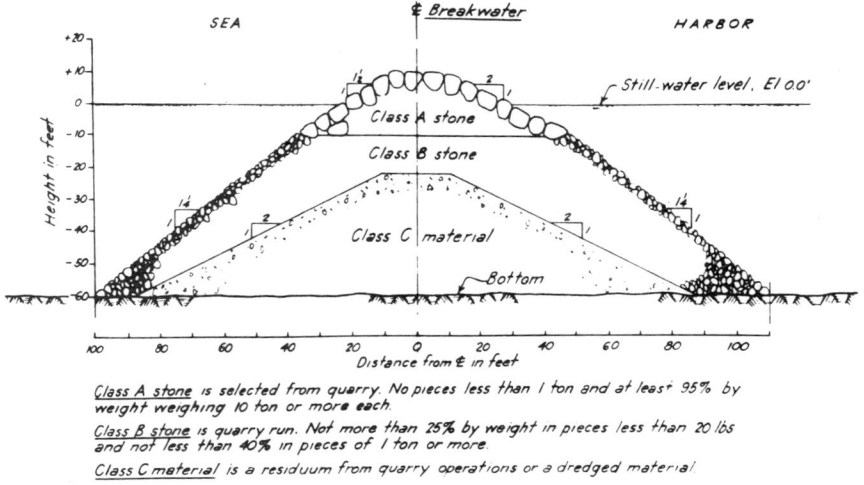

Class A stone is selected from quarry. No pieces less than 1 ton and at least 95% by weight weighing 10 ton or more each.
Class B stone is quarry run. Not more than 25% by weight in pieces less than 20 lbs and not less than 40% in pieces of 1 ton or more.
Class C material is a residuum from quarry operations or a dredged material.

Figure 3.17. Rock breakwater, pile type (35).

Needless to say, good rock placement is important particularly when rock of adequate weight is hard to get and pell-mell design is therefore possible.

In the United States, basically two different designs developed through experience—the filter layer(s) and armor layer (Figure 3.16) and the pile type (Figure 3.17) in which the core fill is stopped a considerable depth below water level and covered with a medium weight rock which forms the base for the heavy armor capping. While most breakwaters of type Figure 3.16 are built with equipment operating from the jetty top, breakwaters of type Figure 3.17 can be built by dump barges and crane equipment operating from barges and pontoons.

The cover layer rubble-mound has one or two filter layers or a secondary armor and a filter course placed between the armor layer and the core. The toe of the mound is designed according to depth. If water is shallow, the mound may be subjected to breaking waves exerting much greater power than nonbreaking waves. Numerous jetties in the United States have been built on the principles described by Figures 3.16 and 3.17.

One weakness in the rubble-mound design was the need for very large blocks when wave action increased beyond about 15 feet. This is explained by research mentioned in the following section demonstrating that block weight depends upon the wave height raised to the third power (19, 20).

Adequate size blocks were often impossible to get from natural sources which usually fail to produce blocks above 20 to 30 tons. In addition, these heavy irregularly-shaped blocks were very difficult to handle. As a solution, very large artificial blocks were manufactured for placement, but then crane equipment able to handle 60- to 80-ton blocks became a problem. Some 400-ton blocks were cast *in place* (orderly) in jetties in the Mediterranean (Figure 3.18), but it soon became clear that the *pell-mell* (disorderly) design was much better than the design based on regular (rectangular) blocks placed in a certain pattern which usually made the slope almost impermeable causing adverse effects on breakwater stability partly due to build-up of hydrostatic pressure inside the armor block layer. Only a few special designs of the old type remain.

On the basis of general experience, research was now promoted, leading to employment of concrete blocks prefabricated in new geometrical shapes—tetrapodes, stabits, tribars, akmon, dolosse, cone, Nagai, etc. Two main advantages with

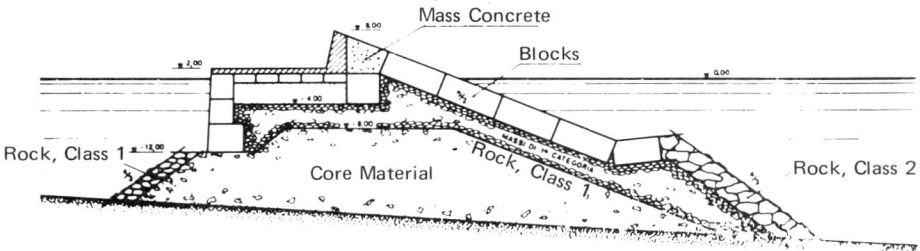

Figure 3.18. Biserte-type breakwater with sloping walls 1:3 capped with 400-ton blocks; new type blocks provide the same stability with a 4/3 slope (14).

these blocks were that they insured better interlocking between themselves as well as high permeability and a pronounced rough surface. Most of the new blocks provided more than 50% void spaces instead of the 20 to 35% afforded by natural parallel-piped blocks.

Design of Rubble-Mound Breakwaters

Rubble-mounds have been and still are constructed in a variety of cross-sections dictated to some extent by site conditions, including character of wave attack, depth and soil conditions.

The basic principle is to build up a core and provide it with a protective covering. The core must prevent wave action as well as sediments from penetrating into the area behind the mound. For this purpose the core usually consists of quarry (waste) material ranging in size from a few pounds to a few hundred pounds and securing good compactness. In certain cases, a sand fill may provide the inner part of the core.

The protective cover, also called armor, must consist of blocks which hinder core material from escaping at the same time as it itself must remain stable against all occurring wave action or at least stable enough to prevent collapse under even the worst conditions (although this may result in some damage).

It is not possible to determine by rigorous analytical methods the forces required to displace individual armor units from the cover layers. It is also impossible to predetermine whether under extreme conditions a larger area of the cover layer will be displaced down the slope en masse or whether individual armor units will be lifted and rolled either up or down the slope. Blocks are never placed with the same degree of relative stability. The wave spectrum in itself is a complex phenomenon, its complexity increasing further when some of the waves break, others only break partially and some do not break at all but establish an oscillatory motion of water particles up or down the structure slope (similar to the motion of a clapotis at a vertical wall).

The following is a review of the U.S. Army Corps of Engineers general practice in designing rubble-mound structures which appeared in "Small craft harbors," *ASCE—Manuals and Reports on Engineering Practice*, no. 50, 1969.

Data needed for designing a rubble-mound structure or a structure of artificial blocks, in addition to wave data, should include, as a minimum: (a) degree of protection desired in lee of the structure; (b) a hydrographic survey of the site; (c) laboratory method giving most uniform results and maximum size of pieces economically available for use as armor units, as well as size and gradation available for underlayer material; (d) the unit weight of water in which the structure is situated (fresh water = 62.4 pounds per cubic foot, salt water = 64.0 pounds per cubic foot); (e) shape and roughness of armor material; (f) a knowledge of interlocking obtained by local placement methods; (g) the degree of allowable overtopping; and (h) degree of permeability permissible.

With these data, the following dimensional features of the structure may be determined: (a) armor stone size and slope of primary cover layer, (b) crest elevation, (c) crest width, (d) underlayers and core, (e) layer thickness and (f) bedding or filter layer size and thickness. The design of the cover layers using concrete components is similar to that for quarry stone structures. Design equation mentioned in the next paragraph is used with the applicable value of K_Δ. However, structural damage to the units may occur if movement is permitted on the slope. The structure may require a concrete cap.

Armor Unit Size and Slope of Cover Layer

The weight or size of the armor units, side slopes, density of armor material and degree of interlocking or wedging between units are interrelated and comprise the principal factors in the design of a rubble-mound structure. Several empirical equations have been derived for determining the size of armor stone required for stability under wave action. Those developed by Hudson at the Waterways Experiment Station (WES) (19, 20) are based on results of over 10 years of model testing as well as a limited amount of preliminary verification by prototype data. The equation developed for determining the weight of armor units for rubble-mound structures is

$$W_r = (\gamma_r H) / [K_\Delta (S_r - 1)^3 \cot \alpha] \quad (3.1)$$

in which W_r is the weight in pounds of the armor unit in primary cover layer; γ_r is the unit of the armor unit in pounds per cubic foot; H is the design wave height; S_r is the specific gravity of the armor unit relative to the water in which the structure is situated, expressed as

$$S_r = \gamma_r / \gamma_w \quad (3.2)$$

in which γ_w is the unit weight of water, fresh water is equal to 62.4 pounds per cubic foot, sea water is equal to 64.0 pounds per cubic foot; a is the angle of breakwater slope measured in degrees from the horizontal; and K_Δ is a coefficient that varies primarily with the shape of the armor units,

roughness of the surface, sharpness of edges and degree of interlocking.

The slope of the cover layer will be determined partly on the basis of rock sizes economically available at the quarry. However, in general, a cover layer slope steeper than 1 to 1.5 is not advisable.

Selection of K_Δ Factor

The various values of dimensionless coefficient K_Δ in Equation 3.1 include all unevaluated variables other than structure slope, wave height and unit weight of armor units and the fluid in which they are placed. These variables include shape of the armor units, degree of interlocking and the wave form at the time it reaches the structure. Equation 3.1 ignores the angle of wave approach which research has proven is not important unless the angle of attack gets below 45°

WES has conducted numerous laboratory tests with a view towards establishing values of K_Δ for different conditions of some of the variables.

The major emphasis of the testing program has been on nonbreaking waves approaching the trunk at 90° with no overtopping allowed. Table 3.3 gives a list of reasonable K_Δ values based on these data, limited data on heads, project model studies using breaking waves and judgment. Because of insufficient data, both model and prototype, a safety factor has been added that decreases the factor value below that which was generally obtained in the model. Tests have indicated that the form of the wave at breaking has a large effect on the stability of the structure; therefore, caution should be used in evaluating this factor. Experience and judgment are necessary in selecting the proper K_Δ factor for use in each case.

Table 3.3 also includes some data on artificial blocks, tribars and tetrapods mentioned later. As mentioned earlier, the K_Δ values of Table 3.3 were obtained by laboratory experiments with uniform waves, and the Hudson formula refers to $H_{1/3}$ in a wind wave train. As explained in the following section, model tests with uniform waves and with nonuniform (wind) waves making H(uniform) equal to $H_{1/3}$ may demonstrate more damage in

Table 3.3. Average K_Δ Values (WES).

Armor	Conditions*			
	1	2	3	4
Rounded stone, 2 layers pell-mell	2.6	2.5	2.4	2.0
Rough stone, 2 layers pell-mell	3.5	3.0	2.9	2.5
Rough stone, 2 layers placed†	5.5	5.0	4.5	3.5
Tribars, 2 layers pell-mell	10.0	8.5	7.5	5.0
Tribars, 1 layer uniform**	15.0	12.0	9.5	7.5
Tetrapods, 2 layers pell-mell	8.5	7.5	6.5	4.5

*Conditions: (1) trunk, nonbreaking waves; (2) trunk, breaking waves; (3) conical head, nonbreaking waves; and (4) conical head, breaking waves.
†Good placement with center line of long diameter of stone placed normal to structure face.
**For special conditions.

---

the case of the nonuniform waves. Comparisons between results of model tests in different scales (45) seem to reveal that no scale effect exists as long as the Reynolds number $N_R = V_R \delta/\nu$ (where δ is the characteristic diameter of unit of primary cover layer, defined as average of x, y and z for quarry stone, ν is the kinetic viscosity of water at 60° F and V_R is the value of water particle velocity parallel to side slope of breakwater measured at a distance R equal to half of characteristic diameter below SWL is equal to or greater than about 3 (10^4).

In this connection, it should be noted that placement of armor units in the prototype may not duplicate the degree of interlocking that may be obtained in the laboratory. In the prototype, although it is possible to set stones or blocks so as to achieve a closely knit structure above the water surface, the same quality construction can rarely, if ever, be attained for that part of the armor below the water surface. Thus, it is considered advisable to use data obtained from random (pell-mell) placement in the laboratory as a basis for K_Δ values. Nevertheless, certain model effects caused by lack of full similarity in test conditions cannot possibly be avoided. The importance of various characteristics of wave spectra and of resonance effects between uprush/downrush period and wave period should be fully realized as discussed later in the section on "Design Wave Height."

It is well established that the head of a breakwater or jetty normally suffers more extensive and more frequent damage than the trunk of the structure. This generally results from several factors. The rounded structure head is subject to a slope segment overtopping under all wave conditions causing a jet effect across a segment; a part of the head is usually subject to direct wave attack regardless of the direction of wave approach; and a wave trough on the lee side may coincide with maximum run-up on the windward side creating a high static head for flow through the structure. Therefore, it is practical to increase the weight of armor units in the jetty head, e.g., by 50%. Model experiments (and experience) with breakwaters in Hawaii (31) showed that considerable damage may occur to a breakwater head if this is not taken into account.

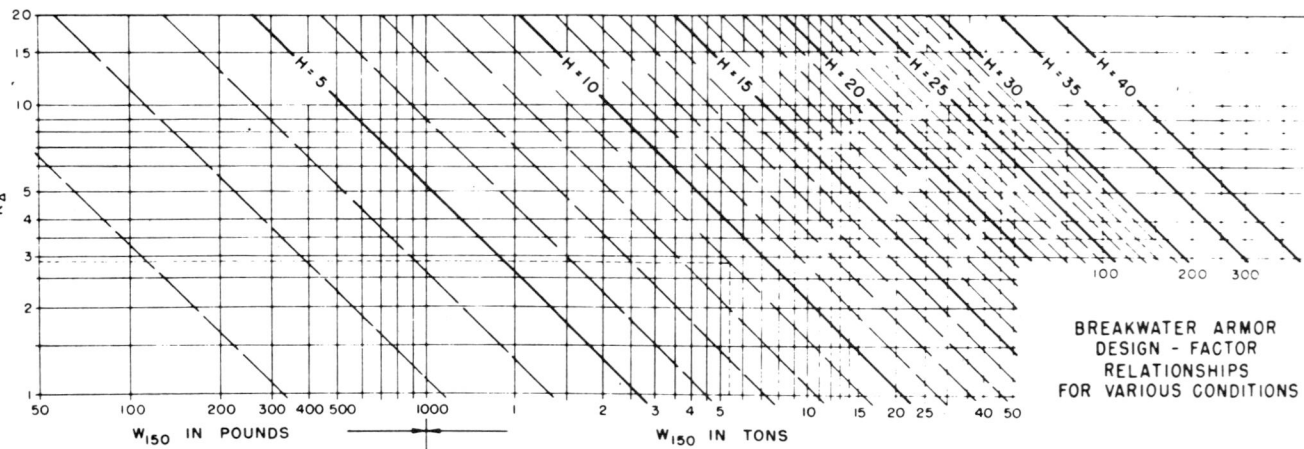

Figure 3.19. Stone size graph (ASCE Manual on Small Craft Harbors).
Problem: For the purpose of illustration the following values have been assumed:

Table 3.4. Example of Computation of Rock Size.

		\multicolumn{16}{c}{γ = pounds per cubic foot}
		150	152	154	156	158	160	162	164	166	168	170	172	174	176	178	180
$\cot \alpha$	1.5	100	95	90	85	81	77	73	70	67	64	61	58	55	53	51	49
	2.0	75	71	67	64	61	58	55	52	50	47	45	43	41	40	38	37
	2.5	60	57	54	51	48	46	44	42	40	38	36	35	33	32	31	29
	3.0	50	47	45	42	40	38	37	35	33	31	30	29	28	27	26	25
	3.5	43	40	38	36	34	33	31	30	28	27	25	25	24	23	22	21
		\multicolumn{16}{c}{Percentage of W_{150}}

Selection of Crest Elevation

The primary function of breakwaters is to provide adequate protection against wave action in harbor areas or roadsteads. Consequently, overtopping can be tolerated only if it does not generate waves in the protected areas that exceed allowable limits as determined by the type of harbor and its designated use. Factors that determine whether overtopping will occur under design conditions and the extent of overtopping when it does occur are the elevation of the crest, the elevation of design still-water level and the height of wave run-up.

As mentioned above, numerous tests have been carried out on uprush on breakwaters of varying geometry, slope frictions and permeability. Since the size of stone in the cover layer of the harbor side can be reduced if no overtopping occurs, the economics of crest elevation should be considered.

Selection of Crest Width

The width of crest depends to a large extent on the degree of allowable overtopping. Where there will be no appreciable overtopping, the crest width is not critical with respect to the forces on the structure. From the standpoint of stability, a

Breakwaters and Jetties 71

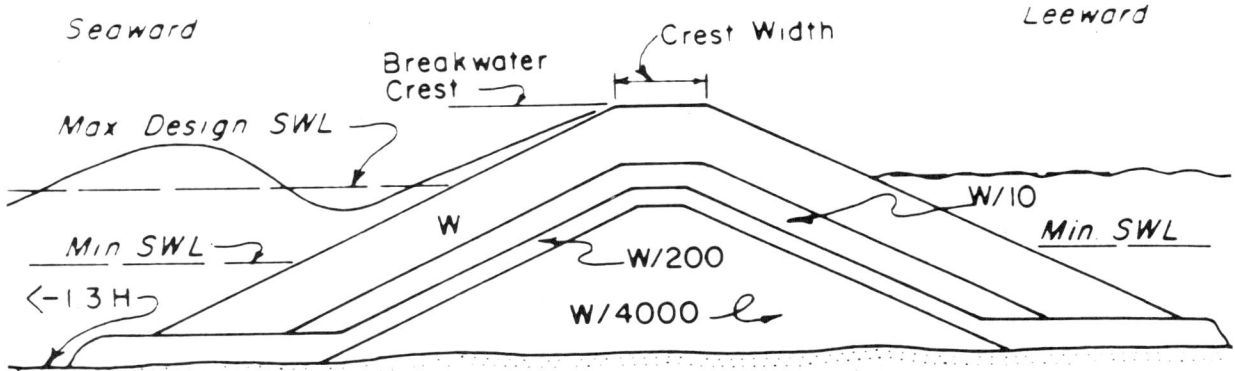

Figure 3.20. Shallow-water breakwater, theoretical designs (39, 40).

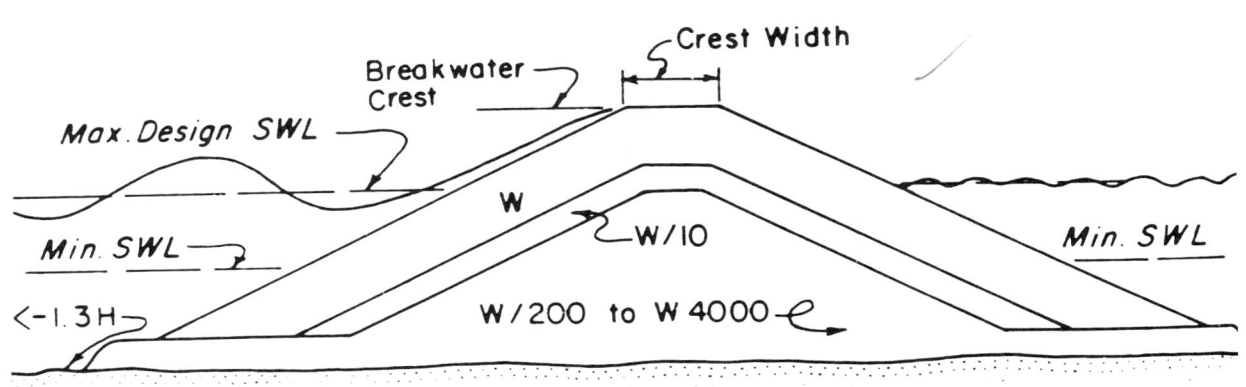

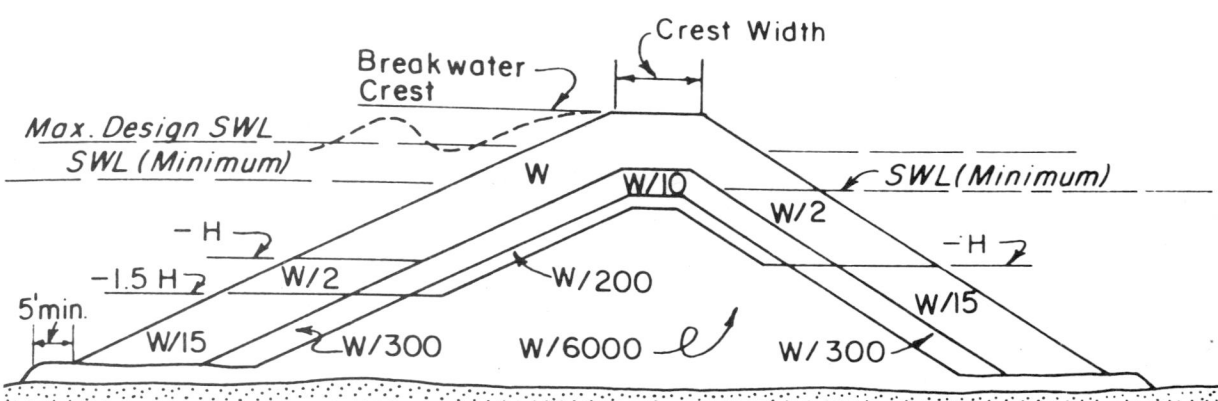

THEORETICAL SECTION
DEEP WATER RUBBLE MOUND BREAKWATER
① NON BREAKING WAVE CONDITIONS
② DEPTH OF WATER > 1.3 WAVE HEIGHTS

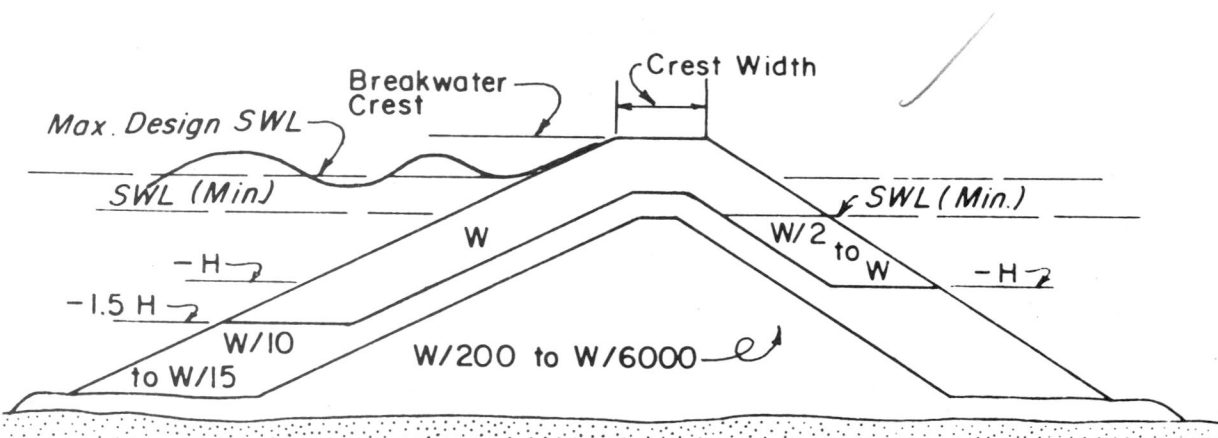

TYPICAL 3-LAYER SECTION OF THEORETICAL
BREAKWATER DESIGN

Figure 3.21. Deep-water breakwater, theoretical designs (39, 40).

combined width of three cap stones is generally desirable. However, where conditions dictate the advisability of building the structure progressively with equipment working from the crest of the completed work, the crest width should be adequate for operating any such construction and maintenance equipment. For a three-stone width, the crest width may be obtained from

$$B = 3k_s (W_r/w_r)^{1/3}$$

in which B is the crest width in feet; k_s is the layer coefficient; W_r is the weight of the armor unit in primary cover layer in pounds; and w_r is the unit weight of the armor unit in pounds per cubic foot.

Primary Cover Layer

Guidance in determining the weight of component W_r and the slope of the primary cover layer is obtained by applying the Hudson equation (Equation 3.1) or by using Figure 3.19 and Table 3.4. W_{150} in Figure 3.19 refers to $\gamma = 150$ pounds per cubic foot. Unit weight of water equals 64 pounds per cubic foot. Table 3.4 shows how data based on $\gamma = 150$ pounds per cubic foot and $\cot\alpha = 1.5$ are converted. The thickness may be determined by Equations 3.1 and 3.2. When the water depth at the structure is less than $1.3H$ and overtopping will occur, the primary cover layer should cover the entire structure (see Figure 3.20, Reference 40). If the depth is less than $1.3H$ and no overtopping will occur, the primary cover layer should extend across the crest and to the bottom on the seaward side while the cover for the harbor side may be determined by wave action within the harbor. When the depth at the structure is greater than $1.3H$ and overtopping will occur, the primary cover layer should extend from $-H$ on the seaward side, across the crest and down to the elevation of minimum still-water level on the harbor side (see Figure 3.21, Reference 40). If the depth is greater than $1.3H$ and no overtopping will occur, the entire harbor side cover may be based upon wave action occurring within the harbor. Except in special cases involving small maximum wave heights, the primary cover layer should have a thickness of two stones.

Secondary Cover Layer

The secondary cover layer is the outer layer extending downslope from the primary cover layer. The units comprising this layer should be half the weight of those in the primary cover layer, $W_r/2$, if the slope of the primary cover layer is maintained for the secondary layer (Figure 3.21). Below the depth of 1.5 to $2H$, the stone size can be further reduced in the secondary cover layer. When the size of stone is reduced in the secondary cover layer, the number of layers, n, should be increased to maintain a thickness at least equal to the primary cover layer to prevent it from sliding. When the primary cover layer consists of formed concrete components and the secondary cover layer is made of stone, the size of units in the secondary cover layer should be based on the weight of quarry stone required for stability in the primary layer, rather than the weight of the concrete components.

Underlayers

The underlayers are placed beneath the cover layers. The individual stones of the underlayers should be large enough to prevent their withdrawal through the interstices of the cover layer and prevent excess movement which may cause subsequent breakage of the armor unit. Unless the stone in the primary cover layer is relatively small, a first and second underlayer will be required for adequate filter action, each layer approximately one-tenth the weight of the stone in the layer above. The second underlayer will be advisable when the design wave is severe—over about 15 feet with frequent occurrences. Generally, the second underlayer can be formed by selecting the larger core material and placing it on the outer surface of the core (see Figures 3.20 and 3.21).

Core

The most frequently used core stone is a quarry-run material, the gradation of which is governed by economics and the desired degree of impermeability. Sand, gravel and other material have been successfully used in core structures. Sand in the lower part of the core of the Los Angeles Long Beach, California, breakwater was placed by hydraulic pipeline dredge. This sand core was, in fact, an artificial shoal, and the stone structure was graded up on the shoal. In some segments, a partially indurated clay from the nearby bay bottom was also used successfully in the core. If fine material is used in the core, the underlayer should be properly graded as a filter to prevent loss of the fines from the core by piping. The height of the core can affect the stability of the cover layers. This effect is a result of the imperviousness of the core causing a reflection of the energy or a buildup of head beneath the cover.

Bedding Layer

Foundations for marine structures deserve as much, if not more, careful study than foundations for land structures. Wave forces acting against a rubble structure have been found to attack the natural bottom and the structure foundation even at depths usually thought to be little affected by such forces. A rubble structure may be protected from settlement, resulting from leaching, piping, undermining or scour, by a bedding layer or blanket.

Experience indicates that using a bedding layer to protect foundations of rubble-mound structures from undermining is advisable except where (a) the depths of water are greater than twice the maximum wave height, (b) the anticipated current velocities are smaller than those necessary to move the average size of foundation material, and the material has sufficient strength to prevent settlement of the individual pieces of stone, or (c) the foundation is a hard, durable material, such as bedrock. Foundations that meet these requirements do not require a blanket. When the rubble structure is placed on a sand foundation, material may be provided to prevent waves and currents from removing sand through the voids of the rubble, thus destroying their support. When large stones are placed directly on a sand foundation at depths insufficient to avoid wave and current action on the bottom (as in the surf zone) and if an adequate bedding layer is not provided, the rubble will settle into the sand until it reaches the depth below which the sand will not be disturbed by the currents. The settlement may be irregular, causing the interstices between the stone to increase in size, thereby making the structure more susceptible to wave damage.

The gradation requirements of a bedding layer depend principally on the littoral characteristics in the area and on foundation conditions. However, quarry spalls ranging in size from approximately 1 to 50 pounds will usually suffice. The thickness of the layer normally depends on the water depth in which the material is to be placed and the size of stone used in the bedding layer. The thickness should not be less than 1 foot to assure that bottom irregularities are covered, or not less than 1.5 times the diameter of the largest stone in the blanket. Beneath the water surface and the landward section where scour might expose the bedding layer, the bedding layer should extend at least 5 feet beyond the toe of the cover stone.

Where there are strong currents and a rubble-mound structure is constructed seaward from shore, a scour hole may form at the outward end of the completed portion of the structure and progress seaward as the construction progresses. This will greatly increase the quantity of material in the structure. The scour can be prevented by keeping a bedding layer a minimum of 50 feet in advance of the unfinished end of the mound. At the Mississippi River-Gulf Outlet where strong currents prevail, the bedding layer was kept a maximum of 100 feet and a minimum of 50 feet in advance of the stone bedding and no scour occurred.

Design of cover layers for rubble-mound breakwaters subjected to nonbreaking waves is mentioned specifically by Jackson in Reference 42. His results also show the influence of the d/L and H/L ratios. For the conditions tested, he found that the stability of rubble-mound breakwaters is not appreciably influenced by relative depth (d/L) and wave steepness (H/L); and the experimental coefficient and the stability number are

Table 3.5. Design Coefficients for Tests on Nonbreaking Waves (42).

Type of Armor Unit	Method of Placing	Number of Layers	K_Δ Average Values Determined Experimentally	K_Δ Values Proposed for Design
Smooth quarrystones	Random	2	2.8	2.4
Rough quarrystones	Random	2	4.6	4.0
Rough and smooth tetrapods	Uniform; Random	2	9.4	8.0
Rough quadripods	Uniform; Random	2	9.4	8.0
Tribars	Uniform	1	28.1	15.0
Tribars	Random	2	11.5	10.0
Modified leadite cubes	Uniform	1	Not recommended	
Modified leadite cubes	Random	2	11.2	7.5
Hexapods	Uniform	1	Not recommended	
Hexapods	Random	2	10.4	9.0
Rough and smooth truncated tetrahedrons	Uniform	2	Not recommended	

good indicators of the ability of a given shape of armor unit to resist the action of wave attack. Furthermore, for the type of test sections and armor units used in these tests on breakwater trunks and for the no-damage and no-overtopping criteria, the design coefficients in Table 3.5 were proposed for use in the design of rubble-mound breakwaters:

The values of K_Δ tabulated in Table 3.5 clearly demonstrate that K_Δ is a function of shape of armor unit and method of placement. The selected design values of K_Δ in the tabulation are conservative and are equal to or less than the values of K_Δ corresponding to the lower-limit curves of the plotted data points. For further information on these tests and the results, the reader should consult Reference 42.

DESIGN WAVE HEIGHT

Breakwater design depends on the selected design wave height. For vertical as well as for a sloping wall, design wave height is usually defined as the height which causes maximum force or pressure on the wall. It may also be defined as the height of the wave that is potentially most damaging to an economically feasible structure. In the case of a nonbreaking wave, the design wave is generally assumed to be the largest wave to reach the structure. For the breaking wave, it is assumed to be the largest wave to break directly on the structure. A detailed wave statistic is therefore necessary.

It is not always the largest wave which exerts the maximum force and causes the maximum damage. It is observed in the laboratory as well as in the field that it may be a certain succession of waves. Field experience has also indicated that most damage often occurs at the end of the storm when waves have become longer but perhaps lower at the same time. The significant wave height has often been used as a basis for design, and wave height in Hudson's design formula (19,20) is $H_{1/3}$.

New laboratory equipment like programmed wave generators and wind-wave generators, have been able to imitate natural wave spectra quite closely. As pointed out in References 7 and 17,

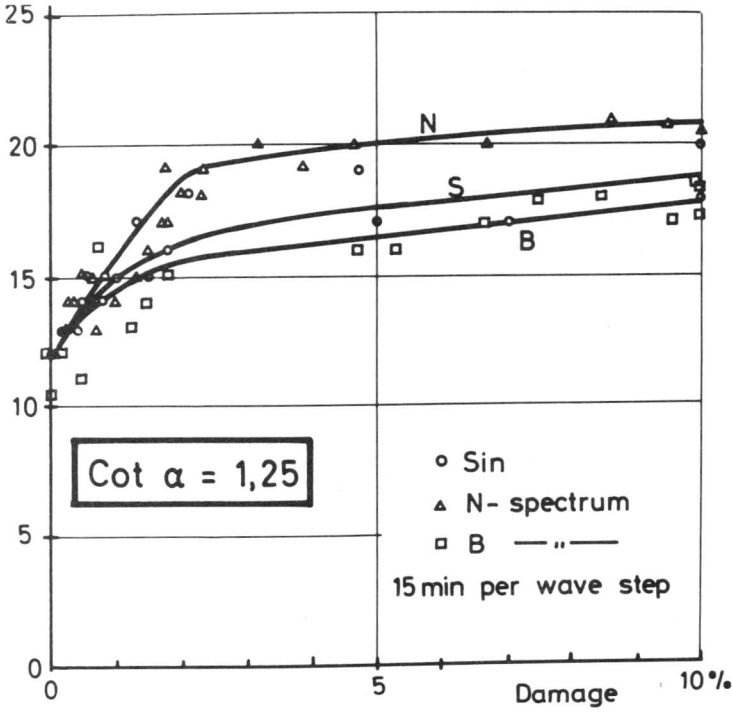

Figure 3.22. Damage curves for tests on rubble-mound using various wave spectra (7).

comparative tests have shown that under certain conditions model tests with more or less regular waves present results that deviate from corresponding tests with wave spectra. As mentioned specifically in Reference 7, stability tests on armor units for the Europort breakwater in Holland showed an increase in damage when regular waves were replaced by irregular waves, the significant wave height, $H_{1/3}$, remaining the same. With a certain depth at the toe, irregular waves caused complete failure while regular waves left the breakwater intact. This question is dealt with more thoroughly in a paper by Johannesson and Bruun presented at the "First International Conference on Port and Ocean Engineering under Arctic Conditions," Trondheim, Norway, August, 1971 (Proceeding available from Gulf Publishing Company, Houston, Texas).

Similar observations have been made in tests with practical breakwaters in Norway. Reference 7 describes basic tests in Norway on irregular waves of various spectra (Figure 3.22). The conclusion of these tests was that there does not seem to exist one single relation which describes the effect of regular waves compared with irregular waves for all kinds of wave spectra. Therefore, it is not always safe to substitute regular waves for irregular waves in a model tank. On the other hand, the tests indicated a relation between stability and run-up rather than the apparent wave height. The run-up is a function of the wave spectrum; compare Figures 3.23a and 3.23b (7).

Downrush and uprush (uprun) seem to be closely related; great care should therefore be demonstrated when tests are run. Detailed information on the actually occurring wave action is needed.

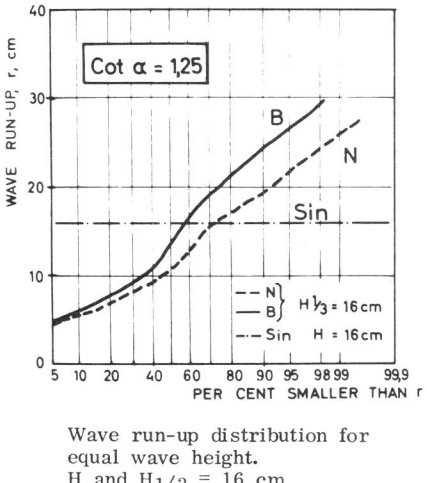 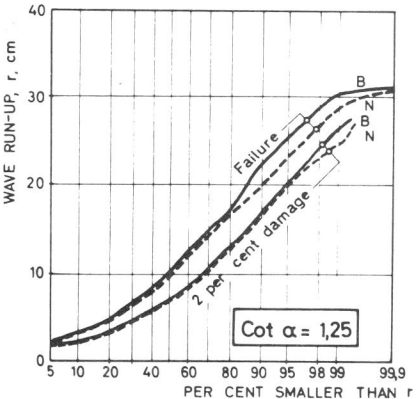

Wave run-up distribution for equal wave height. H and $H_{1/3}$ = 16 cm

Run-up distribution for equal damage. 15 min per wave step

Figure 3.23 (a) Wave run-up distribution for equal wave height (7) and (b) run-up distribution for equal damage (7).

This includes statistical data on frequency of occurrence of waves of a certain height and period and information on the character and type of actually occurring wave spectra including their frequency.

Most often insufficient meteorological (not to speak of wave) data are available for the production of such diagram. Wave recording is a recent invention particularly deep-sea recording (by accelerometer buoys). In the latter case, wave action has to be hindcasted for a certain, usually deep-sea location after which the waves are carried shoreward to the point of particular interest by shoaling and (numerical) refraction analyses. This is usually a laborious and not fully safe procedure which should be checked when possible by actual observation of wave action en route from deep water to the actual point or site of interest. Selection of design sea state for offshore structures is mentioned in the following section.

The complexity of the problem of determining a design wave height increases further in the case of wave breaking. As pointed out by Galvin (16), there is no single procedure for choosing the design wave height in case of wave breaking. Most often it is assumed that the depth at the structure, d, controls the height, H, of waves breaking on the structure according to the relation

$$\beta_b = d_b/H_b = 1.28 \qquad (3.3)$$

obtained from the solitary wave theory. The depth at the toe of the proposed structure is calculated from the hydrography and tidal range usually corrected for estimated storm surge and possible wave set-up (29).

The currently accepted practice (outlined above) may be summarized. Using an estimated water depth at the structure, a breaker height is obtained from Equation 3.3 which is assumed to be the design wave height if it has a significant probability of occurrence. If the height given by Equation 3.3 occurs too rarely, a smaller breaking or nonbreaking design wave height is chosen from the cumulative frequency distribution. There are, however, several problems in using this procedure.

Equation 3.3 is used because periodic waves near breaking are assumed to act as solitary waves. If this is the case, the values of the constant and the definition of the depth in Equation 3.3 may be questioned. The value 1.28, usually rounded off to

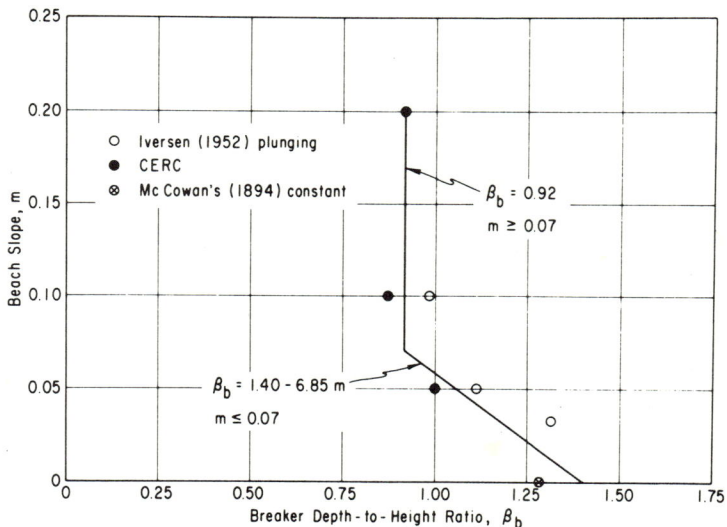

Figure 3.24. Slope dependence of breaker depth-to-height ratio (16).

1.3 in engineering practice, is McCowan's (29) value for the maximum height of a solitary wave, but recent work indicates that this should be 1.20 (16). For either value, the appropriate depth is the depth beneath the trough, d_t, at the breaker position, but the depth used, d_b, is usually measured from the mean water level (MWL) or still-water level (SWL). Usually choosing the larger depth more than compensates for choosing the higher constant in Equation 3.3, so that the measured value is expected to exceed the constant in Equation 3.3.

A second factor to consider is that β_b in Equation 3.3 is not a constant but depends on beach slope and wave steepness. Because Equation 3.3 was derived for constant water depth, a slope effect is not surprising. Galvin continued investigations of earlier data on the slope dependence of breaker depth-to-height ratio. Figure 3.24 shows the results indicating the importance of the breaker depth-to-height ratio (β_b).

The most dangerous type of wave breaking is the plunging when the wave crest travels faster than the wave as a whole. The front of the wave then begins to fall and finally develops a jet of water which strikes the base of the wave entrapping a pocket of air and throwing up a splash which typically rises as high as the crest elevation before plunging. The splash also has a forward speed which carries it some distance shoreward before it touches down in the surf. Observations mentioned in Reference 16 indicate that by the time the main body of the wave has reached the point where the splash touches down, the principal breaking has occurred. Landward from the splash touchdown point, the wave continues as a bore to the run-up limit. The question arises as to which depth should be used as "design depth" for a wave breaking on a structure. It is apparently not sufficient to consider the depth at the toe of the structure because the wave started breaking before it reached the toe. Galvin carried out a considerable number of laboratory tests on the subject. Referring to Figure 3.25 and using the dimensionless distances denoted by

$$\tau_a = x_a/H_b : \tau_b = x_p/H_b : \tau_s = x_s/H_b$$

and $x_d = kx_p$ and β_b (experiments) = 0.92 for $m \geq 0.07$, $\beta_b = 1.40 - 6.85\,m$ for $m \leq 0.07$, m is the

Breakwaters and Jetties 79

Table 3.6. Possible Design Wave Heights for Idealized Example*

Equation number	H_d		Remarks on H_d	$\dfrac{H_d}{g\,m\,T^2}$ †
	k	in feet		
3.3	—	7.8	accepted practice	0.048
3.4	0	9.4	not recommended	0.058
3.4	0.5	10.3	minimum recommended	0.064
3.4	1.0	11.4		0.071
3.4	2.0	14.1	probable spilling breaker	0.088

*Conditions of example: $m = 0.05$, $d_s = 10$ feet, $T = 10$ seconds.
†Inshore breaker type parameter. On plane slopes, plunging usually occurs for $0.003 < H_d/(gmT^2) < 0.068$.

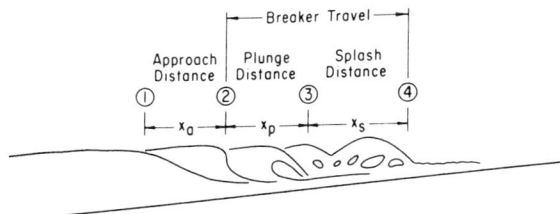

Figure 3.25. Travel of plunging wave (16).

① Point of Initial Instability
② Breaker Position
③ Crest Touchdown Point
④ Splash Touchdown Point

slope and $\tau_p = 4.0 - 9.25\,m$ it is possible to write a relation between design wave height, H_d, and the parameters d_s, m and k. In Figure 3.26, $x_d = k, pH_d = (d_d - d_a)/m$, the subscript β_d indicates the breaker position of the design wave height. Solving for H_d,

$$H_d = d_a / (\beta_d - k\,m\,\tau_p) \qquad (3.4)$$

in which β_d and τ_p can be evaluated in terms of m from the earlier equations.

Table 3.6 (16) shows how H_d varies for selected values of k and how these values compare with the results obtained by the accepted practice of using Equation 3.3.

Since it is assumed that the design wave breaks by plunging, it is useful to check this assumption with a breaker type parameter. Values of the inshore breaker type parameter for the example conditions are shown in the last column of Table 3.6. Waves on plane slopes usually break by plunging when this parameter is in the range 0.003 to 0.068. Jackson (43) carried out experiments on the maximum steepness for plane slopes and breakwaters. The results are indicated in Figure 3.27.

The lowest relative depth used by Jackson was at the customary upper limit of shallow-water waves ($d/L = 0.05$), whereas most of the results of Galvin's study were in the shallow water range ($d/L < 0.05$). The applicable data from Jackson are compared with Galvin's data from 1:10 slopes in Figure 3.27. Also shown are Equations 3.3 and 3.4 for the region between $k = 0$ and $k = 1$ and the theoretical relation of Miche for the maximum breaking wave.

Under shallow-water conditions, the data of Jackson and Galvin show heights greater than those expected from the theoretical relations. Other data in Jackson's paper show that H at the shallow-water limit is greater than the theoretical pre-

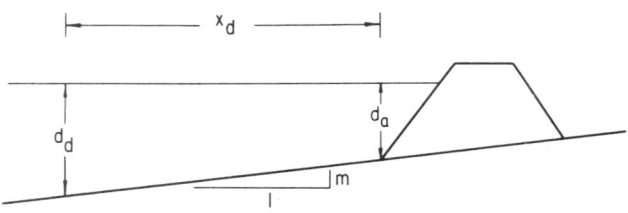

Figure 3.26. Idealized example of structure on slope (16).

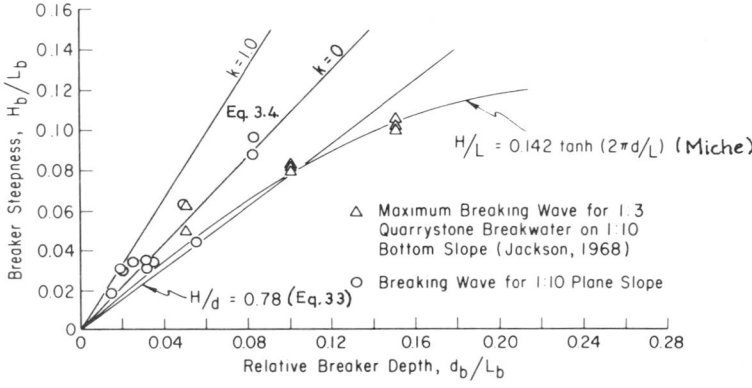

Figure 3.27. Maximum steepness for plane slopes and breakwaters (43).

dictions whenever the seaward bottom slope is 1:10 but not when it is flat. This result is in accordance with Galvin's explanation that breaker travel and the slope dependence of β_b permit waves on moderate or steep slopes to approach closer to shore before breaking (see Reference 16 for further information).

Wave Run-up

When waves propagate toward the shore or toward any shore structure, they finally, whether breaking or not, run up the beach or the structure. Estimates of the run-up size are very important in determining the height of a breakwater as well as in determining the top elevation of a coastal or flood protection structure. The actual wave uprun on a breakwater is a function of geometrical char-

acteristics of structure (height, shape, roughness, etc.), depth at structure and incident wave characteristics. Very little field data are available, but a considerable number of model experiments have been carried out. References 6, 25, 38 and 40 give considerable data. Generally, uprun or uprush is highest with smooth designs compared to rough designs including those which are provided with artificial roughness arranged, for example, by means of blocks of unequal thickness. Various types of (usually patented) blocks are designed particularly for revetments when uprush height is important because flooding is possible. Permeability as well as composite structures including those which have an almost horizontal berm between an upper and a lower slope decrease uprun.

Model tests by Bruun (6) on various types of rubble-mounds and sloping structures of varying

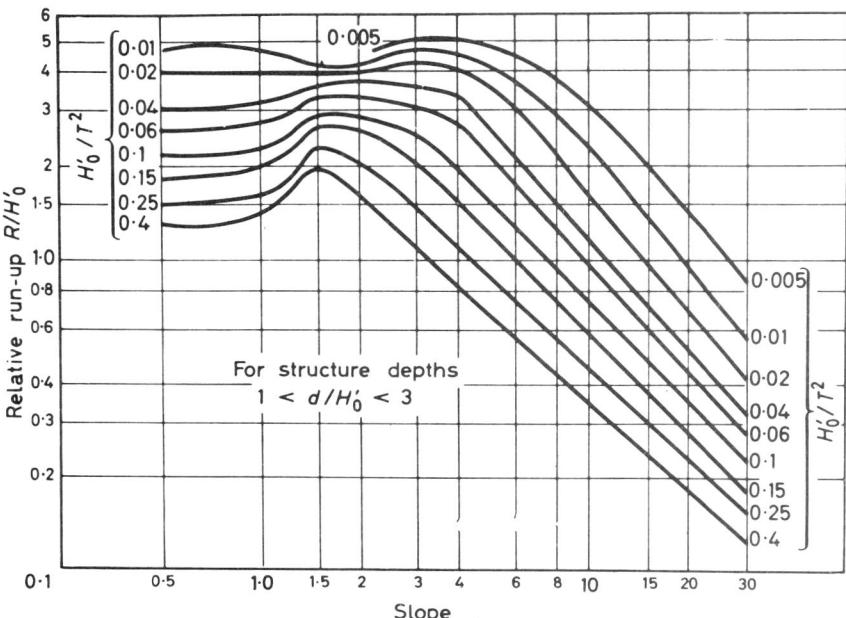

Figure 3.28. Run-up on sloped structures (38, 40).

geometry give overall information on reflection coefficients as well as uprun.

Figure 3.28 (40) is an example of run-up on sloped structures for various H_0'/T^2 ratios. Theories for run-up are usually complicated, particularly for breaking waves.

Le Méhauté (25) considers theories for run-up by nonbreaking as well as for breaking waves. For nonbreaking waves, he refers to Miche's linear theories for uprun on a smooth slope,

$$R/H = \sqrt{(\pi/2\alpha)}$$

where R is the uprun elevation above still-water level, H is wave height at toe of slope and α is the slope angle.

According to Reference 25, for a not too gently sloping beach we may empirically add the superelevation term which is obtained in front of a vertical wall installed at toe depth.

With respect to breaking waves, Miche proposed the equation for maximum H/L ratio,

$$(H/L)_{max} = [\sqrt{(2\alpha/\pi)}] \, (\sin^2\alpha/\pi)$$

Le Méhauté based the following well-fitting formula on a review of existing information:

$$H_b/H_o = 0.76 \, (S^{1/7}) \, (H_o/L_o)^{-1/4}$$

referring to $1/50 < S < 1/5$ and $0.002 < H_o/L_o < 0.09$. Using a bore run-up theory of a nonsaturated breaker (26) combined with the characteristic method, it is possible to calculate the uprun even though a varying friction causes some difficulties particularly when the uprun sheet becomes very thin.

As described in Reference 25, numerical methods for solitary waves have also been developed. The problem becomes increasingly difficult as the wave period decreases (or as the wave steepness increases) due to the influence of the backwash on the following wave. Because the backwash

Table 3.7. Stone Weight Coefficients for "Placed Stone" Jetties (23).

Quarry stone type	n^*	K_Δ Breaking wave	K_Δ Nonbreaking wave
Rough	1	3,6	4,2
Rough	2	5,7	6,7
Rough	3	7,1	8,3

*Number of layers.

causes more energy dissipation in the bore, wave run-up decreases as the wave steepness increases.

Recent Development

Kidby (23) describes experience with jetty construction on the Pacific by the Portland District, U.S. Army Corps of Engineers. Prior to 1949, stone used in constructing and repairing rubble-mound jetties was distributed by using dump cars operating along a railroad trestle constructed to an elevation well above the jetty crest. As the rubble-mound rose and finally emerged from the water, many larger stones were broken by vertical drops to 30 feet.

With the advent of increasingly mobile construction equipment, delivering stone by truck, using the jetty crest as a haulroad, resulted in need for higher and wider crests to provide suitable haulroads. Between 1949 and 1958, all jetty repair work—but repairs on the south jetty at Coquille River—was performed by delivering stone to the advancing end of the jetty by truck, then shoving it off the crest with a dozer. This method produced a pell-mell type of rubble-mound that was an improvement over that produced by using dump cars on a railroad trestle because of the compaction effect produced by heavy hauling equipment passing along the crest. However, side-slope armor stones could not be positioned to obtain desirable contact with adjacent stones throughout the armor layer. Some stones would fall outside the design section, and many would come to rest with their long axis more or less parallel to the length of the jetty.

In 1955, repairs were completed on the south jetty at the Coquille River entrance which was relatively sheltered from heavy seas by offshore rocks so that the contractor was able to construct the jetty to its terminal at an elevation of approximately 15 feet above mean lower low water. The contractor then placed the armor layer along the side slopes and over the crest by crane to comply with the specification requirement that the armor stones be in juxtaposition.

Other jetties were repaired by truck delivery and dozer placement. Practically all these jetties suffered considerable and continuing damage during winter storms except the south jetty at the mouth of the Coquille River. This lead to initiating model tests at the U.S. Waterway Experiment Station using the Hudson formula, $W_r = (\gamma_r H^3)/[K_\Delta (S_r - 1)^3 \cot g\alpha]$, as design formula determining the value K_Δ for "placed stone" jetties—jetties with the stone placed with the long axis perpendicular to the center line of the jetty. Table 3.7 (23) shows the K_Δ coefficient.

These K_Δ values are approximately twice as large as the corresponding values for stones in a normal pell-mell design provided that stones of 75% size are selected weighing 30% more than the 50% size on increase of K_Δ of 1.3 compared to the value for the 50% size. Another result of the model study was that the underwater part of the rubble-mound jetty, although less susceptible to observation and construction control, is nevertheless worthy of great care in its initial design and con-

Figure 3.29. Prefabricated concrete blocks (14).

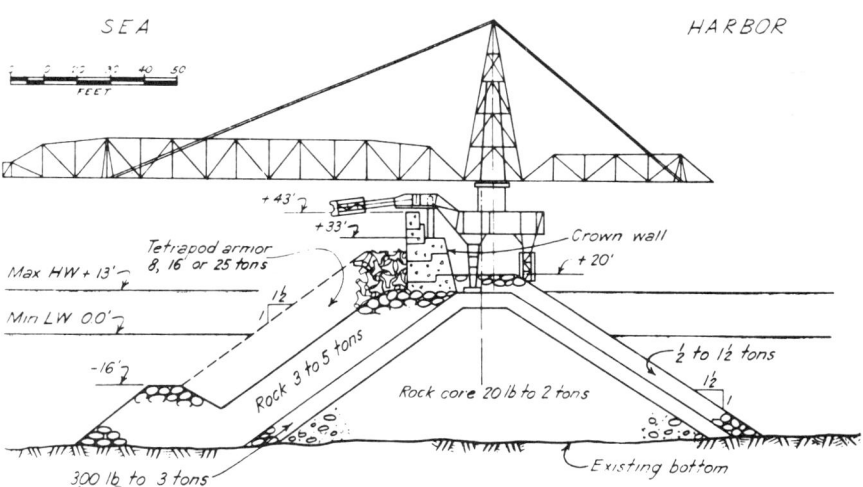

Figure 3.30. Cross-section through breakwater at Rota, Spain. (From article by R.H. Corbetta and H.W. Hunt, Civil Engineering, *October, 1958.)*

struction. Some means of compacting the underwater part should therefore be considered in all new constructions. Dropping a piling or constructing as much of the underwater section as possible using bottom dump barges or other suitable equipment and allowing a storm season to consolidate the mound was suggested.

The knowledge obtained from Coquille River, which was also used for the south jetty of Siuslaw River (23), is, however, a repetition of an old Norwegian experience when gneissoid stratified granite was placed with the long side perpendicular to the center line of the breakwater, thereby increasing stability.

Considerable effort has been exerted to develop concrete blocks prefabricated in more "intelligent" shapes hydraulically. Research was promoted leading to the employment of concrete

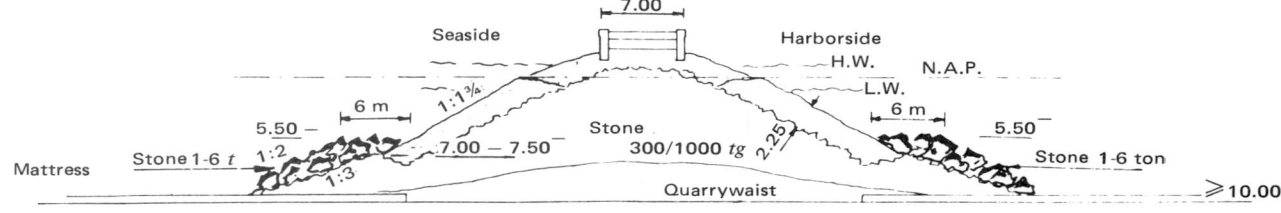
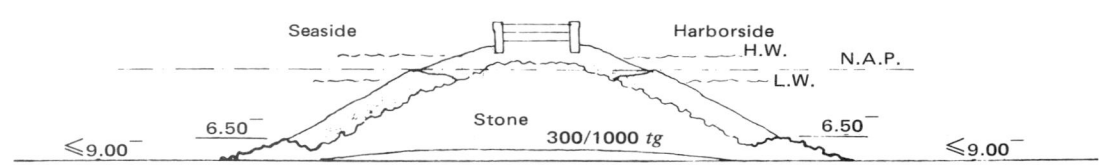

Figure 3.31. Cross-sections of breakwater at Ymuiden (17).

blocks prefabricated in new geometrical shapes called tetrapods, stabits, tribars, akmon, dolosse, cone, nagai, etc. The two main advantages with these blocks were that they insured better interlocking, high permeability and a pronounced rough surface. Most of the new blocks provided more than 50% void spaces instead of the 20 to 35% afforded by natural or parallel-piped blocks placed haphazardly. Their employment, limited to the upper layer of the wall facing the sea, often ensured stability of the entire structure with slopes of 4 to 3, instead of the formerly adopted 3 to 1, even with no exceptionally large weight blocks. With the resulting reduction in total volume, the cost of such structure is obvious. Figure 3.29 gives examples of such blocks.

Tetrapods, invented by Danel (10), have been used in three structures in the United States: Crescent City Harbor, California; Kahului Harbor, Hawaii, and Rincon Island, California. Tribars were used at Nawiliwili Harbor and Kahului Harbor, Hawaii, and at Ventura Harbor, California; quadripods were used at Santa Cruz Harbor, California.

Figure 3.30 is a cross-section through the Port of Rota Naval Base in Spain (35). This principal port of entry for the U.S. bases in Spain was completed in 1958. Figure 3.30 shows a 400-ton crane placing tetrapods. Ten thousand blocks weighing up to 25 tons each were placed on the breakwater at a distance up to 125 feet from the center of the breakwater by the full revolving hammerhead crane. The core consists of soft rock protected with secondary armor layers.

Figure 3.31 shows the use of asphalt in saving block size in a modern design at the harbor of Ymuiden in the Netherlands (also mentioned in Chapter 6). Plans called for enlarging the outer harbor area by extending the two existing breakwaters so that the new entrance lies ¼ mile further into the sea. To realize the plans, new equipment, new materials and new methods were needed (17 and publications in Dutch).

Figure 3.31 shows the new design and Figure 3.32, its method of construction. Two self-elevating pontoons of Texas-tower type with a crane were employed in its construction. The rock mound of 500 to 2,000-pounds rock was placed on mattresses and a quarry waste layer. Stability against wave action of the relatively small rock was secured by means of a layer of stone asphalt which

Figure 3.32. Construction of breakwater at Ymuiden (17).

is a warm-prefabricated mixed material consisting of 50%, 2 to 20 pounds, gravel and 50% asphalt mortar. The single load of asphalt placed by crane was 18 tons. A toe supporting the stone asphalt layer was built with 1 to 6-ton blocks. The crown was covered by concrete blocks.

Economic Feasibility; Optimum Design

Economic feasibility is, needless to say, very important for any practical design whether in harbor or any other engineering field. It affects the choice of design wave height by influencing the type and siting of the structure. Statistically, an "optimum design" may be developed. Thus the design engineer is faced with the problem of choosing a safer design criterion to reduce the damage expectation. On the other hand, the building costs will then increase. The design engineer is then faced with an evaluation of benefits and costs. In so doing the aim will be toward a maximization of overall economy for which the investment is then referred to as being *optimal*. This question has been dealt with by many authors (e.g., References 12 and 17, section by Bischoff van Heemskerck).

As pointed out by all authors on this subject, attention was first focused on the question of what risk should be accepted. This resulted in a method of first developing the building cost and next evaluating the amount of funds which should be set aside to pay the cost of all future maintenance and damage. When sufficient field and laboratory data are available, the relation between the total costs involved and the design criteria may be computed for various designs and plotted in a graph like Figure 3.33 (12). The optimal design criterion corresponding to minimum costs may then be read from the figure.

Purely financial considerations are very important and may be extended into technical fields associated with, but not neccesarily included in, the design. The purpose pursued should be the greatest possible total benefit from the total amount of money available for the investment. In order to establish the most economical height and design of a breakwater, it has gradually become customary to determine the dimensions of a structure and the nature and the rate of damage by means of model experiments. No other method is possible as long as the physical factors which determine the behavior of a structure are not better understood because they are due to the overall complexity of the

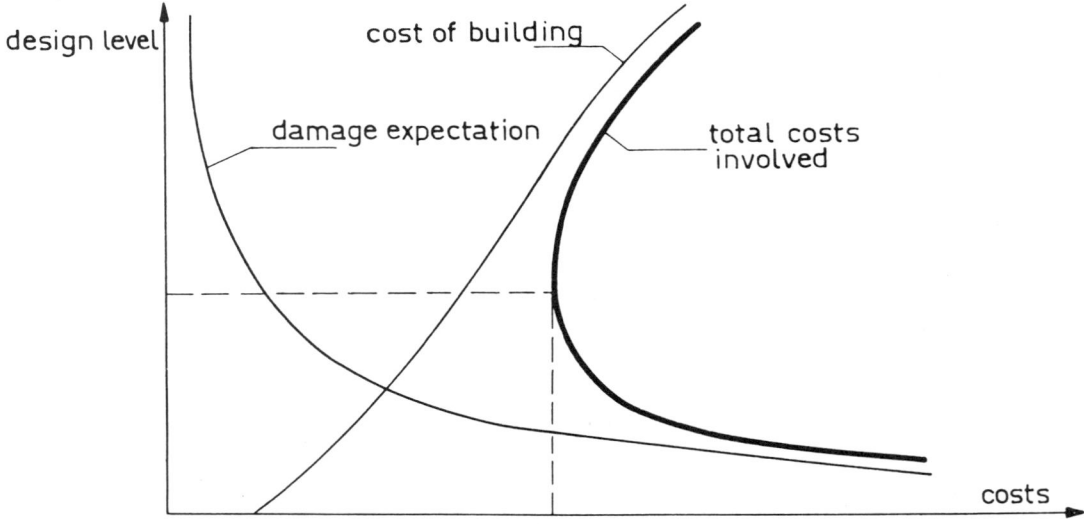

Figure 3.33. Relation between total costs involved and design criterion for breakwater (32).

problem including lack of adequate knowledge of the wave spectrum and its characteristics in all three dimensions or the wave power spectrum in its two dimensions.

With respect to hydraulic model studies, it should be noted that scale effects may exist. Tests at the Waterways Experiment Station (45) proved that any significant scale effects are not very likely in models of a reasonably large scale. For the model tests on rubble-mounds with about 20-ton armor (45), it was observed that no significant scale effect was present in no-damage wave heights obtained from models having a linear scale which corresponds to a Reynolds number N_s of about 3 (10^4) or greater. The surface drag coefficient C_D is a function of N_s, that is, a function of the ratio between viscous and inertia forces. For low values of N_R the viscous forces are predominant and the value of C_D decreases and continues to decrease for increasing values of N_R until a critical value $(N_R)_C$ is reached at which the viscous forces are no longer the predominant ones and the value of C_d is no longer dependent on the value of N_R. The conclusion therefore is that small scale experiments may give results on the conservative side.

Open-Sea and Pier Facilities

Beginning from the deep sea and moving landward, it has become necessary to develop special deep-water mooring systems including buoys and platforms for tankers. Only a relatively few existing ports are able to accommodate vessels with drafts exceeding 50 feet and supertankers of 65 to 90-foot drafts.

Examples of mooring platforms and buoys for tankers are mentioned in Chapter 1. These facilities are becoming more and more popular with increasing tanker sizes. Development within the oil transport industry seems to be toward larger size vessels bringing superloads to terminals for further distribution. *Universe Ireland* (312,000 dwt), bringing crude oil from Kuwait to Bantry Bay in Ireland (mentioned in Chapter 1), is an example of this trend of development. Shallow seas like the North Sea and the Baltic are becoming "second class transport seas" for "smaller vessels" (drafts less than 70 feet). The future bulk terminals will mainly be located in natural harbors like Bantry Bay in Ireland, the Inland Sea in Japan and in deep bay and fjords wherever they might be.

In numerous cases, tanker berths in deeper waters were established as long hammerhead piers. Port Latta in Tasmania was mentioned as an example of this in Chapter 1. The use of steel piles filled with concrete gradually became universal in a number of structural fields including harbor engineering (37). The Port Latta is a particularly interesting case. Reconnaissance of the port site indicated a sloping ocean bottom of continental shelf rock with negligible sand cover. Sonar proved that a berth for 100,000 dwt ore carriers (45 to 50-foot draft) would have to be located 6,000 feet from shore. Economically dredging the rock was out of the question.

Steel box trusses of 200 feet supported on bents with 220-foot spacings were selected as an economical gallery for a mile-long approach conveyor. The hard rock ocean floor, however, presented an unusual design problem for structures built a mile out to sea. Several schemes in both concrete and steel were developed for the four sizes of bent structures plus two protective dolphins required along with different methods of moment connection attachment to the rock. To resist horizontal forces, they had to be designed as cantilevered from the ocean floor with lengths varying from 35 to 85 feet to the support platforms plus some additional superstructures (37).

A modular steel pile and bracing jacket bent design was selected to effect erection economies and speed. ASTM A-411 28- and 30-inch longitudinally welded steel pipe piles were used in 20- by 20-foot modules to build four, six, nine and 20 straight pile bents and 14 all-batter pile dolphins. Piles were fastened to the ocean floor by AP15Lx52 18-inch, 30-foot spud pipes drilled and grouted 15 feet into sound rock and extending 15 feet into the pile which was then filled with concrete. To facilitate this erection procedure in deep water, 32- and 34-inch diameter permanent pile bracing jackets, 20 feet high with 8-inch pipe cross bracing, were designed to act as pile placement templates. Three movable drill platforms were built, and one of these was placed on the ocean floor at each marine substructure site by a 350-ton floating crane. A four-pile bracing jacket template was suspended from this drilling platform and four piles slipped through the 32- or 34-inch jackets and driven to a firm seat on the ocean floor (½ to 3 feet).

A 22-inch rotary drill then drilled holes in the rock for the 18-inch spud through each pile; the spud was placed and grouted through a 4-inch grout hole in its precast concrete fill and the pile filled with concrete. The tops of the jackets were welded to the tops of the cutoff piles and the 1½-inch x 20-foot high annular void between piles and jackets filled with grout. After the concrete developed sufficient strength, the drill platforms were lifted away by the floating crane and 25- by 25- by 4-foot deep reinforced concrete pile caps (preset on shore) were grouted to the piles through shearkey holes in the caps. Thirty piled marine bents were built as were the two batter-pile dolphins built in a similar fashion with 34- by 19-foot 6-inch x 12-foot deep cast-in-place concrete caps; two 2-legged shore bents were cast of concrete. The single 22-inch drill was moved to each of the three drill platforms as jackets and piles were set up and driven (37).

A pier installation like the one described can only be used where wave action is moderate or small making drilling possible. It may involve some delicate soil mechanics problems (see *ASCE Journal of the Soil Mechanics and Foundations Division* November 1969, "Problems in design and installation of offshore piles," by McClelland et al.)

An "all-weather tanker terminal for Cook Inlet, Alaska," is mentioned in Reference 15. Cook Inlet extends approximately 150 miles northeast from the Gulf of Alaska to Anchorage. Following offshore exploration by oil companies, permanent production platforms were installed in the Inlet and submarine pipelines were laid. The Cook Inlet environment includes severe physical problems for marine construction, including the climate itself, high currents, waves and ice problems. As mentioned in Reference 15, Cook Inlet possesses a "Spartan environment" for year-around ship operations. Spring tides plus wind setup or drawdown range from -5.0 to +31.0 feet referenced to a zero datum of mean lower low water. Due to the large tidal prism contained by the long inlet combined with a standing wave effect, the tidal currents may

88 Port Engineering

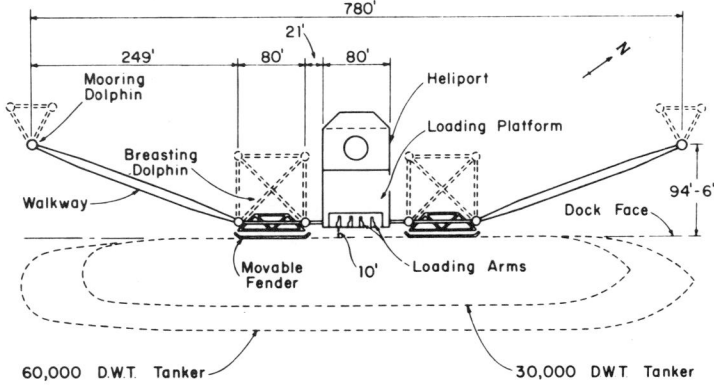

Figure 3.34. Plan of offshore tanker berth (15).

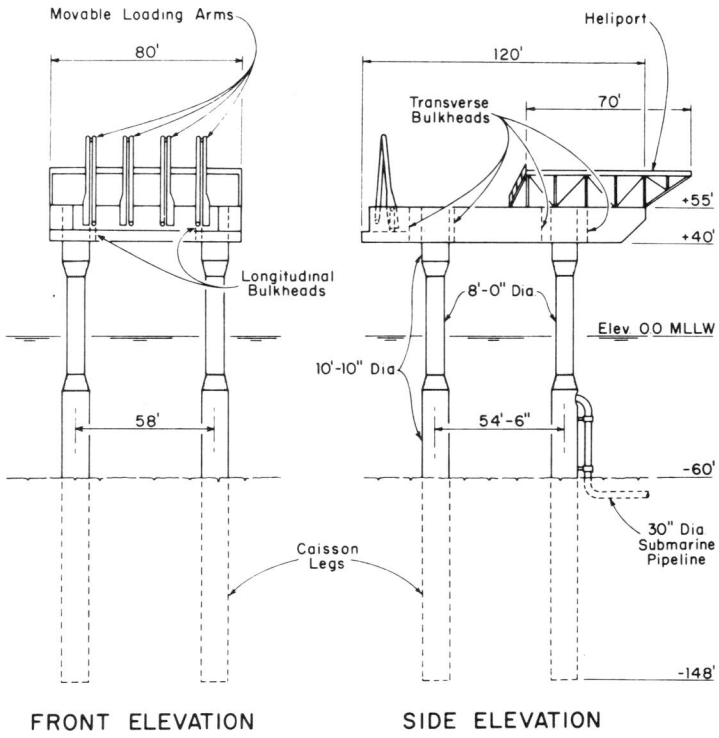

Figure 3.35. Loading platform (15).

Breakwaters and Jetties 89

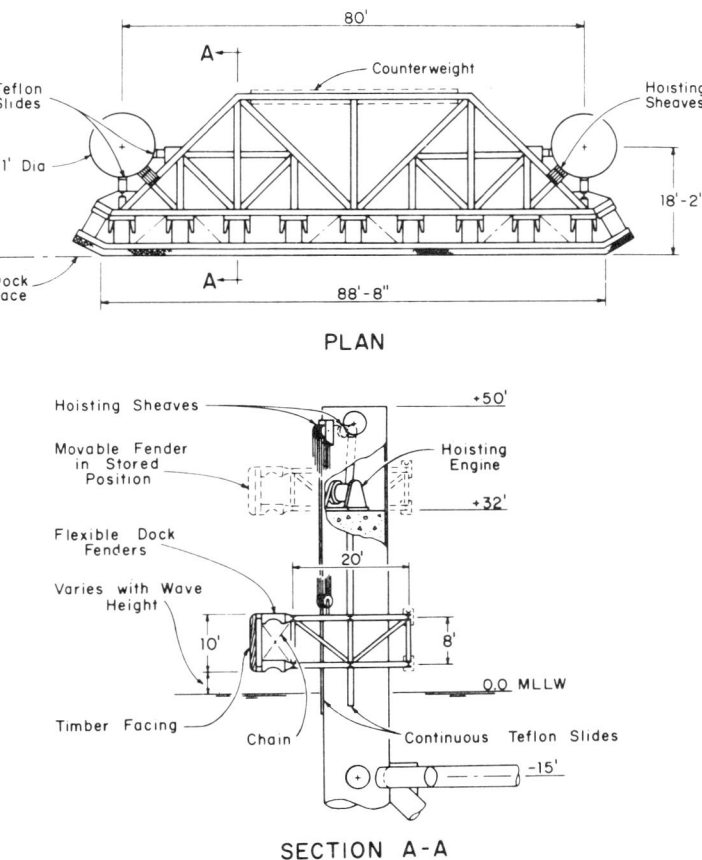

Figure 3.36. Movable fender (15).

attain velocities of up to 8 knots in restrictions and even higher velocities in eddies. The location is susceptible to sudden intense storms reaching almost hurricane force (70 mph.). The design minimum temperature is -50° Fahrenheit. Ice conditions are severe. Due to the extreme range of the diurnal tides, the inlet does not freeze into a continuous ice sheet. Instead, large ice floes of ½ mile or more in diameter travel with the tides at the velocity of the currents. Reference 15 describes how marine terminal sites were investigated along the west side of the inlet where the inlet widens, permitting packed ice fields to disperse into smaller floes. Ice concentrations, however, are heavier on the west side than on the east side.

The survey included comprehensive field and design research. Both structural and operational problems associated with the severe ice conditions led to the adoption of structures with a small number of large diameter circular legs which are able to resist ice forces from all directions and are not so closely spaced as to permit the bridging of ice between adjacent legs. Figure 3.34 shows the plan of an offshore tanker berth for 60,000 dwt vessels. The facility consists of five basic units: a loading platform, two breasting dolphin units immediately adjacent to the platforms and two mooring dolphin units forming the ends of the dock. The critical forces are the ice forces assumed to result from a solid ice field which will prevent a tanker from approaching the berth. Neither berthing impact nor wave force is combined with ice-loading which is as high as 151-kip per horizontal feet ice on permanent members projecting through the ice.

A comprehensive report on sea ice strength by Peyton (33) contains the results from a study of the mechanical and structural properties of sea ice. Some of the most interesting results of this study were the evidence of solid salt reinforcement and the influence of temperature, rate of loading crystal size and orientation of crystals, the history of the ice and depth in the ice sheet.

The basic configuration of the loading platform (Figure 3.35) is that of a barge supported by four 10-foot 10-inch diameter permanent caisson legs which neck down to an 8-foot diameter in the ice zone. The platform barge is designed as a rigid three-dimensional frame to resist full ice force impinging from any horizontal direction. Details of the design including the platform erection procedure is mentioned in Reference 13. Primary structural steel members were fabricated from ASTM A-537 Grade A (low temperature) steel. Below elevation -12 feet, water temperature does not drop below +28° Fahrenheit. In these submerged structure portions, lower charpy impact-value steels are permitted. Pipe piles in the bottoms of the dolphin units are ASTM A-36.

To avoid ice pack formation between the ship and the fender systems which would force the ship away from the dock to the limit of the loading arms, a movable fender system providing uniform energy absorption was adopted (Figure 3.36). The system remains above the water surface by several feet, thus avoiding direct ice forces while remaining in a position to fender effectively an approaching or moored ship. The breasting dolphin units have four 11-foot diameter steel legs joined below the ice level by 4-foot diameter pipe bracing. The two legs adjacent to the dock face project above the water surface to serve as movable fender guides and mooring points (for further information, see Reference 15).

Most open piers are located in areas where wave and current action do not predominate. Protection against impact forces are offered by dolphins and fenders as mentioned in Chapter 4.

Apart from special cases like the Cook Inlet situation, ocean current forces are not very strong. The situation is very different when it comes to wave action. Because of the great increase in the number of coastal works built for oil drilling and mineral exploration, the problem of dynamic forces exerted by water waves on pile structures has experienced growing interest. This brings up the question of correlation of statistics of waves and wave forces on structures. A considerable amount of work has been done on this subject. One of the most recent is by Freudenthal (13).

As mentioned by Freudenthal, correlation between the statistics of the horizontal forces exerted by waves and swell and the statistics of the sea surface elevation is based on the assumption that the total horizontal force per unit length of vertical surface at a specified height above the sea floor can be considered as the sum of a drag force and an inertia force depending, respectively, on horizontal particle velocity $u(t)$ and particle acceleration $\dot{u}(t)$ at that level. Considering that $u(t)$ and $\dot{u}(t)$ are stationary (Bivariate) Gaussian processes, an assumption consistent with the generally assumed linear random model for ocean waves, the spectral density functions $S_u(\omega)$ of $u(t)$ and $S_{\dot{u}}(\omega)$ of $\dot{u}(t)$ can be related to the spectral density function $S_X(\omega)$ of the sea surface elevation with the aid of transfer functions $T_u(\omega)$ and $T_{\dot{u}}(\omega)$ obtained from linear wave theory:

$$S_u(\omega) = T_u(\omega) S_x(\omega)$$

$$S_{\dot{u}}(\omega) = T_{\dot{u}}(\omega) S_x(\omega)$$

A linear combination of the inverse Fourier transforms of $S_u(\omega)$ and $S_{\dot{u}}(\omega)$, which are the autocorrelation or covariance functions $R_u(\tau)$ and $R_{\dot{u}}(\tau)$ of $u(t)$ and $\dot{u}(t)$, respectively, represents a first approximation of the covariance function $R_f(\tau)$ of the wave force f at this level. In the Fourier transform, the spectral density function $S_f(\omega)$ is, in first approximation, a linear combination of the Fourier transforms of $S_u(\omega)$ and $S_{\dot{u}}(\omega)$ of $R_u(\tau)$ and $R_{\dot{u}}(\tau)$ or

$$S_f(\omega) = C_1 S_u(\omega) + C_2 S_{\dot{u}}(\omega)$$
$$= C_1 T_u(\omega) S_x(\omega) + C_2 T_{\dot{u}}(\omega) S_x(\omega)$$
(3.5)

It follows from Equation 3.5 that a close similarity between the spectral density functions $S_f(\omega)$ and $S_x(\omega)$ can be expected when the contribution to the total drag force is small or nonexistent (for instance, in the case of wave forces against sea walls) or when the contribution of the inertia force is small or when both $T_u(\omega)$ and $T_{\dot{u}}(\omega)$ vary rather slowly with ω in the vicinity of the peak $S_x(\omega_0)$. The result of observation analysis suggests that these conditions are almost satisfied even when the contribution of drag and inertia forces are of similar magnitude, with the result that the spectral density function of the wave forces is quite similar in shape to that of the surface elevations. Therefore it can be expected that the same arguments that justify the assumption of a Rayleigh distribution of surface elevations will support the assumption of a Rayleigh distribution of the associated horizontal wave pressures or wave forces so that the probabilistic structure of wave crest and wave forces is, for practical purposes, identical.

The probability levels of the selected design waves are, therefore, identical with the probability levels of the design pressures and design forces exerted by these waves. These probability levels are obtained on the basis of hydrodynamic theories or empirical rules applicable to the various design conditions arising in the design of maritime structures at various ratios of water depth, wave height and wave height to wave length and at various rigidities and geometric configurations, such as standing waves (clapotis), progressing waves, broken waves or dynamic excitation of flexible structure by deformational resonance or by configurational resonance.

The conventional equation used for force calculations, assuming that the total force acting on a submerged body as mentioned above may be obtained by adding inertia and drag components, is:

$$f(z,t) = C_M \rho (\pi D^2 / 4)(\delta u / \delta t) + \tfrac{1}{2} C_D \rho D u |u|$$

in which $f(z, t)$ is the horizontal component of the total force per unit length of pile at elevation z from the bottom, ρ is the mass density of the fluid, D is pile diameter, u is the horizontal component of flow velocity passing the body, $\delta u / \delta t$ is the horizontal component of local acceleration, and C_M and C_D are the mass and drag coefficients, respectively.

The statistical distribution of wave forces on vertical cylindrical piles has been studied by Borgman (4), Brown and Borgman (5), Pierson and Holmes (34), Bretschneider (2) and Bretschneider and St. Denis (3).

Bretschneider considers the probability distribution of peak forces. The most probable maximum (peak) force becomes:

$$f_{m(\max)} = f_{D(\max)} \left\{ 1 + \tfrac{1}{4} [(f_{i(\max)}/f_{D(\max)})^2] \right\}$$

$$\text{for } 0 \leq (f_{i(\max)}/f_{D(\max)}) \leq 2$$

with i referring to inertia forces and D referring to drag forces; otherwise,

$$f_{m(\max)} = f_{i(\max)}$$

$$\text{for } (f_{i(\max)}/f_{D(\max)}) \geq 2,$$

$$f_{D(\max)} = f_{Da}{}^{m_1} \sqrt{(1/A_1)} \, (1_n N)$$

$$f_{i(\max)} = f_{ir}{}^{m_2} \sqrt{(1/A_2)} \, (1_n N)$$

when $\quad f_{Da} = K_1 H_r^2 \,;\, f_{ir}^2 = K_2^2 H_r^2$

$H_r^2 = 1/N \, \Sigma \, H_i^2$ (i indicates individual wave heights)

$$K_1 = \tfrac{1}{2} \rho \, C_D \, D \left[(\pi/T)(\cosh k(d+z)/\sinh k d) \right]^2$$

at $\theta = 0$

$$K_2 = \tfrac{\pi}{4}\rho\, C_m D^2\, (2\pi^2/T^2)\, (\cosh k\,(d+z)/\sinh k\,d)$$

at $\theta = \pi/2$

$A_1'\ A_2'\ m_1$ and m_2 in the equations above are empirical constants. To correlate empirical data on the probability distribution of drag forces and inertial forces with the probability distribution of wave height, the terms *correlation drag coefficient* C_{Dr} and *correlation inertial coefficient* C_{mr} were introduced

$$C_{Dr} = f_{Da}/(\tfrac{1}{2}\rho\, D\, u_r^2) \qquad f_{Da} = \tfrac{1}{2}\rho\, C_{Dr}\, D\, u_r^2$$
$$C_{mr} = (4 f_{ir})/(\pi\rho D^2 \dot{u}_r) \qquad f_{ir} = 4/\pi\, \rho\, C_{mr} D^2 \dot{u}_r$$

f_{ir} is root mean square average of maximum inertial forces. $\dot{u}_r$ is root mean square average of particle acceleration. This assumes that C_{Dr} and C_{mr} are relatively constant or some function of the variables H, T, d, S and D (2).

In Reference 3 the total wave action per unit for vertical height is written

$$f_T = f_D + f_I$$

where the drag force

$$f_D = \tfrac{1}{2}\rho C_D\, A\, |u|\, u$$

and the inertia force

$$f_I = \rho C_M V\, (\delta u/\delta t)$$

and where ρ is the water density, A is the projected area of an element per linear foot of height, V is the volume of an element per linear foot of height, C_D is the drag coefficient, C_M is the mass coefficient, u is the local wave orbital velocity and $\partial u/\partial t$ is the local acceleration.

If, as usual, the element is cylindrical, the projected area per unit height becomes its diameter, D, and the volume, $V = (\pi/2)D^2$.

The total force on a single vertical element (pile) is obtained by integration from sea bed to sea wave surface

$$F_{Dm} = \tfrac{1}{2}\rho \int_o^{z_C} C_D A\, u\, |u|\, dz$$

$$F_{im} = \rho \int_o^{z'} C_M V\, (\delta u/\delta t)\, dz$$

where the upper limit in the first integral is the crest elevation above the sea bed. This is given by

$$z_C = \eta_C + d_t$$

where η_C is the crest elevation above still water in feet, d_t is the total water depth in feet and where z', the limit in the second integral, corresponds to the wave ordinate in that phase position where the integrated acceleration is maximum.

The total water depth is given by

$$d_T = d_0 + a + S$$

where d_o is the depth at mean low water, a is the astronomical or ordinary tide and S is the storm tide or surge.

The total maximum drag and maximum inertial forces on a circular vertical pile are obtained respectively from the following equations

$$F_{im} = \tfrac{1}{2}\rho\, C_M K_{im} D^2 H$$

and

$$F_{Dm} = \tfrac{1}{2}\rho\, C_D K_{Dm} H^2 D$$

where F_{Dm} is the maximum total drag force, F_{im} is the maximum total inertial force, K_{Dm} is given by Figure 3.37 and K_{im} is given by Figure 3.38.

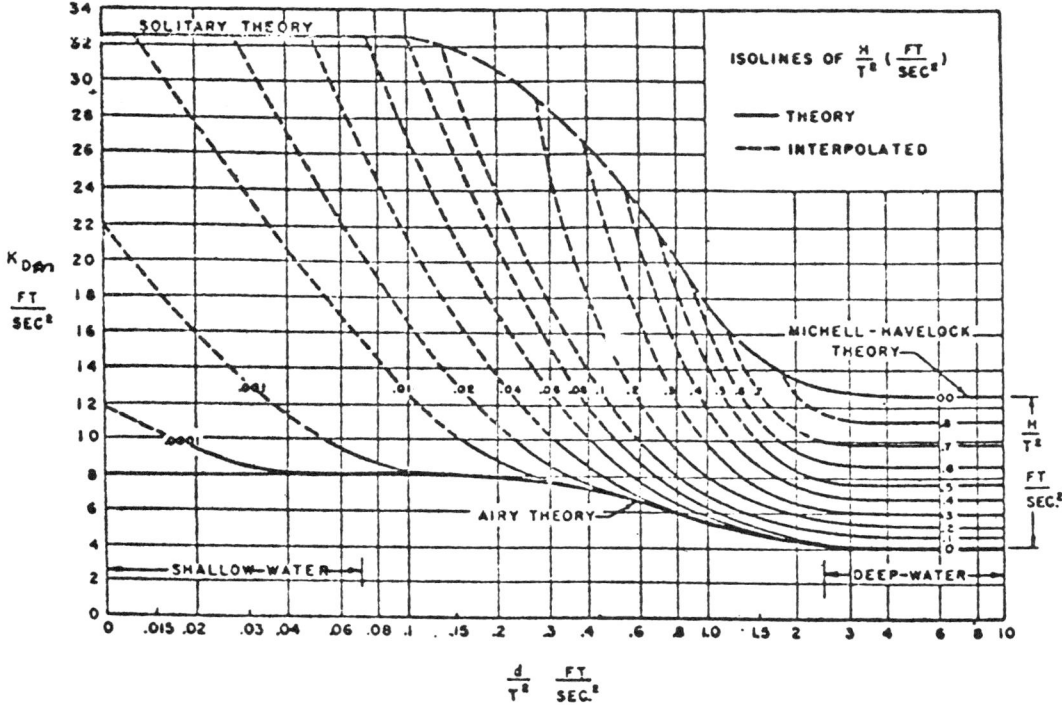

Figure 3.37. Drag force factor at wave crest (3).

Since F_{Dm} and F_{im} are out of phase, the maximum resultant total force F_M is a vector summation of F_{Dm} and F_{im}. Figure 3.39 gives a method of estimating F_M, maximum resultant force.

The corresponding overturning moment about the bottom of a vertical pile extended throughout the full depth is given according to the following equations:

$$M_{Dm} = S_D F_{Dm} \quad \text{and} \quad M_{im} = S_i F_{im}$$

where M_{Dm} is the moment due to maximum drag force and S_D is the corresponding moment arm; M_{im} is the moment due to maximum inertial force and S_i is the corresponding moment arm.

Figures 3.40 and 3.41 give, respectively, approximate values for S_D/d and $S_i/s,d$ as functions of d/T^2 and H/d. The vector addition of drag and inertial moments can also be estimated by use of Figure 3.39, wherein the F-values are replaced by M-values.

It is pertinent to observe that the lower deck of a platform should be at least as high as z_C. Many of the platforms which failed in the Gulf of Mexico during Hurricane Hilda failed because the bottom of the deck elevation (and temporary cellars below the deck) were located below the elevation z_C. Regarding drag and inertial coefficients, see Table 3.8.

Dean and Harleman (11) investigated wave forces on rigid circular members focusing on forces due to small-amplitude waves by shallow-water as well as by deep-water waves. The total force F_T on the piling at any time is the integral of dF_T over submerged length, that is,

$$F_T = \int_o^{h+\eta} dF_T = \int_o^{h+\eta} dF_D + \int_o^{h+\eta} dF_I \quad (3.6)$$

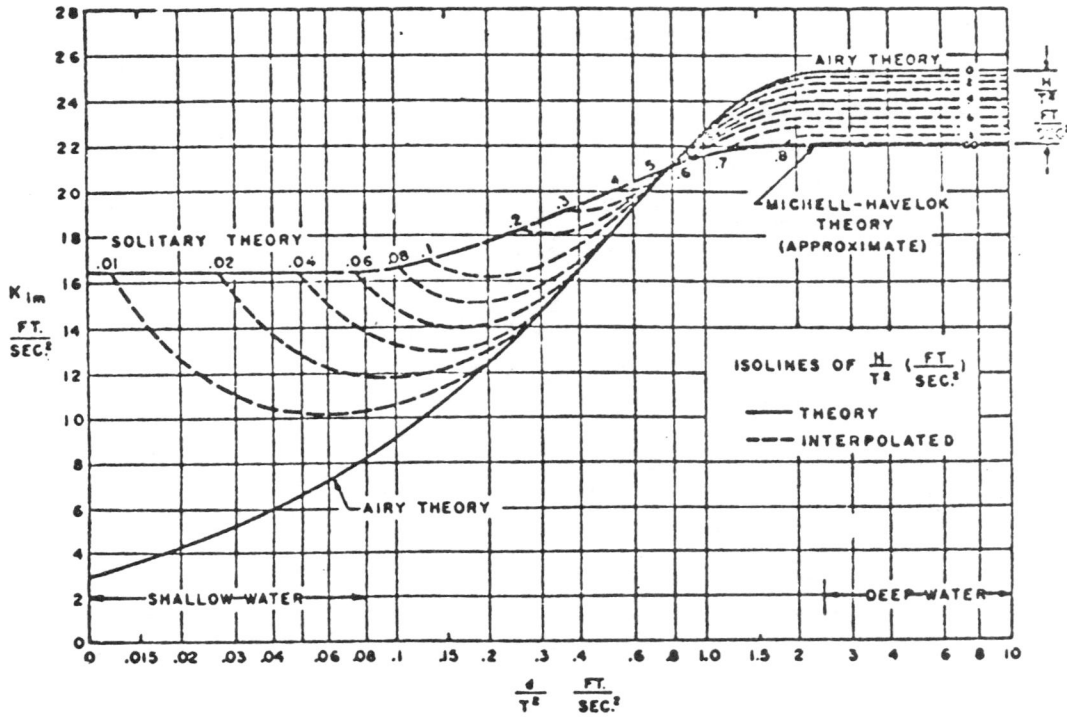

Figure 3.38. Inertial force factor (3).

The components dF_D and dF_I on section ds are defined by

$$dF_D = C_D \rho D (u |u|/2) ds \qquad (3.8)$$

$$dF_I = C_M \rho (\pi D^2 /4) u \, ds \qquad (3.7)$$

With $\eta = a \cos(kx - \sigma t)$, $k = 2\pi/L$ and $\sigma = k \dfrac{L}{T}$ Equations 3.6, 3.7 and 3.8 give

$$F_T = \int_0^{h+\eta} \left(\frac{C_D \rho}{2}\right) Da^2 \sigma^2 \left(\frac{\cosh^2 ks}{\sinh^2 kh}\right) \cos \sigma t | \cos \sigma t | ds$$

$$\int_0^{h+\eta} -\left(\frac{C_M \rho \pi D^2}{4}\right) a \sigma^2 \left(\frac{\cosh ks}{\sinh kh}\right) \sin \sigma t \, ds$$

which, when integrated, and employing the small-amplitude relationship $\sigma^2 = gk \tan kh \, kh$ becomes

$$F_T =$$

$$\gamma \frac{C_D D}{2} \frac{a^2 kh \cos \sigma t |\cos \sigma t|}{\sinh 2kh}$$

$$\left[\frac{1}{2kh} \sinh 2kh \left(1 + \frac{\eta}{h}\right) + \left(1 + \frac{\eta}{h}\right)\right]$$

$$- \gamma \frac{C_M \pi D^2}{2} \frac{a \sin \sigma t}{\cosh kh} \left[\sinh kh \left(1 + \frac{\eta}{h}\right)\right] \qquad (3.9)$$

which is valid for deep and shallow water. The only small-amplitude assumption implied in Equation 3.9 is that the small-amplitude kinematic relationships apply. Equation 3.9 is simplified for shallow- and deep-water waves and for cases in which

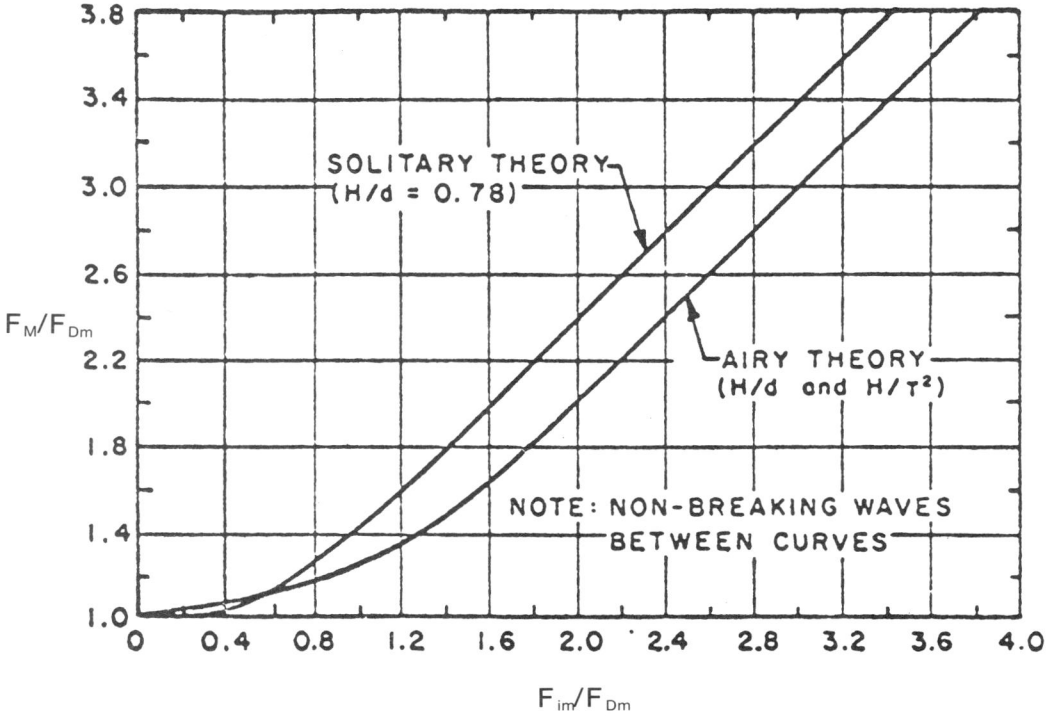

Figure 3.39. F_M/F_{Dm} versus F_{im}/F_{Dm} for the breaking solitary wave and the airy wave (3).

the wave amplitude is small, compared to other pertinent wave dimensions.

Shallow-water conditions, $h/L < 1/20$, imply that $a/L \ll 1$ and the following approximations are valid:

$$\frac{\sinh 2kh \left(1 + \frac{\eta}{h}\right)}{2kh} \cong 1 + \frac{\eta}{h}$$

$$\sinh kh \left(1 + \frac{\eta}{h}\right) \cong kh \left(1 + \frac{\eta}{h}\right)$$

$$\cosh kh \cong 1$$

We then have

$$F_T = \gamma \frac{C_D D}{2} a^2 \cos \sigma t \, |\cos \sigma t| \left[1 + \frac{\eta}{h}\right]$$
$$- \gamma \frac{C_M \pi D^2}{4} a \, kh \sin \sigma t \left[1 + \frac{\eta}{h}\right] \quad (3.10)$$

With the further small-amplitude approximation

$$\frac{\eta}{h} \leqslant \frac{a}{h} \ll 1$$

Equation 3.10 simplifies to

$$F_T = \gamma \frac{C_D D}{2} a^2 \cos \sigma t \, |\cos \sigma t|$$
$$- \gamma \frac{C_M \pi D^2}{4} a \, kh \sin \sigma t \quad (3.11)$$

Equation 3.11 can be written in the alternate form

$$F_T = \gamma \frac{C_D D}{2} a^2 \cos \sigma t \, |\cos \sigma t|$$
$$- \gamma \frac{C_M \pi^2 D^2}{2} \frac{a}{T} \sqrt{\frac{h}{g}} \sin \sigma t$$

96   Port Engineering

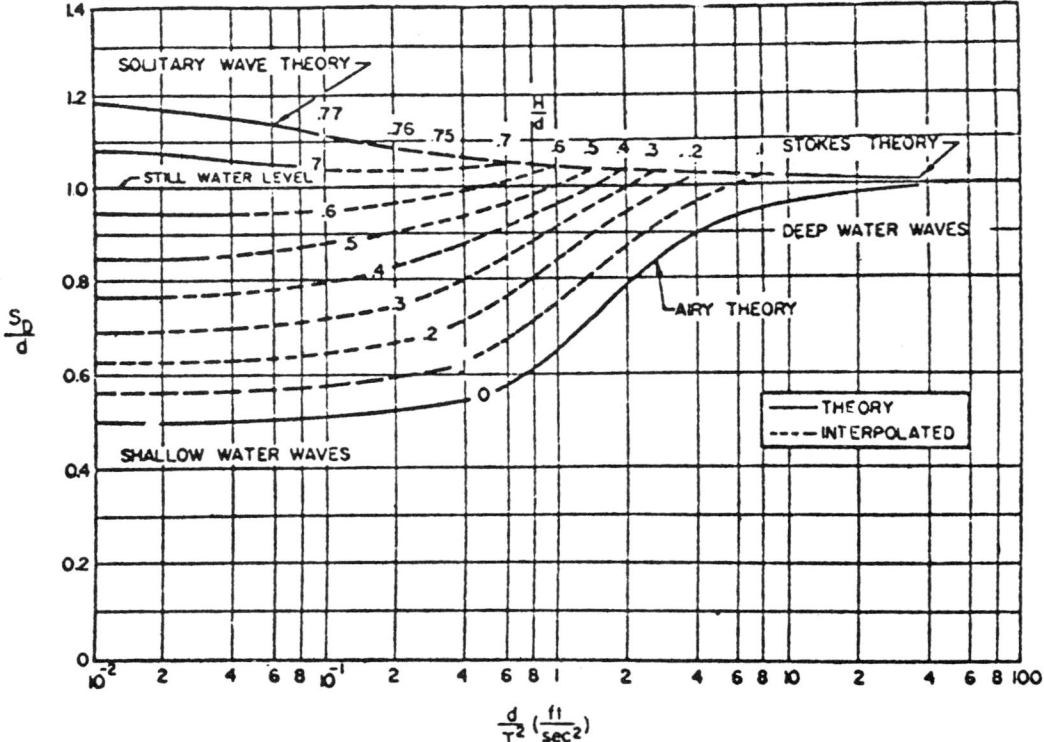

Figure 3.40. Relative lever arm measured from bottom versus relative depth corresponding to maximum drag force (3).

which shows that for this order of approximation and for shallow-water waves the maximum drag force is independent of wave period and the maximum inertia force is inversely proportional to wave period.

Deep-water conditions, $h/L > \frac{1}{2}$, imply $a/h \ll 1$, and the following approximations are in order:

$$\sinh 2kh \left(1 + \frac{\eta}{h}\right) \cong \frac{e^{2kh}e^{2k\eta}}{2} \gg 1$$

$$\sinh kh \left(1 + \frac{\eta}{h}\right) \cong \frac{e^{kh}e^{k\eta}}{2} \gg 1$$

$$\cosh kh \cong \frac{e^{kh}}{2} \gg 1$$

$$e^{2k\eta} \cong 1 + 2k\eta$$

Employing these approximations, Equation 3.9 becomes

$$F_T = \gamma \frac{C_D D}{4} a^2 \cos \sigma t \, |\cos \sigma t\,|(1 + 2k\eta)$$

$$- \gamma \frac{C_M \pi D^2}{4} a \sin \sigma t \,(1 + k\eta)$$

and, with the further approximation of $\eta/L < a/L \ll 1$,

$$F_T = \gamma \frac{C_D D}{4} a^2 \cos \sigma t \, |\cos \sigma t\,|$$

$$- \gamma \frac{C_M \pi D^2}{4} a \sin \sigma t \qquad (3.12)$$

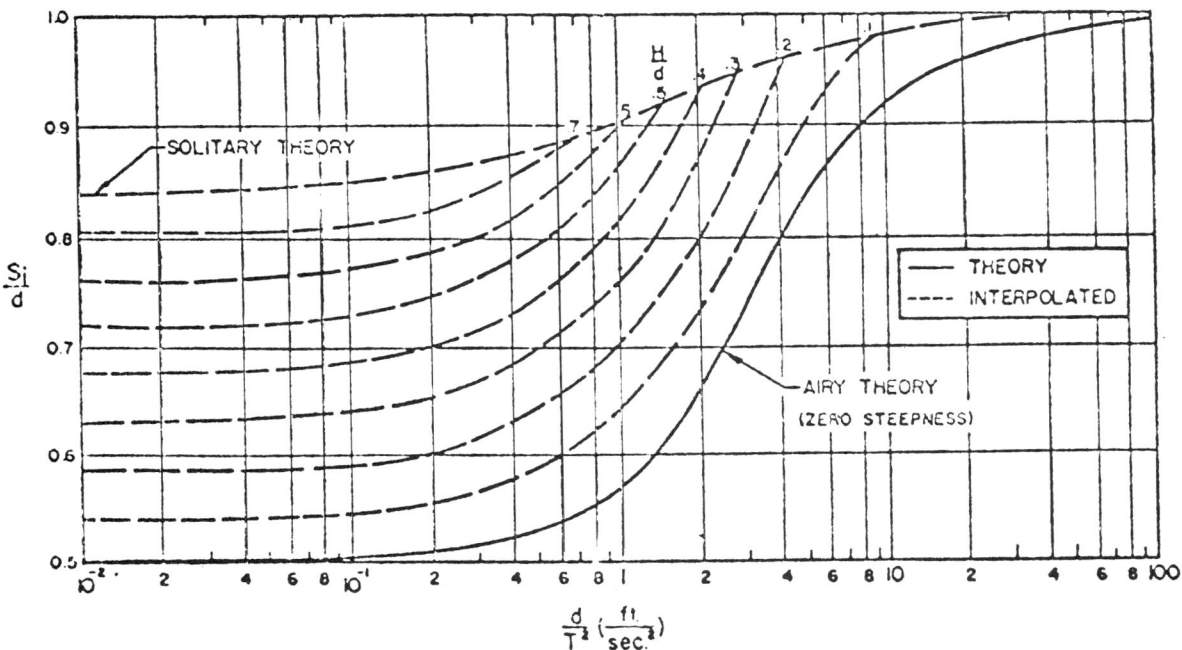

Figure 3.41. Relative lever arm measured from bottom versus relative depth corresponding to maximum inertial force (3).

Equation 3.12 demonstrates that for this order of approximation and deep-water waves, both the maximum drag and inertia force components are independent of wave period.

For further information, the reader should consult Reference 11 which also lists available results of the most significant studies to determine drag and mass coefficients referring to research by Wilson and Reid. Table 3.8 is Table 8.1 from Reference 11.

Averages of the drag and mass coefficients presented in Table 3.8 are $\overline{C}_D = 1.05$ and $\overline{C}_M = 1.40$, but as mentioned in Reference 11, p. 362, the drag coefficient shows an increasing trend with increasing roughness, and the inertia coefficient is influenced by the relative size of pile diameter compared to wave length (D/L).

It should be noted, however, that forces are not in line with the direction of wave propagation. Considerable transversal forces occur (11, 36).

Then forces are cyclic, oscillating with a frequency much higher than that of the imposed frequency. Rance (36) found that, if the parameter for describing the vibration is the normal Strouhal Number, $S = ND/V$ (N is frequency, D is diameter of pile and V is water velocity), S showed remarkable consistency. There was no variation with a/D (a is the semiorbit length) or with Reynolds Number.

The large scatter found in C_M and C_D values may be attributed to deviations about mean forces due to eddy shedding. This phenomenon would also explain the result of negative values of C_M recorded by several authors. Since the predominant linear dimension of the system is the piling diameter, it is reasonable to assume that, for a rigid piling, the axial length of the vortex is proportional to the piling diameter. With this assumption, one would expect that two sections of the same piling separated by many piling diameters would not experience in-phase vortex fluctuations.

Table 3.8 Drag and Inertial Coefficient Values for Circular Cylinders in Accelerating Flows (11).

Authority and date	Nature of experiments	Cylinder diameter	C_D	C_M	Type of flow (remarks)
Crooke, 1955	Model	2, 1, ½	1.60	2.30	Oscillatory
Keulegan and Carpenter, 1956	Model	3, 2½, 2	1.34	1.46	Oscillatory (av. of 29 tabulated values)
		1½, 1¼	1.52	1.51	(av. of 57 tabulated values)
Klim, 1956	Model	1, ½	1.00	0.93	Accelerated, nonoscillatory
Dean, 1956	Model	3	1.10	1.46	Accelerated, nonoscillatory
Wiegel et al., 1956	Prototype	24	1.00	0.95	Ocean waves, west coast
Reid, 1956	Prototype	8-5/8	0.53	1.47	Ocean waves, Gulf of Mexico
Bretschneider 1957	Prototype	16	0.40	1.10	Ocean waves, Gulf of Mexico
Wilson, 1957	Prototype	30	1.00	1.45	Ocean waves, Gulf of Mexico

On the other hand, two sections of the same piling separated by only a few diameters would have a higher probability of in-phase vortex fluctuations. Extending this line of reasoning further, it can be shown that some dimensionless measure of the force scatter should correlate with the dimensionless ratio $\Delta \ell D$ where $\Delta \ell$ is the length of the section of piling to which the force scatter is related. Theoretically, according to Lamb, $C_M = 2.0$ for a right circular cylinder in an ideal potential flow. This was confirmed by Rance (36) and by Jen (22) for forces exerted by uniform periodic waves in relatively deep water, $d/L > 0.175$, and low steepness, $H/L < 0.02$.

Tests by Lebreton and Cormault (24) proposing a mathematical approach to the interaction between a nonviscous fluid with a free surface and an assembly of structures composed of shells, whether fixed or not, partially or totally immersed in the fluid, showed that C_M for horizontal forces upon submerged cylindrical bodies should be equal to 1, as soon as the water height overtopping the pile is more than one diameter of this pile.

For irregular waves in Jen's study (22), the spectral density function of total force $P_{FF}(f)$ was found to be accurately predictable by applying a transfer function to the known spectral density function of the water surface, $P_{\xi\xi}(f)$. For the case of strong inertia predominance, the solution is reduced to

$$P_{FF}(f) = P_{\xi\xi}(f) \left(\frac{(2\pi f)^2 \, m}{k} \right)^2$$

in which $f = 1/T$; $m = C_M \rho (\pi D^2/4)$ and $k = (2\pi/L)$ and f are related by $(2\pi f)^2 = gk \tanh kd$ according to Airy's theory.

For the tests on irregular waves Jen found that the spectral density function of total force $P_{FF}(f)$ was accurately predictable by applying a transfer function to the known spectral density function of the water surface, $P_{\xi\xi}(f)$.

A great number of pier installations and other offshore installations are described in References 8 and 35. Several periodicals like *Journal of the Marine Technology Society, Offshore Engineering,* and *Ocean Industry* bring news regularly about the developments in the field of ocean engineering. The materials used include mainly steel and reinforced concrete but prestressed concrete is gradually moving into this field. Some major pier installations have been built on creosoted piles (New York Harbor) with reinforced concrete decking.

References

1. Brandtzaeg, A. 1965. "General report on breakwaters with vertical and sloping faces. Measurements of waves. Study of wave forces. Methods of calculation." *Proceedings of 21st International Navigation Congress* s II - s 1. Brussels.
2. Bretschneider, C.L. 1965. "On the probability distribution of wave force and an introduction to the correlation drag coefficient and the correlation inertial coefficient." *Proceedings of Coastal Engineering Specialty Conference.* Santa Barbara, Calif.: American Society of Civil Engineers. pp. 183-217.
3. ____, and St. Denis, M. 1967. "Selection of design sea state for offshore structures." *Le Petrole et la Mer.* Section 1(117).
4. Borgman, L. E. 1965. *A Statistical Theory of Hydrodynamic Forces on Objects.* Wave Research Report HEL9-6. University of California, Berkeley: Hydraulics Engineering Laboratory.
5. Brown, J.J., and Borgman, L.E. 1966. *Tables of the Statistical Distribution of Ocean Wave Forces on Vertical Piling.* Tech Report HEL9-3. University of California, Berkeley: Hydraulics Engineering Laboratory.
6. Bruun, P. 1953. "Breakwaters for coastal protection, hydraulic principles in design." *Proceedings of the 18th International Navigation Congress* s II - q 1. Rome.
7. Carstens, T., Torum, A., and Traetteberg, A. 1966. "The stability of rubble mound breakwaters against irregular waves." *Proceedings of 10th Conference on Coastal Engineering* 2:958-76.
8. Cornick, H.F. 1958-64. *Dock and Harbour Engineering,* vols. 1-4. London: Charles Griffin and Co. Ltd.
9. Cote, J.B., and Simard, G.R. 1964. "The breakwater quay at the Bay of Comeau." *The Dock and Harbour Authority* 45 (Apr.): 372-76.
10. Danel, Pierre. 1953. "Tetrapods." *Proceedings of 4th Conference on Coastal Engineering.* University of California, Berkeley: Council on Wave Research. pp. 390-98.
11. Dean, R.G., and Harleman, D.R.F. 1966. "Inter-action of structures and waves." *Estuary and Coastline Hydrodynamics.* Edited by A. Ippen. New York: McGraw-Hill Book Company, Inc., pp. 341-403.
12. Delfth Hydraulic Laboratory. 1969. *Proceedings of Symposium on Research on Wave Action* 1-4.
13. Freudenthal, A.M. 1968-69. "Probalistic evaluation of design criteria for maritime structures." *PIANC Bulletin* 3 and 4(2): 17-31.
14. Gallareto, E. 1967. "Lines for research in breakwater design." *The Dock and Harbour Authority* 48(July): 78-83.
15. Gaither, W.S., and Dalton, R.E. 1969. "All-weather tanker terminal for Cook Inlet, Alaska." *ASCE Journal of the Waterways and Harbors Division* 95(WW2): 131-48.
16. Galvin, Cyril J. 1969. "Breaker Travel and choice of design wave height." *ASCE Journal of the Waterways and Harbors Division* 95(WW2): 175-200.
17. Gerritsen, F.G. 1969. "Design criteria in coastal engineering." *Topics in Ocean Engineering,* vol. 1. Edited by Bretschneider.

Houston: Gulf Publishing Company, pp. 370-411.
18. Hayashi, T., and Hattori, H. 1963. "Effect of the wave pressures and the impulses of breaking waves on the stability of breakwaters." *Proceedings of International Association of Hydraulic Research Congress* (1.5): 33-40.
19. Hudson, R.Y. 1959. "Laboratory investigations of rubble-mound breakwaters." *ASCE Journal of the Waterways and Harbors Division* 85(WW3): 93-120.
20. ____. 1961. *Wave Forces on Rubble-Mound Breakwaters and Jetties.* Misc. Paper 2-453. Vicksburg, Mo.: U.S. Army Waterways Experiment Station.
21. Jarlan, G.E. 1961. "A perforated vertical wall breakwater." *The Dock and Harbour Authority* 42(Apr.): 396-98.
22. Jen, Y. 1968. "Laboratory study of inertia forces on a pile." *ASCE Journal of the Waterways and Harbors Division* 94(WW1): 59-76.
23. Kidby, Harold A., et al. 1964. "Placed-stone jetty, stone weight coefficients." *ASCE Journal of the Waterways and Harbors Division* 90(WW4): 77-85.
24. Lebreton, J.C., and Cormault, P. 1969. "Wave action on slightly immersed structures. Some theoretical and experimental results." *Proceedings of Symposium on Research on Wave Action* 4(127). Holland: Delft Hydraulic Laboratory.
25. Le Méhauté, B. 1963. "On nonsaturated breakers and the wave run-up." *Proceedings of 8th Conference on Coastal Engineering.* Mexico. pp. 77-92.
26. Le Méhauté, B., Koh, R.C.Y., and Li-San Hwang. 1968. "A synthesis on wave run-up." *ASCE Journal of the Waterways and Harbors Division* 94(WW1): 77-92.
27. Lundgren, H. 1962. "A new type of breakwater for exposed positions." *The Dock and Harbour Authority* 42(Nov.): 228-31.
28. ____. 1969. "Wave shock forces and analysis of deformation and forces in the wave and in the foundation." *Proceedings of the Technical University of Delft Conference on Waves* (8).
29. Munk, W.H. 1969. "Solitary wave theory and its applications to surf problems." *Annals of the New York Academy of Sciences* 51(Art 3): 326-424.
30. Nagai, Shoshichiro. 1969. "Pressures of standing waves on vertical wall." *ASCE Journal of the Waterways and Harbors Division* 95(WW1): 53-76. Discussion of this paper by Y. Goda, 96(WW1): 155-57.
31. Palmer, R.Q. 1960. "Breakwaters in the Hawaiin Islands." *ASCE Journal of the Waterways and Harbors Division* 86(WW2): 39-67.
32. Permanent International Association of Navigation Congresses. 1969. "Methods for deciding the limiting design conditions to be allowed for in the satisfactory economic conception of maritime structures." *Proceedings of 22nd Congress of PIANC* s II - s 5.
33. Peyton, H.R. 1966. *Sea Ice Strength.* Report WAG R-182. University of Alaska.
34. Pierson, W.J., and Holmes, P. 1965. "Irregular wave forces on a pile." *ASCE Journal of the Waterways and Harbors Division* 91(WW1): 1-10.
35. Quinn, A. De F. 1961. *Design and Construction of Ports and Marine Structures.* New York: McGraw-Hill Book Company, Inc.
36. Rance, P.J. 1969. "The influence of Reynolds Number on wave force." *Proceedings of Symposium on Research on Wave Action* 4(13). Holland: Delft Hydraulic Laboratory.
37. Soros, Paul. 1969. "Port Latta, open sea terminal." *Civil Engineering* (Jan.): 62-65.
38. Thorn, R.B. 1960. *The Design of Sea Defence Work.* London: Butterworth and Co. Ltd.
39. U.S. Army Corps of Engineers. 1958. *Design of Quarry-Stone Cover Layers for Rubble-Mound Breakwaters.* Research Report 2-2. Waterways Experiment Station.
40. ____. 1966. *Shore-Protection, Planning and Design.* Coastal Engineering Center.
41. ____. 1968. *An Experimental Study of Breaking-Wave Pressures.* Research Report H-68-1. Waterways Experiment Station.
42. ____. 1968. *Design of Cover Layers for Rubble-Mound Breakwaters Subjected to Non-*

breaking Waves. Research Report 2-11. Waterways Experiment Station.

43. ____. 1968. *Limiting Heights of Breaking and Nonbreaking Waves on Rubble-Mound Breakwaters.* Tech Report H-68-3. Waterways Experiment Station.

44. ____. 1968. *Shock Pressures Caused by Waves Breaking against Coastal Structures.* Research Report H-68-2, Waterways Experiment Station.

45. ____. 1969. *Scale Effect Tests for Rubble-Mound breakwaters.* Research Report H-69-2. Waterways Experiment Station.

46. von Karman, T. 1929. *The Impact on Seaplanes during Landing.* Tech Note 32. National Advisory Committee on Aeronautics.

4 planning and layout of ports
wharves, quays, fenders dolphins and mooring devices

Wharves, quays and piers are marine structures which are used for the mooring or tying of vessels while they are loading or discharging cargo and/or passengers. Wharves and quays are backed by warehouse areas, marshaling and storing areas, industry areas, roads, rails, etc.—areas often created by extensive fill operations. It is characteristic for many ports in the United States and many other places in the world where ports are built on the estuary, bay, lagoon or riverside that fill for construction of port areas and areas adjacent to the port come from dredging of port channels and basins.

A pier is usually a rectangular wharf structure which projects out into the water. In the United Kingdom, it is often referred to as a jetty. It may also be called a mole, and, in combination with a breakwater, it is frequently termed a breakwater pier.

Because of its geometry, it can be used for berthing of vessels on three sides. A pier does not necessarily need to run perpendicular to the shoreline or wharf line but may project under any angle. It may also be connected with the shore or general wharf line by a trestle and may thus become T- or L-shaped.

Wharves, quays and piers are often in the general port language combined in one terminology—docks.

Layout of Quays and Wharves

Quays and wharves may be placed in an infinite number of ways—no firm rules exist, but it may be done in a more or less practical way. The two main boundary conditions for a layout are the water area available and its geometry (bay, river, open sea) and the land areas available (for harbor services and transport and for industry which most practically may be placed in the harbor area).

Basically two principles exist, *the parallel quay system* and *the pier system* with piers perpendicular to or at an angle with the shore. T-piers are a mixture of the two systems. These principles are demonstrated in the New York and Newark Port area which is used as an example in the following.

Wharves and Quays 103

Figure 4.1. Parallel quay wall at Port of Newark (Port of New York Catalogue).

Figure 4.3. Erie-Basin Port Authority Marine Terminal (Port of New York Catalogue).

Figure 4.2. New York Port Authority Grain Terminal and Columbia Street Pier (Port of New York Catalogue).

Figure 4.4. Brooklyn Port Authority Marine Terminal (Port of New York Catalogue).

Figure 4.1 shows a parallel quay at the Port Newark, total 707-acre, 36-berth terminal, readily accessible to the entire Port of New York area.

Figure 4.2 shows two piers, the New York Port Authority Grain Terminal and Columbia Street Pier on Gowanus Bay in Brooklyn.

Figure 4.3 shows a more diversified pier system, the Erie Basins-Port Authority Marine Terminal on Gowanus Bay south of the Brooklyn Port Authority Marine Terminal.

Figure 4.4 shows the Brooklyn Port Authority Marine Terminal which is located on a prime sec-

*Figure 4.5. Elizabeth Port Authority Marine Terminal (*Port of New York Catalogue*).*

tion of the port's waterfront in the heart of one of the greatest freight generating centers in the world. It extends southward two miles from the Brooklyn Bridge to and including the Atlantic Basin.

The New York Port Authority's redevelopment program for this facility, which began upon acquisition of the property in 1956, has resulted in the replacement of twenty-five obsolete piers with twelve new piers, plus the rehabilitation of one pier and the improvement of about 60 acres of upland area. These modern piers offer wide aprons and ample shedded space to facilitate the efficient loading and discharge of vessels. Extensive upland areas and broad truck platforms make possible the rapid pickup and delivery of freight by merchants and truckers using the new piers.

Figure 4.5 is the Elizabeth-Port Authority Marine Terminal located on Newark Bay in the city of Elizabeth south of Port Newark. It is the largest waterfront development ever undertaken in the New Jersey-New York harbor.

This new seaport is being developed on 919 acres of reclaimed meadowland as the world's largest and most modern containership terminal. Thirteen deep-water vessel berths, supported by some 297 acres of paved cargo area, huge modern cargo distribution buildings with rail sidings and truck-high platforms are already in operation. Ten giant gantry cranes, each 150 feet high and mounted on rails, rapidly move containers to and from the vessels.

The facility includes the operations base of Sea-Land Service, Inc., a pioneer containership company. The firm's 111-acre terminal includes six berths and a marshaling yard for 2,000 containers. Atlantic Container Lines and Moore-McCormack Line occupy a six-berth terminal and 93 acres of upland area. International Terminal Operating Company provides service to other containerships operating at a three-berth, 85-acre public terminal.

When completed in 1975 at a cost of $175,000,000, the Elizabeth-Port Authority Marine Terminal will have 793 acres of transit and open storage area and distribution building space. The facility is expected to handle nearly 9,000,000 tons of general cargo a year, providing jobs for about 5,000 people earning an estimated $37,500,000 annually.

Because of the large scope of this development, which involves the eventual construction of almost 5 miles (8 kilometers) of quay, the study of the wharf design was an exhaustive one intended to eliminate the more expensive types of constructions from further consideration. This procedure and the ultimate result are mentioned in the following section giving examples of designs of quay walls.

Figure 4.6 shows a closer view of the southern part of the Brooklyn Port Authority Marine Terminal which comprises the Møller Steamship Company pier installation which was built by the New York Port Authority as part of its redevelopment of some two and a half miles of waterfront south of the Brooklyn Bridge. The $95-million redevelopment program included the construction of new piers to replace narrow, obsolete piers.

The wharf structure (Figure 4.6) is a steel sheet piling ZP 38 anchored to a steel sheet piling of ZP 27 by 3 5/8-inch tie rods. It is designed for a water depth of 35 feet plus 2 feet overdredging.

No general rules exist for length of basins. Quinn (26) only mentions piers with one or two berths on either side of a pier. Fugl Meyer (10), on

Figure 4.6. Moller Steamship Company Terminal, Brooklyn Port Authority Marine Terminal (Figure 4.4) Port of New York Authority.

the other hand, says that "the length of a basin should not exceed 2,000 meters, elsewise transportation and navigation is impeded." The basins should not be curved as this makes berthing inconvenient. A slight concavity is less inconvenient.

Convex quays for larger ships are only practical when floating fenders or other contrivances are used.

The minimum length of a quay should be sufficient for mooring the longest ship expected to arrive. At medium-sized ports with 9 meters of water depth, such a ship may be 160 meters long, and adding 20 meters at both ends for moorings, the total minimum length should be 200 meters.

If the port work is carried out in connection with rail traffic and by means of cranes, one berth is generally uneconomical. Figuring that a large and a small ship are to be accommodated at a quay, the ships being 150 and 110 meters long respectively, and calculating with three mooring distances of 20 meters, the quay for the accommodation of the two ships should be 320 meters long. This gives a reasonable apportionment of transit sheds and open spaces for storage. Six to seven hundred meters is a suitable length for a basin. The interspacing of 20 meters may serve as a reserve which occasionally may be used.

With respect to basin widths, Fugl Meyer (10) considers the following traffic situations in a basin with quays at both sides in order to arrive at some definite figures:

1. Maximum ships at both quays with two rows of lighters on the outer side of each ship and a fairway twice the breadth of a large ship between the moored vessels.
2. Smaller cargo ships at both quays with one row of lighters on the outer side and a fairway four times the breadth of a smaller ship so that two ships are able to pass one another.
3. The necessity of widening the basins at a river port so that a row of dolphins can be placed in the middle as moorages for ships discharging directly to the river lighters and other river craft. If such dolphins are placed in the basin, an additional width is required exceeding the width necessary for situation 1. The addition will be one ship of maximum size and a river craft on either side of it. Two fairways are necessary, and in this case they must be twice the width of the ship expected.

The following designations are used for figuring the required width of the basin in the above three situations:

B = 22 meters, width of a large ship
b = 14 meters, width of a local ship
c = 7 meters, width of a lighter
f = 10 meters, width of a river craft
Situation 1: $4 \times B + 4 \times c$ = 116 meters
Situation 2: $6 \times b + 2 \times c$ = 98 meters
Situation 3: $7 \times B + 6 \times f$ = 214 meters.

The basins are often narrower at the inner end, widening at the end where they join other basins. If the basin is 110 to 120 meters wide at the inner end, the basal quay is able to berth local ships up to 1,500 BRT, and if the basin is 300 to 400 meters long, it is usually 10 meters wider at the outer end. Many river ports consist of a number of piers protruding from the shore, like teeth of a comb. Such piers are often so short that they can accommodate only one ship at each quay. The width of such basins, which corresponds to the distance between the piers, does not necessarily have to include a fairway. In Great Britain and the United States, the width between piers varies between 60 and 200 meters.

Wherever the width of an ordinary port basin is less than 80 meters, the narrowness causes complaints as tugboats maneuver with difficulty and the exchanging of lighters is complicated, especially if work is proceeding on both sides of the basin.

Although it is important for a basin to be sufficiently wide for the demands of today's traffic and expected future traffic, it should not be prodigiously wide. In fact, it should be designed as narrow as possible in order to decrease the internal transportation distances and limit investments and maintenance.

In regard to basin depths, Fugl Meyer (10) rightfully claims that the necessary depth of the basins in a port cannot be determined solely by the maximum draught of the arrivals. It is more practical to have sufficient depth to accommodate the largest conceivable arrival. This raises the important question of what depths are wanted versus what depths are possible.

Most ports want as much depth as possible because they may then accommodate as large vessels as possible which is usually an advantage for trade and commerce. Chapter 2, section 1, includes Figures 2.1, 2.2 and 2.3 which were constructed from dimensions of ships in service in

1967 and 1968 to show the draught and beam against the dead weight tonnage of typical oil tankers, bulk carriers and general cargo vessels. In various catalogs such as *Ports of the World* (24), harbors are listed giving a great variety of information on their capabilities including length of berths at various depths, usually at mean low water or at mean lower low water. Information is also given on special installations such as those for bulk carriers. What kind of depth(s) is wanted is one thing; what is possible within reasonable economic limits is another.

The proximity of the port to the deep-water ocean is of major interest. If the distance to the 60-foot contour is 10 miles across a continental shelf area or an estuary, the port will be able to accommodate all general cargo vessels and some bulk carriers but not large tankers or bulk carriers of draughts exceeding 50 feet. An example of this is the Port of Antwerp now aiming to maintain at least 40-foot official depth at all tides in its navigation channel and 50 feet in some new dock basins. For example, it is always possible to dredge channels all the way out to a 100-foot depth, but this could be very expensive. Even if initial dredging could be financed, maintenance costs may be prohibitive (see Chapter 9). The cost/benefit ratio used by the U.S. Army Corps of Engineers as mentioned in Chapter 2 is helpful in determining the economic limit of a navigational dredging project.

Many large ports have official depths of 28, 30, 32 and 35 feet. For ports in developing countries where economy plays an important role, depths of 28 and 30 feet are usually accepted. The new container port facility at Newark (Figure 4.5) has a 35-foot channel; Antwerp, a 40-foot channel and Europe-port in Holland, a 72-foot channel. The future trend will be toward increasing depths but within practical and economic limits. Some ports have made 42 feet their targets. For large tankers, draft limit in 1970 was 80 feet, but it may soon become 100 feet accommodating the vessel at offshore mooring installations.

In open tidal ports with a highly fluctuating water level, the surface of the quay may be built slightly above highest high water. A daily rise and fall of the tide of 15 to 18 feet or more may occur. Such fluctuation complicates and delays loading and discharging and increases the cost of the quay construction. Consequently, it is often necessary to close a series of basins by means of sluices and thus maintain a constant water level in the closed port section. In tidal ports depths are almost always calculated with the lowest low-water line as zero line. In closed docks or in ports with a stable water level, the quay surface should never be less than 2.5 meters above water level (10). Ports with locks are common in England, France and in the Low Countries in Europe (7), but not elsewhere. They are now replaced with open tidal ports if at all possible.

Design of Wharves and Piers

As explained in Chapter 2, the design of interior harbor structures may play an important role for the wave situation in the harbor if the harbor is located on an exposed shore or is subject to other kinds of wave action like long period waves and boat waves of magnitude as may happen in estuaries and inlets. Hydraulically, one may distinguish between reflecting walls which may be vertical gravity walls, caissons or sheet pile walls and open energy absorbing walls like pile and trestle structures which may be backed by rubble-mounds, revetments or sheet piles. Crib structures are "in between." They are vertical but open and absorb some wave energy. Open structures are of particular importance when soil conditions necessitate the use of long piles to be driven down to bed rock or other solid foundation or down far enough to provide the necessary friction to support the structure. This is often the case in New York harbor. In the Port of Oslo, Norway, very steep rock slopes call for very long steel foundation piles.

One can also distinguish between various kinds of walls by the way in which forces by earth and work loads exerted on the wall are absorbed: by gravity in gravity walls, caissons and cells; by active and passive earth pressures in sheet pile structures with anchor plates; by compression and/or friction forces in pile structures; by a combination of passive earth pressures, compression

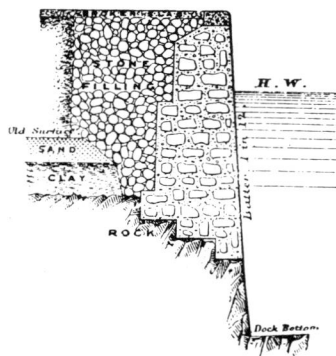

Figure 4.7. Masonry type gravity wall at Androssan, (6), hard and durable rock (7).

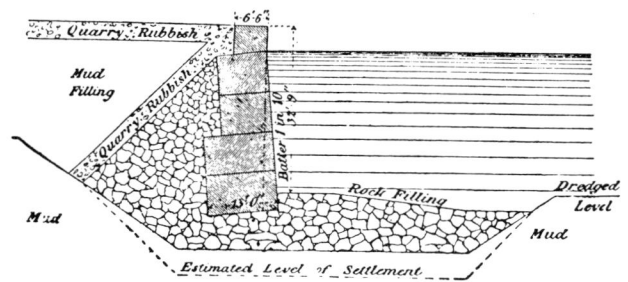

Figure 4.8. Concrete block wall in Algeria (7).

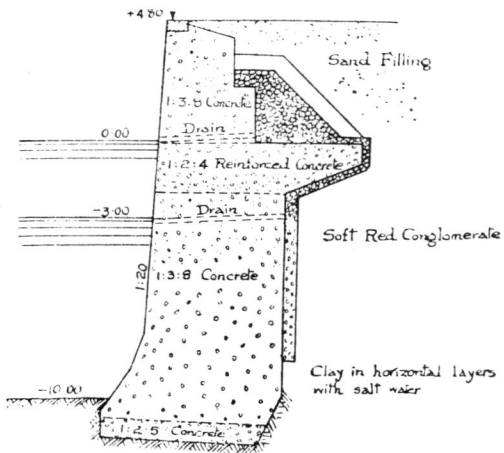

Figure 4.9. Reconstructed mass concrete wall at La Plata (7).

and, next, in relation to the way earth pressures and work loads are absorbed. Structures of various material are also mentioned.

Walls Classified According to Hydraulic Performance

Examples of Impermeable, Fully Reflecting Walls

The oldest type is the hewn natural rock block wall. The oldest known wall of this type is the breakwater piers at Tyre. The harbor of Alexandria had similar single walls but also double block walls with rubble filling between the walls, providing 200 feet wide breakwater piers.

Later, masonry (Figure 4.7) and concrete block walls like Figure 4.8 and mass concrete walls like Figure 4.9 replaced natural rock walls. This type of gravity wall is rather common in Europe and in Latin American countries but not in the United States. Individual blocks in block structures may weigh from 50 to 200 tons. These walls are usually placed on a rock fill with a toe protection extending out in front of the wall and possibly also with a rock fill behind the wall to reduce the lateral earth pressure and to drain the wall through "weep holes" in the structure. Some

and/or friction forces in sheet pile structures with relieving platforms where required by soil conditions and water depth. One may also distinguish between various structures based on the material used for their construction—gravity walls built by natural rock, masonry or concrete and caissons built of reinforced concrete or steel sheet piling, wooden, reinforced concrete, prestressed concrete or steel sheet pilings and pile structures of wood, reinforced concrete or steel with deck of wood or reinforced concrete.

In the following, examples are given of various types of structures. These are classified, first, in accordance with the hydraulic capabilities of the walls because this, as described in Chapter 2, is very important for wave motion in the port basin

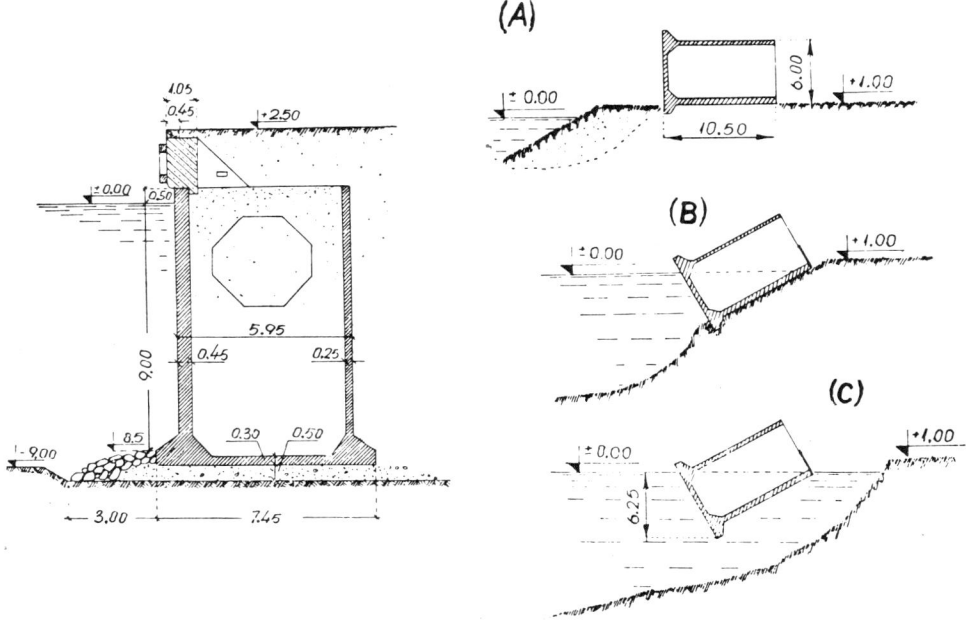

Figure 4.10. Quay wall at Gdynia, Poland, and method of launching caissons (7).

block walls may lean slightly backward. Blocks above low water may be cast in place. Most mass concrete walls are cast in an excavated (dry) construction pit.

Reinforced concrete caissons and steel sheet pile walls have been used extensively for constructing wharves and quay walls. Concrete caissons are usually cast in dry on the construction site, launched and then sunk in place after which construction work is completed by cast in place. A great variety of casting, launching and placing procedures exist. Figure 4.10 shows how caissons were launched during the construction (pre-World War II) of the harbor at Gdynia (Gdansk) in Poland. These caissons were cast on dry land and launched by dredging out a harbor basin. Caissons have been used widely in modern designs. In connection with the construction of a port at Sheibah on the coast of Kuwait (1964-66), three deepwater berths were provided. According to information by KAMPSAX, Copenhagen, the natural soil consists of up to 1 meter of calcareous sand and shell conglomerate, about 3 meters of calcareous sand and about −10-meter elevation of the so-called "gatch" consisting of sand in a cohesive matrix of calcareous clay and gypsum. This soil is suitable for direct foundation, and, as piling would be very difficult, a caisson quay structure was chosen. Mean sea level is at +1.5 meters, lower low water at −0.6 meter and higher high water at +3.0 meters.

The harbor was placed outside the shoreline at 6- to 7-meters natural water depth, and the deepwater quays constitute the inner side of the 200-meter wide sandfilled harbor mole. Depth at the quays was 11.5 and 10 meters. No breakwater protection was provided in this first stage of harbor development. In Figure 4.11 the caissons are 20.8 meters long, 8.5 meters wide (including heel and toe—11.2 meters wide) and 13.8 meters (12.1 meters) high. Made of reinforced concrete, they are placed on a 65-centimeter thick stone bed. The caissons were filled with sand and the joints between them were filled with graded gravel and

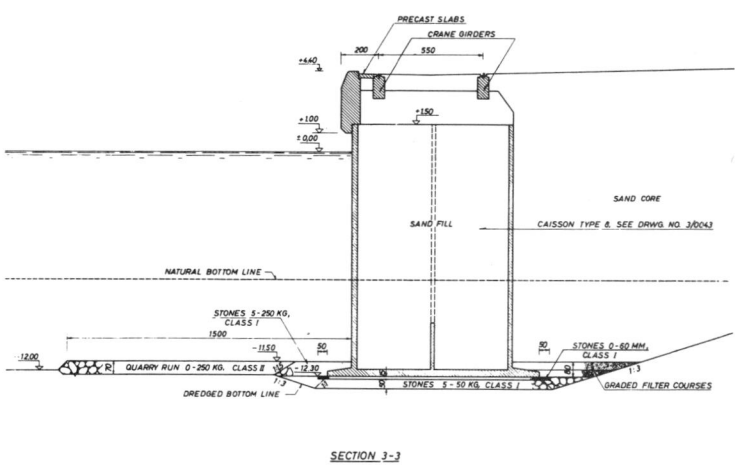

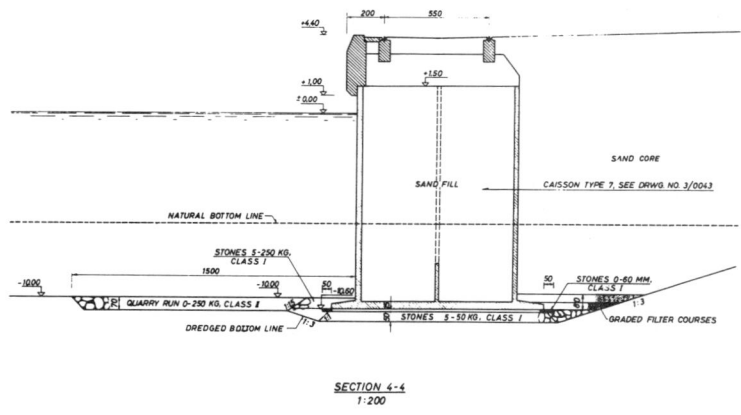

Figure 4.11. Reinforced concrete caissons at the Port of Sheibah, Kuwait (KAMPSAX, Copenhagen).

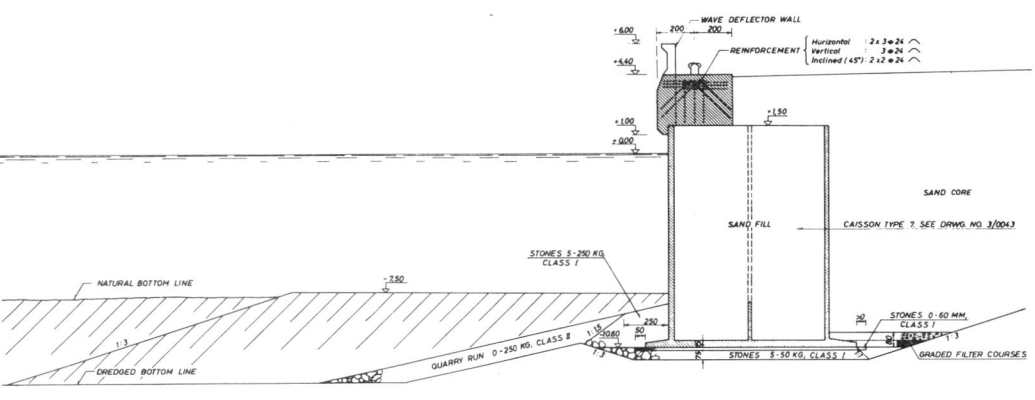

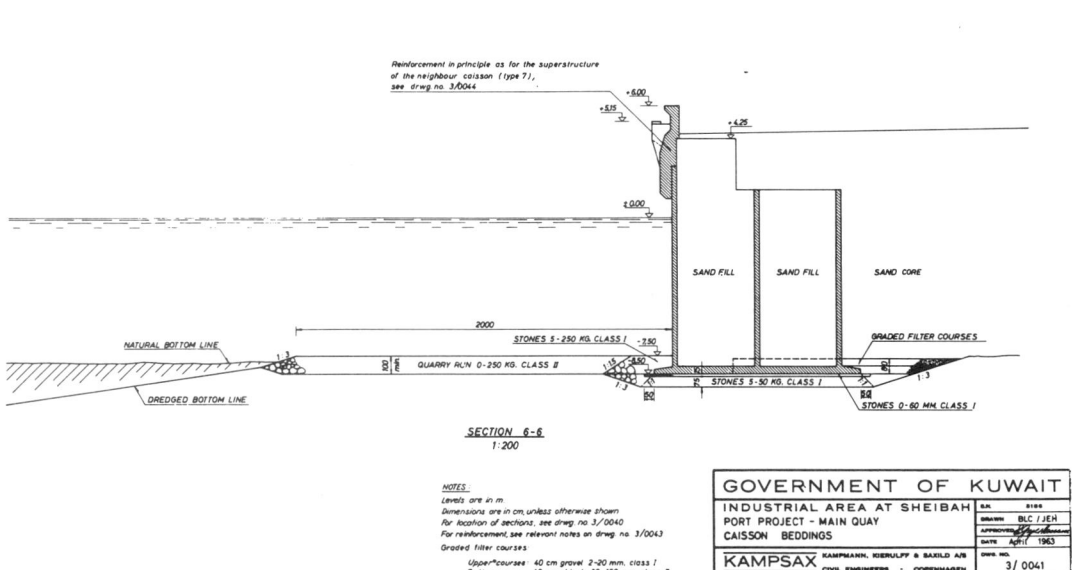

Figure 4.11 continued.

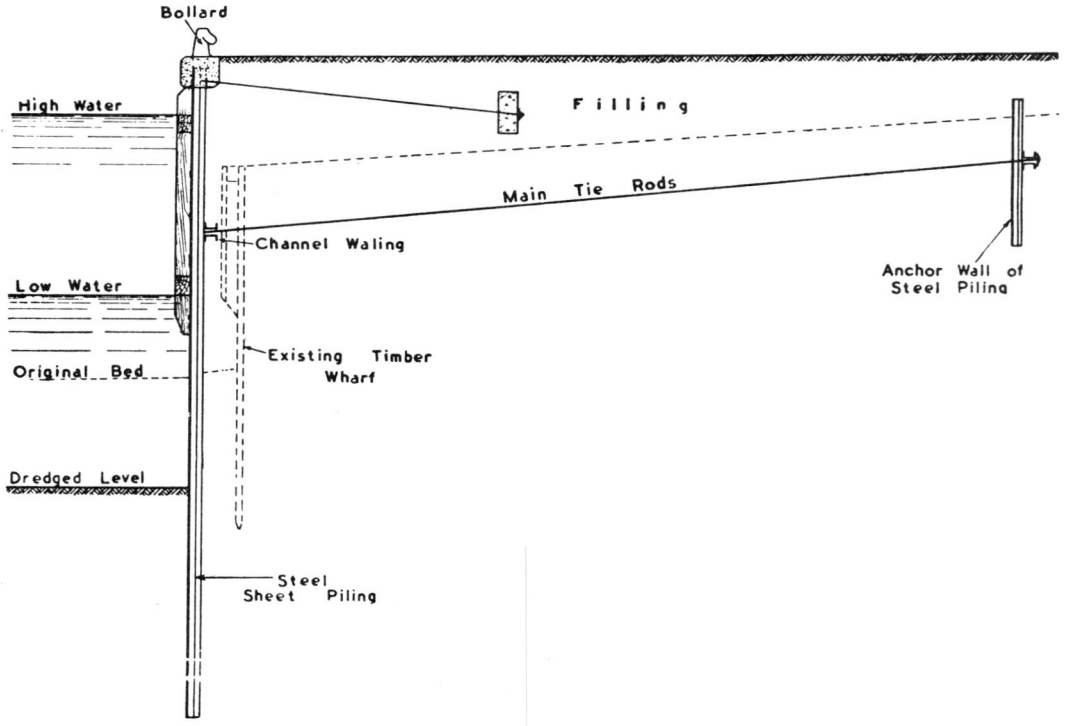

Figure 4.12. Steel sheet pile wall (7).

closed by plain concrete placed in a vertical grooved lock between each pair of caissons.

The superstructure consists of a front wall and crane beams resting on crossbeams, all of reinforced concrete. The top structure level is +4.4 meters. The fender works consist of 25-centimeter diameter rubber fenders.

In the solid type of dock construction, steel sheet pile cells are quite commonly used where water depth does not exceed 50 feet and the bottom conditions are suitable for the support of gravity type structures. The cells are generally capped with a concrete slab and bulkhead wall above water level. Cells utilize flat web-steel piling which acts in tension to retain the fill inside, thereby forming a gravity wall of sufficient weight and shearing strength to resist overturning or sliding at the base. Cells may be circular in shape or they may have circular ends and straight walls. The cir-

cular type is used more often because each individual cell may be filled to the top and remains stable in itself. Therefore, it may be used as a base on which to construct the next cell.

The most common type vertical impermeable wall is the sheet pile wall. The first sheet pile walls were made of wooden boards and planks placed and driven behind kingpiles to limited depth only. Generally, all wood exposed to the open sea water was protected against marine borers and gribbles. Now sheet pile bulkheads may be constructed of steel or concrete sheet piling which may be supported by tie rods attached to an anchor plate (or to anchor piles) located at a safe distance in the back of the face of the bulkhead, as shown in Figure 4.12, or by batter piles along the rear of the piling. In shallow installations and where the bottom is of good supporting value, the sheet piling may be driven deep enough to act as a cantilever without the benefit of additional support.

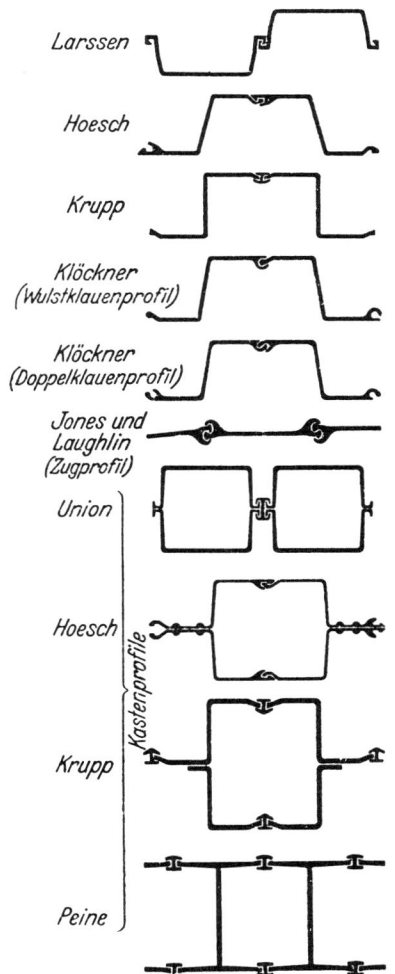

Figure 4.13. Various steel sheet pile profiles (reference Taschenbuch fur Bauingenieure; Springer-Verlag, Berlin).

The need of greater depths initiated development of various types of steel sheet pilings including Larssen, Krupp, Hoesch, Bethlehem, Belval and Peiner (Figure 4.13). With the exception of the Larssen profile which has its lock in the middle of the combined cross-section, profiles are shaped to provide maximum resistance. They have locks which are sandtight but not necessarily watertight. The steel sheet pile wall, however, suffers from corrosion caused by galvanic action by which iron ions are exchanged for hydrogen ions developing rust and decreasing the steel cross-section, weakening the structure. A cathodic protection (mentioned in more detail later) has been developed in recent years by changing the direction of the electric current to the steel and not away from it (9, 26).

Examples of Open, Not Fully Reflecting Energy-Absorbing Walls

Figure 4.14a shows a quay on reinforced concrete piles and cylinders of reinforced concrete used for supporting the deck of a wharf. The particular design shown in Figure 4.14b uses cylinders 0.82 meters thick with 9.0-meter external diameter. In both cases, piles or cylinders were driven down with the help of heavy "Benoto" grabs dropped through the hollow piles taking the ground away from below the piles. In the case of the 9.0-meter cylinder, the central core of ground material remains intact, adding stability and saving useless earth-moving.

Figure 4.15 shows a cross-section of a typical Norwegian "pillar-quay" built of reinforced concrete, cast underwater using a special technique. The pillar is often placed on a prepared concrete foundation or directly on the (clean) rock bottom. Pillars are up to 50-60 feet long and up to about 3 feet in diameter. The deck is also poured of reinforced concrete and fenders established as shown in Figure 4.15 or by piles (wood or steel) driven independently in front of the quay. This "mushroom-design" has proved to be practical as well as economical for conditions of medium depth in Norway, but great care is necessary to secure a first class concrete.

Most open quays are built on piles driven down in the ground. These piles may be wood, reinforced concrete, prestressed concrete, steel or sometimes steel piles filled with concrete. Some of the new pier installations in New York are built on creosoted wooden piles with reinforced concrete

114   Port Engineering

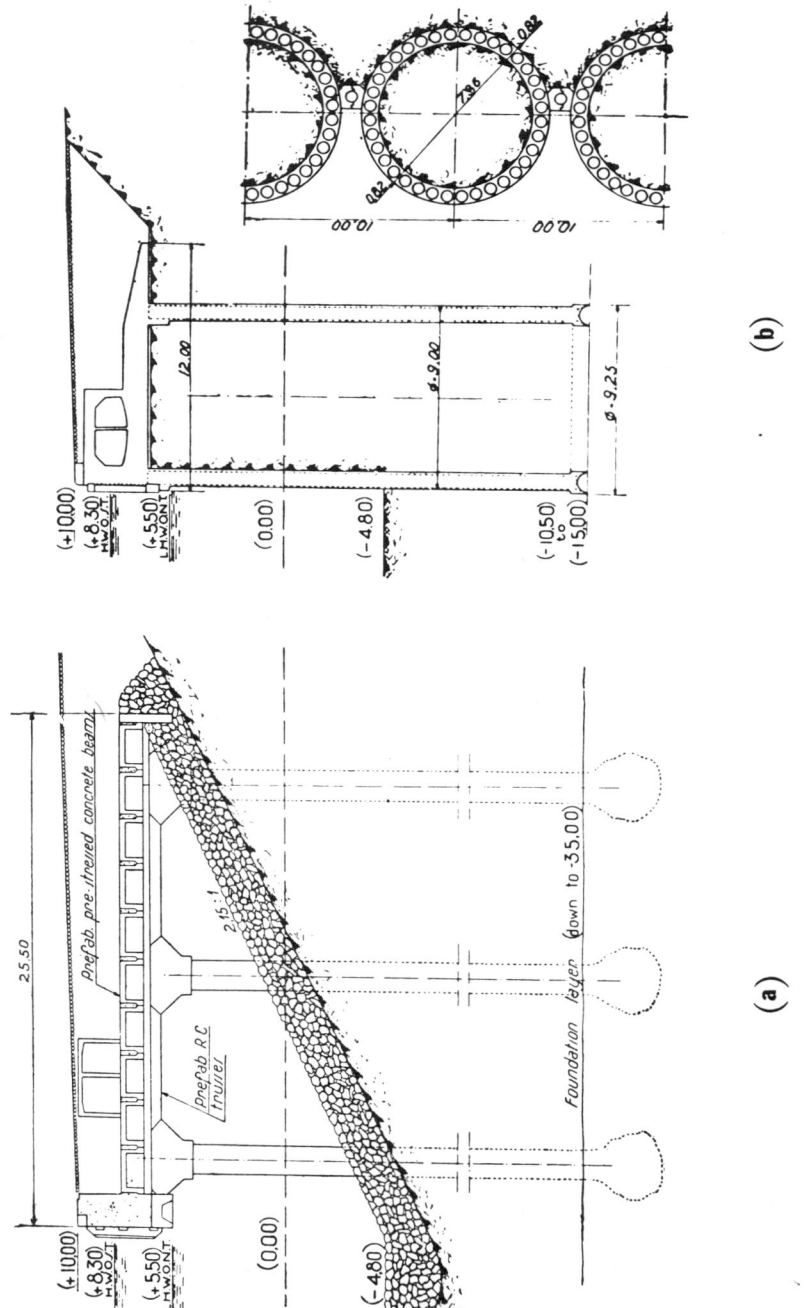

Figure 4.14. Joanne's-Couvert quays on inner basins at Le Havre, built by Benito process: (a) on piles, (b) on cylindrical piers (7).

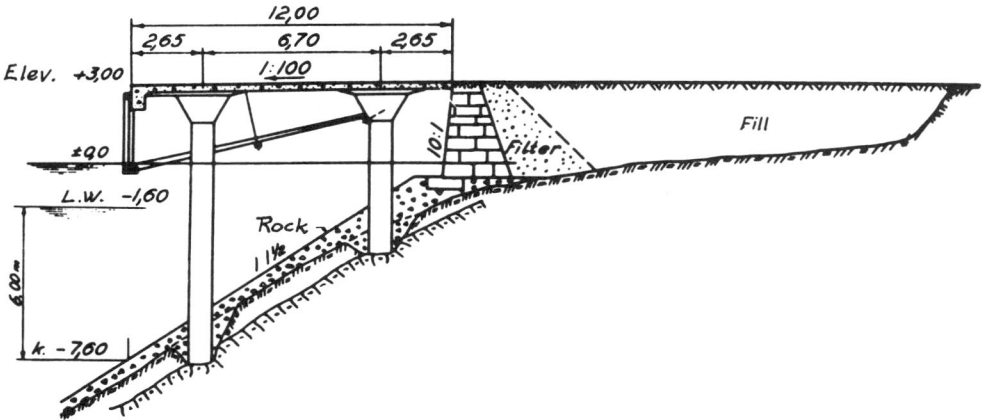

Figure 4.15. Norwegian pillar-quay.

decks. In Los Angeles, plastic sheets have been placed as protection on wooden piles (32).

Most structures are built of reinforced concrete. An interesting reinforced concrete design has been constructed at the Scandia-Harbor in Gothenburg, Sweden, where reinforced concrete piles were carried down to the rock Pile diameter was decreased below the bottom. Figure 4.16 (KAMPSAX) is an example of an open design of reinforced concrete which will be built on the tidal mudflats of Bandar Shahpour, Iran. Four new deep-water berths will be placed to the west of the present harbor jetties of Bandar Shahpour.

The natural soil consists of marine estuarine deposits of clays, silts and sand of low bearing capacity to very considerable depths. The quay structures accordingly will be founded on friction piles brought down approximately to elevation −25 meters (mean sea level at +0.5 meters, lower low water at −2.9 meters, higher high water at +3.8 meters).

The quays will be placed as close to the reclaimed harbor areas as possible. As reclamation near the natural big depths of the navigational channel would be impossible, it was decided to place the quays on natural soil levels of about ±0 meters where settlements for reclamation to future ground level, about +4.5 meters, should not exceed 1 meter. In order to reduce post-construction settlements, the reclaimed areas will be preloaded for at least six months with fill material.

The dredging will be carried down to −12.5 meters for three berths and to −13.5 meters for the fourth berth. For stability reasons, the dredged slope will be kept at 1:3 and the quay front will be placed about 60 meters outside the frontline of the harbor areas. The quay structures consist of a 27-meter wide reinforced concrete platform supported on vertical and raked precast concrete piles. The platform is connected to shore by 30-meters long approach bridges and provided with expansion joints at approximately every 180 meters. Total length of quays is 549 meters + 196.5 meters.

The main fenders consist of 80-centimeter diameter rubber fenders fixed to a shield of Azobé planks on Basralocus piles. These fenders are placed at 16-meter intervals. In between there are Basralocus fender piles to protect the concrete piles against floating items and to prevent small boats from being caught below the platform deck.

Driving reinforced concrete piles in hard bottom causes problems. The point of the pile may be damaged, but it can be protected by a "shoe." Cracks may develop in the pile. In all cases it is best to jet the pile down in hard bottom or to puncture the bottom before the pile is set in the punctured hole and grouted. It is also difficult to

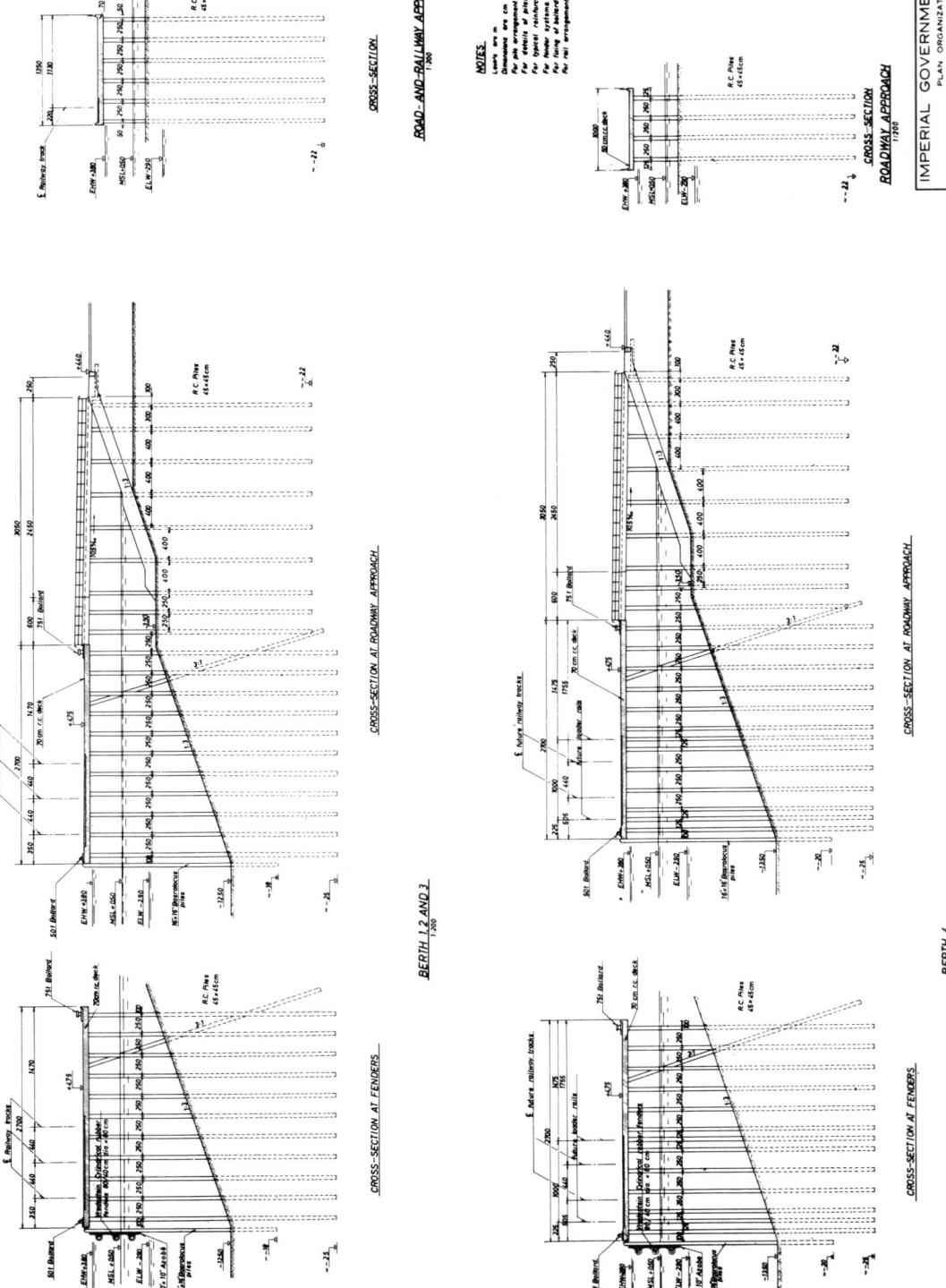

Figure 4.16. Open pier of reinforced concrete for Bandar Shahpour, Iran (KAMPSAX, Copenhagen).

drive heavy piles over a certain length (50-60 feet), and it is difficult and not always safe to put them together by a steel collar. Such difficulties may be avoided by steel piles which are able to withstand heavy driving and are easy to prolong by welding.

Corrosion presents a problem, and it may become necessary to take special precautions against it by special, usually metallic (patented), coatings or by a cathodic protection which involves the applications of a counter electric current opposing that responsible for corrosion, thus rendering the whole structure cathodic. As explained in Reference 9, the essence of the cathodic protection is that it prevents iron ions from leaving the surface of bare metal and becoming ultimately oxidized, thereby forming rust. Two methods of applying the necessary superimposed current are possible in practice. Structures of iron or steel, either wholly immersed or partially immersed or buried in the ground, may have a cathodic current of sufficient density and electromotive force impressed upon them either by using external anodes of magnesium, aluminum or zinc, or anodes of scrap iron or graphite may be used, the necessary current being supplied by an external generator. In both cases the external anodes are sacrificed and corrode away.

Steel pipes have minimum exposed surface and therefore are more suitable than steel profiles, particularly when they are filled with concrete after driving. Special piles are produced (mainly in Germany), but in many cases four U-profiles are welded together to form a box (12). The piles are usually pointed by a cast iron shoe or a point which is particularly suitable for driving in bed rock. Figure 4.17 shows an example of using steel pipes with 22-inch exterior diameter and 1/2-inch wall thickness. Piles are hollow and only filled with concrete on the uppermost 3 feet. The reinforced concrete deck is 33 feet wide. A similar structure was built at the Port of Aquaba, Jordan of German Krupp piles (KP nr. 34) of maximum 20-inch cross-section and 5/8-inch thickness. This pier also has a reinforced concrete deck, and the two piers are backed by steel sheet piling (3).

Figure 4.18 shows a cross-section of an open pier built for the Southern Peru Copper Company at Ilo, Peru (26). Five-foot steel cylindrical piles filled with concrete are placed up to 62-foot depths at the outer end of the pier. Since using conventional piling was not feasible, and since the large earthquake forces had to be considered in the design of this heavy pier structure, it was decided to use concrete filled steel cylinders founded directly on the rock bottom. These 5-foot cylinders have 1/4-inch steel walls in the straight section, flaring out into a bell section of 3/8-inch steel walls, 11 feet in diameter at the bottom.

Each of the 30 pier bents is composed of three heavily reinforced cylinders which are capped with a large transverse reinforced concrete girder. Each bent was designed as a rigid frame to take the force of an earthquake (0.1 g) and the lateral docking and wind forces from a 40,000-dwt vessel.

The pier was constructed by the overhead method, that is, without the use of floating equipment. This procedure consisted of using a pair of heavy steel mats designed to rest on top of the cylinders after they had been braced and concreted, to support a large crane and to permit it to advance offshore as work progressed by picking up the rear mat, swinging it around and placing it in position on the cylinders in the next bent in front and then walking forward onto this mat. The cylinders were of welded construction, and the bottoms of the belled-out sections were cut to fit the contours of the rock bottom.

A relatively small prestressed concrete wharf design that is a very elegant and practical as well as an effective and economical breakwater wharf was built at Beaver Harbor, New Brunswick, Canada, on a small inlet connected to the Bay of Fundy (23).

The new breakwater/wharf (Figure 4.19) is 40 feet wide and extends 406 feet from the end of the rubble fill approach. The Bay of Fundy, which experiences some of the largest tides in the world, has an extreme tidal range of 25 feet at this site. Thus, it was necessary to establish the wharf deck 28 feet above low water. The piling consists of 14-inch concrete filled steel pipe. Along the seaward side of the structure, vertical and batter piles are installed in pairs at 6-foot centers. Along the

118 Port Engineering

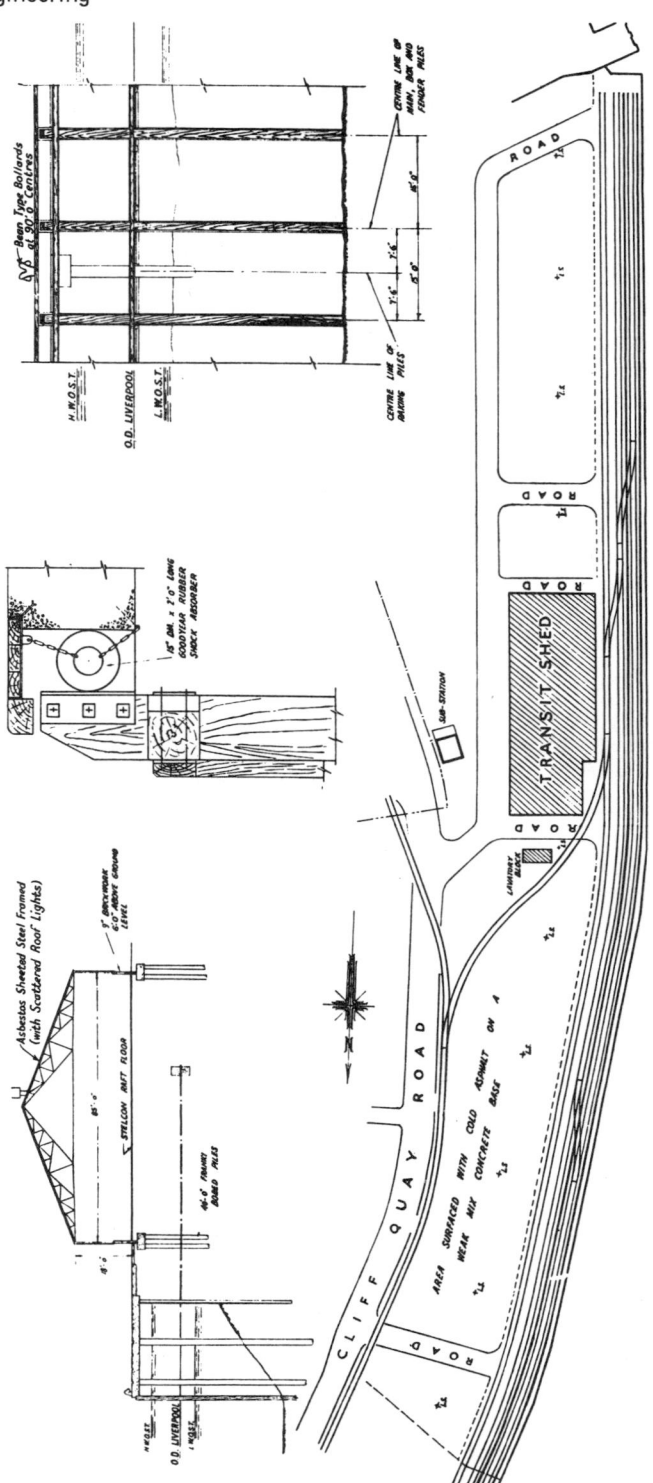

Figure 4.17. Open pier on steel piles Ipswich, England (3).

Wharves and Quays

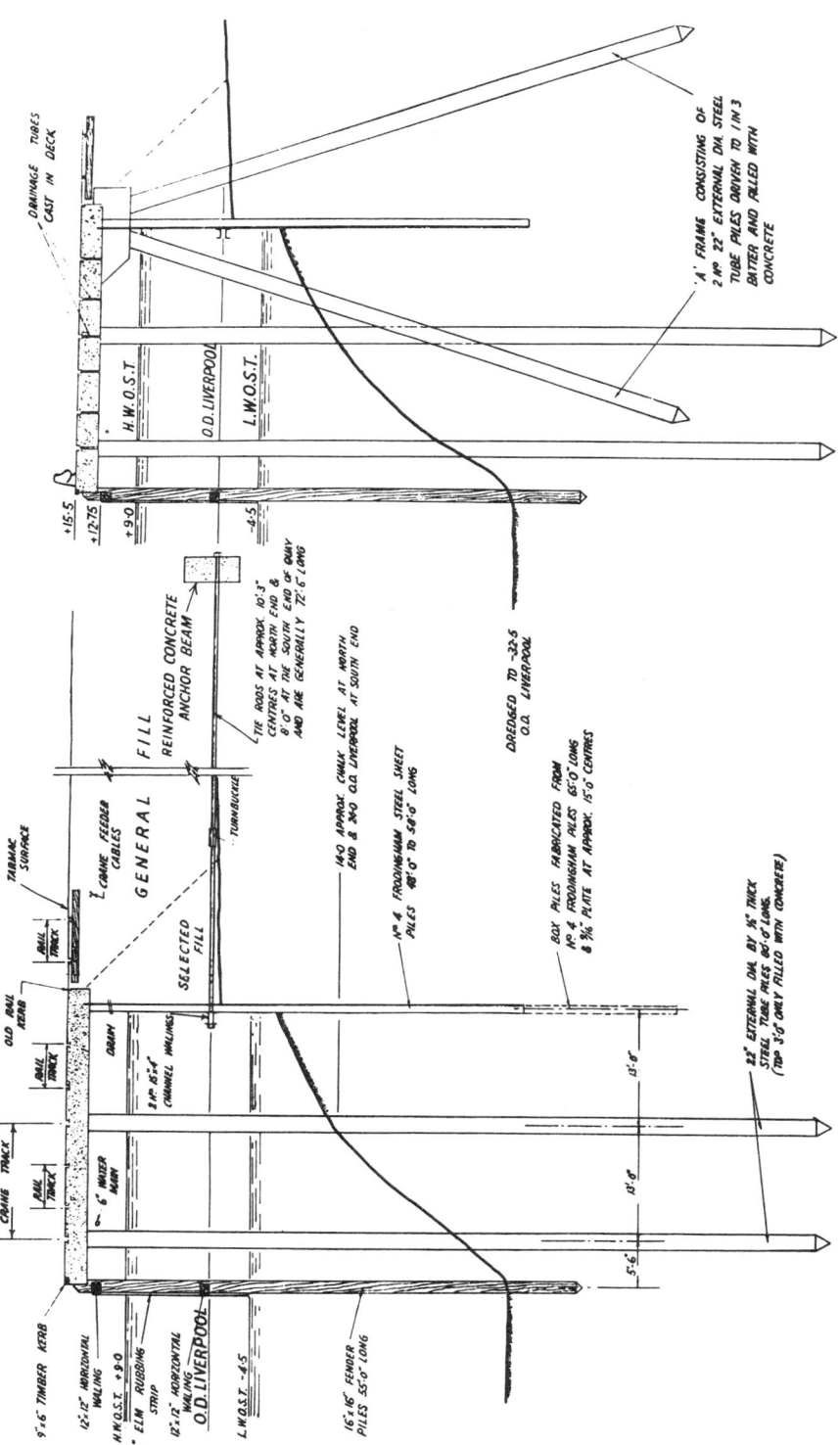

Figure 4.17 continued.

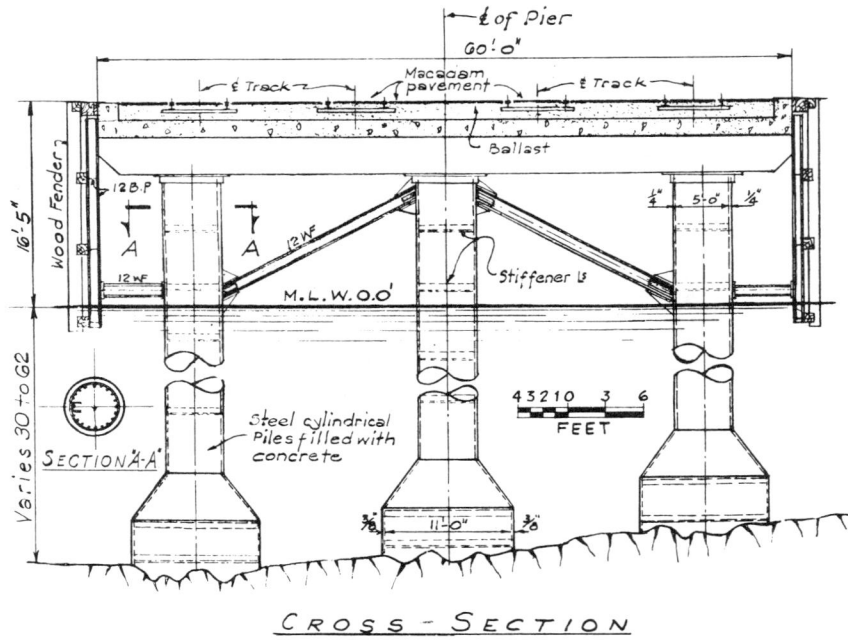

Figure 4.18. Cross-section of pier for the Southern Pier Copper Company at Ilo, Peru (26).

shoreward side, or the berthing face, vertical piles are installed at 16-foot centers. The batter piles act in compression under mooring or berthing forces. From a point approximately 16 feet below the mud line to the underside of the pile cap, the piles have 3/8-inch walls. For economy the wall thickness of the pile lower sections embedded in the ground is reduced to 1/4 inch. To protect the piles from corrosion in the splash zone, they are enclosed in a 21-inch asbestos-bonded, asphalt-coated corrugated culvert pipe with the annular space between the pipe pile and the enclosure filled with concrete. The corrugated pipe extends from 2 feet below the low water level to the underside of the pile cap. The thicker walled piles include an allowance for corrosion in the submerged zone extending from the bottom of the corrugated pipe to the mud line.

To support the wharf deck, the piles are capped with cast-in-place, reinforced concrete beams running continuously along each side of the wharf. Transverse beams are placed only at the ends of the structure. The wharf deck consists of prestressed concrete channels spanning 37 feet across the wharf and topped with 4 inches of cast-in-place concrete. The deck is designed for the more critical live loading of 300 pounds per square foot or H20-S16 highway truck loading.

Prestressed concrete sheathing is installed on the seaward side and on the offshore end to act as a breakwater. These sections are driven 9 feet into the underlying soils to provide toe embedment. A gravel berm covered with rip-rap prevents erosion on the seaward side of the sheathing. The sheathing, 2 feet 2 inches wide by 1 foot 4 inches thick and of tongue-and-groove section, is designed to withstand the forces resulting from an 8-foot wave.

The joint between the prestressed deck channels and the pile cap beam is achieved by extending reinforcement into the cast-in-place edge closure. Along the seaward face, the edge closure also

Wharves and Quays 121

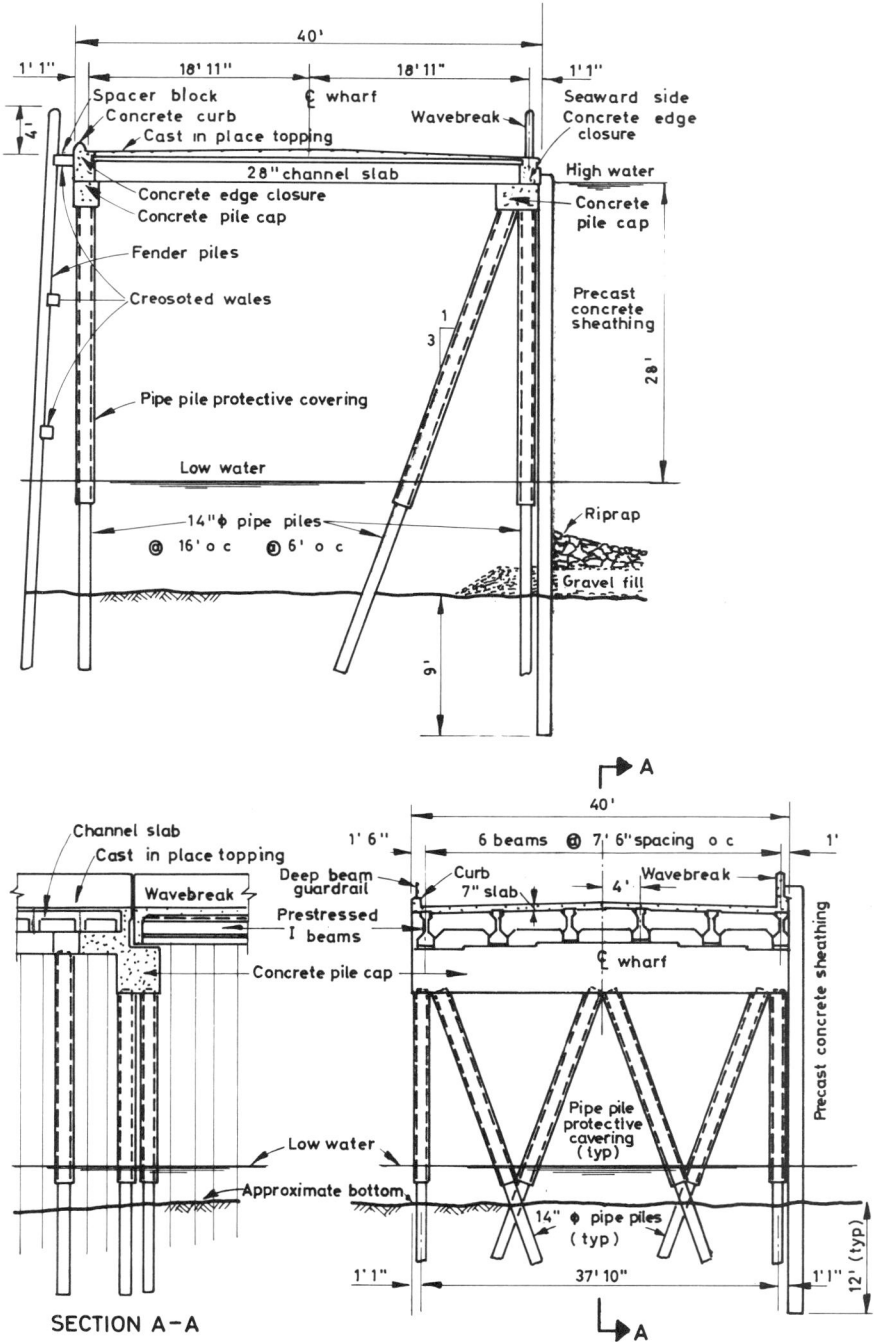

Figure 4.19. Prestressed concrete breakwater wharf at Beaver Harbor, New Brunswick, Canada; section through main wharf and approach spaer (23).

engages reinforcing steel extending from the prestressed sheathing. The combination of channels, topping and edge beams forms a very rigid flat plate which assists in the lateral distribution of berthing or wave forces. Wharf traffic is protected from wave action during high tides by a 4-foot high reinforced concrete wave break constructed on the seaward side of the structure.

Fendering consists of a wood springing system with creosoted Douglas fir piles at 5-foot centers. The piles are driven some 16 feet into the subsurface soils and are bolted to creosoted wales at elevation +27.3, +18.5 and +7.0 feet. The upper wale is connected to the concrete edge closure at 10-foot centers with creosoted spacer blocks. The fendering continues across the end of the wharf to provide a temporary mooring point for vessels waiting to moor alongside the wharf or to discharge fish catches for the cannery.

The pipe piles were driven using an internal drop hammer and a scow mounted Link Belt LS98 crawler crane. The piles along the seaward side were positioned by threading them through a template fabricated from a discarded crane boom. The template was held in position by connecting one end to a previously driven pile and the other to temporary timber spud piles. The template held nine vertical and nine batter piles. For the majority of the piles, the contractor field-welded the pile sections into their final lengths on shore and floated them out to the template. Where the final pile length exceeded 100 feet, the pile was unwieldy with the driving equipment available, so the pile was partially driven and a field splice made.

Just before driving the bottom 2 to 3 feet, each pile was filled with dry concrete. An 8,000-pound ram on the end of a line connected to the crane was lowered inside the pile and the driving commenced. By varying the height of the drop, the driving energy could be adjusted easily to suit the soil conditions. For further details on this design including its decking and sheathing, see Reference 23.

Another prestressed concrete wharf of interesting design was built in North Vancouver, British Columbia (25). Prestressed concrete was chosen for extension to a wharf of a deep-sea bulk loading terminal because of its many advantages over other structural systems. Load carrying capacity, ease of erection, fire resistivity, cost and resistance to deterioration were all factors leading to this choice.

With reference to Figure 4.20, ninety-six 80-foot long, 24-inch, octagonal, through-voided concrete piles with 14-inch hollow cores and 6,000 psi concrete were used in the substructure. Each pile contains 16 strands, 1/2-inch diameter, 270 ksi, stressed to apply 415 kips per pile.

The main deck consists of 72 panels, 6 feet wide by 27 1/2 feet long and 1 foot 4 inches thick, haunching to 2 feet thick at the supports. Haunching of these panels eliminated the need for deflected strand, thus permitting the entire 550-foot long deck to be post-tensioned from one end to form a continuous, ductile horizontal beam. Resistance to seismic and ship berthing loads was economically and efficiently achieved in this manner. An additional advantage was the increased capacity to absorb vertical loads both from concentrated wheel loads up to 50 tons and from storage loads up to 500 pounds per square foot.

The panels were pretensioned for construction and handling loads. The end bearing of these slabs was achieved by casting the haunched ends into the second stage casting of the pile cap. Seventeen conveyor deck trislabs, 8 feet 5 inches wide by 26 feet 8 inches long with 14-inch deep ribs and 2-inch flange thickness, were precast using 6,000 pounds per square inch concrete. They are prestressed using fifteen 1/2-inch diameter, 270 kips per square inch strands with an initial prestress of 390 kips per slab. The panels are designed for a wheel load of 4.5 kips or 100 pounds per square foot of uniformly distributed load.

The approach ramp uses twelve 4-foot wide by 3-foot deep precast, prestressed concrete bulb tees 70 feet long. They use eighteen 1/2-inch diameter, 270 kips per square inch strands with an initial prestress of 470 kips and 6,000 pounds per square inch concrete. Bearing for these beams was achieved by again casting their ends into the second stage of the two-part cast-in-place pile cap. Shear connection between the bulb tees and the 6-inch cast-in-place deck was achieved through

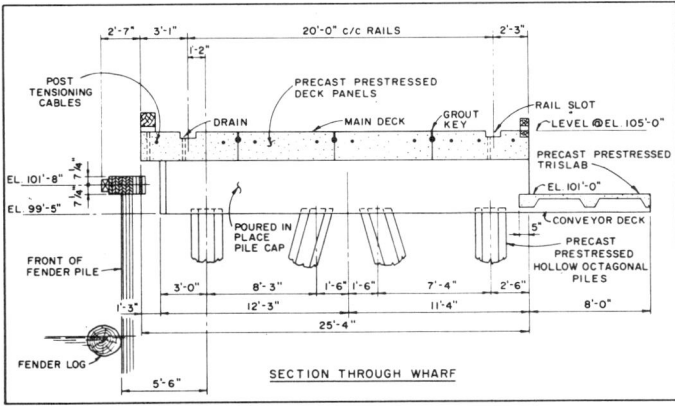

Figure 4.20. Cross-section of prestressed concrete wharf in North Vancouver, Canada (25).

mild steel projecting into the deck and a rough top flange. This structure was designed to take wheel loadings, but provision was made to incorporate it into a future storage area at which time additional supports will be built at the mid-span of the beams. Prestressed concrete piles have also been used for major wharf installations in San Francisco, and it is without question that prestressed concrete will invade the port engineering field at an increasing rate in the future.

Walls Classified According to Method of Absorbing Earth Pressures

The vertical impermeable designs shown in Figures 4.7 to 4.12 are subject to active earth pressures and mainly vertical work loads. They absorb these forces by compression and friction forces and, in the case of sheet pile walls, by passive earth pressures. If foundation material is weak, gravity walls must have a wide footing, or the weak material must be removed and replaced by better material. Most walls are placed on a mattress of coarse (rock) material. It is very difficult to place sheet pile walls in weak material for they must either be carried down to firm bottom, or the weak material must be replaced by better material which has a reasonable friction angle. Sheet pilings in soft

material of low friction angle are subject to higher pressures, and passive earth pressures are lower. In sedimentation geology, it often happens that soft layers of low friction angle and low shear stress cover layers of better material. It will then become necessary to absorb gravity forces by carrying them down to firm ground. Another problem arises if the material behind the wall has such a low friction angle that it may exert excessive horizontal pressures on a sheet piling, or when its slope angle is so low that the slope would extend "far out" in the harbor basin. In such cases relieving platforms are practical.

Figure 4.21 represents a form of wharf wall which may be regarded as standard design for this type if the soil is of poor quality and cannot be relied upon to develop sufficient resistance for anchorage ties or if long tie rods are inconvenient. In this design, the top of the front sheet piling, which may be of reinforced concrete or of interlocking steel, is held by the reinforced concrete "relieving platform," and the horizontal forces necessary to sustain the sheeting are combined with the vertical forces derived from the weight of the superimposed filling on the platform and that of the superstructure to produce compression in the front raking piles and tension or compression in the rear ones. Where the soil is capable of being

124 Port Engineering

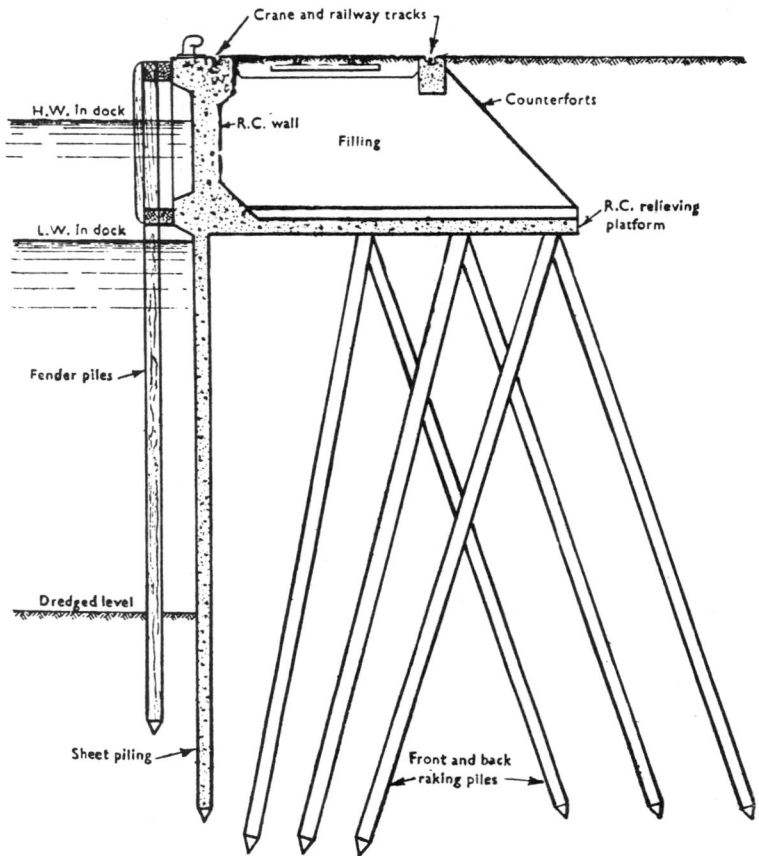

Figure 4.21. Quay wall with relieving platform on raking piles (7).

stable at a reasonable slope, it may be economical to locate the sheet piling at the rear of the wharf, and the section of the sheet piling can then be lighter, due to the smaller height of the soil retained.

The quay walls used for the Port Elizabeth Port Authority Marine Terminal (Figure 4.22) are also of the relieving platform type. As described in detail in Reference 4, because of the large scope of this development which involves the eventual construction of almost 5 miles (8 kilometers) of quay, the study of the wharf designs was an exhaustive one. This study was intended to eliminate the more expensive types of construction from further consideration and thus narrow the field, for later and more detailed studies, to those types which offered the greatest potential for economy. Also, variation in subsurface conditions of the site made it obvious that no one design would be the economical choice at every location. It was also realized that the development of new or improved designs or construction methods, as well as changes in the competitive bidding market, would make additional, more refined studies necessary as the development of the terminal progressed.

For the purpose of the study, controlling design criteria were established. The wharf structures were to be designed for a uniform live load of 500 pounds per square foot (2,417 kilograms per square meter), as well as for applicable railway and highway truck loading. Limiting pile load capacities were established as 30 tons for timber bearing piles, 100 tons for steel H or pipe bearing piles, 150 tons for precast concrete bearing piles and 200 tons for concrete caisson piles. These capacities were established on the basis of long experience with those types of piles in the adjacent Port Newark area. The nature of the subsurface material is such that friction piles would be of such low capacity as to be unworthy of consideration.

The study encompassed all conceivable basic designs, as well as many variations of those designs. The types of construction considered may be broadly characterized as follows:

1. High-level platforms supported on bearing piles or caissons.
2. Relieving platforms supported on bearing piles.
3. Straight-wall steel sheet pile bulkheads.
4. Cellular steel sheet pile bulkheads.
5. Concrete crib construction.

In general, it may be said that three of these basic types offered approximately equal low cost—the concrete relieving platform on timber piles, the high-level concrete deck on timber piles and the cellular steel sheet pile bulkhead.

The first major problem to be faced prior to the beginning of channel dredging operations in 1958 was disposing the organic silt and peat, the first material to be removed. This material, amounting to some 6,500,000 cubic yards (4,880,000 cubic meters), made up the top 15 feet (4.6 meters) of the cut and was not desirable as subgrade fill on the terminal site. One possibility was to pump the material to nearby spoil areas (if such could be found) away from the site. Alternatively, this material could be placed in barges and towed out to sea for dumping. Since the latter possibility apparently would cost approximately $1.00 per cubic yard more than the cost of pumping it into a nearby disposal area, the obvious answer was to search out adequate spoil areas which were found. Dredging and reclamation were combined in a fortunate way as described in Reference 4.

In 1960, the first two wharf construction contracts were awarded. This work provided for the construction of the 800-foot (244-meter) berth at the west end of the main channel and the adjacent four berths totaling 2,400 feet (731 meter) in length along the south side. In this portion of the channel, the relatively high elevation of bedrock precluded the use of steel sheet pile bulkheads, and the high-level type of construction was eliminated because of the difficulty of relocating trackage or of making other possible future modifications. A review and refinement of the earlier construction study led to choosing the concrete relieving platform supported on timber piles (Figure 4.22).

The wisdom of eliminating the high-level wharf was apparent only five years later when it became necessary to install foundations and rails for wharf cranes to facilitate container operations by Sea-Land Service at these berths. A relatively simple modification of this structure (Figure 4.22) served to provide the crane supports. Crane supports are also being installed in adjacent berths to the east in a similar manner.

A vertical wall will cause almost full reflection of wave motion, and it may therefore be necessary to cover the front face with rip-rap. Such design was employed at Newton Creek, New York (18). In this case, however, the rubble fill was also necessary in order to relieve the platform from some of the backfill pressure and keep the horizontal thrust within safe limits. Another type of wall, which in principle is very similar to Figure 4.21, was built in Copenhagen on ground of poor bearing quality (7). A modified form of mass concrete gravity wall, it consisted of a comparatively thin vertical wall stiffened by counter forts of buttresses with platforms, all of concrete. The general principle underlying this form of wall is the utilization of the weight of the earth superimposed on the platforms to increase stability against overturning. Great care must be taken as to the type of back-filling material used and the method of placing. If the material is porous, adequate drainage facilities must be provided.

The quay walls built recently (1968-69) during the expansion of the port of Ravenna on the

126 Port Engineering

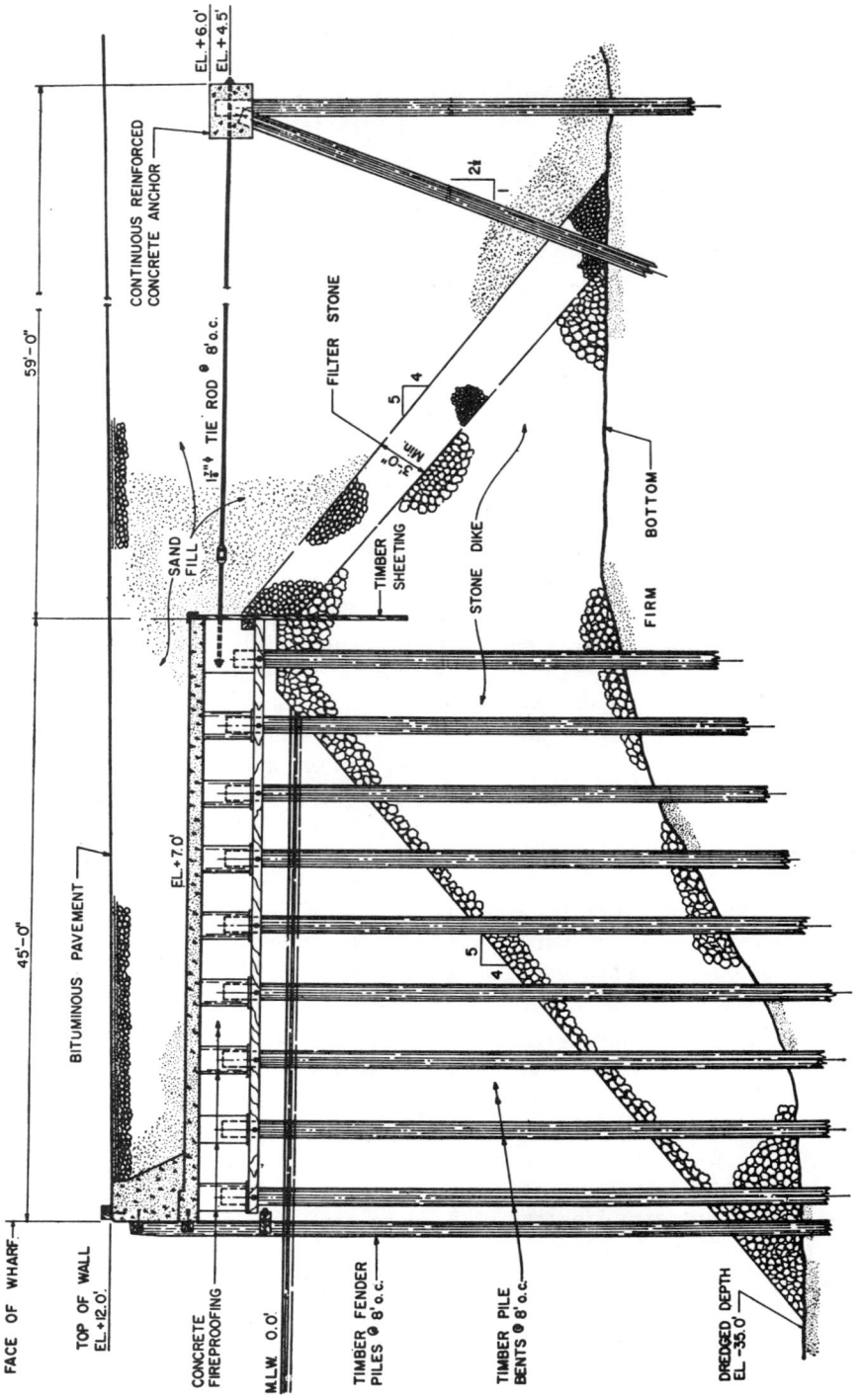

Figure 4.22. Port Elizabeth Marine Terminal Wall (4).

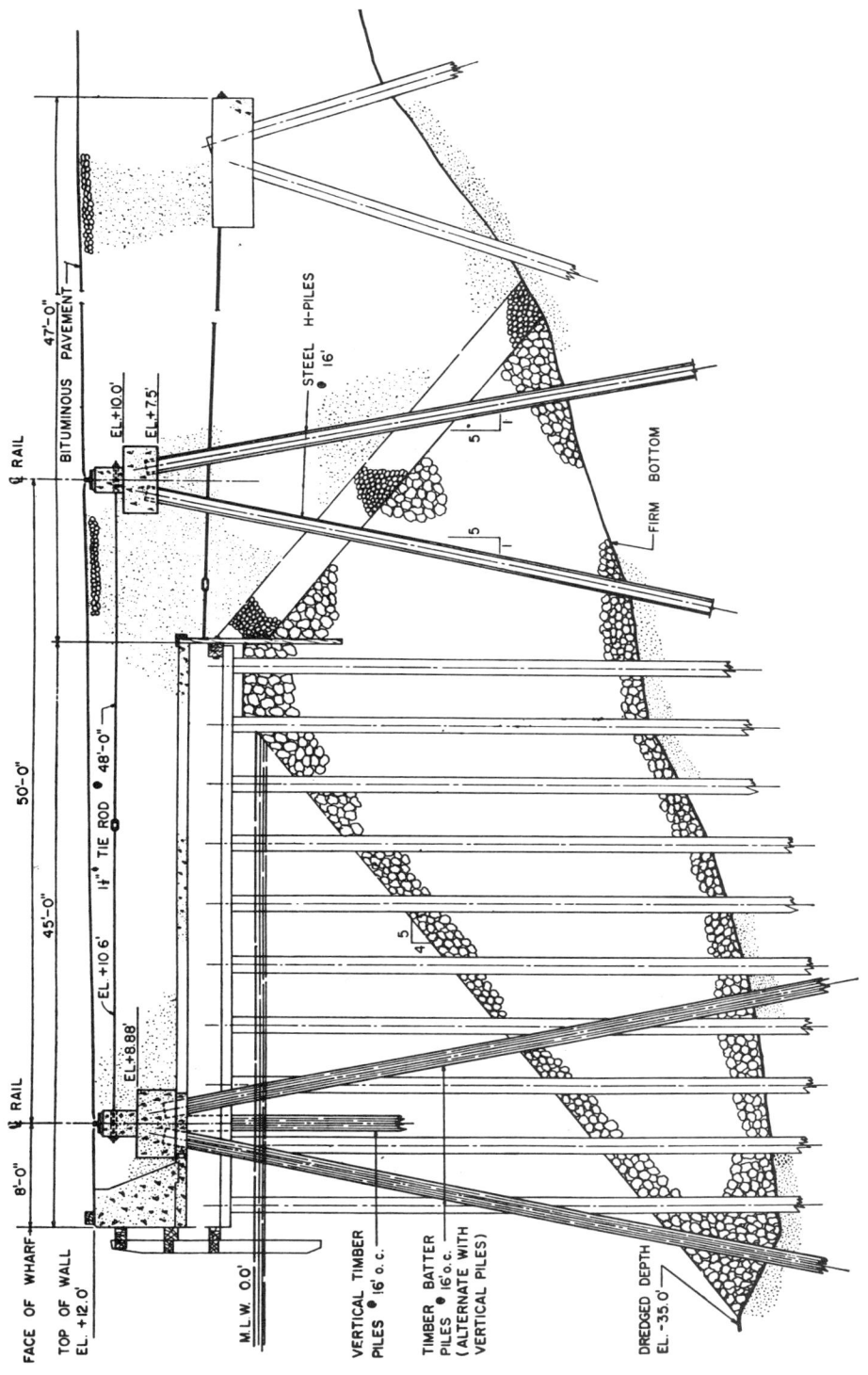

Figure 4.22 continued.

Table 4.1. Impact Velocities and k-Values (21).

dwt	Impact velocities (m/sec.)	k
20,000	0.11 – 0.3	0.50
40,000	0.09 – 0.27	0.50
60,000	0.08 – 0.25	0.45
80,000	0.08 – 0.25	0.35

Adriatic coast in Italy represent an interesting example of the application of the so-called "bentonite" process on a relieving platform design. The inner harbor at Ravenna is formed by the existing Candiano Canal which was deepened to −9.4 meters by dredging and pumping the material to form new industrial areas. Furthermore, an evolution basin and quay walls having a length of about 2,000 meters have recently been completed. The walls were built by employing continuous concrete vertical diaphragms, the concrete being placed inside a deep excavation, executed with the bentonite (slurry) system. The vertical loads were distributed only upon the vertical diaphragms and upon reinforced concrete piles by a powerful superstructure in reinforced concrete so that the diaphragm resists only the horizontal thrust of the ground under the superstructure.

Foundation of pile structures is mentioned specifically in Appendix 1. For estimating ultimate and allowable loads on axially loaded piles, a static formula (for clay and homogeneous sand) and a semiempirical pile driving formula (for sand) are proposed, including a criterion for determining the maximum allowable driving energy to avoid overdriving of concrete piles. It is suggested that settlement estimates of pile groups are obtained from an empirical diagram for sand and from the consolidation theory for clay and fine silt. For both friction and point-bearing piles, load tests are recommended.

Appendix 2 mentions anchored bulkheads. The free earth support theory together with Rowe's moment reduction curves (for sand) are recommended as the basis for designing anchored bulkheads. For homogeneous soils with $c = 0$, simple diagrams for calculating the necessary driving depth below the dredgeline, the anchor pull, the length of the anchorage and the maximum free earth support moment are presented. The application of the proposed design methods is illustrated by numerical examples dealing with both sand and clay.

Berthing and Berthing Forces on Structures

The final movement by a vessel just before mooring at quay wall or pier is called the berthing maneuver. The basic principles involved in such maneuvers are described in Appendix 3 by Prof. Vasco Costa. Reference is also made to Chapter 2 which gives a few examples on approach and berthing maneuvers.

The theory outlined by Appendix 3 allows computation of the amount of energy which has to be absorbed during an impact by a berthing vessel on a structure including its fender system. The simplified equation (Equation 7 of Appendix 3),

$$W = \frac{mu^2}{2} \cdot \frac{1}{1 + (a/k)^2}$$

was found. Figure 14 of Appendix 3 shows the influence of the direction of the velocity in the amount of energy to be absorbed by the fender. The mass m includes the mass of water which moves with the vessel,

$m = m(\text{ship}) + m(\text{hydrodynamic mass})$
$m = (C_m)(m_s)$, when $C_m = $ "mass-coefficient".

C_m is a function of the vessel geometry, water depth and the way the impact is absorbed. An approximate expression (31) for C_m is

$$C_m = 1 + (2D/B) \tag{4.1}$$

where D is water depth and B is beam width.

According to Equation 4.1, the hydrodynamic mass is equal to ship mass when its draft equals

Table 4.2. C_w Coefficient for Wind Forces (31).

Wind Direction	C_w		
	Max.	Min.	Mean
Crosswise	1.40	0.80	1.11
Bow	1.04	0.62	0.82
Stern	1.02	0.64	0.77

half of its beam width. In order to compute the energy at impact, the velocity u must be known. It depends upon several factors, including ship characteristics, winds and currents and the human factor. With increasing size of vessel, u must necessarily decrease. For larger vessels (more than 20,000 dwt), it should not exceed 1 foot/second and be smaller (less than 1/2 foot/second) for heavy bulk carriers. The figures of Table 4.1 give impact velocities and k-values for vessels $>$ 20,000 dwt (21). In cases where tugboats are used, values are less.

The energy absorption of the quay wall is handled by fenders. Some energy is absorbed by rolling, deformation and vibration of the vessel. These energy losses are usually relatively small and can be ignored.

Forces on Vessel at Berth

A vessel moored at a quay wall may be subjected to forces by winds, currents, waves and other accidental forces such as those caused by passing vessels.

Forces by wind may be computed as

$$F_{wi} = C_w \gamma_w A_w (V_w^2/2g) \quad \text{kilograms}$$

when C_w is a wind force coefficient, γ_w is the specific weight of air (1.225 kilograms per cubic meter) A_w is the area exposed to wind forces (square meters), V_w is the wind velocity (meters per second), g is acceleration of gravity (9.81 meters per second per second).

For a nonobstructed vessel, C_w may have approximately values as indicated in Table 4.2 (31).

The maximum wind velocity occurring as gustiness should be used for computation.

Forces by currents may be computed as

$$F_c = C_c \gamma_w A_c (V_c^2/2g)$$

The current force coefficient, C_c, is a function of the geometry of the vessel and of the water depth. C_c increases with decreasing depth and for crosscurrents is approximately 1.5 for deep water and up to 6.0 at the quay wall. For parallel currents C_c has the order of magnitude 0.2–0.6 (15).

Wave forces are often the most important problem, particularly when they occur as long period waves causing surge (Chapter 2).

The wave force parallel to a vessel at berth may be computed as

$$F_{wa} = mg\, a\, k\, \epsilon\, \beta\, \cos\beta t$$

when m is the moving mass (ship mass plus added mass), a is $H/2$ is half wave weight, $k = 2\pi/L$' $\epsilon = (1/kD)$ (sinh kd - sinh kh/ cosh kd), D = ship's draft, h = keel clearance of vessel.

$$\beta = \frac{3(\sinh kl - kl \cosh kl)}{(kl)^3}$$

$2l$ = length of vessel.

Factor ϵ is approximately 1 for long period waves and for long short period waves.

β is a function of the ratio between ship's length and the wave length. Wave forces perpendicular to a vessel at berth are complicated. Model experiments are necessary to get a quantitative evaluation. Experiments are usually also necessary in order to evaluate the ability of mooring devices for surge motion. For further information on berthing forces, the reader is referred to References 19, 20, 21, 27, 31 and 34.

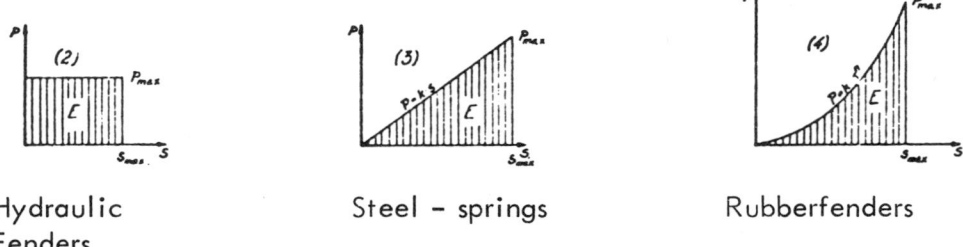

Figure 4.23. Deformation diagrams for fenders.

Fenders

A fender system is supposed to assure safe berthing without damage to vessel or wall and to absorb forces which might occur while the vessel is moored at the quay wall. Only part of the forces between vessel and wall is absorbed by the fenders. The forces in the mooring system are suppose to take care of most of the forces working parallel to the wall, but they are unable to handle forces perpendicular to and against the wall.

Fenders may be divided into two main groups: (a) *protective fenders*, which are supposed to function as an energy absorbing protective pad between the vessel and the wall available at all times, and (b) *impact fenders*, which are supposed to absorb impact particularly during the berthing maneuvers.

The absorption of energy by a particular fender may be compacted from its deformation diagram:

$$\text{Absorption } E = \int_0^s F(s)\,ds$$

when $F(s)$ = force, and s = travel distance of fender.

Figure 4.23 shows examples of such diagrams for three different systems—hydraulic, steel springs and rubber. The best system in principle is the linear spring system. The hydraulic system may be a little hard to the vessel, and the system indicated as "rubber" (not necessarily just rubber) is often too "ship-friendly" on the cost of the quay wall. However, not all rubber fenders have this characteristic.

The protective fenders are usually wood or rubber. The wooden fenders may be arranged as shown in Figure 4.24 with horizontal and vertical members. Exposed timber members may be provided with a relatively thin protection of hard wood which may be fastened to the main vertical members by spikes. Creosoted camels (floating timber) or hard wood had been used much earlier (34).

Various kinds of rubber fenders are used as protection. Hollow round or square rubber fenders can be hung on the wall (Figure 4.25). Solid rubber members or tubes may also be used on the front side or behind or between other members (see Figures 4.26 and 4.27). Old tires may serve the same purpose. They may be hung up directly on the wall or be put together as "Cordkapp fenders"—horizontally or vertically. The fenders mentioned above all have energy absorption diagrams like rubber fenders in Figure 4.23. Figure 4.28 is an example of a deformation diagram for 12 by 12 inch rubber block fenders.

Damage to a quay wall usually results from impacts during the berthing maneuver. Heavy protective fenders also function as impact fenders, but typical fenders must have a stronger design.

Energy absorption of impacts may be provided by compression bending or shear of rubber materials, compression of steel springs, hydraulic compression systems, gravity systems, pneumatic systems and hydropneumatic systems.

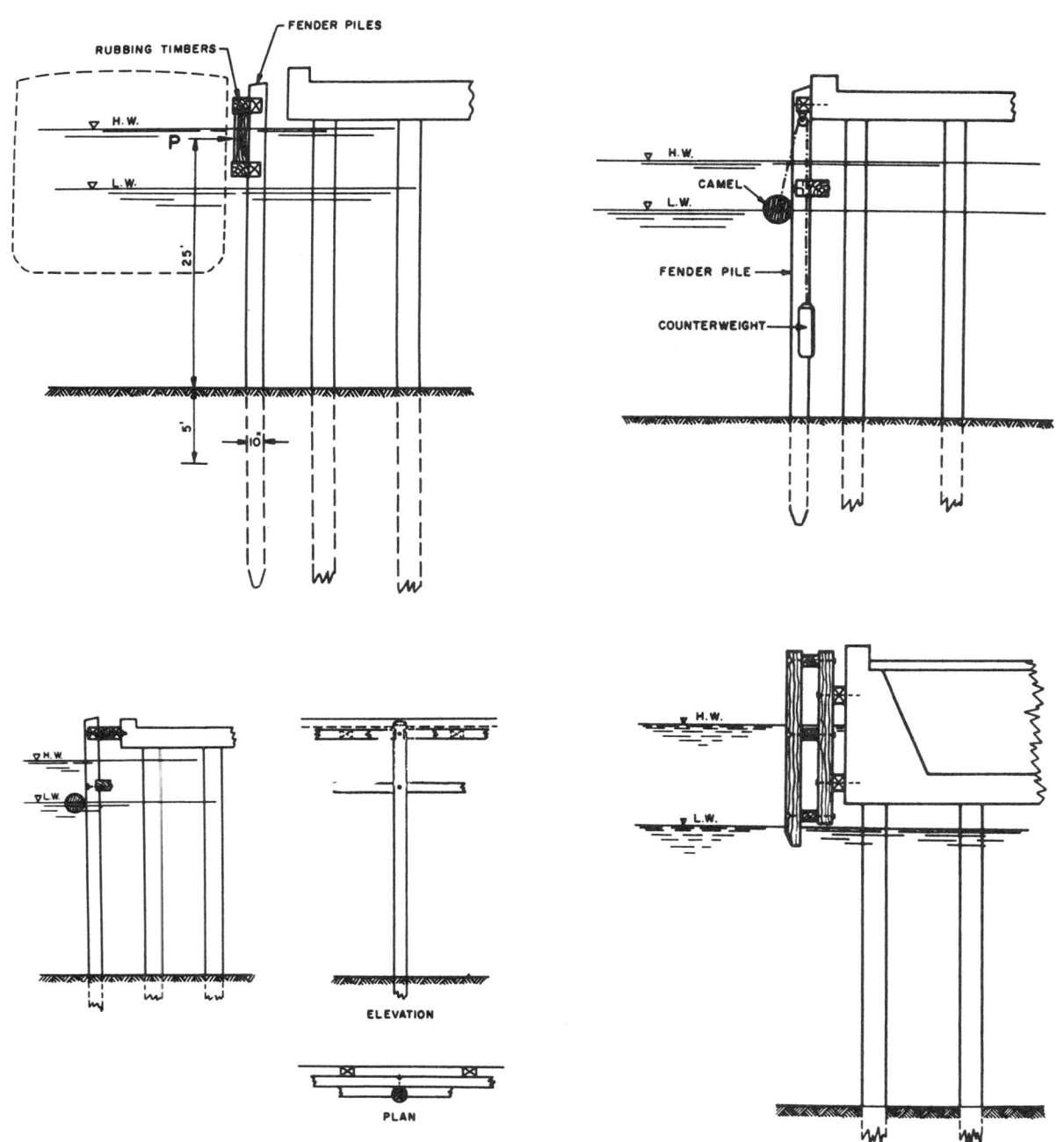

Figure 4.24. Wooden fenders (34).

132 Port Engineering

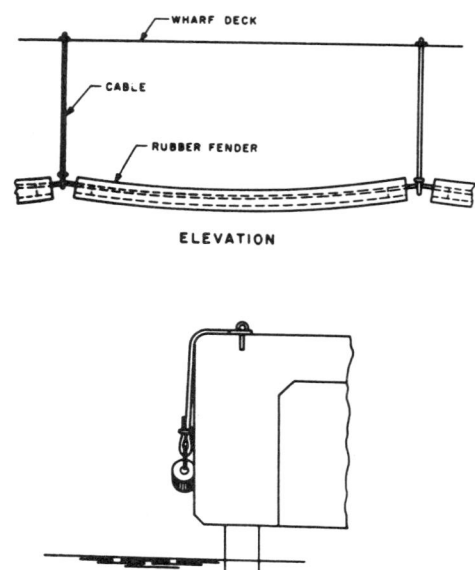

Figure 4.25. Rubber tube for fendering (34).

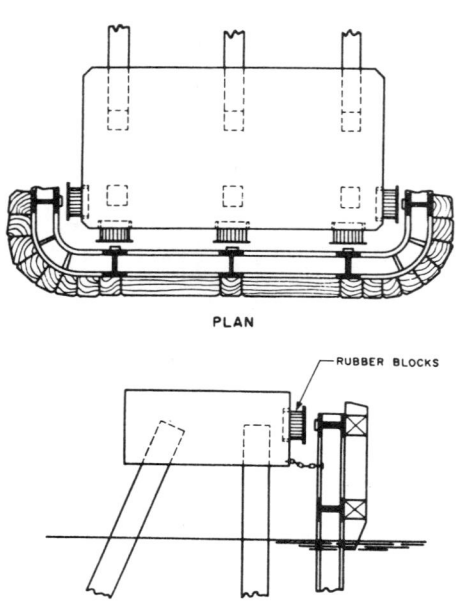

Figure 4.27. Rubber block between dolphin and fender pile (34).

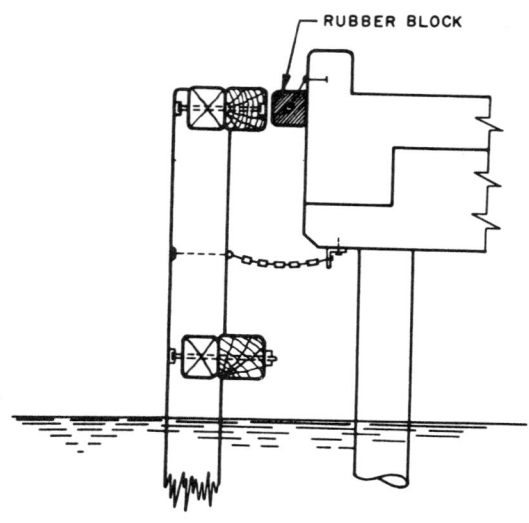

Figure 4.26. Rubber block between fender pile and wall (34).

Figure 4.29 shows the "Raykin" rubber fender when the rubber is put to work mainly in shear. The resilient unit is built of steel and rubber sandwiches bolted together to form an arched beam. Each sandwich is a rubber block vulcanized to two steel plates. The unit may be attached vertically or horizontally to the face of the wharf, and in front of them there are timber or steel piles carrying the rubbing timbers. Raykin fenders may be damaged by overloading them.

The Japanese V-shaped Seibu-fender absorbs the energy by compression and bending. It is used where very heavy bulk carriers load or discharge; Narvik ore-port Norway is a typical example. The Lord fender (Figure 4.30) absorbs the energy by bending.

The gravity fender system works on the pendulum principle and depends on heavy chains. Limited use has been found in the Brooklyn Naval Yard and in tanker berths where it has proved to be a satisfactory answer to the problem of avoiding heavy jarring from glancing blows.

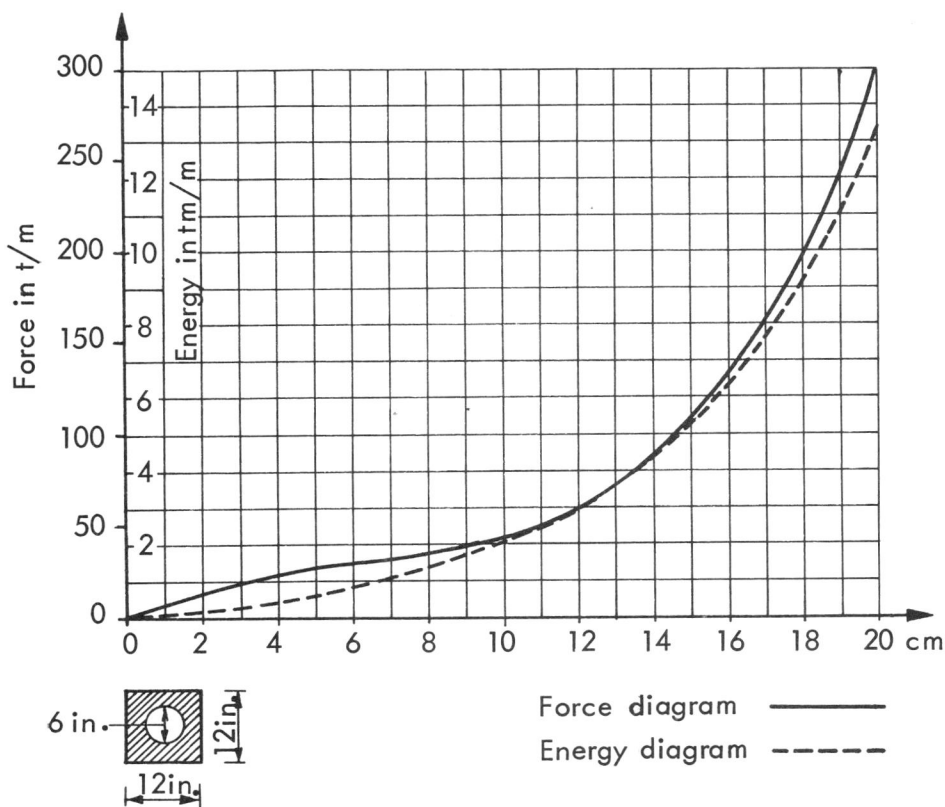

Figure 4.28. Deformation diagram for 12 inches by 12 inches Butyl rubber fender (reference commercial catalog).

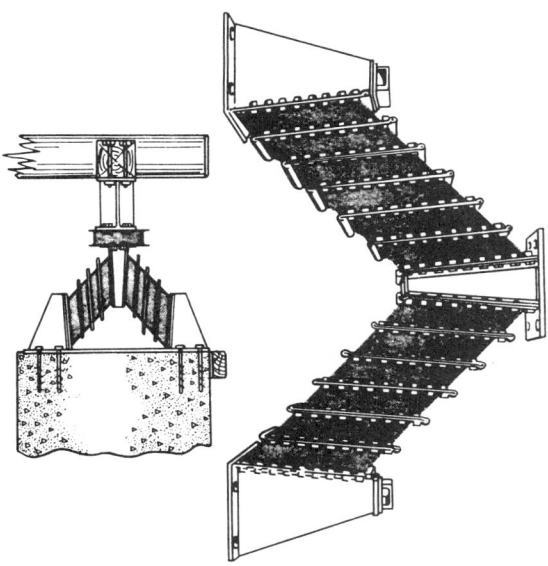

Figure 4.29. Raykin fender (34).

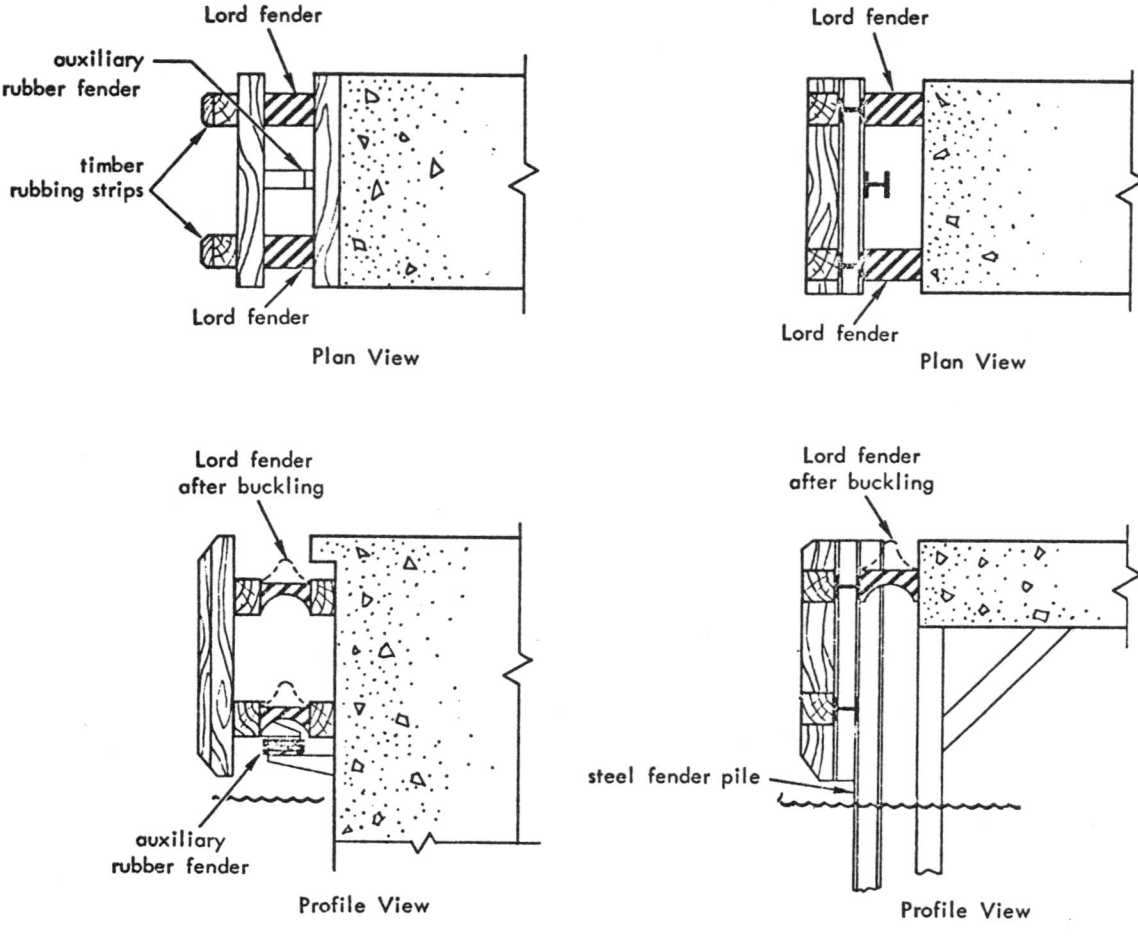

Figure 4.30. Lord fender.

Spring, hydraulic and hydropneumatic systems are most suitable for ferry berths. Hydraulic systems have also been used in ferry-rings for offshore platforms.

Table 4.3 gives an impression of the energy absorbing ability of various fender systems.

A new principle in fendering, which may prove to be valuable particularly for breasting dolphins, was announced recently. The new fender design (28), which utilizes the torque principle, is called "Cambridge fenders" because it is based on research work on plastic deformation of metals at Cambridge University, England. Each fender consists of timber pads or rotating pneumatic fender units carried between the extremities of a pair of torque arms. These torque arms are rigidly attached to a vertical torque tube which rotates in journals fixed to dockside or dolphin. The impact energy of the ship is absorbed by the torsional deflection of a bar concentrically mounted within the torque tube with one end fixed to the dock side. Two identical units are fitted to one of the

Table 4.3. Energy Absorption of Various Fender Systems.

Type of fender	Energy absorption
Rubber	
1. Hollow, cylindric or rectangular members (radial forces)	Up to 10 tons meter per meter for diameters up to about 0.5 meter
2. Axial forces on rubber blocks	Up to 19 tons meter
3. Lord fender	Up to 7 tons meter
4. Raykin fender	Up to 30 tons meter
5. Seibu	For example: About 80 tons meter for 3-meter length and 1-meter height
Gravitation	Variable, several hundreds tons meters if desirable
Hydropneumatic	Variable up to say 30 tons meter
Spring	Unlimited within practical limits

dolphins of an oil tanker terminal. In the installation at Grays Thurrock, England, the torque arms are 5 feet long, and the timber fender they support is 30 feet high. Energy absorption at the full deflection of 36 inches is 560 tonf, and the maximum load exerted on the ship is 30 tonf. This design is suitable for 25,000 dwt, but according to Reference 28, it may easily be expanded to 100,000 dwt or more.

For further information on fender systems, the reader may consult References 8, 17, 21, 22, 23, 26, 29 and 34.

Dolphins

Dolphins are commonly used in combination with piers and wharves to shorten the length of these structures. *Breasting dolphins* are designed to take the impact of the ship when docking and to hold the ship against a broadside wind. *Mooring dolphins* are designed for mooring and not for impacts of ships. They are located some distance behind the face of the dock, about 45° off the bow and the stern of a vessel (bulk carrier) of standard size, so that the mooring lines usually will be not less than 200 feet nor more than 400 feet long. Dolphins may also be used just as navigation markers.

Design may be of the flexible or the rigid type. Wool-pile clusters like Figure 4.31 for mooring are examples of the former type. Large steel cylinders and groups of steel pipe piles have also been used to provide flexible dolphins mainly for mooring.

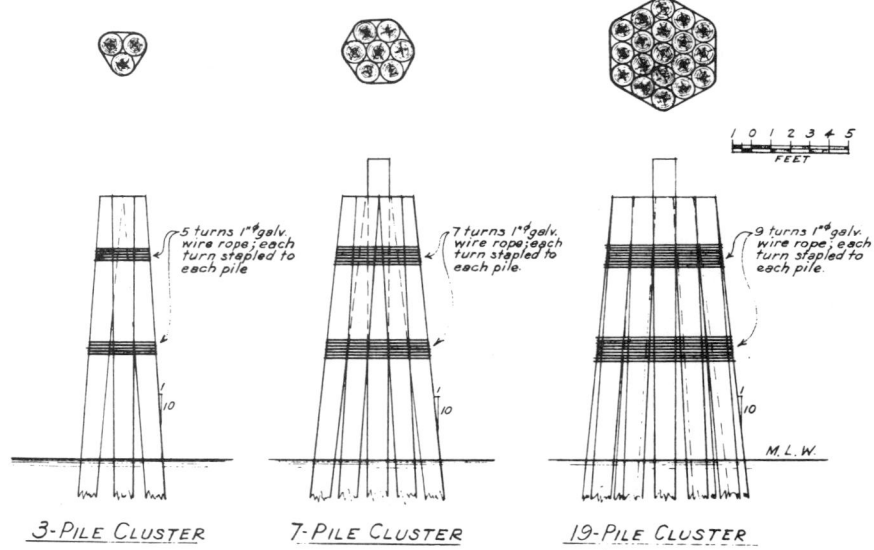

Figure 4.31. Flexible wood pile dolphin (26).

Breasting dolphins are much heavier because they must stand up to heavy impacts. Heavy sheet pile cell dolphins are also well suited as turning dolphins for warping or turning the ship around at the end of the dock. As the ships have become larger, the design of dolphins has turned to using heavy concrete platform slabs supported by vertical and batter piles, usually of steel, although precast concrete is also used (26).

At Kalundberg tanker terminal in Denmark, a heavy concrete block arranged for impacts is able to slide on the top of the concrete slab, thereby providing certain flexibility. When the block has slid too far, it is lifted back by a crane.

Figure 4.32 is a breasting dolphin designed for Cook Inlet. It consists of four vertical 11-foot diameter steel legs joined below the ice level by 4-foot diameter pipe bracing. The two legs adjacent to the dock face project above the water surface to serve as movable fender guides and mooring points. The breasting dolphin unit resists horizontal shear and overturning forces by means of six 24-inch diameter piles in the bottom of each leg. A 4-inch diameter horizontal pipe separates the top of the fronttubes and serves to maintain the 80-foot center to center spacing of the vertical fender guides.

Figure 4.33 shows a heavy 5-foot diameter mooring dolphin built for mooring of floating dock under difficult soil conditions in the Martinscica Bay, Yugoslavia (14).

For further information on dolphins, the reader is referred to References 9, 16, 21, 26 and 34, including a great number of special catalogs from companies producing fenders. Berthing for large oil tankers is mentioned specifically in Reference 20 from the PIANC Congress in 1957.

Moorings

A vessel may be subjected to the following motions as shown in Figure 4.34: heave, yaw, pitch, sway, roll and surge. Although all movements may occur for a vessel moored at a quay wall, it is the surge motion parallel to the quay wall which causes trouble. As described in Chapter 2, the surge motion is usually caused by the pene-

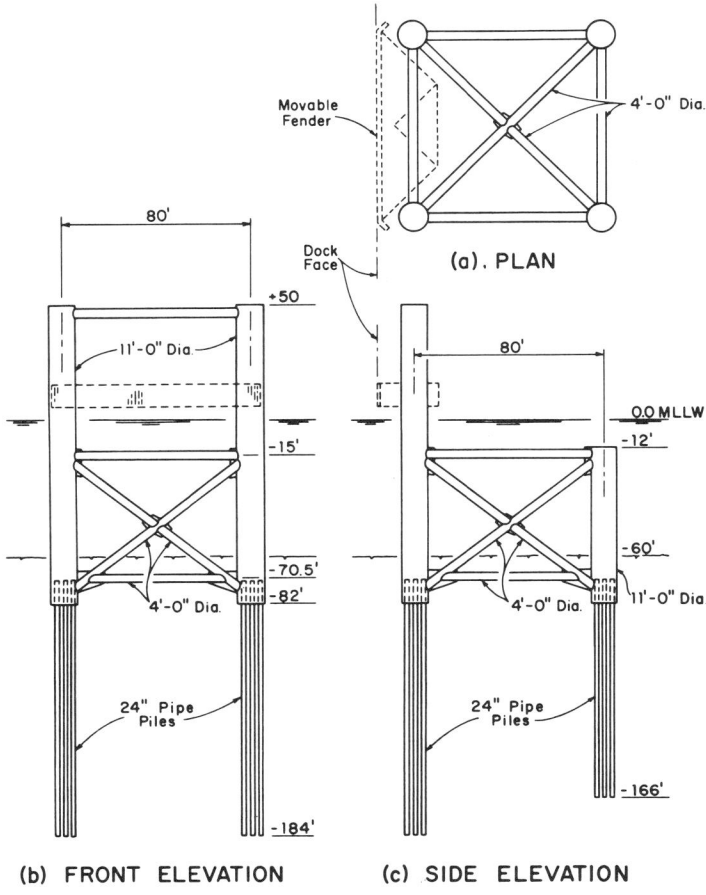

Figure 4.32. Breasting dolphin units (11).

tration of long period waves in the harbor basin. A very comprehensive literature on the computation of mooring forces is available (13, 19, 33, 34, 35).

The basic equation (34) is

$$M'_x \ddot{x} + N'_x \dot{x} + R_x x = M'_x \dot{U} + N_x U \quad (4.2)$$

where x is the variable horizontal surge translation on mass-center of ship from rest position in head sea; $\dot{x}$ and $\ddot{x}$ are the corresponding velocity and acceleration; M'_x is the total mass in movement (mass of vessel + added mass); N_x is the linear damping coefficient in surge motion; R_x is the horizontal resisting force to surge motion in x direction, e.g., in the form of mooring devices; U is the horizontal component of mean velocity of water mass displaced by ship; and $\dot{U}$ is the corresponding acceleration. R_x may be approximated as $R_x \sim k' x^n$ where n is a numerical exponent and k' a factor where values depend on the degree of tightness (or slackness) and elasticity of the combined mooring lines.

There is no exact solution to Equation 4.2. Using small amplitude theory, the approximate solution may be obtained by solving the equation

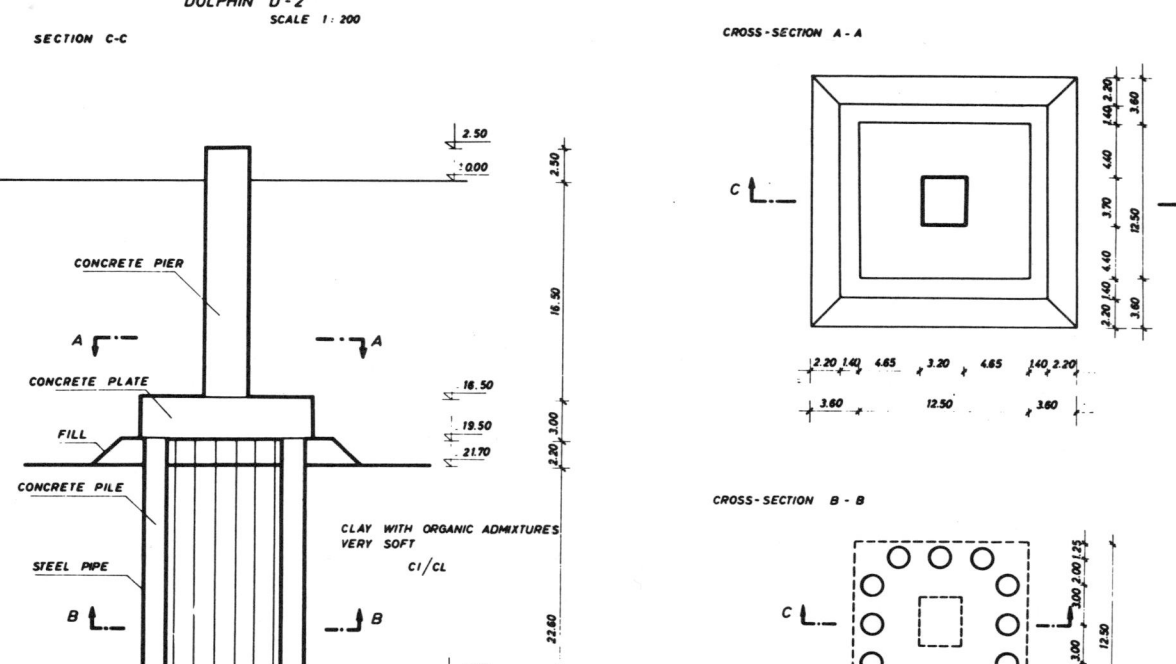

Figure 4.33. Heavy mooring dolphin built in Yogoslavia (14).

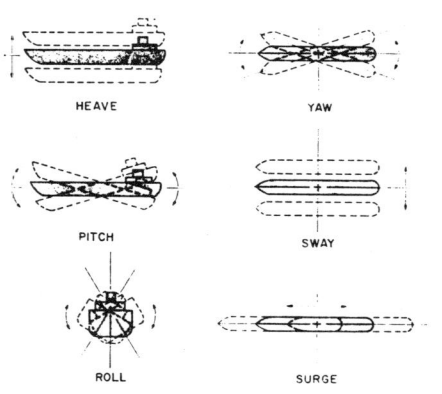

Figure 4.34. Various movements of vessels (22).

$$\frac{C}{\epsilon \beta g} \left(\frac{K' x_o^n}{(M'_x) w} R_n - w x_o \right) = \frac{H}{2} \qquad (4.3)$$

where $C = L/T$ = wave celerity and the other notations are those mentioned above under wave forces on vessel, $\epsilon = (1/kD) (\sinh kd - \sinh kh/\cosh kd)$; $\beta = [3 (\sin kl - kl \cos kl)]/(kl)^3$; D is vessel draft; $k = 2k/L$; $2l$ is vessel length; $w = 2\pi/T$; x_o is maximum movement of vessel from its mean position; $R_{(n)}$ is the coefficient which is a function of n. For $n = 1$, $R_{(n)} = 1$. For $n = 2$, $R_{(n)} = 0.8488$. With $n = 1$,

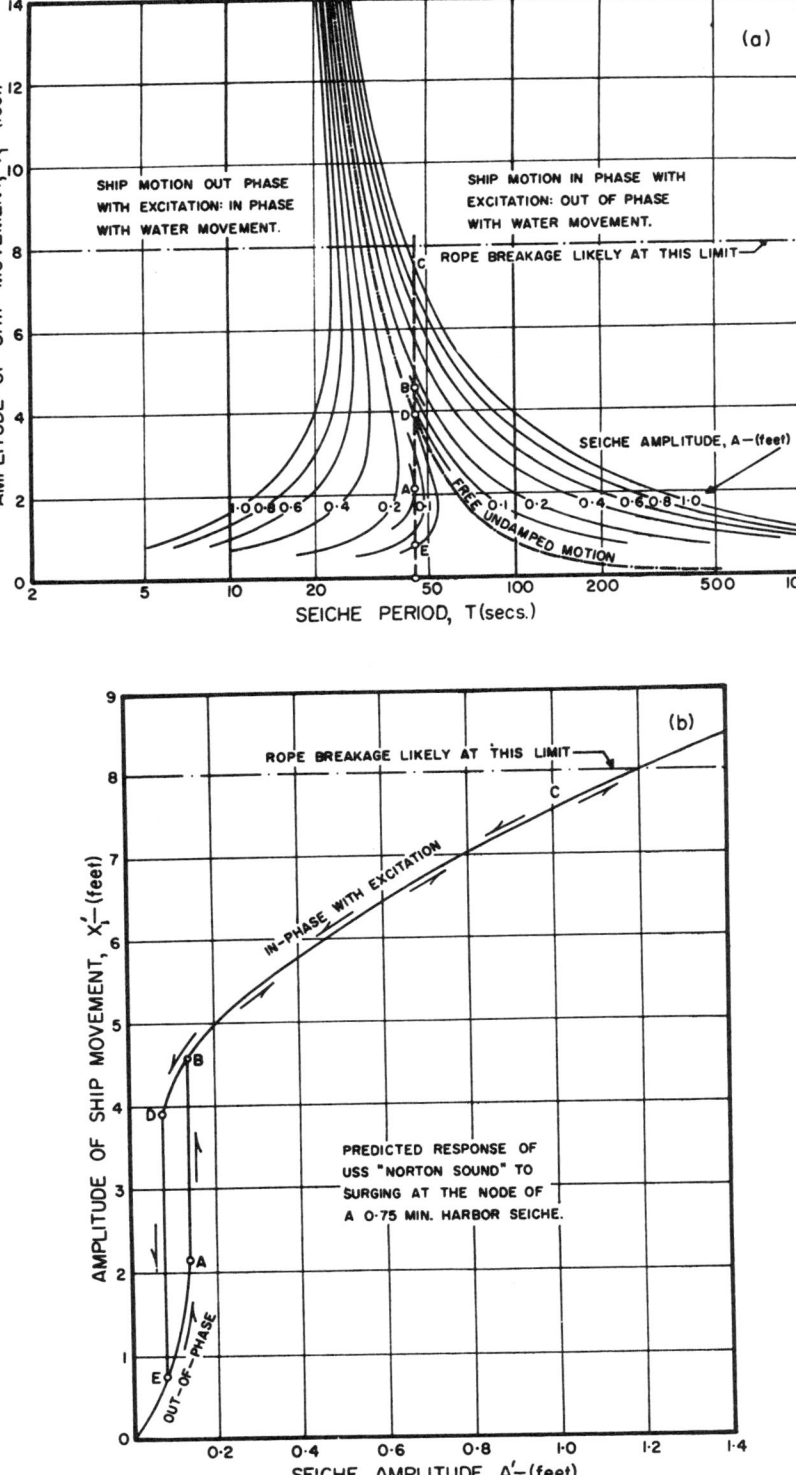

Figure 4.35. Surging response of USS Norton Sound to nodal stimulus of 45 seconds seiche (34).

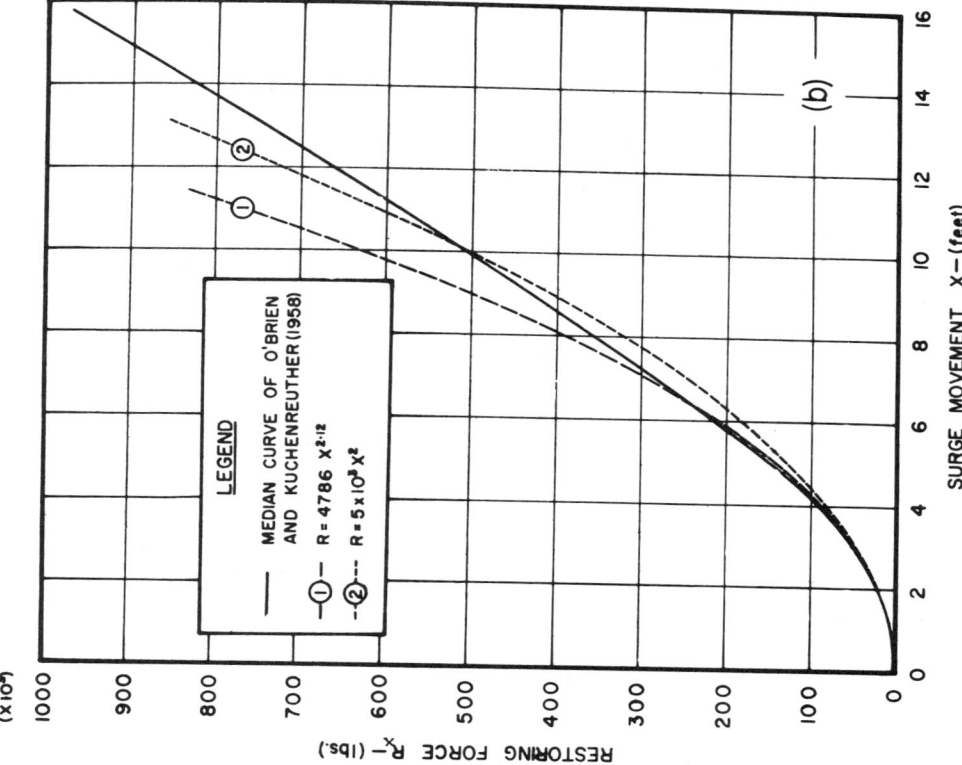
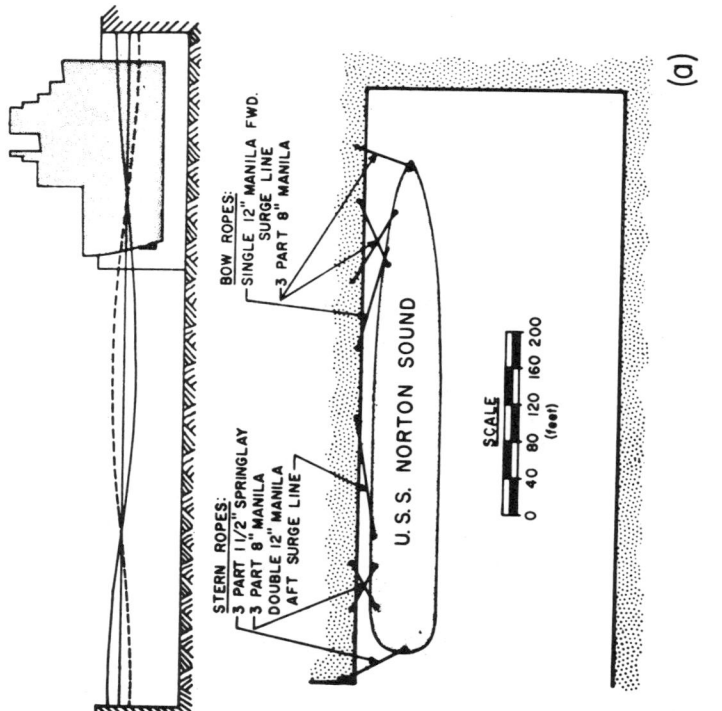

Figure 4.36. Mooring conditions of USS Norton Sound in Port Hueneme showing relationship between combined rope tensions (one end) and ship movement under conditions of loose moorings (34).

$$x_o = -\frac{H}{2}\frac{\beta g \epsilon k}{p^2 - w^2}$$

when $p = k'/(M'_x + M)$.

The solution to Equations 4.2 and 4.3 may be presented in diagrams like Figure 4.35 which refers to research mentioned in Reference 34 and indicates the surging response of USS *North Sound* to natal stimulus of a 45-second seiche. Figure 4.36 shows mooring conditions and gives values for the restoring force as a function of surge movement.

If the resonance period(s) is included in the wave spectrum, a dangerous situation may occur. In order to avoid resonance, one may use hard or slack moorings. For smaller vessels, it is most practical to use hard mooring in order to lower the resonance period. For larger vessels, the problem is more complex because slack moorings may cause resonance with long period waves.

Because surge velocities are always small, the degree of damping is almost negligible. Disregarding the damping makes it easier to compute the maximum amplitude of the undamped oscillation, x_o'. According to Reference 34, it is

$$X_o' = \left(\frac{(\sigma/w)^2}{\Delta'(n)}\right)\frac{1}{n-1}$$

where $\sigma = 2k/T$, and $\Delta'(n)$ is a numerical function of (n) differing slightly from $\Delta(n)$.

The maximum horizontal force which the mooring ropes collectively will be required to withstand are:

$$(R_x) \max = k'(X_1')^n$$

where X_1' refers to the amplitude of the undamped forced oscillation, and k' is a nonlinear spring. It is necessary to resort to mooring-line geometry in order to determine the maximum horizontal pull $(R_h)_{max}$ along the actual horizontal projection of the line of a rope or cable. Thus, for any particular mooring rope of initial length, h, in horizontal projection streched by surge movement

Wharves and Quays

of the ship to another horizontally projected length, H, it is, according to Wilson (34), possible to show that

$$\frac{X_1}{R_x} \sim \frac{(H-h)(1+\sin^2\tau)}{R_h}$$

where X_1 is the forced oscillation part of x with amplitude, x_1, and τ is the angle of the obliquity which the rope makes with the longitudinal axis of the ship. This gives

$$R_h \sim R_x \cos\tau (1 + \sin^2\tau) \sim R_x \cos\tau (2 - \cos^2\tau)$$

where $(H - h)/X_1 \sim \cos\tau$.

The problem is very complex and in order to obtain reliable results on the actual forces to be expected, hydraulic model experiments are preferable.

Mooring Facilities, Wires and Ropes

Mooring is provided by wires or ropes attached to pollards, bollards and rings which are usually fastened to concrete blocks or other heavy elements included in the quay wall. Figure 4.36 shows an example of a mooring arrangement including bow and stern lines, surge (spring) and side lines.

Bow, stern and side lines keep the vessel at the quay. Surge (or spring) lines hinder surge motion parallel to the quay. Forces to be absorbed are exerted on the vessel by winds, currents, waves (short period for smaller vessels, long period for larger vessels) and occasionally by other kinds of waves like tsunamis and ship waves. In order to absorb the forces, cables should be in as horizontal a position as possible, which is difficult where the tidal range is high. Moreover, it is an advantage that mooring cables be made of the same material, arranged symmetrically, if forces are mainly of symmetrical character.

Mooring ropes are available in many types of lay construction, mainly of steel and natural or

Table 4.4. Weights of Mooring Cables (Equations 4.4 and 4.5).

Material	Construction	Constant of proportionality (per foot per square inch)	
		In air, C_a	In water, C_w
Steel wire	6 x 24 fiber core flattened strands	1.80	1.45
	6 x 37 galvanized hawser	1.55	1.20
	6 x 24 (seven-fiber core) galvanized	1.40	1.05
Nylon rope	three-strand towline	0.29	0.028

synthetic fiber materials (34). Individual wires or fibers are woven together into strands which are woven into ropes according to specific lay patterns. In "regular lay," the wires or fibers of the strands have a directional twist which is opposite to that of the strands themselves. The lay is "right hand" if the twist of the strands appears clockwise when looking along the rope; "left hand" if the twist is counter-clockwise.

The wires in steel ropes may have different grades of strength and may be galvanized for protection against corrosion. A steel wire rope usually consists of six strands, each containing 19, 24 or 37 individual wire filaments built around fiber (or steel) cores. Fiber ropes usually consist of three strands (plain-lay), but may be obtained in four strand (shroud-lay) or nine strand (cable-lay) construction.

Typical fiber materials are manila, sisal, coir, nylon, saran, dacron, rayon and prolene (polypropylene). Manila hemp is grown in the Phillippines; sisal fiber in Mexico, East Africa and Java and coir in India. The remaining fibers are synthetic products which provide certain desirable properties not found in natural fibers.

Manufacturers' data on weights of mooring ropes in air and water, when plotted against nominal diameter, show a square-power law relating weight to diameter for both steel wire and fiber mooring ropes, wet or dry. In general, the weights of mooring line per unit length, w, in water and, w_a, in air, may be expressed in terms of nominal diameter, d, by

$$w = C_w d^2 \qquad (4.4)$$

and

$$w_a = C_a d^2 \qquad (4.5)$$

in which C_w and C_a are the constants of proportionality in the respective relationships.

The values of C_w and C_a in Table 4.4 apply to a few representative cases. Reasonable average values of the constants of steel wire mooring ropes are $C_a \cong 1.23$ pounds per square inch.

In Figure 4.37, rope manufacturers' data for the breaking (ultimate) strengths, T_u, of steel wire and fiber mooring ropes are plotted as functions of nominal rope diameters. The distribution of plotted points of like type closely parallel the series of diagonal lines which represent square-power relationships.

$$T_u = C_u d^2$$

Each line carries the value of C_u listed at the top of Figure 4.37. Obviously for steel, nylon, dacron

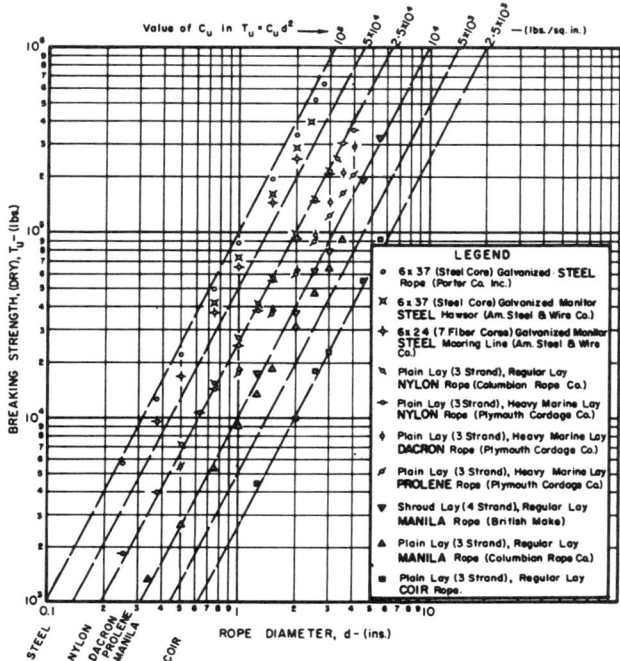

Figure 4.37. Relationship of ultimate (breaking) strength to nominal rope diameter (33).

and coir ropes, the square-power law is a good approximation to the test data; only in the cases of manila and polyprophylene (prolene) ropes is there some departure.

Next to steel, nylon ropes have the greatest strength for their size and would be valuable for certain types of mooring because of low weight. Dacron, prolene and manila ropes may be of value in instances where less elasticity is required than nylon. Manila and coir ropes have been used extensively in harbor moorings; manila being a favorite. Coir ropes, with greater elasticity but less strength than manila, have been widely used for "springs" or "strops" to which steel wires are connected for cushioning the effects of surge in harbors.

With fiber ropes, there is generally a difference between the ultimate strengths of the wet and dry rope. For nylon rope, wet strength is commonly rated from 5 to 19% lower than dry strength. Prolene rope has a wet strength which is about 5% greater than its dry strength. Dacron rope has effective equality between wet and dry strengths. Suitable values of C_u for mooring ropes of different materials are summarized in Table 2 of Reference 33. For further information on mooring ropes, the reader is referred to Reference 33 and its references.

Mooring Facilities on the Quay

Bollards and rings are usually placed just inside the front edge of the quay. Local experience and taste characterize the shape of the bollards.

Wooden poles are still found as bollards in smaller harbors, particularly in yachting and fishing sections.

Still used in Europe, *stone bollards* replaced the wooden bollards at an early stage when wooden walls were replaced by stone retaining walls.

Found in diverse shapes in practically all old ports, *cast iron bollards* may break at the moment

144 Port Engineering

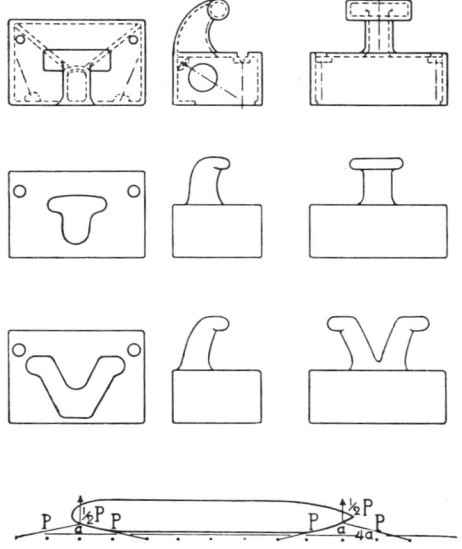

Figure 4.38. Different type of bollards (10).

when they are indispensable because cast iron, like stone, is not a very reliable material.

Cast steel bollards are a natural part of the modern quay outfit. Figure 4.38 shows three ordinarily used shapes. Rings are generally placed in pairs in hairpin-shaped anchorages. The mooring is easily effected by using one ring as a traverse for the other or by using a pipe as a traverse.

The bollards should be constructed in such a manner that the mooring itself or its anchorage breaks before the stability of the quay is threatened. The calculation of the pull transferred by the ship's wire to the bollard should be based on the force with which the wind acts on the ship, as described in the previous section dealing with berthing and mooring forces. For further information, the reader is referred to References 8, 10, 16, 26 and 34.

Pontoon-Wharves and Piers

A review of the development of structures in the field of port engineering would not be complete without mentioning the modern pontoons used as floating piers and wharves in marinas. Development of small craft harbors is mentioned in References 1 and 2. A few extracts on structures should be mentioned here.

The earliest type of flotation unit is an ordinary timber log. Although logs are still the least expensive type of flotation in some areas, their tendency to become "water logged" and sink after a few years makes them undependable. Except in usual circumstances, their use is not recommended.

Figure 4.38 shows various types of pontoons or floats now in use. A common lightweight solid used for flotation is expanded polystyrene. Various densities can be obtained, but the type used for flotation weighs approximately 2 pounds per cubic foot. The logs may be used whole or sawed into planks and either doweled or strapped to the deck frame. Styrofoam is completely impervious to water. One styrofoam installation has been in existence in Los Angeles Harbor for 16 years with little sign of deterioration.

Several other foams exist, but they all seem to attract a rapid growth of marine plant and animal life in sea water. These aquatic growths are not considered too objectionable, except for their appearance and the danger of fouling propellers. Most of these growths periodically die and drop off without damage to the float. Also, exposed foams are subject to vandalism because they can be cut easily with a knife. It has been alleged that fish and birds damage synthetic floats by nibbling or pecking at the marine growth attached to them. However, no evidence of such damage to dock supporting floats has been presented.

The relative softness of the synthetic materials described, as well as their attraction for marine life, have given rise to the use of exterior coating or sheathing. One successful coating now in use is an epoxy paint that bonds firmly and presents a tough, flexible surface that has the appearance of concrete. It attracts less marine life, and what clings to it can be readily wiped off. The coating is also impervious to hydrocarbons. A better but more costly protection is sheathing with a fiberglass-reinforced polyester resin.

Wharves and Quays 145

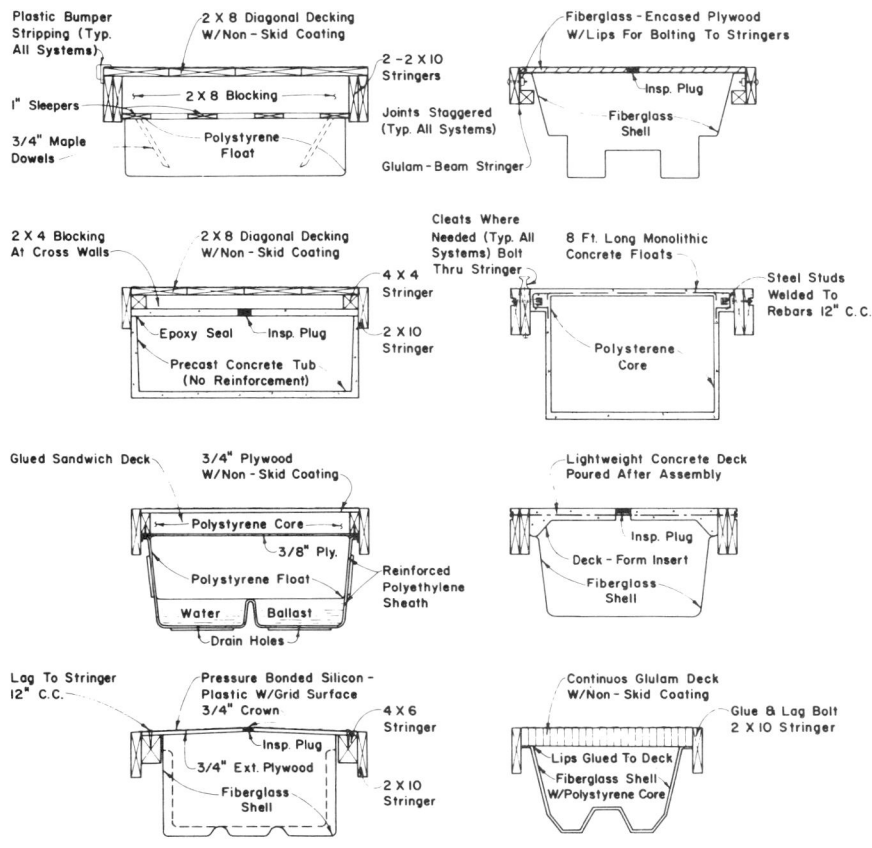

Figure 4.39. Various types of floats (2).

One objection to lightweight floats is their responsiveness to wave action. They tend to roll and pitch with the waves, giving a sense of insecurity to those who are not good sailors.

The number and variety of shell type floats available indicate a need for subhead classification. Such floats will have one common characteristic—all can be ballasted with sand or water to provide for corrective leveling of the deck after installation. However, they are subject to leakage and loss of buoyancy if the shell becomes permeable for any reason. They must be provided with accessible adequate diameter inspection holes for periodic checking.

The most commonly used synthetic shell floats on the market are probably those made of fiberglass-reinforced polyester resin. They are exceptionally tough for their weight and are unaffected by hydrocarbons, salt water or any of the common contaminants found in a small craft harbor. The coatings in which glass fibers and resins are sprayed into an external form and then rolled smooth tend to be resin-rich, to contain air bubbles and to fail through cracking and pinhole leaks. Each pontoon should therefore be pressure-tested, and any of the defects should be corrected before acceptance. Success has been achieved with exterior steel dies and interior solid rubber dies that force all the resin out of the wall, except that resin needed to bond the glass fibers.

A few manufacturers are offering prefabricated steel and aluminum floats. To be competitive, the shells are folded and welded into rectangular units, usually of thin gauge sheets with stiffening baffles for greater strength. Preservative coatings are usually factory-applied to both sides of all corrodible metals. Because of their high corrosion rates in a saltwater environment, most metals are not recommended for seacoast installations. Certain alloys are being offered that may overcome this objection.

Advocates of concrete floats point to the maintenance-free permanence of concrete construction and the sense of stability that the heavy mass of the concrete gives to a floating pier or dock. Various types have been used for a number of years with varying degrees of success. Several early failures have led to the banning of such floats by some authorities. The best units are those made by reliable manufacturers of concrete products, using steel molds and pouring and launching techniques that have been developed through long experience. Internal vibration has proved essential in obtaining the required leak-proof compaction of the concrete. Precise design and control of the mix is mandatory to prevent shrinkage cracks and honeycombing. Lightweight aggregates are used to keep the dead load to a minimum while retaining adequate wall thickness. Care must be used to prevent segregation of the aggregates through excessive vibration, and proper curing is essential.

Successful concrete floats have been made with and without reinforcement. When no reinforcing is used, certain parts of the float will be stressed in tension. Accordingly, the float must be designed so that at no point will the allowable tensile strength of the concrete be exceeded. Care must be used in transporting and launching these floats to prevent their cracking either through impact stresses or temperature changes. Once in the water and decked over, there is little danger of damage except by accident. The small amount of wave action to which any well-planned marina is subjected will not exert stresses that will crack the shell, and adequate deck framing will assure that no torsional or impact loading can occur. Under normal circumstances, the pontoon should strengthen with age indefinitely. Type II cement (Portland Cement Association specifications) should be used in a saltwater environment, preferably with approximately a 4% air entrainment additive.

When concrete floats are reinforced, a galvanized wire mesh is normally used. Because of the thin walls, the reinforcement must be kept to a small diameter and placed near the center of the section. For this reason, it adds little to the strength of the section, and its chief value is its ability to diffuse temperature differentials and hold the unit together even if it cracks.

Figure 4.40 shows various kinds of deck framing and float connections. Anchor piles are the simplest and most commonly used anchorage systems. They require firm but penetrable substrata, a bottom depth of not more than 30 feet at highest water level and moderate horizontal loading. The reader is referred to the ASCE Manual (2) for further information on details regarding floating docks for marinas.

Other types of pontoons exist. Figure 4.41 shows a barge dock adapted to 47-foot variation in river level. This new barge dock for the Shell Oil Company at Wood River, Illinois, on the Mississippi River provides a water level dock despite 47-foot variation in river level. A minimum of maintenance difficulty is reported (6). It can take up to 15 inches of deflection without damage to barge or structure if fendering is provided. It can be prefabricated elsewhere, and its cost was estimated to be the lowest of alternatives studied. The Wood River facility receives barge tows up to 750 feet long with capacities to 90,000 barrels.

A brand new type of facility also arranged for pleasure is shown in Figure 4.42 depicting an underwater observation tower built for Okinawa Tourism Development Corporation by Hitachi Zosen's Innoshima shipyard, which is an important part of the marine park around Bushima Misatei. Through the viewing windows of this cylindrical metal tower, which is embedded on the sea bed, tourists can see coral reef and tropical fish in their natural underwater environments.

Wharves and Quays 147

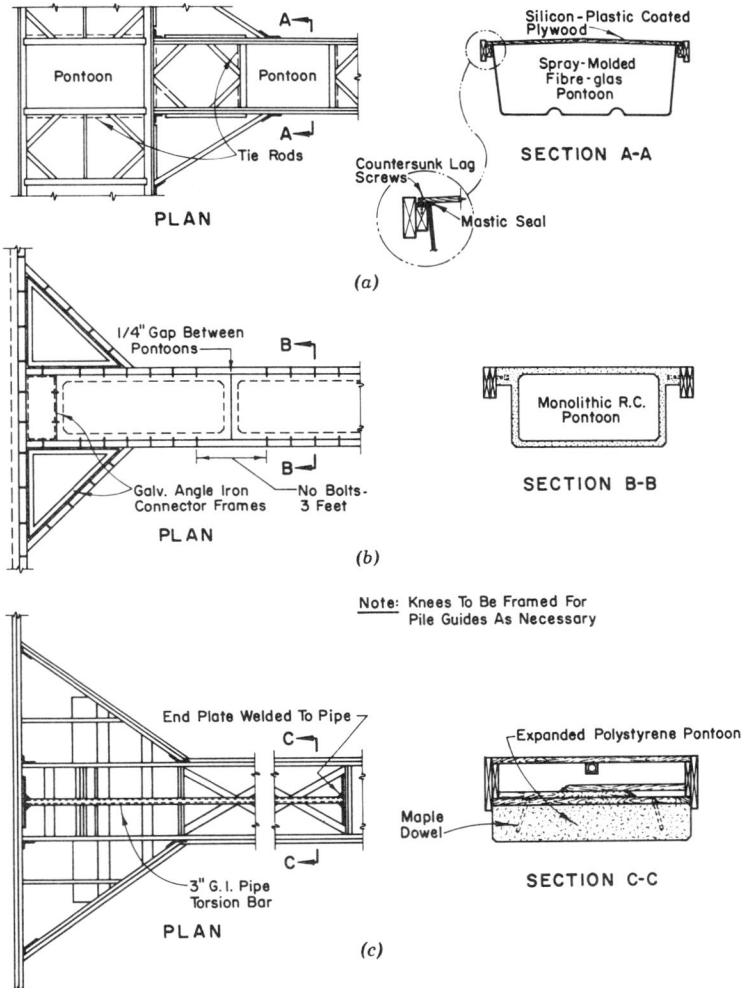

Figure 4.40. Deck framing of floats (2).

Transport Equipment

Port engineering is a changing field, old principles are replaced by new. For this reason, the old loading system mainly used in European ports (and quite effective compared to the old, almost obsolete American burtoning system) should only be mentioned briefly (10). Chapter 5 gives information on the new system(s) which the port planner now has to consider.

Cranes which are bound to crane rails are characteristic for all major ports outside the United States. Their shapes and radii are closely connected with the water depths, the types of ships to be served and the types of transit sheds used.

The history of cranes dates far back. Before the last World War, the famous old crane at Danzig (Gdansk), constructed in 1441, was still in use. At the close of the last century, crane outfits were

148 Port Engineering

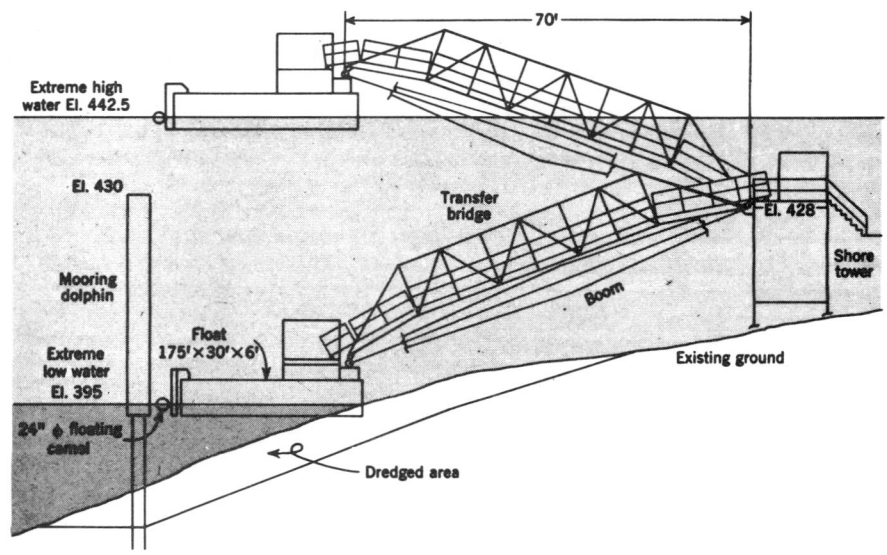

Figure 4.41. Barge dock adapted to 47 feet variation in river level (6).

Figure 4.42. Underwater observation tower built in Japan (5).

Wharves and Quays 149

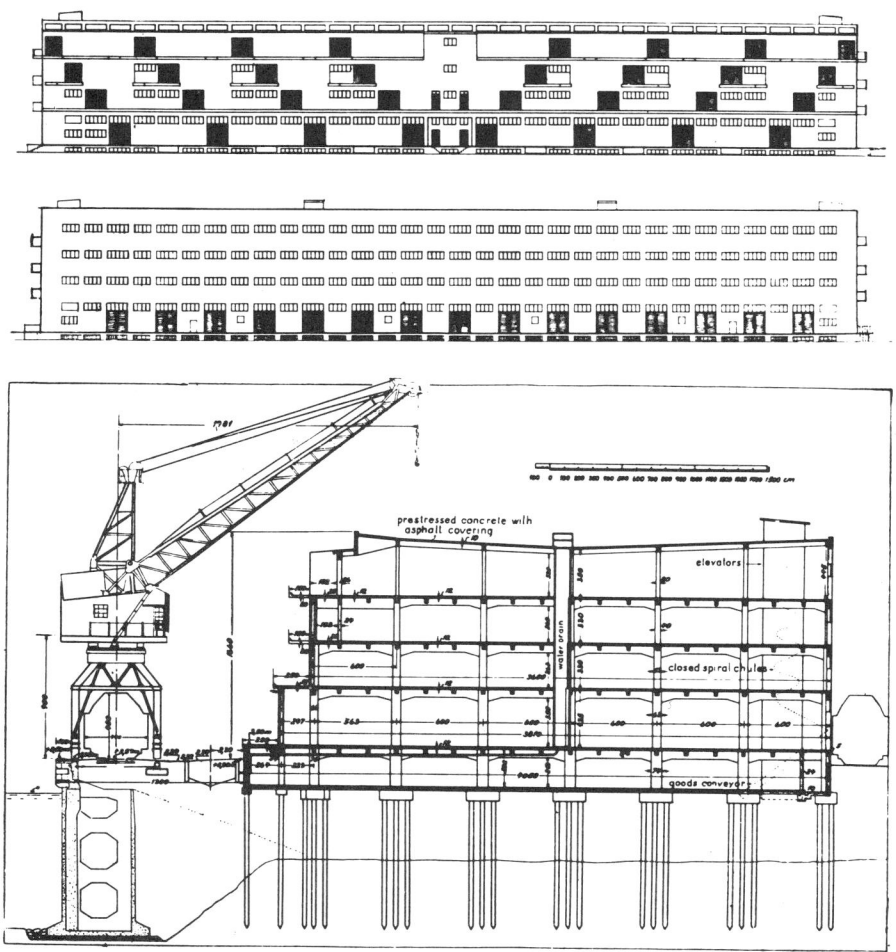

Figure 4.43. Level-luffing crane at a multidecked transit shed at the Port of Copenhagen (10).

found in the majority of the main ports. The cranes were driven by steam or hydraulic power; they required piping and steam-emitting central stations. Hydraulic cranes are still found at a few ports. After the first electric crane was installed at Hamburg in 1892, the idea was adopted by many other ports. Since then, electric cranes have dominated because they are handier and more economical than all other types.

The cranes were installed on portals moving on rails along the quay. The continental cranes were able to slew, hoist and lower. In addition to this, British cranes were able to luff while the burden was kept level automatically. In this way the crane driver could swing the burden around, drawing it near to or pushing it away from himself, besides lifting or lowering it. With two universal handles, the driver could reach any point within the reach of the crane. Furthermore, he could drive the crane along the rails on the quay. Because this movement involved a danger for the persons and goods on the quay, it was not used during the discharging unless a special guard was placed on the quay to warn the traffic.

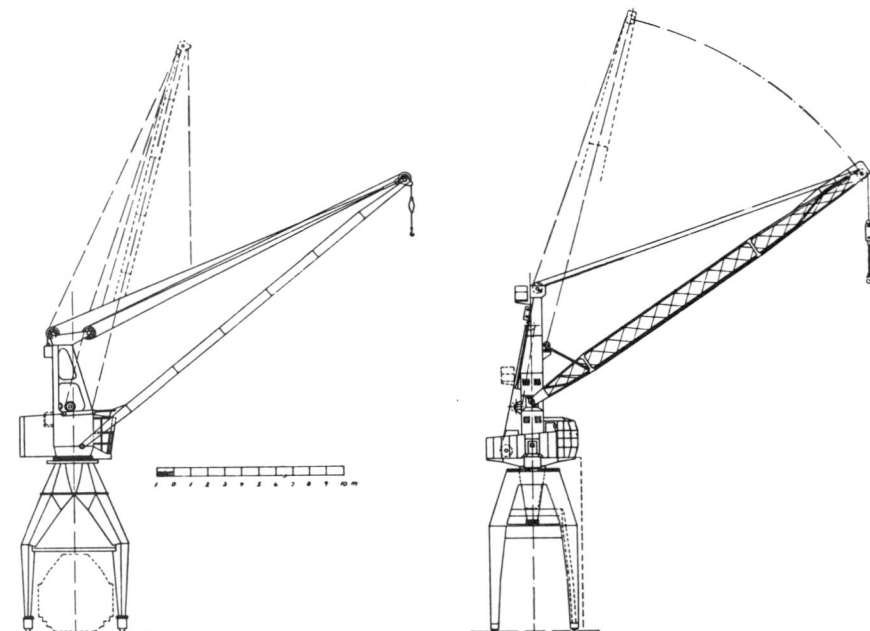

Figure 4.44. German level-luffing cranes (10).

This principle of crane functioning is the standard of all cranes of today. There are many varying systems of cranes but the main attributes as described above are still used. The lifting capacity of cranes varies greatly, from 3 to 50 tons, and, in the case of floating cranes, capacities may be from 100 to 500 tons. Common lifting radii are 20 to 40 meters.

The so-called level-luffing cranes are characterized by the hook preserving its height automatically as long as the driver does not hoist or lower the hook by turning the wire drum. The luffing movement theoretically requires no force and is powered only by a motor of a few horsepower. The luffing system is used widely. Figure 4.43 shows a level-luffing crane at a multi-storied transit shed at the Free Port of Copenhagen (10). The waterside of the transit shed is constructed so that the lowest platform can be reached anywhere by the crane's hook. There is a platform lengthwise along the first floor, two-thirds of which is covered by balconies projecting from the second and third floors. Each of the three uppermost floors has a balcony area on which the goods may be landed, this area being one-third of the total front length. The distance in this case is 13 meters but varies greatly depending upon the number of railway tracks on the quay.

Figure 4.44 shows two typical examples of German level-luffing cranes. The substructure is made of welded sheetiron boxes giving the cranes a pleasant streamline shape. The portal is profiled to span one or more railway tracks, but the substructure narrows considerably in the direction of the crane driver's cabin. The driver's house is made as narrow as possible, and part of the machinery is placed above the driver's level.

The manufacturers constructed test portals one-third their actual size and tested them in every conceivable manner before commencing production. As the actual crane portals are very light, they are stabilized by casting concrete into the lower part of each crane leg.

Some of the German cranes are three-legged. Two of the legs run along the rail on the quay, and only one leg runs on the rear rail. In this way, minimum obstruction is caused to the traffic on the quay, and the three legs are always firmly supported by the rails even if the rear rail were to sink some centimeters on certain stretches. The four-legged box portal is very stiff, causing the crane to rock when only a fraction of a centimeter of the rail sinks under one of the legs. This is avoided by the usual structural steel constructions as their elasticity brings all four crane legs in contact with the rails simultaneously.

The superstructure of all ordinary cranes is connected with the substructure either by a circular line of rollers on the latter or a circular rail attached to the substructure and four or six wheels attached to the superstructure; the wheels run on this rail. In both cases the circular support must be large enough for the superstructure to rest stably on it, that is, the superstructure should transfer vertical pressure to its support among the whole circle of rollers or on all wheels, whatever the wind pressure or load situation may be.

On the crane to the left in Figure 4.44, the superstructure is connected with the substructure by a double ball bearing circle which is able to stand tension on one side and pressure on the opposite side.

In the example to the right in Figure 4.44, the jib and the machinery are installed in a revolving column which is supported by a spheric ball bearing at its base, and under the driver's cabin it is held in position by a vertical ring. On this ring run some cast steel wheels fastened to the column. The ball bearing carries the weight, and, together with the wheel-ring, it keeps the column in a vertical position.

The cranes are bound to their rails and cannot be used as intensively as mobile cranes which can be directed from one berth to another according to the requirements. This is a main objection against the old system.

A ship with five holds often requires seven cranes—one for each hold besides an additional crane for each of the two largest holds where supplementary gangs may be at work. When a quay is long enough for the berthing of several ships with five holds, the number of cranes on the quay should be five times the number of berths plus at least two additional cranes.

Each crane on a quay, handling 500 tons of goods annually per linear meter, is used only 50% of the total working hours of a year. At many ports it has now turned out that cranes only work from 10 to 20% of the total working hours.

Some ports prefer half-portal cranes. The front legs of the crane move on a rail close to the edge of the quay, and the leg-less side of the half-portal runs on a rail placed on a small balcony above the ground floor at the front of the transit shed. There are special supports for the rear rail across the open storage spaces between the transit sheds. Half-portal cranes cause no obstruction to the traffic on the quay and no danger of colliding with men or vehicles, but the unavoidable bridges across the open spaces are an encumbrance and the crane-portals limit the stacking height of the goods on the quay and may be obstructive to mobile cranes.

Crane rails have had to follow modern crane developments, employing higher pressures and higher precision requirements. The large rigid gantries, in particular, require important foundations (30).

Mobile cranes, however, have now often replaced cranes on rails and are commonly used in developing countries at new port installations. In the United States, the antique burtoning system is almost abandoned and replaced by very effective mobile cranes and other equipment for handling containers. Some years ago, 500-ton per meter (150-ton per foot) handling capacity was considered high. Now, capacity has reached far beyond that (see Chapter 5). With respect to special equipment for handling bulk loads, refer to References 9, 10, 16 and 26.

In the past, most arriving cargo spent considerable time in warehouses and transit sheds of common dimensions—100 to 130 feet wide and 300 to 400 feet long (Figure 4.45). Some was stored in open areas. Common figures could be that 25% of the arriving goods were picked up directly, 55% passed through the transit shed and 20% was stored in the open air (10). At new instal-

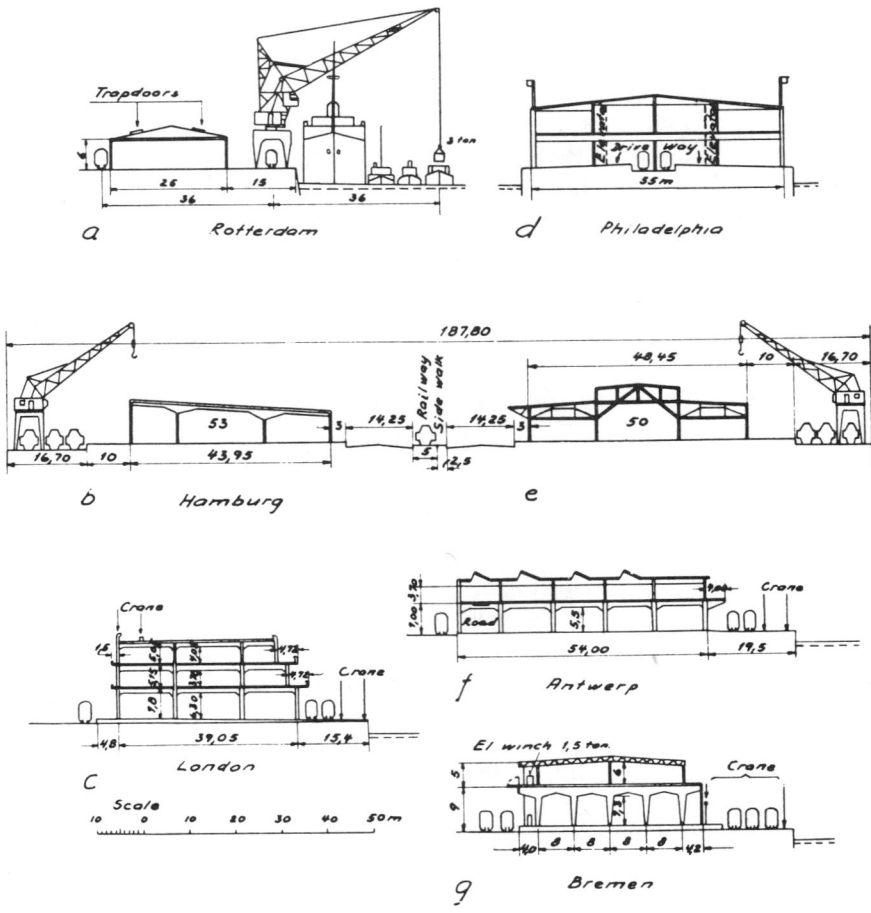

Figure 4.45. Transit sheds and quay arrangements (10).

lations this situation has changed considerably. An increasing quantity of discharged material is left for only a relatively short time in the open air, and less and less material passes through sheds. Reference is made to Chapter 5 which mentions the modern requirements to transit and storage *areas* (rather than sheds).

References

1. American Society of Civil Engineers. 1964. "Small craft harbor development." *ASCE Journal of the Waterways and Harbors Division* 90(WW3):11-114.
2. ____. 1969. "Small Craft harbors." *Manuals and Reports on Engineering Practice* (50).
3. Anonymous. 1960. *The Dock and Harbour Authority* 41(475 and 478).
4. ____. 1967. "Elizabeth container facility New York." *The Dock and Harbour Authority* 48(565):200-08.
5. ____. 1969. *The Dock and Harbour Authority* 50(590):366.

6. ____. 1970. "Barge dock for 47 feet variations in river level." *Civil Engineering* (March):81.
7. Cornick, H.F. 1957. *Dock and Harbour Engineering,* vol. 1. London: Charles Griffin and Co. Ltd.
8. ____. 1959. *Dock and Harbour Engineering,* vol. 2. London: Charles Griffin and Co. Ltd.
9. ____. 1962. *Dock and Harbour Engineering,* vol. 4. London: Charles Griffin and Co. Ltd.
10. Fugl-Meyer, H. 1957. *The Modern Port.* Copenhagen: Danish Technical Press.
11. Gaither, W.S., and Dalton, R.E. 1969. "All-weather tanker terminal for Cook Inlet." *ASCE Journal of the Waterways and Harbors Division* 95(WW2):131-48.
12. Holst, E. 1961. "Piers and wharves on concrete-filled tubular steel piles driven to rock." *Proceedings of 20th International Navigation Congress* s II:201-15.
13. Kilner, F.A. 1960. "Model tests of the motion of moored ships placed on long waves." *Proceedings of 7th Conference on Coastal Engineering* (Aug.). The Hague, The Netherlands. Also, 1961. University of California, Berkeley: Council on Wave Research. pp. 723-45.
14. Kleiner, C.E., et al. 1968. "Construction of dolphins in the Mortinscia Bay." *Proceedings of the 5th International Harbor Congress.* Paper 2-KL-PIN. Antwerp.
15. Langer, R.M., and Wilson, B.W. 1963. "Discussion of proceedings paper no. 3313 by Shu-t'ien Li." *ASCE Journal of the Waterways and Harbors Division* 89(WW2):63-70.
16. Larras, J. 1961. *Cours d'Hydraulique Maritime et de Travaux Maritimes.* Paris: Dunod.
17. Lee, T.T. 1965. *A Study of Effective Fender Systems for Navy Piers and Wharves.* Tech Report R312. U.S. Naval Civil Engineering Laboratory.
18. Netch, G. 1969. "Newton Creek docking facilities." *Civil Engineering* (June):64-67.
19. O'Brien, J.T., and Kuchenreuther, D.I. 1958. "Forces induced on a large vessel by surge." *ASCE Journal of the Waterways and Harbors Division* 84(WW2-1571).
20. Permanent International Association of Navigation Congresses. 1957. "Berthage for large oil tankers." *Proceedings of 19th Congress of PIANC* s II - q 2.
21. ____. 1961. "Terminals, etc." *Proceedings of 20th Congress of PIANC* s II - s 1.
22. ____. 1965. "Motion of seagoing vessels under the influence of waves." *Proceedings of 21st Congress of PIANC* s II–s 2.
23. Ponder, C.A., and Belyea, P.S. 1969. "Prestressed concrete simplifies construction of breakwater/wharf." *Civil Engineering* (Jan.): 58-60.
24. *Ports of the World.* Published yearly by Benn Brothers (Marine Publications), Ltd., London.
25. Prestressed Concrete Institute. 1969. *PCI Bridge Bulletin* (Sept.-Oct.).
26. Quinn, A. De F. 1961. *Design and Construction of Ports and Marine Structures.* New York: McGraw-Hill Book Company, Inc.
27. Russell, R.C.H. 1959. "A study of the movement of ships subjected to wave action." *Proceedings of the Institution of Civil Engineers* 2(Apr.). Also, Discussion. 1960 15(Apr.) : 435-50.
28. Shelbourne, Hugh. 1969. "Fendering for the bigger ships." *The Dock and Harbour Authority* 50(585):112-14.
29. Shu-t'ien Li. 1961. "Operative energy concept in marine fendering." *ASCE Journal of the Waterways and Harbors Division* 87(WW3):1-28.
30. Thues, G. 1968. "Enkele kraanbaantypes in de Haven van Antwerpen." *Proceedings of the 5th International Harbor Congress.* Paper 4-THU. Antwerp.
31. Vasco Costa, F. 1964. "The berthing ship." *The Dock and Harbour Authority* 45(525):90-94.
32. Whiteneck, L.L., Wake-Man, C.M., and Stover, E.H. 1962. "Plastic barriers preserve wood piling." *The Dock and Harbour Authority* 43 (June):58-60.
33. Wilson, Basil W. 1967. "Elastic characteristics of moorings." *ASCE Journal of the Waterways and Harbors Division* 93(WW4):27-56.

34. Wilson, Levinton and Baker. 1958. "Berthing and cargo handling in exposed locations." *Proceedings of Princeton University Conference.*

35. Woodruff, G.B. 1962. "Berthing and mooring forces." *ASCE Journal of the Waterways and Harbors Division* 88(WW1):71-82.

5 planning and layout of ports transportation systems

This chapter deals with general aspects of the transportation problems associated with harbors. The merchant marine's keen competition has developed new modes and new equipment for transport. Ship owners and ship research institutes have undertaken exhaustive studies and created a basis for prediction of future trends in shipping. Attempts to forecast the future of shipping were difficult enough in the days when political and economic factors used to play on the freight markets with about equal force. Now, forecasting is doubly difficult because the economic factors themselves are increasingly affected by unpredictable government intervention in economic affairs, nationally and internationally.

Earlier private entrepreneurs took decisions to invest their own money in ships, based on intelligent guesswork of the future state of the market. No decision today can be taken without a study of such factors as the tax implication of the investment, the cheap credit policy of the shipbuilding country and, in some countries such as the United States the size of the subsidy obtainable from government. For governments investing in state-owned fleets, the motives may be among several: the hope of earning foreign currency as distinct from profits, the availability of a national fleet in case of war, the satisfaction of national pride, the use of shipping as an instrument for political influence and means of assisting exports through lower freight rates. Unfortunately, once the taxpayer's money has been invested in ships for these types of purposes, governments tend to avoid operational losses by flag discrimination. In the old days, the movements of the freight market in time of peace were largely influenced by such factors as the trade cycle or the failure of crops. Now, such factors are far less important compared to the success or failure of governments in arranging international trade.

Despite some flag discrimination, international shipping has remained as the nearest approach in the world to a general free international market and, as such, is extraordinarily efficient. Increasing specialization of ship types is now tending to split that market into several separate compartments which hardly compete with one another.

Port functions may be classified as follows:

Primary: The transfer of cargo (and/or passengers) between ocean carrier and land or inland carrier.
Secondary: Long-term storage of cargo,

156   Port Engineering

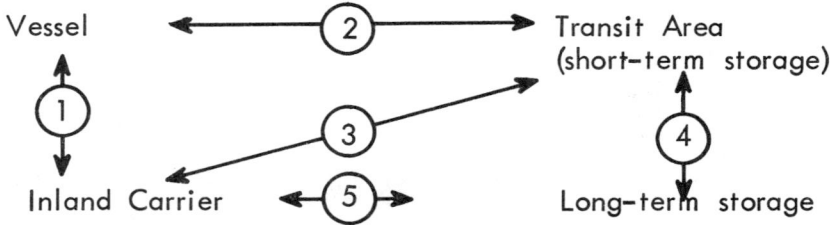

Figure 5.1. Basic types of cargo transfer within ports.

              Marketing and/or processing of cargo,
              Collection of customs.
Auxiliary: Vessel servicing (commissary, fuel, repairs),
              Land traffic servicing,
              Other (Naval operations, pleasure craft).

Transportation vs. Transfer

Transfer of cargo is an element of ocean transportation. It is frequently the most costly element between the points of origin and destination, despite the fact that it does not contribute to the movement of cargo between these points. Transportation between terminals differs basically from transfer within terminals in that the efficiency of the former is measured in ton-miles per hour and that of the latter in tons per hour. Similarly, costs are computed in dollars per ton-mile for transportation and dollars per ton for cargo transfer.

The distance cargo moved within the port has relevance only insofar as it affects cost. Developments of modern handling techniques and equipment have resulted in a trend toward decreasing the importance of the distance factor in cargo transfer operations. This trend is of major significance in the design of port terminals, which are no longer transit sheds and some relatively minor storage areas but now include large, open parking areas for unitized cargo, trailers, etc., with accompanying transport arteries and handling equipment as mentioned later.

Types of Transfer

Figure 5.1 illustrates the five basic types of cargo transfer within ports.

The transit area is generally the space where movements 1, 2, 3 and 4 take place. In addition, the transit area must accommodate the cargo stored for short-term periods, prior to departures and after arrivals of vessels.

In many terminals, short-term storage and transfer of cargo in the transit area are intermingled with such "secondary functions" as long-term storage, marketing and even processing. Unless imports and exports are moved to and from inland points under bond, customs inspection will also take place in the transit area. These "secondary functions" are incompatible with efficient cargo transfer and often complicate the handling and flow of materials through the transit area.

Types of Cargo

Bulk cargo whether liquid or dry, has the advantage of uniformity and is predominantly handled in large quantities, permitting use of mechanized handling (pipelines, belt conveyors, etc.). For most bulk cargos the ocean vessel is the container, as are the railroad cars, trucks or barges used by inland carriers. To date, the greatest strides in improvement of cargo handling methods have been made in the field of bulk materials.

General cargo consists of the packaged goods, separate units of various sizes and shapes, usually comprising the "high value" commodities of ocean transport. Due to problems of packaging, lack of

Table 5.1. Percent of Round-Trip Time Spent in Port for Different Trades and Types of Ships (4)

Type of ship and trade	%Round-trip time In port	%Round-trip time On loading/ discharging	%Port time Gross loading/ discharge time*
Liner			
U.S. East Coast/ Far East	43	29	67
U.S. East Coast/ West Africa	49	35	72
Europe/Great Lakes	40	24	60
U.S. East Coast/ Europe	40	25	62.5
U.S. Gulf/ South America	49	22	45
Tanker average	10	8	80
Bulk ship average	15	13	85

*Gross loading/discharge time includes meal hours, rigging time and other dead time during the working period.

uniformity and drawn-out labor-management conflicts, much less progress has been made in the past on handling of general cargo.

Several years ago, the advent of the forklift truck and the stevedore's pallet greatly accelerated horizontal movement of general cargo. The level-luffing crane (Chapter 4), in conjunction with the stevedoring pallet, have added speed in vertical and horizontal movement, within a limited radius, which shaped developments in European ports. Complete palletizing in conjunction with side-port loading of vessels have resulted in efficient general cargo operations. Development of the cargo container revolutionized terminal operations in several locations.

The *container* eliminates from general cargo operations two of the main problems of the past: packaging and lack of uniformity. It reduces the role of the ocean and land carrier to merely carrying—*not* containing and protecting of the cargo too. It enables the terminal to deal with general cargo as a uniform commodity, regardless of the content of each container,—provided that the secondary functions of the port can be reduced or relocated to a point where they do not interfere with transfer operations.

Conventional Transport

A conventional cargo liner spends between 30 and 50% of her total round-trip time in port (4). Cargo handling expenses therefore amount to between 40 and 60% of her gross freight income. The relative magnitudes of port time for different trades are described in Table 5.1.

Table 5.1 proves that cargo liners are in a far worse situation than ships for bulk and tank cargoes. To some extent, new and better cargo handling and transportation systems have now been developed and are still improving.

General Cargo Terminals

Vessel loading and discharge of general cargo for transfer (1), Figure 5.1, (direct ship to inland carrier) differs in basic terminal requirements from transfer (2) (vessel to transit storage). For instance, if cargo is placed directly on railroad cars, extensive apron, storage and marshaling tracks are required to supply shipside operations. In U.S. ports, steel, heavy machinery and lumber are frequently handled in this manner; however, most other general cargo imports and exports earlier had to go through a transit shed or yard for short-term storage and customs inspection and sorting (see Chapter 4). The container system is changing the pattern, however, and comprises a major rationalization of the overall handling procedure.

Transit areas are greatly affected by the type of vessel loading method. Multi-story transit sheds in conventional European port operation offer large floor areas for storage of cargo near the berths, accessible through balconies or terraces within reach of gantry cranes. Frequently, multiple railroad tracks and roadways on wide aprons between the vessel and the shed are installed to accommodate direct ship to inland carrier transfer. The cranes thus permit simultaneous operations of transfer (1) and transfer (2) (Figure 5.1) at different hatches of the same ship. Transfers (3) and (4), however, are more difficult to make from multi-story sheds, as elevators, chutes or roof-mounted cranes must be used to transport the cargo between the upper floors and truck or railroad cars.

In U.S. ports where burtoning was predominant, operations at shipside were not as flexible as those in the crane-equipped European ports. But the extensive use of pallets and forklift trucks allows high-speed horizontal movement within the single-story transit shed, which greatly accelerates and simplifies sorting of cargo and transfer operations (3) and (4) (Figure 5.1).

The development of container facilities in the United States was an enormous advance.

Inland carrier services at general cargo terminals have changed drastically due to the increase in cargo distribution by truck. In many ports piers originally designed for delivery of 60% to 80% of the cargo by rail or lighter are now congested as trucking space is not available. In many cases, the delivery of import cargo is further complicated by the practice of long-term storage in the shed or by "marketing" of a large shipment to many different consignees while cargo is in transit. Thus, the stacking of cargo in shed or yard is often governed by factors other than handling and storage efficiency. The design of transit areas depends not only on the predominant characteristics of anticipated commodities, but also on the "housekeeping" of the terminal operator.

Trucks are generally serviced at tailgate height platforms on the inshore side of transit sheds. While most modern terminals now have ample maneuvering and parking space for trucks in the transit area, access to terminals through existing narrow and congested streets in many major ports remains a perennial problem. The planning of truck routes between terminals within the same port and the improvement of street connections to arterial highways is usually beyond the jurisdiction of the port agency that operates the terminals and requires coordination with other city planning.

Rail connections to terminals are generally governed by the location of existing rights-of-way. Service via the connecting rail line is often supplemented by "belt" lines or lighterage. However, in many, if not most ports, there is now a trend toward more distribution of general cargo from central rail terminals to ocean terminals by truck.

As mentioned earlier, the efficiency of the conventional system of handling general cargo increased very considerably when container operation was introduced. This system, in certain respects, is still in its infancy, but it is making continuous progress. Particular problems that seemed impossible to solve by unitization are in fact being solved in this way in one case after another.

Unitization of Container Systems

As mentioned in Chapter 1, the key word to rational modern cargo handling is *unitizing*. Before any improvement can be obtained, the cargo must be consolidated into larger units suitable for mechanical handling.

There are two main systems of unitized cargo: the *container system* and the *pallet system*. The characteristic difference between the two systems is the size of the unit. Containers for an integrated container system will have a capacity of about 1,000 cubic feet and upward and a maximum weight of up to 30 tons; the pallet accommodates between 40 and 120 cubic feet and has a weight between 0.5 and 2 tons. The difference in size and weight imposes different requirements on the handling equipment, on quay and shed and on the ship.

As expressed in Reference 11, the most important savings associated with containers appear to be those arising from a reduction of ship turn around time and in cargo handling costs at ports. It follows from this that the greatest potential gain from the use of containers arises on sea routes where these costs represent the largest proportion of the total port-to-port costs. The length of voyage is therefore a factor in this as well as the rate of turnaround and level of labor costs. At one end of the scale come voyages between ports with slow turnaround, high labor costs and comparatively short sea voyages. These would be where the greatest benefits would be likely to occur. At the other end would be voyages between ports with fast turnaround, low handling costs and long voyage distances. Few of the world's sea routes, however, fall at these extremes.

Container transport being a high capital cost system it has to be intensively utilized to be economic, and a corollary of this is that it has limited flexibility and needs a fairly high level of throughput to sustain it. Other factors such as the composition of the cargo, the degree of balance of flows, the extent of necessary inland groupage and the seasonality of the trade will also be important in determining the net savings from containerization. Thus, there may always be a place on some routes for other less capital intensive forms of unitization, including ships catering for both containers and pallets, and in the early years converted conventional ships may have a useful part to play.

There will also be savings in inland transport costs which will arise from transporting homogeneous containers instead of a heterogeneous collection of break-bulk cargo. Some reduction in the cost of both road and rail haulage could be expected, but whereas the cost savings by road may be no higher than 25%, the possibilities for savings by rail over the longer distances and on the dense volume routes could well be greater than this. The British Railways "freightliner" system, substituting the costly and time-consuming marshaling of wagons with a regular and speedy 24-hour door-to-door transit within Great Britain, reduced the handling of goods to the bare minimum.

However, it should not be forgotten that pallet ships have some advantages over container ships in certain conditions, particularly on those routes where the trade volumes are comparatively small and seasonal, of the type not easily packaged and of low value and where the distribution system at one end of the chain is unsophisticated.

In this respect, it must be noted that although the choice between container and pallet ships may often be in balance, particularly on shorter hauls, the inland transport cost savings emerge in full only with containerization. The inflationary trend in labor costs lends support to the more capital intensive system in the end.

The reduction in manpower requirements of goods-handling can be very substantial indeed. According to Reference 11, at one port in the United Kingdom following the introduction of a new deep-sea service, cargo, which would on conventional services have taken perhaps 120 men five or six days to unload, was handled by 13 men in one 12-hour shift. Elsewhere, the entire job of placing containers from vehicles into the marshaling area, unloading and loading a short-sea cellular vessel and loading the containers onto road vehicles is done by one man. Overall, it appears that the reduction in manpower required to handle a given volume of traffic at the port may be 90% or more, even allowing for labor employed in stuffing containers in depots in or adjacent to the port. Similarly, the through freightliner train can reduce the number of men employed in railway yards.

The biggest overall concern is the effect containerization will have on the manning of vessels. With the smaller fleets required, many floating personnel will be without a job. Containerization will solve problems of staff shortages. There will, of course, be feeder services, though limited by the attraction of shore transport with its faster delivery to its destinations (18).

Terminals for Unitized Transport

Container Load and Load off and Roll-on/Roll-off Traffic

While technological developments in shipbuilding made almost revolutionary progress during the past decades, the techniques applied in general cargo handling remained nearly unchanged due to the conventional loading systems of mixed cargo vessels. The seaports were unable to introduce any technical or organizational innovations because, regarding their quantitative and qualitative investment programs, they were absolutely dependent upon the various types of vessels.

Container traffic by the lift-off and lift-on system (Lo/Lo) and by the roll-on/ roll-off system (Ro/Ro) are the criteria of a new orientation in the organization and mechanization of cargo handling emanating from the ship. The new development is based on the following aspects (11).

1. Increasing volumes, homogeneity and high-grade quality of the general cargo to be handled.
2. Highly developed economies at the termilal points of such traffics.
3. Excellent results in the exchange of goods between the economies concerned.
4. Full-time employment in these economies.
5. Rising wages and stagnant growth of productivity in conventional cargo handling; thus, tendency to substitute or reinforce manpower by capital investments.
6. Marked infrastures for supplies and deliveries from and to the interior.
7. Marked infrasturctures of the ports.

Container traffic and roll-on/roll-off traffic may be considered a delayed industrialization process in the field of transporation. Preplanning of the various operations (prestowage of containers), standard operations, integrated information, process supervision and control are signs of industrializing transportation and of the change from more or less handicraft undertakings to mechanized port industries.

The counterpart to the container traffic overseas is the roll-on/roll-off traffic in the coastal and short distance trade. What both modes of transportation have in common is that, instead of individual handling, the goods are packed in units and, as such are handled by one or more carriers. For cost-saving reasons, the chassis is left behind in one case and shipped along in the other.

Container System

There are two main systems of container transport: the "port-to-port" system and "door-to-door" system, the difference clearly defined by the terminologies. The port-to-port system compared to the door-to-door system suffers from too much handling and storage. It is some kind of "compromise" between the new and the old system "making boxes larger." It is "a negation of the container system," which, among other things, should reduce the intensive character of labor in port operations, and, finally, the ultimate aim should be door-to-door operation which does not suffer the drawback of either an inland depot or port working (15). The vessel may bear its cargo on a trailer to be pulled to the door. It may bear trailer and cargo together over the ramp, and they wheel themselves to the door or the vessel, or it may bring its cargo forth as barges or pontoons loaded to capacity for towing to "the door."

The possibility of being able to attract a full load of full containers, outwards and homewards, is one of the first things to be established. The development has not always been as fast as desirable.

As an example, Reference 15 reported that in Japan the Container Association is disappointed that Yokohama, for example, which handles 60%

Transportation Systems 161

Figure 5.2. Conventional cargo handling at Antwerp.

Figure 5.3. Container handling system at Baltimore (1).

Figure 5.4a. Container vessel en route (The "Atlantic Saga", Atlantic Container Line, Gothenburg).

of the containerized cargo imported in that country, still works mostly on the pier-to-pier system instead of on the more desirable door-to-door basis "and that in 1964, 70 per cent of Yokohama's incoming containers were empty ones!"

Containerization is making rapid progress, however. In Reference 11, it is mentioned that according to recent figures, it seems that 42 shipowners already have 145 container ships and that 130 ships are under construction or on order (1968-1969).

In the United States, there are 17 ports equipped, including New York (nine gantries), Oakland (four gantries) and Seattle (four gantries). The number increases continually.

Great Britain is also equipping several ports. Apart from Tilbury, Harwich and Felixstowe,

Figure 5.4b. Container vessel "La Pampa" (2).

which are the best-equipped ports, the following ports are also becoming equipped: Grangemouth, Liverpool, Southampton, and on the East coast, Hull and Grimsby. More ports have been added to this list recently.

Others include: in Belgium, Antwerp; in the Netherlands, Rotterdam; in Germany, Hamburg and Bremerhaven; in Sweden, Gothenburg; in Denmark, Copenhagen and Esbjerg (Ro/Ro); in Poland, Gdynia; in France, Le Havre, Marseilles and Dunkirk; in Spain, Barcelona; in Italy, Genoa, Leghorn and Trieste; in Japan, Yokohama, Tokyo, Osaka and Kobe; and in Australia, Sydney, Melbourn and Freemantle; in Norway, Oslo. Some South American ports are preparing for containerization, too.

Examples of Container Ports

Figures 5.2 and 5.3 give an impression of the difference in operation of the conventional system and the container system. Figure 5.4a shows a 14,000 dwt container vessel *The Atlantic Saga* of the Atlantic Container Line en route from the U.S. East Coast to Scandinavia. The 24,800 dwt bulk carrier *La Pampa* (Burnes Markes, Ltd., London) was launched in 1970 from Harland and Wolf, Belfast. It is an open type bulk carrier with five cargo holds, two of which are designed to carry containers (Figure 5.4b).

With respect to container ports, they all have certain features in common. The heavy equipment needed for handling of containers has forced a certain amount of "standards" upon outlays and design of container ports. In Japan efforts have even been made to standarize container berths as shown in Figure 5.5 with dimensions as indicated in Table 5.2.

As an example of an ultramodern container port, the Elizabeth container facility in New York should be mentioned (17). Chapter 4 gives certain details on layout and wharf designs.

In designing the Elizabeth Port Authority Marine Terminal, the Port of New York Authority took into account the possible future demands of containerization and amended their plans as work

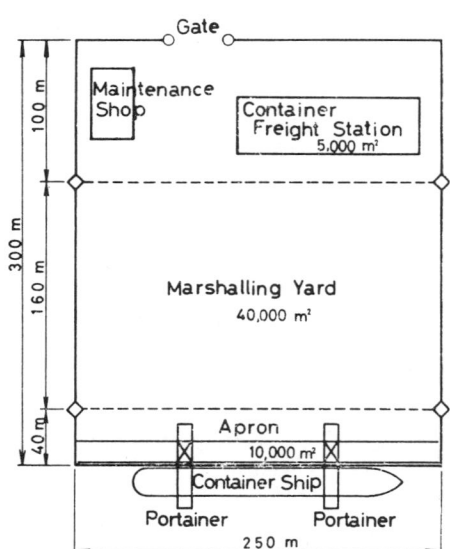

Figure 5.5. Standard container ship berth in Japan (11).

**Table 5.2
Specification of Standard
Container Ship Berth in Japan (11)**

Properties	Measurements
Depth	-12 m
Length	250 m
Width	300 m
Marshaling yard	40,000 m²
Portainer	2 for 8' x 8' x 40'
Capacity	30 tons
Loading-unloading cycle	3 minutes

on the terminal progressed to fit in with current trends.

The planning and design of the Elizabeth Port Authority Marine Terminal anticipated the demands of containerization, and the development will provide facilities to meet the long-range needs of the concept. The terminal is located on Newark Bay and is approached from Ambrose Channel via Newark Bay Channel. The controlling channel depth is 35 feet below mean water level. This depth is considered adequate for the large 30,000 dwt, 30-foot draft container vessel of the type *Sea Witch* (Sea/Land Company) carrying 928 twenty-foot containers when fully loaded. When completed in 1975 at a cost of $175 million, the terminal will consist of 919 acres (371 hectares), and it will provide 28 efficient wharf-type berths backed by open transit areas along newly dredged channels. The area will include about 4.5 million square feet of distribution buildings in addition to special cargo handling, administration and service facilities. Efficient road and rail networks designed to meet projected traffic loads will serve the entire complex. The terminal was built with quays and spacious paved open areas, both of which are vital to container ship operation. The quay permits a continuous flow of trailers to shipside in an assembly line fashion, reducing loading time to a minimum. The paved areas enable the ocean-going trailers to be parked near the vessel berth, eliminating delays in transferring them from more distant points. Each of the berths provided in the terminal is supported by as much land as is required for containers, usually a minimum of 12 acres per berth. Roadways are as much as 100 feet wide, and an additional 50 to 72 feet allocated as a setback for those buildings with loading docks. Roads of the terminal are supplemented by direct rail connections and sidings to the distribution buildings and other terminal structures. Its system of trackage may be utilized in container-on-flatcar as well as on trailer-on-flatcar movements and for conventional cargo.

As mentioned in Chapter 4, an exhaustive study of wharf designs is intended to eliminate the more expensive types of construction from further consideration.

A similar but smaller container terminal has been built at Oakland, California, (9) in the San Francisco Bay and in San Francisco (14). It has nine ship berths for containerized and break-bulk cargo and will give the city the West Coast's largest container port facility. The corresponding Honolulu terminal is of modest size but is modern and efficient (Figure 5.6).

Figure 5.6. Container terminal at Honolulu, Hawaii (Port Brochure)

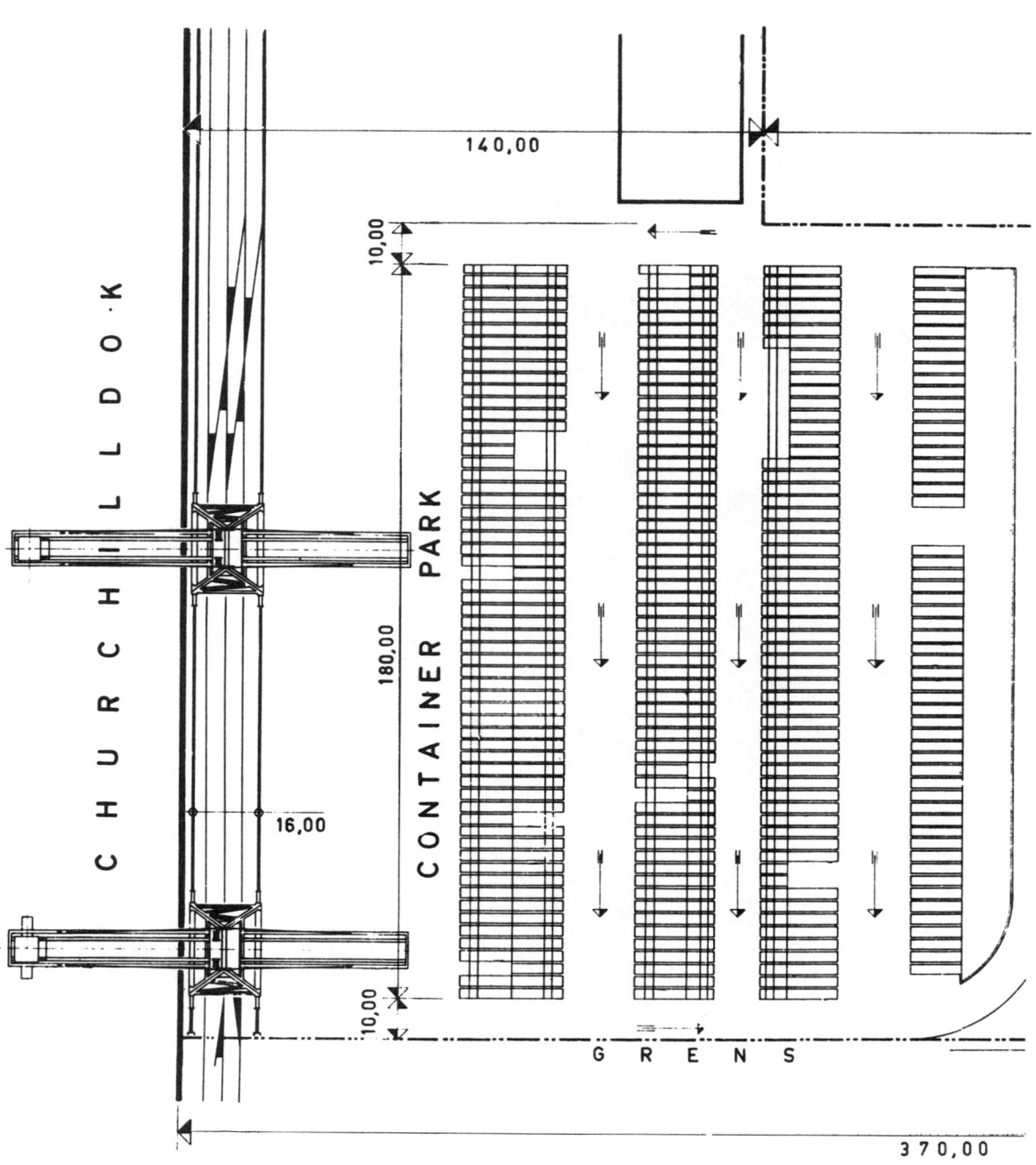

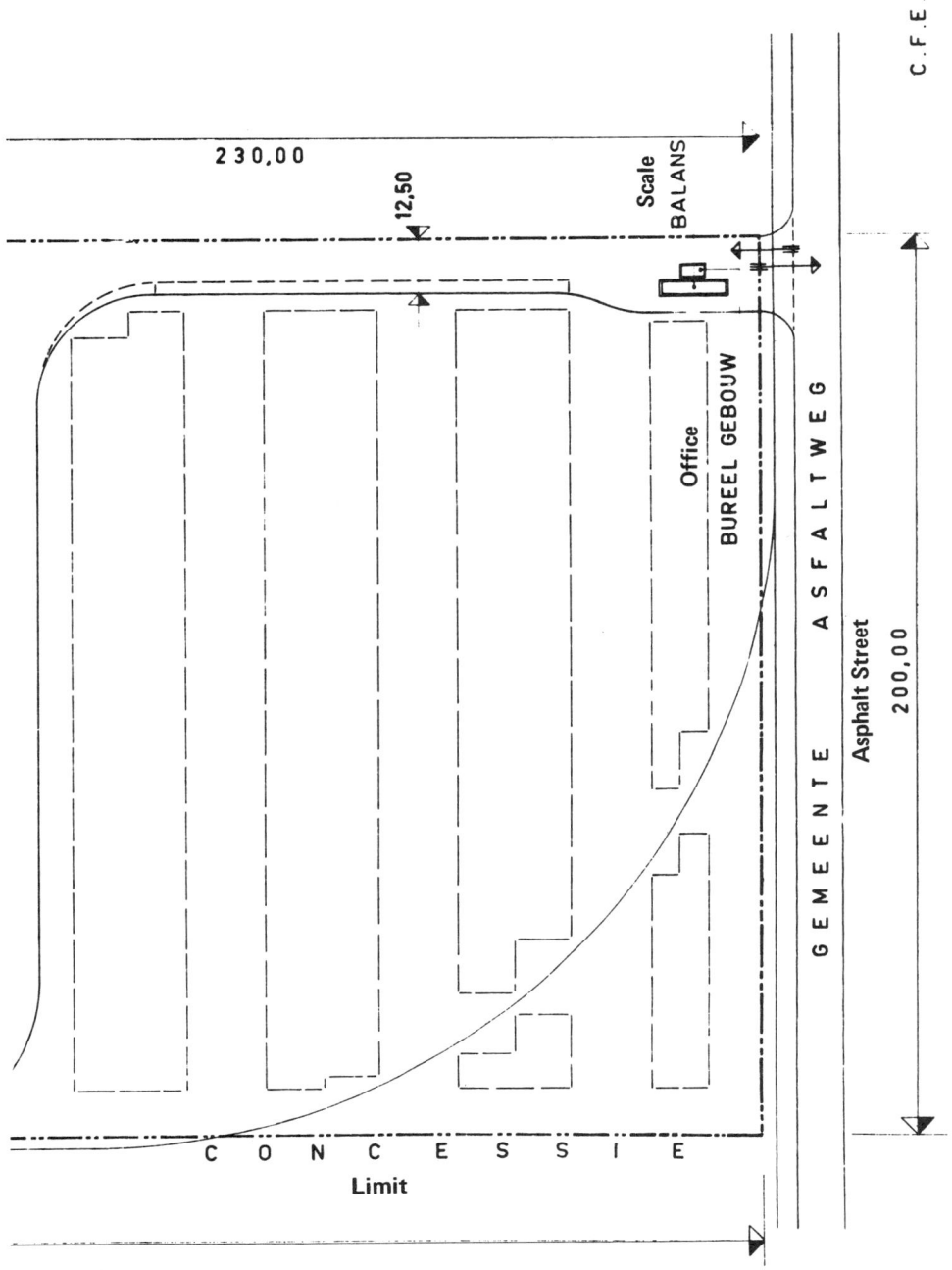

Figure 5.7. Container terminal at Antwerp, Belgium (Port Brochure).

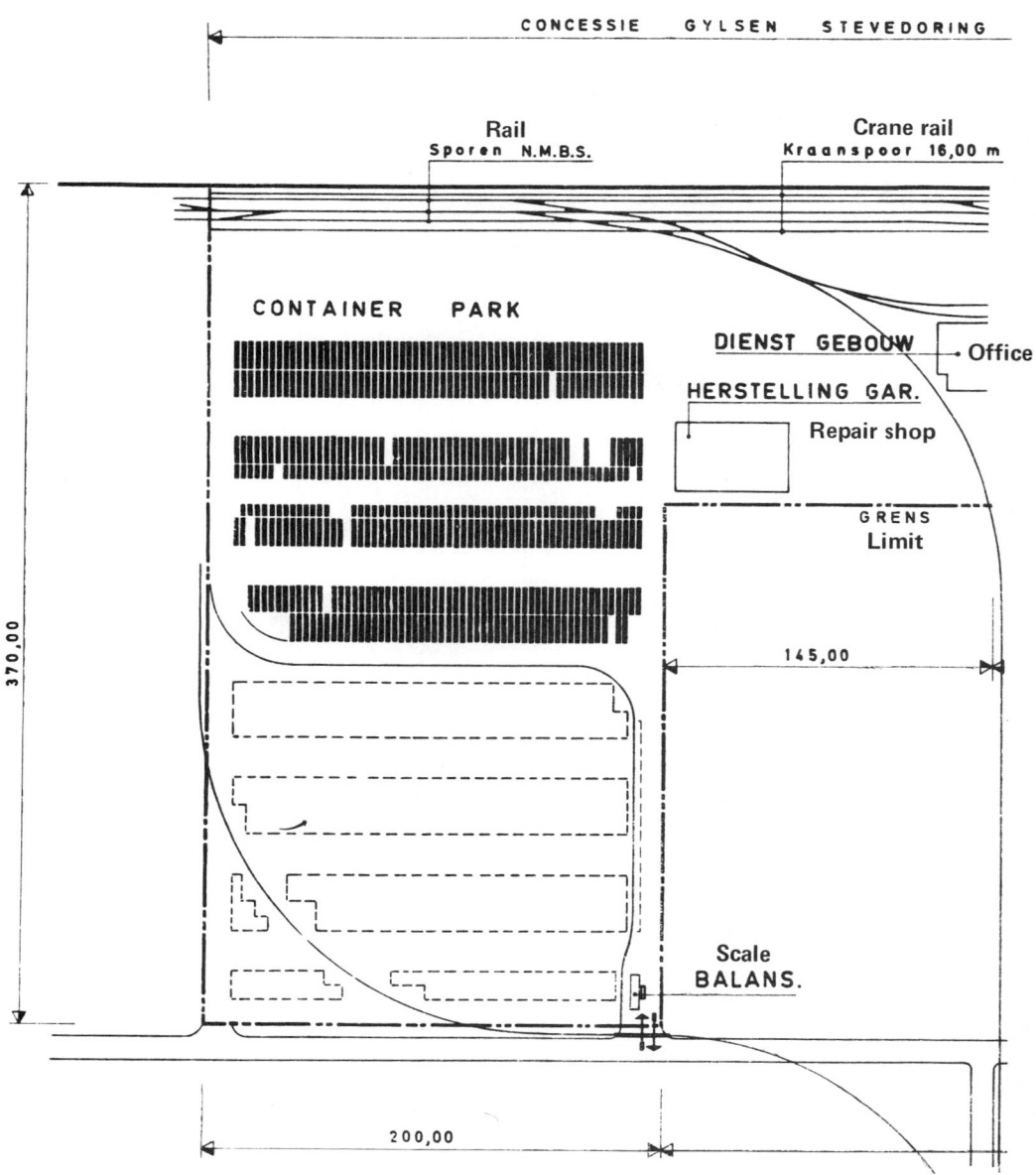

Figure 5.8. Container terminal at Antwerp, Belgium (Port Brochure).

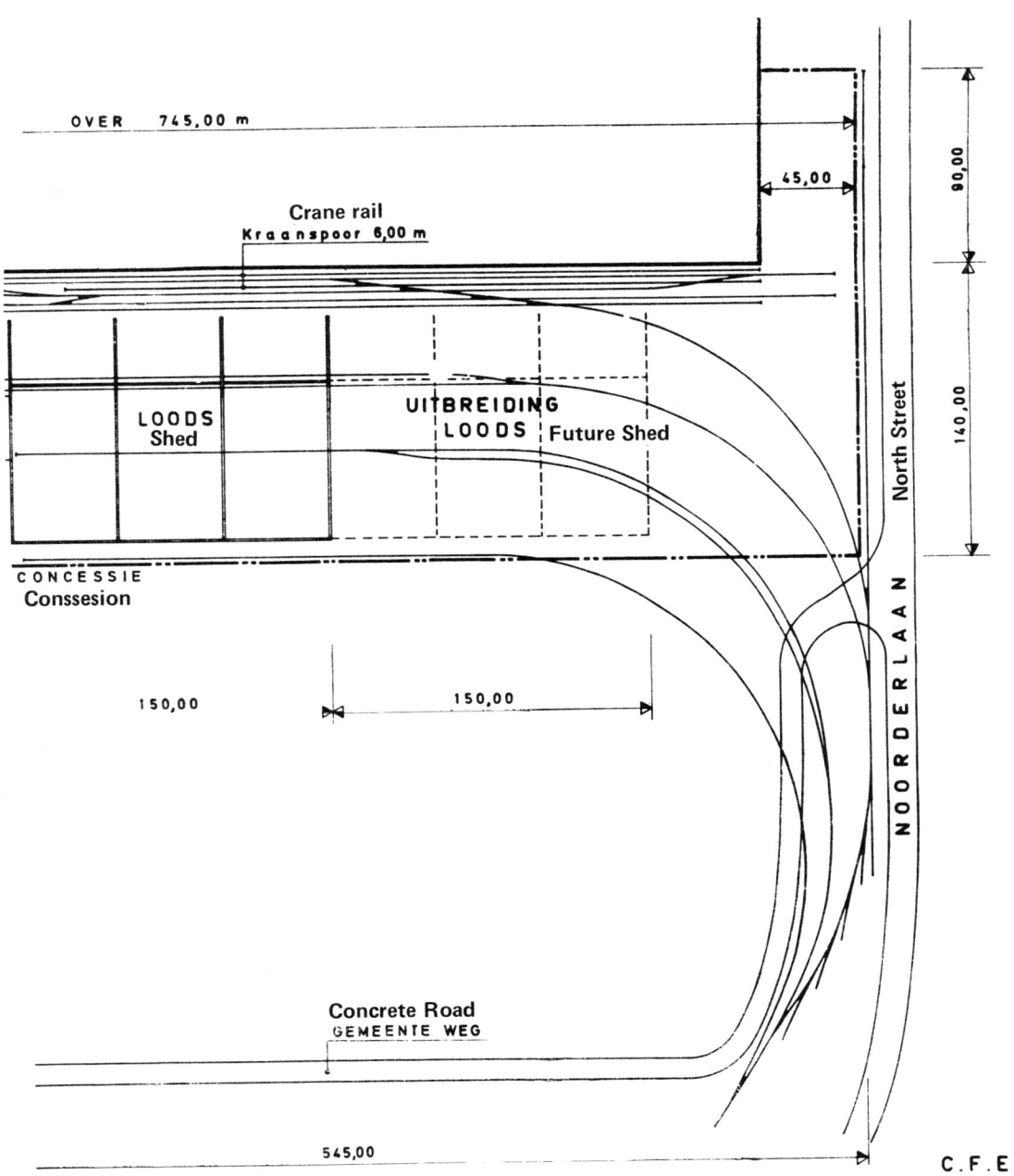

Figure 5.8 Continued

The Port of Antwerp completed a new comprehensive container facility recently (12). Established for more than 60 years in the port of Antwerp and highly specialized in the handling of general cargo and iron and steel (the latter being the leading export traffic in Antwerp), Stevedoring Company Gylsen decided in the early 1960s to concentrate all its activities in the sixth Harbor Dock. In 1964 operations started at this new port terminal, Gylsen, which offers a total quay length of 1,200 meters, i.e., seven modern berths for large vessels. The total surface of the terminal amounts to 120,000 square meters. Three sheds with a surface of 11,300 square meters each provide ample storage capacity for general cargo. About 100,000 square meters have been equipped for open air storage and are presently used for storage of containers, cars, harvesters, logs, etc. As far as the technical equipment is concerned, 18 cranes with a capacity of 5 tons per 32 meters have been installed. The quay apron—with a depth of 43 meters—is equipped with three railway tracks so that loading and discharging operations may proceed simultaneously in or out of railway cars, trucks and barges as well as on and from the transit sheds.

The rapid development of the activities at this terminal have necessitated a further expansion of port facilities. Negotiations with the Antwerp Port Authority have resulted in the building of a new Terminal in the Churchill dock, which was finished in the second half of 1968.

This port terminal, Gylsen II, offers a total quay length of 745 meters and has been conceived for the handling of containers, unit loads—especially iron and steel—and also provides a berth for RO/RO.

The new port terminal is situated in the immediate neighborhood of the railway shunting yard, Antwerp-North—the largest in Belgium—as well as of the highways to Germany, France and Netherlands. The Churchill dock being at short distance of the new lock at Zandvliet and therefore of the new canal with the Rhine, the location of this terminal may be considered as extremely favorable as well for maritime as for inland water traffic.

With regard to the container operation, the initial stage covers the building of a container park with a total surface of 74,000 square meters and a storage capacity of 1,600 containers (20-foot units) (Figure 5.7). Two container cranes with a capacity of 45 tons will enable a rapid and safe handling of all container operations. The container berth will offer 200 meters of quay length whereas the remaining 500 meters of quay wall will be equipped for the handling of unit loads and iron and steel.

For this purpose, six cranes with a capacity of 10 tons per 45 meters and two cranes with 5 tons per 32 meters have been installed to grant the maximum efficiency in the loading of iron and steel products ex barge, ex railway truck or truck and from quay. It has to be mentioned that the two container cranes as well as the eight other shore cranes cover the full quay length of 700 meters. Therefore, it may be said that unit loads up to 45 tons can be loaded in any ship. The container cranes are indeed equipped as well for operations with a hook or even with a grab.

Special attention has been given to the quay equipment of this unit load berth. The main characteristic certainly consists of building a transit shed, which in the initial stage will offer a covered surface of 11,250 square meters (Figure 5.8). The basic idea is to discharge the iron and steel products under cover to protect them against the prevailing weather conditions and to improve the qualitative aspects of the cargo handling operations.

For the same reason, the shed is being equipped with three roll bridges with a capacity of 10 tons each. As a rule, all horizontal transport from the shed to the crane will be realized with the roll bridges. The tracks of these bridges are indeed extended onto the apron so that the cargo can be put immediately under the hook of the crane. With this new method, a considerable improvement must be reached in the horizontal transport of iron and steel in comparison with the presently prevailing system.

As it is shown in Figure 5.8 the steel quay will be served by seven railway tracks: four on the fore-apron for direct loading ex railway car, two in the shed and one behind the shed. It is therefore obvious that the unloading of railway cars and trucks will be possible in all weather conditions without any damage occurring to the cargo.

The whole terminal will be controlled by radio in order to arrive at a perfect coordination of all participating elements on board as well as on the quay in the loading and discharging operations.

Handling of Containers

C.J. Evans in his article, "Container handling in ports" (3), gives a thorough review of various methods of handling and storing containers in ports and the factors which affect the choice of method for any individual port.

In the LO/LO system, containers are loaded and unloaded by crane. Containers must be brought to the shipside and removed at the correct intervals to suit the crane's capacity, and storage areas and equipment must be provided to enable this to be done.

Efficient loading and discharge of containers can be achieved by specially built equipment, including quay cranes (portainers), and either tractors and trailers, straddle carriers or travel lifts, lifter transporters, sideloaders tractor/trailers and Goliath cranes, etc., or by large gantry cranes extended by a cantilever boom to be used for loading and unloading of containers between the stocking area and the ship. Containers do not need protection against rain and, therefore, contrary to pallets, need no shed space.

The handling and storing of containers in a port is still only one step in the process of handling freight from its origin to destination. As mentioned earlier, the ideal method would be the door-to-door method by which containers are transported direct from factory or inland depot to the ship, and then when the ship reaches its port of destination, the container is transported direct to destination or depot where it is unpacked. The empty container must then either be filled, transported to another point for filling or returned by sea empty. This ideal method is, as already mentioned, very rarely achieved in practice. The nearest approach is the RO/RO (roll-on roll-off) trailer truck operation, but even in this method, it is impractical for trailers to drive from their origin straight onto the ship. Due to vagaries of road traffic, the trucks could not be expected to arrive at the correct time, and a storage area is required to park the trucks as they arrive in such a manner that loading of the ship can be accomplished in the shortest possible time.

In both LO/LO and RO/RO, the object of the organization of the port area and handling of containers is to achieve the fastest possible loading and unloading of the ship, and thus keep the ship's turnaround time to a minimum.

The majority of these systems are designed for handling containers at high speed to give loading and unloading rates of perhaps 20 to 40 containers per hour, or 400 to 1,200 tons per hour. This is fine in the major ports handling a million tons per year and upwards, as it will enable one berth to handle say one-half to one million tons per year and thus replace perhaps four to five general cargo berths of the 100,000 to 150,000-tons per berth type (about 500 tons per meter or 150 tons per foot).

With respect to the actual mechanical handling of the container, there is now on the market a large range of container handling equipment each having its own advantages and disadvantages. The method of handling containers, the choice of equipment and the layout of the container berth are all interdependent and are discussed later (3).

Where *high-speed cranes* are employed, it is most important that the movement of containers to and from the dockside is completely integrated with the crane's capacity. Equipment used for moving containers was outlined earlier. Figures 5.9 and 5.10 show overall systems. Figure 5.11 shows two coupled containers cranes.

Methods of stacking may be summarized as follows.

1. Containers stored on trailers in the port area.
2. Containers stored on the ground, either one high, two high or possibly even up to

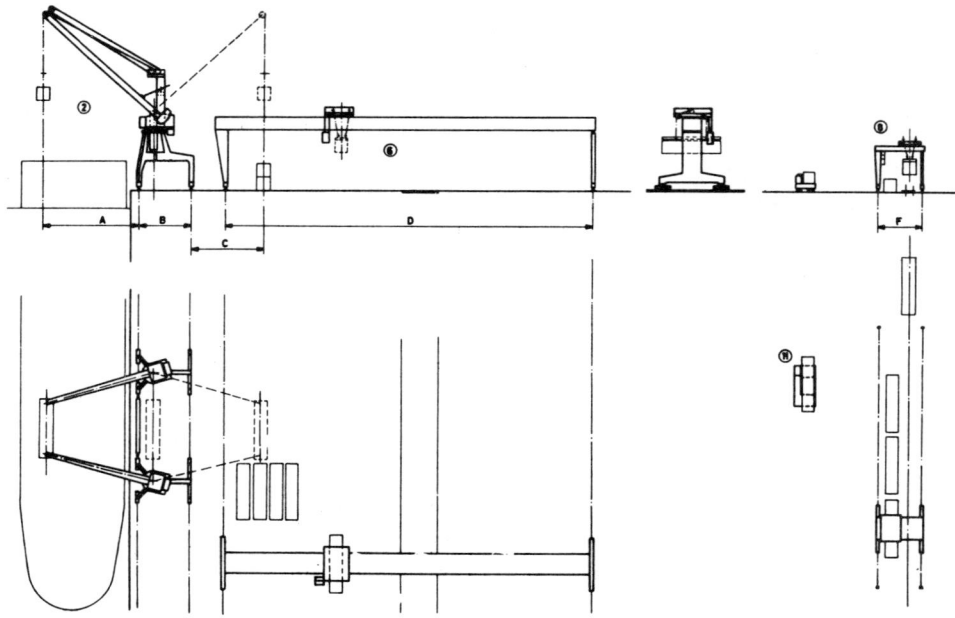

Figure 5.9. Container handling system (10).

six or seven high. Methods of moving containers in stacking may be one of the following:
a. Lifted on the trailer from stacked position by lifting equipment (straddle carrier, side loader, portal crane, yard loader and transported by motive unit attached to trailer).
b. Transported from stacked position to crane by lifting equipment.
c. Lifted direct from stacked position into ship.

In the trailer system, containers are driven on trailers into the parking area of the container port where they are stored on the trailer, the motive unit being detached and used to tow another trailer out of the park. When a ship is being loaded or unloaded, the motive units tow the containers on the trailers to the shipside where it is lifted on, and the trailer is either returned empty to a parking spot or receives a container from the ship and then drives off either to a parking area or direct to its destination.

In the trailer-stack-trailer system, the container is brought into the port area by trailer (either road or rail), lifted off the trailer or railtruck by one of the many types of equipment available and stacked in the storage yard. For loading onto the ship, the container is transferred from its stored position onto another trailer, not necessarily the same type, and then transported onto the trailer to the container crane.

The trailer-stack-carry-to-crane system is similar to the previously mentioned system, except that from the storage yard the container is lifted and carried to the crane by the same piece of equipment.

The trailer-stack-direct-lift system can only be used with a Goliath type of crane. In addition to loading and unloading ships, this type of crane straddles the stacking area and the access lane for

Transportation Systems   173

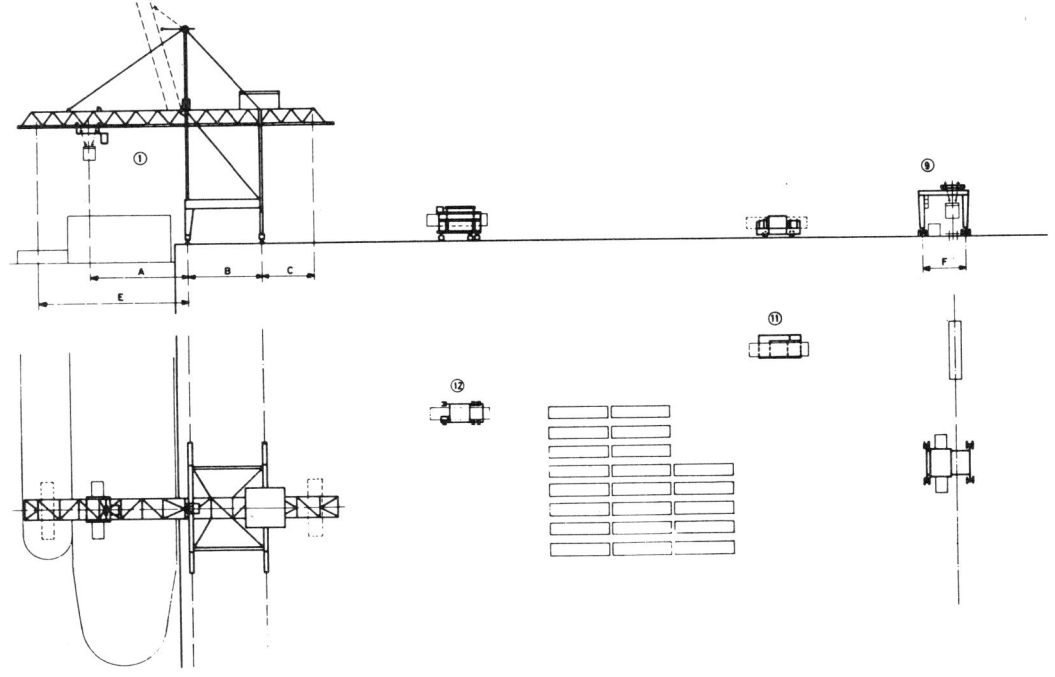

Figure 5.10. Container handling system (10).

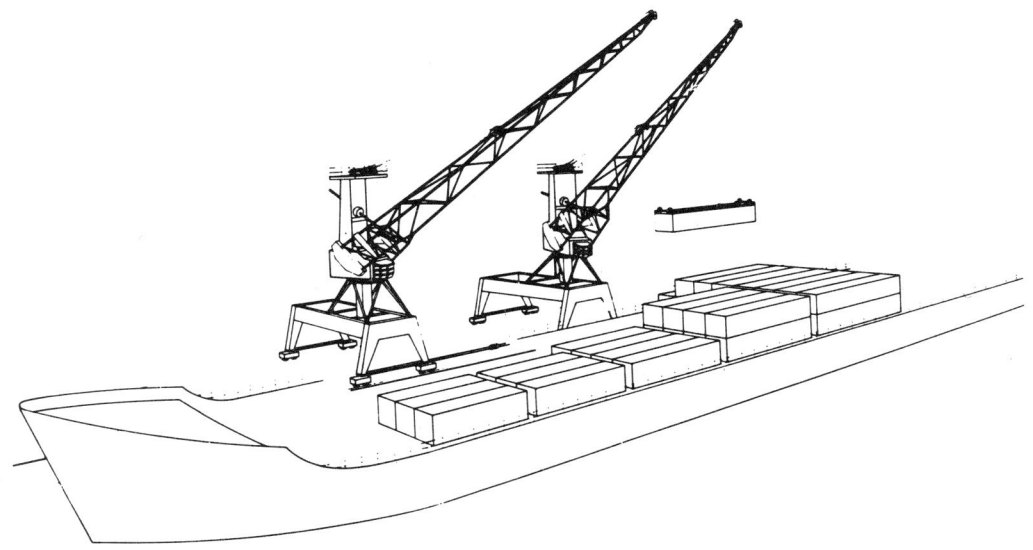

Figure 5.11. Coupled container cranes (10).

the trailer—road or rail. The Goliath then takes the container off the trailer and stacks it or loads it straight onto the ship and also loads directly from the stacking area. Containers can be stored several high with this system so that land requirements are small, but great care is necessary in stacking containers so that containers are in the position for loading without movement of the Goliath crane and that containers at the bottom are not required before those on the top row. Sorting into the correct order can sometimes be done in between loading and unloading.

The crane loading and unloading *low-speed system* is the type of container operation that exists where the number of containers being handled does not justify the normal type of high-speed container crane. It occurs at present at a number of ports where containers and general cargo are carried on one ship, with possibly less than 50 containers to be handled at one port. As the length of time that the ship has to remain in port is generally governed by other factors such as general cargo handling, the rate of unloading and loading is not critical and could perhaps be of the order of five to ten containers per hour. The method of unloading or loading would probably be a scotch derrick, or in some cases, by ship's crane.

For further information on equipment, the reader may consult References 4, 5, 10, 11 and 13 and numerous articles in *The Dock and Harbour Authority* through recent years. A great many commercial catalogs exist.

Roll-on/Roll-off System

There are several ways in which containers can be handled in this type of operation. In most cases, the method of handling containers and design of the berth and layout of the port area is inextricably tied up with the design of the ship. A large number of new ships and new berths for this type of operation have been built or are under construction, which shows the importance of this type of operation. It will undoubtedly increase throughout the world, especially as feeder services on short sea routes from main container transshipment ports.

Figure 5.12 shows schematically various types of RO/RO installations, all of which are in use (11). Figure 5.13 is a large "bacon container terminal," provided for the handling of bacon traffic between Denmark and Great Britain and located at Grimsby, Great Britain.

Basically, there are three methods of handling containers on a roll-on/roll-off service:

1. Trailer and tractor unit drives on, remains on the ship during its voyage and drives off at the other end. This can only be economic on very short sea journeys as the tractor unit is idle and utilizing ship's capacity during the sea journey. No special facilities or equipment are required in the port area except sufficient land for parking the trailer while waiting to drive on.
2. Trailer unit only remains on ship during sea journey. In this case, the tractor unit simply tows the container on its trailer from the storage area onto the ship and drives off leaving the container on its trailer. A further set of tractor units is required at the destination to tow the containers off the ship and to reload the ship for its return journey. The trailer may be of two types: (a) normal road trailers suitable for driving on public roads and (b) special small trailers suitable only for use in the port areas. The former is heavier and takes up more room on the ship but would be used where the container is driven some distance to the port and will be driven inland some distance to its destination. The latter would generally be used where the inland depot is in the port area so that the container is only handled in the port area, or where the container is delivered by rail and transferred to the trailer in the port area. This type of trailer is generally much lighter and cheaper than the normal road trailer and takes up less ship capacity. In the former method where the road trailer is driven on and off the ship, no special

Transportation Systems 175

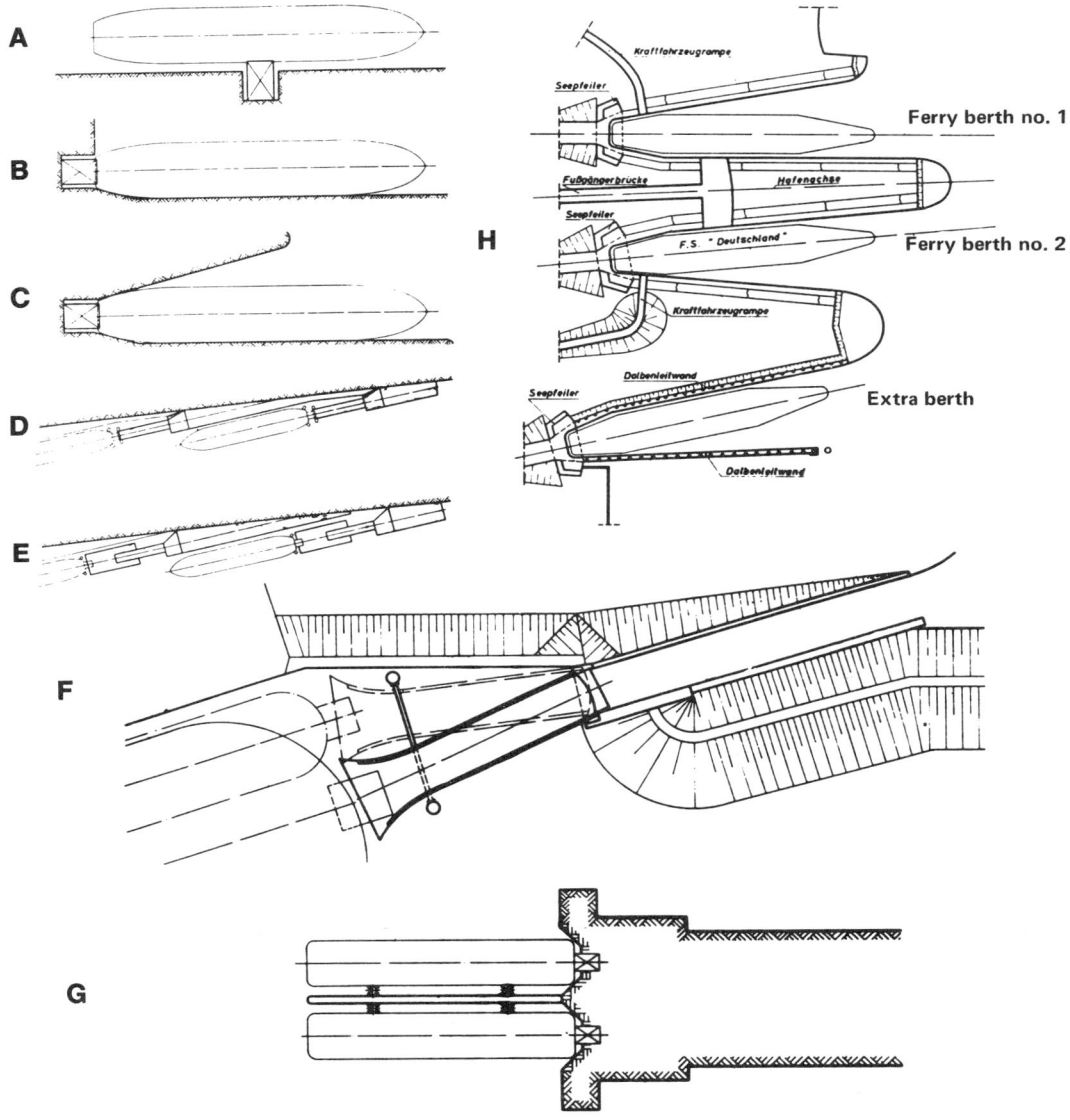

Figure 5.12. Various types of RO/RO installations (11).

equipment is required. Where the small trailer is used, equipment may be required for transferring the container from rail or road trailer to the special trailer or to load onto the trailer if the container is normally stacked on the ground.

3. Neither the trailer or tractor unit remains on the ship. In this case, either a straddle type carrier must be used to drive the container onto the ship and stack it on the ship, or the ship itself must have lifting equipment which can lift it off a

176 Port Engineering

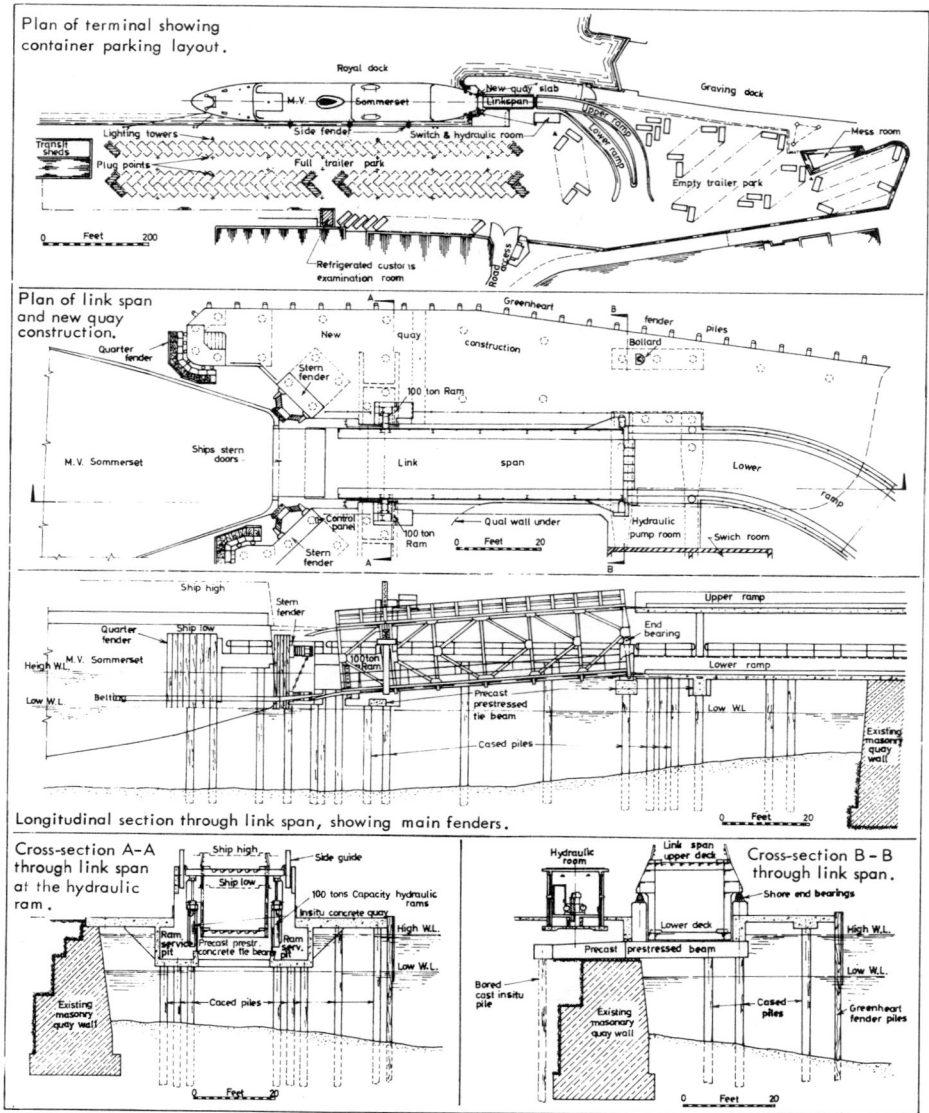

Figure 5.13. The Grimsby Bacon container terminal (The Dock and Harbour Authority, May 1967).

trailer and stack it. This type of operation is generally more efficient from the ship's point of view as it enables containers to be carried two high, and there is no wastage of space by trailers or tractors. It does, however, require more expensive container handling equipment.

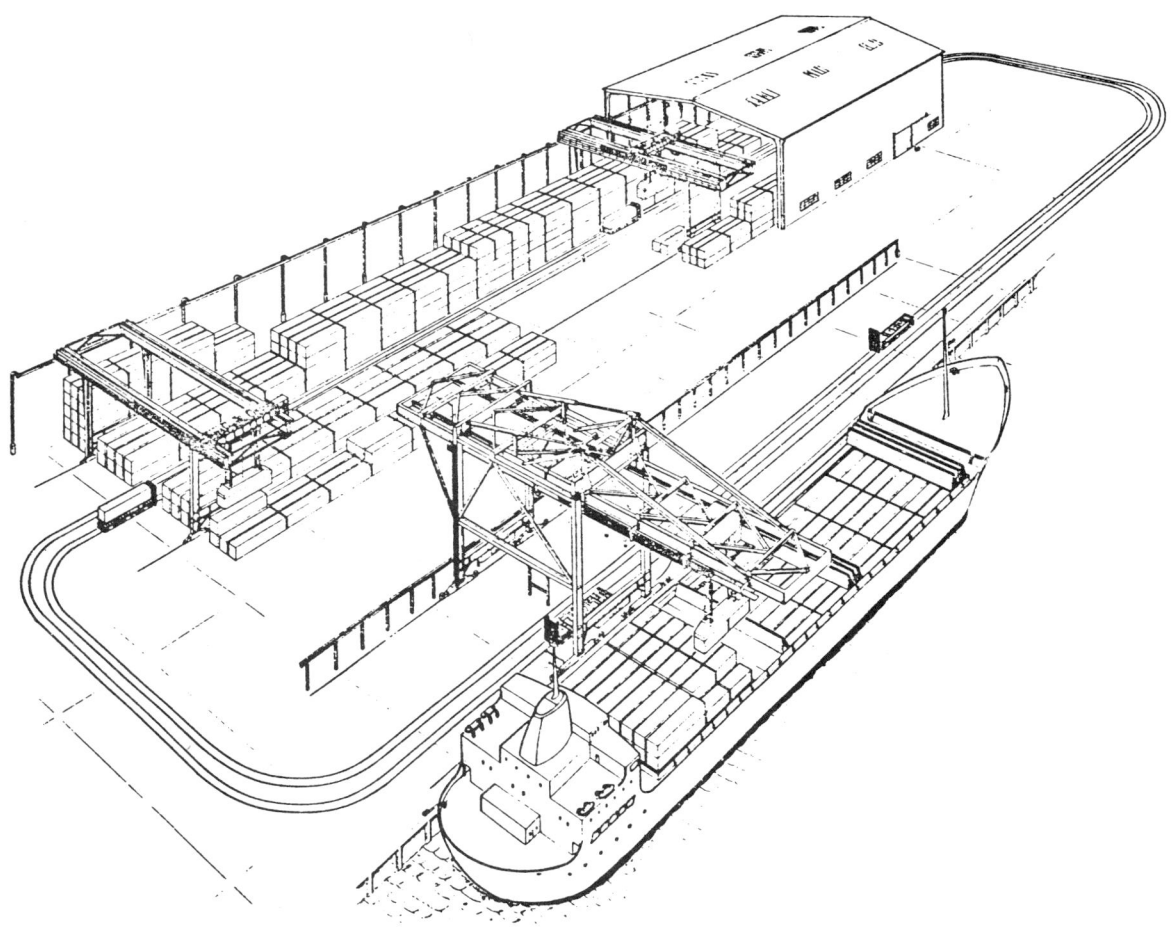

Figure 5.14. Completely automated port system (3).

The Future Development

The main development likely to occur in the future is complete automation of the container handling operations. Computers are used at present to control the movement of containers, and their use is likely to increase in the future in more sophisticated operations.

Systems have been developed to *store containers* in multi-story cells, served by automatic lift and container transfer units, controlled either manually or by computer.

This type of store uses very much less land for a given number of containers than present methods of stacking, but the more important advantage is that each container is immediately available and its position in the system accurately defined. The service lift and transfer and transport equipment can be keyed into a computer control system giving a completely automated operation (Figure 5.14).

Another new development is the automatic horizontal transportation of containers. A number of systems have been or are being designed, although these are all basically similar and consist of trolley or bogey, rail mounted, which carries the container between dockside crane and inland depot or store, and can be remotely controlled so

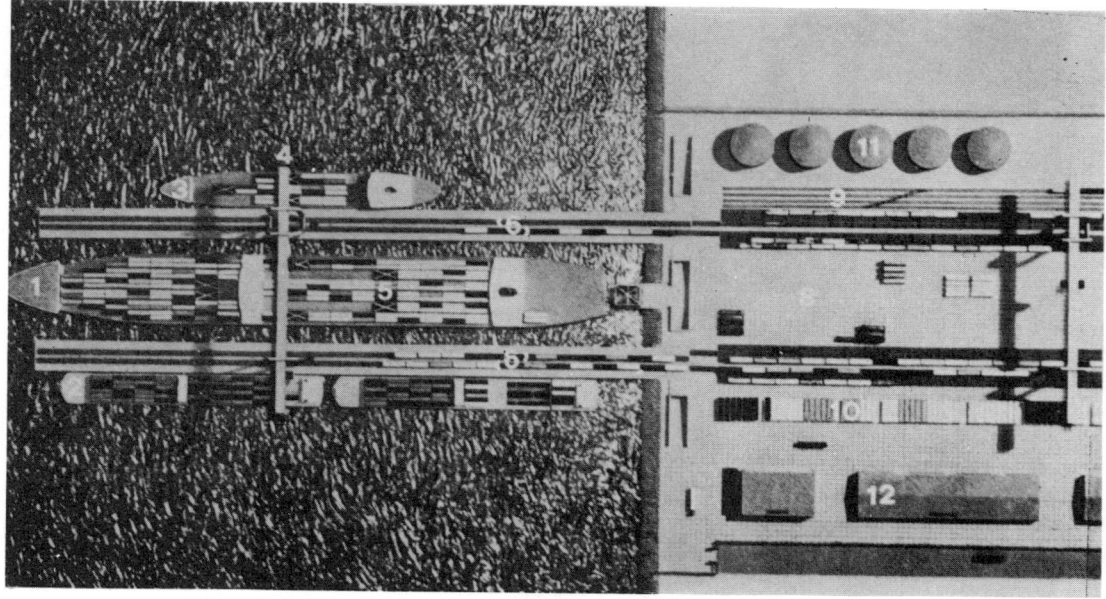

Figure 5.15. The Meeusen trans-ocean terminal (1).

that no driver is necessary. This can be coupled into the multi-story system.

Thus, the possibility of a fully automated port operation with the handling of containers centrally controlled by push button and computer operated coming into use within the next few years cannot be ruled out. However, it would seem that it can only be economic where there is lack of storage area—and land values are very high—and where there is a very high volume of containers to be handled and the quick selection of individual containers is important. This type of operation can only be expected to occur in very few ports throughout the world, and the majority of container ports will undoubtedly develop with less automated systems. But the present type terminals may not be able to cope with the increased number of containers and might have to be rebuilt.

A Dutch firm, Meusen Consultants Systems, designed a new type container ship and terminal (1). The ship could carry some 1,500 forty-foot containers which would be moved on board vertically be means of lifts and horizontally by conveyor belts. A terminal has been designed which consists of two jetties, a bridge crane and a number of conveyors (Figure 5.15). The transoceanic liner is berthed between the jetties, while smaller ships and barges are moored alongside. The main beam of the crane is fitted with extensions at either end protruding beyond the jetties and permitting direct transhipment operations by means of winches to the required loading position to avoid traveling of the crane. On either side of the crane track on each jetty, conveyor belts are installed carrying the containers to and from the stacking area. Suspended from the crane are two hoisting trolleys lifting the pair of containers between the liner and each of the jetties or directly to the smaller vessels.

The RO/RO system may have only relatively limited uses as an economic principle. The greatest benefits realized must be to car and passenger-car-

Figure 5.16. LASH-vessel "Acadia Forest" (A/S Molash Shipping Co., Norway).

cargo ferries, all sailing on short voyages and to strict schedules where cargo may have to be shut out. By employing roll-on/roll-off vessels instead of conventional vessels, a greater percentage of cargo can be loaded in the same amount of cargo-work hours allotted, that is, without affecting times of departure. Ferries, in general, do not carry many tons of cargo on a voyage so that the potential cargo space lost from stern-loading causes little concern.

Special Vessels

A number of special vessels have been developed. In the barge carrying type of container vessel the normal container has been replaced by barges. Up to now (1970), only the LASH (lighter aboard ship) has been commissioned (Figure 5.16).

One major advantage associated with the LASH system is that it does not need a (special) port installation. The barge containers are floated (towed) to the vessel and lifted aboard by large gantry cranes (500 tons). In the beginning of October, 1969, the world's first LASH-ship, the *Arcadia Forest*, was delivered to the Norwegian Molash Shipping Co., Inc. It was designed in the United States and built in Japan. The same company has ordered another vessel of the same type, and American companies recently ordered 11 vessels. Similar vessels are planned to be built by Dutch companies. Several other advantages are associated with the LASH-vessels. The turnaround time is reduced to a few hours. Ship size is not limited by depths at quay walls in any harbor, and expensive harbor installations such as jetties, wharves, piers,

180 Port Engineering

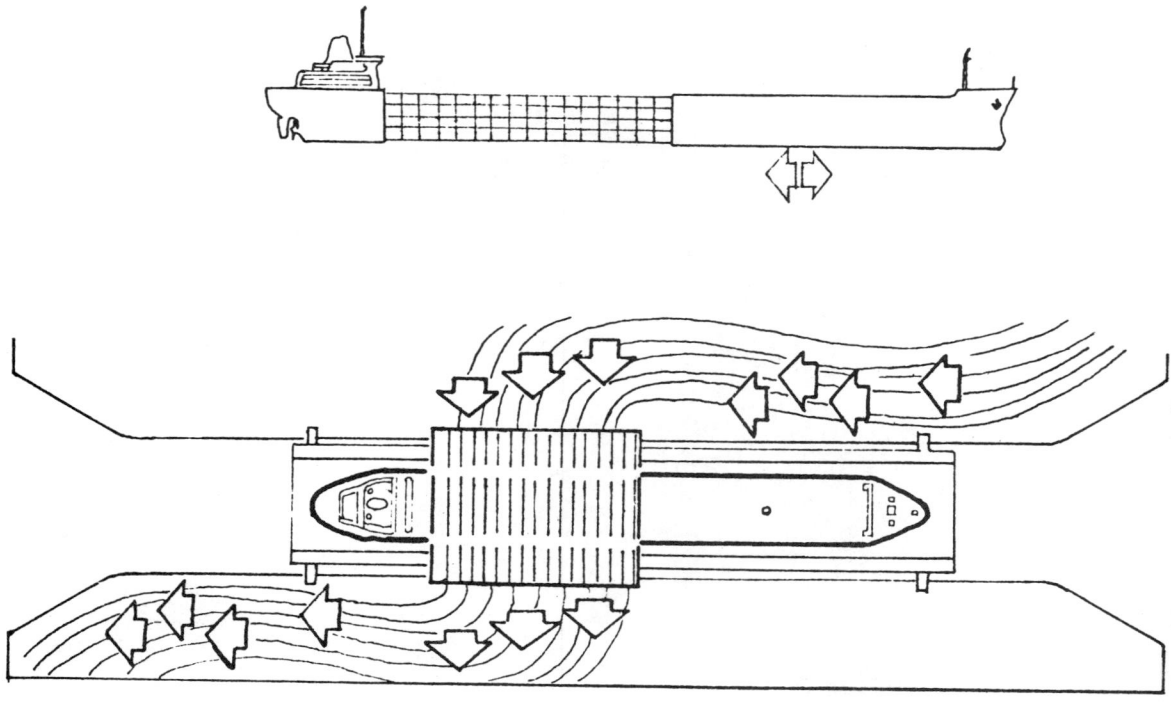

Figure 5.17. Box vessel by Vessman for loading and unloading by rolles conveyor.

sheds, etc. are unnecessary. Afterunloading (and before loading), barges are towed on rivers and waterways to their final destination. Even though the LASH system at first view seems to be most suitable for transport in developing countries, which have few harbor installations—if any—but often large river or lagoon systems, the fact is that the first LASH-vessel (s) was put in use on transatlantic transport from New Orleans to Central—European river ports. There is considerable economic savings involved in the barge system because of the low costs of river transport; e.g., on the Mississippi and on the European rivers through the Low Countries, Germany and all the way up on the Rhine to Switzerland.

The M/S *Arcadia Forest*, Figures 5.16, is 43,000 dwt (38,900 BRT). Its main dimensions are 780 x 60 feet. The barges are 13 x 30 x 61 feet. Their weight is 82 tons and loaded, approximately 450 tons. The vessel has a 500-ton gantry crane. Service speed is 18 knots at 37 feet draught. The type of vessel is rather expensive to build, however.

Another project comprises the construction of an ocean-going catamaras-type vessel. The twin-hulled ship has a bow section that can open like a bear trap and admit a load of 10 barges into the space between its hulls. Once inside, the barges are lifted mechanically and locked into place. Such a "straddler ship" can cross an ocean, release its barges, pick up another set and be on its way back in a matter of hours. Since the ship would scarcely ever be at reast, provisions have been made in the design for the accomodation of permanent crews and their families.

Several other ideas have been developed. Figure 5.17 shows a Norwegian "box-vessel" (Vessmann) by which boxes are moved directly into the hull in one side and moved out at the other side on some kind of roller conveyor. This system—if ever built—would be extremely effective. Regarding new types of vessels, see Reference 2.

Tozzoli (17) describes the benefits of containerization as "dramatic" and reports that Sea-Land Service, Inc., which has pioneered ocean container freight between New York and Europe, finds that a properly designed and located container terminal has an annual capacity of 500,000 tons per ship berth, which is five times the capacity of a berth operated in the traditional way. Because man-handling of cargo is reduced, the cost of both damage and pilferage is lessened.

Pallet System

Pallet operations are, as previously mentioned, suitable for smaller ships and smaller unit loads (0.5 to 2 tons). According to Reference 18, one of the most prominent advantages of palletization is the comparatively small cost of conversion, if conversion is effected at all. Any conventional freighter is suitable to carry pallets, although space may be wasted through loading such, and spaces suitable to load pallets, limited. With palletization, the cost of a paper pallet is five shillings, and yet, despite its cheap cost, it is strong and instantly disposable, thus culminating all problems of storage and space at the "other end." For instance, there must be occasions when containerized ships will be obliged to make a return voyage with empty containers, with the consequent loss of potentially valuable cargo space. Add this invisible loss of profits to the cost of container hire and construction, for a company which can ill afford the capital to invest in containers and their subsequent demand on new vessels, and it is obvious that palletization is the humbler but highly effective alternative for those firms with less capital to invest.

As mentioned earlier, one advantage associated with the pallet system is that it does not require nearly as much expensive equipment as the container system. Forklifts are relatively inexpensive. According to Reference 4, "an actual line carrying 1,500 pallet loads per ship, each ship calling weekly, acquired 35 forklifts at $15,000 for one of the two terminals, and 3 forklifts plus 4 electrical handtrucks for each of two ships. The total investment in cargo handling machines was about $600,000. Forklifts for the other terminal were provided by the stevedore. The pallets, which are often criticized as costing too much, required a rather modest investment for this particular line. Ten thousand steel pallets were purchased at a total price of $100,000. In other cases, expendable pallets measuring 40 by 48 in. may be had at $2.50." Furthermore, when it comes to the quay and shed, the containers will require a much larger area than palletized cargo. A fully door-to-door containerized service will not require any shed on the quay, whereas it will be necessary to have a shed in case any stuffing or unstuffing of container cargo is to take place in the port. A pallet load will generally have no protection against rain and will need shed space. A cargo volume corresponding to 800 twenty-foot containers is about 750,000 cubic feet when the cubic of the pallets is included. Ashore, palletized cargo will be stacked about 12 feet high, requiring shed area of 2.5 to 3.5 acres, depending on the need for forklift driving alleys. Two and one-half acres will be sufficient when only 30% of the area is reserved for driving alleys, 3.5 acres corresponding to 50% driving area. When the cargo consists of a small number of large shipments to a limited number of ports, 30% driving space will be sufficient; otherwise, about 50% will be required (4).

The most efficient way to load and discharge pallets is by forklifts, which handle them through combined side door and side hatches (Figures 5.18 and 5.19). By combining the side door with the side hatch, it is possible to handle pallet loads through the opening, independent of the ship's relative height to the quay. A forklift working on a deck below quay level may go up with its fork through the side hatch and pick up pallet cargo which has been placed in the side opening. In this way, the second and even the third 'tween deck compartment may be served through the same side hatch, provided the ship is not too low in relation to the quay.

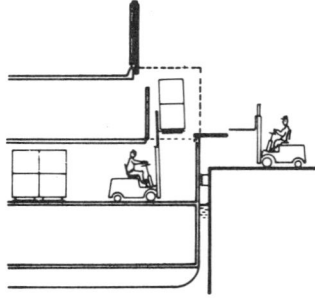

Figure 5.18. Discharge of pallet loads (4).

Figure 5.19. Photo of operation outlined in Figure 5 (20).

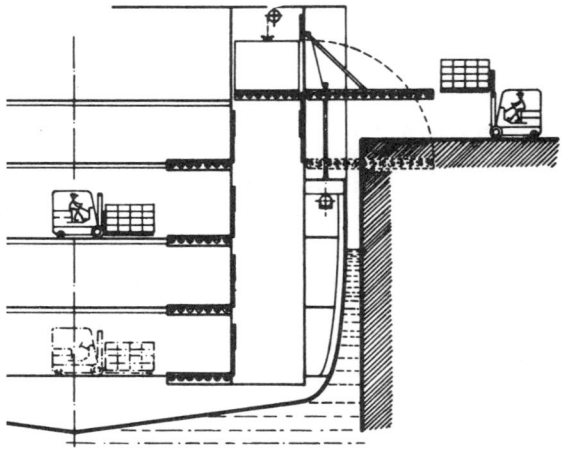

Figure 5.20. Pallet loads being handled from one dock to another (4).

When the side door opening has a width of about 17 feet two forklifts may work simultaneously (Figures 5.19). By this method, the first and second or the second and third 'tween deck compartments may be loaded and discharged at the same time. For this purpose, the 'tween deck side hatch cover should be divided in two equal parts. When working, one should be open to give access to the compartment below, the other closed to allow the forklift which is working in the upper compartment to drive to the side opening.

With a low tide and deep-loaded ship, the second and third 'tween decks may not be reached from the quay, and forklifts on board the ship must handle pallet loads from one deck to another through hatches. However, this method becomes impractical with large ships, which may have four and five 'tween decks. For these ships, it is better to load and discharge the lower compartments by a pallet elevator (Figure 5.20). When the pallet elevator is combined with automatic roller tables, cargo delivered at the ship's side opening is fed automatically into the preselected compartment.

A ship, fully equipped with side doors and elevators designed for mechanical cargo handling, will not need any conventional hatches or any lifting equipment; the hull construction will thereby be simpler than for any ordinary ship. As an example, Figure 5.21 shows a design of a pallet carrier for the North Sea trade. Although all commodities which can be handled by forklifts are suitable for side door operations, it has been assumed for the calculations of this paper that the pallet ships will have one swinging derrick for heavy lifts and one hatch through which these lifts can be loaded into the lower hold. Even if pallet ships without ordinary hatches have been in service for some time, it may be a little too unrealistic

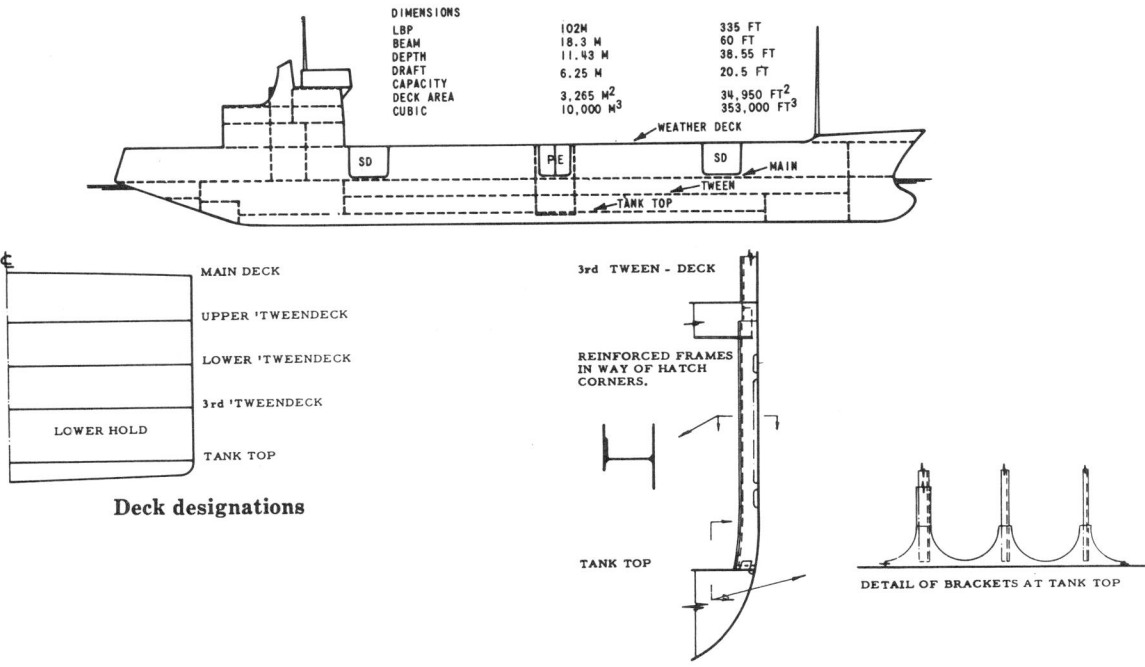

Figure 5.21. Design of a fast-running, 350,000 cu. feet pallet carrier for North Sea trade. Cargo-gear: 2 side doors and 1 pallet elevator; no lifting rig (4).

to base the cost calculations on the assumption that the pallet ships will be completely without conventional cargo hatches and gear. It will be sufficient to install combined side openings/side hatches in one side of the ship only, and thereby it will be necessary always to berth with the same side to the quay. This can be accomplished by installing a bow thruster. (Port managements are not always too happy about such a procedure.) Acceleration forces increase the load on the pallets when a ship meets sea. This means that the 'tween deck heights should be kept within a reasonable limit to avoid damage to pallets.

As mentioned earlier, palletization is particularly suitable for short routes; e.g., in coastal trade and on seas like the North Sea between the Scandinavian countries and England. It still remains debatable whether palletization is economical on long voyages, but palletization comes as a blessing to those companies engaged in coastal and short sea trades. But because as many goods can be palletized as can be containerized, palletization, if fully adopted, will reduce the home trade fleet, and as a result, place even more seafarers out of a job. On shorter routes, there may be a definite need for "combines" as shown in Figure 5.22, a Norwegian design of a LO/LO-RO/RO pallet vessel.

Dimensions of Unit Loads

The employment of all kinds of sophisticated containers is increasing. Such containers carry a wide range of goods and materials, including loose consignments of cases, cartons, bales, drums, pieces, etc.; unit loads of the kinds which can be handled conveniently by forklift trucks (e.g., palletized loads, cases with bottom battens and packages strapped into cube loads, without pallets);

Figure 5.22. LO/LO-RO/RO—Pallet vessel (Norwegian design).

Table 5.3. ISO Standards for Containers (18 and others).

Length (ft)	Volume	Weight (kg)	
		Empty	Loaded
20	1,100 ft³ (31 m³)	1,850	20,320
30	1,600 ft³ (46 m³)	2,600	25,400
40	2,200 ft³ (62 m³)	3,200	30,580
40 (insulated)	2,050 ft³ (58 m³)	4,350	30,480

and bulk materials. The work of correlating the dimensions of containers, unit loads and pallets has been difficult. Efforts have been made by the International Standards Organization (ISO). Table 5.3 indicates some results.

The maximum density of cargo (pounds per cubic feet) decreases as the length of container increases. In the United Kingdom, a further limit is put on the pay load of 40-foot containers by the maximum which may be carried by road without special authorization.

There are, however, many dimensions differing from those sizes mentioned in Table 5.3. In the United States, lengths of 12, 24, 27 and 35 feet are common. Statistics demonstrate that the average net weight of 20-foot containers for eastbound transatlantic transport is of the order of 11 to 11.5 tons and for westbound transport, 11.5 to 12 tons. Most containers are built of wood and steel and sometimes aluminum. Empty containers take up space; efforts have therefore been made to develop folding containers (Figure 5.23). For pal-

Figure 5.23. Model of folding container (Dock and Harbour Authority, February 1968).

lets there is even more confusion in dimensions. Table 5.4 gives an impression of dimensions of pallets used at various places in the world.

There are now available in many developed countries a variety of pallets made of various materials which would meet the specifications of individual shippers. These include: (a) all timber construction of varying strengths, (b) bitumen paper reinforced with wire, (c) mild steel, (d) wire and wood block, (e) fiberglass and wood and doubtless many others. Several are manufactured in various sizes, while some are collapsible, which gives the advantage of reducing the required storage space. The user's choice will be governed by his specification, package sizes, load factor, transit conditions and a host of other factors, not forgetting cost.

The planning of and preloading of pallets involves a considerable amount of detailed study and experimenting if one is to arrive at an optimum load. The optimum figure will vary with different products, as will the actual method of stowing the block stowage on the pallet. While cartons are of regular shape, their size differs between products as does density and rigidity of pack within the carton. With powdered products in paper or polythene bags, much can be done to press the bags

Table 5.4
Pallet Dimensions

Type	Dimension (M)
Europe	0.80 x 1.20
Australia	1.15 x 1.15
Hunsa	1.15 x 1.80
North Sea	1.20 x 1.80
Stevedore	1.20 x 1.60
Coaster	1.10 x 1.60
Industry	1.00 x 1.20
Pacific	1.00 x 1.20

Table 5.5. Capacity, Manning and Cost per Ton for Ship and Shore Mounted Gear (4).

Costs in U.S. $		Conventional		Palletised				Container	
		1 shore crane	10 pairs of derricks	1 shore crane	10 pairs of derricks	8 revolving cranes	2 pallet elevators +3 sidedoors	1 shore crane	2 gantry cranes
A Initial price		140,000	175,000	140,000	175,000	280,000	200,000	800,000	900,000
B Capacity, tons/hour		15	150	40	400	400	300	200	400
C Tons/year handled	D x B	30,000	140,000	80,000	140,000	140,000	140,000	580,000	560,000
D Hours/year in use	C/B	2,000	930	2,000	350	350	465	2,900	1,400
E No. of operators, signalmen		2	20	2	20	8	0	1	2
F Hourly pay/operator		3.5	3.00	3.50	3.00	3.00	-	4.00	4.00
G Total operator cost/hour	E x F	7	60	7	60	24	0	4	8
H Total operator cost/year	G x D	14,000	56,000	14,000	21,000	8,400	0	11,600	11,200
J Depr. & interest/year	0.15 A	21,000	26,200	21,000	26,200	42,000	30,000	120,000	135,000
K Power, maintenance etc.		3,000	15,000	6,000	15,000	15,000	10,000	20,000	30,000
L Total cost per year	H + J + K	38,000	97,200	41,000	62,200	65,400	40,000	151,600	176,200
M Total cost per ton	L/C	1.27	0.69	0.51	0.44	0.47	0.29	0.26	0.32

Notes: 1 ton = 1 longton or 100 cu. ft. The calculation for shore cranes is based on a fixed number of working hours per year, while for ship's gear the basis is the carrying capacity and the roundtrip time.

With portable remote control, signalmen not required.

into a more suitable shape for palletizing. Expendable wooden pallets of conventional dimensions may come as low as about $2.50 a piece (4). Various pallet boxes exist—large pallets are approaching small containers in volume as well as in design. Large pallets called "flats" are built of steel with a capacity up to 20 tons (8 x 20 feet) and may be handled by normal container handling equipment.

The value of containerization for the shipper and receiver is greatly diminished if handling, loading and unloading costs at the start and end of the container transport cannot be reduced, because no mechanical handling is possible for various reasons, such as loss of space in containers, one-way expendable pallets costly, etc.

The one-way expendable pallet offers a solution for loading and unloading containers rapidly at both ends. It is wrong to assume that the container replaces the pallet. In fact, the container has one big disadvantage—it is too large to be used for factory or warehouse internal movement. It is not really a unit load to be formed at the end of the production line or to be broken up when transport or consumer packs are placed on the shelf in the shop. The container is just another vehicle, mode of transport or part of the ship's hold. Although "stuffing" and "unstuffing" containers manually is a laborious job, the advantages of no handling in ports may, for the time being, permit manual instead of mechanical stowage—if shippers participate in the savings in port handling and more rapid turnaround of ships. Besides, new techniques and equipment are being developed to speed up stowage in containers (conveyors, etc.) where pallets cannot leave the factory. There still remains the problem of unloading at the other end, often more costly and more difficult to organize than loading.

Comparative Cost Figures for Various Systems

The article by Getz et al. (4) gives an interesting analysis of the unit cost of handling cargo by a variety of mechanical gear installed on the ship or on the quay. Table 5.5 is an evaluation of the cost per ton for hoisting cargo on board and ashore (1967-1968 figures). Costs of gangs, forklifts, etc., is not included. However, within each of the three groups—conventional, palletized and containers—these other costs per ton will be fairly constant (4).

The basis for the ship-borne equipment is a relatively small 6,000 dwt liner on an eight-week round trip. Provided the ship is always fully loaded, the 6,000 tons must be loaded and discharged twice for every round trip; in other words, the gear must handle 24,000 tons each time. Six round trips per year give roughly 140,000 tons for the gear to handle in a year. The capacity figures are true today—not maximum values.

The resulting figures of cost per ton show clearly that, for conventional work, ship's gear is the best solution, while mechanized production puts shore or ship-borne equipment on fairly equal terms. Actually, the shore crane will win here if a higher utilization is obtained, and this should be quite possible with smart administration of a large port.

In a lecture given by Axelson, General Manager of the Port of Gothenburg, Sweden, at the International Container Symposium, London, May 28-29, 1968, a comparison was made from the harbor-management viewpoint of the berths in Gothenburg (Scandia Harbor) and their various methods of cargo handling traffic. The figures compared are the annual capital costs for the harbor per ton of goods handled, and the annual capital costs are taken as 10% of the investment costs. The results arrived at in this comparison are shown in Table 5.6 (11).

In connection with Table 5.6, it should be noted that the berths under items 3, 4, and 6 have a reserve capacity which, when utilized, can bring down costs still further. The figures speak for themselves, giving a clear impression of the advantages of the LO/LO and RO/RO systems compared to conventional systems.

It should still be noted that the figures in Table 5.6 do not indicate a comparison between the total cost for the different transport systems, but they do show clearly that, from the harbor-management viewpoint, there is every reason to encourage traffic with containers and other units, provided that the underlying volume of traffic is

188   Port Engineering

Table 5.6 Annual Capital per Ton of Goods Handled at Scandia Harbor (11).

Type Ship	Type berths	Cargo handling	Traffic	Annual cost*
1. Conventional	Modern	Almost all conventional	European	1.45
2. Truck-on/truck-off	Modern		European	1.25
3. RO/RO	Special		Mostly trailer, European	0.70
4. RO/RO	Special	Container and flats	European	0.65
5. Conventional	Modern	Almost all conventional	Transoceanic	2.20
6. LO/LO and RO/RO	Special	containers and flats	Transoceanic	0.95

*Annual capital cost in dollars per ton of goods handled.

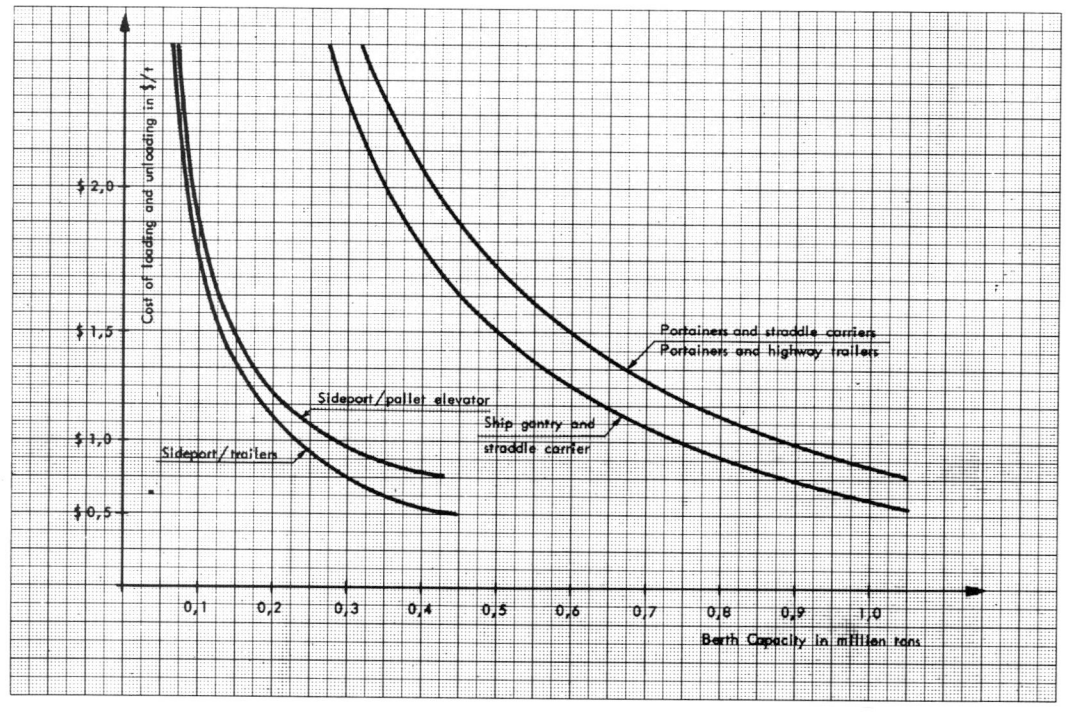

Figure 5.24. Costs in dollars per ton for different methods of loading and unloading at various berth capacities (R. Holm).

sufficient for the larger capacity of a container harbor to be used.

According to Reference 11, the experience gathered up to now (1968-1969) of the transoceanic container traffic in the Swedish Scandia Harbor indicates that it is possible to handle 750,000 tons of goods annually through a container berth with the lift-on/lift-off system, which is now in general use in the container harbors. Further development in handling methods should increase these figures still further.

A comparison of approximate nature between all fixed and variable loading and unloading costs per berth for pallet transport and container transport is shown in Figure 5.24. A capacity of up to about 250,000 tons is assumed for pallet transport and a capacity of up to about 1,000,000 tons for container transport. It may be seen that the pallet system is most advantageous at the relatively small berth capacities. Capital costs are, needless to say, highest for the container transport, but variable expenses seem to be three to four times higher for pallet transport than for container transport. For further information on the economics of the transport problem, the reader is referred to articles in PIANC report (11) and their references.

Application of Queuing Models to Ship Turnaround Time

Queuing theories and models are applicable to a great number of transportation problems whether they are associated with telephone services, parking problems or arrivals of airplanes or vessels. Two basic elements are necessary for the application of the queuing model to a waiting-line problem (6): an arrival function and a servicing function. From the information source and an appropriate model, useful results pertaining to the amount of delay to be expected and the length of queues may be calculated. Ship turnaround time involves the arrival from sea of ships expecting to use port facilities and the duration of occupancy of a berth (serving time).

Experience shows that the sequence of arrival of vessels often may be confidently described as a Poisson function. With respect to servicing time, it is usually possible to describe berth occupancy as an Erlangian function, which is better suited to represent servicing times that are more regularly spaced in time than those represented by the Poisson distribution.

Through the choice of the Erlang K-value (explained later), a service time distribution may be described as anything from the purely random negative-exponential type to the completely regular constant servicing time type. As K increases, there are fewer very long or very short values of servicing time.

The essential parameters for the queuing model are: λ is the mean arrival rate (ships per hour); μ is the mean servicing rate (ships per hour); N is the number of "servicing channels" (berths); and ρ is the utilization ratio equal to $\lambda/N\mu$.

No feasible mathematical solution is possible in the case of a multiple channel, an unlimited queue with exponential arrivals and Erlangian servicing situation. Three courses are available for analysis, however (6).

1. Consider the port as comprised of 10 single-channel systems (with negative exponential arrivals and Erlangian servicing) and compute the delay per channel (berth) from the equation:

$$W'_q = \frac{\rho^2 (K+1)}{2K\lambda(1-\rho)}$$

2. Consider the port as a multi-channel facility with the servicing time distribution of each channel as negative exponential having a mean value equal to the observed mean and compute the delay in the arrival queue by the equation:

$$W''_q = \frac{L''_q}{\lambda} = \frac{\rho}{\lambda(1-\rho)} \frac{e_N(\rho N)}{D_{N-1}(\rho N)}$$

in which e_N is the Poisson function, and D_{N-1} is a function of cumulative Poisson functions (8).

3. Consider the servicing time as constant ($K = \infty$) and compute delay in the arrival queue by the equation:

$$W_q''' = \left[\left(\frac{\rho^N}{1-\rho}\right)\left(\frac{e(1-\rho)N}{\sqrt{(2\pi N)}}\right)\right]\left[\frac{(1-\rho^{N-1})}{\mu(1-\rho)(N+1)(1-\rho^N)}\right]$$

The first term is an approximation of the probability of any waiting where the number of service channels is large. The second term is a general approximation for multiple channels with Poisson input and constant service time (6).

In order to give the reader a more practical feeling for the problem, the article, "Forecasting delays to ships in port," by J.D. Mettam (7), published in the April, 1967, issue of the *Dock and Harbour Authority*, London, with permission from the author, is reprinted in full below.

The subtitle of the article is "A description of the application of mathematical analysis of queuing problems, as they apply to ships in port, to the planning and design of ports."

Except for passenger ships or ferries on scheduled services, the pattern of arrival of ships at a port is normally random. When they arrive, they may be able to move directly onto a berth or they may have to wait until other ships are clear before they can do so. The amount of cargo which each ship carries and the time required to handle it will also vary so that the delay to vessels waiting for berths will be the resultant of two variable functions. Operational research workers have developed mathematical techniques for analysing queueing problems of this nature. The purpose of this article is to show how these techniques may be applied to the planning and design of ports to forecast realistically the likelihood of congestion and costly delays as ships wait for berths. Some general conclusions are also drawn.

The following symbols, units and definitions have been adopted for this paper:

N = the number of effective berths in the port or in that part of it which is being analysed as a single operating unit; the number of berths which can be analysed in this way is limited in practice by the fact that the analysis requires that any ship can be sent to any berth in the group.

n = the total number of ships arriving in the period considered, treated hereafter as a full year of 365 days.

λ = the average rate of arrival of ships (number per day).

t_w = the time (in days) waiting for a berth, that is the time from moment of arrival in port to commencement of movement into berth.

T_w = the average waiting time for all ships during period of study.

t_b = the berth service time in days, that is the time when the berth is effectively occupied by each ship including transit time between the berth and the point where an incoming ship will have to pass an outgoing ship.

T_b = the average berth service time.

μ = rate of servicing = $1/T_b$ (No. per day)

θ = average berth occupancy (per cent)

$$\theta = \left(\frac{100}{N}\right)\left(\frac{nT_b}{365}\right) = 100\frac{\lambda T_b}{N}$$

ψ = traffic intensity = $\lambda T_b = N\theta/100$

If it is assumed, firstly, that the actual rate of arrival is a random function following Poisson's law, and secondly, that the service time in berth varies according to a negative exponential distribution then a queueing analysis may be carried out using Erlang's formula. These two assumptions imply idealised distributions of the form shown on Figures A and B (Figure 5.25 and 5.26). Actual distributions will vary in form but cases which have recently been studied in detail show reasonably good agreement in both respects. The nature

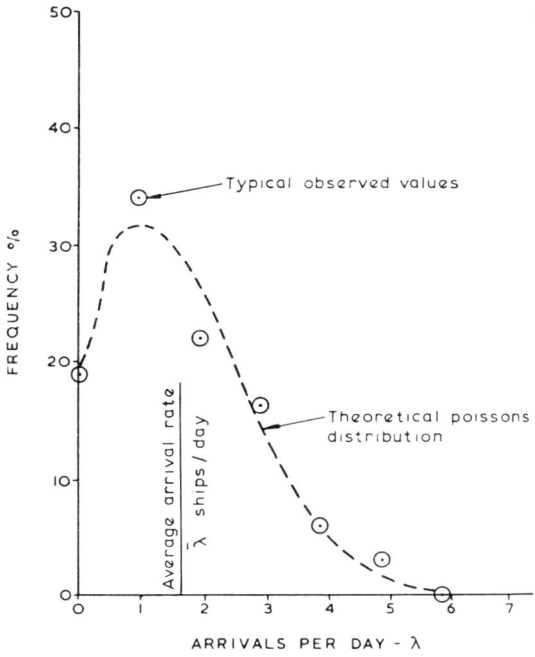

Figure 5.25. Frequency distribution of ship arrivals.

of the analysis is such that a very close fit is not essential.

In cases where the berth service times do not follow the simple negative exponential curve sufficiently well, it becomes advisable to consider whether a better fit would be obtained by using one of a more complex series of curves known collectively as the K curves. These are purely theoretical curves based on the assumption that the service time is split into two or more phases following one another and that the ship does not leave the berth until all phases are complete. K is the number of phases, each of which has a negative exponential distribution. As K is increased the effect is to make the total service time more uniform until finally with $K = \infty$ all service times are identical. In the general case the total service time probability $P_o(t)$ is given by

$$P_o(t) = e^{-K\mu t} \sum_{n=o}^{K-1} (K\mu t) \frac{n}{n!}$$

When $K = 1$ this reduces to $P_o(t) = e^{-\mu t}$
When $K = 2$ the probability is $P_o(t) = e^{-2\mu t}(1 + 2\mu t)$

The distributions of service times corresponding to $K = 1$ $K = 2$ and $K = \infty$ are shown in Figure B (Figure 5.26), all being plotted for the same average berth service time T_b. It will be seen that the typical distribution for the case studied approximates more closely to the $K = 2$ curves than to $K = 1$, particularly for short service times. The reason for this is not clear. There are indeed three phases included in service time in as much as the movements in and out of berth require varying times which are to an extent independent of the service time at berth, but the time required for these moves is generally very small compared with the

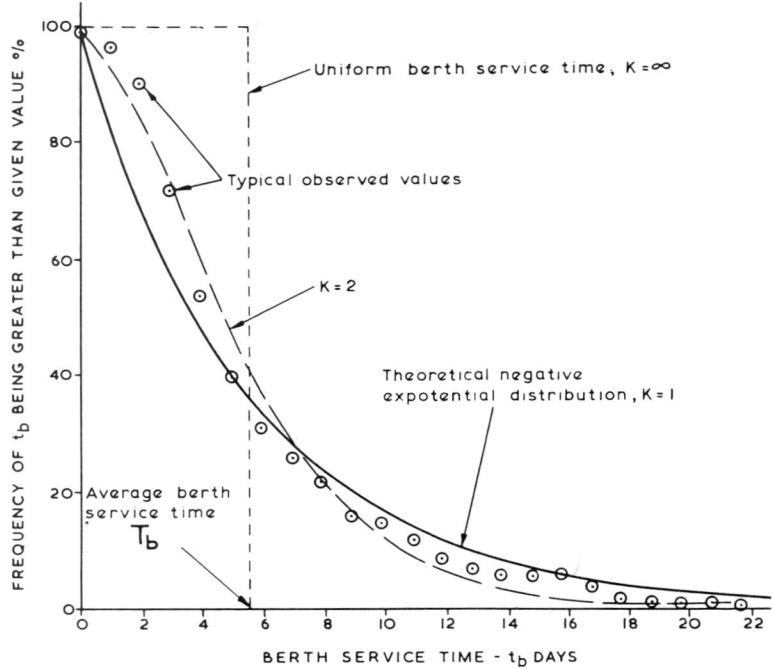

Figure 5.26. Cumulative frequency distribution of berth service times.

time at berth. Perhaps the real cause is that there is in practice a lower limit of service time due to the fact that it is not worth calling at port where waiting times are high with only a small amount of cargo. If this is the reason, provision of more adequate facilities would reduce waiting time and could encourage quick calls rather than transshipment of small cargoes. This would improve the fit of service times to the $K = 1$ curves.

It was therefore decided in this particular case to adopt $K = 1$, which gives conservative (higher) estimates of waiting times, and which also allows the use of the relatively simple Erlang's formula. Using the symbols defined above, this formula may be written as illustrated in the box at the bottom of this page.

$$\frac{T_w}{T_b} = \frac{\psi^N}{N\left(1 - \frac{\psi}{N}\right)\psi^N + N \cdot N!\left(1 - \frac{\psi}{N}\right)^2\left(1 + \frac{\psi}{1} + \frac{\psi^2}{2} + \frac{\psi^3}{3} \cdots \frac{\psi^{N-1}}{(N-1)!}\right)}$$

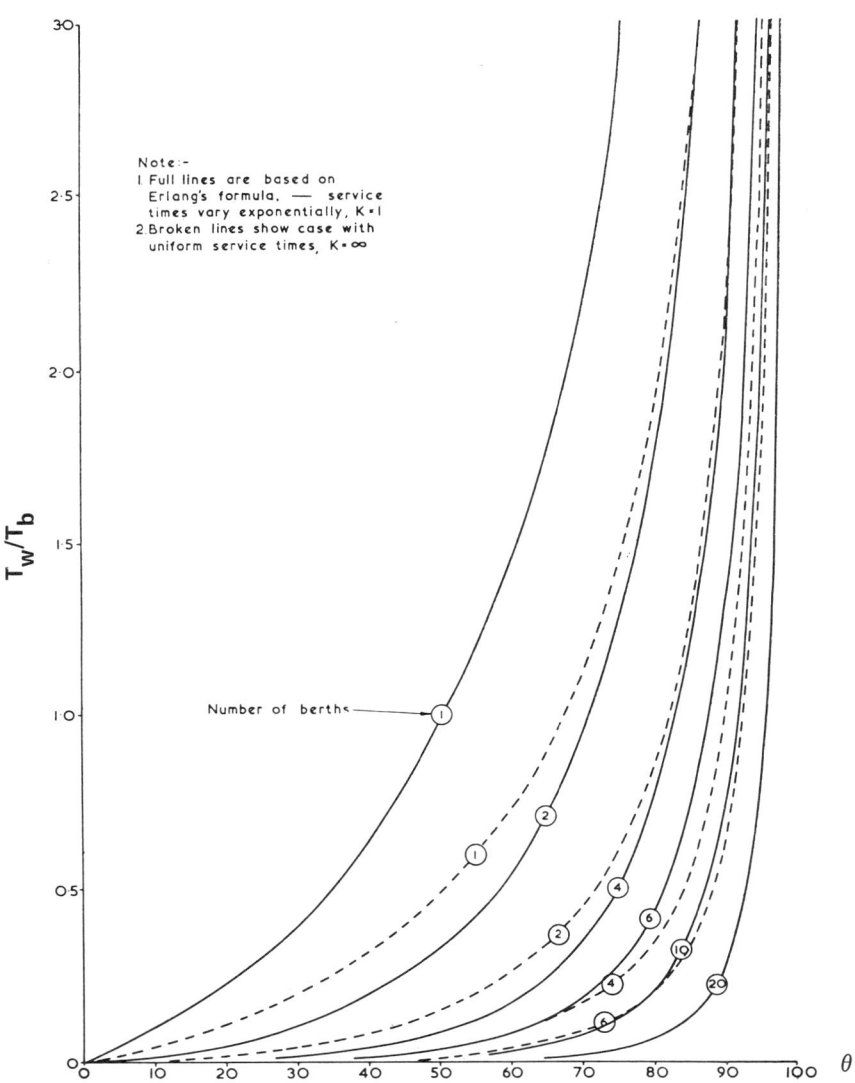

Figure 5.27. Relation between Tw/Tb and θ for various different numbers of berths.

This formula is happily not as difficult to use as it might appear on first sight. Since $\psi = N\,\theta/100$, graphs can be plotted to show the relationship between T_w/T_b and θ for various different numbers of berths N. Figure C (Figure 5.27) shows a series of such graphs prepared for numbers of berths varying between 1 and 20. The graphs in full lines on Figure C (Figure 5.27) relate to the $K = 1$ curve for service times. Higher K values would give reduced waiting times. Broken lines have been added on Figure C (Figure 5.27) to show for one, two, four and six berths the effect on waiting times of the extreme case when waiting times are constant ($K = \infty$). It will be seen that delays are half those for $K = 1$. This case could occur only when identical ships carrying identical cargoes are handled with identical equipment, which must also be uniformly reliable and served by ideal dockers! It may perhaps be approached sometimes in the case of crude oil tankers of a single fleet. More normally the true position even for oil tankers will lie between $K = 1$ and $K = \infty$ and will be close to $K = 1$ for general cargo ships.

The curves on Figure C (Figure 5.27) may be used for calculating the delays arising from making alterations to an existing system, for example, by increasing the amount of cargo handled or by changing the number of berths. They can also be used to consider seasonal effects, such as heavy seasonal rain, causing delays in handling cargo which leads to increased values of T_b. This method is not, however, very accurate unless the seasonal change is fairly small and operates over a long enough period to allow a new steady state to become established. In practice, when considering a large port operating initially at very high berth occupancies and changing to even worse conditions for a few months each year, there is a danger of exaggerating delays. Build-up of extra queues of waiting ships will occur more slowly and the full build-up may not be completed before conditions improve again. Unless conditions are very bad indeed, recovery will be more rapid than the build-up of queues.

The procedure for using the curves to forecast delays is as follows:

1. Analyse records of existing ship arrivals to establish the following data:
    a) number of ships calling each year, n;
    b) average tonnage of cargo carried per ship;
    c) average berth service time T_b.
    d) the average rate of arrival λ;
    e) the effective number of berths available for the traffic being studied (that is, exclude the berths which may be reserved for repairing ships, etc.), N.

2. Estimate the rate of handling cargo at each berth. An average rate can be determined for the portion of service time spent actually loading or unloading cargo and it will be helpful to convert this into an equivalent rate related to the total service time. It will then be seen that the total cargo handled is a product of the handling rate, T_b and n. It is also proportional to the product of N and θ, and consequently the cargo handled in the port is roughly proportional to the average berth occupancy. (This is a slight over simplification because the service time, as defined, includes periods of transit to and from the berth when no cargo handling is taking place.)

3. For any given future traffic and number of berths, it is possible to prepare a forecast of queueing delays. The procedure would be:
    a) decide tonnage of cargo to be handled and effective number of berths, N;
    b) consider whether the average amount of cargo carried per ship is likely to change and thence determine the number of ships, n, which will arrive in port;
    c) if the average amount of cargo to be handled from each ship is unchanged and no new factors arise in the nature of cargo or method of handling the cargo, the average time at the berths will probably be the same. For any significant changes the average service time T_b must be recalculated;
    d) the new annual berth occupancy θ is calculated from the above factors;
    e) the corresponding value of T_w/T_b can be read off from Figure C (Figure 5.27) using the curve for the appropriate number of berths;
    f) the average waiting time, T_w, may be determined and multiplied by n to determine the total number of ship-days wasted in waiting for berths;

g) The cost of delays may be assessed, based upon actual costs or demurrage charges as appropriate.

The cost of the delays to ships waiting for berths can be used in the cost/benefit analysis for comparing the economics of developing additional facilities, or of continuing to operate existing facilities with increasing congestion. Some inaccuracies are inherent in adopting Erlang's analysis based on simplified assumptions for the form of the two variables, but in practice it is believed that the errors will not be found to be serious and the method described will be a valuable tool in analysing the economics of investment in ports.

Even without using the detailed analysis outlined above, it is possible to use Figure C (Figure 5.27) to provide some interesting pointers to fundamental principles in port planning. For example:

(1) assume that a T_w/T_b ratio of 0.5 is taken to be the level of delays acceptable to users. It will be seen from Figure C (Figure 5.27) that a dock system with 20 berths will not reach this limit until the berth occupancy is as high as 93 per cent. The corresponding limited berth occupancies with 10, 4, 2 and 1 berths are respectively 88, 75, 59 and 35 per cent. The throughput per berth is proportional to berth occupancy and the larger port will therefore be capable of higher throughput per berth than smaller ports, with similar delays to ships. There will, on the other hand, be a risk of very severe congestion if something goes wrong, say a strike or bad weather. Even a moderate increase in berth occupancy, which would be required to clear extra cargo during the recovery period, would put the operation on to the steep part of the graph with correspondingly high waiting periods. Provided that berth occupancies are not allowed to reach quite such a high level, it will, however, be possible to operate a large port more intensively than a smaller one. Other things being equal, it will therefore prove more economic to expand an existing port rather than build a new port.

(2) Other things are, of course, not usually equal and in particular specialised berths are now needed for rapid handling of bulk cargoes and containers. When a highly mechanised berth is developed for a single class of traffic, it must be considered as an isolated unit even if it forms part of a large port. Such a facility cannot derive any benefit from being built near other different facilities, as far as delay to ships is concerned, though it may well benefit in other respects such as sharing facilities and services. Figure C (Figure 5.27) shows that operation of a single berth will result in heavy delays to ships unless it is worked to a very low berth occupancy or very short berth service times. If the amount of traffic to be handled is fixed, a low berth occupancy can be achieved by installing sufficient mechanical handling equipment. This is in contrast to a normal general cargo berth where the rate of handling cargo is determined more by the traditional practice of the port, or the nature of the relations between management and unions.

(3) If it is difficult to achieve sufficiently rapid rates of cargo handling at a single berth, an installation with two berths will be found much more efficient. With proportionately similar delays (for example, $T_w/T_b = 0.5$), the single berth can be operated at only 35 per cent occupancy while each of the two berths can be operated at 59 per cent occupancy. With equal handling rates, the combined capacity of the pair of berths is therefore more than three times that of the single berth perhaps.

It might be argued that these three points are self evident or that a well-developed engineering instinct will reach the same conclusions without

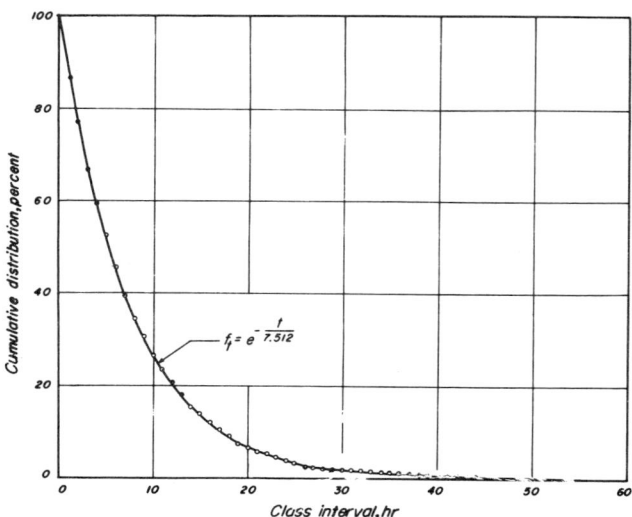

Figure 5.28. Cumulative distribution of ship arrivals at bar for entry to Port of Bangkok (6).

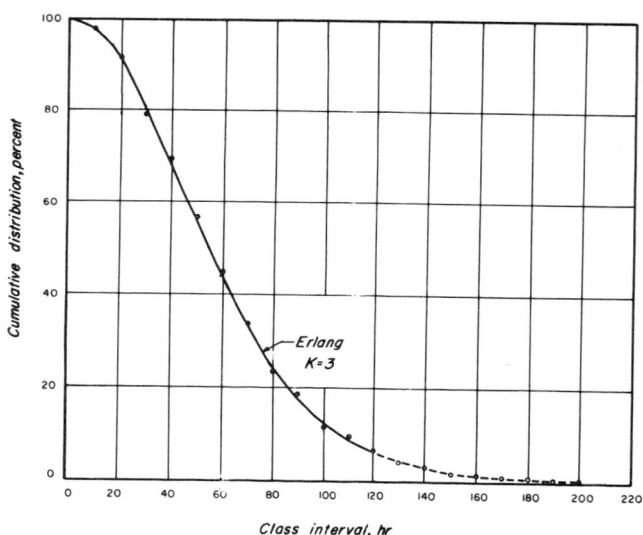

Figure 5.29. Cumulative distribution of time spent at berth by ships at Port of Bangkok (6).

recourse to mathematics. Taking the first point, all port engineers and managements are already aware of the tendency for large ports to get bigger, and this growth is not solely due to the factor mentioned above. Regarding the second point, many terminals for oil or grain which have been built with two berths have been found to have advantages of flexibility of operation. A recent visit to a number of container berths handling considerable quantities of cargo in the United States emphasized the third point in that it was difficult to observe the actual unloading and loading of ships because the berth occupancies were very low.

However, it is always useful to have a simple graphical picture of the influence of a common factor on a group of principles which might otherwise appear to be unrelated. Figure C provides just a simple picture in addition to forming the basis for a quantitative assessment of the probable cost of delays.*

Figure 5.26 uses $K = 1$ and $K = 2$, while Figure 5.27 considers $K = 1$ and $K = \infty$. High K values (as for oil tankers) are needless to say an advantage.

For comparison of the previously mentioned, Figure 5.28 shows the cumulative distribution of ship arrivals at bar for entry to the Port of Bangkok (6). Distribution = exp. (-t/7.512) when the mean duration between successive arrivals is 7,512 hours, and Figure 5.29 depicts the cumulative distribution of time spent at berth by ships at Port of Bangkok (6) with $K = 3$, which was chosen for $K = 2$ or $K = 4$. A x-square analysis was performed to compare to observed frequency distribution with the postulated Erlangian function (6).

Port Transportation Studies

Port studies may be of local or of more "universal" character. The local studies are part of the local planning undertaken by Port Authorities,

*End of article J.D. Mettam article.

Port Committees, etc., in order to forecast future needs. The navigation studies by the U.S. Army Corps of Engineers may be local in character, but they consider overall justification and economy. The most important overall studies are those undertaken or initiated by the United Nations and by the International Bank of Research and Development (IBRD).

The trend in these studies may be understood from some remarks by P. Engelman (IBRD) on the Panel on Long-Range Port Planning regarding the relation between ocean-port commerce and inland distribution systems and the possibilities of interaction between port development and "regional" transport planning.

We speak of "cargo through-put" as a basic measure of port capacity because ocean-port commerce is predominantly "through-traffic." Except for entrepot trade and the commerce that has its origin or destination in the immediate vicinity of ocean-port terminals—in most cases a small part of the total port traffic is distributed and collected via the road, rail and inland or coastal waterway connections in the ports' hinterland. The total volume and the flow patterns of this traffic are a function of the transport network outside the port area and will vary with the service characteristics of all connecting transport modes.

Therefore, when major capital investments are studied for the construction of public port terminals or related channel and harbor improvements, it is often desirable to assess alternatives in the context of "regional" transport facilities and services. Such assessments may involve comparisons of various terminal locations and, possibly, various types of terminals, in combination with alternative connecting routes and modes of inland transport. By weighing the total investment required for new or improved channels, ports, railroads, highways and related equipment against the benefits that would result from this investment to the economy of the "region," an optimum solution for the anticipated traffic can be found.

If the port under consideration serves a "region" that is also the tributary area of other ports, such assessments become somewhat more complex: differences in the service characteristics of ocean shipping to and from competing ports must then be taken into account, along with the operating conditions and alternative investment possibilities within each port. Thus, the scope of these assessments will necessarily be broader and the viable alternatives may become more numerous; but the same principles will apply—provided, of course, that the sponsor of the study is interested in comparing total costs with total benefits, in terms of the economy of the "region" served by the ports.

However, not all investments in port development require such assessments. In many instances it may be evident that the inland connections serving a port have adequate capacity and that only the terminal needs expansion. Furthermore, in highly industrialized areas, there is much transport activity that is unrelated to ports, such as traffic between and within industrial centers and traffic resulting from the increasing mobility of industrial populations; these frequently overshadow the land transport needs of port-oriented commerce. But one cannot always assume that the inland distribution system in such areas will have sufficient capacity to serve port traffic with efficiency. Nor can affluence justify the general assumption that port development planning, when isolated from "regional" transport planning, will result only in minor diseconomies. It is therefore surprising that, in the more industrialized areas of the Western Hemisphere, examples of recent studies that combine port development with regional transport planning are relatively few and far between (1967).

In countries where industrialization is only beginning, the assumptions based on affluence are not commonly made and economic development often depends in large measure on the expansion of export trade; port-oriented traffic is therefore likely to be given priority over other transport needs. Investment capital for development being less than abundant, there has also been a growing awareness of the need for the planning of all transportation investments on a regional or national scale; this has been encouraged by the international and bilateral agencies that are engaged in financial and technical assistance. As a result, studies which contain elements of port and other transport planning in developing countries have been more frequent in recent years; specifically, these have been of two types:

a) feasibility studies for the construction of new ports and new inland links in undeveloped regions; and
b) transport sector surveys on a "regional" or national scale.

Feasibility studies are designed specifically for each project because the economic and physical environment of the particular case determines the scope of the investigations and the approach that will lead to meaningful answers; it is therefore difficult to give an outline for this type of study in general terms.

The second type of study that involves port development as well as *"regional" transport planning*, the *"transport sector survey,"* differs from the type described above in both purpose and scope. While feasibility studies prepare and assess one project or a group of projects to the point where an investment decision can be made, the "sector survey" has a broader focus and is concerned with the total transport system of an entire country, or of a "region" that covers a large part of one or more countries, or even several entire countries as a group.

Typically, the objectives of such a survey are (1) to formulate a program of public investments in transport for a period of five to fifteen years, based on a ranking by economic priority of specific projects in all modes of transport, (2) identify means of improving the operation and administration of each existing transport mode in the country or "region" and (3) prepare recommendations for future government policies in the transport sector, with special emphasis on effective coordination of transport developments.

Examples were given of both types of studies, and it was finally concluded that:

The two types of studies outlined above have been found useful for developing countries in the planning of investments for the transport sector; with some modifications, these methods can also be applied effectively on port development and transport planning for more industrialized countries. In Great Britain and the Netherlands, for instance, transport development programs are underway which involve studies of equivalent scope.

Several of these studies are now (1970) in progress. Future emphasis will probably concentrate mainly on the regional studies.

References

1. Anonymous. 1968. "Baltimore faces the future with confidence." *The Dock and Harbour Authority* 49(Dec.):223-24 and 295-96.
2. ____. 1970. "Ship building and ship repairing." *The Dock and Harbour Authority* 51 (Jan.):393-94.
3. Evans, C.J. 1968. "Container handling in ports." *Proceedings of the 5th International Harbor Congress.* Paper 4-EV. Antwerp.
4. Getz, J.R., et al. 1968. *Design of a Cargo Liner in Light of the Development of General Cargo Transportation.* Trondheim: The Ship Research Institute of Norway. pp. 1-15.
5. International Cargo Handling Co-ordination Association. 1969. *Proceedings of the 9th International Conference (ICHCH) in Gothenburg, Sweden.* London: Central Office of ICHCH, Abford House, Wilton Road.
6. Jones, John H. 1968. "Ship turn-around time at the Port of Bangkok." *ASCE Journal of the Waterways and Harbors Division* 94(WW2):135-48.
7. Mettam, J.D. 1967. "Forecasting delays to

ship in port." *The Dock and Harbour Authority* 48(Apr.):369-402.
8. Morse, P.M. 1958. *Queues, Inventories and Maintenance*. New York: John Wiley and Sons, Inc.
9. Nielsen, E.F. 1969. "Container port engineering for the Port of Oakland." *Civil Engineering* (Jan.):40-43.
10. Ordemann, H. 1968. "Erfahrung in der Weiterentwicklung der Container-Lader fur Seeshiffe." *Proceedings of the 5th International Harbor Congress*. Paper 4-ORD. Antwerp.
11. Permanent International Association of Navigation Congresses. 1969. "Development conditions of container transport. Organization of the chain of transport. Economic and social aspects." *Proceedings of 22nd Congress of PIANC* s II - s 1.
12. Port of Antwerp. 1968. "Container and specialized steel terminal in the Churchilldock—Antwerp." *Proceedings of the 5th International Harbor Congress*. Special Paper. Antwerp.
13. Ratinckx, F. 1968. "Enkele aspekter van de container-portaalkranen in de haven van Antwerpen." *Proceedings of the 5th International Harbor Congress*. Paper 4-RA. Antwerp.
14. Sembler, E.C. 1967. "Eight-berth marine terminal in deep mud bay." *ASCE Journal of the Waterways and Harbors Division* 93(WW3):23-29.
15. Tooth, E.S. 1966. "Containerships in the ocean trades." *The Dock and Harbour Authority* 47(July):73-76.
16. ____. 1967. "The ISO Container Committee." *The Dock and Harbour Authority* 48(March):359-61.
17. Tozzoli, A.J. 1969. "Planning and construction of the Elizabeth N.J. Port Authority marine terminal." *Civil Engineering* (Jan.):34-39.
18. Turner, N.T. 1969. "For and against in containers, pallets and roll-on, roll off." *The Dock and Harbour Authority* 50(Dec): 389-90.

6 littoral drift and sedimentation problems

This chapter does not intend to mention basic aspects of littoral drift and sedimentation technology but to review the state of the art and recent technical developments in these fields. Littoral drift problems on seashores and sedimentation problems in estuaries and rivers are mentioned separately, emphasizing technological aspects of direct interest for the engineer who must solve the actual problems. By-passing technique and tracing of material transport (Appendix 4) are mentioned separately.

Littoral Drift

It has been known for about 30 years that longshore drift of alluvial material is related to the longshore flux of energy. Several formulas for computation of littoral drift magnitude (Q) as a function of longshore energy flux (E) exist. In Chapter 7 it is explained that the relationship, $Q = E \sin \alpha_o$, when Q is quantity of littoral drift, E is deep-water energy of wave action and α_o is the deep-water angle of incidence, could explain the shoreline geometry of many curved shores (5).

The so-called "Los Angeles formula" (3, 5, 30),

$$Q = \Sigma \tfrac{1}{2} k_1 \, we \, \sin 2\alpha_b$$

when Q is the total longshore material transport per year, w is the total work accomplished by all waves of a given period and direction in deep water during an average year, e is the wave energy coefficient at the breaker line for waves of a given period and direction, or the ratio between the distance between orthogonals in deep water and at the shoreline, α_b is the angle between wave crest at the breaker line and the shoreline, k_1 is the factor depending on dimensional units and empirical relations—it varies with beach slope, grain size, and other undetermined variables, is able to explain a number of shore features including cuspate forelands (see Figure 6.1a) like Dungeness, England, (Figure 7.7) and the size of the angle between two headland shores because two different angles of incidence (α_1 and α_2 in Figure 6.1b), will give the same amount of drift according to this formula (5). This is explained in detail in Chapter 7.

Generally, all formulas for calculating the rate of sand transport are of the type

$$Q_{\text{longshore}} = (k) E^n_{\text{longshore}} \quad 0.5 < n < 1$$

Inasmuch as the k-factor varies considerably with shore characteristics including material and profile, it is necessary to check available literature

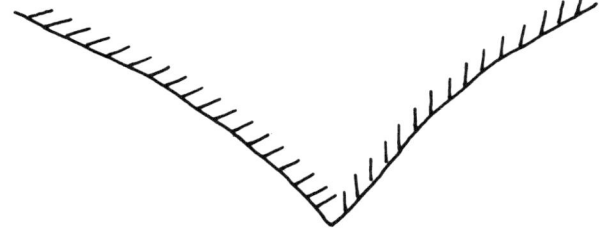

Fig. 6.1 a

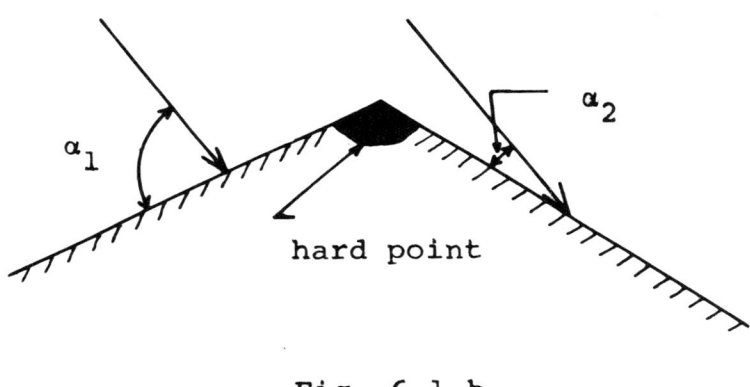

Fig. 6.1 b

Figure 6.1. (a) Cuspate foreland, an equilibrium feature (Chapter 7) and (b) headland in littoral drift equilibrium (Chapter 7).

on this subject in detail before any formula of this type is used. The reader is referred to numerous articles in *Proceedings on the Coastal Engineering Conferences* (Americal Society of Civil Engineers), to the *Japanese Harbor Engineering Manual* by the Bureau of Construction of Harbors, Tokyo, and most recently to papers published in the *Proceedings of the PIANC* (Permanent International Navigation Congress), 1969, II - s 4. The paper by F. M. Abecasis et al. in these proceedings (1) reviews some of the existing formulas including the following by the U.S. Army Corps of Engineers:

$$Q = 1.4\,(10^{-2})\,(H_o^2)\,(C_o^2)\,k^2 \sin\alpha_b \cos\alpha_b$$

when Q is the littoral drift quantity in meters³ per second, H_o is the wave amplitude in deep water, C_o is the wave celerity in deep water, k is the refraction coefficient, α_b is the breaker angle. This formula suffers from lack of consideration of sediment characteristics and assumes "normal littoral drift sand." Under average conditions it does, however, give figures for the quantity of drift of the right order of magnitude. It is necessary to know the wave energy input in great detail.

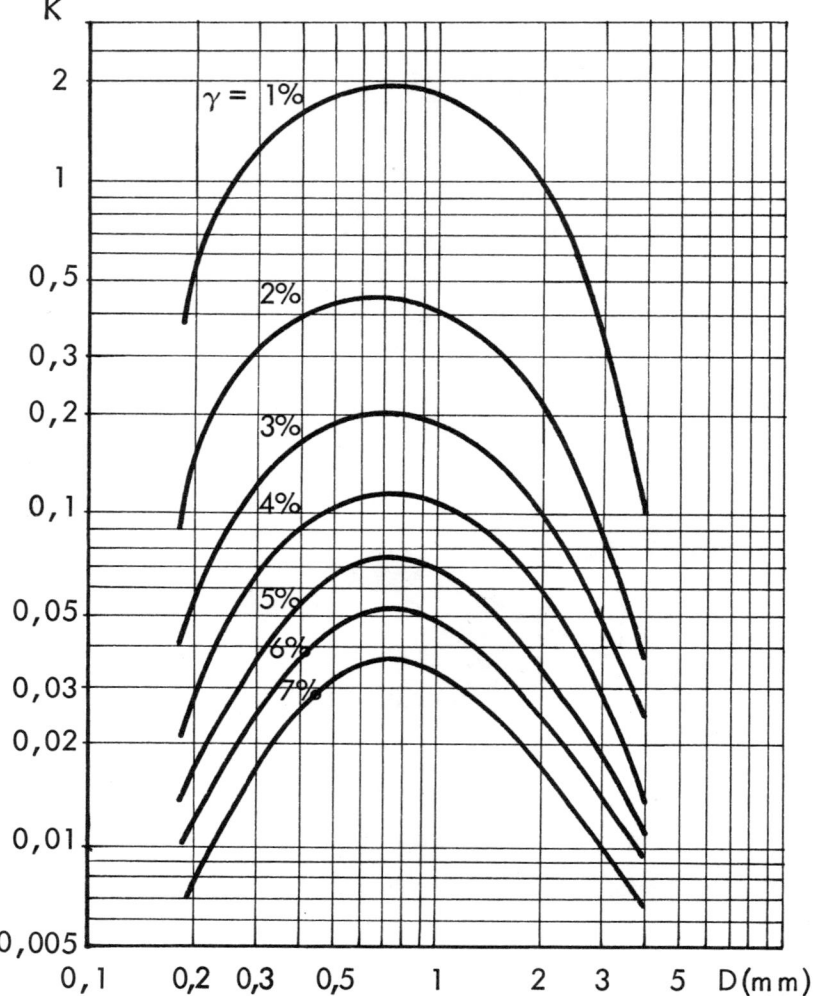

Figure 6.2. The k-factor by Bonnefille et Pernecker as function of γ_0 and D (1).

The formulas by Larras and by Bonnefille and Pernecker mentioned in Reference 1 (*see also*, J. Larras, "Cubes de sable charriés par la houle parallèlement a la cote," *Annales des Ponts et Chausees*, March-April 1966, and R. Bonnefille and L. Pernecker, "Etude théorique et expérimentale du transport littoral." *Bulletin de la Direction des Etudes et Recherches, Electricité de France*, no. 3, 1967) are almost identical and do not suffer the above mentioned drawback.

The formula by Bonnefille and Pernecker has

$$Q = k\left(\frac{\gamma_o}{2.75}, D\right)(H_o^3/T)\,[f(\alpha)/f(20°)]$$

where Q is the littoral drift quantity in meters³ per day, k is a function shown graphically in Figure 6.2–it depends on wave steepness, deep-water wave steepness γ_o and median grain diameter of

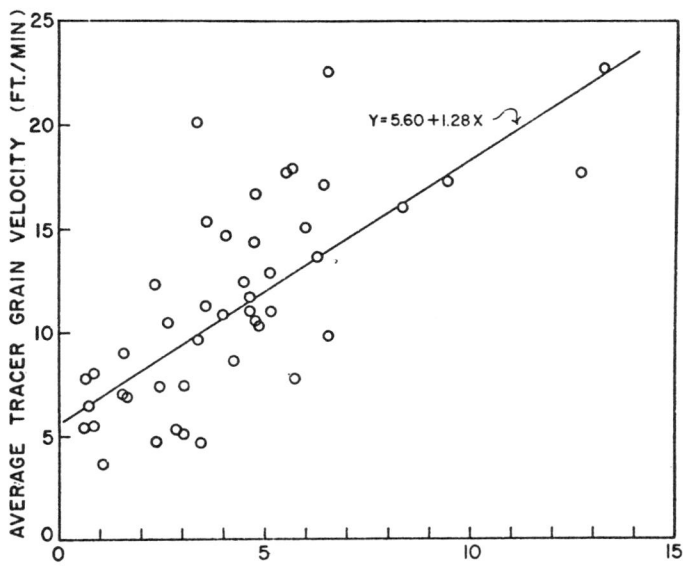

Figure 6.3. Correlation between longshore wave energy and tracer grain velocity (23).

material D, H_o is deep-water wave height, T is wave period, $f(\alpha) = \sin(7\alpha_o/4)$ (see Chapter 7), $f(20°) = f(\alpha)$ for $\alpha_o = 20°$.

The difficulty with such formulas is that they represent an integration of major order disregarding all details. It is, therefore, a matter of "good luck" that they give a useful result. Bijker in Reference 4 suggests a more detailed method of semi theoretical nature and computes the quantity of drift $Q_i, i+1$ between two depths h_i and h_{i+1}, as shown at the bottom of the page, when c_{i+1} and c_i are the wave celerities corresponding to depths h_{i+1} and h_i and k_{i+1} and k_i are the corresponding refraction coefficients. For computation, a "characteristic wave period," based on experiments, was found to be 1.2 (T_m), where T_m equals the mean zero crossing period, k_m is the refraction coefficient and ϕ_m, the angle between wave crests and the shoreline referring to the mean depth of the section under consideration.

Others attempted to investigate the relation between the longshore energy flux and the material transport considering the migration of single grains. No distinction was made between material transport in suspension and as bedload. Two examples, both using fluorescent tracers, should be mentioned here.

Figure 6-3 (23) shows the relation between average tracer velocity and alongshore energy computed as

$$E_i = 1/10 \, \omega \, H_b^2 \, (L_b/T) \sin 2\phi$$

referred to as Adachi's formula (2). E_i is the alongshore energy in foot-pounds per minute per foot

$$Q_{i,i+1} = \frac{(h_i^2 + 1)(c_{i+1})}{k_{i+1}^2} - \frac{(h_i^2)(c_i)}{k_i^2} \quad k_m^2 \sin 2\phi_m,$$

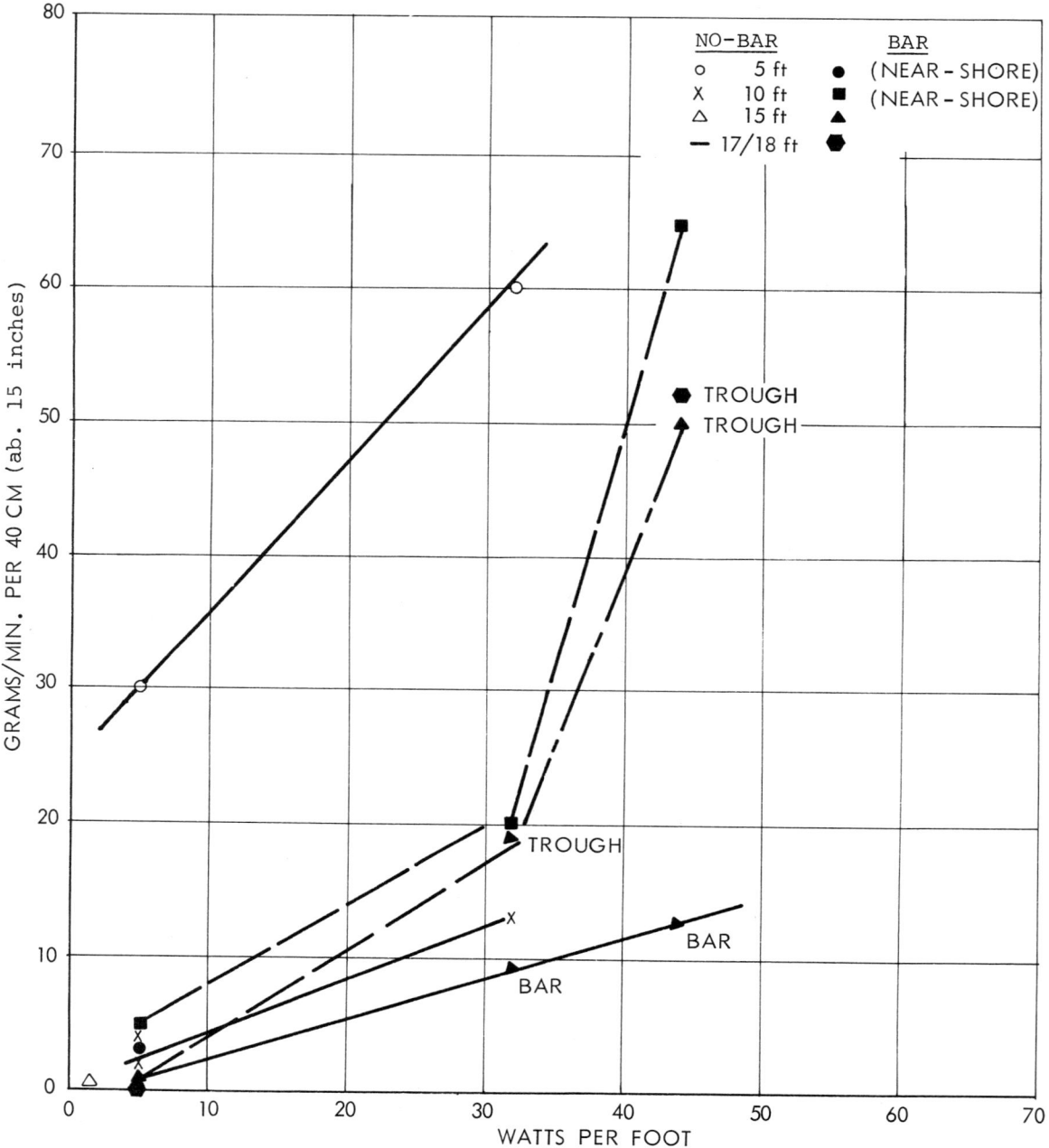

Figure 6.4a. Longshore drift as function of longshore wave energy (Bruun, 1969, (12) and Thornton, 1969, (53)).

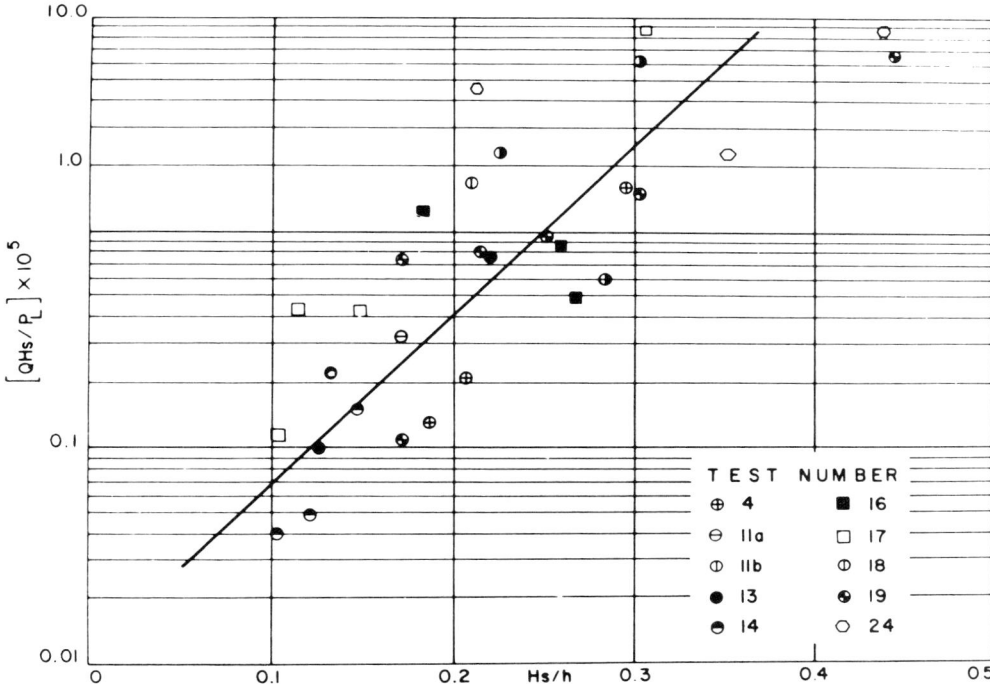

Figure 6.4b. Longshore drift as function of longshore wave energy (Bruun, 1969, (12) and Thornton, 1969, (53)).

of beach; ω is specific gravity of sea water; H_b is average breaker height; L_b is wave length at breaking; T is the wave period; ϕ is the angle of incidence at wave breaking.

It may be noted that there seems to be a trend towards a linear relationship between grain velocity and alongshore wave energy calculated for the surf zone for a great number of places on the California shore. Ingle does not specify to which sections of the nearshore bottom profile his results refer. Such research was undertaken by Bruun using fluorescent tracers (10). Figure 6-4a shows longshore drift as a function of longshore wave energy for various depths and sections of the bottom profile, including trough as well as bar. Based on these tests, Bruun concludes that longshore transport apparently increases with longshore energy whether the trough or the bar section is considered, but that not enough results are available to draw any wide-range conclusion. The importance of the longshore currents combined with stir-up activity by the waves may be noted from the results for the higher wave energy levels.

Thornton (53) continued the experiments. Results indicated in Figure 6.4b also show that the bedload transport is related to the depth of water and longshore energy flux. Inman and Komar's simultaneous field measurements of the energy flux of breaking waves and the resulting longshore transport of sand in the surf zone made along three beaches for a variety of conditions (26) confirmed that the longshore transport of sand is directly proportional to the longshore component of wave power. The velocities measured by Ingle (23) and by Bruun (10) have the same order of magnitude for the same energy level. Ingle noted that when average median grain diameter exceeded 0.2 millimeters, grain velocity tended to drop and generally was less than 12 feet per minute longshore.

It is clear that the configuration of the beach and bottom profile is important for the mode as well as for the quantity of littoral drift. So far, this situation has not been considered by any of the existing formulas.

From laboratory as well as field experiments, it is known that waves with a high steepness ratio (Ho/Lo)—that means storm waves—mainly cause transport of material from the beach and toward the sea (erosion). Waves with a low steepness ratio (Ho/Lo) cause mainly shoreward movement. In the laboratory, the transition from "bar profiles," associated with high steepness ratios, to "swell profiles," which have no bar but a berm or platform on the beach, takes place at Ho/Lo ratios of about 0.024 to 0.028. In the field, a similar tendency is noted, but the Ho/Lo ratio for transition is much lower. There seems to be no general rule for its value (see Chapter 7 when Reference 12 gives results from investigations of fluctuations of beach and bottom profiles on the Danish North Sea Coast and at Mission Bay, California, which confirm the quantitative similarity between laboratory and field results. In California there were certain indications that profiles in Mission Bay decreased steepness already at $Ho/Lo = 0.01$).

The laboratory experiments also clearly indicated the difference between suspension transport, which is mainly a result of wave breaking causing heavy turbulence, and bedload transport by a combination of wave induced and other currents. This is mentioned in more detail in Chapter 7.

The influence of coastal structures on the development of beach and bottom profiles depends upon the reflection of wave energy, including the downrush which causes extra stir up of material in front of the wall. Breakwaters and sea walls, particularly of the vertical fully reflecting type, often cause considerable erosion and perhaps, final collapse of the structure. As explained in Chapter 3, it is necessary to provide toe protection in front of such structures if they are erected on alluvial or other kinds of erosive material. In coastal protection technology, energy-absorbing structures are preferable. In harbor engineering, reflection shall also be as small as possible to avoid adverse conditions for navigation.

Currents in the nearshore zone are mainly tidal currents, or they are caused by wave breaking setting up longshore currents by the inflow of water and momentum caused by the breaking waves.

Various theories for longshore currents, including the momentum approach by Putnam et al. (48) and by Eagleson (19) and the continuity approach by Bruun (6) and by Inman (25), exist. According to Galvin (20), the continuity approach, which lets water flow in by wave breaking and out by the "rip-currents" (which are transversal currents passing water from wave breaking out again), seems to be the most applicable and reliable approach, particularly for bar profiles. But the problem of longshore currents by wave action is very complex, and no theoretical approach can ever be appointed to be just right.

It is not known how far out in the ocean the longshore littoral transport of material extends. If the definition of littoral drift is associated with wave action and longshore currents by waves, the area inside the 30-foot contour is the most active on exposed shores like the Atlantic and Pacific Coast, but as proven by Trask (55), drift still by-passes the southern California promotories up to 60 feet deep. Sand is stirred up by wave action at much greater depth as demonstrated by vessels steaming in the North Sea during heavy storms, getting sand on their deck at 100-foot and even greater depths. A considerable transport may also take place in large sand waves or sand humps migrating by current action on the bottom. This is mentioned later in this chapter with reference to the situation in the Elbe River in Germany and in more detail in Chapter 7 referring to American, Dutch and Danish examples.

Littoral Barriers on Shores

Definition

A littoral barrier is an obstruction to normal littoral drift along the shore. It may be natural, like a tidal inlet (Figure 6.5); a promontory extending far out into the sea in deep water, like some of the headlands in California (55), Hawaii, India, Italy, Portugal and Spain; or a shore-parallel

Littoral Drift 207

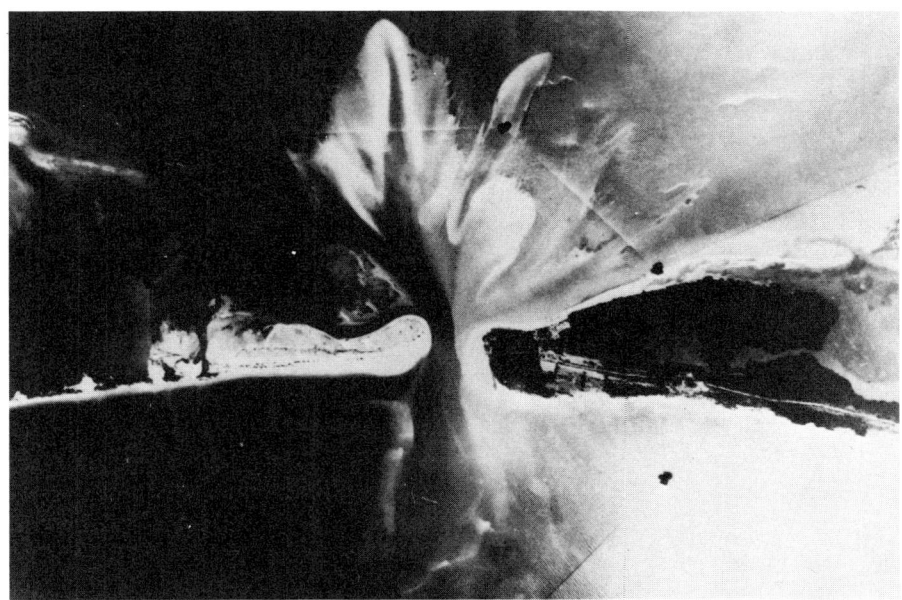

Figure 6.5. Red-Fish Pass, Florida Gulf coast (7).

island, which by wave diffraction at both ends of the "breakwater" causes littoral transport in opposite directions toward the middle of the shore behind the island, causing the formation of a "tombolo" as explained in Chapter 7. Man-made barriers include jetties and groins, dredged channels and man-made sand traps of many kinds.

Practical Examples

A group of "intentional barriers" in the form of T-groins are located at Deerfield Beach, Florida (13). These groins are so short that they only obstruct a smallpart of the littoral drift but they have succeeded in creating a number of "tombola" as explained in Chapter 7 with reference to Figure 7.36. Figure 6.6a and 6b shows a dreadful example of a littoral barrier, the Port of Hirtshals on the Danish North Sea coast. A heavy littoral drift, perhaps 500,000 to 1,000,000 cubic yards per year comes from the west by strong wave action. The harbor was completed in the 1930s, but even before its completion, large quantities of sand had deposited on its updrift (west) side in "tongues" along the jetty. Most of the sand did by-pass the updrift jetty with its sand catch extension and was deposited partly in a smaller shoal just inside the jetty and partly by a large clockwise eddy current in a large shoal on the downdrift side (see Figure 6.6b where the breaking waves clearly indicate where the shoals are located). The downdrift shoal with depths between 10 and 20 feet is gradually growing larger by deposits ranging between 50,000 and 200,000 cubic yards per year. Continued maintenance dredging is necessary in the about 25 to 28-foot deep entrance channel to the port. The order of magnitude of the annual dredging is 150,000 to 250,000 cubic yards per year with some increasing tendency. This case is now subject to further study. The solution to the problem seems to be a trap arrangement that means increased dredging at proper places to decrease the possibility of rapid shoaling of the entrance channel. A detached shore-parallel breakwater on the updrift side as built at Ventura, southern California, may be a useful (but rather expensive) improvement. Full transfer of material may then be

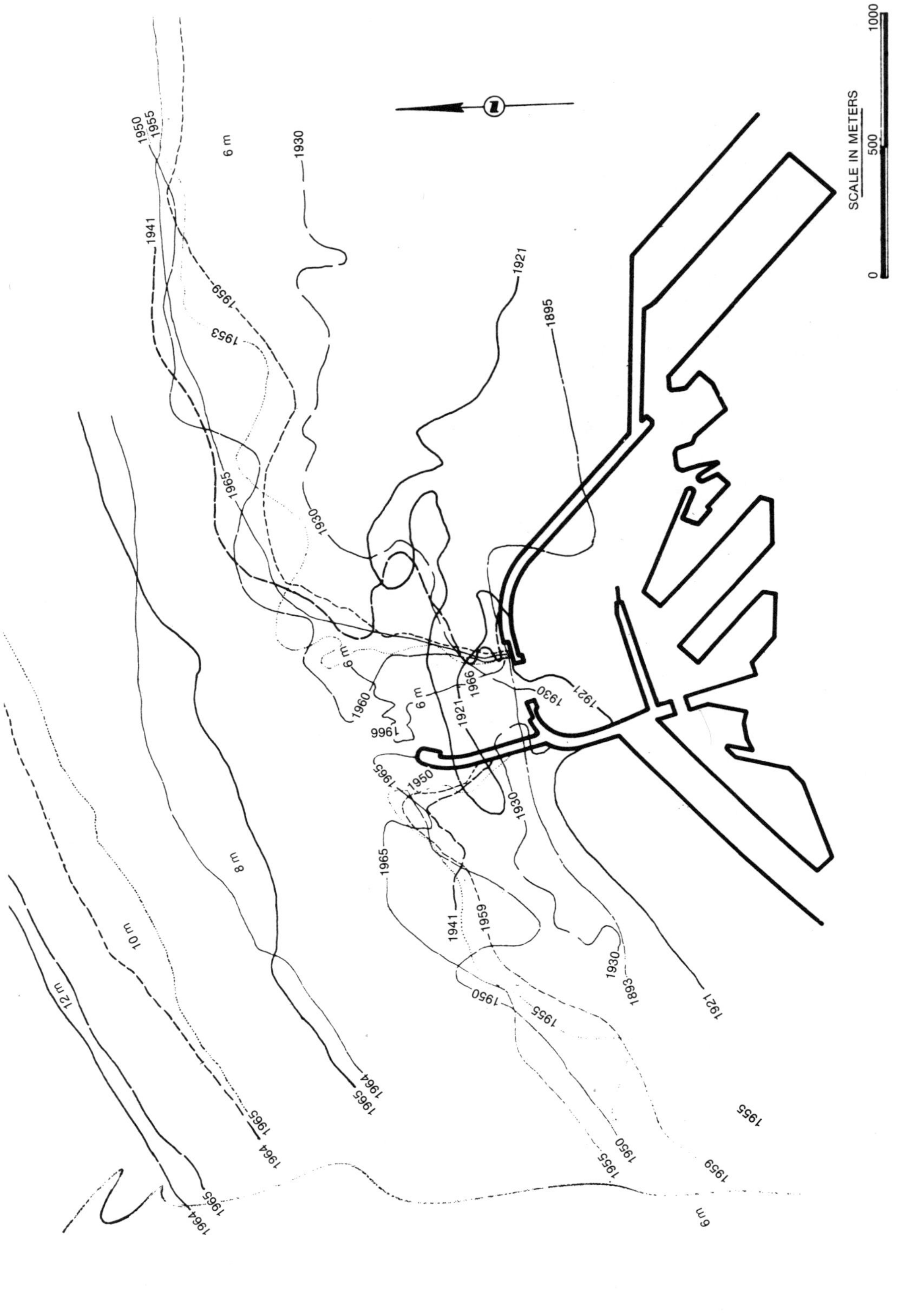

208   Port Engineering

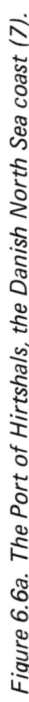

Figure 6.6a. The Port of Hirtshals, the Danish North Sea coast (7).

Littoral Drift 209

Figure 6.6b. The Port of Hirtshals, the Danish North Sea coast (7).

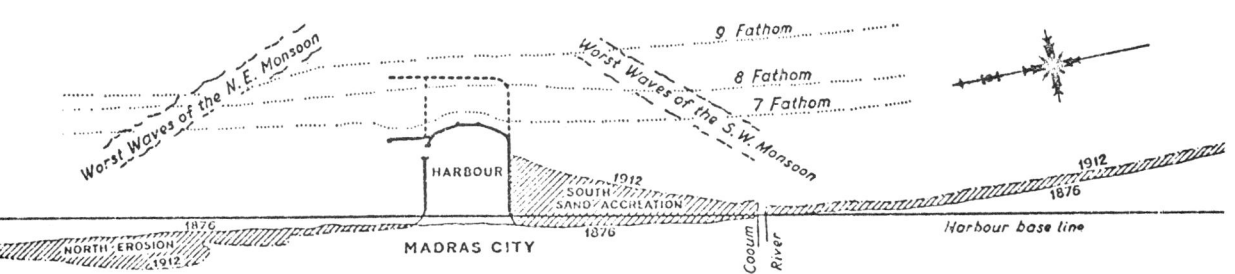

Figure 6.7. The Port of Madras, India (16).

210 Port Engineering

needed. Further extension of the updrift jetty will have time-limited effect only; but due to economy it is the most likely solution which at the same time will protect the entrance better for wave action.

A third good example is the Port of Madras, India (Figure 6.7). The harbor breakwaters extend outward about 1,000 meters (3,300 feet) from the original low water shoreline (1876). Up to 1913, a large triangular area of sand, about 260 acres, had accumulated on the south side of the harbor. On the north side, a considerable shoreline recession had taken place. The old entrance to the harbor was centrally situated with respect to the breakwater, facing east, and the sand drifting northward found slack water between the pier heads and settled there. The result was that, before the entrance was closed, it was shallowing at the rate of about 1 foot per year. In 1902 the project of a northeast entrance was started, including a 400-meter (1,300-foot) long sheltering arm, which was completed in 1911. The result of closing the old entrance and extending the eastern arm was continued deposition along the whole eastern jetty face, which would have become more and more pronounced if it had not been checked by comprehensive dredging operations. Another sheltering arm was later built at the southern (updrift) corner of the harbor, where accumulating sand is checked by a suction dredger mounted on the arm, which pumps the spoil into hopper barges moored inside the harbor. All these difficulties could probably have been avoided by model experiments in advance, but the hydraulic model technique was unknown when the harbor was first built in 1800s. For further details on the Port of Madras, the reader is referred to H. F. Cornick's book (16). A new large breakwater expanding the harbor considerably northward is being completed.

A similar situation exists at the Santa Barbara Harbor in California. Reference is made to Trask (54) and to several other ports in California, such as Ventura and Channel Islands harbors.

Source and Drain

Sediment-transport problems on seashores and their relation to man-made structures can most often and most conveniently be explained by the terminologies *source* and *drain*.

A *source of materials* is a coastal zone, submerged or emerged, which delivers materials to other coastal areas. A source might be an area where erosion takes place—a shoal in the sea, located on the downdrift side of a jetty-improved inlet; the shallow area in front of an inlet that has been closed; a river that transports sand material to the littoral coastal zone; or sand drift from dunes to the beach. Artifical nourishment to a beach is also a source.

A *drain of materials* is a coastal zone where materials are deposited. Natural drains include marine forelands of any kind, such as spits, recurved spits, tombolos, cuspate forelands, angular forelands, etc. (See Chapter 7.) The drains may also be a bay, inlet, or shoal. Artificial drains include man-made constructions such as jetties, groins, dredged sand traps, inadequately designed and inadequately constructed harbors, etc.

In practical coastal engineering and littoral drift technology, the following rules are valid:

1. Coastal protection should be built so that it functions as a drain. It should, therefore, have a source but not a drain on the updrift side. If there is a drain, the coastal protection cannot be expected to work satisfactorily unless materials are supplied artificially to the shore.
2. A harbor (or an improved inlet) on a littoral drift coast should not act as a drain. It is, therefore, desirable to have no source area or only a limited source area on the updrift side or on either side of it. It is best if it has a drain on the updrift side or on both sides.

If these two simple terminologies were always remembered and used for planning harbors on littoral drift shores, many problems of sedimentation and many costly mistakes could have been—and can still be—avoided.

Littoral Drift and Coastal Structures

By-passing by Nature

By-passing is the way that material, after a short interruption caused by an inlet, pass, chan-

Littoral Drift 211

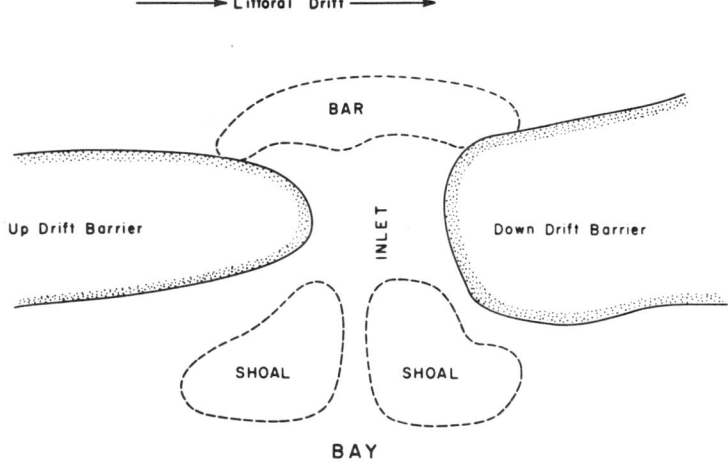

Figure 6.8. Coastal inlet with predominant bar by-passing (8 and 12).

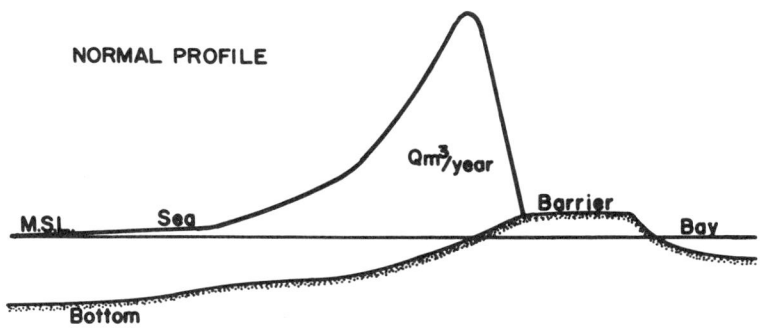

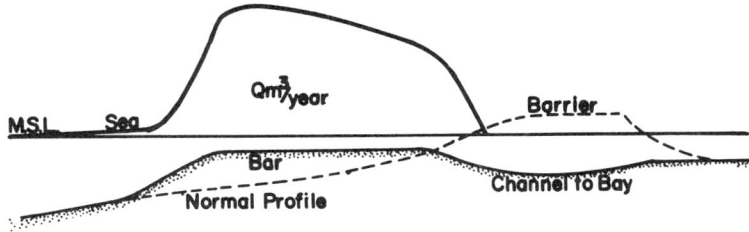

Figure 6.9. The principle involved in by-passing on a submerged bar (8 and 12).

nel, jetty or other kind of *littoral barrier*, is given back to the normal littoral drift zone a short distance downdrift from the littoral barrier. If nature did not by-pass sand across inlets, passes and channels on seashores, a number of *marine forelands* including barriers, spits and entire peninsulas would not exist (see Chapter 7). A typical example of this is Florida, which was built of sand washed down by rivers and streams from the Appalachian highland and carried southward, crossing estuaries and tidal inlets, for final deposition in the huge barrier and ridge systems.

The two main principles in sand by-passing by natural action are by-passing on an offshore bar and by-passing by tidal flow action. Most cases present a combination of these two methods (7, 12).

Bar By-passing—Limited Tidal Action

The Principle Involved

Figure 6.8 shows a barrier with an inlet. Littoral drift material passes along the barrier. At the downdrift end, it continues on its way across the inlet on a submerged bar, the extent and depth of which depends on the amount and character of the material which by-passes and the intensity of wave and current action. By increasing amounts of littoral materials, the bar area increases and depths decrease. Increased wave action results in a smaller and more streamlined bar with greater depth. Stronger longshore currents also produce a narrower and more streamlined bar with perhaps one predominant channel, while weaker longshore currents may result in more and shallower channels. The mechanics of bar by-passing may be a more or less continuous process, or it may partly take place in greater irregular sand waves or humps which migrate across the inlet on the bar.

From this, it is clear that if satisfactory natural by-passing is to be established, the criterion must be that the longshore drift capacity be kept on the same level, regardless of the existence of the inlet. Knowing the distribution of littoral drift and longshore currents at different depths in the normal beach and bottom profile, it is possible to estimate the necessary depth for a certain width or the necessary width for a certain depth of the bar, both for a certain wave action and longshore current action (Figure 6.9). Meanwhile, wave and current action varies, causing irregularities in by-passing. Experience demonstrates that such by-passing cannot exist without considerable wave action and that the depth over the bar is usually limited to the breaker depth for normal and predominant storm waves. Width of the bar is, as previously mentioned, mainly a function of the velocity of the longshore current.

It is obvious that man has few chances to arrange satisfactory navigation and bar by-passing conditions simultaneously because breaking waves necessary for by-passing are hazardous to navigation. This is the reason why inlets with bar by-passing are usually only useful for small crafts. Navigation improvements have only limited interest and are often very difficult to justify and finance. Examples of inlets with bar by-passing include unimproved as well as improved conditions.

Unimproved Conditions

Figures 6.10 and 6.11 show Matanzas and Ponce de Leon inlets on the Florida east coast, where littoral drift is about 400,000 to 500,000 cubic yards per year to the south. Both of these inlets are very old and have probably been almost stationary where they are now located for hundreds of years. The normal tidal range is about 3 feet, but tidal prisms are rather small in both cases.

Matanzas Inlet, with 3 to 5-foot depths on the bar, is an example of very irregular bar by-passing. A shifting channel sometimes gets too close to the downdrift beach, causing serious erosion of this beach. This happened in the period from 1955 to 1958. The inlet is not very useful for navigation because of its ocean side shoals.

Ponce de Leon Inlet has a half-moon shaped bar 8 to 10 feet deep. This bar is very unstable because of shifting channels, and sand transfer is very irregular causing irregular erosion of New Smyrna Beach on the downdrift side. An improvement of bypassing based on the depressed weir system (Chapter 8) is being completed.

Littoral Drift 213

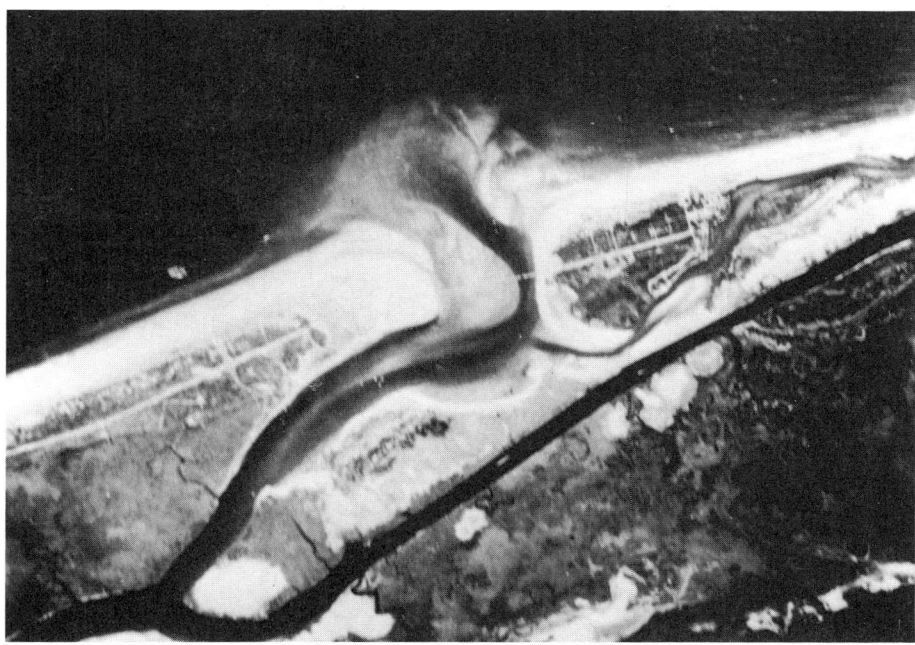

Figure 6.10. Matanzas Inlet, Florida (8 and 12).

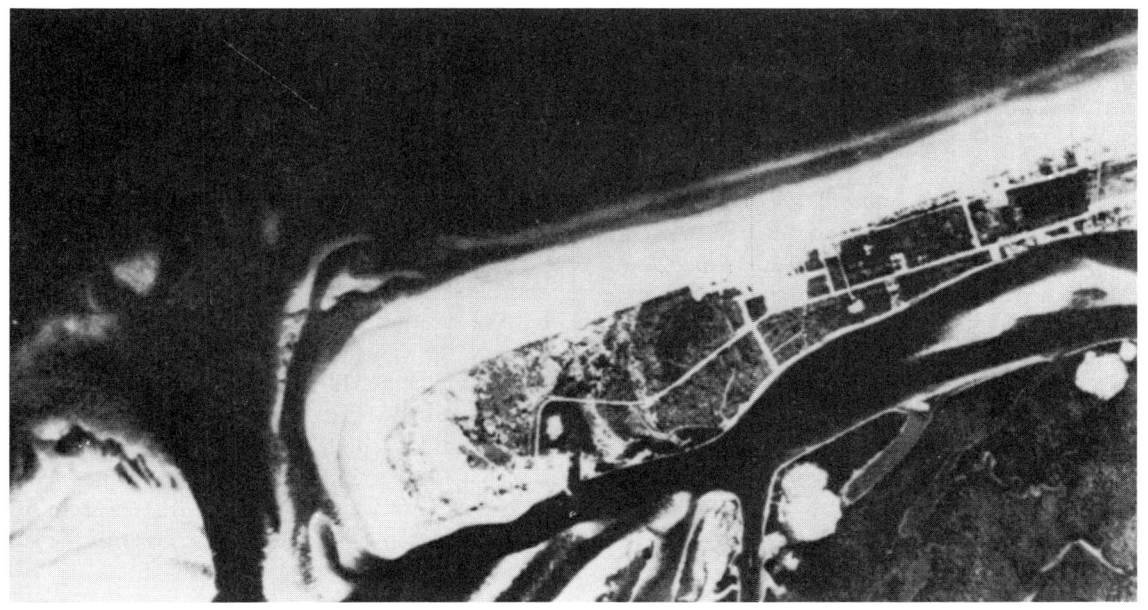

Figure 6.11. Ponce De Leon Inlet, Florida (7 and 8).

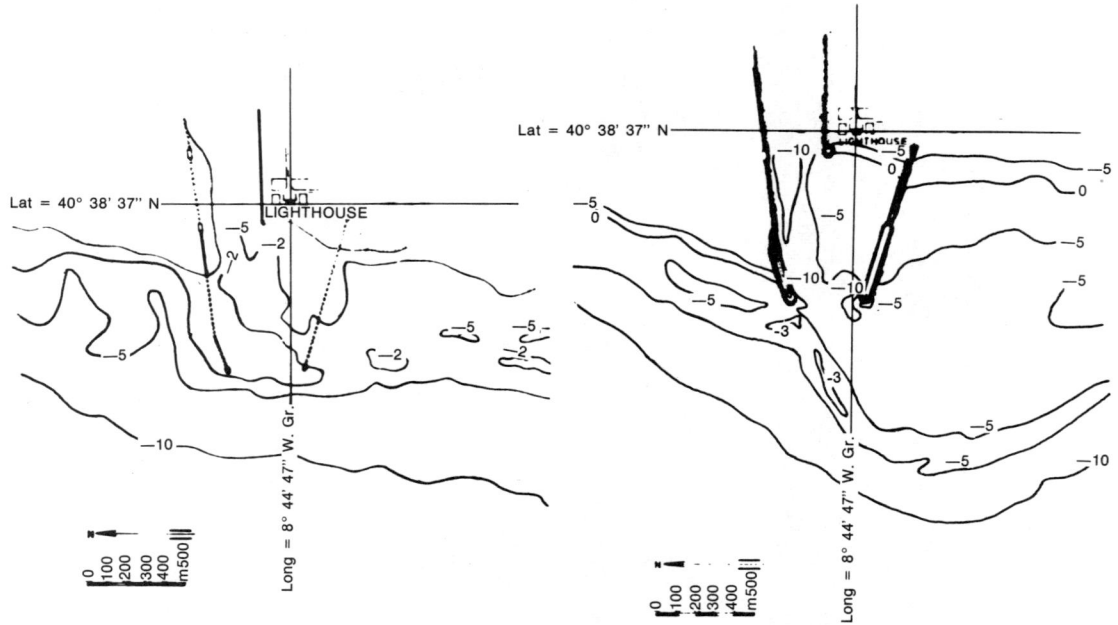

Figure 6.12. The development at Aveiro Harbor, Portugal, between 1950 and 1968 (1).

Improved Conditions

The inlet of Aveiro on the Portugese coast north of Mondego River, as described by Abecasis et al. (1), shows a similar development on a larger scale, but tidal flow resulting in a half-moon shaped bar is of more importance (Figure 6.12).

The history of the inlet dates from the tenth century and shows a number of migrating as well as stable periods. Attempts to stabilize the inlet started in the seventeenth century, but only one project, an artifically cut inlet completed in 1808, gave a long-range result. During the following 140-year period, sand migrated on a bar across the inlet in a predominantly southward direction. During years of normal weather conditions, the entrance was merely fixed by a jetty built along the southern bank extending to the low water line. Navigation in the inlet was considerable even if the configuration of the shoreline at the entrance was changeable and the original project was not well maintained.

From 1949 to 1959, the improvement of the entrance, consisting of two converging jetties 800 meters long, had a beneficial effect on the access conditions which used to be at levels of -2 meters below tide. As explained by Abecasis et al. (1), the jetties developed into a severe littoral barrier causing strong accumulation of sand on the updrift (north) side (Figure 6.12). The shoreline moved seaward almost to the extreme end of the jetty bottom profiles, steepening considerably. Southwest of the entrance, a large shoal accumulation took place, apparently a result of an eddy current, as is well known from other harbor installations under similar conditions, e.g., the above mentioned Hirtshals, Denmark (7). As a consequence of the various accumulations updrift, erosion became serious in an extensive area south of the jetties and has at this time extended about 10 kilometers downdrift (south) where the shoreline has receded up to 150 meters from 1954 to 1969. This trend continues.

Littoral Drift 215

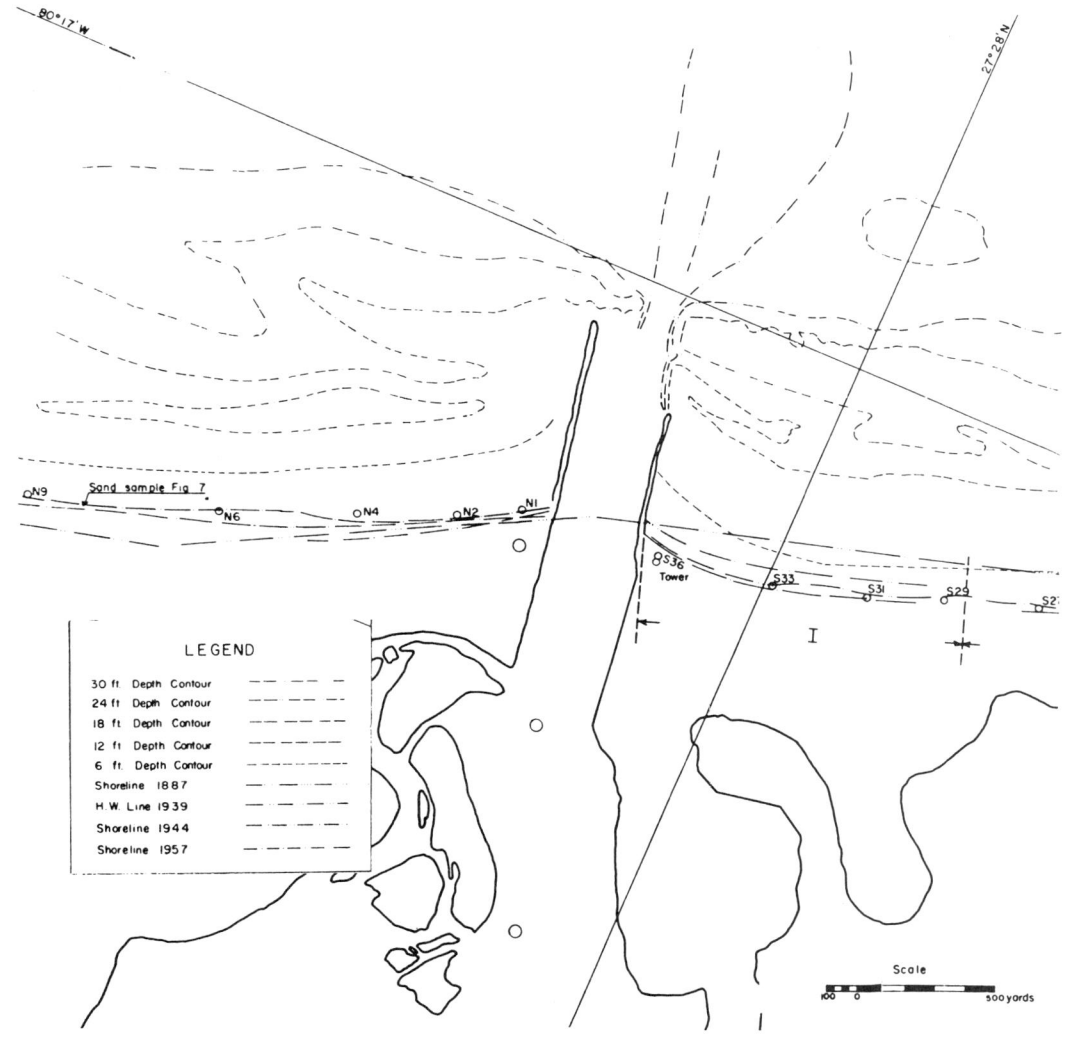

Figure 6.13. Ft. Pierce Inlet, Florida (7, 8, and 15).

Model tests are now being performed in Portugal to develop a protection scheme which includes structural works as well as artificial nourishment based on material dredged in the entrance as well as material transferred across the entrance. According to Reference 1, a similar situation is developing at the Figueira da Foz entrance south of Aveiro.

The Fort Pierce Inlet on the lower east coast of Florida (Figure 6-13) should be mentioned here even though tidal currents play an important role in its natural transfer arrangement. Meanwhile, it is unlikely that sand would be transferred without the existence of a rather wide rock reef with 10 to 12-foot depths on the downdrift side of the inlet.

Investigations concluded by the Coastal Engineering Laboratory of the University of Florida (15) show that out of a littoral drift of some 200,000 to 250,000 cubic yards per year, only about 20,000 cubic yards are deposited on the up-

216   Port Engineering

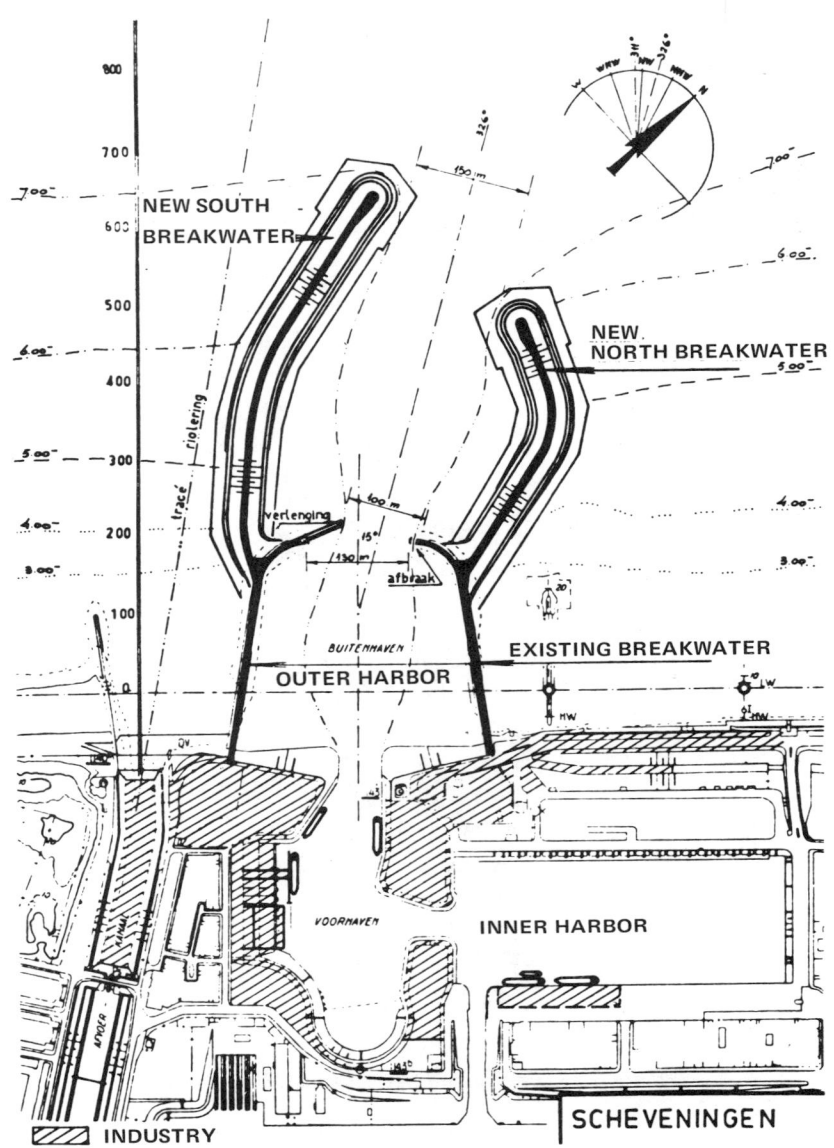

Figure 6.14. The Port of Scheveningen, Holland (Port of Scheveningen brocure).

drift side, while about 160,000 to 200,000 cubic yards pass through or over the 2,000-foot updrift jetty. Approximately 40,000 cubic yards of this quantity are dredged or deposited on bay shoals; 120,000 to 160,000 cubic yards are jetted out in the ocean again by the very strong ebb currents (5 to 6 feet per second). Part of the material jetted out, perhaps 40,000 cubic yards, is lost to deep water; about 20,000 cubic yards are washed back into the inlet channel through the south jetty; and about 100,000 to 150,000 cubic yards are evidently given back to the downdrift side but apparently

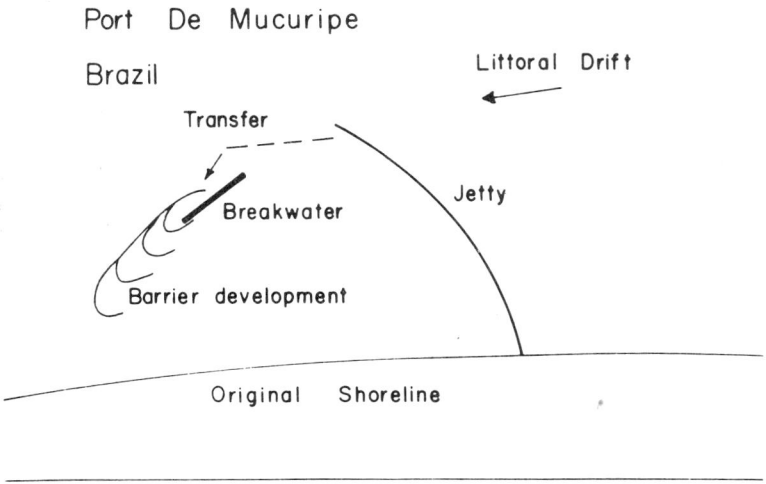

Figure 6.15. Port De Mucuripe, Brazil (12 and 58).

not until some few miles farther downdrift. Leeside erosion, in the amount of about 100,000 cubic yards per year, occurs in the first two to four miles south of the inlet, according to the 1958 survey.

How this by-passing mechanism works is not known, but there is evidence that the flat rock reef with depths of 10 to 12 feet beginning at the extreme end of the 1200-foot south jetty and extending downdrift plays an important role in this transfer action. For further information on this interesting problem, see References 7 and 15. Sand nourishment from offshore source was initiated south of the entrance in 1970 using a submersible crawler type hydraulic dredge unit which pumps material directly to the beach.

By-passing at Harbors

Figure 6.14 shows projects for breakwaters now (1970) under construction to improve the fishing port of Scheveningen on the Dutch coast (refer to Port of Scheveningen brochure). The alignment of the jetties was determined by model experiments intending to secure maximum material by-pass by flood currents and minimum deposit in the harbor entrance.

Interesting examples of giving nature a hand in by-passing are shores suggested for Port De Muccuripo, Brazil, and for Santa Barbara, California, the former shown in Figure 6.15 (12, 58). Material accumulated at the extreme end of the updrift jetty will be pumped across the harbor entrance to the outside of a smaller breakwater where it will be transferred downdrift by the gradual development of a barrier.

Another interesting case of by-passing sand at a harbor by natural action is found at the La Guaira Harbor, Venezuela. This harbor has the extreme end of its nail-shaped updrift jetty located at 18-meter (60-foot) depth. There is considerable littoral drift from east to west caused by heavy wave action (waves up to 20 feet from north east). Some years ago, a tanker ran aground midway out on the jetty in 30 to 40 feet of water and accumulated in a short time a great amount of sand behind it, demonstrating the heavy drift. So far, there has been no accumulation at the extreme end of the jetty, and it is believed that the great depth may be responsible for this. The material disappears downslope.

218   Port Engineering

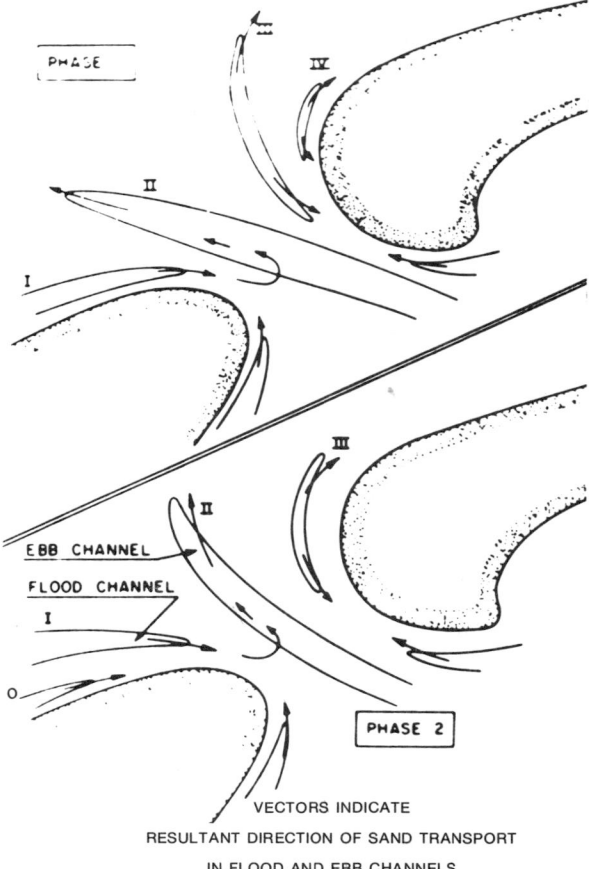

Figure 6.16. Migration of tidal channels (12).

Principles Involved in By-passing by Tidal Flow Action

Unimproved Inlets

In general, sand transfer by tidal flow takes place in two different ways, namely by migration of channels and bars and by transport of sand by tidal flow in the channel. Tidal channels in inlets, particularly those running between the gorge and the ocean, are subject to migration. This means that they change location continuously, moving from one side of the inlet to the other. In Figure 6.16, this principle is demonstrated by Phases 1 and 2 of a tidal channel system. Channels in Phase 1 are numbered I, II, III and IV. In Phase 2 the locations of these channels have changed compared to Phase 1, and a new channel, 0, has developed. In this example, the channels move from left to right, and bars or shoals between the channels move in the same direction with the result that a bar occasionally joins the downdrift coast by waves and littoral currents.

In most cases, migration of tidal channels takes place in the direction of the littoral drift. Sand is transported over the bar under the influence of waves and deposited on the updrift bank of the channels, thus forcing the shifting.

In the vicinity of tidal inlets, the generally strong tidal currents in the inlet change the littoral drift pattern entirely. Along the uninterrupted coastline, wave action is generally the predominant cause for the transportation of material. In the vicinity of tidal inlets, however, transport of material takes place under the combined effect of waves and tidal currents.

In tidal rivers, estuaries and inlets, tidal channels can usually be identified as either *flood* or *ebb* channels. Flood channels carry predominantly flood flow, causing a resultant sand transport in a bayward direction; they usually have a shoal at the end. Ebb channels carry predominantly ebb flow and have a resultant material transport seaward and a bar or shoal at the end. See Figure 6.17 where different types of ebb and flood channels have been indicated (57).

Jetty-Improved Inlets

During the first phase of a jetty improvement, a great amount of sand is generally accumulated along the updrift beach. With an increasing amount of accumulation, by-passing of material gradually develops. Adequate by-passing in such cases needs considerable wave action to move the flushed material shoreward again. The presence of a specially shaped breakwater may develop an advantageous diffraction and refraction wave pattern for moving sand back to the beach.

At tidal inlets, material is often accumulated on the inner shoals, and this decreases the amount

Sketch of the mutual evasion of flood- and ebb-channels by means of a forked tongue

Sketch of a mutual evasion with flank attack of flood-and ebb-channels

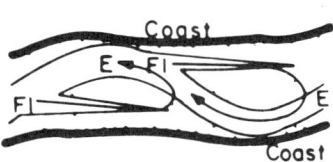

Sketch of so-called circulating sand currents, the sand moving up-stream in flood-channel, downstream in ebb-channel

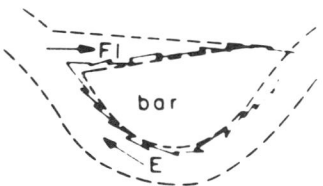

Sketch of the true up-and down-stream movement of the sand in so-called circulating sand currents. A grain of sand may come back to its original place; dredging may be of small avail.

Figure 6.17. Ebb and flood channel characteristics (12).

of material available for by-passing. It sometimes provides a convenient source for artificial by-passing by pumping material from the shoal to the downdrift side. Examples of inlets with by-passing by tidal flow action include unimproved as well as improved conditions.

Unimproved Inlets

Examples of predominant tidal flow by-passing are the two groups of estuaries which form the southern part of the Dutch coast (12, Figure 6.18). The southernmost inlet, the Wester Schelde, forms part of the seaway to the port of Antwerp, Belgium. Its tidal prism is about 1,600 feet miles and the cross-section near the entrance about 865,000 square feet. The mean tidal range in this area is 10 to 12 feet.

Large quantities of sand are by-passed across this wide estuary by the tidal flow. However, the downdrift shore is insufficiently nourished, primarily because of a deep tidal channel close to the shoreline which carries the material away.

The next inlet to the north, the Ooster Schelde, has almost the same size as the Wester Schelde, but tidal currents, although equal in strength, are less concentrated, apparently result-

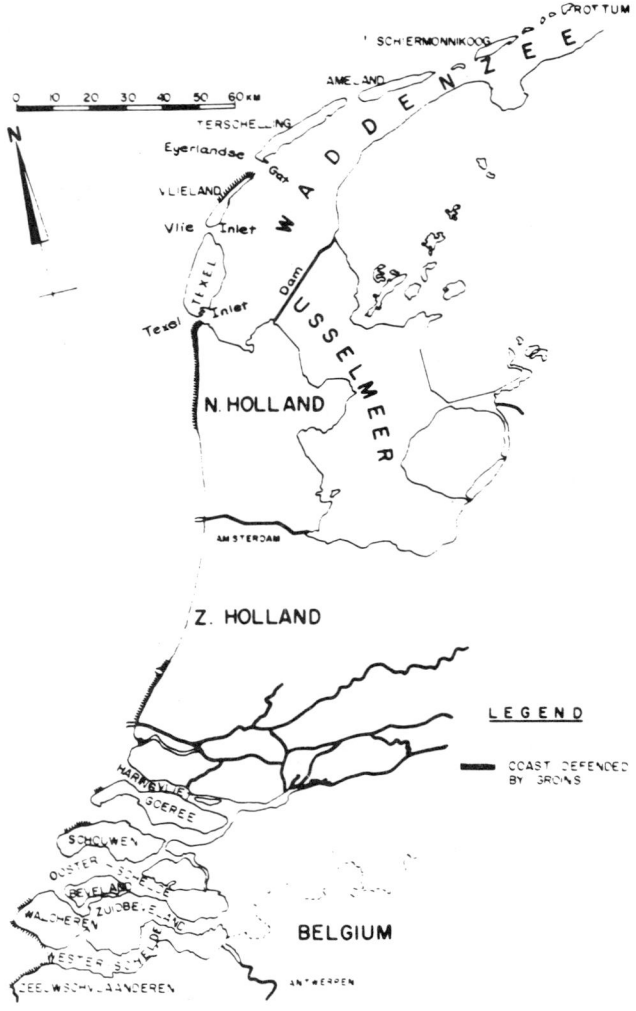

Figure 6.18. The Dutch coastline (12).

ing in better sand transfer that sufficiently nourishes the downdrift island coast.

Farther to the north, the size of the inlets decreases. Therefore, the ratio of littoral drift to tidal flow increases, resulting in improved by-passing.

At the northwest group of tidal inlets on the Dutch coast, a chain of barrier islands is located at a varying distance from the mainland. The area between the islands and the mainland is called Wadden. The Wadden Sea is formed of tidal sand and mud flats which are dry at low water. Numerous tidal channels exist. Tidal range is 5 to 7 feet.

Free development of the Texel Inlet has been hampered by a heavy protection along its south bank, which is responsible for the formation of a very deep channel (maximum depth over 150 feet), with high concentration of currents and adverse effects on by-passing.

The inlet of Vlie, which has had more freedom in its development, adequately presents by-passing, even if it has almost the same flow

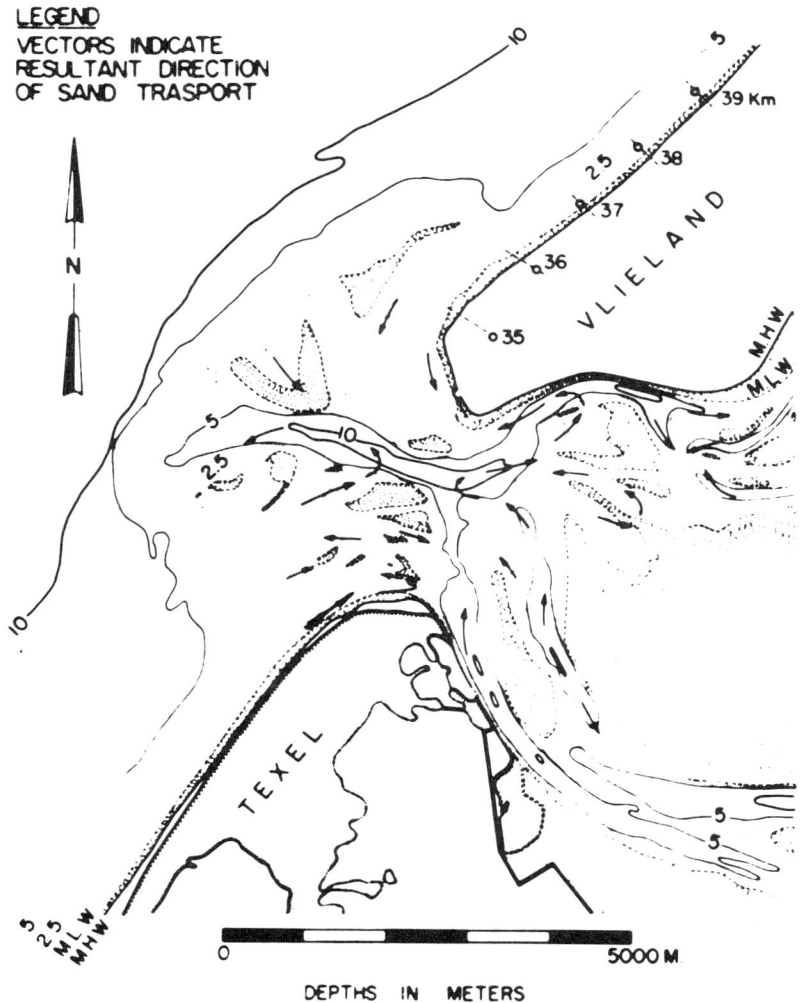

Figure 6.19. Resultant sand transport vectors in "Eyerlandse Gat," North Holland (12).

capacity as the Texel Inlet. The flow capacity of the Eyerlandse Gat is only about one-fifth of the capacity of the adjacent inlets, which indicates a higher degree of bar transfer. The direction of the resultant sand transport in the flood and ebb channels is shown by means of arrows in Figure 6.19, indicating the zig-zag movement of the sand in the inlet. Transfer is adequate, but nourishment of the downdrift shore takes place intermittently in the form of sand waves with decreasing amplitude downdrift as demonstrated by detailed surveys.

Another example of sand transfer by combined action of tidal currents and waves is Graadyb on the Danish North Sea near the northernmost inlets in the Frisian Island group at the Port of Esbjerg.

Figure 6.20. General principles of material deposition at improved tidal entrances (12).

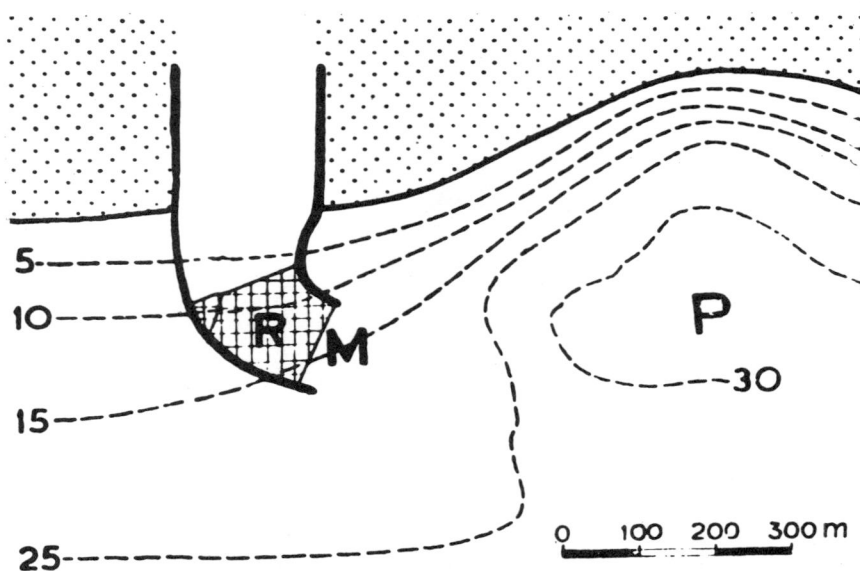

Figure 6.21. Entrance of Abidjan Harbor, Africa (12).

Improved Inlets

Figure 6.20 shows general principles on deposition of material at tidal entrances. Figure 6.21 is the harbor entrance at Abidjan, Ivory Coast, Africa. A cut was made to connect the ocean with a lagoon to accommodate 27-foot depth vessels. Sand coming from the west is deposited by the flood current at M; the ebb current, which is strongly concentrated at that point, transports it in the direction of P, where part of it settles in a deep hole in the sea bottom.

The harbor at Abidjan has been investigated by hydraulic model studies in the Hydraulic Laboratory at Delft, Holland (59). A satisfactory solution for sand by-passing was obtained.

In a similar case at Lagos (59), it became necessary to pump sand across the downdrift barrier to provide nourishment for the eroded beaches.

By-passing at Harbors

A good example of by-passing at harbors is Zeebrugge Harbor, Belgium (Figure 6.22). This harbor, protected by a 4,500-foot long nail-shaped jetty, was for a long time greatly bothered by silt deposits amounting to about 5 million cubic yards

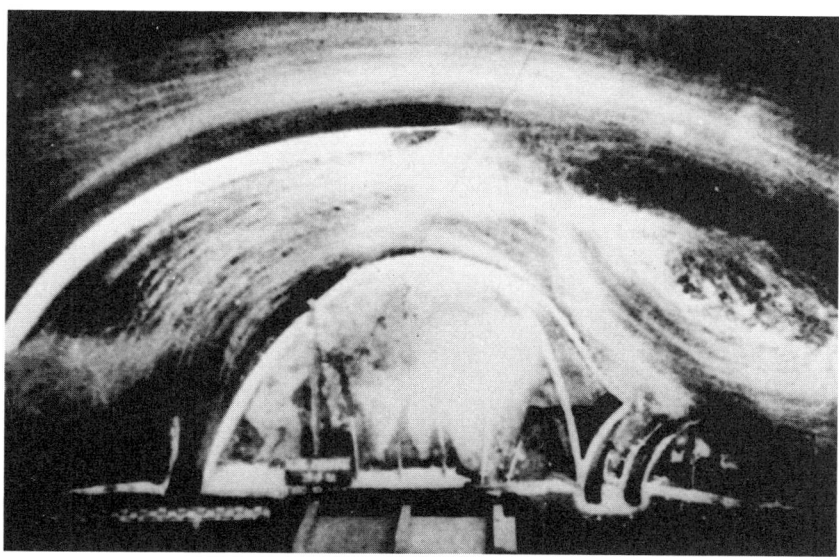

Figure 6.22. Zeebrugge Harbor, Belgium (7 and 12).

per year. The tidal range is about 12 feet, with the tidal currents outside the harbor up to 5 to 6 feet per second. For some time, the harbor was equipped with a 1,300-foot opening (clairevoie), permitting tidal currents to flow through the harbor basin. This was unsatisfactory. Heavy deposits, mainly silt, continued, and subsequent dredging endangered the economy of the harbor.

In order to improve this situation, model experiments were carried out after World War II in Belgium (Waterbouwkundig Laboratorium) and in Holland (Waterloopkundig Laboratorium). An experiment with strong flood currents is shown in Figure 6.22. Construction of the big circular jetty on the shoreside eliminated a large silt-depositing eddy current in the harbor basin. The amount of silt deposits was reduced to less than 50%. The remainder of the material, mainly silt, bypasses the harbor with the tidal currents.

Importance of M_{mean}/Q_{max} Ratio for By-passing

The dimensionless parameter, M_{mean}/Q_{max}, seems to be significant for the by-passing procedure itself (12). The value of this ratio indicates whether by-passing is a predominantly *bar-bridge* or a predominantly *tidal flow* transfer, by which material is flushed out of the inlet by ebb currents carrying the material in a downdrift direction.

M_{mean} is the (net) predominant drift quantity assuming definite predominance from one side; Q_{max} is the maximum discharge per second during spring tide.

From the experience of by-passing at those inlets, the following rule may be used as a guide: $r<10 - 20$ indicates predominant tidal flow by-passing; $r> 200 - 300$ indicates predominant bar by-passing. That M_{mean} is small compared to Q_{max} does not necessarily mean that conditions are very advantageous or even ideal for tidal flow by-passing. A large Q_{max} and a smaller M_{mean}/Q_{max} may still mean unsatisfactory by-passing if the tidal flow is not properly utilized.

The parameter, $r = M_{mean}/Q_{max}$, also plays a role in the stability of tidal inlets as mentioned in Chapter 8 on tidal inlets.

In the case of a navigation inlet, the value, M_{mean}/Q_{max}, should be kept low to allow sufficient depth in the channels across the outer and inner shoals. When the bottom of the inlet consists

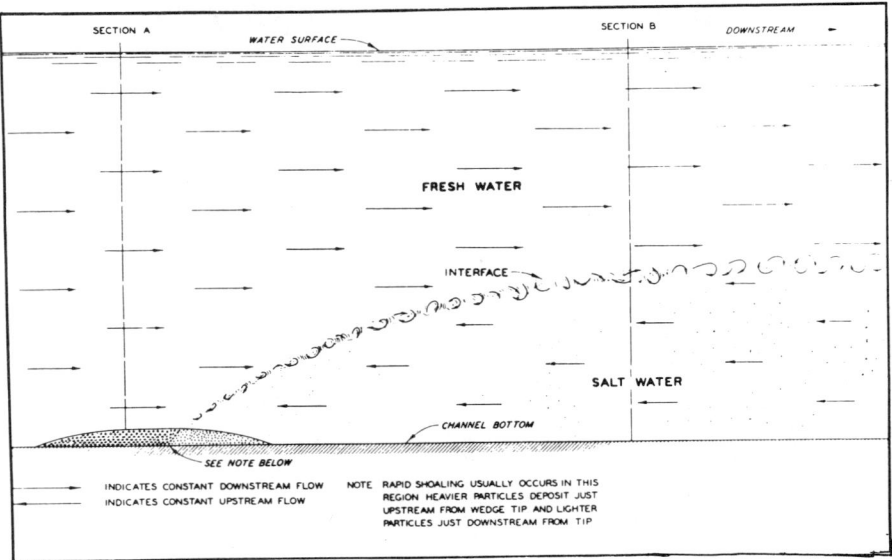

Figure 6.23. Conditions typical of a highly stratified estuary (28 and 40).

of rock, the size of the gorge cannot adjust itself to its natural dimension in alluvial material. Velocities in such inlets may be much higher than at inlets in alluvial material. By-passing, for this reason, may be very inadequate because of strong currents which push the material out to sea beyond the littoral drift zone so that nourishment material for beaches in the surrounding area is lost. An example of this is the Bakers Haulover Inlet on the southeast coast of Florida at Miami. Maximum current velocities reach 7 to 8 feet per second in the rock gorge.

The ratio, $(M_{max}-M_{mean})/M_{mean}$, describes the littoral drift irregularity which, together with the E_{wa}/M_{mean} ratio and the absolute values of M_{max} and M_{mean}, describes the littoral drift conditions. E_{wa} is the total longshore flux of wave energy.

The smaller $(M_{max}-M_{mean})/M_{mean}$ is, the better conditions exist for satisfactory continous by-passing under equal flow conditions. When the coefficient is large, the by-passing might still be adequate but irregular, with intermittent supply of sand to the downdrift beach.

A great number of examples on actual ratios are given in Reference 12 by Bruun and Gerritsen. Information on quantities of drift as related to tidal inlets is given in Chapter 8 (Tables 8.1, 8.6 and 8.9).

By-passing Plants and Arrangements by Man

Chapter 8 includes a review of sand by-passing plants and arrangements as of January 1, 1968. It is noted that material by-passing by means of permanent or semipermanent by-passing arrangements is now undertaken or planned in numereous cases. The most flexible arrangments avoiding fixed plants and replacing them by traps to be dredged at regular intervals seem to be the preferable design for future by-passing. The reader is referred to References 7, 8 and 9 for more detailed information on by-passing of material by man.

Tracing

Very important progress in littoral drift technology became possible with the introduction of

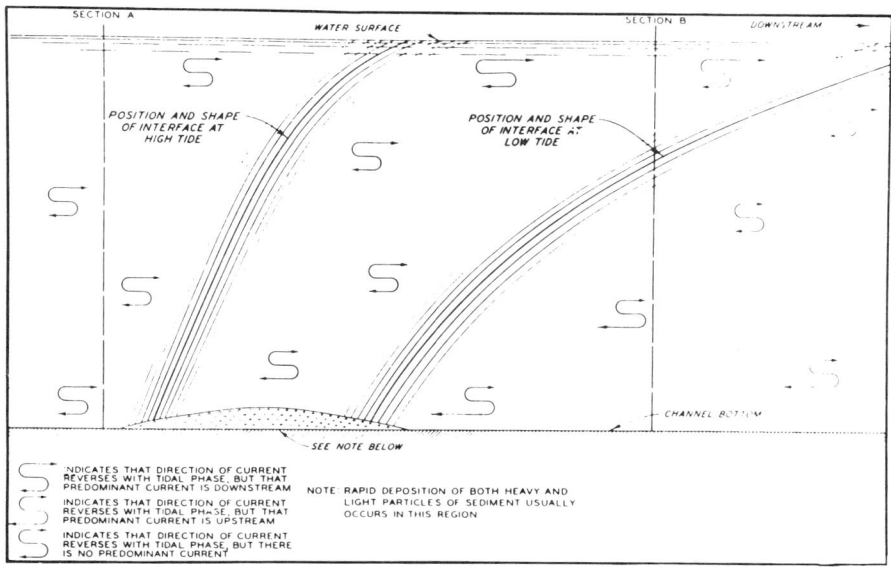

Figure 6.24. Condition typical of a partly-mixed estuary (28 and 40).

the *tracer* technique. Various tracers and examples on their application are mentioned in Appendix 4 by P. Bruun (11) published in *Engineering Geology*, vol. 4, pp. 73-88, Elsevier Publishing Company, Amsterdam.

Sediment Problems in Estuaries

Flow in Estuaries

The sediment problem in estuaries is related to the penetration of salt water below fresh water upstream. If ρ is the density of fresh water, $\rho + \Delta\rho$ the density of sea water and ρ_m the average density of the two liquids, the "densimetric velocity" of the saline bottom wedge moving upstream in case of a tideless sea is

$$V_\Delta = \frac{\Delta\rho}{\rho_m} \sqrt{(gh)}$$

where g is the acceleration of gravity, and h is the water depth.

Tidal and estuary hydraulics is reviewed briefly in Chapter 8. More detailed information is given in Reference 18 by Dronkers, in Reference 31 by Larras, in Reference 51 by Simmons and in Reference 22 by Harleman and Ippen. Shubinski et al (50) gives a comprehensive description of computer simulation of estuarial networks. The digital computer is one of the most useful tools available for the analyses of hydraulic behavior and water quality in large estuarial networks. In evaluating shoaling patterns in an estuary, one has to classify the estuaries according to the degree to which salt water and fresh water mix. A rough approximation of the mixing type of a given estuary may be established by dividing the volume of fresh water which enters the system during a tidal cycle by the tidal prism. If the result is of the order of unity or more, the estuary is likely to be of the highly stratified type.

The highly stratified type has a predominance of fresh water over tidal flow. Fresh and salt water remain separate. The saltwater wedge (Figure 6.23) penetrates into the estuary to a distance which is a function of channel depth, fresh-water discharge and density differences. The highly stratified estuary is characterized by rapid bottom and

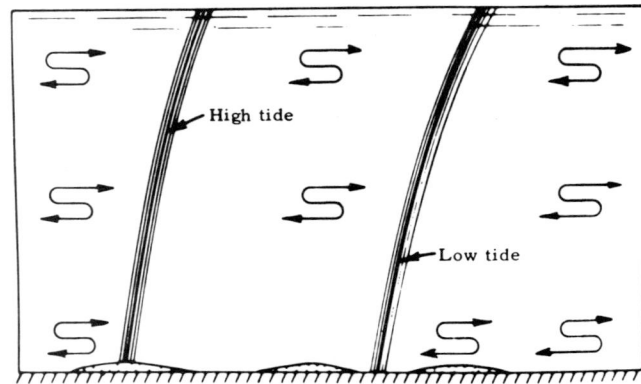

Figure 6.25. Condition typical of a well-mixed estuary (28).

surface currents and a relatively small diffusion from the lower saltwater layers into the upper fresh-water layers.

The wedge is finally "arrested," the length of penetration of the wedge being dependent of density differences, depth, width, bottom topography, river flow, viscosity, etc. (27, Chapter 11, and 29). Of these factors, depth is the most important. Any deepening of channels in the lower reaches of tidal rivers and estuaries to improve navigability will affect the salinity distribution upstream, and small changes of the channel depth may cause large changes in intrusion length.

Where fresh water moves over a saline arrested wedge, mixing occurs where the velocity of the fresh water exceeds a limiting, rather low, value. This mixing process by diffusion and the turbulent shear flow and any stop of movement of the water causes settling of suspended materials, part of which "flocculate," which, as explained in the following section, means that single particles join and become one larger and heavier particle.

The simple arrested wedge, which occurs when a river discharges in a tideless sea, becomes a more complex phenomenon in a practical sea subject to tidal action. In such estuaries, the current system is mainly dependent upon factors like (a) tidal action causing a fluctuating water table, (b) density differences, (c) river currents, (d) estuary geometry causing eddies and countercurrents, (e) turning of currents by Coriolis force and (f) wind-stresses, wave action including mass transport by waves.

Figure 6.24 shows the conditions typical of a partly mixed estuary. In the partly mixed estuary, the ratio of fresh-water discharge to tidal prism is normally in the range about 0.2 to 0.5. The interface between the fresh(er) water in the surface strata and the salt(ier) water is not nearly as well defined as in the highly stratified type, but the interface is indicated by a transition in the vertical salinity profile and/or in the vertical velocity profile. In the region of saltwater intrusion, the direction of the current near surface and bottom reverses with tidal phase. The net current is downstream above the interface and upstream below the interface.

Local salinities over the entire intrusion length vary little from surface to bottom, due to rapid vertical diffusion and mixing by high turbulence and convective currents. Velocities do not exhibit extremes as in the case of the stratified estuaries, although surface currents are strongest at ebb tide, and bottom currents are stronger during flood flow.

This situation develops further in the well-mixed estuary, Figure 6.25, when tidal forces predominate over the fresh-water flow and mixing is predominant. In the well-mixed estuary, the ratio of fresh-water discharge to tidal prism is usually of

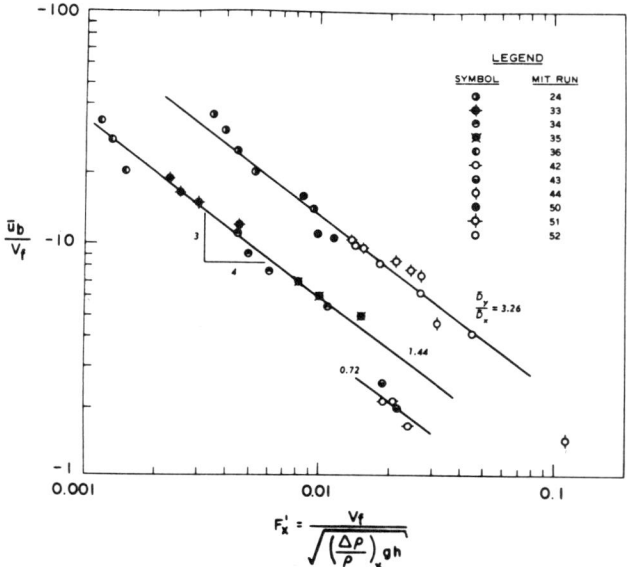

Figure 6.26. Bottom velocity correlation for idealized estuary (22).

the order of 0.1 or less. Salinities decrease progressively from sea water at the entrance of fresh water in the upper reaches. Currents reverse with tidal phase throughout the estuary.

As mentioned in Reference 56, an empirical relationship exists between salinity at low water, ebb flow velocity and channel depth, enabling calculation of the average longitudinal salinity distribution. Reference 22 reviews rational methods of predicting the change in estuary regime which apply to estuaries in which the salinity distribution is of the partially or well-mixed type and therefore is useful in the project planning stage and as a basis for evaluating the needs for more detailed studies.

Results of two-dimensional salinity and velocity distributions in an idealized estuary demonstrated that an unique correlation exists between the velocity ratio U_b/V_f (U_b is the average horizontal velocity near the bed over a tidal period, and V_f is the average fresh-water velocity in the estuary) and the densimetric Froude number F_x^1 defined as

$$F_x^1 = V_f / \sqrt{[(\Delta\rho/\rho)_x g h]}$$

when $(\Delta\rho/\rho)_x$ is the relative density difference between the fresh-water and the average density at a section x within the region of salinity intrusion, and h is the channel depth. The time-averaged velocity distribution exhibits the characteristic velocity reversal—a net seaward flow along the surface and a net landward flow near the bottom. The correlation, Figure 6.26, gives a quantitative relation for the decrease of the near bottom velocity in the upland direction. Figure 6.27 shows examples on the use of this concept on flume experiments and reveals a unique relation between the location of the null point (where U_b changes direction from upstream to downstream) and the longitudinal salinity distribution. Reference 22 further mentions application of the velocity predominance and null point correlation to velocity data for the Savannah and Delaware estuaries mentioned later in this chapter.

Shoaling of Estuaries

Most undisturbed estuaries are characterized by entrance bars and shoals crossings within the

228   Port Engineering

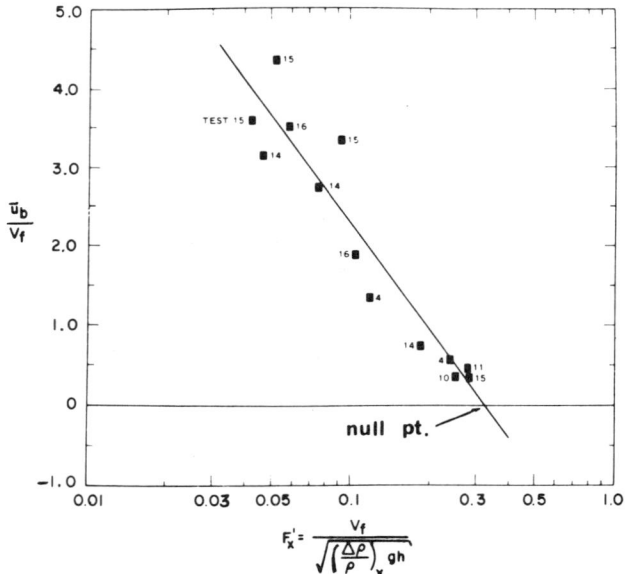

Figure 6.27. Bottom velocity correlation for salinity flume (22).

system. Sediments may deposit on the shoals during periods of relatively low fresh-water flow just to be flushed out on entrance shoals during periods of relatively high discharge. The sea shoals may then be worn out by wave action. This situation is typical for some locations in India and the Arabian Sea as well as in the Bay of Bengal. Materials may deposit during the late or after the monsoon period to be eroded again when the monsoon starts as later explained in more detail.

Generally, depositional mechanism in an estuary follows the patterns of energy distribution. The most common trend is that, first, the sediment was eroded; next, it proceeded from the area of higher energy content per unit flow volume to areas of lower energy content. High sediment concentrations may come into an estuary either from entering rivers or from the sea by tidal flow. Most estuaries are characterized by a number of circulation systems, and these features tend to cause entrapment of particles.

The existence of essentially closed circulation systems for suspended matters is due to the character of water movements in estuaries and in tidal areas, and these features tend to cause entrapment of particles. Water passes freely through these areas, but particular matter is caught or its escape to open water is retarded. One example is the movement of suspended sand in front of beaches under the influence of wave and surf action. This process, however, is restricted to a rather narrow strip of water. Two other mechanisms cover greater areas. One is the general accumulation of fine-grained material by tidal action. The other is the entrapment of suspended matter in river mouths and the consequent formation of areas of great turbidity.

With respect to the entrapment of sediments in shoals, all estuaries have in common a net inflow of water in the bottom strata and a net outflow of water in the surface strata. The sedimentation pattern also has common features particularly when the partly-mixed and the well-mixed types are compared. Figures 6.23, 6.24 and 6.25 indicate principal patterns. In the highly stratified type, the main accumulation takes place at the tip of the saltwater wedge where fresh and salt water has its main collision. The partly-mixed estuary drops the main part of its material in the zone of tidal shifting of waters limited by the low tide downstream boundary and by the flood tide upstream flow boundaries. In the well-mixed estuary, sedimentation takes place within the entire zone of mixing without concentration in any large area but with a great number of individual shoals, their location being determined by local (eddy) currents and the accompanying shear forces and formation of pockets.

Bedload will be transported only during those phases of combined tidal and density-generated currents when the necessary entrainment velocities are exceeded. Suspended load is subject to diffusion processes, possibly flocculation and settling. As a general rule, sediments deposited on the bottom in an estuary will averagely be transported upstream and will accumulate near the ends of the intrusion zone and create shoals which will also form at any place where the net bottom velocity is zero. The intensity of shoaling will be most pronounced near the end of the intrusion for stratified estuaries and will be more evenly distributed in partly and well-mixed estuaries. As a consequence of this situation, the major portion of sediments introduced into an estuary during normal conditions will be retained therein.

Because of the behavior of sediments, the fine-grained suspended matter reacts with a certain inertia to changes of current velocity (46). Usually there is a time lag between the turn of the tide, when current velocity is zero, and the moment at which the lowest figures for suspended silt are found. This lag can be explained by the fact that in a period of decreasing current velocity, some time is needed for the material to settle. Contrarily, when the current increases, it takes time before the material is suspended.

The lag effect has been used to explain why, in many tidal flat areas, the amounts of fine-grained suspended matter are often considerably higher than in the adjoining open sea. Further, it has been used to explain why, proceeding landward in a tidal flat area, the grains in the bottom sediment gradually become smaller.

The decrease of grain size on the bottom is primarily a result of the reduced average and maximum current velocity from the open sea toward the coast. In a tidal area connected with the sea by tidal inlets between barrier islands, it is evident that in and near the inlets, the bottom will consist of coarse sand, because fine sand and silt are winnowed out by the strong currents. Near the coast and on tidal flats where currents are weaker, fine-grained matter prevails—the coarse sand cannot reach these places, but the fine materials can.

In a steady state, one might expect a decrease of fine-grained matter in suspension toward the coast or no concentration differences at all. That the concentration of suspensions increases toward the coast has been demonstrated extensively for various parts of the tidal flat areas (Wadden) along the North Sea coasts of Denmark, Germany and the Netherlands, as well as on the eastern seaboard and in the Gulf of Mexico in the United States. The increase is found during calm weather as well as during storms.

The phenomenon has been explained on the basis of the lag effect mentioned earlier. When water is carried landward through a tidal channel with the flood, it is traveling in a large channel, its flow is much faster than farther landward, and it contains the amount of silt appropriate to the turbulence caused by this flow rate. As the current velocity gradually decreases, part of the silt content, being too high in relation to the slower flow rate, will sink to the bottom. Because silt sinks slowly, it will be transported farther into the flood direction than if sinking took place more quickly.

After the turn of the tide, the water mass will move in an opposite direction. However, the slow reaction of silt on the decrease of current velocity causes the silt to settle in places where the current is too weak to carry it away. Therefore, if ebb and flood are symmetrical, a certain fraction of silt is left on the bottom. The process repeats itself every tide. As a result, the bottom in the inner parts of the area becomes very silty, and there is a very high concentration of suspended matter in the water. In the steady state, the inward residual movement of silt is balanced by the loss of silt seaward due to the silt gradient in the water.

The most common suspended material in tidal estuaries is clay-silt mixtures. With respect to its depositional behavior, experiments by Partheniades (38 and 39) with kolinite clay-silt suspensions in a rotating annular apparatus revealed the following important depositional characteristics of fine sediments.

1. For given geometry, sediment and flow conditions, the suspended sediment concentration reaches, after a period of relatively rapid deposition, a constant value, called "equilibrium concentration," which is very nearly a constant fraction of the initial concentration.
2. The ratio of the equilibrium concentration to the initial concentration appears to correlate very well with the average shear stress around the channel boundary, provided that the speeds of the channel and the ring rotating in a direction opposite to that of the channel are adjusted so that the sediment deposits uniformly across the channel. These speed combinations presumably also yield a similar pattern of shear stress around the channel.
3. The secondary currents generated by the rotational motion also have a significant effect on the equilibrium concentration and the rate of deposition.
4. A size analysis of a sample of material obtained at equilibrium concentration showed that most of the deposit material comes from the size fractions corresponding to the larger clay particles and suggests that flocculation is more important as a settling agent than the initially higher particle weight and settling velocity of the silt particles.

Generally, flocculation seems to be an important problem in tidal estuaries. Flocculation is associated with the deposition of clay minerals, including fine particles of mica and certain metallic oxides and hydroxides. It further seems to depend on the relative distribution of various mineral components, and different flocculation rates are obtained for different mixtures. The electrochemical forces producing flocs increase substantially as particle sizes decrease (27, Chapter 15).

Most of the material which flocculates is derived from erosion of cohesive sediments, mainly clay. Cohesive material forms a considerable part of the material moving in an estuary. The Task Committee on Erosion of Cohesive Materials of the ASCE in their report published in the July, 1968, issue of *ASCE Journal of the Hydraulics Division* admits that the properties which control erosion resistance of cohesive sediments have still not been conclusively defined, and that a major effort should be undertaken to define those properties—whether chemical, physical or environmental—that determine the resistance of a cohesive sediment to flowing water. The mineralogy of the clay fraction and the role of different cat-ions associated with the clays causing flocculation need investigation. Also, the influence of suspended sediment and its effect on the viscosity of the water producing erosion has to be better understood. Cohesive soils have bonds which are related to the soil mineralogy and chemistry. Consequently, the Task Committee concludes that water quality can play an important role in changing these bonds by chemical action.

With respect to the area distribution of sediment transport by density currents in an estuary, field research on a coastal plain estuary mentioned in Reference 37 demonstrated that the transport in a partly-mixed estuary is directed downstream mainly over bordering shoals and upstream in the central channel as mentioned earlier. Rates of net transport are greatest in the upper estuary just above the channel floor. Downstream transport over shoals by density currents is strengthened by wave agitation and tidal turbulence; upstream transport is augmented in the upper estuary by tidal flow that produces differential settling of suspended particles. Sediment transport is partly entrapped on shoals in the middle estuary, where upstream and downstream density currents meet. Another part is deposited in the basin where tidal flow is diminished. Suspended sediment that accumulates near the estuary head does not form major shoals; instead, it is actively recirculated by moderate tidal turbulence and advective density, mixed and carried upstream in the central channels. This experience is similar to the results of investigations in the Mersey River (England) mentioned in the following section.

For further information on basic sedimentation in estuaries, the reader is referred to References 14, 22, 27, 31, 33, 41, 42, 46 and 51 and to papers from the Tidal Hydraulics Session of the Hydraulic Division ASCE meeting in New York, October 1968, published in *ASCE Journal of the Hydraulics Division*, January, 1969. It should be mentioned, in this respect, that tracing has become a very important tool in research on estuaries and sediment transport along shores. Appendix 4 reviews the application of tracers in coastal engineering.

Influence of Man-Made Changes in Shoaling

An important engineering problem in tidal waterways is the change in estuary shoaling pattern which inevitably accompanies man-made changes in estuary geometry in flow rates. Such measures include structures to reduce the tidal flow, diversion of additional fresh-water flow into the estuary, deepening and narrowing the channel. Hydraulic model experiments have been used to test methods of correcting or improving shoaling problems, but usually these studies have been undertaken after the change which caused the problem has been made.

When channels were dredged, flow pattern and quantity changed. Consequently, shoaling changed too. This was particularly true for rivers when sediment load was largely clay or other lightweight materials as the Charleston Harbor, the Savannah River and the Mississippi River entrances mentioned in a following section. Often the dredged channels became sediment traps, or existing shoals shifted to another area upstream or downstream or both where they became an even greater nuissance than they were before. It became common practice in dredging estuaries to dump the material dredged in the entrance area or elsewhere in deeper holes.

This, however, often proved to be a severe mistake, as demonstrated in the now classic experiment with radioactive Sc^{46} in the Thames River in Britain, mentioned in Appendix 4. For tracing of *silt movement*, this particular isotope was selected as a suitable gamma-ray source, with a convenient half-life of 85 days. The tracer material which had a density similar to that of Thames mud consisted of soda glass containing about 1.5% of scandium oxide. These experiments were arranged to demonstrate with certainty whether or not landward transport of silt takes place in the main shipping channel abreast the entrance to the Tidal Basin of Tilbury Docks, at the upper end of Gravesend Reach, 26 miles below London Bridge. Immediately before the test, a systematic survey was made of background activity using Geiger counters on the bed of the estuary between 8 and 38 miles below London Bridge. The Scandium 46 glass was mixed with mud from the river. During the next three weeks of tracing, one surprising result was that in the tidal basin at Tilbury Docks, 12 miles from the injection point, where siltation necessitates considerable dredging, the activity gradually increased to three times the background value. From the total number of observations, it was clear that silt moved toward the head of the estuary where there is a net movement of water close to the bed. This, in turn, indicated what later was proved in so many similar cases that dredged material should never be put back in the estuary but should be pumped ashore. This method of operation is now gradually becoming the practice in the United States where reasons for conservation of biological life speak for the same procedure.

From this, it is also clear that dumping downstream as well as "agitation" (stir-up) dredging are most likely poor practices in estuaries. Likewise, any other source of supply of material to an estuary should be limited, if possible. Such sources of material are marsh areas, material from eroding shores, organic material resulting from biological cycles of estuarine plant and animal life, industrial and sewage wastes of any kind and wind-born sediment. In the Potomac River in Maryland, surveys proved that a very essential contribution to suspension load in the river was erosion material from construction sites, particularly clay minerals. As mentioned earlier, such minerals tend to flocculate. Some coarser material is also washed down in the river, but an essential difference in hydraulic transport between granular and colloial materials, however, exists, which lies in the property of the latter to flocculate and to form aggregates of multiples of particles in interaction with the suspending fluid, while granular sediments remain single regardless of flow conditions. The internal shear stresses generated by the flow will promote flocculation by increasing the collision rates to a certain critical shear as previously mentioned (39). Beyond a certain critical shear, the flocs are reduced to a limiting size for a given shear, since interfloc erosion reduces the size as rapidly as the floc grows. Thus, the size of sediment unit—hereby, the settling velocities—is governed by the flow conditions themselves which man may change in one direction or the other, but most often with the result that sedimentation increases due to higher input of material because of dredging operations.

General Principles of Improvement

Improvements usually include attempts to maintain a channel of a certain width and depth in a fixed position, making initial as well as maintenance costs as small as possible. Natural estuary channels are usually winding. It is difficult to avoid such a tendency because any stream in alluvial material is subject to variations in bottom and bank resistance causing meandering flow. General principles of meandering are mentioned in Reference 34. Meanders and their bearing on river training are mentioned in Reference 24; Professor Engelund of Denmark developed new theories (report of 1971 from Hydraulic Laboratories Technical University of Denmark). A comprehensive review of laboratory contributions to channel stabilitation with special reference to meandering is given by Margaret Petersen in Reference 45. A navigation channel must not be too winding, and radius of curvature must, for safety reasons, stay above certain limits. But sinuosity cannot be too mild, because if it is, the channel will simply start making its own meanders which will not necessarily suit navigation (see Chapter 2).

Any navigation channel must maintain certain regularity in its horizontal as well as cross-sectional geometry. Estuaries usually have more than one channel, and flow distribution in these channels may be very skewed with prodominance for either ebb or flood flow. In nature this usually means a very complex situation with respect to material transport by which the same sediment circulates in the estuary in the way that flood channels discharge sediment in ebb channels and vice versa. Any improvement on one channel is likely to affect one or more other channels, either by producing more sediment transport by increased flow or, the opposite, by creating a trap for sediment so that the associated channel(s) start to scour.

Any improvement for navigation, therefore, should usually concentrate on one main channel. In estuaries it is the ebb channels which usually carry most flow. Ebb currents flow from a narrow to a wide body of water and tend to concentrate more on the ocean side than flood channels where mode of flow is the opposite. Consequently, they are also easier to train and regulate for flushing of sediments in entrance channels to be used for navigation. This may be done by first selecting the channel which is most suitable for training and next by attempting to concentrate the flow in this channel, cutting off "uneconomic branches" and "organizing" the flow in the main channel by training walls, spurs, dikes, dams, etc. Sometimes, proper placement of spoil banks will suffice, but material in these banks should be coarse enough to stay on the banks. Fine material may erode and be carried back in the estuary channel(s). Often training may be accomplished by dredging the favored channel, gradually giving it more and more opportunity to take over the leading role, letting the other channel(s) deteriorate. As previously mentioned, it had earlier been normal practice to spill material from dredging in the estuary in the estuary itself, but modern tracing techniques proved in several cases that this may be a very dangerous practice since the dumped material upsets the local equilibrium condition with the result that it is carried away and perhaps returned to the main channel or to other places where it is not welcome. The example from the Thames River is very descriptive and grave in this respect. It is always best to spill dredged material on dry land or in marsh areas behind dikes, which is gradually becoming recognized practice in the United States.

By orienting the channel perpendicular to the depth contours, currents will tend to follow the channel. This is also an advantage with respect to wave action, because it causes least sediment transport by wave action to the channel from the sides.

Optimum conditions may be obtained if the predominant direction of wave propogations is identical with the direction of flow of the tidal currents. Training of an estuary channel is, however, a very delicate process, and the possibility of errors by putting training walls in a wrong location of a wrong configuration and at a wrong distance apart has often proved fatal to stability. Spur groins of jetties from the side and properly aligned training walls and not just straight parallel walls may prove to be a great advantage. They require meticulous planning, including field and hydraulic model studies as dredging operations for maintenance and dredging of sediment traps to store unavoidable deposits.

The situation in the Mersey River estuary (mentioned later) is a good example of a long time "learning by hard experience" improvement of a complex estuarine case.

The problem of providing sediment traps is common for tidal inlets on littoral drift shores, estuaries and any combination of these two types of entrances. The first section of this chapter explained natural and artificial by-passing modes and techniques. Chapter 8 gives further details on improvements. Figure 8.7 shows a trap inside a depressed weir in the updrift jetty at Hillsboro Inlet, Florida. At Bakers Haulover, Florida, bed material sucked in by flood currents deposits on bay shoals from where it may be transferred by pumping downdrift. A similar situation exists at Ft. Pierce (Figure 6.13). The situation becomes more difficult when a good part or even most of the material travels in suspension as is generally the case in estuaries. It will then be more difficult to place the trap(s) for most effective operation. Dredging of a deeper channel will always improve tidal flushing, but it also almost inevitably increases input of material because the inflow of saline water increases, which in turn makes the saltwater penetrate further upriver in the highly stratified estuary, causing even more siltation by flocculation. The situation develops similarly in the partly and in the well-mixed estuary. In all cases, penetration of more salt water will cause an increase of siltation and thereby increase maintenance costs. But the difficulties with deposits may be handled in a more practical way, resulting in better conditions for navigation by regularly scheduled maintenance operations, from sections of the river or estuary where traps were established for permanent maintenance operations. These traps may be just dredged areas without any structures, or they may be arranged in connection with training walls. As an example of the above mentioned difficulties, the classical example at Liverpool in Mersey River (47) should be mentioned.

The Mersey estuary at Liverpool Bay is a well-mixed estuary suffering severe siltation problems which man tried to cope with, but with insufficient knowledge and experience until he realized the rules of the game. Figure 6.28 (47) is a key plan of Liverpool Bay, and Figure 6.29 (47) shows the upper estuary of the Mersey. The tidal range at spring and neap is 30 feet and 16 feet, respectively, at the mouth. The outer estuary, Liverpool Bay, consists of extensive sand banks, large areas of which are exposed at low water. Shipping bound upriver for the Narrows (Figure 6.28 and 6.29) crosses the bay by the main navigation channel, which has been trained by two jetties over a distance of 9 miles. The Narrows is a single, deep, 6-mile long channel, 3000 feet wide at its narrowest part, having depths up to 60 feet at low-water spring tides. Beyond the Narrows lies the upper estuary which reaches a maximum width of 18,000 feet and extends for a distance of about 26 miles upstream. At low water, almost the whole tidal basin dries out, the downstream section between Dingle and Eastham now being characterized by the three channels of Carston, Middle Deep and Eastham. Further upstream, the low-water channels meander through large areas of sand and mud, constantly changing their course and frequently covering considerable distance before finally flowing into the Eastham channel (Figure 6.29).

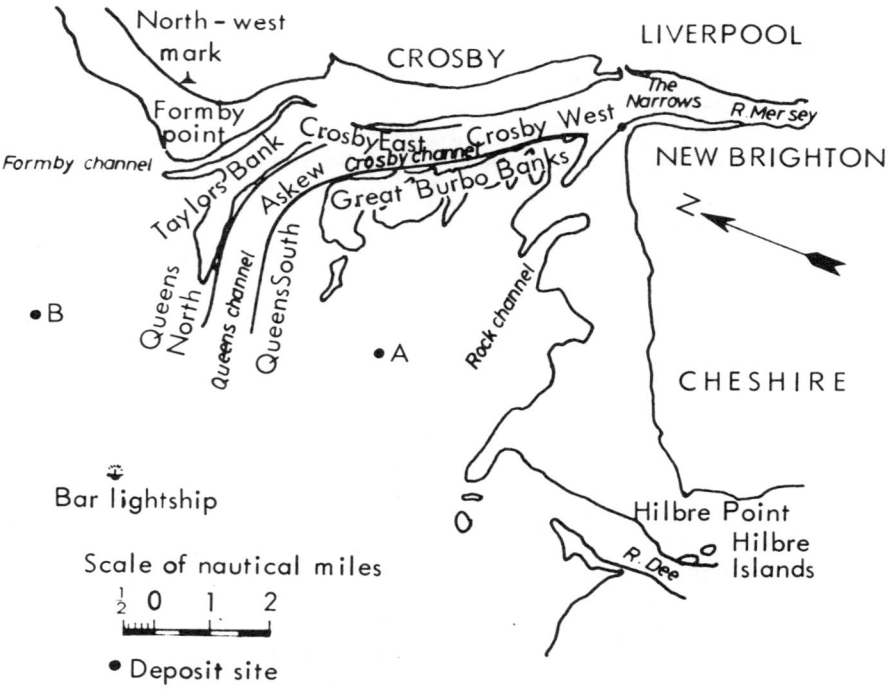

Figure 6.28. Key plan of Liverpool Bay (47).

The Narrows and the main shipping land through Liverpool Bay are maintained by the large tidal volume of the estuary flowing in and out of these channels on the flood and ebb tides. It is known that the capacity of the estuary, defined as the volume of water between the bed of the river and the highest level reached at all points by a spring tide, has decreased considerably since the 1861 survey due to heavy siltation between Rock Light and Runcorn (Figure 6.29). This deterioration took place even though between 1897 and 1955 over 400 million cubic yards of material were removed by dredging from the area upstream from Rock Light.

A second problem is concerned with fluctuations in the depths and extent of the bars in the Eastham and Carston channels (Figure 6.29). In July, 1953, deepening of the Eastham channel was begun to allow large tankers to use the new Queen Elizabeth II oil dock, and since then the dredging on Bromborough Bar has greatly increased. It was, therefore, necessary to establish the reasons for this and to suggest ways in which depths might be improved.

Comprehensive field and laboratory research as described in Reference 47 was carried out to clarify the problem and to develop proper remedies for it. Two models corresponding to Figures 6.28 and 6.29 were built in different scales and molded to different situations with movable or fixed bed. Fluorescent tracer experiments were undertaken in the upper estuary model. One of the first conclusions of the study was that the main reason for upper estuary siltation was not a cyclic change but the increase in human activity, including dredging and training walls both in the upper estuary and in Liverpool Bay. Probably during the period 1906 to 1931, the main reasons for the capacity loss were the stabilization of the low-water channel in the upper estuary and the effect of

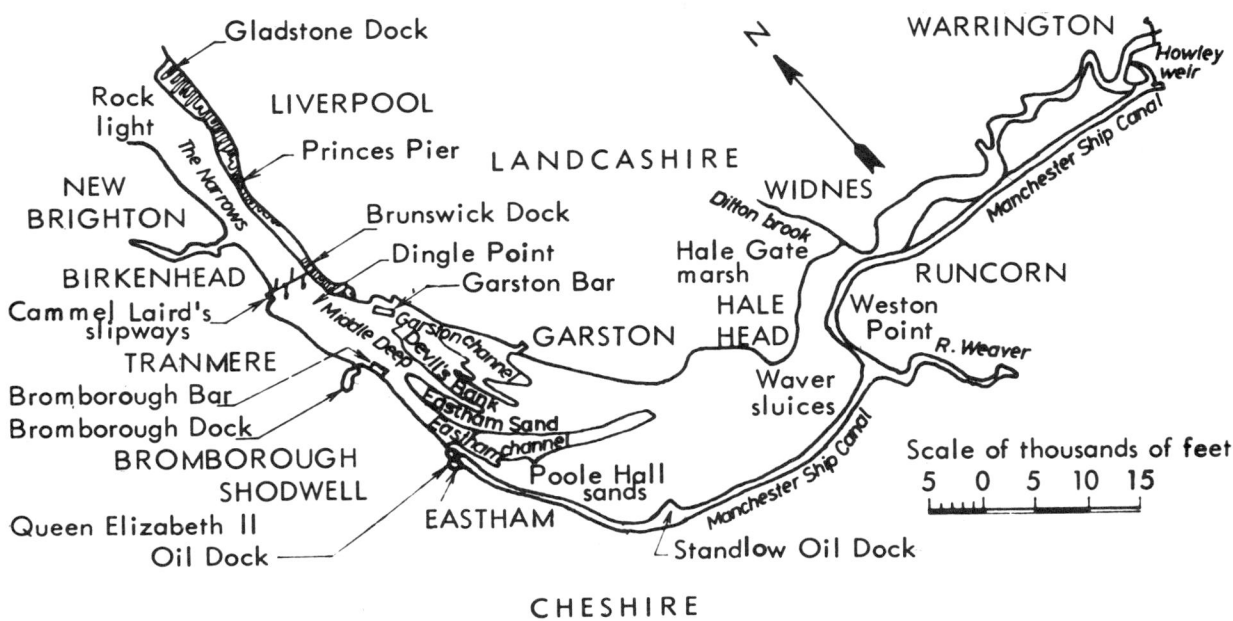

Figure 6.29. Key plan of the upper estuary of the Mersey (47).

training works constructed in the bay up to that time. After 1931, however, most of the deterioration was likely to have been associated with sea channel training as explained next.
the capacity loss were the stabilization of the low-water channel in the upper estuary and the effect of training works constructed in the bay up to that time. After 1931, however, most of the deterioration was likely to have been associated with sea channel training as explained next.

The canalization efforts of the main shipping channel in Liverpool Bay increased velocities and depths in the channel. The material that was eroded during the process of deepening was transported both upstream and downstream. The proportion moving upstream increased the sediment load at the mouth, and since tidal discharges at this section had remained unchanged, deposition occurred. However, the quantity of material eroded from the sea channels is not in itself enough to account for the total accretion in the upper estuary. Other factors, including increase of sand from external source, have been acting.

The construction of the West Crosby revetment (Figure 6.28) increased the extent of the flood drift in the area behind the wall toward the main channel so that more material could now be brought up to the back of the wall than could be carried away by the ebb. Some of this material is carried over the wall and is likely to be retained in the channel. As most of the sand is transported in the layers close to the bed and the direction of the main ebb stream in these layers is down the channel parallel to the training, this leaves only surface water, carrying very little material in suspension, to flow out of the Crosby channel over the Burbo banks (Figure 6.28). Next, bed levels in the channel are considerably lower than the top of its revetment. For these reasons, the training walls have had the effect of holding the load in the main channel. The discharges in this channel as well as the supply of material to the mouth thereby increased, which tended to cause progressive deterioration in the upper estuary. As maintained in Reference 47, these effects have not and could hardly have been foreseen from the information available to the designers. Although the training works in the bay have contributed to upper estuary siltation, other factors, such as restriction of low water, channel movements (meandering, see Reference 24 and 45), revetments and training walls and large scale dredging, have also had a bearing on the problem.

The fluorescent tracer experiments in the upper estuary model, with particular reference to the problems associated with the Bromborough Bar, illustrated the siltation mechanism. Model tests further showed how depths could be increased by constructing training walls in the Eastham Channel. The test, however, did not justify a suggestion on constructing an island in the wide part of the upper estuary (Figure 6.29) since the tests indicated that the long-term hydraulic efforts would be undesirable.

The tests also revealed that persisting poor conditions on the Bromborough Bar since 1953 might well be due to the excessively high dredging rate. The model showed that the ruling depth over the bar under the most unfavorable conditions that could be foreseen was 5 feet. Although not proven, it was considered possible that the high rate of dredging on the bar aggravated the problem and was one of the more important factors preventing a natural return of better conditions. The results of the tests justify the possibility of discontinuing or at least limiting the dredging on Bromborough Bar for an experimental period. Furthermore, actual dredging techniques could become an advantage by substituting trailing suction-type dredgers for the bucket dredgers.

The investigation confirmed the still not fully recognized truth that it is safer to pump dredged material ashore. Dumping in the bay or in the estuary could easily become an agent to keep the siltation running a little faster.

Detailed silt measurements carried out later (21) showed that, at positions along the boundaries of the Mersey, the quantity of silt in suspension increased linearly with tidal range and is greater in winter than in summer. When compared with measurements taken away from the shorelines, the results showed that the silt patterns at the boundaries of the estuary can be very different from those occurring at nearby river positions, even when these river positions are only a few hundred feet from the shore stations. It can, therefore, be very misleading if the results of silt measurements at the estuary boundaries are used to determine the general pattern of silt movement. Similarly, it is likely to be dangerous to infer a silt pattern at the boundary from measurements taken in mid-river.

Based on overwhelming experience, it may be stated that it is not possible in any improvement of an estuary to do away with the dredging requirement, but one can move it from one section to another. For this transfer, one uses either training or trapping for ebb currents or training or trapping for flood currents, concentrating the interest on one or the other. The conservative and generally accepted practice has been to rely on training of ebb currents for flushing because they were the strongest, disregarding that bottom currents may be more material-laden due to saltwater intrusion and therefore more practical to train. Sand traps were, however, almost always arranged for trapping of material carried by flood currents because this material mainly moved as bedload transport from the sea, possibly in the form of major sand waves traveling on the bottom, such as happens in the Watten Sea in the German Bay (32, 40, 44). But the major part of the silt load may also come from the sea as it happens in the Thames River and at Cochin, India (40). If siltation is decreased by traps, it is often the flood (density) currents which deserve the main interest.

The most radical method of improving an estuary is to hinder sediments from penetrating into its empire. As almost all rivers carry sediments and the main parts of the seashores carry littoral drift material, the only way in which sediments could be prohibited from entering an estuary would be by hindering production of sediment or by trapping it before it entered the main waters of the estuary. On the riverside clearing (settling) basins could be built, and nature has actually provided

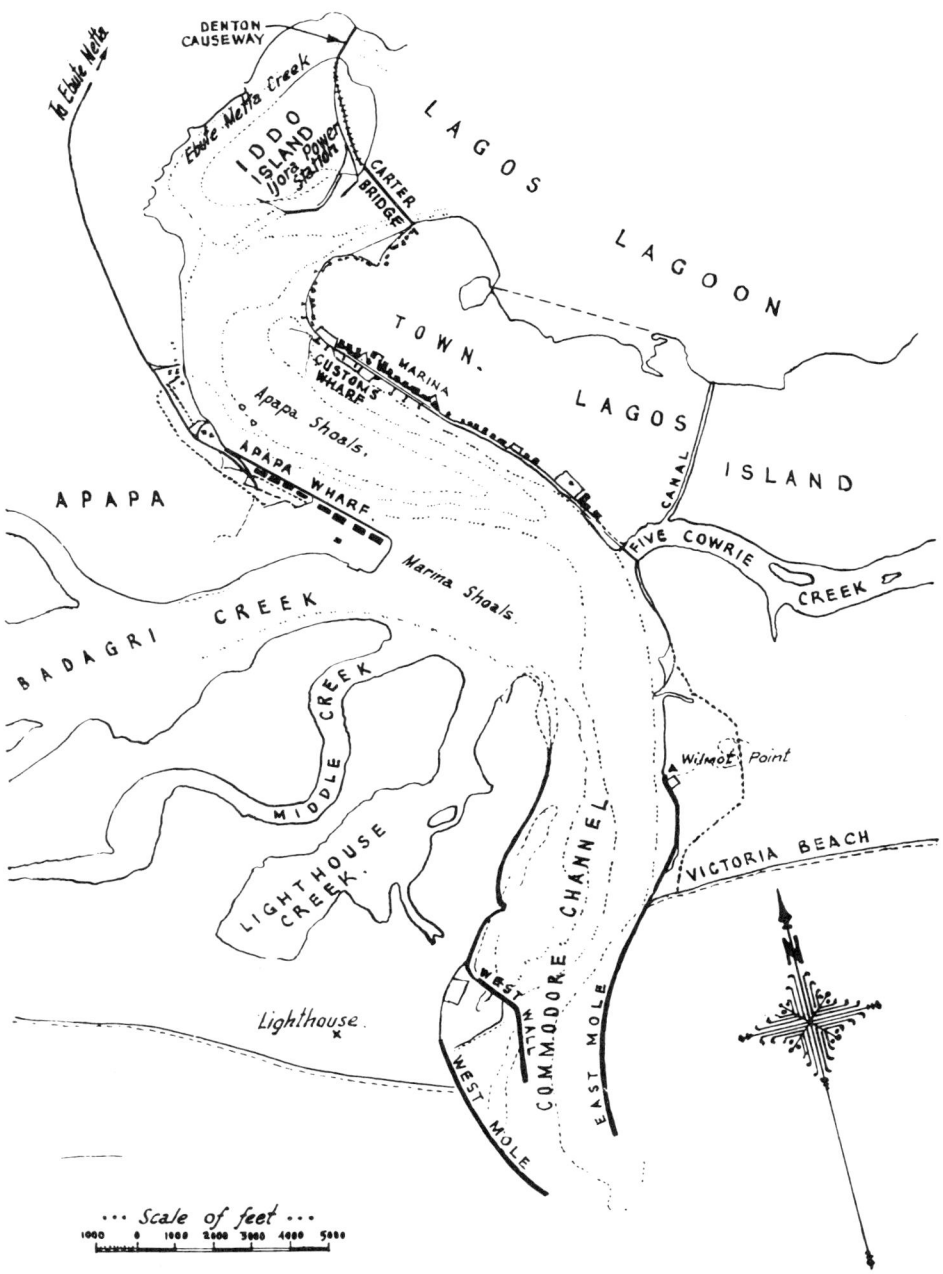

Figure 6.30. The harbor at Lagos, Nigeria (31).

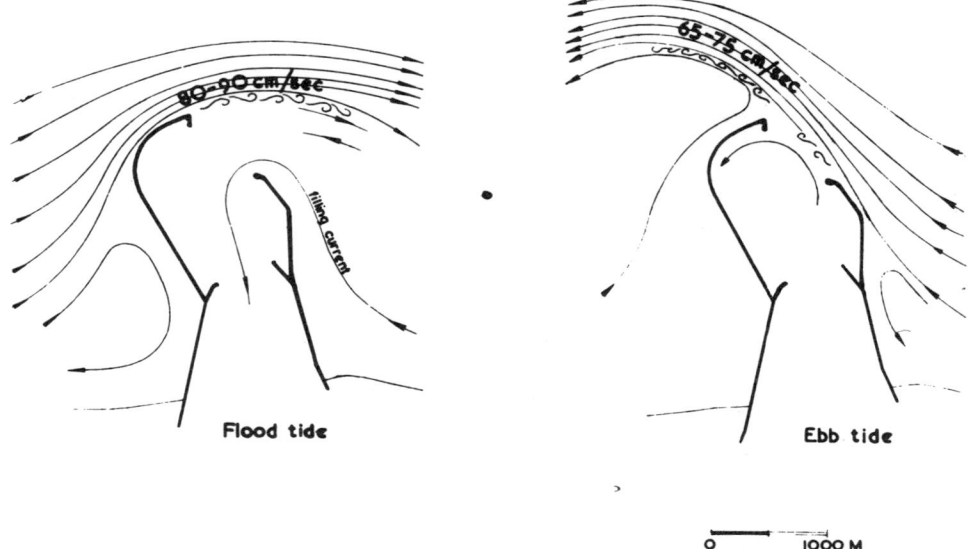

Figure 6.31. The harbor at Ymuiden, Holland (42).

such basins in the form of lakes and lagoons, but they will be filled up sooner or later unless they are cleared of deposits. Thus, several estuaries in India on the Arabian Sea as well as on the Bay of Bengal have gradually been filled with material, and the establishment of hydraulic power plants for gradual release of water has made the situation even worse. On the seashore, jetties may be built— and are effective if it is mainly sand which enters the estuary from the littoral drift zone. If it is silt jetties may improve the situation, but they can hardly block fine sediments from entering. They are, however, able to concentrate the flow and so are other types of regulatory works like spurs, training walls, dikes, etc. They have also been used widely.

The harbor at Lagos (Figure 6.30) is an example on how jetties simultaneously may function as sand traps for sediments from the sea and as training walls for utilizing the flushing ability of ebb currents which, because of predominantly fresh water over tidal flow, are very strong (3 to 4 knots) in the rainy season. They are always stronger than flood currents and run 1 to 2 knots most of the year. The outer harbor functions as a sediment trap mostly for sand.

The situation at Ymuiden Harbor in Holland (Figure 6.31) is not nearly as fortunate (42, section by Volbeda and Stelling). This harbor is provided with locks for navigation as well as for discharge of fresh water from the interior of Holland. The quantity of fresh-water flow exceeds the tidal flow in the relatively small area between the locks and the ocean. The plan of improvement, now almost completed, includes a new configuration of the entrance as shown in Figures 6.31 and 6.32. Flood currents running north by-pass the harbor without bringing too much sediment into the front port, but silt-laden sea water meets fresh water directly and does not enter the port but by-passes the harbor as shown in Figure 6.31. A countercurrent carries silt-laden water into the area inside the jetties. The silt content of the sea water is 130 miligrams per liter, and most of this settles when it meets the fresh-water flow from the gates and sluices inside the protecting jetties, which amounts to approximately $4(10^6)$ cubic meters per tide, thus exceeding the saltwater quantity. The sedi-

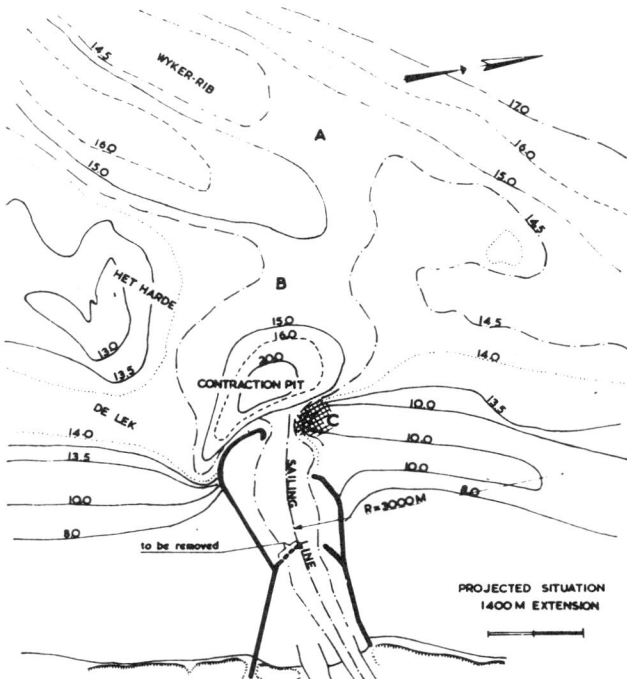

Figure 6.32. Improvement of the harbor at Ymuiden, Holland (42).

mentation rate in the old port was about 1.8 million cubic meters per year. This was almost all silt because little sand entered the port due to low entrance velocities. The newly completed (1970) entrance is expected to increase siltation by about 50%, partly because tidal inflow increases linearly with the enlargement of wetted surface and partly because depth increases. Seiches in the old port area caused by the oscillation in the North Sea (mentioned in Chapter 2) also contributed to siltation in the old port area and may continue doing so in the new port area. A total of $2.5(10^6)$ cubic meters siltation is therefore expected in the new port. With respect to sand deposits, the curved part of the south jetty will guide the northgoing flood currents as shown in Figure 6.31. Because of the retracted position of the northern jetty, the flood current is not able to carry sand to the harbor basin. Some sand will undoubtedly deposit on the shore side of a line of eddy or harbor area in any quantity, but a shoal may develop outside the harbor as shown in Figure 6.32 at point C.

Other problems in Holland are associated with maintaining the Rotterdam Waterway. The difficulties encountered are responsible for the establishment of the huge harbor installation "Europort" at the entrance to the waterway, with an entrance depth through dredged channel of 72 feet (see Chapter 9 which mentions dredging equipment for this project).

Several harbors are located along the Rotterdam Waterway in open communication with the river. These harbors are subject to siltation resulting from water flowing into the harbor basin, where silt and fine sand particles settle down. The water movement toward the second petroleum harbor originates for about 85% from differences in the specific gravity of the river water at low and high tide and for the remaining percentage by tidal movement. Reference 17 describes how, by ap-

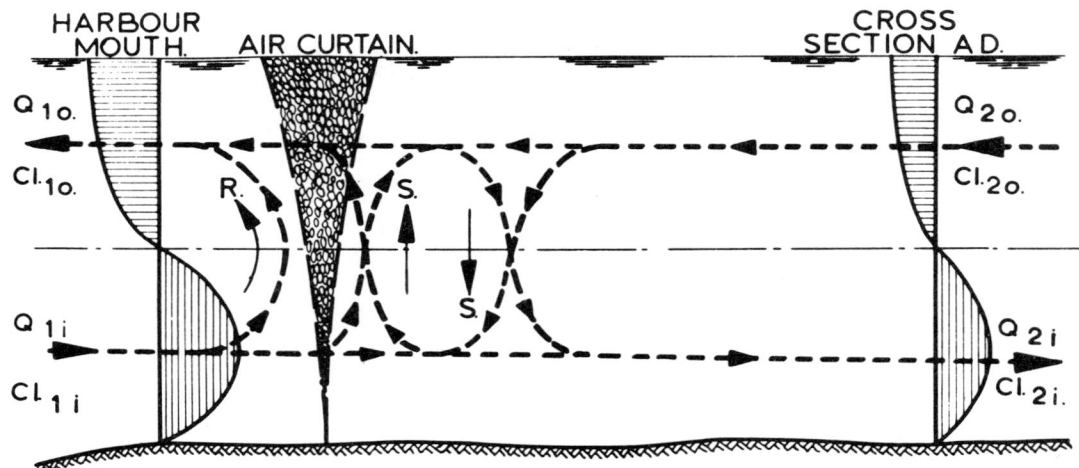

Figure 6.33. Airbubble screen in the harbor at Rotterdam, Netherlands (17).

plying an air bubble screen, reduced exchange is caused by differences in density. The pneumatic breakwater blowing silt-laden density currents up from the bottom to the surface was designed for 160 cubic meters of air per minute during five hours operation per tide, Figure 6.33 (17).

Hydraulic model experiments described by Simmons (52), with special reference to the conditions in the Hudson River, (mentioned in the following section) proved that pneumatic barriers offer a means for altering the salinity and hydraulic regimens of estuaries in the interests of reducing saltwater intrusion, reducing shoaling of critical areas and improving flashing characteristics.

Generally, it may be said that hydraulic model experiments are of great value in solving problems at estuaries and tidal inlets or at least for securing information useful for planning and for further field experience. Such models will have to be calibrated on a "time history" basis as model laws are difficult to establish for a great variety of conditions and changes in currents and sediments loads, making it impossible to fulfill model laws, including requirements to flow and sediment transport similitude. To the purely hydrodynamic difficulties are added problems like flocculation which are very difficult to imitate, but the result of flocculation tests may still be useful for qualitative evaluations. Reference is made to the Mersey River model test (47).

Major Examples on Estuary Shoaling and Improvements for Navigation

As an example of a *highly stratified estuary*, the Southwest Pass of the Mississippi should be mentioned (28, 51). For river stages of less than 10 feet at New Orleans, the tip of the saltwater wedge is located far upstream, 100 to 135 miles for minimum stages, and for such conditions, no significant shoaling takes place in the jetty and bar channel. For stages at New Orleans between 10 feet and 20 feet, the tip of the wedge is located within the jetty and bar channel, and a very rapid shoaling (1 to 2 feet per day) may take place in the area on either side of the tip. In order to handle this very hazardous situation, continued dredging is necessary. Figure 6.34 (28) shows the magnitude of shoaling which occurred in a two-week period during which dredges could not operate in the area because of hazards to navigation. The river stage during this period varied from 16.5

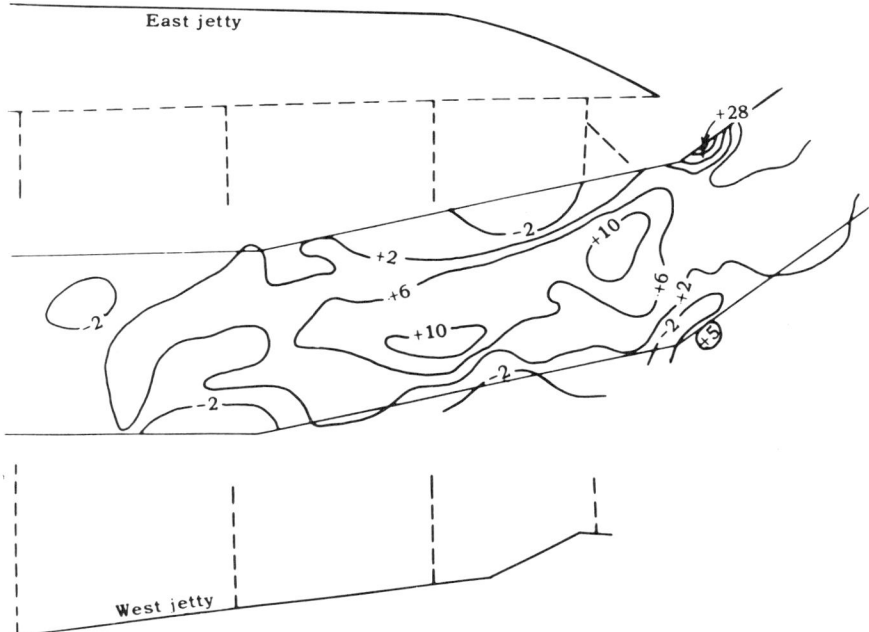

Figure 6.34. Shoaling for two-week period, Southwest Passage, Mississippi River (28).

to 17.5 feet. From Figure 6.34, it will be noted that filling the channel amounted to as much as 28 feet in one area, with an average of about 6 to 7 feet for the entire area of shoaling.

Another example of a *highly stratified estuary* is the Port of Cochin on the southwest coast of India which has a 450-foot wide, 16,000-foot long approach channel, 37 feet deep at low water (40). This channel passes through a crescent shaped bar, 4,000 feet from the entrance with a depth of 10 feet at low water (Figure 6.35). The tidal prism is approximately $50(10^6)$ cubic meters. During the monsoon period, the fresh-water flow exceeds the tidal prism in quantity.

A peculiar feature of the Cochin coast is the presence of mud banks, probably derived from river discharges north of Cochin. These mud banks travel from north toward south, particularly during the monsoon period when heavy wave action stirs them up. Before the entrance channel was dredged, it was expected that little silting would take place, but the situation developed very differently. The annual dredging of the approach channel has been about 2 million cubic yards and about 1.5 million cubic yards in the inner Mattencherry channel (Figure 6.35). This silt comes almost entirely from the offshore mud banks and is mainly brought in by the flood currents. The mechanics of the siltation apparently is that silt and clay on the sea bed is disturbed by wave action during the monsoon, causing a heavy concentration of silt which is carried by flood currents toward the entrance. By the time the sediment reaches the port entrance, most of the material moving in suspension flocculates, and the silt load is confined to the bottom, which has a high concentration in a 3-foot thick layer. Considerable siltation takes place in the Mattancherry channel (Figure 6.35), which, because of its location on the convex side of the entrance channel, becomes the natural intake for sediment at flood tide. The ebb tide, which is equally distributed between the Mattencherry and the Ernakulam channels, is not able to remove the material brought in by the flood current in the

242   Port Engineering

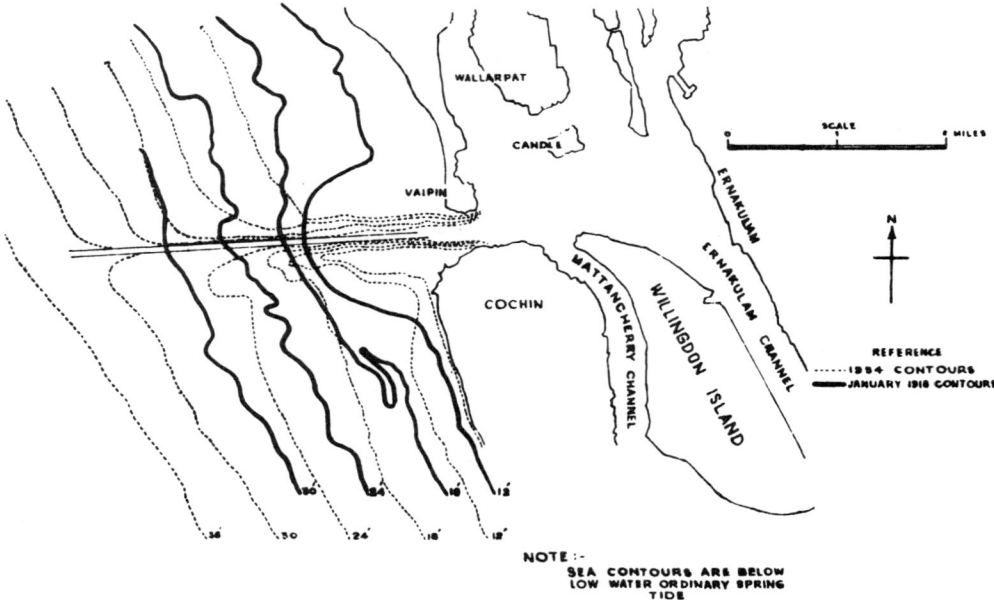

Figure 6.35. Port of Cochin, Southwest India (40).

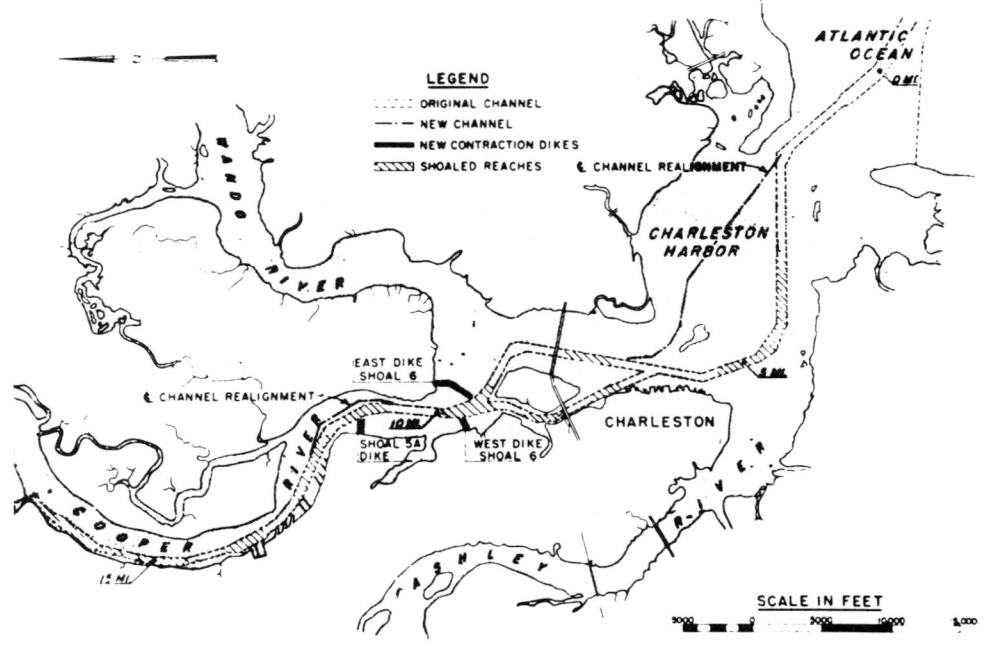

Figure 6.36. Location map of Charleston Harbor (40).

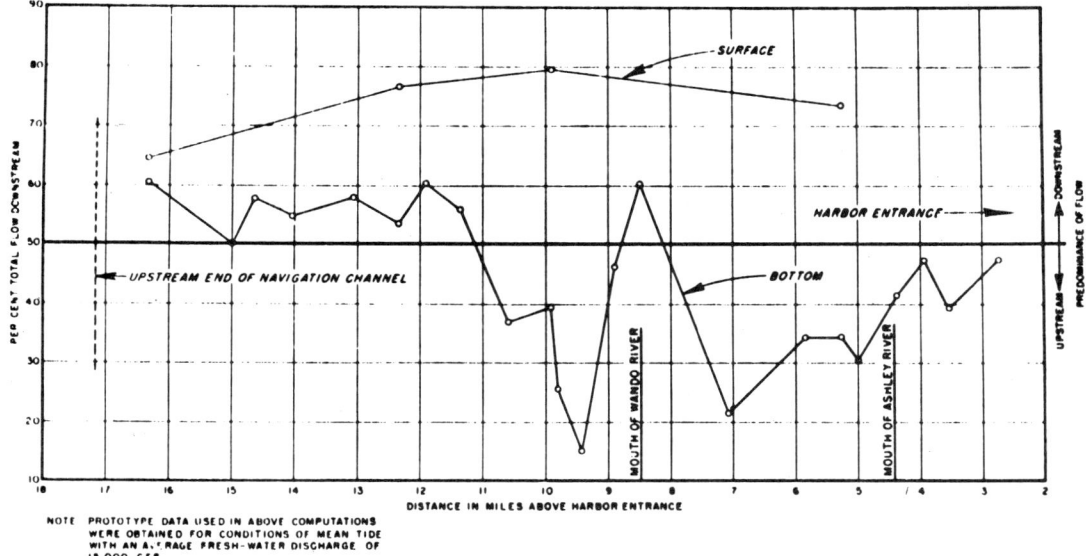

Figure 6.37. Predominance of flow in surface and bottom strata, Cooper River, Charleston Harbor (40).

Mattencherry channel. Thus, the material from the sea bed, disturbed by wave action, is carried by the flood currents from the main source of siltation, as is also confirmed by model experiments.

An interesting detail to be noted is the relation between tidal prism and gorge area which is almost linear. The tidal prism during spring tide is approximately $6(10^7)$ cubic meters, and the corresponding gorge area is approximately 5,000 square meters. This gives a mean maximum velocity of approximately 0.7 to 0.8 meters per second, which is somewhat lower than the mean maximum velocity of approximately 1 meter per second found in tidal inlets mentioned in Chapter 8. The difference is explained by the difference in bottom conditions and flow pattern in an entrance which carries density currents causing flow in two opposite directions in the same cross-sectional area. This situation necessarily requires a larger cross-sectional area than a unidirectional current system. Furthermore, bottom conditions (soft, silty material) probably have a similar effect.

In the more complicated *partly-mixed estuaries*, shoaling develops at each nodal point for predominance of bottom flow. As an example, Charleston Harbor, South Carolina, consists of three large rivers—the Cooper, Ashley and Wando (Figure 6.36)—of which only the Cooper contributes a significant source of fresh water (40, section by Schultz and Simmons). Figure 6.37 shows a plot of bottom and surface flow predominant along the Charleston Harbor (Cooper River) navigation channel. This figure reveals that flow at the surface is predominantly downstream throughout the harbor. At the bottom, however, the flow is predominantly upstream up to the Ashley River, at which point the upstream and downstream flow is essentially in balance. Upstream from the effects of the Ashley River the predominance of upstream flow is reestablished and prevails to the mouth of the Wando River, where in a short region bottom flow is predominantly downstream. The predominance of upstream flow at the bottom is reestablished beyond the mouth of the Wando River and prevails for several miles before a definite nodal area comes into existence. According to References 28 and 40, the turbulence associated with channel bifurcations and junctions, together with the fact that salinity varies with tide phases which are appreciably less in the Ashley and Wan-

244 Port Engineering

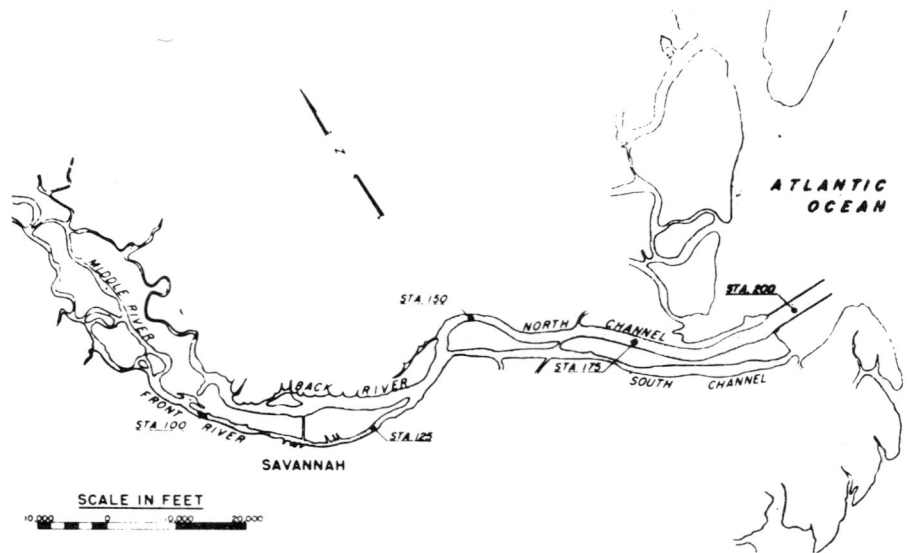

Figure 6.38. Location map of Savannah Harbor (40).

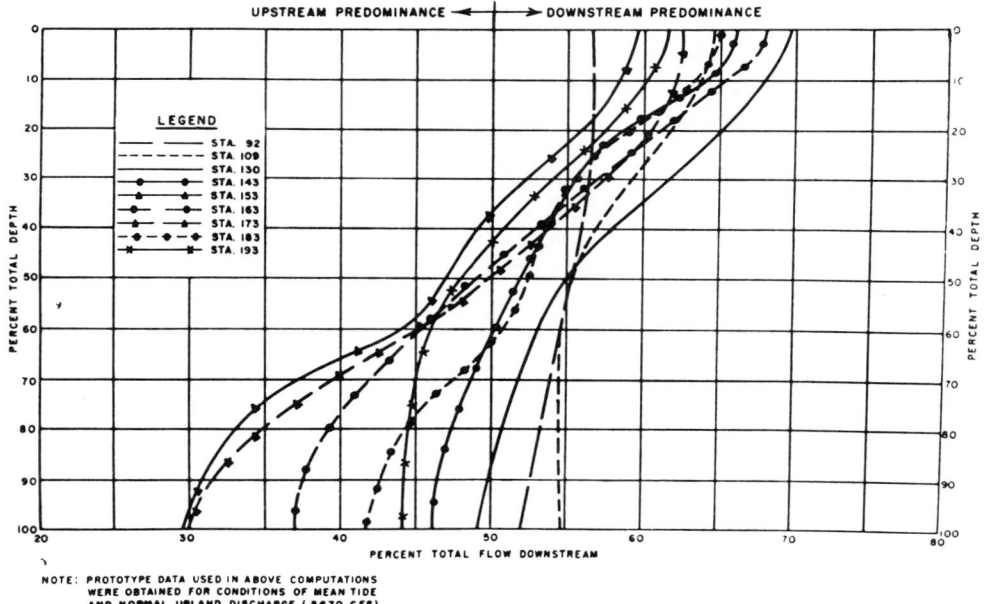

Figure 6.39. Flow predominance curves, Savannah Harbor, (27 and 40).

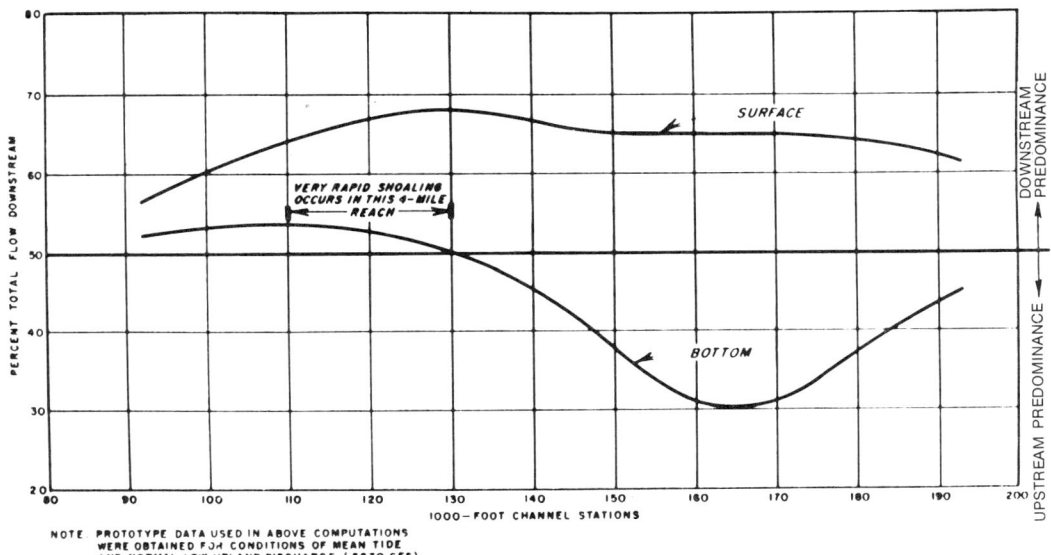

Figure 6.40. Predominance of flow in surface and bottom strata at Savannah Harbor (40).

do Rivers than in the Cooper River, is responsible for the local interruptions in the flow-predominance pattern. Vertical density gradients are greatly reduced at the junctions of the larger tributaries, with the result that the predominant upstream flow at the bottom is halted temporarily. The upstream predominance of bottom flow is quickly reestablished as soon as the effects of the tributary are passed. As demonstrated by Figure 6.36, shoaling in Charleston Harbor is heaviest in isolated reaches extending to and into the entrance—that means, in reaches far downstream from the range of movement of the interface. The controlling features appear to be the strong predominance of upstream current on the bottom in combination with such factors as excessive cross-sectional area, eddy and crosscurrents, and other physical parameters.

As another example of a partly-mixed estuary, the Savannah Harbor in Georgia should be mentioned (40, section by Schultz and Simmons). Figure 6.38 maps the location. Figure 6.39 presents flow predominance curves for various locations in Savannah Harbor (27, 40). At station 130, which is in the upstream limit of saltwater intrusion, all or most of the time, flow is predominantly upstream in the bottom 10 to 15% of the channel depth and predominantly downstream in the remaining 85 to 90% of the depth. At all other stations which are downstream from the intrusion limit at all times, flows are predominantly downstream from the surface to about mid-depth and are predominantly upstream from about mid-depth to the bottom.

Figure 6.40 (40) presents a different method for plotting the results of the above mentioned. The percentage of total flow downstream at surface and bottom for each station is plotted against channel stations. The resultant diagram indicates those harbor regions in which the currents at the depths under consideration are predominantly upstream or downstream and in what degree.

For the conditions described by Figures 6.39 and 6.40 sediment entering the upstream end of Savannah is moved. The average annual shoaling in Savannah Harbor presently amounts to 7.5 million cubic yards. Due to dredging, the major shoaling areas have shifted upstream. More than 80% of the

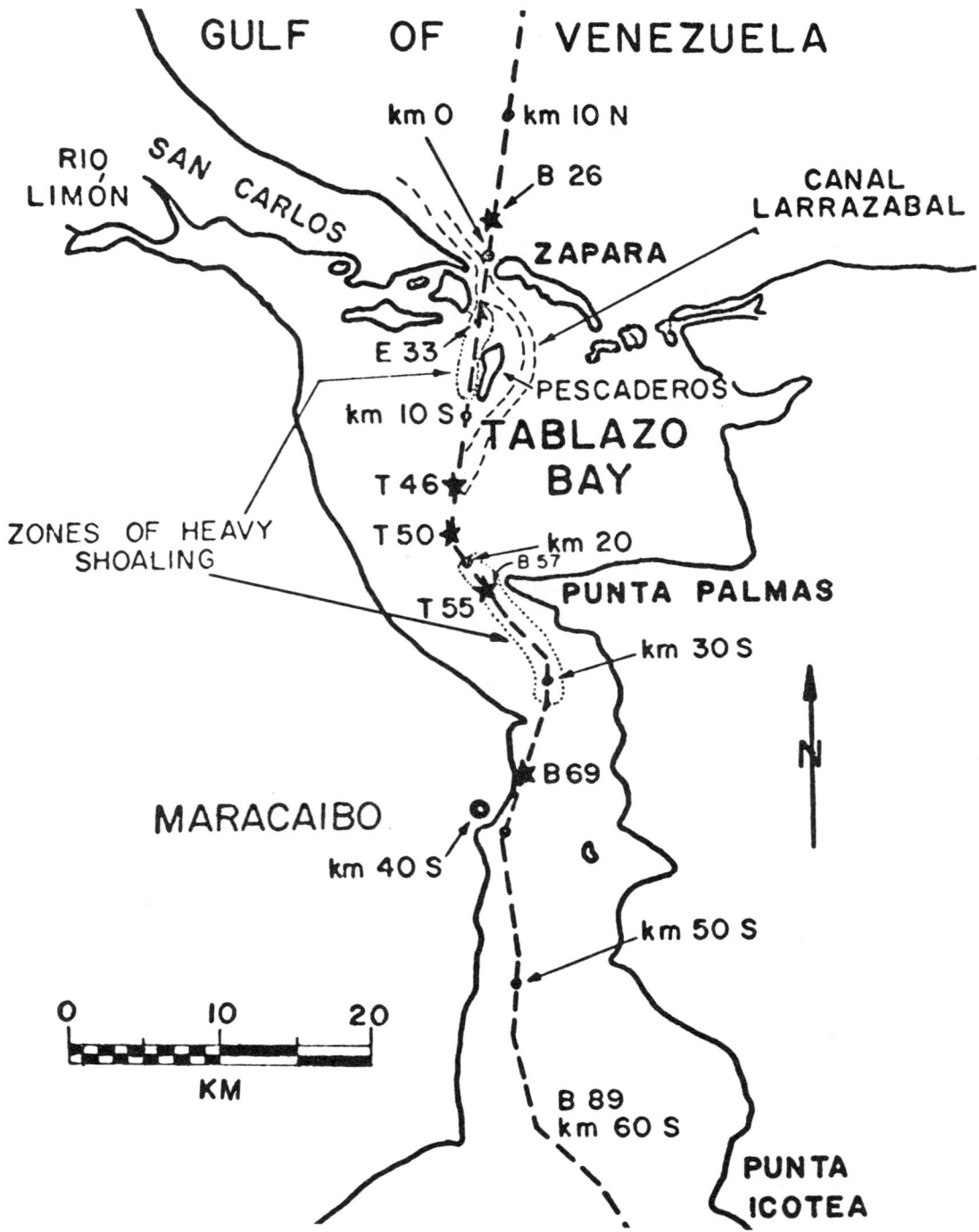

Figure 6.41. The Lake Maracaibo estuary and channel (38).

total shoaling occurs in a very short reach of the channel which brackets the nodal point for bottom flow predominance (Figure 6.40).

While the Savannah and Charleston Harbor estuaries have shoaling patterns controlled by the salinity intrusion, Maracaibo estuary (38) apparently is subjected to "tide-controlled" shoaling. Figure 6.41 shows an outline of the problem area at Maracaibo, which, with its marginal swamps, covers about 18,000 square kilometers and is connected to the Gulf of Venezuela by the Straits of Maracaibo and the broad and shallow Tablazo Bay, both of which have a surface area of approximately 1,100 square kilometers. The Straits of Maracaibo are approximately 40 kilometers long, and their width varies from about 18 to 7 kilometers. A natural channel about 3,000 feet wide and 38 to 58 feet deep runs through this zone. The distance between the northern end of the straits and the Gulf is about 24 kilometers through Tablazo Bay, where the depth varies from 2 to 15 feet, except within certain natural channels where it may exceed 20 feet.

A navigable channel leads from the Gulf to the lake. Its width is 800 feet within the bay and the straits and 1,000 feet within the Gulf. Its original depth in 1954 was 35 feet below mean sea level, but it was increased to 45 feet between 1960 and 1963. The total length of the navigable channel is about 100 kilometers.

With the constructing and deepening of the new channel, heavy shoaling started, requiring frequent dredging to maintain the desired navigation depth.

Within a 50-kilometer sedimentation zone, shown in Figure 6.41, there are two sections of extreme shoaling—(a) the first 10 kilometers of the interior channel; i.e., from the entrance to Tablazo Bay to the southern tip of the island of Pescaderos and (b) the 15-kilometer segment between 20 kilometers south to 35 milometers south (i.e., a little north of Punta Palmas to about midway between Punta Palmas and the city of Maracaibo). The sediment in the first shoaling zone is of the sandy loam type, composed of 50 to 65% fine sand, 20 to 35% silt and 5 to 15% clay. Within the second heavy shoaling zone, the sediment is much finer and of the sandy clay loam type with an average composition of 30% clay, 55% silt and 15% fine sand. Moreover, the latter sediment bears a striking similarity to the Gulf sediment and to that dredged from the exterior (within the Gulf) part of the channel. Very little sedimentation takes place south of the second shoaling zone. From dredging records, it appears that the shoaling rates are higher for the 45-foot channel than for the 35-foot channel.

The salinity of the lake water increased at substantial rates after the channel construction. From 1957 to 1962 the chlorinity at a reference point in the lake increased from 500 to 2,200 parts per million, and by 1966 it had already reach 5,000 parts per million. This is an indication of substantial salinity intrusion into the lake through the navigable channel.

The salinity intrusion into the lake, the similarity of sediment in the shoaling zones with that in the Gulf of Venezuela and the intense littoral transport along the coast suggested that the sediment originates from the Gulf and is transported to the shoaling zones by the net upstream bottom flow. This hypothesis was confirmed later by extensive field investigations and analysis of filed data on suspended sediment concentrations, salinity and velocities. These investigations disclosed that the estuary is of the partially-mixed type. A high salinity near bottom zone exists continuously through all seasons along the channel to the lake. Within a zone a substantial suspended sediment concentration was encountered at the upstream end of the second shoaling area. From this area to the lake, no measurable suspended sediment was detected.

From the velocity and sediment concentration data, the sediment discharge rate in pounds of dry material per foot per second was computed. The sediment transport rate through station T-50 (Figure 6.41), computed on the basis of average data for the five-month period from February to June, 1965, is equivalent to a deposition rate of about 0.008 feet of wet, low density mud per day over the second shoaling zone. This rate agrees with similar figures computed from the dredging data.

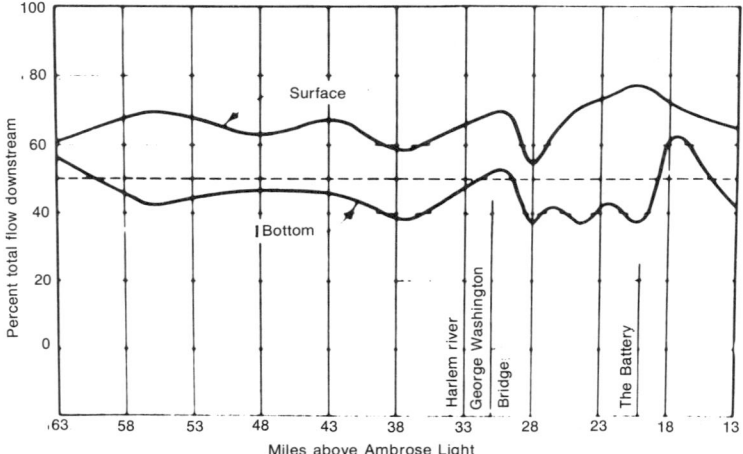

Figure 6.42. Flow predominance, surface and bottom, Hudson River, fresh-water discharge, 6,000 cubic feet per second (51).

In the Maracaibo estuary, no null point really exists, since, even at the entrance to the lake 60 kilometers south, strong net bottom currents have been detected. The heavy shoaling takes place in a zone where a strong upstream net bottom flow exists.

It should be noted that there is significant tidal energy dissipation in the Maracaibo estuary. The tidal height diminishes from 4.6 feet at the entrance near Zapara Island to 2.3 feet at Punta Palmas to about 8 inches near the lake (Figure 6.41). This dissipation is partly due to the sudden flow expansion in Tablazo Bay and partly to the shallow depth of the bay. The coarser part of the sediment, originating mainly from the coastal sandy littoral transport, requires relatively high shear stress and flow velocities for its resuspension and transport; therefore, it deposits in the first shoaling zone after its entrance to the interior navigable channel. The finer part of the sediment is transported further upstream to the second shoaling zone, where the tide-induced shear stresses are not sufficient for its resuspension. Comprehensive dredging by sidecasting is now being undertaken in the channel as described in Chapter 9.

Generally, it may be stated that in the well-mixed estuary shoals normally form in regions of low current velocity (excess cross-sectional area) and at places where local slowdown of current velocities takes place because of islands, strong curvatures, outlets of tributary streams, etc. The predominant vertical circulation pattern, however, makes it difficult or impossible for sediments to move through an estuary and out to the ocean by itself. As an example of such combining features of the well-mixed and the partly-mixed estuary, upper New York Bay and the Hudson River should be mentioned. While bottom flow in the Narrows is predominantly upstream, it is mainly downstream in upper New York Bay because of the mixing effects of the East River and Kill Van Kull. Figure 6.42 (51) shows that in the Hudson River, for a fresh-water discharge of 6,000 cubic feet per second, the bottom flow is predominantly upstream from the battery 60 miles upstream from Ambrose, except for a local area in the vicinity of the George Washington Bridge. The cross-sectional area of the channel at the George Washington Bridge is about 20 to 25% less than the average for this reach of the Hudson River, so local current velocities and turbulence are well above normal. Furthermore, the Harlem River, which is a relatively small stream connecting the Hudson and East Rivers, joins the Hudson River just upstream

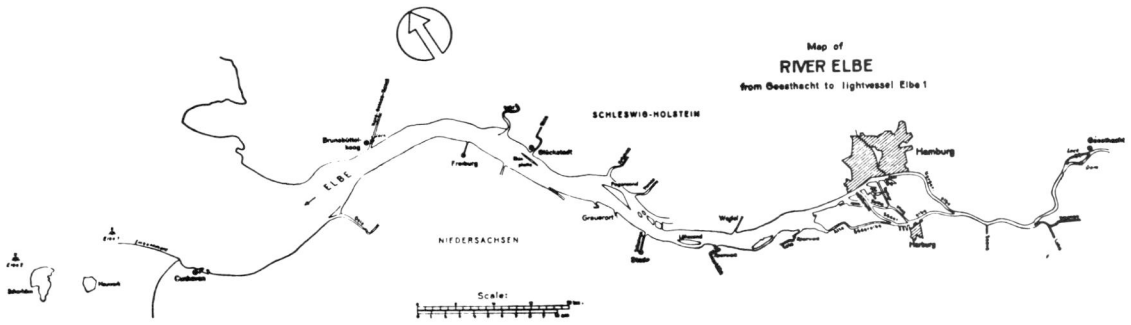

Figure 6.43. Elbe River, Germany (42).

from the bridge. The combined effects of this small tributary and the abnormal turbulence are such that the upstream predominance of bottom flow is interrupted locally. However, as in the case of Charleston Harbor, the upstream predominance is quickly reestablished and prevails for many miles upstream.

Very complex and difficult situations exist in the San Francisco Bay (41, section by Einstein and Krone) and Columbia River entrances (35), which are being investigated in comprehensive field and laboratory experiments in order to provide the best possibilities for improvements of depths which at present (1970) is 45 feet, allowing navigation by vessels of 40-foot draft.

Another complex case is presented by the condition in the Elbe River in north Germany (42, section by Niebuhr et al.). The improvement of this large estuary of the well-mixed type with an approximate 8-foot normal tidal range and a 9-foot spring tide range at Hamburg (Figure 6.43) started about 1,000 years ago by constructing dikes along the river. The main problem was countless sand banks. Before the turn of the century, the depth of the navigable channel to the important Hamburg seaport was brought up to 8 meters below mean high water. The need for greater depth increased rapidly, however. In this respect, it is fortunate that immediately adjacent to the Elbe estuary and close to the port of Cuxhaven (Figure 6.43), the 20-meter depth contour funnels in from the North Sea. This makes it possible to establish harbor basins in the shallow areas offering a safe natural access for vessels requiring a 20-meter draft.

Generally, the attempts to improve the Elbe as well as the Ems and Weser navigable channels included dredging in conjunction with regulation measures such as the construction of groins and embankments. The principles applied were increase of the tidal flow volume by removing all obstacles, such as a secondary branches, narrows sharp bends; formation of the river course widening gradually in the shape of a funnel from upstream to downstream with easy bends, and creation of a cross-section adapted to the volume of tide available from time to time, so that the current velocity required for self-cleaning the river was afforded.

An interesting question came up during these studies—namely whether flushing by currents should concentrate on ebb or on flood currents. The most natural answer to this question seems to be to use the ebb flow which, in the case of an estuary, would supposedly be more voluminous than the flood flow. In the case of the Elbe and other German estuaries (42), the situation is more complicated because littoral drift, which partly takes place in the form of large sand waves traveling on the bottom of the seashore, feeds material to the flood currents at the entrance (see Chapter 7 for details of sand wave movements). Even though ebb flow is higher quantitatively than the flood flow, density currents make the inflow of

250   Port Engineering

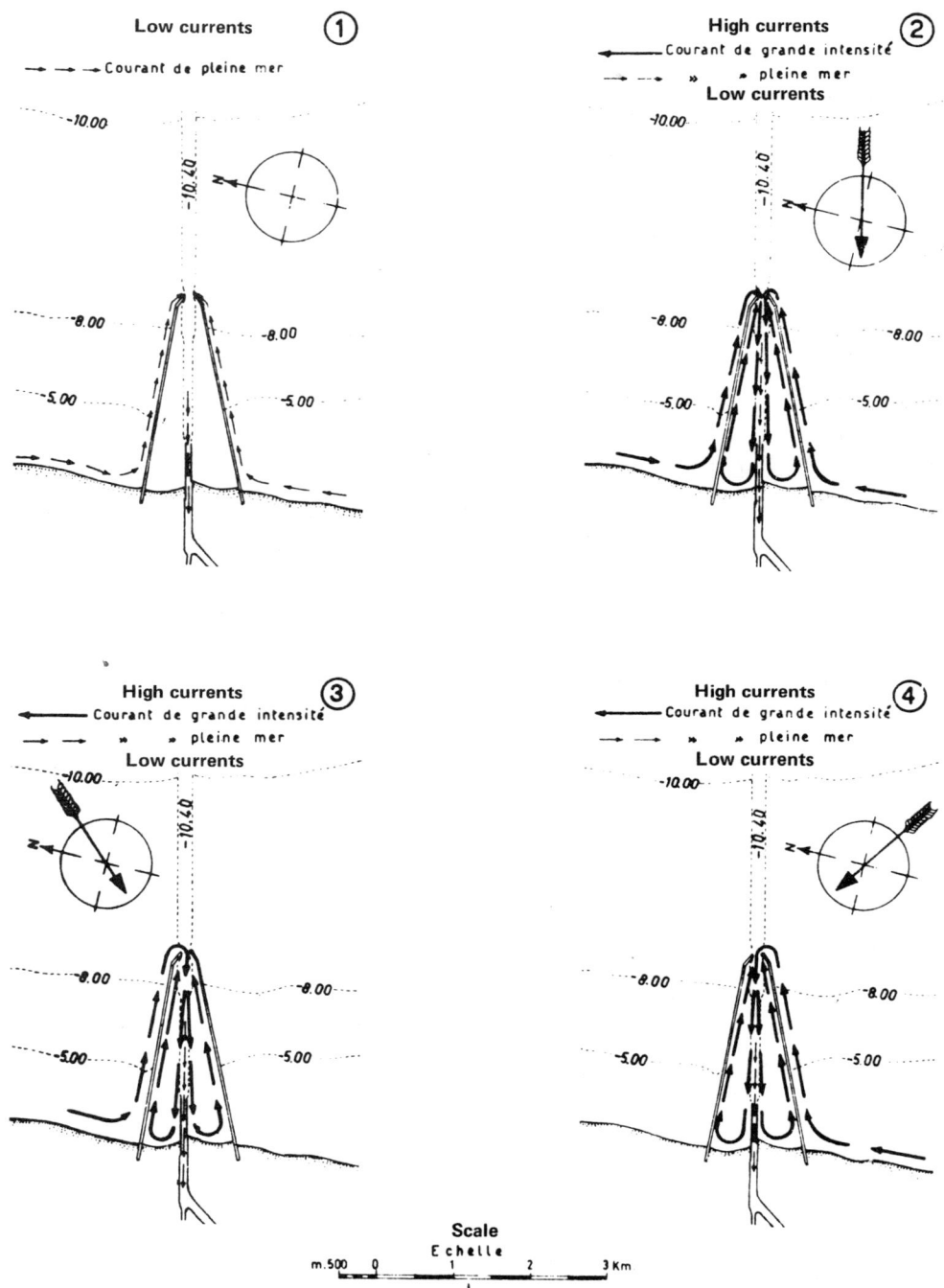

Figure 6.44. The Port of Ravenna, Italy (43).

bottom waters more predominant in large ranges of the river because the bottom density currents brake the ebb tide current in the lower part of the cross-section. Therefore, it is more logical to use the flood currents as flushing agents carrying the bottom material to sand traps established at strategic points. Although density currents are only involved to a minor extent in the case of inlets in Florida, the same principle is utilized there. Reference is also made to the preceeding section, including Figure 6.13, and to Chapter 8. The Elbe has been dredged to 11 meters below low tide up to Hamburg, and work is in progress to deepen it to 12 meters.

The consequences of the improvements have so far been an increase of tidal ranges from 6.5 to 8 feet at Hamburg, corresponding to changes in the tidal prism and displacement of the brackish water zone upstream. The increase in the tidal range is mainly caused by lowering of the low-water level. The improvements have had a beneficial effect on the stability of the navigation channels, particularly in the entrance and outer sections of the river, where sand movement in and out is considerable but, unfortunately, very irregular. Even if the increased tidal prism has caused an overall general improvement of this section, it cannot adjust itself to meet any situation, and the unavoidable fluctuations in sand supply must therefore be equalized by dredging operations to maintain a continuity in the navigation conditions.

In order to plan thoroughly for the future, a very comprehensive research program has now been initiated, including collection of all kinds of hydrographic data pertaining to the estuary, concentrating on the origin of the material transported by the estuary flows, including the movement of sand waves on the bottom of the North Sea in the entrance areas (32).

The Port of Ravenna on the Adriatic Sea presents a rather unique case (43, section by Migliardi, et al.). The sea is almost tideless, but as a result of a very gently offshore slope (Figure 6.44), the pileup by wind may reach 3 to 4 feet above mean sea level. This, together with waves up to about 10 feet proceeding over a shallow bottom, causes a rather strong longshore current which carries a considerable quantity of material, sand and silt. The now almost completed harbor of Ravenna (Figure 6.44) is protected against waves and sediments by two converging jetties, each having a length of 2,595 meters. Because the bottom is generally formed by a very small layer of sand disposed over a very deep layer of mud, the jetties are founded on a mattress of sand, obtained ·by dredging the soft layers and filling the excavation with about 13 feet of sand. The inner harbor is formed by the existing Candiano Canal deepened to about 31 feet by dredging and spoiling the material to form new industrial areas.

Figure 6.44 also shows (schematically) the drift pattern at the harbor for various winds. Because of the composition of the bottom, wave and current action stir up considerable amount of material. Part of this material penetrates through the narrow entrance into the outer harbor due to density currents, a situation similar to the Ymuiden case. Dredging operations are, therefore, necessary in order to maintain sufficient depth in this well-mixed estuary in an astronomically tideless, but actually wind tidal estuary.

Texas has some estuary problems of great concern and shares its problem with Mexico's Gulf Coast and with similar salt marsh areas in the Caribbean and elsewhere. As explained by Lockwood and Carothers in Reference 36 some of the bays and lagoons in Texas are too salty while others have too much fresh water. Fresh-water inflows into the lagoons have, historically, wide seasonal variations, ranging from severe droughts to major floods. In places these estuaries are being choked with pollution and spoil from dredging operations, increasing pollution. The Texas Water Development Board has recognized the possibility of serious damage to the estuaries and to fisheries by major but inevitable modifications of the river flows. The obvious solution to the problem would be to increase inflow of Gulf water into the estuaries to substitute for large quantities of fresh water. This exchange would be accomplished by using tidal inlets which would also permit migration of fish.

Lockwood and Carothers (36) estimated the annual inflows needed through seven new inlets to approximately 35 million acres-feet (approx. 40 billion cubic meters, 40 (10^9) cubic meters). These proposed inlets, together with existing inlets, are only spaced 25 to 30 miles apart because the efficiency of mixing between Gulf and estuary water is greatly decreased if distance is greater. With present limited Gulf water, together with river developments, hypersalinities may be expected at several bays, which necessitates a rather close spacing to replace the fresh-water flow. A similar situation exists on the approximately 50 miles of lagoon-shore in Mexico south of Brownsville (Texas)—Matamoros (Mexico) where the Laguna Madre has almost dried out and is only opened up occasionally by hurricane tides. Low tidal ranges and heavy littoral drifts prohibit maintenance of a permanent entrance(s) by nature.

References

1. Abecasis, F.M.N., Castanho, J.P., and Matias, M.F. 1969. "Coastal Regime." *Proceedings of 22nd Congress of PIANC* s II - s 4. Paris.
2. Adachi, S., Sawaragi, T., and Ogo, A. 1959. "The affects of coastal structures on the littoral sand drifts." *Coastal Engineering in Japan* 2:86-98.
3. Beach Erosion Board. 1950. *The Source, Transportation, and Deposition of Beach Sediment in Southern California.* Tech Memo 22. U.S. Army Corps of Engineers.
4. Bijker, E.W. and Svasek, J.N., 1969. "Littoral drift as a function of waves and currents." *Proceedings of 22nd Congress of PIANCs* II - s4(58):155-80. Paris.
5. Bruun, P. 1954. "Forms of equilibrium of coasts with a littoral drift." *Coast Stability.* Copenhagen: Danish Technical Press.
6. _____. 1963. "Longshore currents and longshore troughs." *Journal of Geophysical Research* 68(4):1065-77. Theory expanded statistically in Chiu and Bruun. "Computation of longshore currents by breaking waves." *Engineering Progress at the University of Florida* 18(3).
7. _____. 1966. *Tidal Inlets and Littoral Drift.* Oslo: University Book Company.
8. _____. 1967. "Bypassing and backpassing." *ASCE Journal of the Waterways and Harbors Division* 93(WW3):101-28.
9. _____. 1968. "Shore protection in harbor construction with special reference to littoral drift shores." *Proceedings of the 5th International Harbor Congress.* Antwerp.
10. _____. 1969. "Quantitative field research on littoral drift using tracers." *Proceedings of the 22nd Congress of PIANC* s II - C 4:155-80. Paris.
11. _____. 1970. "Use of tracers in harbor, coastal and ocean engineering." *Engineering Geology,* vol. 4. Amsterdam: Elsevier Publishing Company. pp. 73-88.
12. _____, and Gerritsen, F. 1959. "Natural bypassing of sand at coastal inlets." *ASCE Journal of the Waterways and Harbors Division* 85(WW4):75-107. *See also,* Bruun and Gerritsen. 1960. *Stability of Coastal Inlets.* Amsterdam: North Holland Publishing Company.
13. _____, and Manohar, M. 1963. "Coastal protection for Florida." *Engineering Progress at the University of Florida* 17(8).
14. Burns, R.E. 1963. "Importance of marine influences in estuarine sedimentation." *Proceedings of the Federal Inter-Agency Sedimentation Committee.* Misc. Pub. 970(64): 593-98.
15. Coastal Engineering Laboratory of the University of Florida.. 1958. "Coastal engineering study at Ft. Pierce." *Engineering Progress at the University of Florida* 12(9).
16. Cornick, H.F. 1959. *Dock and Harbour Engineering,* vol. 2. London: Charles Griffin and Co. Ltd.
17. de Nekker, J., and Knol, J. 1968. "Results of experiments with an air-bubble screen against siltation in the Rotterdam Harbor." *Proceedings of the 5th International Harbor Congress.* Antwerp.
18. Dronkers, J.J. 1969. "Tidal computations for rivers, coastal areas, and seas." *ASCE Journal of the Hydraulics Division* 95(HY1):29-77.
19. Eagleson, P.S. 1965. *Theoretical Study of*

Longshore Currents on a Plane Beach. Tech Report 82. MIT: Hydrodynamics Laboratory.
20. Galvin, Cyril J. 1967. "Longshore current velocity: a review of theory and data." *Review of Geophysics* 5(3):287-303.
21. Halliwell, A.R., and O'Dell, M. 1969. "Differences in silt pattern across an estuary." *The Dock and Harbour Authority* 50(585):125-29.
22. Harleman, D.F., and Ippen, A. 1969. "Salinity intrusion effects in estuary shoaling." *ASCE Journal of the Hydraulics Division* 95(HY1):9-27.
23. Ingle, James C. 1966. *The Movement of Beach Sand.* New York: Elsevier Publishing Company.
24. Inglis, C.C. 1947. *Meanders and their Bearing on River Training.* London: The Institution of Civil Engineers, Maritime and Waterway Engineering Division.
25. Inman, D.C., and Bagnold, R.A. 1963. "Littoral processes." *The Sea,* vol 3. New York: Interscience Publications. pp. 529-33.
26. _____, and Komar, P.D. 1969. "Longshore transport of sand." *Proceedings of the 11th Conference on Coastal Engineering.* London. pp. 298-306.
27. Ippen, A., ed. 1966. *Estuary and Coastline Hydrodynamics.* New York: McGraw-Hill Book Company, Inc.
28. _____. 1966. "Salinity intrusion in estuaries" and "Sedimentation in estuaries." *Estuary and Coastline Hydrodynamics.* New York: McGraw-Hill Book Company, Inc. pp. 598-629 and 648-72.
29. Keulegan, G.H. 1966. "The mechanics of an arrested saline wedge." *Estuary and Coastline Hydrodynamics.* Edited by A. Ippen. New York: McGraw-Hill Book Company, Inc. pp. 546-74.
30. Larras, Jean. 1957. *Plages et cotes des Sables.* Paris: Publishing House Eyrolles.
31. _____. 1964. *Embouchures, Estuaries, Lagunes et Deltas.* Paris: Publishing House Eyrolles.
32. Laucht, H. 1968. "Ursachen und Zicle der Hamburger Kustenforschung und der Elbmundung." *Hamburger Kustenforschung.* Heft 1. Hamburg: Freie und Hansetadt.
33. Lauf, George F., ed 1967. *Estuaries Pub.* 83. American Association for the Advancement of Science.
34. Leopold, L.B., and Wolman, G.M. 1957. *River Channel Patterns Braided, Meandering and Straight.* Geological Survey Prof. Paper 282-B. Washington D.C.: U.S. Government Printing Office.
35. Lockett, John B., and Kidby, Harold A. 1961. "Prototype measurement of the Columbia River estuary." *ASCE Journal of the Hydraulics Division* 87(HY1):57-83.
36. Lockwood, M.G., and Carothers, H.P. 1967. "Preservation of estuaries by tidal inlets." *ASCE Journal of the Hydraulics Division* 93(HY1):133-52.
37. Nichols, M., and Poor, G. 1967. "Sediment transport in a coastal plain estuary." *ASCE Journal of the Waterways and Harbors Division* 93(WW4):83-95.
38. Partheniades, E. 1970. Discussion of Proc. Paper 6340 by D.R.F. Harleman and A. Ippen, "Salinity intrusion effects in estuary shoaling." *ASCE Journal of the Hydraulics Division* 96(HY1):264-88.
39. _____, and Kennedy, John F. 1967. "Depositional behavior of fine sediment in a turbulent fluid motion." *Proceedings of the 10th Conference on Coastal Engineering* (10):707-29. Tokyo. *See also,* Staff Pub.136. MIT: Hydrodynamics Laboratory.
40. Permanent International Association of Navigation Congresses. 1957. "Siltation in coastal works, in estuaries, in channels, in tidal basins, in enclosed docks and in maritime channels." *Proceedings of 19th Congress of PIANC* s II- c 3. London.
41. _____. 1961. "Methods of determining sand and silt movement along the coast, in estuaries and in maritime rivers. Use of modern techniques such as radioactive isotopes, iuminophores, etc." *Proceedings of 20th Congress of PIANC* s II - s 5. Baltimore.
42. _____. 1961. "Orientation and layout of ac-

cesses to seaports and the improvement of the channel as far as deep water—increasing the depth and maintaining it—influence of currents, waves and wind and of the transport of bed material." *Proceedings of 20th Congress of PIANC* s II - s 2. Baltimore.

43. _____. 1969. "Coastal regime, carriage of material by swell and currents. Model studies and on site observations. Influence of port structures. Coastal defence works, breakwaters." *Proceedings of 22nd Congress of PIANC* s II - s 4. Paris.

44. _____. 1969. "The problem of bed-load in canalized rivers and in sections of a partially canalized waterway, in particular at the mouth of tributaries." *Proceedings of 22nd Congress of PIANC* s I - s 5. Paris.

45. Petersen, M.S. 1966. "Laboratory contributions to channel stabilization." *ASCE Journal of the Waterways and Harbors Division* 92(WW1):87-108.

46. Postma, H. 1967. "Sediment transport and sedimentation in the estuarine environment." *Estuaries*. Edited by George H. Lauf. Pub. 83:158-279. American Association for the Advancement of Science.

47. Price, W.A., and Kendrick, Mary P. 1963. "Field and model investigation into the reason for siltation in the Mersey estuary." *Proceedings of the Institution of Civil Engineers* 24:473-518. London.

48. Putnam, J.A., et al. 1949. "The prediction of longshore currents." *Transactions of American Geophysical Union* 30:337-45.

49. Schultz, E.A., and Simmons, H.B. 1957. *Fresh Water-Salt Water Density Currents, a Major Cause of Siltation in Estuaries*. Tech Bulletin 21. Committee on Tidal Hydraulics, U.S. Army Corps of Engineers.

50. Shubinski, R.P., et al. 1965. "Computer simulation of esturial networks." *ASCE Journal of the Hydraulics Division* 91(HY5):33-49.

51. Simmons, H.B. 1966. "Field experience in estuaries." *Estuary and Coastline Hydrodynamics*. Edited by A. Ippen. New York: McGraw-Hill Book Company, Inc. pp. 673-90.

52. _____. 1967. "Potential benefits of pneumatic barriers in estuaries." *ASCE Journal of the Hydraulics Division* 93(HY3):1-16.

53. Thornton, E.B. 1969. "A field investigation of sand transport in the surf zone." *Proceedings of the 11th Conference on Coastal Engineering*. London. pp. 335-51.

54. Trask, Parker D. 1950. *Applied Sedimentation*. New York: John Wiley and Sons.

55. _____. 1955. *Movement of Sand Around Southern California Promontories*. Tech Memo 76. Beach Erosion Board, U.S. Army Corps of Engineers.

56. Van der Burgh, P. 1968. "Prediction of the extent of salt water intrusion into estuaries and seas." *Journal of Hydraulic Research* (4):267-88.

57. Veen, John van. 1950. "Ebb and flood channels in the Dutch tidal waters." *Koninklyk Nederlands Aardrykskundig Genootschap, Tweede Reeks* 98(3).

58. Vincent, G.E., and Gamot, J.P. 1957. "Defense des port maritimes contre l'ensablement." *Les Energies De La Mer, France*. pp. 590-99.

59. Waterloopkundig Laboratorium. 1952. *History and Description of Hydraulic Model Investigations*. Delft, Holland.

Note: Furthermore the reader is referred to a number of papers on estuary problems which will be printed in Volume 4 of *Proceedings of the 14th Congress of the International Association for Hydraulic Research* (Paris, 1971).

7 coastal geomorphology vs. port engineering

Coastal geomorphology is the field which describes the development of a coast or a coastal zone under the influence of acting forces by winds, waves and currents, including development in all dimensions, all movements (progradation and retrogradation) and mineralogical, chemical and biological features which are associated with morphological development. Coastal geomorphology is a multifield composed of geology, geography and geophysics, including hydrodynamics, wave current and wind mechanics. In the port engineering field, it is particularly important to predict future shore development. As an example, a port should neither be built on a shore with heavy erosion and littoral drift nor on a shore with heavy accretion. However, some ports were built that way.

The old Roman Naval Port Ostia on the Tiber sanded up completely. In Ireland attempts to maintain the harbor at Dublin at the entrance to Liffey River involved considerable difficulties for which reason a harbor was built at Howth in 1807-17. Also a disappointment, it had to be abandoned. Next a harbor was built at Kingstown. It was successful because of relatively less material transport by flood currents to the entrance and the existence of a slow flushing ebb current through the entrance.

Some ports, built on exposed shores, were destroyed by the sea. A unique example is the destruction of Port Royal at Jamaica in 1692 by an earthquake causing a severe landslide which took the port with it. Such a slide would not have occurred had the bottom profiles not been weakened by the high steepness caused by sea forces. Similar slides take place rather often in Norwegian fjords due to excessive river material accumulation on steep slopes.

The normal case of port installation destruction is that the barrier or inlet shore, or any other shore of alluvial material upon which the port was built, erodes away. This has happened in many estuaries and at numerous tidal inlets all over the world necessitating comprehensive coastal protection measures. Examples are Den Helder in Holland, Thyboroen Inlet in Denmark and Absecon Inlet in New Jersey.

The field has acquired increasing interest during recent years. At earlier times consideration of development up to 40-foot depth sufficed; it is now, due to the still increasing demands for greater navigation depths, often indispensable to consider development up to at least 60 to 80 feet. This may sound rather innocent because of the relatively small depth increase, but the distance from the 50-foot to even the 60-foot contour may be much longer than the distance between the shoreline and the 50-foot contour. This is a typical situation for many sandy shores. As an

Table 7.1
Areas and Depths of Important Shelves

Name of Shelf	Area (1000 km²)	Depth (m)
Northwest European	1050	Mostly less than 100
Norwegian	93	200-300
Barents	830	200-300
North Siberian	1330	50% less than 50
Iceland-Faeroe	115	200-300
Newfoundland	345	150-200
Florida-Texas (Gulf)	385	Mostly under 50
Campeche (Yucatan)	170	Mostly under 50
Guiana	485	Mostly under 50
South Brazilian	370	Mostly under 50
Patagonian	960	50-100
Agulhas	75	Mostly more than 100
Zambezi	55	Mostly under 50
Bombay	230	50-100
NW Australian (incl. Sahul)	590	50-100
Arafura	930	50-100
South Australian	320	50-100
Tasmanian	160	50-100
Queensland	190	Mostly under 100
Burma	290	Mostly under 100
Sunda (Borneo-Java)	1850	50-100
Tongking-Hongkong	435	Mostly under 100
Tunghai	915	Mostly under 100
Okhotsk-Sakhalin	715	50-100
Bering	1120	50% less than 50

Source: Krummel, O. 1897. *Handbuch der Ozeanographie*. 2 vols. Stuttgart.

example, at St. Augustin, Florida, the 50-foot contour is about 10,000 feet from shore, but the 60-foot contour is about 30,000 feet. If there is a bottom erosion outside the 50-foot contour, this would be of no immediate concern, unless it causes a strong bottom drift which would block any deep-water navigation channel. Continued erosion could, however, eventually cause too steep—and therefore unstable—bottom profiles resulting in shoreline recession. This recession could develop very quickly as a result of one particular severe storm (or an earthquake, as at Port Royal). If the offshore bottom also is accreting, the situation is much worse for developing future navigation channels. This happens particularly at the entrance to estuaries and major tidal inlets such as the Golden Gate.

The configuration of rocky shores is mainly a result of geological factors. A very slow adjustment process occurs as a combined result of tectonic movements, weathering, wear and tear and reactions to sea level fluctuations relative to land. The latter process may cause development of terraces (abrasion platforms), as seen in Southern California, and continental shelves usually at depths varying between 70 and 100 fathoms. Table 7.1 shows areas and depths of important continental shelves. It may be seen that average depth generally is less than 100 meters (330 feet) and in a good many cases is even less than 50 meters (165 feet), although depth at the outer extremity is usually of the order of 200 meters (660 feet).

Shelves of limited width may consist of two parts—an inner abrasion platform, the depth of which is of particular importance in port engineering, and an outer constructional form built up of material eroded during the formation of the inner part. The best example of a constructional form (with subsidence of the sediments) is the shelf off the east coast of the United States, that, to a high degree, was built up of eroded material from the Appalachian rocks. The coastal shelf of the Gulf of Mexico is the same type and has been formed by a great mass of material brought down by the Mississippi River and other streams.

The shores which the port engineer is particularly interested in are those which were built up of alluvial materials like sand, clay and gravel because they are relatively "soft" and erode (or accrete) much faster than rocky shores, making it possible to observe their movements from year to year and perhaps to relate their behavior to the physical forces to which they are exposed. One may distinguish between the "static description" of a shore development, which may include evolutionary theories, and the "dynamic description." The former is typical for descriptive research like geology and geography; the latter belongs to the physical or engineering approach when any development is considered in relation to the acting forces.

Static and Evolutionary Descriptions

The classical description of a shore referred to the way it presented itself geologically or geographically without consideration to "forces involved." Shores were divided into "flat shores" (gently sloping shores) and "steep shores." Later detailed studies on the geometrical shape of these shores, including the offshore abrasion platforms, were added (43). It was the American, William Morris Davis, who about 1900 first introduced the basic scientific principle of considering any feature in nature's morphology as only one picture of a development which is active and ever changing. For Davis, "structure, process and stage (s)" were the essential features to be considered for any deeper understanding. A consequence of this method was the time-classification of the features as "old," "mature" and "young."

Davis's theories, when used on seashore phenomena, resulted in the classification of all shores into two catagories, namely (a) shores of emergence and (b) shores of submergence (20). Shores of emergence are characterized by barrier and lagoon systems, offshore bars, ridge and dune systems, all demonstrating that the quantity of material above and below the water table is increasing either because the shore is coming up or because the water is coming down. It should be noted, however, that shores of no relative movement between sea and land may have the appearance of shores of emergence just because material is accumulated. This is explained in the section on development of beach and bottom profiles. The U.S. eastern seaboard from Sandy Hook to Key West is an example of a shore of emergence, presenting itself today as a result of outpour of material derived by erosion of the Apalachian Highland and the lowering of sea level which took place when the latest glacial stage developed. When the ice with its marginal moraines standing on Long Island finally melted approximately 20,000 years ago, the sea level started coming up again and an erosion cycle, still continuing, followed gradually, encroaching more and more upon the appearance of the shore as a shore of emergence.

Shores of submergence are often characterized by deep fjords, drowned valleys and open bays, all depending upon the geomorphological and geological structure of the shore. An example is the Norwegian Coast, which was heavily submerged as a result of the enormous compression by the ice cap. This was also true of Greenland. Supposedly a solid island, Greenland consists mainly of narrow shores with an ice-filled saucepan between them, the bottom of the pan being below sea level due to the load of the ice.

Davis's classification, although it is able to explain some coastal features on the large scale, does not consider the result of rapid shore development due to imbalance between the material brought to the shore and the material carried away from the shore. The result of this imbalance is that shores of Davis's emergence type may erode and look as if they were submerging. And, vice versa, shores of the Davis's submergence type, because of rapid accumulation, may have the appearance of shores of emergence. Erosion and accretion can, in the geological time scale, be classified as "stopwatch" phenomena. As explained later, it is still true that a relative rise of sea level, compared to land, tends to cause erosion while a relative lowering of sea level, compared to land, tends to cause accumulation.

Rapid shore development by accumulation or erosion is not least typical on the eastern seaboard from Long Island southward. Because of its barriers, hundreds of miles long, and its huge spit and barrier systems, the eastern seaboard is an El Dorado of coast researches. No wonder that the United States should be in a leading position in respect to coastal morphology, its greatest contribution being D.W. Johnson's *Shore Processes and Shoreline Development*, 1919 (35), which presents itself as a comprehensive encyclopedia in descriptive coastal morphology and geography.

Dynamic Approach

The dynamic approach considers the development of a shore, including its horizontal and cross-sectional geometry, erosion and accretion, and mineralogical composition in relation to acting forces by winds, waves and currents. The dynamic approach may also be classified as the physics or engineering approach because it combines movement of material (mass times travel distance) with work by forces (by wind, waves and currents). In order to utilize this approach, much data composed of exact topographical surveys and surveys of winds, waves, currents and sediment movements are necessary. Attempts are then made to relate these factors.

The dynamic approach has progressed considerably. The first progress made—merely of philosophic or speculative nature—was based on assumptions which sounded likely. It is surprising to see how speculative wave energy assumptions related to material transport (thereby to shoreline movements) and reasoned in shoreline configurations by later research proved to be "reasonably right." Although considerable progress has been made on how to relate wave and current energy in the nearshore zone to material transport, still much remains to be done. On a shore composed of alluvial material, most material transport takes place at and inside the breaker zone when water movements are very turbulent and the current system is very complex. Therefore, it must be considered unrealistic that it should be possible to establish simple and unique relationships between "forces" and "work by forces" in the nearshore zone. The complexity of nature's operation undoubtedly prohibits that. On the other hand, it is highly likely that it is possible gradually to build up a still increasing "file of experience and data" which will make it still more possible to predict littoral drift movements as well as shoreline and profile movements when wave and current data are available. The difficulty mainly lies in the recording procedures, and the problems involved are so complex that the instrumentation needed could influence the field test. Modern tracing techniques as explained in Appendix 4 have improved chances of success and will probably greatly improve the status of actual knowledge on these problems in years to come. Chapter 6 gives examples of field and laboratory tests.

Coastal morphology, as it presents itself today, is mainly a result of the speculative but still improving reasoned approach. The following sections deal with the configurative development of shoreline and beach and bottom profiles.

Erosion and Accretion

Shore erosion arises when more material is eroded away than deposited. Waves causing erosion are generated by transfer of wind energy to the water by interfacial shear stress. Waves may also be generated by other means, such as underwater earthquakes, but these occur infrequently.

Coasts may be rocky and sandy. The former type does not create any erosion problem. The latter type, however, is constantly in transitional movement and may have to be protected against erosion.

Usually there are two types of erosion: (a) natural erosion from natural causes such as storms, tides, and rise in sea level and (b) man-made erosion resulting from improperly designed and incorrectly located coastal structures, or caused by inlets and entrance channels. Both result from disturbance of natural equilibrium between supply and loss of material. The former may be either a very slow process, such as is caused by the slowly rising sea level, or a sudden one from storms, showing the appearance of devastation. Man-made erosion is a process caused by man's interference with natural shore processes, such as inlet improvement by dredging and/or construction of jetties and training walls and coastal protection which blocks the natural movement of sediment along the shore. It is mentioned later how one can distinguish between natural and man-made erosion by studying the development of beach profiles.

In the section on shoreline configuration development, various littoral drift formulas relating drift quantity to longshore wave energy input are considered, and it is shown how various forms of equilibrium may be developed by using these equations. Although forms may be eroding or accreting, they keep their configuration or tend to approach a configuration which results from an equilibrium condition between acting forces and material movement which leaves the shoreline configuration unchanged. Any deviation from the equilibrium form will cause movements deviating from those associated with the equilibrium conditions.

The configuration development of eroding profiles is mentioned in the section on the development of beach and bottom profiles. Man-made structures may influence the shoreline configuration considerably as explained in the section on the influence of port installations on shore configuration.

Shore accretion is just the opposite of erosion because more material is deposited than eroded. As explained in the section on shoreline configuration and as mentioned earlier, the equilibrium forms associated with accretion may be computed, based on assumptions of material movements versus equilibrium configuration. The development of accreting profiles is mentioned in the section on the development of beach and bottom profiles. Man-made structures may influence the shoreline configuration considerably as explained in the section on the influence of port installations on shore configuration.

Natural erosion is usually a rather slow geological and climatological process, or perhaps a sudden one caused by extreme storms and storm tides. Although it may amount to average shoreline recession of a few feet per year, great deviations may occur because of changes in the actual weather situation. Figure 7.1 shows schematically the erosion situation by annual shoreline recessions in Florida, 1963 (17). It may be seen that shoreline recessions vary greatly. On the majority of the shores, it is between 0 and 3 feet per year. At some places, it is much higher—even up to about 20 feet per year. These terrific erosion rates are caused by littoral drift barriers which could be natural inlets but usually are man-made. Another reason for erosion, as mentioned earlier, is sea level rise.

Influence of Rise in Sea Level

Changes in sea level have produced great changes in land area due to low relief. Present studies indicate a general rise in sea level of approximately 1 foot in 100 years with a noticeable increase in recent years along the U.S. East Coast (24), probably due to the melting of midlatitude ice caps. Between 1940 and 1960, the sea level in northeast Florida rose by about 1/6 inch per year, while the upper Gulf Coast experienced about 1/8-inch rise per year. The slowly rising sea level is encroaching on land causing shoreline recession.

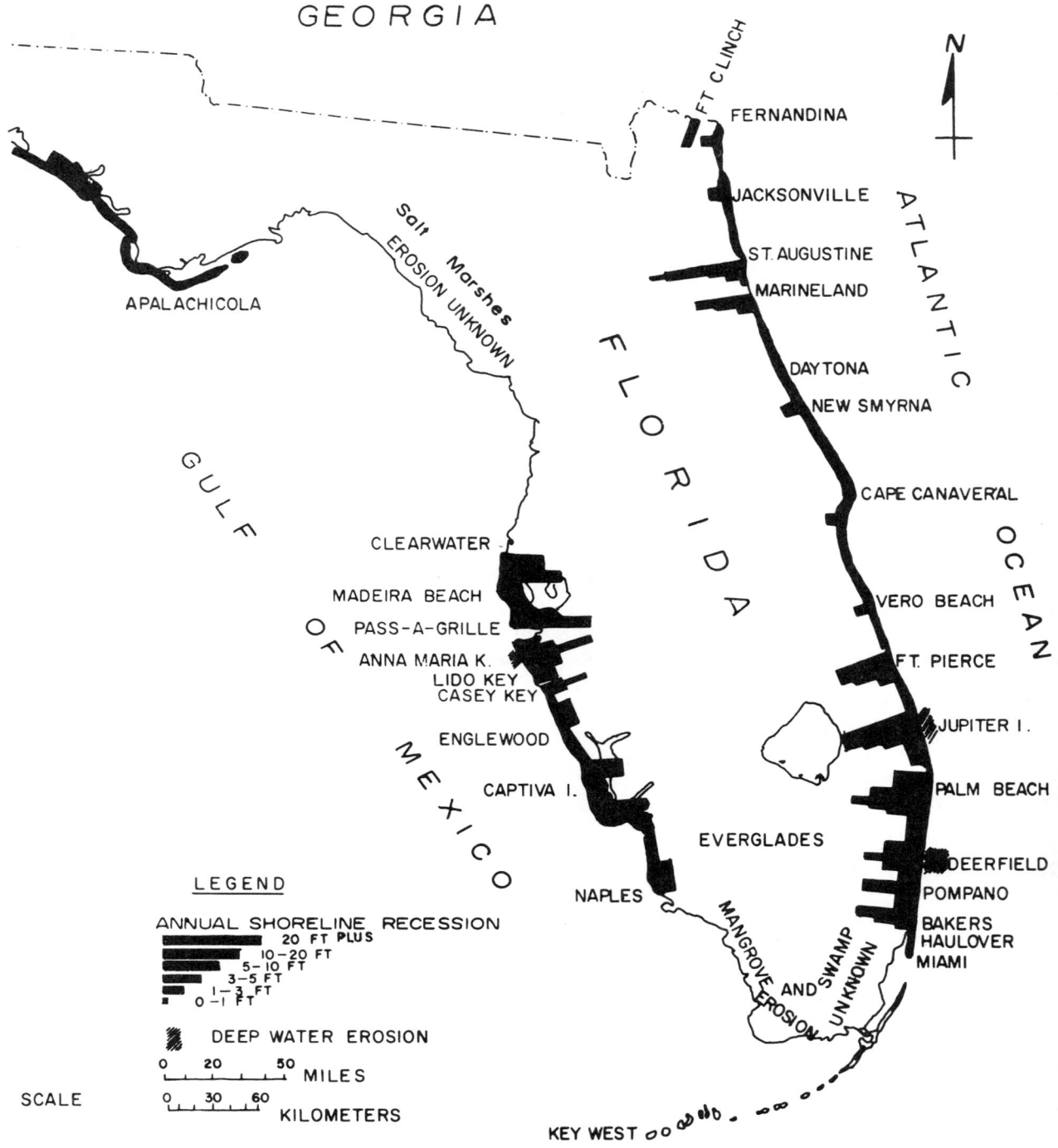

Figure 7.1. Erosion situation in Florida, 1963 (17).

Coastal Geomorphology

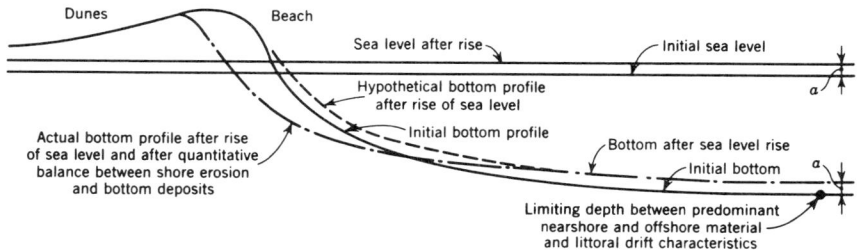

Figure 7.2. Influence of sea level rise on the development of offshore profiles (14).

Referring to Figure 7.2 and Reference 14, one can consider an equilibrium profile (nonchanging form). If the water table rises a millimeter, the quantity of material needed to re-establish the same bottom depth over a width of shelf, b, is b times a.

Now, one can consider a shoreline that is in longshore quantitive equilibrium, which means that the same quantity of material that is passing in from the updrift side is also passing out downdrift. The quantity, $(b)(a)$, must be derived from erosion of the shore, giving rise to a shoreline recession, x. If the elevation of the shore is e, the quantity eroded above sea level is $(x)(e)$. Meanwhile, in order to reestablish the original equilibrium bottom profile, the entire profile must be moved shoreward by the same distance, x, up to depth, d, at distance, b, from the shoreline. The balance between eroded and deposited quantities by the two independent movements is expressed by

$$x e = a (b - x) d$$

and

$$x(e + d) = a b \qquad (7.1)$$

To test the validity of this concept on a short-term basis, it will be necessary to look for a coastal area at which the phase difference between rise of sea level and its influence on erosion is relatively small. This, as previously mentioned, will be true for an area with a steep, offshore bottom. Another assumption is that the edge of the continental shelf is no nearer the shore than at approximately the 18-meter (60-foot) depth on the exposed Pacific or Atlantic shores, which seems to be the outer limit for short-term (not in geological sense) material exchange between beach and offshore areas.

Such a situation exists along the southeast coast of Florida between Palm Beach and Miami. Yet, part of the shore has rock reefs; and in the Hallandale-Miami Beach area, a rocky, gently sloping "platform" exists between 12 and 20-foot depths. The distance on the 18-meter (60-foot) contour from the shoreline is approximately 2,000 meters. In Equation 7.1, x denotes the shoreline recession per year, a is the sea level rise per year, b = 2,000 meters, e describes about 3 meters (10 feet) and d = 18 meters (60 feet), yielding $x(3 + 18) = 2,000a$.

Referring to the preceding section on rise of the sea table, a rise of 1.2 milimeters per year gives x = approximately 11 centimeters = 1/3 foot per year. This figure is not in agreement with recent experience. Most likely the 2,000-meter shelf is not wide enough to reflect very small but tough, long-term rises. In long-term periods, material is probably "tipping over" the edge of the shelf to deep water, thereby increasing erosion. It is more likely that this shore development reflects the short-term rapid rises of sea level. Using the 6-millimeter average figure for the rise in recent decades gives x = approximately 57 centimeters per year = 2 feet per year. With a 15-meter (50-foot) depth on this short-term basis, x = approximately 2.4 feet.

The 2 to 2.5-foot shoreline recession per year is a realistic value when the shores not affected by inlets or groins are considered, but it should still be borne in mind that even on a short-term basis, it is possible that (fine) material disappears in the deep waters past the shelf edge, causing an increase of the shoreline recession. Similar reasonings were used in Reference 14 for the other Florida shores. shores.

Model experiments described in Reference 53 on the effect of tidal action on wave-formed beach profiles give certain information on the behavior of profiles with a fluctuating water table. These results should not be transferred, uncritically, to field (prototype) conditions. Although they do not interfere with the previously noted approach, they are mainly of a qualitative nature, as are experiments by M. Schwarts, carried out at the Colombia University (thesis).

An analytical approach based in part on the results from the southeast coast of Florida will be made. Assuming an equilibrium profile, as indicated in Figure 7.2, following the equation,

$$y^{3/2} = p x \qquad (7.2)$$

in which y is the depth at distance x from the shore, and using the results from the southeast coast of Florida where a rapid rise in sea level of a millimeters causes a shoreline recession of $100\ a$, the intersection point between the old and the new profile corresponding to the rise a is found by means of Equation 7.2 and

$$(y + a)^{3/2} = p (x + 100a)$$

The mathematical expression for the intersection point is complex, and it is easier to find the point using a numerical method.

For the steep profiles on the southeast coast of Florida, $p \sim$ approximately 0.04 (x and y in the metric system). With a rise of 1 meter, that is 6 millimeters per year in 167 years or 1.2 millimeters per year in 830 years, the theoretical shoreline recession will be approximately 100 meters (335 feet). The intersection point between the old profile without rise in water level and the new profile corresponding to 1-meter rise in water level is at a distance of approximately 135 meters (450 feet) from the original shoreline and at a depth of approximately 2 meters (7 feet) in the original profile (235 meters from shore in the new profile at a depth of 3 meters or 10 feet).

A 0.3-meters (1-foot) sea level rise that may come in 50 to 100 years may cause shoreline recessions of more than 100 feet on the southeast coast where many beaches at this time (1971) are too narrow to meet that kind of development. This unfortunate situation can only be adequately handled by means of artificial nourishment with suitable sand material. The latest records of sea level movements on the east and west coasts (1969) bear witness to slow rising.

Man-made erosion is a result of man-made littoral barriers, including port installations like breakwaters, jetties and dredged channels. The man-made littoral barrier interrupts the natural longshore drift, causing accumulation on the updrift side and erosion on the downdrift side. Examples of man-made erosion are given in the section on the influence of port installations on the coastal morphological development.

Shore Geometry

Shoreline Geometry

The geometrical shape of a shoreline is usually defined as the geometry of the intersection line between the water table and the shore. As the water table is subject to fluctuations by tides, there is only one definition of shoreline geometry when the slope of the beach and bottom profile in the tidal zone is steep at the same time as the tidal range is so limited that the location of the intersection line is only influenced slightly by tidal fluctuation.

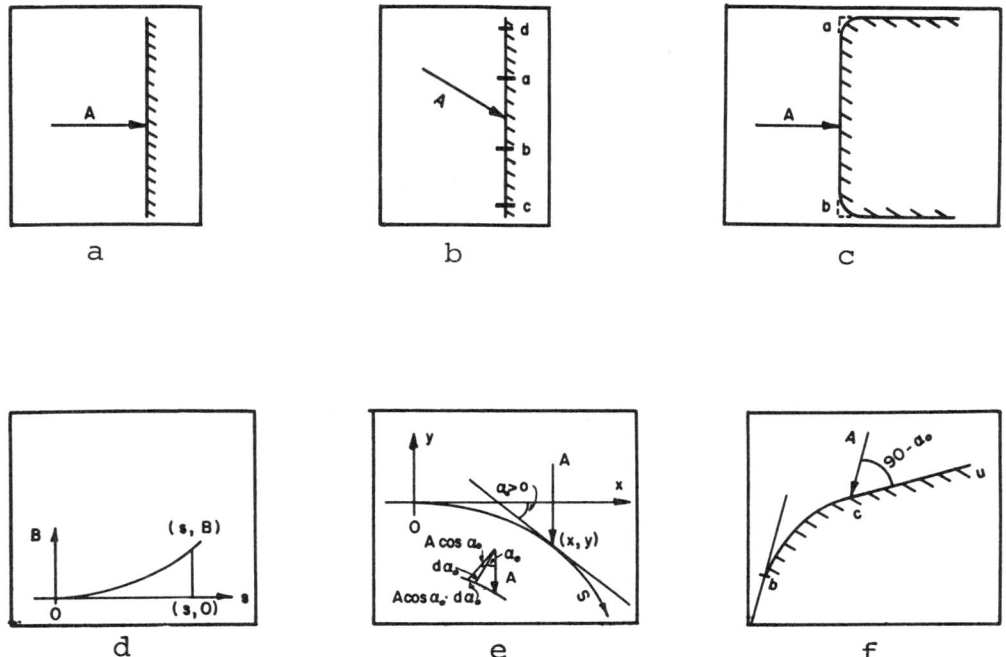

Figure 7.3. a. Straight coast of unlimited length subject to wave action perpendicular to the shore (9 and 11). b. Straight coast of limited length subject to wave action under an angle with the shore (9 and 11). c. Island shore subject to wave action perpendicular to the shore (9 and 11). d. Littoral drift mass-curve (9 and 11). e. Computation of shoreline (9 and 11). f. Free end of shore of limited length subject to wave action under an angle with the shoreline (9 and 11).

In order to discuss the geometrical shape of a shoreline, it is necessary to refer to a configuration which is possible to define and describe geometrically. This does not mean that the shoreline is stationary; it may move, but during its movement its geometrical shape remains the same, although the actual dimensions may change. For example, it may be a circle; during its movements, it stays a circle, but the diameter of the circle may increase or decrease and the center may also move. Therefore, it is logical to introduce the terminology *equilibrium form*. A shoreline has an equilibrium form when it maintains its geometrical form.

Simplified Theory

Figure 7.3a shows a straight sand or shingle coast of *infinite length*. The direction of wave propagation is as indicated. The littoral drift at b must be equal to the littoral drift at a; therefore, the coast is in stable equilibrium.

If the length of the coast in Figure 7.3b is limited from d to c, it will be eroded. The erosion will be greater at d and will decrease towards c. As a consequence of this condition, the coastline will be reoriented to "face" against the waves.

Figure 7.3c shows an island. If the direction of wave propagation is not perpendicular to the coastline a-b or if the corners at a and b are not absolutely sharp, erosion will begin.

The assumption is now made that the relationship between the littoral drift and the deep-water angle a_o can be illustrated by a sine curve (9, 11). The terms "neutral (or nodal) point of littoral drift" and "mass curve of littoral drift" are introduced. A neutral point is the point of a coastline where the resulting littoral drift is equal to zero. In Figure 7.3e, point O is a nodal point. The "mass-curve of littoral drift," Figure 7.3d, is the curve which will result, when in a right-angled coordinate system, the length of the coast from the nodal point is taken as the abscissa and the ordinate is the quantity of material (sand, gravel, etc.) which, in a given period, is eroded between the nodal point and the point in question. The nodal point has the coordinates 0, 0. From the coast with length s, B cubic meters of material are eroded; dB/ds is equal to the erosion per meter of the coastline. When the mass-curve is a straight line, dB/ds is constant; that is, the eroded quantity per meter of the coast is the same at all points, which again means that the coastline maintains its form. Figure 7.3e shows a coastline with $dB/ds =$ constant. This coast is composed of the same sort of material (sand and gravel) everywhere and is attacked by waves perpendicular to the coastline at the nodal point o. The eroded material can pass freely at any point. From the above, it is noted that for the point x, y, which is the distance s from O on the coastline,

$$k s = A \sin a_o$$

where k is a constant. A can be identified as the wave effect, and a_o is the deep-water angle of the waves. Solution of the differential equation gives the curve:

$$x = \frac{A}{k} \left(\frac{\sin 2\alpha_0}{4} + \frac{\alpha_0}{2} \right)$$

$$y = \frac{A}{k} \left(\frac{\sin^2 \alpha_0}{2} \right) \qquad 0 \leq \alpha_0 \leq \frac{\pi}{2}$$

These are equations of a cycloid, with the diameter of the corresponding circle being $A/2k$. Naturally, all equilibrium forms are uniform.

In Figure 7.3f, A inclines toward the coastline. The form developing is that given by the above equations between the angles $(90 - a_o)°$ and $90°$. Several typical examples, all from the Danish Seas, are shown in Figure 7.4, including configurations of islands, peninsulas, headlands, etc. (9, 11).

In References 9 and 11 is mentioned how it was possible to produce the island or corner configurations in model basins using sand as model material. The scale was about 1:500, and the 0.18 to 0.2 millimeters sand used would therefore correspond to shingle.

As explained in References 9 and 11, the theory and reasoning explained for a convex form (e.g., an island) may also be used for a concave (bay) form by changing land and sea (Figure 7.5a). It is very difficult to find areas in nature where a bay shoreline like this can be investigated. The initial condition must be an indentation with vertical sides and infinite length in one direction. Figure 7.5b shows the bay of Vemmingbund in Denmark. From the figure it will be seen that the coastline deviates from the theoretical form between 40° and 70°—the actual form having sharper corners. Figure 7.5c shows Abbotts Lagoon on the U.S. Pacific Coast. Here the same deviation from the theoretical form exists as in Figure 7.5b.

In order to investigate the problem more distinctly, studies were conducted in two small oblong sand bays in the Nissum Inlet on the west coast of Jutland in Denmark. The bays were a reasonable size in proportion to the wave length—width, 10 to 30 times the storm wave length. The form of the shoreline was measured every month during a period of about 2 years. Figure 7.5d shows a characteristic measurement where the black points indicate the shoreline. A groin was built in the neutral point to isolate the test area. Included in the figure is a theoretical equilibrium form, and one can see that the theoretical form again has a shorter radius of curvature than the actual, between 40° and 70° angle of incidence. The curvature is smallest between 40° and 50°,

Coastal Geomorphology

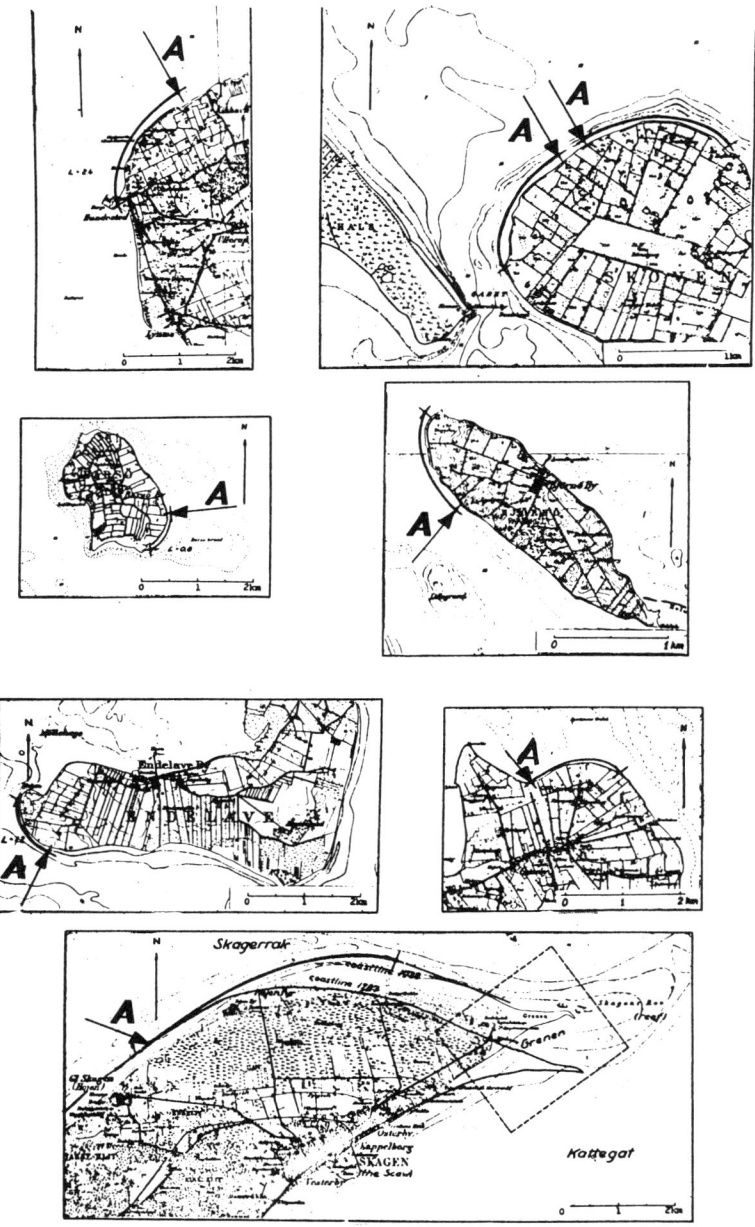

Figure 7.4. Configuration of various islands, peninsulas and headlands in Denmark (9 and 11).

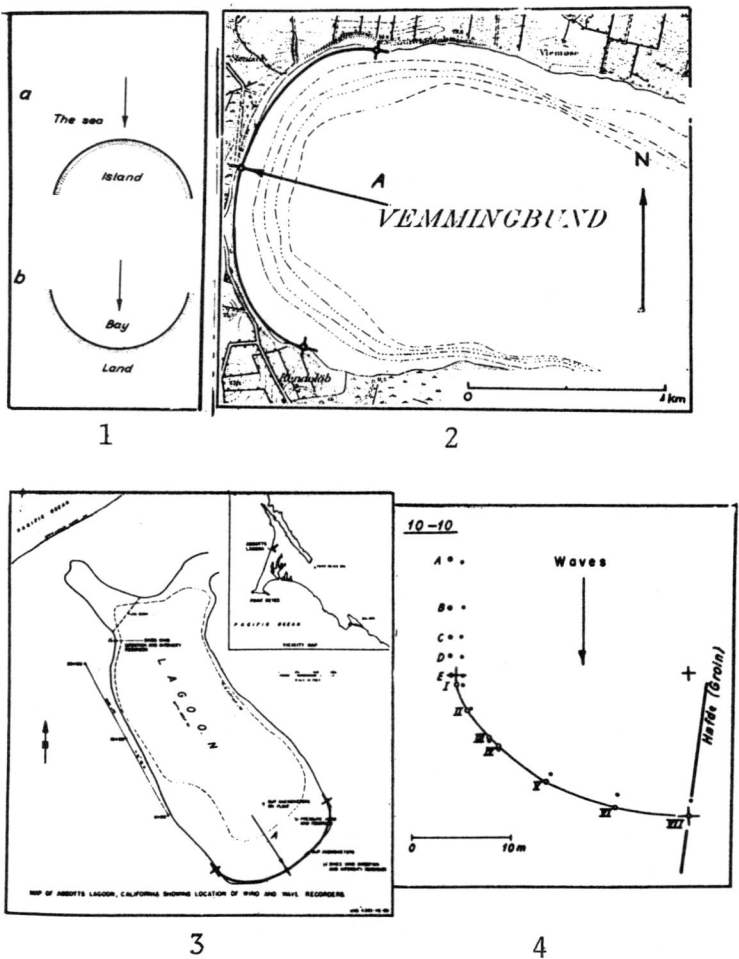

Figure 7.5. a. Island shore, bay shore (9 and 11). b. Vemmingbund Bay, Denmark (9 and 11). c. Abbotts Lagoon, California (9 and 11). d. Field test on bay shoreline (11).

which indicates that the littoral drift may have had its maximum rate between 40° and 50°.

Various other relationships between longshore energy and littoral transport exist. They all have in common that they give maximum material transport for angles of incidence of approximately 45°. As explained in Reference 11, an "apparent maximum" at 90° for island forms must be sought in the influence of currents which concentrate along the island "corners."

It is unrealistic to expect that the littoral drift should be related uniquely to just the angle of incidence of the wave action. Chapter 6 explains how the actual drift capacity depends upon wave, profile and material data. The actual maximum seems to occur at or close to the angle of incidence

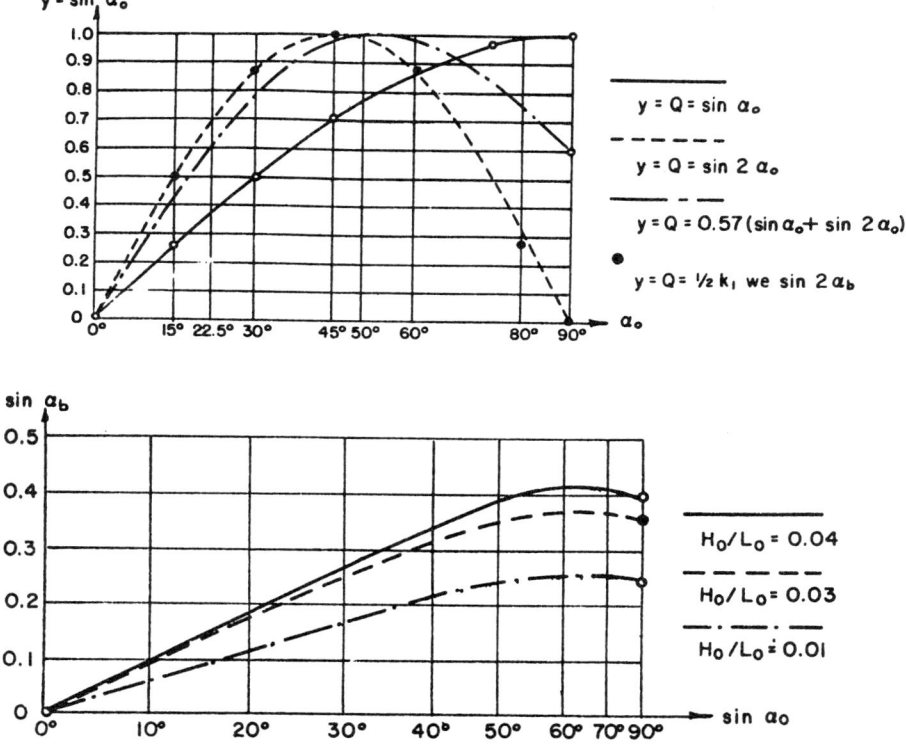

Figure 7.6. Relationship between littoral drift capacity and angle of incidence of wave action (11).

which gives maximum current velocity. This is the reason why one may obtain maximum at a great variety of angles depending upon the shore configuration horizontally as well as vertically. On the other hand, for straight shore lines, the maximum usually occurs between 45° and 50° angle of incidence, which is also true for laboratory experiments in a number of instances (9, 11).

Figure 7.6 shows the relative magnitude of drift as a function of angle of incidence under various assumptions. The black points correspond to the Los Angeles formula: $Q = \frac{1}{2} kwe \sin 2\alpha_b$ (Chapter 6), when $\sin 2\alpha_b$ has been converted to $\sin \alpha_0$ for wave steepness ratio $H_0/L_0 = 0.04$. The dot and dash curve, $y = Q \sim 0.57 (\sin \alpha_0 + \sin 2\alpha_0)$, was derived from field experiments on bay forms, previously mentioned (9, 11).

It is interesting to note that certain shoreline configurations may be explained from the relationships shown in Figure 7.6. Assume that a shoreline turns so that it is able to carry more and more material. Still maximum capacity is reached at a certain angle. If the material is fine sand, it may take a very long shoreline to reach maximum capacity. If it is coarse, such as gravel or shingle, the maximum capacity may be reached rather rapidly. When the shoreline has turned until the angle of maximum capacity has been reached, any further turning in either direction will cause less capacity. This means material will be dropped. Dropping may be in the form of an extension of the shore or it may take place in shoals. In some cases the material is partly used for an extension and partly shuffled over on the other side of the extension tip

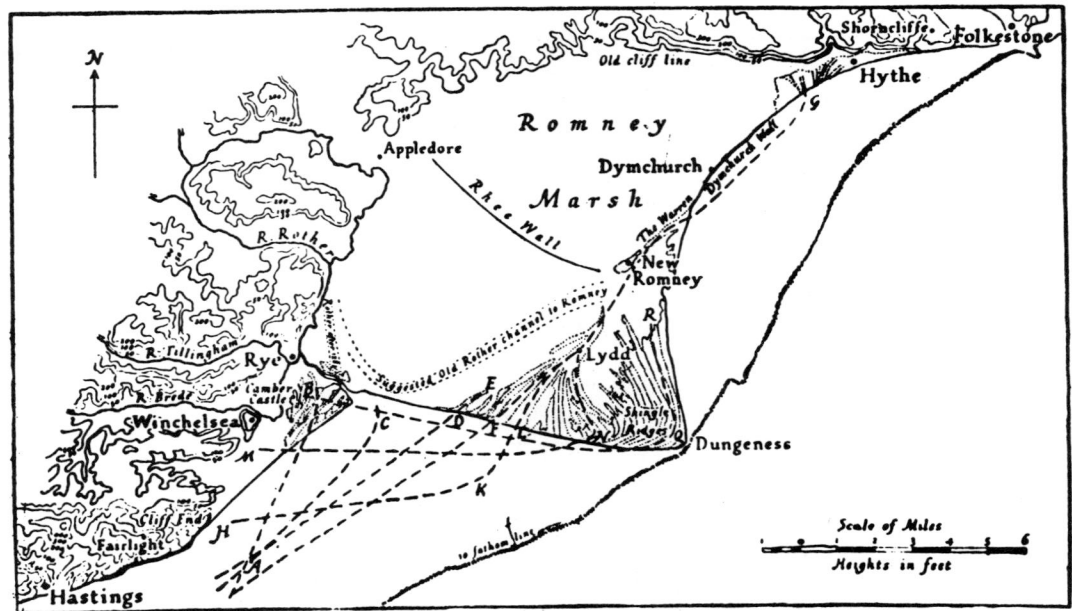

Figure 7.7. Dungeness, Kent (49).

for building up a new shore which is mainly influenced by wave action from the opposite side. This development may be understood from an example, the shingle foreland Dungeness at Kent in England (Figure 7.7), the history of which is explained by J.A. Steers in Reference 49, p. 60, as follows:

Associated with the whole question of wave action and beach-drifting is another interesting matter first pointed out clearly by Lewis. If an inspection be made of the main spits of shingle around our coasts on large-scale maps it is clear that many of them have a tendency to run somewhat outwards and away from the main trend of the coast. This is especially plain in Cardigan Bay: both Morfa Dyffryn and Morfa Harlech, the two main coastal forelands, are good illustrations. On the east coast, Blakeney Point and Scolt Head Island also exemplify the same feature. Again, on the south coast, Dungeness and the smaller Hurst Castle spit trend outwards from the coast, and it would be easy to cite a number of other instances. Many beaches between headlands are arranged, too, so as to show a clear tendency to run at right angles to the main direction of wave approach, a characteristic discussed more fully below.

While mentioning Lewis's views on the development of Dungeness in Kent, one of the biggest and most interesting marine forelands of this type existing, Steers stresses Lewis's contention that the sharp turn of this headland into the sea may be explained by the fact that "shingle ridges show a tendency to turn at right angles to the dominant wind and waves" (see Reference 49, p. 324).

The history of the development is given full mention in Reference 49, pp. 318-31. Roughly, it may be explained as follows: If, as in the case of Dungeness, α_o for the big waves is greater than about 50°, the quantity of littoral drift is presumably below maximum (see Figure 7.7). Meanwhile, the littoral drift is saturated very rapidly where the material is gravel and shingle, which mainly migrate on the beach. This material will deposit very quickly if a slight decrease in the littoral drift forces takes place (Figure 7.7).

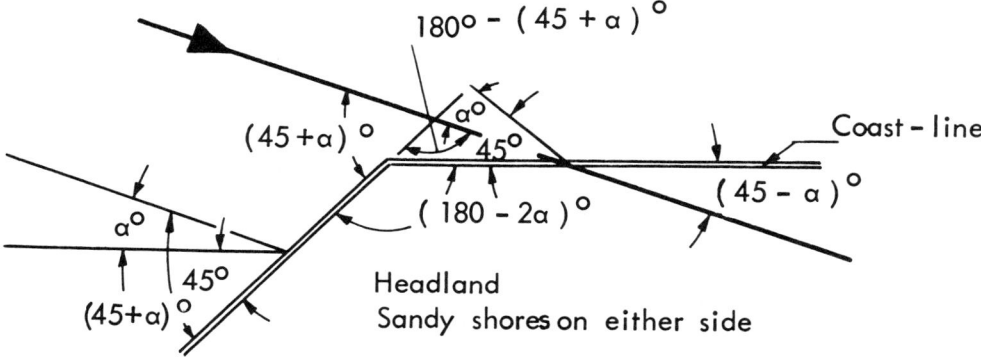

Figure 7.8. Headland shores, schematic.

If the shoreline turns out, still more material can be transported, but at last the value of α_o, which gives the maximum littoral drift, will be passed. Deposits then take place, giving rise to a sudden turnout of the shoreline until it is perpendicular to the wave propagation. The development is shown by the letters (alphabetical order) in Figure 7.7, and the parallel nature to the above mentioned will be noted. A development similar to this may take place at any shingle beach where the wave propagation is oblique to the shoreline.

Consider a situation like the one depicted in the schematic Figure 7.8, showing a headland with sandy shores on either side. In this case the magnitude of drift is assumed to depend upon $\sin 2\alpha_o$ (9, 11), which means that the quantity of drift is equal for angles of incidence of $(45° \pm \alpha°)$. If the headland shall maintain the same angle between the two shorelines, this angle must consequently be $(180 - 2\alpha)°$. If this assumption is used for various headlands on the Danish North Sea Coast and in California when surveys demonstrate that the angle between the shoreline has been constant (which in some cases may have been influenced by the geological structure), one may get relatively small deviations ($\pm 10°$) if an energy vector based on the most predominant severe storms input of energy is considered. This is only mentioned as an example to show how it is possible, at least "superficially," to interpret nature's development, based on very simple geophysical reasonings and "facts."

General Equation for Shoreline Configuration

As mentioned in the proceeding section, Figure 7.6 shows various dependencies between littoral drift quantities (Q) and deep-water angle of incidence (α_o), including $y = Q \sim \sin \alpha_o$ (full line), $Q = \sin 2\alpha_o$ (dotted) and $Q = 0.57 (\sin \alpha_o + \sin 2\alpha_o)$ (dot and dash). Also indicated are some black points originating from References 8 and 11, which refer to the semiquantitative mathematical approach mentioned in Chapter 6 and above as the Los Angeles formula, because it was produced by district engineer office of the U.S. Army Corps of Engineers, using methods developed at Scripps Institution of Oceanography. If it is assumed that the rate of littoral drift varies with the longshore component of energy for waves with a given energy content, measured along the crest, then

$$Q = \tfrac{1}{2} k_1 \, w \, e \, \sin 2\alpha_b$$

where Q is the littoral drift factor, the total amount of sand moved in littoral drift past a given point per year by waves of given periods and direction; w is the total work accomplished by all waves of a given period and direction in deep water during an average year; e is the wave energy coefficient at the breaker line for waves of a given period and direction (it is the ratio between the distance between orthogonals in deep water and at

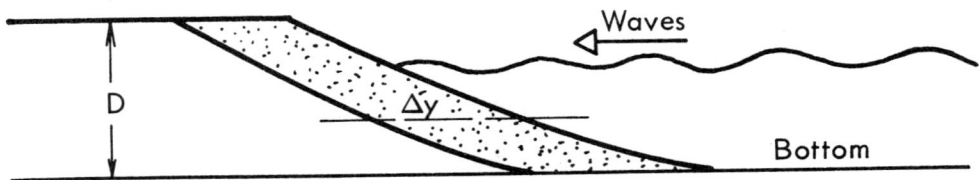

Figure 7.9. Erosion at equilibrium profile (42).

the shoreline); α_b is the angle between wave crests at the breaker line and the shoreline, or the angle between orthogonals and the normal to the shoreline; k_1 is the factor depending on dimensional units and empirical relations (it varies with beach slope, grain size, and other undetermined variables).

As explained in Chapter 6, this equation does not yield quantitative results because of limited present knowledge of wave action in the littoral zone. However, it is of some value for comparative purposes. Fortunately, the quantity of material moved in littoral drift can be measured indirectly at certain points where the longshore currents are blocked by man-made obstructions such as groins, jetties and breakwaters, if the accretion rate upcoast from the barrier is assumed to be equal to the littoral drift rate. As also explained in Chapter 6, it has become possible to evaluate at least the order of magnitude of drift. Because the k_1-factor in the Los Angeles formula varies considerably with shore characteristics including material and profile, it was recommended in Chapter 6 to check all available literature in order to compare the particular situation in question to similar conditions, thereby obtaining the most reliable basis for comparison.

With respect to coastal morphological development, it is theoretically not necessary to know actual quantities in order to explain the development of shore configuration; only the relative magnitudes must be known. The formula most suitable for a coastal morphological mathematical handling is not the Los Angeles formula, because of its variety of ingrediences, but the French formula (41, 42):

$$Q_s \sim H_o^2 T \sin 7/4 \, \alpha_o$$

which gives results very similar to the formula developed by Bruun (9, 11):

$$Q_s \sim E_0 \, (0.57) \, (\sin \alpha_o + \sin 2\alpha_o)$$

when $Eo = H_o^2 T$ (wave effect), leaving the "constant" out which, if known, would give the actual quantities. The former formula gives the maximum at 52°, the latter at 54°.

It is now assumed that the wave direction remains constant (or in effect that there is a predominant wave energy direction). Further, it is assumed that the drift transportation along a curved beach is given by the same formula as that on a straight beach with the condition that the angle of wave incidence varies along the shoreline. Under these conditions, the discharge is assumed to be given by

$$Q_s = KgH_o^2 T \sin 7\alpha_o/4$$

for $\alpha_o < 25°$, the case which occurs most often in nature.

According to Reference 42, it may then be deduced that

$$\frac{\partial Q_s}{\partial x} = \frac{7K}{4} \, gH_0^2 \, T \cos (7\alpha_0/4)$$

Now, considering an axis, OX, parallel to the initial straight beach, and a perpendicular axis OY,

$$\frac{\partial Q_s}{\partial x} = \frac{7K}{4} \, gH_0^2 \, T \cos (7\alpha_0/4) \, \frac{\partial \alpha_0}{\partial x} \, xH_0^2$$

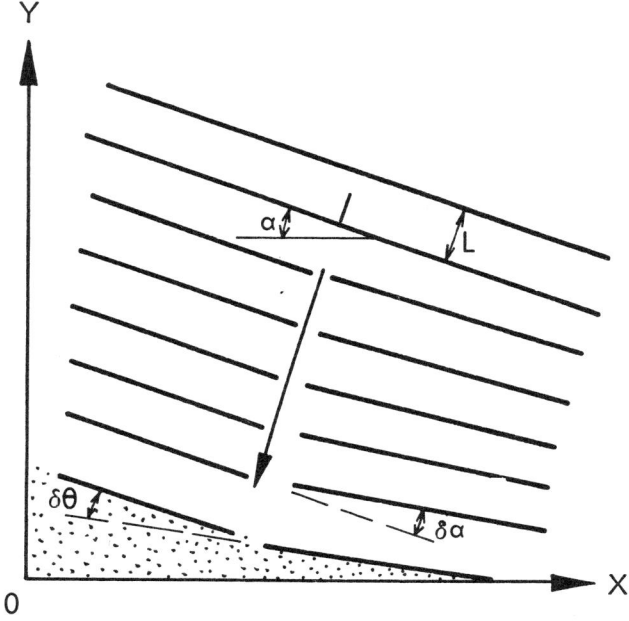

Figure 7.10. Accumulation form, theoretical computation (42).

The quantity of sand deposited or removed on a length of beach is D (∂x) (∂y), where D is the vertical distance between the top of the beach and the lowest line where material is moved (see Figure 7.9); ∂y or Δy would be the difference, $y_1 - y_2$, of the ordinates of the shoreline at the same horizontal level, after and before the elapsed time involved. This volume is equal to the difference, ∂Q_s, of discharge entering and exiting the length, ∂x, during the considered time, ∂t. Hence,

$$\partial x \, (\partial y) \, D = \partial Q_s \partial t$$

Then if θ is the angle of the shoreline with the OX axis (Figure 7.10), $\tan \theta - \partial y / \partial x$, or insofar as $\theta = \tan \theta, \theta = \partial y / \partial x$.

Now $\partial \alpha / \partial x$ represents the variation of the angle of the wave incidence with the shoreline along ∂x because of the curvature of the beach. This curvature is defined by the variation of $\theta = \partial y / \partial x$). Hence,

$$\partial \alpha / \partial x = \partial \theta / \partial x = (\partial / \partial x) \, (\partial y / \partial x) = \partial^2 y / \partial x^2$$

Since α is small, $\cos 7\alpha_o/4 = 1$.
Finally, the equation for $(\partial Q_s / \partial x)$ becomes

$$D \, (\partial y / \partial t) = (7K/4) \, gH_0^2 \, T(\partial^2 y / \partial x^2)$$

or putting $A = (7 \, K/4 \, g H_0^2 \, T \, (1/D)$

$$\frac{\partial y}{\partial t} = A \frac{\partial^2 y}{\partial x^2}$$

As mentioned in Reference 42 this is the classical one-dimensional differential "heat equation." Thus, the variation of a shoreline is analogous to heat variation in a rod. The solution for this relationship is known and may be defined when the boundary conditions are given. Some particularly interesting solutions are mentioned in a following section on the influence of shore installations like jetties and breakwaters on the development of shoreline configurations.

272   Port Engineering

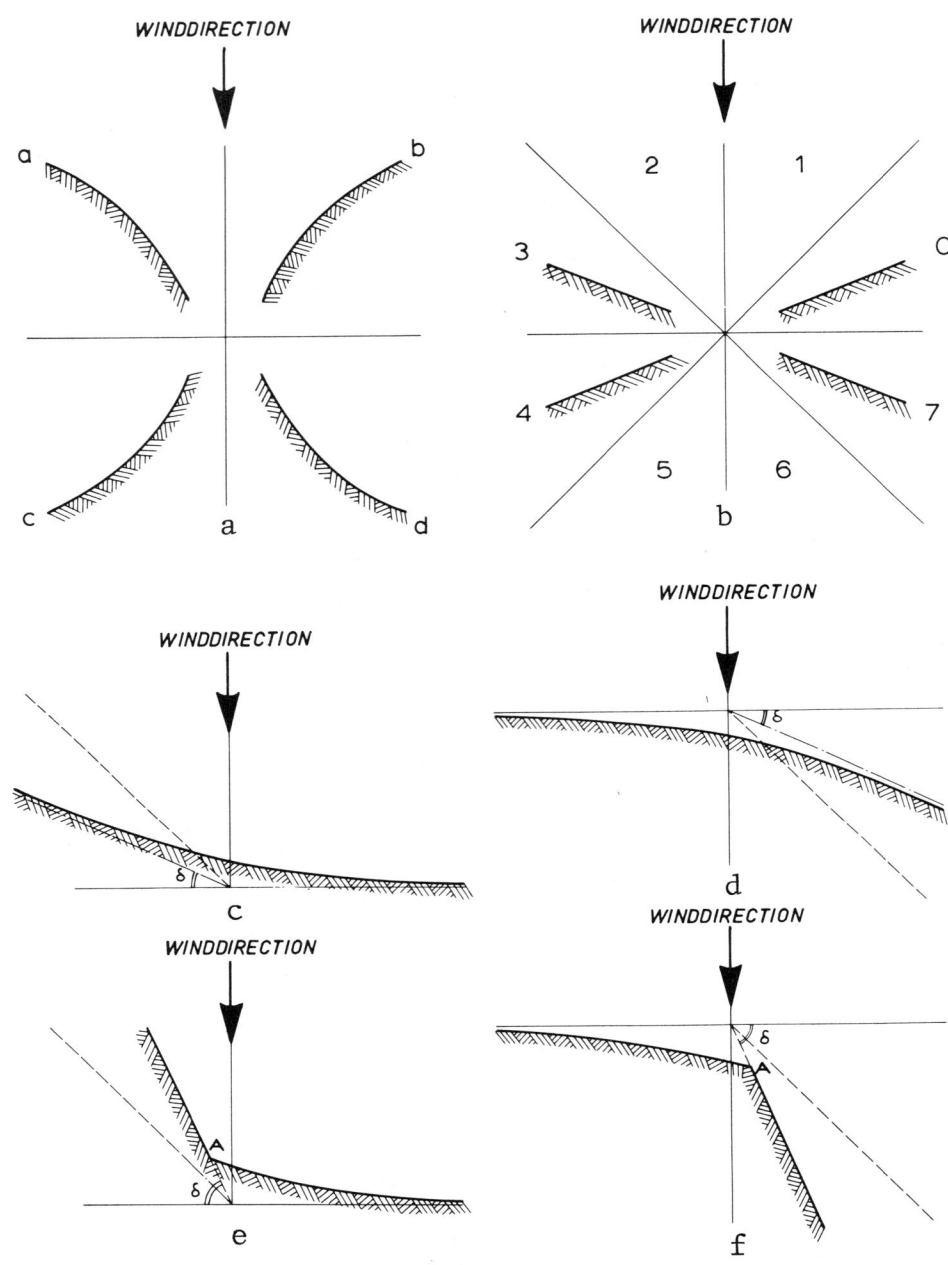

Figure 7.11. Forms of equilibrium by Grijm (27).

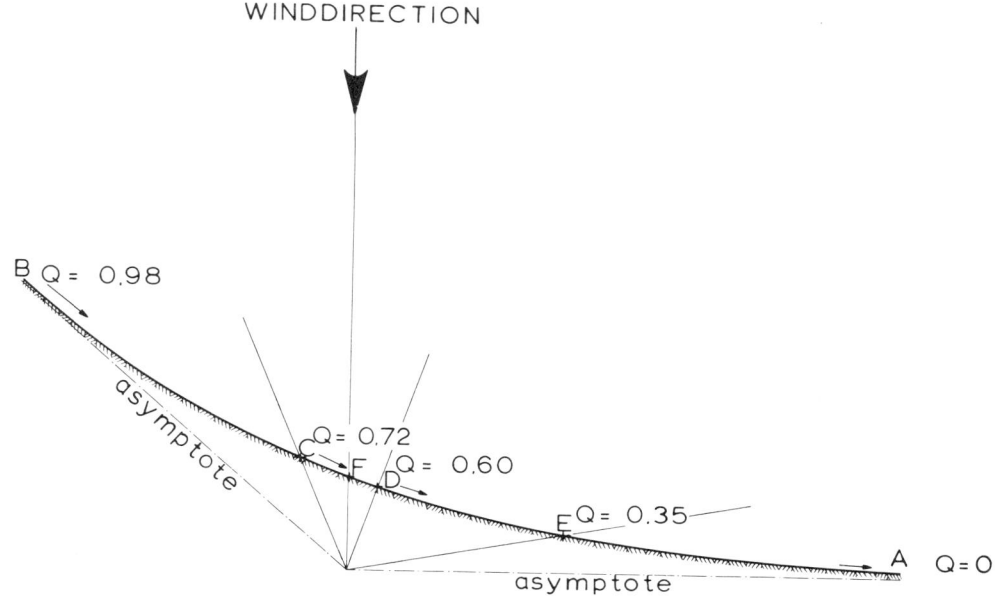

Figure 7.12. Shoreline configuration versus relative drift quantities (27).

Other authors have, under varying assumptions, put up equations for equilibrium conditions for shorelines. Grijm (26, 27), using $a \sin 2\alpha_o$ relationship, developed several forms of equilibrium. Those of Figure 7.11 included curved forms (Figure 7.11a), asymptotes, indicating maximum drift like Figure 7.11b, and headland and bays forms like Figures 7.11c, d, e and f.

Figure 7.12 by Grijm (27) shows the result of calculating relative littoral drift magnitude. With this one solution of the littoral drift equation by Grijm ($\sin 2\alpha_o$ relationship), it is possible to construct shorelines of different types. Figure 7.12 may be interpreted as the shoreline of a bay or, by mirroring it, as the shoreline of a headland. Likewise it can be used to construct a symmetrical delta, a river entrance (ignoring nearshore river currents), etc.

Development of Beach Profiles

The interest in and the study of the development of beach profiles is by no means of recent origin. As mentioned in Reference 44, Fenneman's "Development of the profile of equilibrium of the subaqueous terrace" (25) has been a source of inspiration to many researchers in coastal geomorphology. Likewise, mention should again be made of Davis's grouping of coasts into coasts of emergence and coasts of submergence, each with its specific shape of the beach profile (20).

With a certain amount of justice, it may be contended that the greatest contribution toward the study of beach profiles has been made by engineers. The reason is obvious, for in all marine construction works, such as jetties, groins, dams or sea walls, a thorough knowledge of the shape and development of the beach profile is imperative. Consequently, depth soundings have been taken all over the world where such soundings are of special interest.

As far as laboratory research is concerned, it may be appropriate to mention experiments with "equilibrium profiles" made by Johnson (36) and by Keulegan (38, 39). In Europe similar experi-

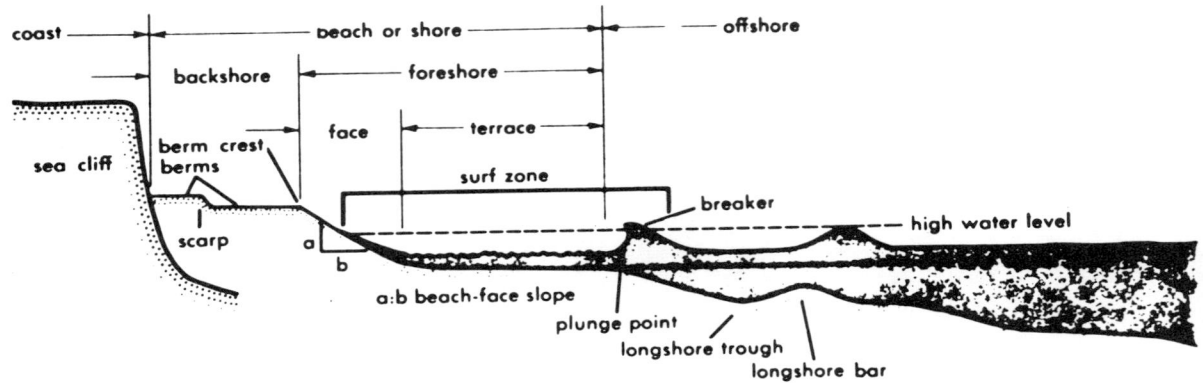

Figure 7.13. General characteristics of beach and bottom profile (D.L. Inman).

ments were made in England and in Denmark by the author, (11).

Laboratory tests have been simulated by extensive studies of the development and fluctuations of beach profiles in nature. Reference 7 deals particularly with the development of bars, and Reference 5 deals with the seasonal fluctuations of beach profiles.

Coast Stability by Bruun (11) covers very thoroughly the development of erosion and beach profiles on the Lime Fjord Barriers on the Danish North Sea Coast, and *Coast Erosion and the Development of Beach Profiles* by Bruun (12) compares the development of beach and bottom profiles on the Lime Fjord Barriers with the development of beach and bottom profiles at Mission Bay, southern California, and relates the results to available wind and wave records. Inman and Rusnak (33) measured actual changes in the level of the sandy bottom at La Jolla, southern California, periodically over an interval of about three years up to 21 meters depth (70 feet).

More recent research, including major field contributions by Harrison and Krumbein (28) following a geological approach and laboratory research by Kemp (37) clarifying details on mechanism of the up-and-down rush and its relation to the transition zone between bar (storm) and step (swell) profiles and research on the equilibrium characteristics of sand beaches in the offshore zone by Eagleson et al. (22), is mentioned in detail in the following sections which deal with the most important contributions to research on the behavior of beach and bottom profiles, a field which has been of great importance for the development of coastal morphology.

Figure 7.13 shows the general characteristics of a beach and bottom profile, including the corresponding terminologies.

Equilibrium Profiles of Beach and Offshore Bottom

Definition of Equilibrium Profiles

In the laboratory an equilibrium profile is a profile which maintains its form. The initial condition is a "vertical wall." In the field an equilibrium profile is a statistical average profile which maintains its form apart from smaller fluctuations including seasonal fluctuations. One must distinguish between a *summer* profile and a *winter* profile.

The form of the actual profile in the field depends on such factors as wave characteristics and their mutual ratios, direction of wave propagation and change in wave action. Different waves, for instance, try to destroy the system of bars not belonging to their peculiar profile and build up a new system of bars. It must also be assumed that the profile is a function of grain size, grain size distribution and specific gravity. Where bedrock

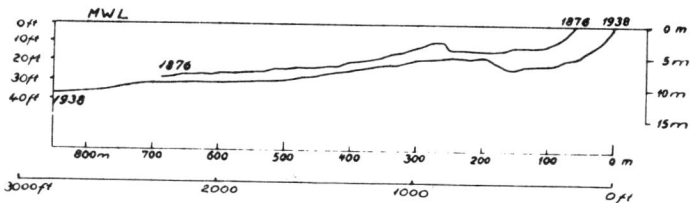

Figure 7.14. Beach profiles at Lyngby on the Danish North Sea Coast (11).

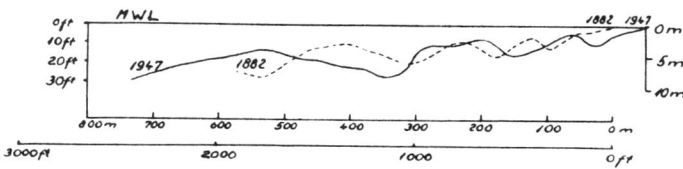

Figure 7.15. Beach profiles at Old Skaw at the northern tip of Jutland (11).

exists, bars cannot be formed. In addition, the coastal currents, especially the longshore current due to the wave breaking, may play a role.

Ultimately, the form depends on the initial conditions. On very steep coasts, a single bar may appear, or perhaps none at all. The number of bars depends on the magnitude of littoral drift. When the drift increases, the possibility of bar formation will also increase, but it cannot be maintained that a profile with, for instance, three bars carries more material than a profile with only one bar, because many other factors may influence the magnitude of littoral drift.

Considerations on the basis of the development of beach profiles seem to show that one can distinguish between profiles in another way; that is, between the overnourished, the sufficiently-nourished and the undernourished profiles (11, 17). The overnourished profiles are fed with more material than the waves can shape into a beach profile. These, therefore, are irregular and often behave as irregular shoals.

There are two different types of sufficiently nourished profiles. At one of them, the profiles are not fed with more material than the waves can shape into a profile having the same "equilibrium form." At the other, the loss of material equals the supply of material, and the profile retains the same equilibrium form.

The undernourished beach profiles are eroded; that is, the coastline retrogrades. The undernourished beach profiles will always keep an equilibrium form, but the form may change from one locality to another, depending on the general conditions mentioned earlier.

Figure 7.14 shows a beach profile at Lyngby on the Danish North Sea Coast in 1876 and 1938. This profile, undernourished to a small degree, has only one bar and is situated close to the nodal point for the nearshore littoral drift on the North Sea Coast (11). Figure 7.15 shows typical beach profiles at the Old Skaw, the northernmost part of the Danish North Sea Coast. This profile is undernourished, the retrogradation of the shoreline being about 3 feet per year, but the littoral drift is very heavy and probably exceeds 1 million cubic meters per year (11). Profiles along the Florida shores are mainly of the eroding type, but some of them are eroding so slowly that they come close to the sufficiently nourished type (17).

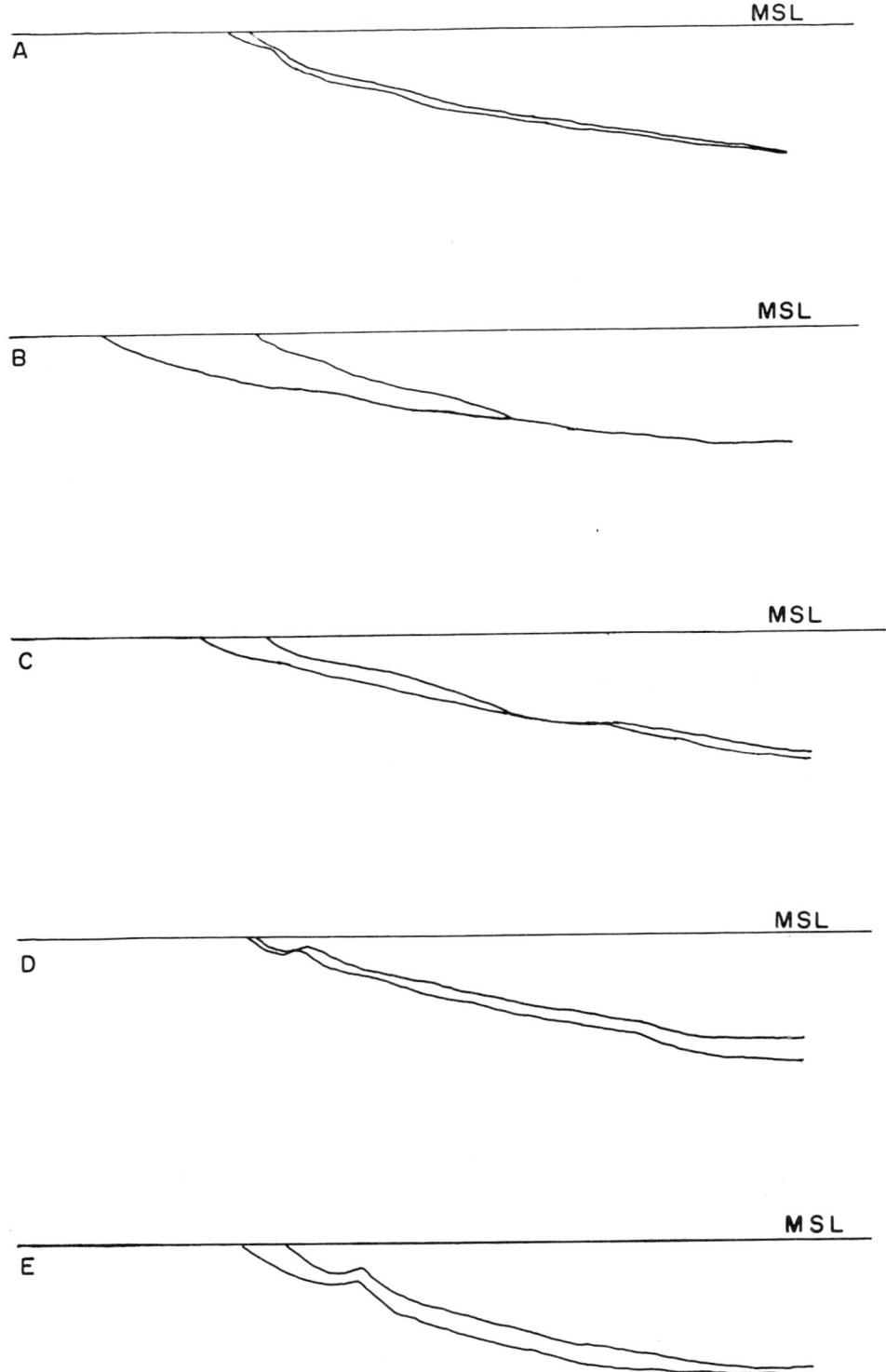

Figure 7.16. Beach profiles on Florida shores (17).

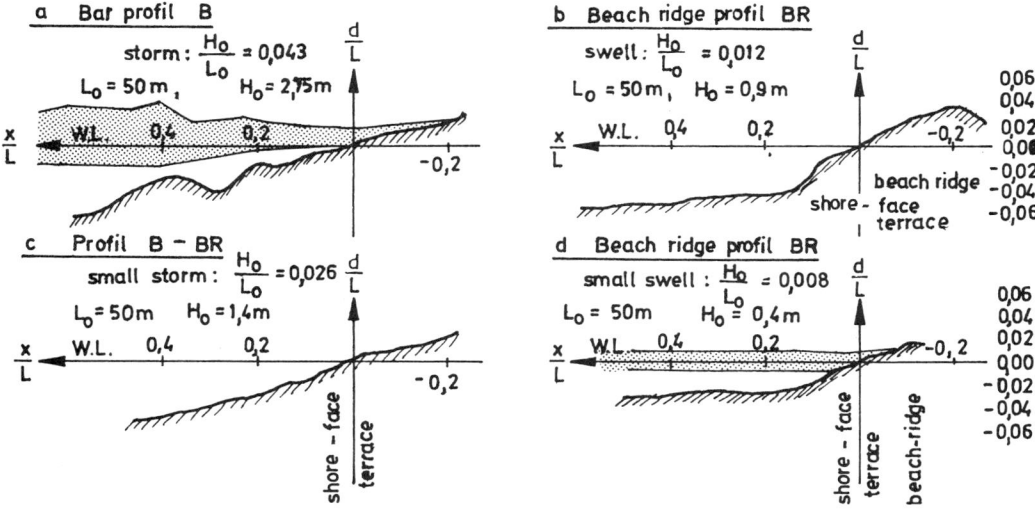

Figure 7.17. Laboratory experiments on beach profiles (11).

Eroding Bottom Profiles

Figure 7.16 indicates schematically various eroding beach profiles in Florida. Profile A shows how an equilbrium profile (upper East Coast) recedes from erosion (e.g., erosion caused by a slow rise in sea level), while profile B is a typical example or erosion caused by a jetty improvement at an inlet. Profile C shows schematically beach profile development at Jupiter Island, 2 miles south of St. Lucie Inlet. Material eroded from the beach is deposited offshore and does not migrate southward fast enough to balance the deposition. Profile D shows the development one mile farther south where deep-water erosion takes place and the profile as a whole steepens. In this case, the shoreline recedes slower than the offshore bottom. Profile E describes the beach profile development at Anna Maria Key on the Gulf Coast. Profiles up to 20 feet deep have steepened so much that they are becoming unstable, causing rapid shoreline changes. Artificial nourishment from Tampa Bay has been undertaken on the southern part of the island and at Holmes Beach; more extensive operations are planned.

Overnourished profiles occur at the end of a "littoral drift line," that is, at a tip or a spit which still receives material. In such case profiles are often very irregular because they become "disorganized" by receiving more material than the waves can shape in a permanent profile. Overnourished profiles also occur on the updrift side of a complete littoral barrier as a major headland extending to deep water. In such case the profile will usually steepen and keep a permanent shape of maximum steepness.

From this it seems that progradation (accretion) of a coast may take place with or without equilibrium profiles, while retrogradation (recession) of a shoreline can only take place with equilibrium profiles having a maximum steepness corresponding to the quantity of littoral drift. An actual equilibrium profile, therefore, should be defined as a stable profile with maximum steepness (see the section below on fluctuations of beach profiles from one period to another).

Laboratory Investigations on Equilibrium Profiles

Laboratory experiments (1, 11, 36) have shown the following:

1. Waves with high steepness ratios produce a bar profile (Figure 7.17a). Waves with low steep-

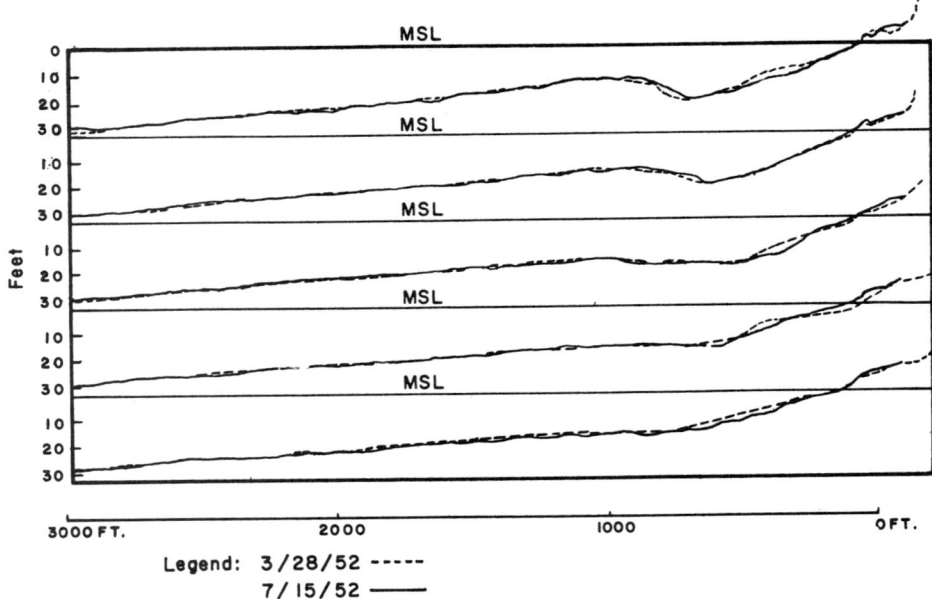

Figure 7.18. Beach and bottom profiles on the Danish North Sea Coast (11).

ness ratios produce a beach ridge profile (Figure 7.17 c, d).
2. Waves with high steepness ratios erode the beach; waves with low steepness ratios build up the beach.
3. Waves with high steepness ratios can be identified as winter waves; they form a storm or winter profile. Waves with low steepness ratio can be identified as summer waves; they build up a swell or summer profile. The intermediate profile occurs at a steepness ratio of about $H_o/L_o = 0.026$ (Figure 7.17b).
4. There are two types of littoral drift—bed load transport on the beach itself (beach drift), due to uprush and backwash, and suspended load transport in the breaker zone, due to the breaking waves and the generated longshore currents.
5. In equilibrium storm profiles, transport is mainly of material in suspension. In equilibrium swell profiles, transport is mainly beach drift. The transition between these different types of transport is sudden and occurs at a steepness ratio of about 0.026 (Figure 7.17b).
6. The transport along summer profiles is much greater than that along winter profiles for waves with the same energy content. The peak transport occurs at a steepness ratio of 0.02 to 0.025 and is almost entirely beach drift.
7. The transport rate decreases very rapidly for steepness ratios less than 0.02.
8. The transport rate increases with an increase in wave energy, other conditions remaining the same.
9. The transport occurs almost entirely in the area shoreward from the breaker.

Short-Period Fluctuations

Investigations have been carried out at many places all over the world, (19, 21, 46). Figure 7.18 shows five profiles on the Danish North Sea Coast sounded about 330 feet apart. Simultaneous levels were taken on the beach itself. The soundings were carried out to the 300-foot depth contour about 3,300 feet from the shoreline (11, 13).

The dotted lines show the profiles on November 15, 1951. The profiles are summer profiles with beach ridges on the beach itself. Although the

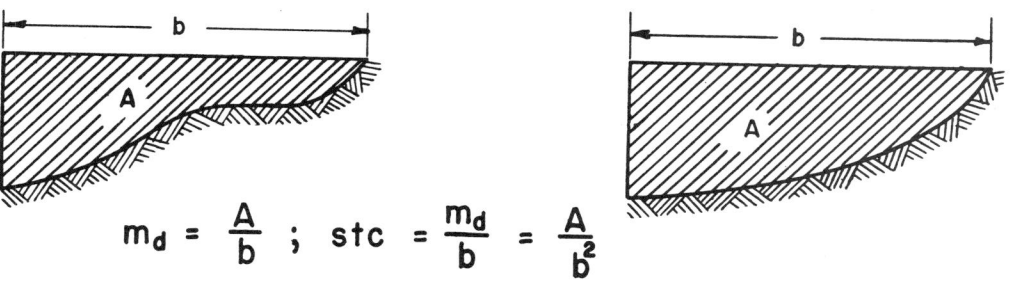

Figure 7.19. Definition of mean depth and steepness characteristic (11 and 12).

bar has migrated toward the shoreline, it is still there, as the summer waves possibly should have acted for a much longer time to carry material from the bar to the beach.

The profiles from the soundings on January 23, 1952, are shown with full lines. Several severe gales occurred between November and January. It can be seen that the difference between the summer profile and the winter profile is that the summer profile has a beach ridge and at the same time is steeper than the winter profile. The accumulations in the outer sections of the beach profiles must have been caused either by sand moving from the bottom outside the 30 feet or by sand waves moving longshore.

Long-Period Fluctuations.

Long-period fluctuations are a result of an integration process by nature in which the results of wave and current action over a long time period are accumulated and the difference between two separate periods may be traced by comparing profile changes and changes in the acting forces. There are very few places in the world where surveys have been carried out over a very long time period permitting studies on such long-period fluctuations. One place is the Danish North Sea Coast at the Lime Fjord Barriers (11).

In order to study the fluctuations of profiles on a long-term basis, the terminologies "mean depth" and "steepness characteristics" were introduced. The *mean depth* (md) is the average depth of the water area over the profile length. The *steepness characteristic* (stc) of the beach profile is the ratio of the mean depth to the profile length. The reason for which the terminology steepness characteristic is introduced is that the two different profiles in Figure 7.19 have the same steepness, b/a, because the depth contour considered is situated the same distance from the shoreline, though the lower in reality is much steeper than the upper.

For the surveys from Denmark, standard deviation calculations of the mean depth and the steepness characteristic of the single beach profile, based on repeated soundings of the same profiles show that both of these are so small that they can be neglected. Bruun (11) shows that if the mean depth or the steepness characteristic of the single profile is taken as a representation for a coast stretch of about 600 yards situated on both sides of the particular profile, the standard deviation in determining the average mean depth is about 5% for the 0 to 20-foot area, about 2% for the 20 to 30-foot area, and about 2% for the 0 to 30-foot area. The corresponding values for four lines (2,400 yards) are about 5, 1 and 1%; and for 16 lines (10,000 yards), about 3, and less than 1%. This refers to specific conditions on the Danish North Sea Coast and may not necessarily be transferred to other shores. However, the order of magnitude of deviations is transferable to shores which are equally exposed.

From numerous investigations with beach profiles, it is known that it is the strong onshore gales which cause the beach profiles to flatten. In Refer-

Table 7.2 Comparison of Winter and Summer Profiles, Mission Bay (12)

Season	0 to 20 feet				0 to 30 feet			
	Area sq yds	Width yds	md ft	stc × 10^3	Area sq yds	Width yds	md ft	stc × 10^3
Winter	1,120	350	9.6	9.3	3,625	655	16.6	8.7
Summer	1,155	335	10.2	10.4	3,690	645	17.1	9.2

Table 7.3 Comparison of Winter and Summer Profiles Danish North Sea Coast at Bovbjaerg

Season	0 to 20 feet				0 to 30 feet			
	Area sq yds	Width yds	md ft	stc × 10^3	Area sq yds	Width yds	md ft	stc × 10^3
3/28/52 Winter	2,390	525	13.6	8.7	5,850	795	22.1	9.3
7/15/52 Summer	2,370	495	14.4	9.7	6,000	785	22.9	9.7

ence (11) Bruun explains how it was possible for a group of beach and bottom profiles on the very exposed Danish North Sea Coast to demonstrate that years with relatively many storms caused a relative flattening of the profiles while years with relatively few storms increased steepness. As mentioned in Reference 12, the same tendency was recorded for profiles in Mission Bay, California, when summer (lower steepness ratio of waves) and winter profiles (higher steepness ratio of waves) were compared. The steepness characteristic was always highest during the summer period, as noted in Tables 7.2 and 7.3.

The change from eroding (flattening) profile to building (steepening) profile does not take place at the "laboratory ratio" of about 0.026 but at a much lower ratio. In the Mission Bay case, Bruun found indications that wave steepness of 0.001 to 0.0015 increases steepness at least to the 30-foot depth at the same time as waves with a steepness ratio of approximately 0.01 tended to decrease steepness.

There is no general rule for the relationship between beach slope and sand size. This depends upon wave characteristics, grain size and distribution of grain size (permeability), specific gravity and local factors of mineralogical and geological nature. Figure 7.20 shows the relationship between beach slope and sand size at mid-tide level for Pacific Coast beaches (3).

From Tables 7.2 and 7.3, it may be seen that the areas are only slightly different. The width, mean depth and steepness characteristic are all less for the winter profile than for the summer profile, just as in the laboratory.

Trask (52) carried out a comprehensive study on changes in configuration of Point Reyes Beach, California, 1955-56. The abstract of his report is given in full in order to leave the reader without any doubt of the complexity of the problem be-

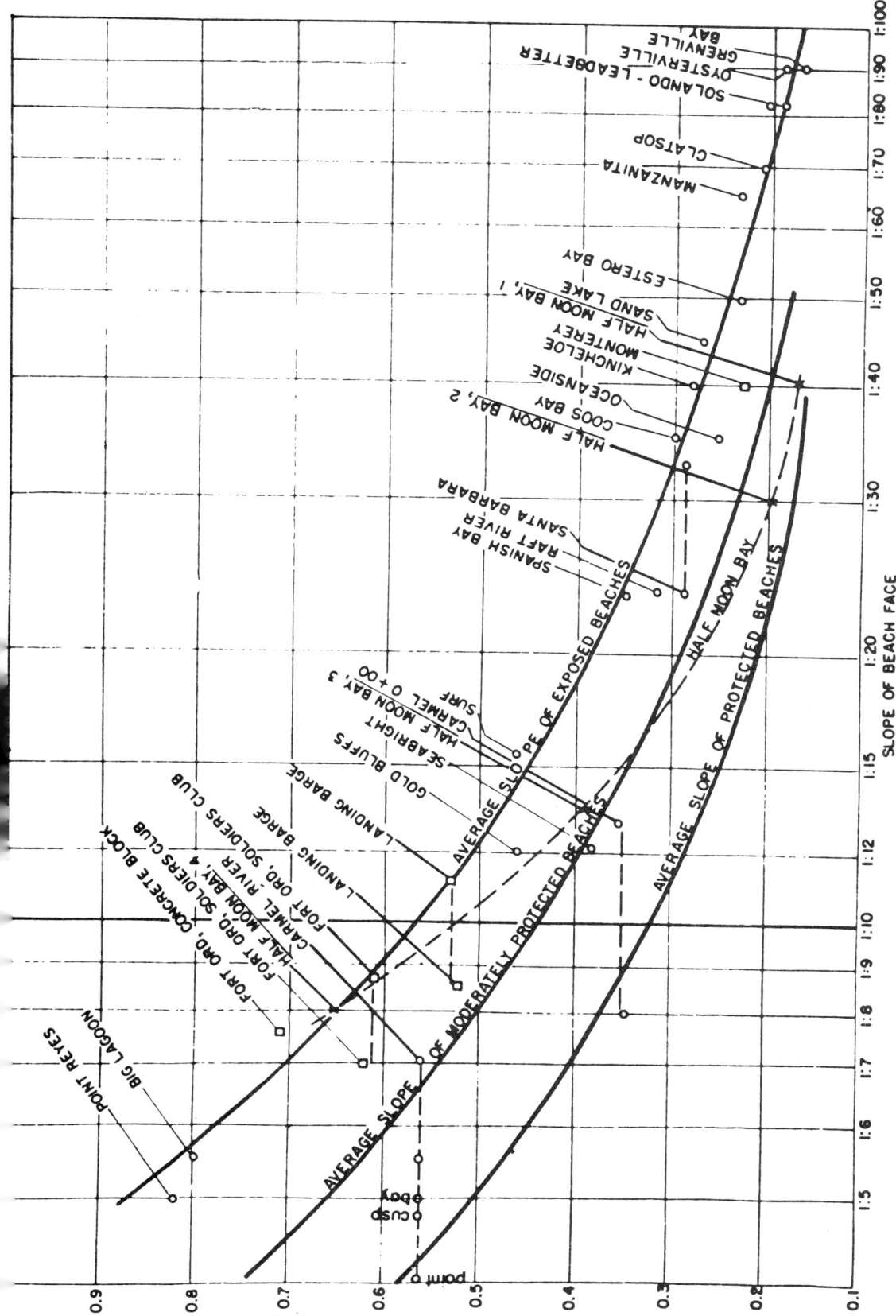

Figure 7.20. Relationship between beach slope and sand size at mid-tide level for Pacific Coast beaches (3).

cause all phenomena are three dimensional—not two-dimensional as in the wave tank.

Point Reyes Beach is a highly variable beach, characterized by steep slopes, high berms and prominent cusps. It has been surveyed in the present study 8 times between August 1955 and June 1956. The sands are coarse, ranging from a mean of 560 microns (0.38 phi units) in February to 770 microns (0.84 phi units) in October. Intervening months have intermediate grain size. The general variation or standard deviation of the samples on the beach ranges generally from 0.30 to 0.35 phi units, which indicates that the median diameter of two-thirds of the samples on the beach at any one time ranges within 20 to 25 per cent on either side of the mean for the beach. At times the beach is more variable than indicated above, and gravels with phi diameters of minus 3 (8 millimeters) are found on the beach. The sediments at all times are more poorly sorted than normal beach sands, as the mean coefficient of sorting ranges generally between 1.27 and 1.30, in contrast with 1.20 or less for many beaches. No distinctive difference in sorting is observed between seasons. The sediments are evenly skewed.

The sediments on the lower foreshore are more coarse grained and better sorted than the sediments on the upper foreshore or berm. The deposits in the swales or bays between cusp points are more fine grained than on the foreshore or on the berm adjacent to the cusp points. The cusps range in height from 12 to 17 feet above mean low water and average 15 feet. The horizontal interval between cusps ranges between 60 to 250 feet, with an average of 160 feet. The cusps change location on the beach from time to time. The average position of the cusps ranges within an interval of 50 feet measured normal to the coastline, and the maximum variation in position occurred within a period of 6 weeks between May and June 1956. Individual cusps or parts of the beach may advance or retreat a maximum distance of 160 feet. The cusps are actively eroded at times, particularly when low berms form on which the waves cut scarps as much as 5 feet in height in the preceding berm. At other times the cusps and beach are built up rapidly. As much as 8 inches of fill in 4 hours and 12 inches in 18 hours has been observed. The maximum fill at any one place in an interval of 6 weeks is 7 feet and the maximum cut is 10 feet. The winter months are periods of active cutting and summer months a period of fill. The slopes on the beach are generally steep. In the swales between cusps the slopes are commonly 4 to 8 degrees, and on the slopes of the points of the cusps, from 6 commonly 4 to 8 degrees, and on the slopes off the points of the cusps, from 6 to 15 degrees, with an average of about 10 degrees on the upper foreshore near the "Reference Point." Where the berm is being actively eroded, slopes greater than 45 degrees or 100 per cent have been observed.

The situation at Point Reyes belongs to the more extreme cases. In Florida seasonal fluctuations of the shoreline vary between 10 feet on the Gulf Coast to up to about 60 feet on the Atlantic.

Exchange of Material Between Beach and Offshore Areas

D.L. Inman (32) studied the formation and occurrence of sand ripples generated by oscillatory wave motion at La Jolla, California, to better understand the role ripples play in the sorting and transportation of sediments. The observations, which extended from the surf zone to depths of about 170 feet, were made by swimmers equipped with self-contained underwater breathing apparatus. The wave length, crest length, height and symmetry of the ripples were measured and these parameters compared with the size of the sand and with the orbital displacement and velocity of the wave motion generating the ripples.

It was found that ripples were always present on sandy bottoms when the significant orbital velocity had a value between about 1/3 and 3 feet per second. The type of ripple was related to the size of the sand and the nature and rigor of wave motion. The ripple wave length ranged from 0.14

feet in fine sand to over 4 feet in very coarse sands. The heights of the ripples ranged from about one-fourth to one-sixteenth of the ripple wave length.

In areas of abundant sand, the largest and least dense material occurred on the ripple crests and the finest and heaviest in the trough. Over rocky bottoms where there was little sand, the relationship was frequently reversed. The ripple crest consisted of sand washed from among the rocks, while the coarse material remained in the trough. Other research has proven that ripple marks exist even in the deepest waters which demonstrates that currents of 1/3 to 1-foot, probably of tidal origin, are active.

With respect to material exchange between beach and offshore bottom, the movement of material from the shore for depositing in the offshore area is probably a slow process by which various kinds of currents, including longshore currents, rip currents and density currents, are active. With respect to material exchange between the shore and the offshore bottom, little is known about the rate of this process because many factors are involved, including the character of shore material and the characteristics of wave and current activity. Most likely, a distinction will have to be made between a short-range process of "fluctuation nature" and a long-range geological adjustment process. With respect to littoral drift material, the observations by Parker Trask (51) are of particular interest.

Trask explains that present data clearly indicate that sand does move around the rocky California promontories. Meanwhile, it seems to be clear that a little sediment is transported beyond a depth of 18 meters (60 feet).

Inman (31, 33) reports that bottom surveys at Scripps Institution of Oceanography, La Jolla, California, indicate that most seasonal, offshore-onshore interchanges of sand occur in depths of less than 9 meters (30 feet), but that some seasonal effects may extend to greater depths. Inman describes the areal distribution pattern (for this particular location) that shows a pronounced alinement of sediment properties generally parallel to the beach. There are numerous possible interpretations of the alinement and banding of sediment attributes. Surf beats may be one explanation. Another may lie in the seaward transportation of sediment by diffusion, resulting from a horizontal gradient in concentration of suspended material from the surf zone, where concentrations are high, to offshore areas, where they are relatively low. In addition to seaward transportation by diffusion, it is well known that a net onshore transportation of sediment occurs along the bottom because of the differential between onshore and offshore velocities associated with the orbital motion of nearshore waves. Bruun (11, 12) described deep-water erosion on the Danish North Sea Coast of up to 20-meters (70-foot) depth.

From these studies, a reasonable assumption seems to be that with sandy shores of exposed Pacific or Atlantic type, the 18-meters (60-foot) depth contour forms some kind of limit between "nearshore" and "deep-sea" littoral drift phenomena, which, in this respect, means that short-term exchange of shore material and offshore bottom takes place inside (although not always up to) this depth. It should not be forgotten that the slope of the offshore bottom must be of significant importance. A very gentle slope will undoubtedly slow down transversal migration of material by giving rise to a considerable phase difference between "action" (rise of sea level) and "reaction" (shore erosion). On the other hand, a very steep, offshore bottom will have the opposite effect, manifested in a relatively quick response (in the form of erosion) to rise of water table. Inasmuch as the slope and width of a littoral drift zone are closely connected, it could be expected that a wide "shelf" would demonstrate considerable phase displacement and higher stability than a narrow shelf. A narrow shelf may develop an "equilibrium profile" to a considerable depth indicating displacement of material from the shore to the offshore bottom. If the offshore bottom, such as the southeast coast of Florida, at about 18-meters (60-foot) depth, turns over to a steeper slope, the tendency to transfer material to deep water by the assistance of gravity forces may be detectable in the shore stability as an increased shoreline recession.

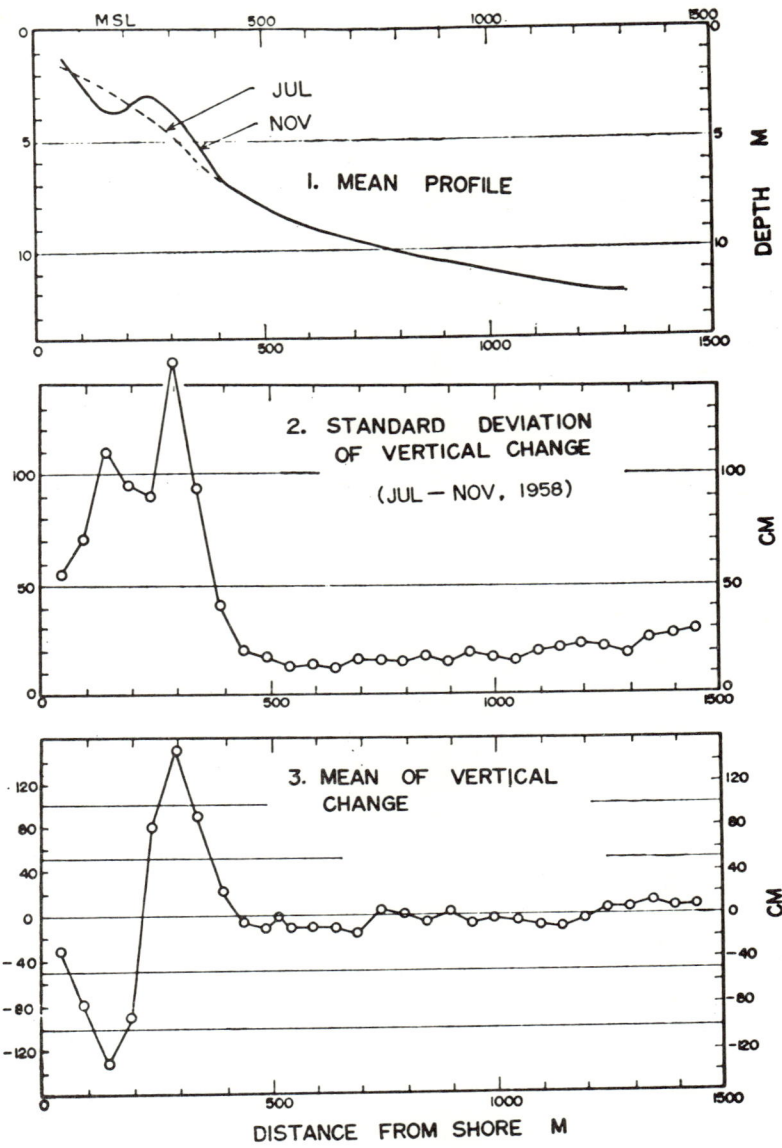

Figure 7.21. Profile data from surveys at Tokai, Japan (30).

Comparing Fluctuations of Bottom Profiles

With respect to short-term fluctuations of the offshore bottom, considerable information is available in reports on field surveys, (11, 12, 19, 30). Laboratory experiments on beach and bottom profiles are also numerous, but so far only relatively little information is available on the movement and exchange of material within the various profile sections. The theoretical and laboratory experiment results (mentioned in Reference 34 on location of a "nodal point" for offshore and onshore movements) are not well confirmed in the field at this time. Meanwhile, modern tracing techniques

Table 7.4 Mean Dimension of Vertical Short-term Seasonal Fluctuation.

Place	0-6 m (0-20 ft)	6-9 m (20-30 ft)
Danish North Sea Coast	0.40 m	0.70 m
Mission Bay, California	0.25 m	0.45 m
Tokai, Japan	0.0 m	0.15 m

have opened new possibilities, particularly when combined with continuous surveys from pier and offshore tower installations such as attempted at Katwijk in Holland.

The various bottom sections must be considered in relation to the action of waves and currents. Three examples, mentioned next, are all based on statistical work published in References 11, 12 and 30. The three shores are located on the Danish North Sea Coast at Bovbjaerg, at Mission Bay, southern California, and at Tokai, Japan. These shores are exposed to wave action from medium (Tokai) to very heavy (Bovbjaerg).

In the North Sea profiles, bar crest is approximately at elevation 4.0 meters (13 feet) below mean sea level, in the Japanese profiles, at approximately 3.0 meters (10 feet) below mean sea level, while the California profiles have no bar at all. Table 7.4 gives the mean value of the vertical fluctuations within the 0 to 20-foot and the 20 to 30-foot contours of six profiles on the Danish North Sea Coast, five in California and 16 in Japan.

Figure 7.21 shows the mean profile at Tokai, the standard deviation of vertical change and the mean of vertical change and the mean of vertical seasonal change, (30). Comparing Figure 7.21 with Table 7.4, it is interesting to note that the average value of the mean of vertical change landward of the 6-meter (20-foot) contour is zero and that little fluctuation takes place seaward of the 6-meter (20-foot) contour at Tokai.

Detailed studies of the situation on the North Sea Coast and at Mission Bay reveals a similar situation, but the short-range (seasonal) deviation line for the nearshore/offshore drift is located farther seaward than at Tokai and perhaps even farther seaward on the very exposed Danish North Sea Coast. Table 7.4 reveals, in both cases, that the mean seasonal fluctuation is less for the 0 to 6 meter (0 to 20-foot) area than for the 6 to 9 meter (20 to 30-foot) area. This means that although the actual fluctuations in the single points are highest on the 0 to 6-meter (0 to 20-foot) area, they are plus-minus and tend to equalize. We do not get zero result, as at Tokai, because the 6-meter (20-foot) contour is not the limiting depth for seasonal fluctuations which also take place outside the 6-meter (20-foot) contour. The field information available is not sufficient to determine the limiting depth for short-term fluctuations, and, in the North Sea, it is obvious that migrating sand waves along the bottom as described in References 11 and 13 exist outside the 6-meter (20-foot) depth contour. As a matter of fact, recent surveys have demonstrated that migrating sand waves may be found at all depths in the North Sea depending upon the magnitude of tidal currents.

Field examples (33) based on three-year records of accurate sounding offshore at La Jolla Beach gave the results listed in Table 7.5. It may be seen that fluctuations still take place at the 70-foot depth and probably further down up to 100 feet or more.

Uprush/Downrush and Profile Development

Kemp (37) investigated in more detail the mechanics associated with the formation of and changes in the bottom profile. In his experiments each wave period was kept constant while a series of runs was made using different wave heights, starting with low waves and increasing the wave height for each run. Beach material was 0.9 milli-

Table 7.5
Tests on Bottom Fluctuations

Depth	Level change (ft)	Sand level occurrence*
70	0.15	61
52	0.16	88
30	0.29	100
18	0.62	100

*In % of observation time.

meters pumice. The following observations in detail were made: (a) wave height, (b) distance from breaking point to limit of uprush, referred to below as the "breaker distance." (c) time for the wave to travel from the break point to the limit of uprush, (d) type of flow in the zone shoreward of the breakers and (e) regularity of the shoreline in plan.

The time of uprush mentioned in (c) above is expressed in terms of the wave period, as the *phase difference* between breaking point and beach crest. The phase difference was found to be the dominant factor in the relationship between the waves and the beach profile, and resulted in the following classification of wave/beach conditions. Figure 7.22 shows phase difference plotted against breaker distance for varying periods and wave heights.

Increase in wave height produces an increase in the breaker distance. Figure 7.22 shows that initially the phase difference or time of uprush remains constant at a value of approximately 0.4 T, even though the breaker distance increases. This is *the surge condition*, which causes the development of a step type or "surge profile" (Figure 7.23).

As the breaker distance is further increased, a critical point is reached at which the phase difference ceases to be constant. Thereafter, the phase difference increases with increase in wave height.

The behavior of the wave and the beach profile in the initial zone of constant phase difference resembles the behavior of a simple pendulum. An increase in incident wave amplitude produces an increase in wave surge velocity. The beach crest retreats and steepens, but the time of the surge remains constant, and the surge profile sustains.

Negligible mixing or interchange takes place between the water seaward of the breaker point and the shoreline. The motion is characteristically oscillatory. In the field some exchange may take place in rip currents, but they are not very predominant until the surf condition mentioned below has been reached.

With further increase in wave height, a point is eventually reached at which the beach crest to breaker distance ratio no longer satisfies the surge condition. The crest height ceases to increase and later begins to diminish. With the retreat of the beach crest and the seaward movement of the break point, the time taken for the wave to reach the crest increases. The time available for backwash before the next wave breaks is consequently reduced. As a result, the backwash is not completed before the next wave plunges. This is the point of demarcation between the surge zone, with its stable oscillatory flow conditions, and the transition zone of behavior characterized by unstable flow and lateral circulation.

The instability of the flow pattern under transition conditions inevitably results in local lateral circulations being set up. This enables the lack of coincidence between the completion of the backwash and the next plunge to be replaced by a continuous and self-perpetuating pattern of flow

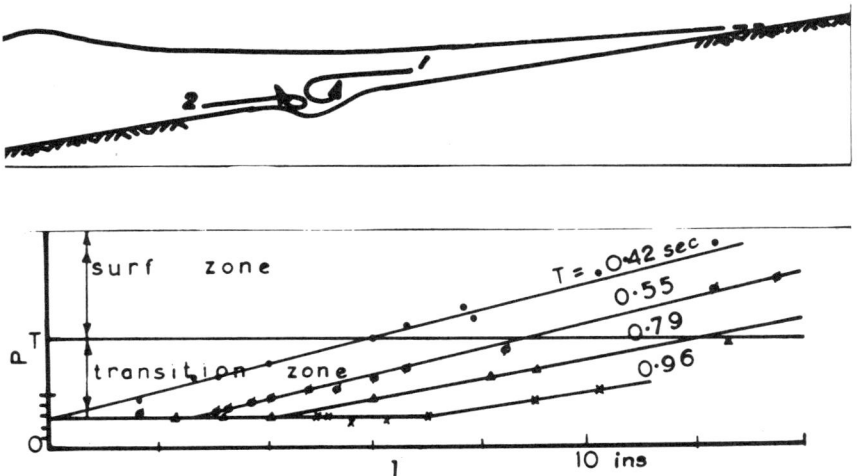

Figure 7.22. Phase difference P versus breaker distance (37).

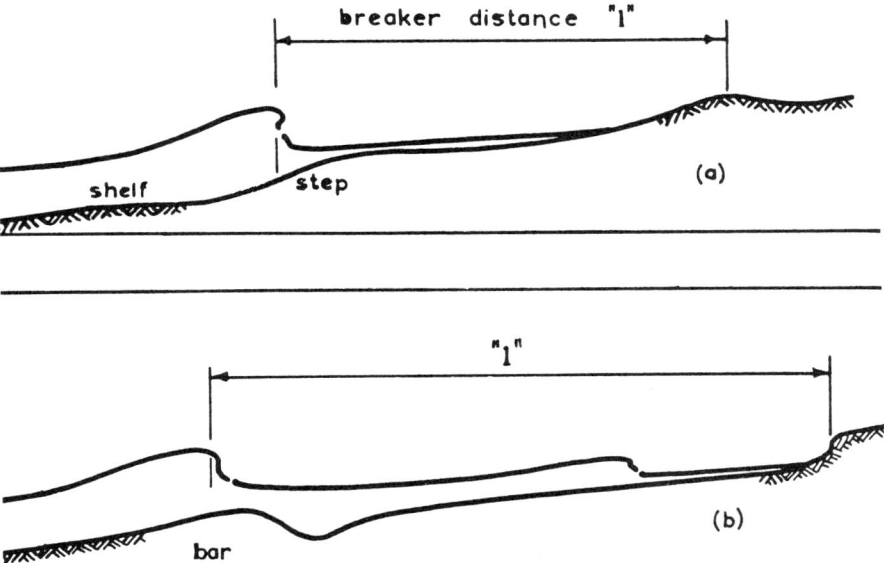

Figure 7.23. Schematic step and bar type profiles (37).

between the break point and the shore. This horizontal flow pattern is the origin of the beach cusps mentioned in the section on horizontal shore configuration.

Transition conditions are characterized by some interchange between the water in the zone seaward of the breakers and the nearshore zone. As the phase difference increases, the partly oscillatory nature of the onwash and backwash with limited interchange of water through the breakers gradually gives way to continuous flow into and out of the breaker zone. Continuous flow conditions become fully developed when the phase difference becomes equal to the wave period. This is the point at which the *bar type* or "surf profile" achieves full development (Figure 7.23).

The flow conditions for phase differences greater than the wave period, T, is classified as the "surf condition" by which beach cusps disappear. The change from step to bar type profile is therefore a function of phase difference. With respect to the question of whether the results of such model experiments may be applied to natural beaches, Kemp says that in attempting to relate and apply the parameters to beaches of fine sand, it is possible that the immobility of such beaches under the action of small waves may obscure the wave/beach profile relationship. In models, fine sand beaches, not formed initially to the correct equilibrium slope, may be only partially adjusted by subsequent wave action. Similar natural beaches may develop a profile characteristic of a dominant wave with only significant movement in the breaker area. Similarly on shingle beaches, if the waves are relatively small compared with the size of the beach material, the beach may behave as a permeable wave absorber. In his paper (37), Kemp further discusses principles of model similarity and the pertaining parameters involved in simulation of nature in tests on profiles.

Headland Influence on Bottom Profile Development

A headland protruding from the general shoreline presents a complete or partial littoral barrier to the longshore littoral drift. The result is that accumulation to capacity takes place on its updrift side while erosion may take place on its downdrift side. This in turn results in a steepening of updrift profiles and a flattening of downdrift profiles.

Theoretical Approaches to Offshore Bottom Configuration

Attempts have also been made to compute the geometrical shape of a (beach and) bottom profile under wave action. The assumptions for such computation must be of a very idealized nature. Basically there are two different approaches to this problem—one is of the more "speculative type," and the other is the detailed hydrodynamic approach considering elementary equilibrium conditions for single grains located on the bottom.

An example of the former is Bruun's approach (11, 12). Reference 12 gives a brief description of this approach.

(I). a. The profile is formed by the shear stress due to the wave action and is at right angles to the shore line. The material detached by the oscillating water is removed by longshore currents. As the shear stress due to wave action in general—and partially during storms—is far greater than the sheer stress originating from the longshore currents, this assumption seems logical.

b. In the equilibrium profile the shear stress per unit bottom area may be assumed to be constant, i.e., the "condition" at the bottom is the same ($d\tau/dx = d\tau/dt = 0$). Confirmation of this assumption only can be attained by experiments. One obtains $\tau = K\rho u_{ave}^2$, where ρ is the density, K the resistance coefficient and u the water velocity. If τ is assumed a constant, then $u_{ave} \sim H\pi/T$, sinh $2\pi y/L$ is also constant where T is the wave period; H, the wave height; L, the wave length; and y, the water depth.

c. dE_1/dx = constant, where E_1 is the transported wave energy per unit area of the wave, and x is the distance from the shoreline. The loss of energy is made up of a loss by bottom friction, a loss by spilling of the wave and a loss by internal friction (very small). The correctness of this assumption can only be proved by experiments. Calculations give:

$$x = L_0 \sqrt{2\pi y} \left[2\left(\frac{2\pi y}{L_0}\right) + \frac{1}{3}\left(\frac{2\pi y}{L_0}\right)^2 \right.$$
$$\left. + \frac{43}{180}\left(\frac{2\pi y}{L_0}\right)^3 \cdots \right]$$

where y is the water depth and L_0 the deep water wave length. The series is convergent for $y < l_0/8$, i.e., for storm waves on the Danish west coast out to depths of about 40 feet where $L_0 \sim 300$ feet. Since $y \ll L_0$, the equation may be reduced to

$$y^{3/2} = px \text{ where } p \text{ is a constant.}$$

(II). If it now is assumed that the loss of energy is due only to bottom friction and that this loss per unit area e_t, is constant, then

$$\tau = k\rho u_{ave}^2$$

where K = constant $(a/R)^{3/4}$, a is the length of the ripple marks and R, the half amplitude of the oscillating water motion at the bottom $(R \gg a)$ [2]. Calculations then give:

$$y^{3/2} = p \frac{x}{T^{2/3}} \quad (y < \text{about } L_0/8)$$

This profile is similar to the one above. Certainly the profile depends on the wave period T, but as the profile mainly is shaped by storm waves and as the variation in T for these is small, the profile in reality will be the same as that given by (1).

(III). If dE_1/dt and e_t are both assumed constant then:

$$y^2 = \frac{px}{T^{2/3}} \quad (y < \text{about } L_0/8)$$

Coastal Geomorphology

If the loss of energy is mainly due to friction loss at the bottom, the assumption dE_1/dx equals constant seems to be most logical. If the energy loss is primarily due to some other circumstance, especially to spilling of the wave, the assumption dE_1/dt equals constant may be more logical. So there is more reason to expect to find the profile $y^{3/2} = px$ nearest to the shoreline but outside the bar—and the profile $y^2 = px$ more distant from the shoreline; this is the case, as investigations with beach profiles mentioned below show that the profile is flatter than $y^{3/2} = px$ at greater depths but follows this equation in shallow water.

These calculations give the slope of the profile but naturally it cannot be maintained that the profile is "computed."

Keulegan and Krumbein (39) give a calculation of a beach profile using the solitary wave theories of Boussinesq and Russell, and tests concerning the energy loss in a solitary wave. They found the equation:

$$y^{7/4} = \frac{x}{4.86} \sqrt[4]{(v^2/g)}$$

where y is the water depth; x, the distance from shoreline; v, the kinematic viscosity; and g, the acceleration of gravity. The assumptions made in the derivation, however, seem to differ from actual conditions.

As explained in References 11 and 12, the steep "equilibrium profiles" on the Danish North Sea Coast and in Mission Bay, California, seem to follow the $y^{3/2} = px$ relations.

An example of a detailed hydrodynamic approach is given by Eagleson, Glenne and Dracup (22). The result of their approach and computations is revealed in Figure 7.24 and may be summarized as follows, referring to a single grain of

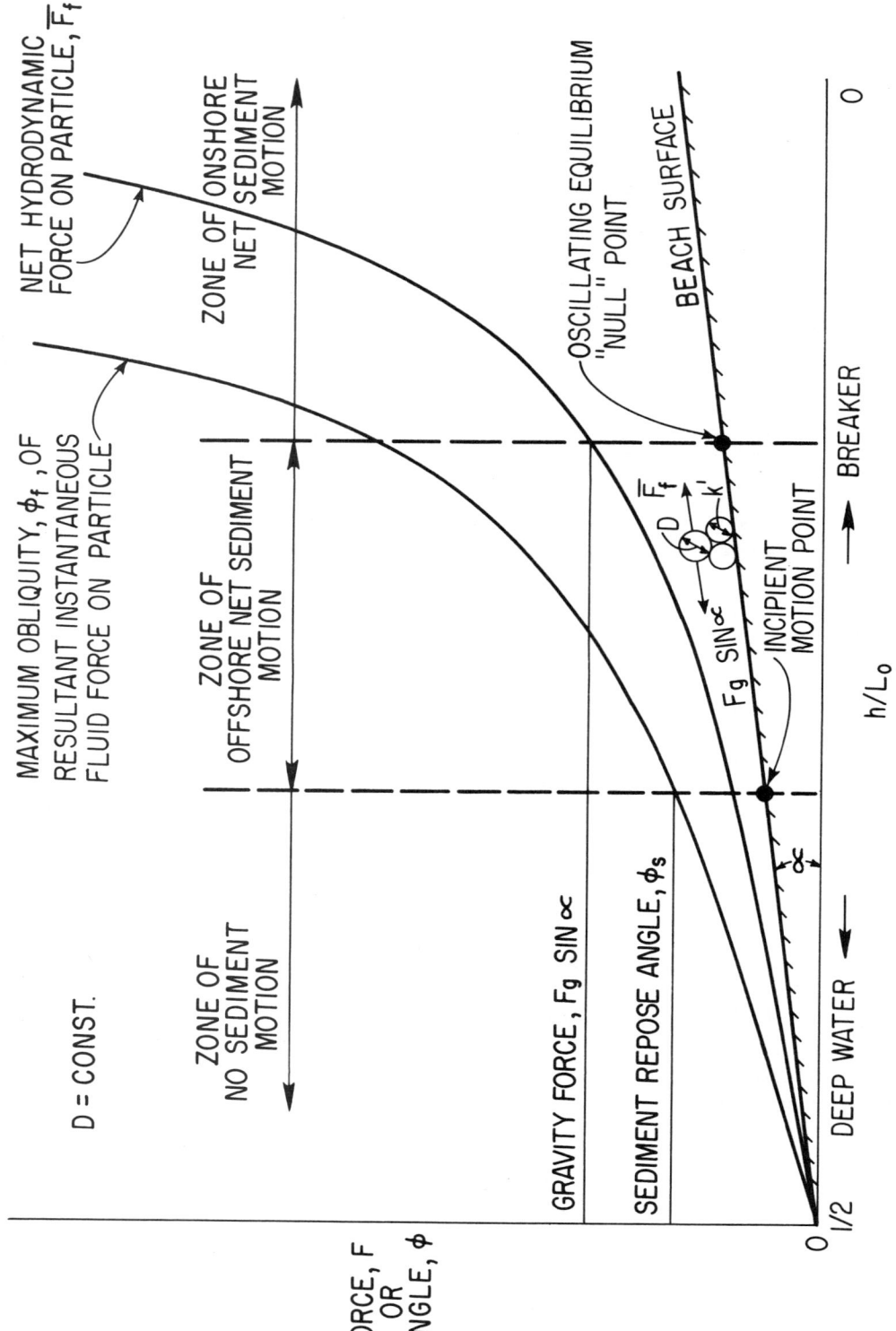

Figure 7.24. Stability situation for single grain on slope (22).

Coastal Geomorphology   291

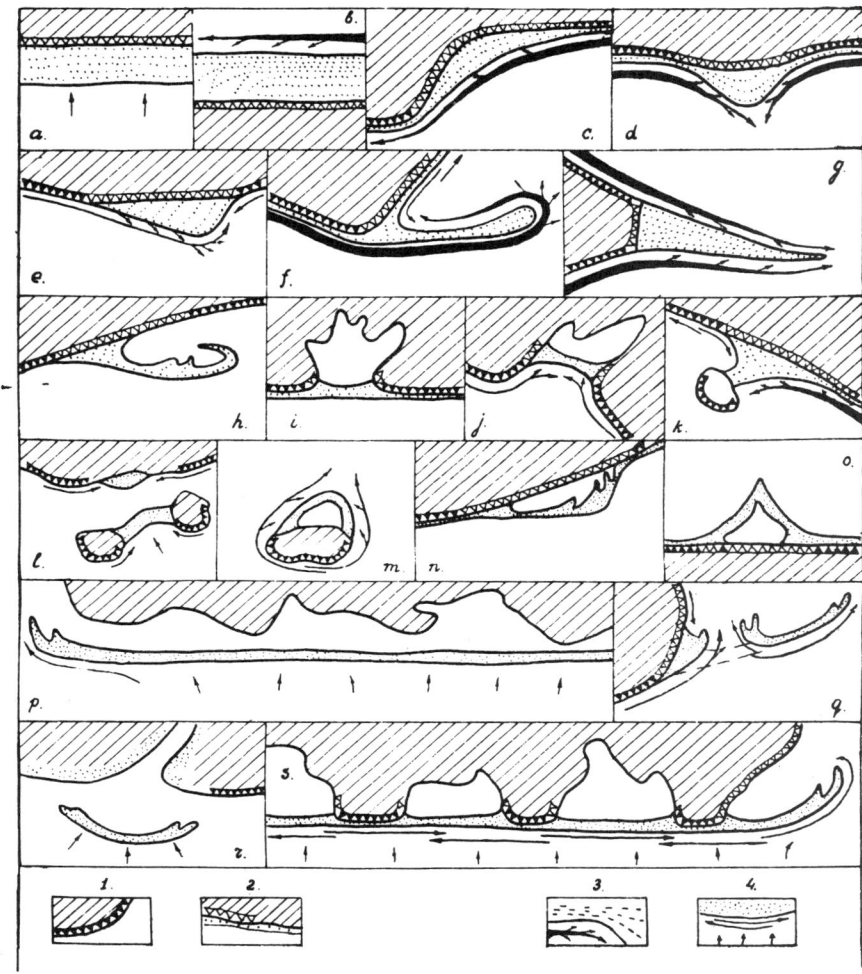

Figure 7.25. Accumulation forms (54).

well-defined grain size geometry and specific gravity located on a straight slope on other grains as indicated in Figure 7.24 and subjected to a specific wave action:

1. There is a point of "incipient motion" when the forces are just able to establish motion.
2. The motion may be either up- or downslope. Wave motion in the nearshore zone is always assymetrical with a tendency to shoreward predominance (as demonstrated by field as well as laboratory experiments). At one point,

theoretically speaking, an equilibrium condition between forces working upslope and forces working downslope exists. The direction of movement of any grain depends upon the location of the point of incipient motion and the point of equilibrium condition compared to each other. If, as shown in Figure 7.24, the point of incipient motion is located at greater depth in the profile than the point of oscillating equilibrium, material will migrate in an offshore direction from points inside the point of oscillating equilibrium but

Figure 7.26. Cuspate spit (45).

Figure 7.27. Barrier island, lunate sand key and lunate bar (45).

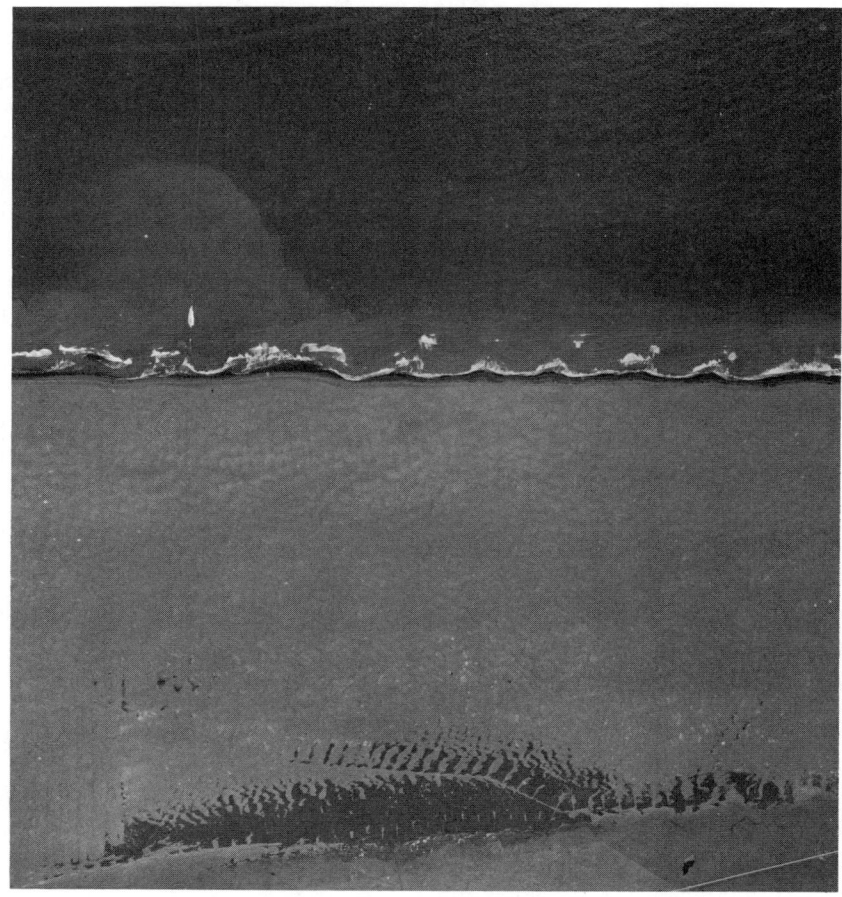

Figure 7.28. Beach cusps on the south coast of Iceland.

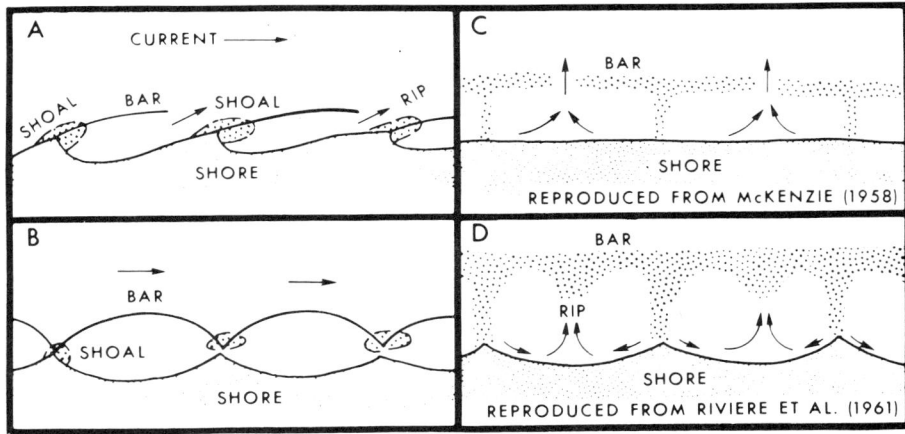

Figure 7.29. Typical effects of cusp-type sand wave on beach topography (47).

onshore inside the said point. This means that the profile, as a whole, flattens (winter profile). If the opposite is the case and the point of incipient motion is located at less depth in the profile than the point of oscillating equilibrium, all motion inside the point of incipient motion will be toward the shore, which means that the profile steepens (summer profile).

Although this theory, because of its very ideal assumptions, may seem "unrealistic," it still has some practical aspects and confirms to some extent the old (about year 1900) Italian "theory" by Cornaglia that a "null point" (referring to oscillating equilibrium) exists, which apparently makes steep littoral drift shores more attractive for harbor development than flat shores. As proved by numerous failures and as explained in a following section, the situation is not nearly as simple.

Horizontal Geometry and Profile Geometry Principles

Wave action penetrates unobstructed on the free open shore but refracts and/or diffracts in shoaling water and when it meets hindrances which may also cause absorption of wave energy as well as reflection or reflection and transmission of wave energy. The steepness ratio of waves changes by shoaling as well as by diffraction and/or refraction. This in turn means that waves, when subject to lowering of their steepness ratio, may change character from eroding to accreting type as far as beach geometry is concerned. Combining the principles of littoral drift direction and profile geometry, it is possible to explain the configuration of almost all "marine forelands" found in nature. Several books have been written on coastal morphology describing the great variety of types (35, 41, 44, 45, 54). Figure 7.25 shows examples which include the most common types like cuspate forelands (Figure 7.25d), tombolos (Figure 7.25k), angular forelands (Figure 7.25o) and barriers and spits of various kinds (Figure 7.25g, s), including the recurved type (Figure 7.25h). Figure 7.26 shows cuspate type foreland from Florida. Figure 7.27 is an example of interference of inlet currents and ocean currents causing bar formation. Regarding beach forms, the *beach ridge* results from action of waves of low steepness ratio as explained in the preceding section on beach geometry. Beach cusps (Figure 7.28, from the Icelandic South Coast) may originate from a certain regularity in

294 Port Engineering

Figure 7.30. Sand waves on the bottom at Skagen, Denmark.

Coastal Geomorphology 295

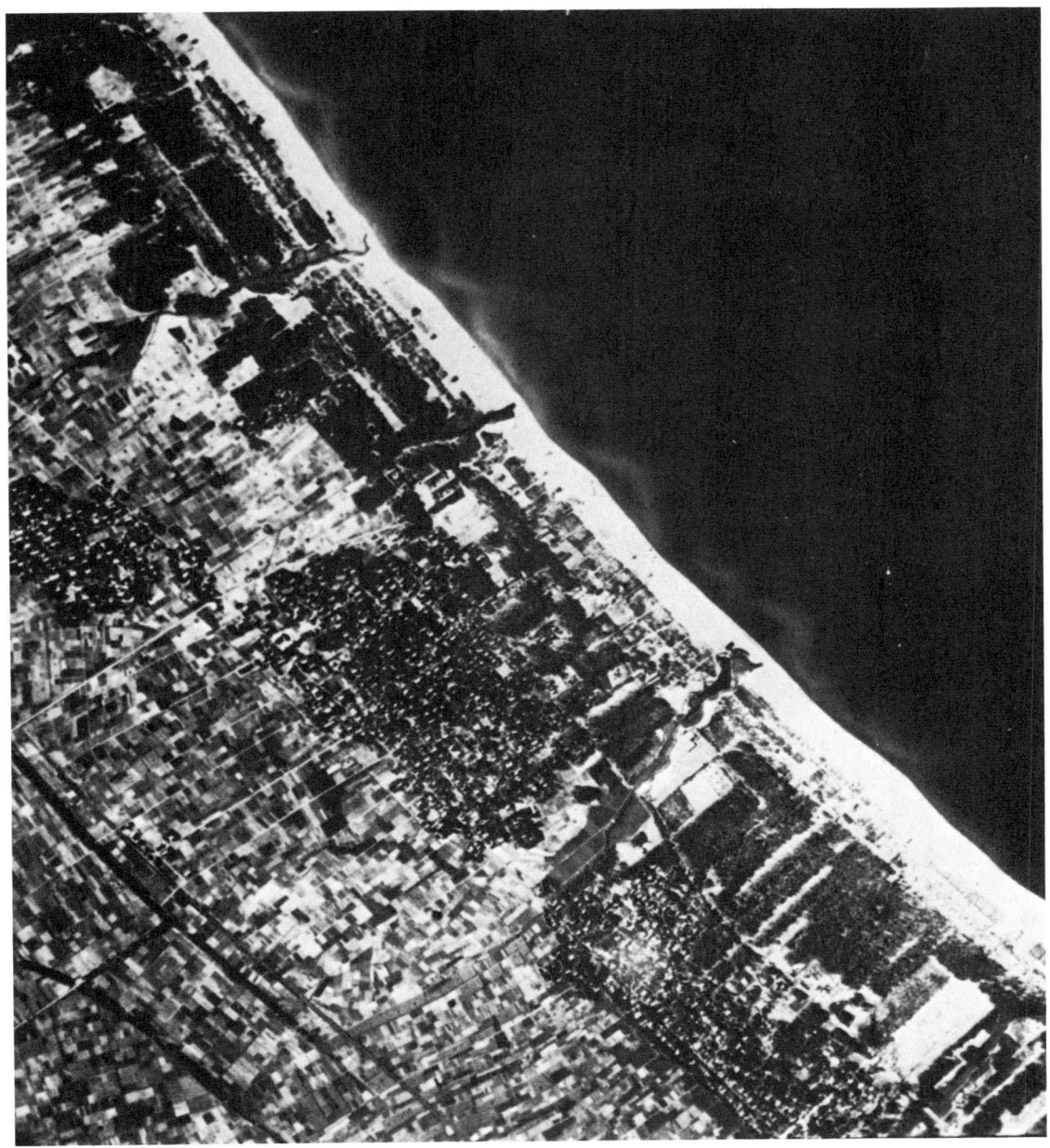

Figure 7.31. Sand waves on the bottom at Kaike, Japan (30).

Figure 7.32. Sand waves on the bottom at Lido Key, Florida Gulf Coast.

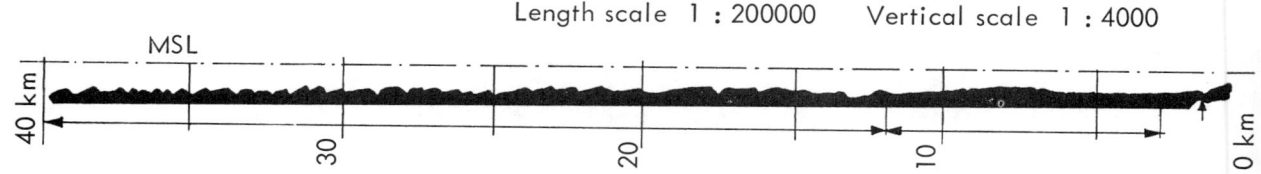

Figure 7.33. Sand waves on the bottom of the sea off the Dutch coast between Hook van Holland and Den Helder (50).

the uprush and downrush pattern. Reference is made to the preceding section on profile geometry which mentions Kemp's (37) research on profile geometry versus uprush and downrush modes related to wave period and beach slope. The large type of cusps (Figure 7.29) seems to be related to the current pattern, partly the longshore current (Figure 7.29A and B) and partly to the formation of rip current (Figure 7.29C and D). The undulations, meandering and fluctuations of the longshore currents may give rise to some very beautiful "guirlanders" (festons) of a great variety of length up to 3,000 meters (see Figures 7.30 and 7.31).

Some sand wave phenomena, as in Figure 7.32, may be seen as a result of the interaction between flow and boundary, perhaps following the principles developed by Engelund and Hansen mentioned by Bruun in Reference 16. This is also true for wave phenomena on the bottom-like, migrating sand waves (13, 50).

Thierry and van der Burgt wrote the following in their report to the 17th International Navigation Congress (see Figure 7.33).

It is quite probable that there is not only a sand drift along the natural coast curve between Hook of Holland and Den Helder and presumably along the other parts of the Netherlands coast, on the beach and in the breaker zone, but also that sand is being carried towards the coast from the sea bottom far off-shore.

The sand drift, which has its resulting component in the northerly direction, may be divided into:

a. sea drift from far off-shore—40 km and more—to about 12 km off-shore, where the slope of the sea bottom is about 1 in 4500, the depth decreasing from 23 to 17 m below water,
b. coastal drift from about 12 km to 3 km off-shore, where the slope of the bottom is also 1 in 4500, the depth decreasing from 17 to 15 m below low water,
c. breaker drift in the breaker zone, 2.5 to 3 km wide from the coast, including the part where the sea bottom slopes under 1 : 225 from 15 m to 4 m below water and the steeper part up to the back shore,
d. wind drift on the beach, where the elevation is over 1 m above the mean sea level.

The sand, which is brought towards the coast by these four kinds of drift, will move north as a local widening of the beach and will, as it passes by, be seen as a temporary advance and retreat of the shorelines.

These waves and bars are probably a tidal current phenomena, also explainable by the theories of Engelund and Hansen mentioned earlier.

In the North Sea waves of 10-meter height have been found in water of 30 to 60-meters depth. Very large waves are also found on the bottom of Cook Inlet, Alaska. The above mentioned waves have similar dimensions as those which travel on the bottom of the Mississippi (40). Sand waves traveling along the shore with crests perpendicular to shore are described in Reference 13 with reference to the Danish North Sea Coast. They may be a result of longshore wave currents because they seem to travel in the direction of the littoral drift. Sand waves traveling on the bottom in the Elbe River estuary (Germany) were mentioned in Chapter 6, where it was also explained that they caused large scale shoalings. They are mainly moving with flood currents. With the still increasing navigation depths for bulk carriers, it is necessary to pay much attention to these waves which are impossible to stop unless very extensive structures are built. Research on the migration modes, including magnitudes of these waves, is an important aspect of the Elbe River research program. They are a major concern when they occur in areas where pipelines for crude oil or gas have been placed, as in the North Sea.

Influence of Port Installations on Coastal Morphological Development

The erection of any structure of a littoral drift or any other sediment transportation shore immediately creates a problem in interference with natures order. Using a well-established terminology, the structure is said to present a "complete littoral barrier" if it blocks the littoral drift completely and a "partial littoral barrier" if it only blocks part of the littoral drift.

The situation which then develops may best be understood by the two terminologies *source* and *drain*. A *source on a littoral drift shore* is a coastal area which delivers material to other areas, e.g., a shoal in the sea, an erosion shore or a river

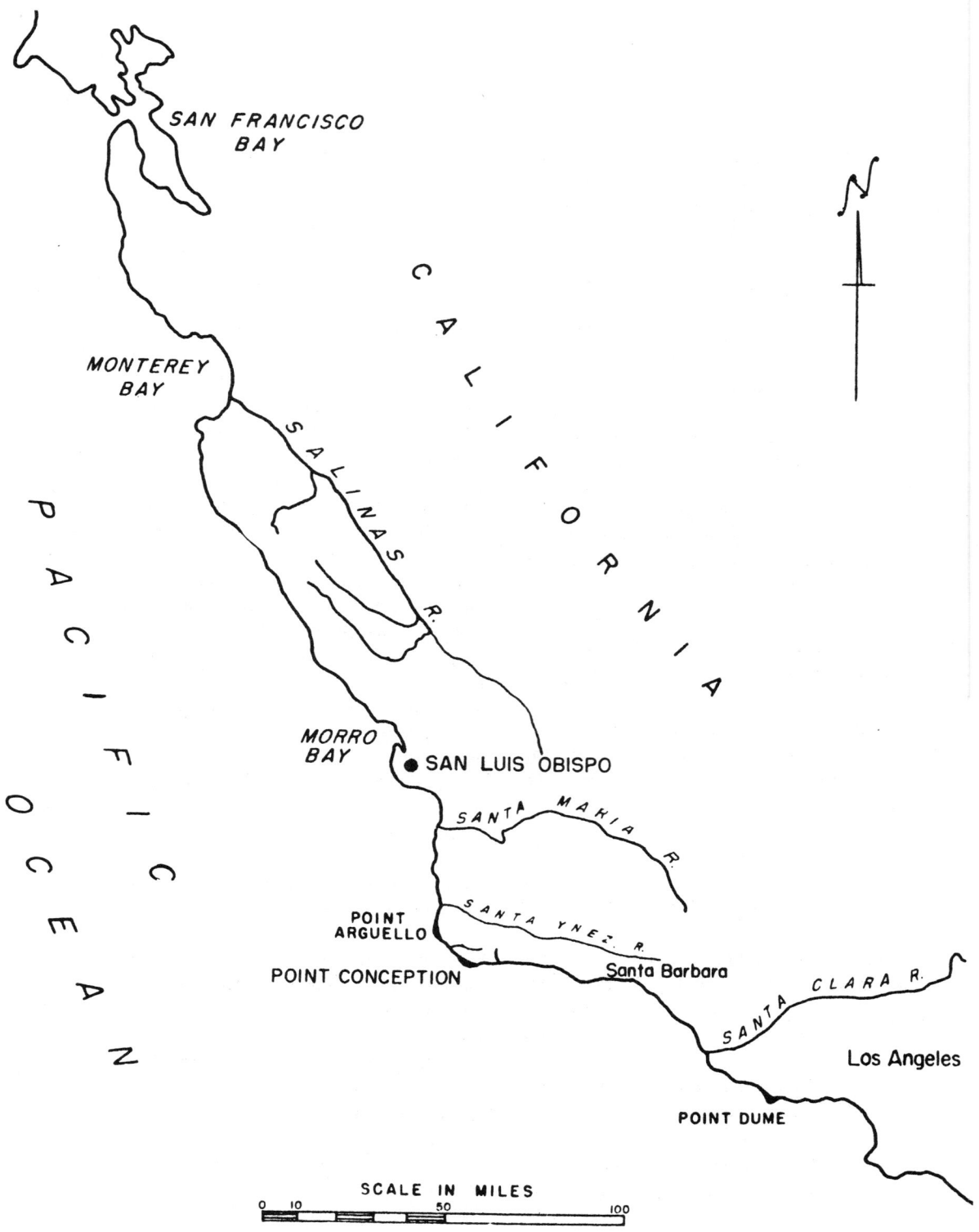

Figure 7.34. California headlands (51).

Coastal Geomorphology 299

Figure 7.35. The headland "Portland" (Dyrholaey), Iceland south shore.

carrying sediment to sea. A *drain on a littoral drift shore* is a coastal area where sediment is deposited, e.g., inlet, bay or sea shoals, cuspate foreland, spits, recurved spits, etc. Coastal protection should be built so that it functions as a drain and, therefore, should have a source on the updrift side. For proper functioning of coastal protection in a drain area, artificial nourishment is necessary. On the other hand, an improved inlet or a harbor should have no source or only a limited source on the updrift side. In any case, it will cut off sediment supply to the downdrift side and cause erosion. Thus, coastal protection problems are the reverse of harbor problems in this respect.

Development of Shoreline Geometry

Natural Barriers

Natural barriers are headlands protruding into deep water as many rocky headlands do. Reference 51 describes the situation at headlands in California. The research indicated very clearly that sand moves around these rocky California promontories. Furthermore, the data showed that the sand moves in three well-defined zones: (a) the beach and surf zone, (b) an active zone extending to a 30-foot depth and (c) an intermediate zone extending to a depth of about 60 feet. Relatively little sediment is transported in the passive zone beyond a depth of 60 feet. The mechanics of movement are different on each zone of migrating, but the sand definitely moved in each zone. The promontories only affect the sediments in the active zone, as water greater than 30-foot depth is not found as the base of any promontory studied.

Natural barriers are headlands protruding into deep water as many rocky headlands do. Reference 51 describes the situation at headlands in California. The research indicated very clearly that sand moves around these rocky California promontories. Furthermore, the data showed that the sand moves in three well-defined zones: (a) the beach and surf zone, (b) an active zone extending to a 30-foot depth and (c) an intermediate zone ex-

Figure 7.36. Man-o-war rocks, Dorset, England (49).

tending to a depth of about 60 feet. Relatively little sediment is transported in the passive zone beyond a depth of 60 feet. The mechanics of movement are different on each zone of migrating, but the sand definitely moved in each zone. The promontories only affect the sediments in the active zone, as water greater than 30-foot depth is not found as the base of any promontory studied.

Promontories or headlands, whether they present complete or partial littoral barriers, may cause a development like the one seen in Figure 7.34, which demonstrates a sawtooth configuration shore where material piles up against the headland on its updrift side and the predominant wave action usually is not far from being perpendicular to the direction of the shore and another straight shore downdrift which is often almost parallel to the direction of wave propagation. Reference is made to the preceeding section and to Figure 7.8 which indicates a method of (or a philosophy for) computing the headland angle. The final result is the characteristic sawtooth configuration with angles between shorelines of usually 100° to 120°. The headland geology may influence the development of the configuration, particularly if rock extends on either side of the promontory. An example of this, the headland Portland on the Icelandic south coast (Icelandic: Dyrholaey), a lava and basaltic mass which earlier was undoubtedly an island as indicated by some old records (Figure 7.35). This caused the formation of a tombolo between the island mass and the mainland. The shore toward the west (left on Figure 7.35) consists of a coarse lava sand, about 0.5 millimeters in diameter. The drift is slightly eastward. The downdrift shore is rocky (including basalt) for some ¾-mile

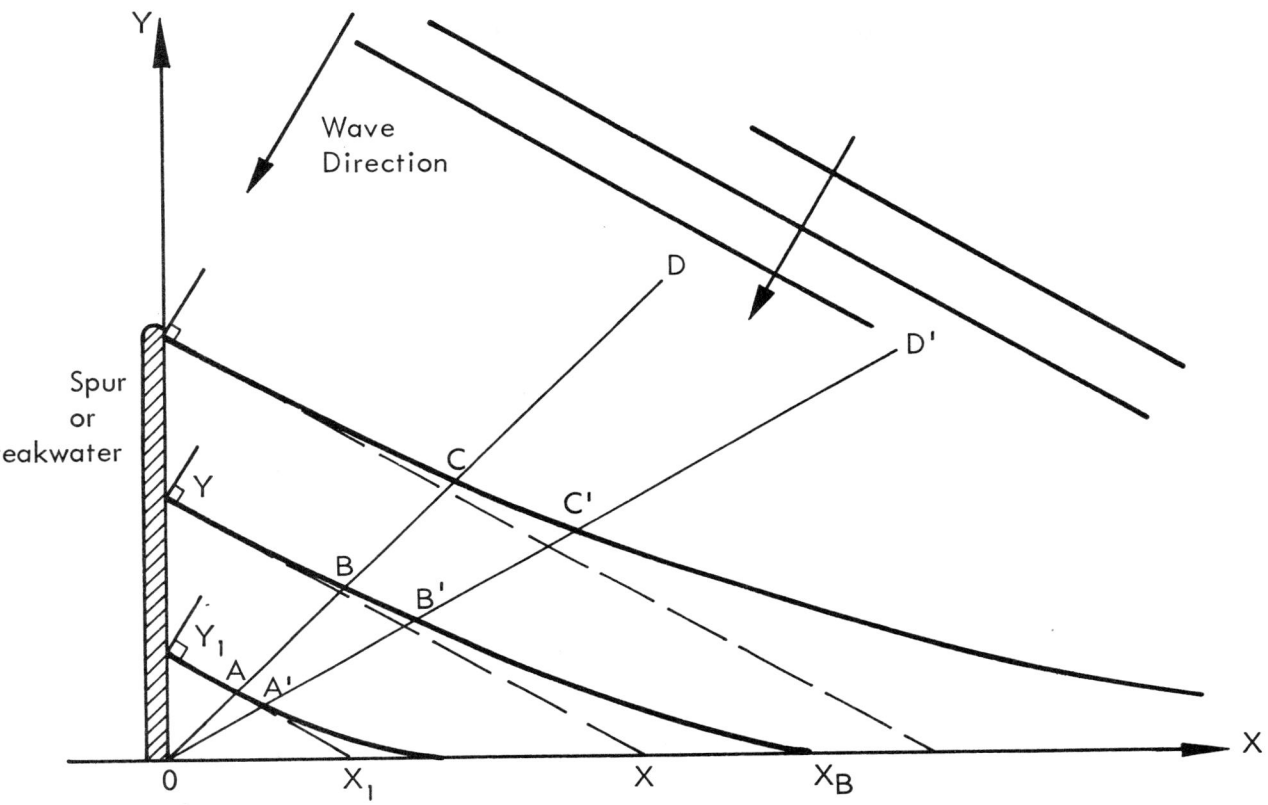

Figure 7.37. The approximate form of the shoreline given by Equation 11 (42).

distance and then becomes sandy and later rocky again. The Man-o-war rocks (Figure 7.36) are examples of how a shore-parallel rock formation may cause the development of a tombolo.

Man's interference with nature has largely been to create littoral barriers by breakwaters and jetties, whether perpendicular or parallel to the shoreline, which resulted in a development very similar to the development demonstrated by nature. Before examples of that are given, some theoretical, partly speculative, aspects of shoreline development will be mentioned.

Computation of Shoreline Development

In preceeding sections on shoreline development on a free, unobstructed shore, an expression was developed which gives the relation between shoreline configuration and littoral drift capacity based on the littoral drift formula:

$$Q = K f(L_o / H_o)(H_o^2 T) \sin(7/4 \alpha_o)$$

$$dy / dt = A (d^2 y / dx^2) \qquad (7.3)$$

when $A = (7 K g H_o^2 T)/4D$.

Consider the case when a breakwater perpendicular to shore presents a complete littoral barrier. According to Le Méhauté and Brebner (42), the solution to Equation 7.3 is

$$y = \frac{\tan\alpha_0}{\sqrt{\pi}} [\sqrt{4At} (e^{\frac{-x^2}{4At}}) - x \sqrt{\pi} E(x/4At)]$$

where $E(x/At)$ is Fresnels' integral used in probability calculation given by

$$E(\frac{x}{4At}) = E(u) = \frac{2}{\sqrt{\pi}} \int_u^\infty e^{-u^2} du$$

Many tables give the value of $E(u)$ or more often $\phi(u) = 1 - E(u)$ as given at the bottom of the page.

Figure 7.37 gives the approximate form of the shoreline given by the above solution. Integration of the curve along the Ox axis gives the total accumulation of sand. It must be noted that, consequent on the limit condition hypothesis, the tangent to the shoreline near the spur or breakwater, OY, is parallel to the incident wave crest. These curves, representing the shoreline at any time, t, are similar with respect to the center O; that is, one may draw any lines OD and OD' such that $OA/OA' = OB/OB' = OC/OC'$. When $t = t_1 = A/4 = 7/16\ CgHo^2 T$, $OY^1 = \tan\alpha \cdot /\sqrt{\pi}$ and at any time t, $OY = (\tan\alpha \cdot /\pi)\ 2\sqrt{(at)}$, and the sand reaches a length OY, which may be the end of the spur in time

$$t = \frac{(OY)^2 \pi}{4A \tanh^2\alpha}.$$

Hence, it is possible to forecast the shoreline at any time t with

$$\frac{OB}{OA} = \frac{OB'}{OA'} = \frac{OY}{OY'} = \sqrt{\frac{t}{t_1}}$$

or

$$\frac{OA}{\sqrt{(t_1)}} = \frac{OB}{\sqrt{(t_2)}} = \frac{OC}{\sqrt{(t_3)}} = \cdots$$

It may be shown that the ratio of the area between the shoreline at any instant, the spur or breakwater and the OX axis (the initial shoreline) to the area of the corresponding triangle OXY, where XY is parallel to the wave crest, is 1.56; that is,

$$\frac{\text{Area } OX_B Y}{\text{Area } OXY} = 1.56$$

Further, it is relatively easy to calculate sand discharge by measuring the variation of the triangles similar to OXY. Finally, $OX_B = 2.7(OX)$, which gives the limit where spur or breakwater effects are felt.

As explained in Reference 42, the above theory may be applied in a number of cases of accretion or depletion, including updrift accumulation and downdrift erosion, updrift or downdrift depletion because of dredging, updrift or down drift accretion because of accumulation, accretion by dumping in a single point or depletion by constant dredging of sand at a given point.

In most practical cases, the obstacles only stop the drift partially, which is considered next.

Obstacles Partially Stopping the Drift (42)

In the previous case, when OY reaches the length of the obstacle, the sand begins to pass the spur or groin after time

$$t' = \frac{(OY)^2 \pi}{4A \tan\alpha_0}$$

ϕ $\frac{u}{(u)}$	0.1	0.2	0.3	0.4	0.5	0.7	0.9	1.2	2	∞
	0.112	0.223	0.328	0.428	0.520	0.667	0.796	0.910	0.995	1

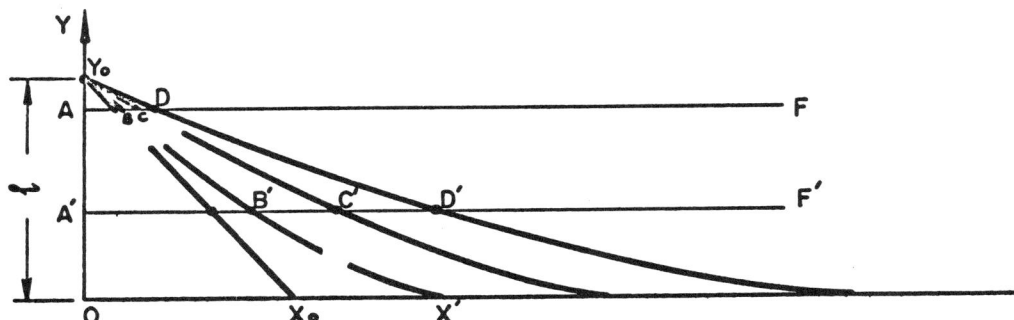

Figure 7.38. Computation of shoreline on the updrift side of jetty which is not a complete littoral barrier (42).

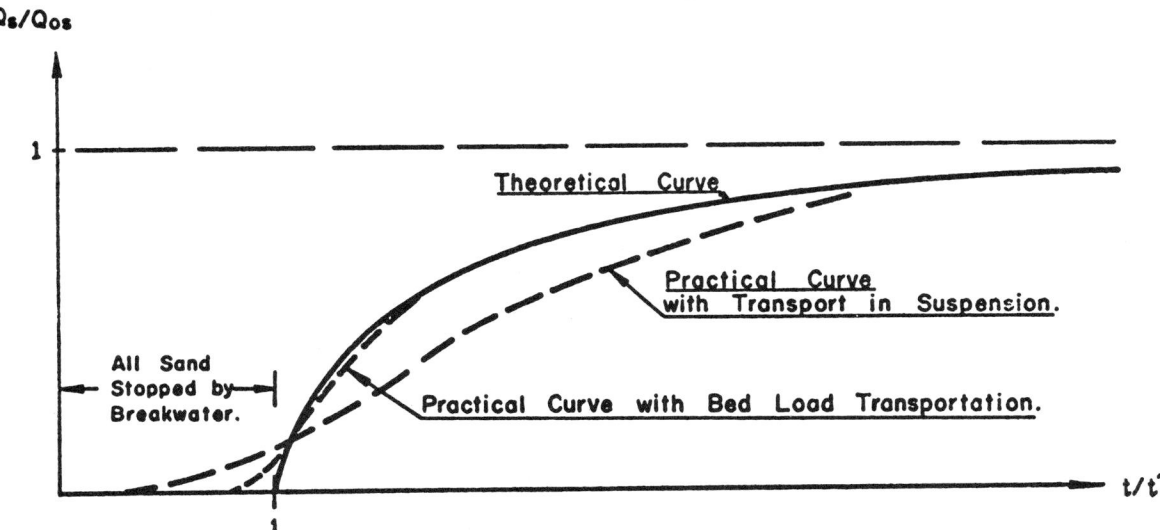

Figure 7.39. Qs/Qos as function of t/t' (42).

In this case OY becomes a constant, which is the boundary condition: let $OY = \ell$ when $t = t'$.

In this case the shoreline equation becomes more simply:

$$y = \ell E\,[x/\sqrt{(4At)}]$$

or

$$y = \ell\,(2/\sqrt{\pi}) \int \tilde{\tilde{u}}\, e^{-u^2}\, du$$

where $u = x/\sqrt{(4At)}$ and $y = \ell$, when $z = 0$, for any value of t.

Figure 7.38 gives the form of the evolution of the shoreline for this case. These curves are similar with respect to the OY axis, i.e., for any line AF or AF' parallel to the OX axis,

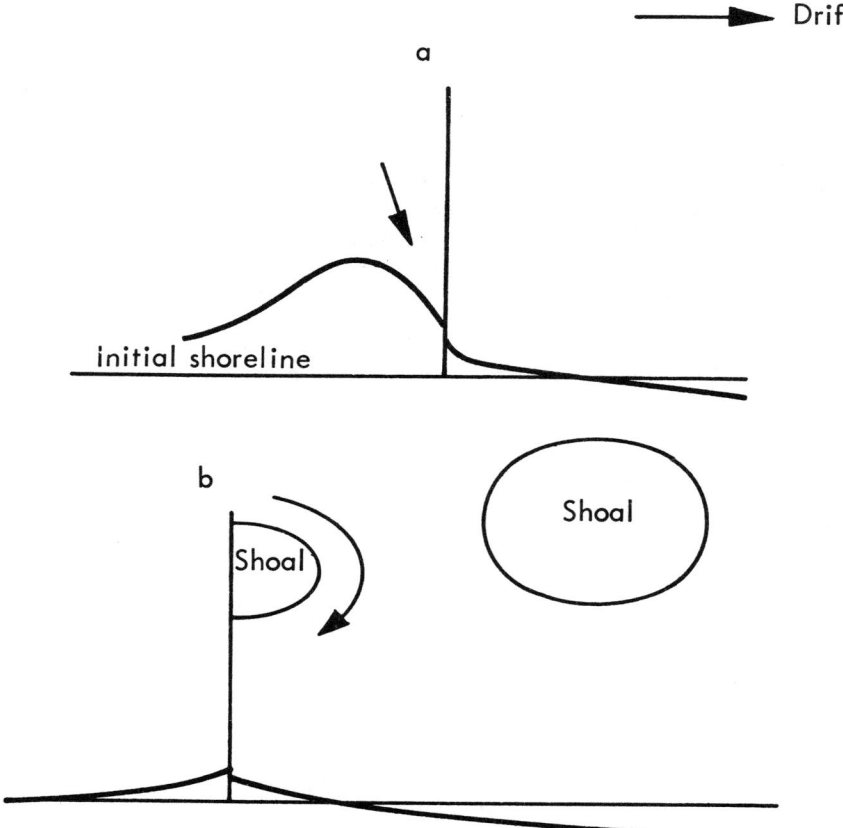

Figure 7.40. a. The influence of concentration of wave energy along vertical jetty. b. Shoal formation in case of fine material and strong currents.

$$\frac{AB}{A'B'} = \frac{BC}{B'C'} = \frac{CD}{C'D'} = \frac{AD}{A'D'} = \cdots$$

The surface between the shoreline and the OX axis is OY_oX'; its area is given by $2\ell\sqrt{(At/2\pi)}$ The triangular area OY_oX_o is given by $(\ell/2)\sqrt{(\pi At)}$ where X_oY_o is tangent to the shoreline at the point Y_o. Hence,

$$\frac{OY_oX'}{OY_oX_o} = \frac{\pi}{4} = 1.27$$

and

$$OX' = 2OX_o.$$

The discharge of sand as by-passing the groin is given by the expression:

$$Q_s = Q_{os}\left(1 - \frac{\ell}{\tanh\alpha_o[\sqrt{\pi A(t - 0.38t')}]}\right)$$

$$Q_s = Q_{os}\frac{0.638}{\sqrt{(t/t' - 0.38)}}$$

where Q_{os} is the discharge on the initially straight

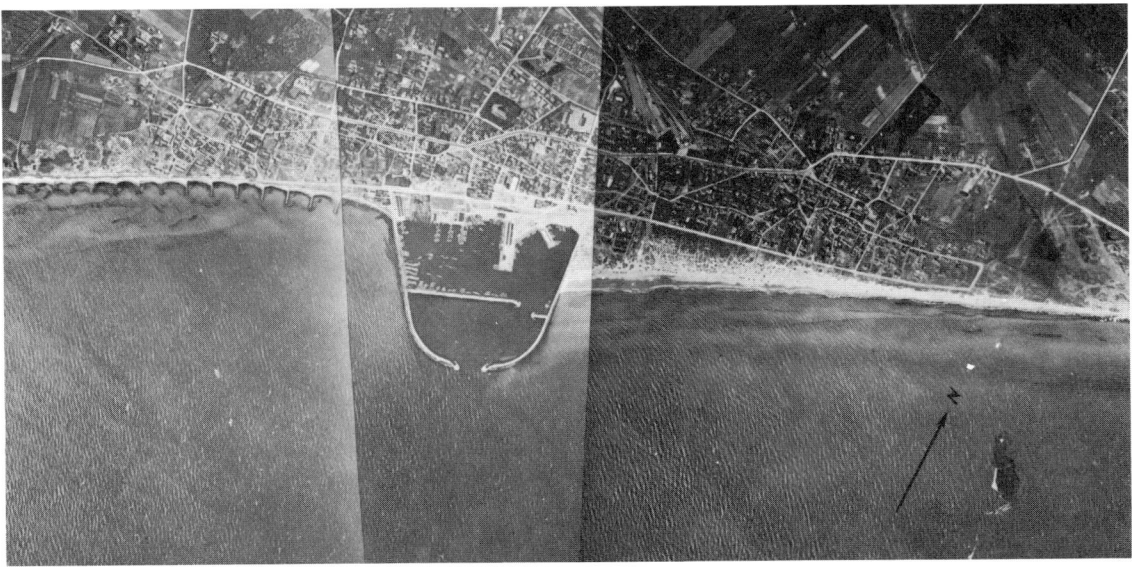

Figure 7.41. The Port of Skagen (the Skaw), Denmark (1930).

beach. The variation of t/t' with Q_s/Q_{os} is as given at the bottom of the page.

The variation is shown graphically in Figure 7.39.

Finally, the shoreline may be deduced at any time t_3 by similarity about the OY axis with the shoreline at time t_2 by the relationship

$$\frac{AB}{\sqrt{(t_2 - 0.38\, t')}} = \frac{AB}{\sqrt{(t_3 - 0.38\, t')}}$$

Reference 42 mentions how it is possible to study a number of other cases in detail, like sudden dumping of material in a given point and erosion and accretion between two obstacles. Figure 7.40a shows the influence of concentrations of wave energy along a vertical jetty. Figure 7.40b indicates how shoals form in case of fine material and strong currents.

Practical Examples

Figure 7.41 from the Skaw Harbor, Denmark (northernmost tip of Jutland), is a typical case of a harbor which functions as a complete littoral drift barrier, thereby causing serious erosion downdrift. Groins, built on the downdrift side, delayed shoreline recession without stopping it, due to the lack of artificial nourishment for feeding the groins. The harbor has now been expanded considerably, and a good part of the eroding shore has been protected by the new harbor installations (see Figure 10.5).

Figure 7.42 shows the situation at Conneaut Harbor, Ohio, when the west breakwater has

t/t'	1	1.25	1.5	2	3	4	5	∞
Q_s/Q_{os}	0	0.298	0.394	0.500	0.607	0.667	0.704	1

Figure 7.42. Conneaut Harbor, Lake Erie, Indiana (29).

trapped a great quantity of sand and gravel, creating a beach more than 2,000 feet long and 700 feet wide near the wall, tapering off westward to a beach about 50 feet wide. A considerable amount of sand has passed over the west breakwater to form a protected beach inside the harbor. The east jetty has had little effect on shore processes except to protect a very small beach just east of the Conneaut River mouth. The "slope" of the updrift shoreline toward a more or less complete littoral drift barrier is usually between 1 in 2 and 1 in 4. At Fairport, Ohio (Figure 7.43), two large breakwaters protect the harbor from storm waves and sedimentation. The west breakwater, which is about 3,900 feet long, has trapped, on its west side, one of the largest beaches on the Ohio shore

(29). The beach is more than 7,500 feet long. The updrift (west) shoreline has the characteristic feature of a slightly curved line. As it is often true in similar cases, the accumulation changes over in erosion at the end of the accumulation area. This is probably caused by an increase in drift capacity in the transition area up against the barrier due to refraction of waves, increasing their transport ability. The situation depicted in Figure 7.41 is another example. Erosion in this case started about 1 mile updrift.

Development of lee-side erosion is peculiar in this respect because it usually does not start immediately after a littoral barrier has been built. It may take a few years before it is felt. The reason for that may be sought in the steepness ratio of the

Coastal Geomorphology 307

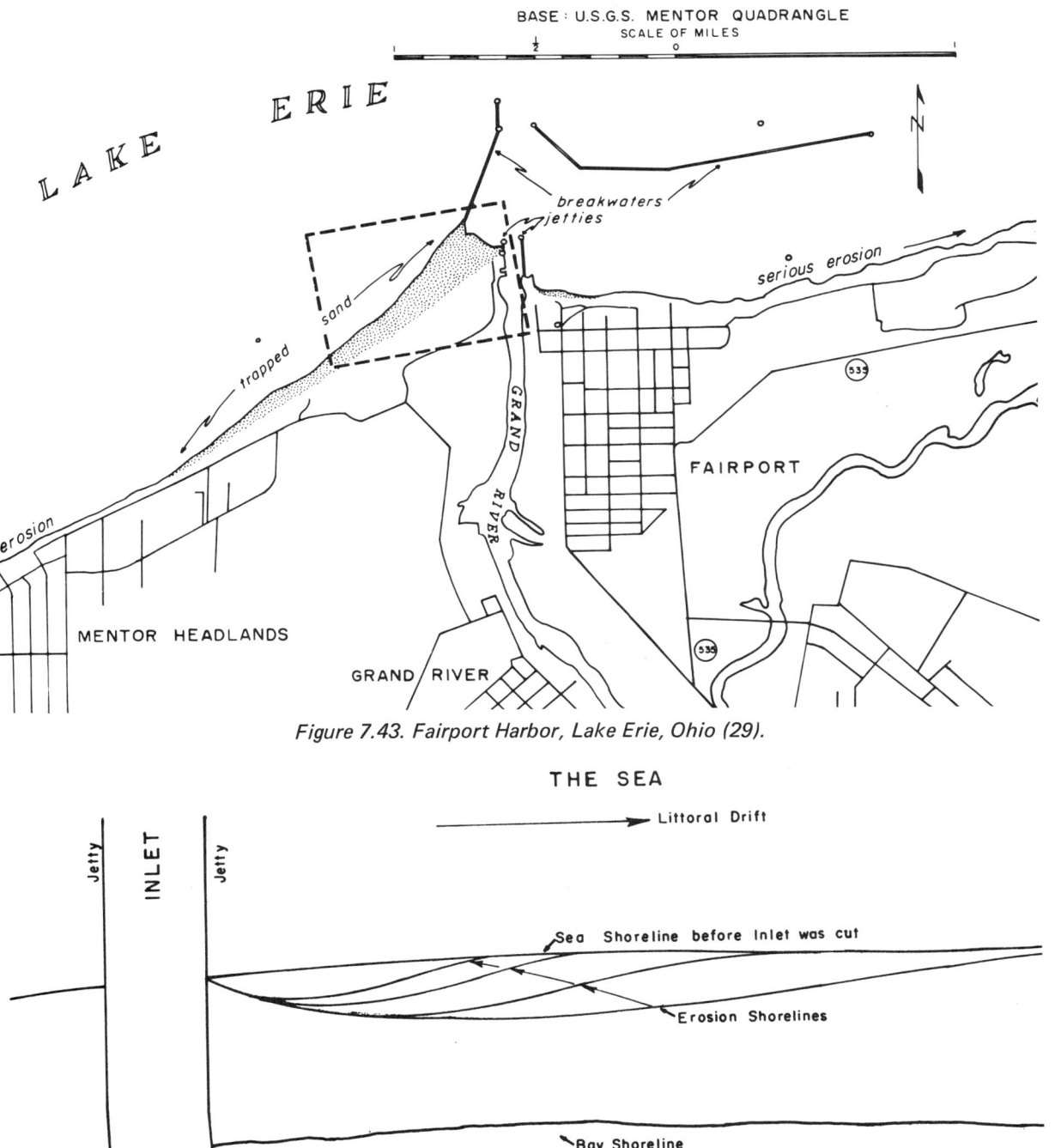

Figure 7.43. Fairport Harbor, Lake Erie, Ohio (29).

Figure 7.44. Shoreline development downdrift at Fort Pierce, Florida, schematic (18).

308   Port Engineering

Figure 7.45. Santa Monica Breakwater, California (Cassidy, Shore and Beach, October, 1961).

Coastal Geomorphology 309

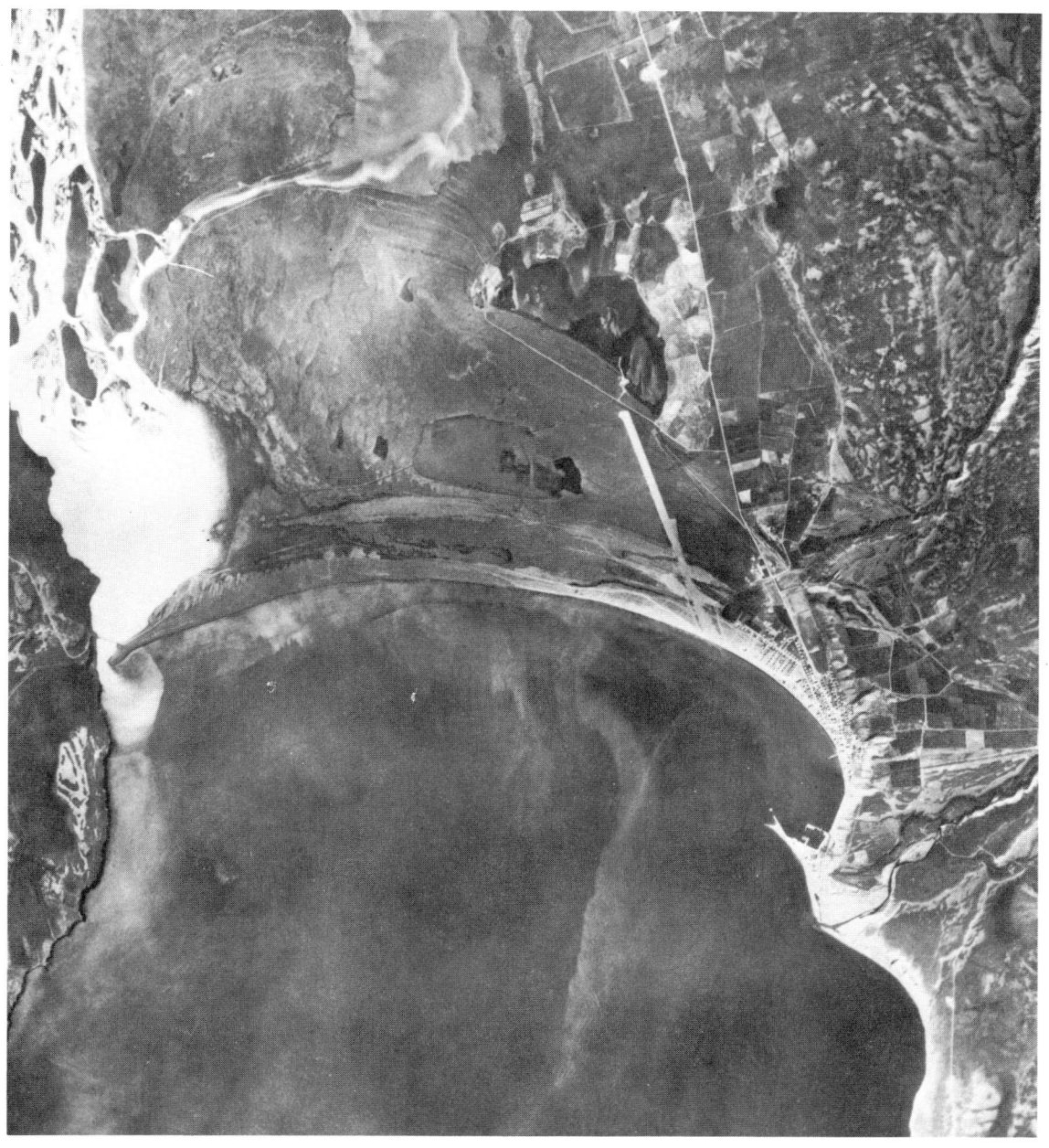

Figure 7.46. Aerial photos from Skagafjordur, Iceland.

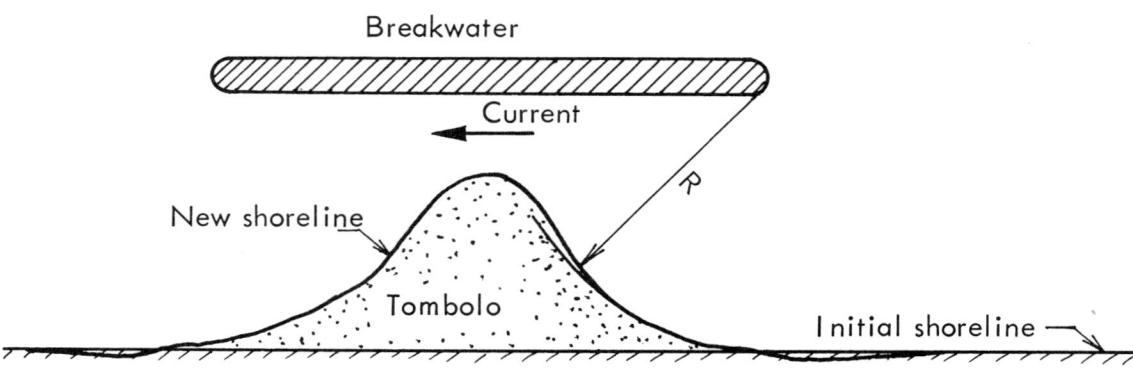

Figure 7.47. Shoreline configuration behind breakwater (schematic).

waves due to wave diffraction decreasing in the downdrift corner, making the waves less erosive at the same time as a local reversal of drift direction takes place. This may cause a temporary and "apparent" improvement by accumulation downdrift, which does not last very long. The imbalance of drift quantities soon makes itself felt, and erosion starts at the local neutral point and proceeds from there on downdrift. Figure 7.44 depicts such a situation with special reference to the condition at Ft. Pierce, Florida (18).

The shore-parallel breakwater is man's tombolo generator. The Santa Monica breakwater (Figure 7.45), the Port Huneme breakwater and the Ventura Harbor, all in California, are classical examples. Figure 7.46 shows an example with a shore attached breakwater (Iceland). The shorelines behind these breakwaters developed a form which is mainly a result of the diffraction pattern causing shoreline configurations which conform with the predominant pattern of wave crests. As the wave heights decrease with decreasing diffraction coefficient, a tendency to a slightly steeper angle higher curvature may develop. Figure 7.47 explains this situation.

Shores of materials like silt and clay may behave very differently because there is no "fixed" relationship between drift quantity and longshore energy. The quantity of material depends upon many factors, like wave characteristics, material characteristics, water viscosity, profile characteristics and the availability of material for stirring up a suspension transport. Lee-side erosion, however, also occurs under these conditions, but the profile development may be very different. However, when this occurs at exposed coasts, most shores of fine material will provide themselves with a cordon of coarser material like sand or gravel or mixtures of these, after which shoreline configuration will develop just like sandy shores, but it may be subject to major changes during extreme conditions. On very exposed sandy shores, a very substantial amount of material travels in suspension which does not hinder the shoreline in developing "normal configurative features." In addition to that, the travel modes of suspended material may play an important role particularly for the offshore bottom development. This is mentioned later under the development of bottom profiles as a result of man-made structures.

The development of shoreline configurations at tidal inlets differs from the normal development at breakwaters because of inlet current influence. Figure 7.48 schematically shows current situation, shoreline and shoal geometry at a tidal inlet. Currents will tend to draw water from the adjoining

Coastal Geomorphology 311

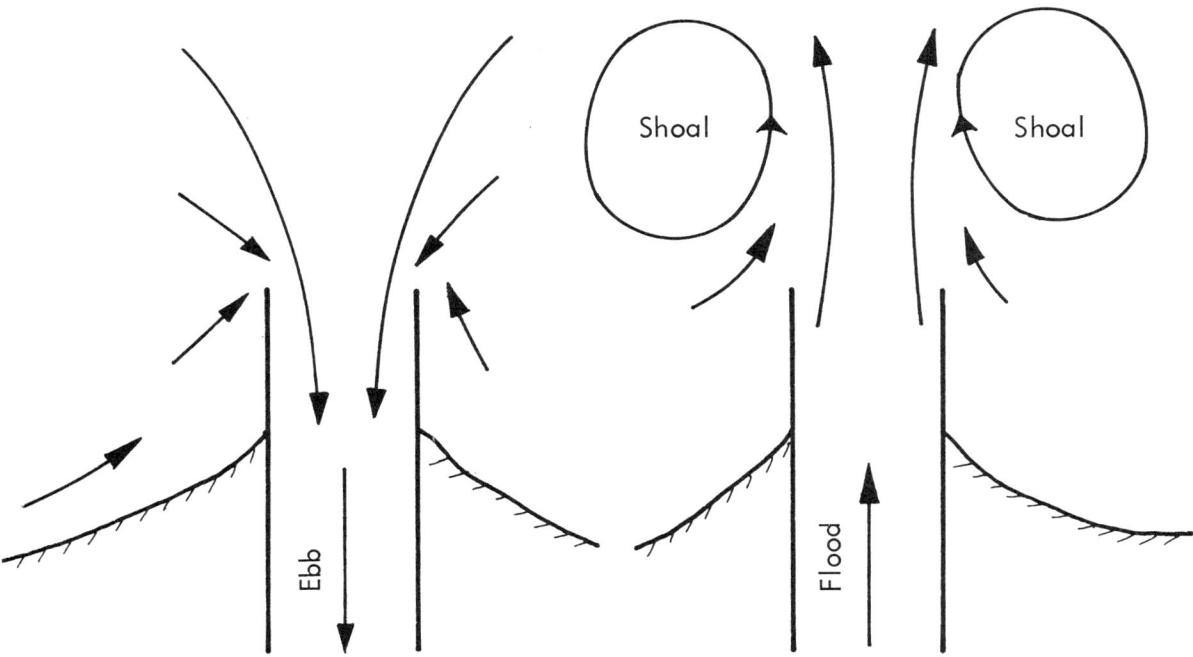

Figure 7.48. Shoreline and shoal development at tidal inlet (schematic).

nearshore areas to the inlet. This may result in an increase of the natural accumulation angle between the new shoreline and the old shoreline undisturbed by the inlet. The ebb current will cause the formation of ocean shoals which will be assymetrically located with respect to the inlet's centerline in case of a predominant drift in one direction, causing mainly or wholly downdrift shoal formation (see Figure 6.13 from Ft. Pierce, Florida).

Figure 6.20 showed shoreline and shoal configuration at inlets of varying entrance geometry. As mentioned in the following section, bottom geometry is greatly influenced by currents at tidal inlets, particularly when material is fine.

In the case of the shoreline configuration up and downdrift at Palm Beach Inlet, Florida (Figure 8.6), updrift jetty is filled to capacity, and the updrift shoreline is nearly straight. Most wave action has a low steepness ratio (swells), and this favors beach drift and consequent relatively steep profiles. At Palm Beach Inlet ebb eddy-currents developed a large shoal downdrift and offshore of the entrance, similar to the situation at Ft. Pierce.

In case a series of groins (small jetties) are built on such shore, a guirlande (festoon) shoreline configuration may develop.

Influence of Man-made Structures

As mentioned in the preceeding section, waves' steepness ratio decreases when they diffract as it happens on the downdrift side of an obstruction. The result is that eroding (profile steepening) waves, which initially make profiles, steepen close to shore because of the low steepness ratio of the waves (Figure 7.17). As already explained, the first reaction may not last very long. Soon the lack of material supply to downdrift profiles makes itself felt and erosion starts concentrating mainly on the nearshore part of the profile. This development results in the formation of some kind of a "platform" (see Figure 7.49) which schematically shows depth contours up and downdrift of a lit-

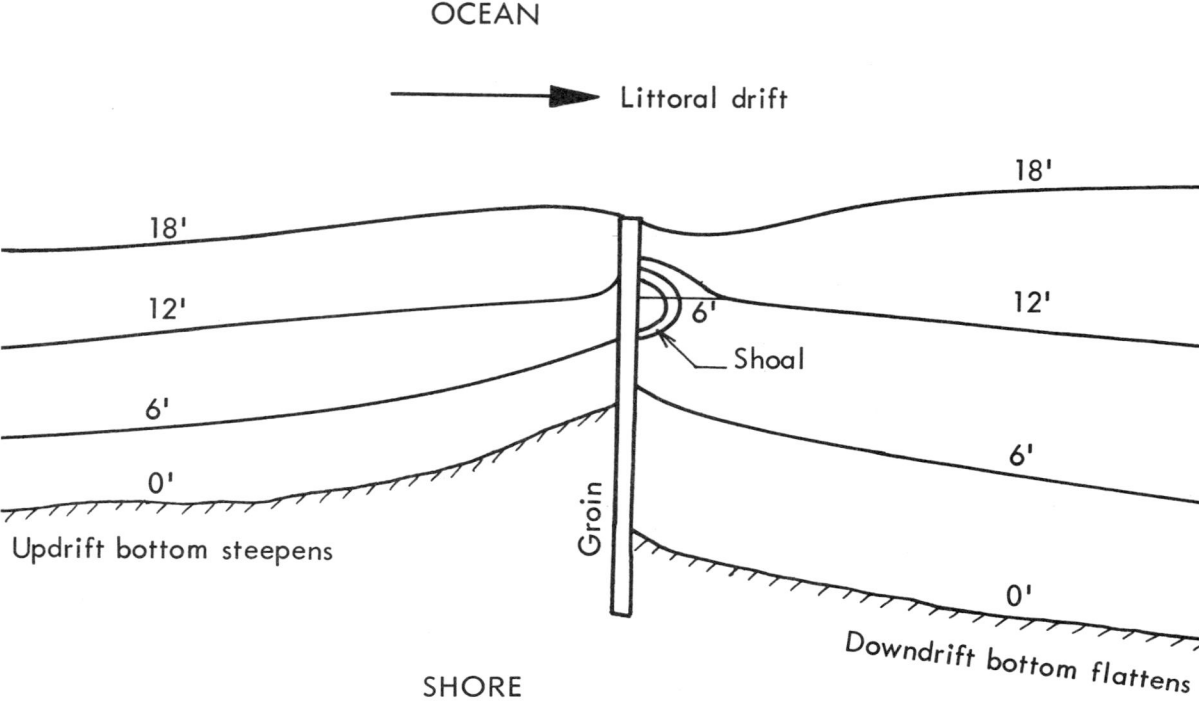

Figure 7.49. The development of bottom configuration downdrift of littoral drift barrier (schematic).

toral barrier in the form of a jetty. Figure 7.50 shows a practical example, the development of bottom configuration downdrift of the Aveiro Inlet in Portugal (see also Figure 6.12).

As already mentioned, current action and suspension material on exposed shores complicate the situation. Figure 6.6 shows a practical example: the Port of Hirtshals on the Danish North Sea Coast, which has large shoals in the offshore area downdrift due to large eddy currents.

Reestablishment of Natures
Morphology when Disturbed by Man

In Chapter 6 it is explained how, by transferring material past a littoral barrier, it it possible to reestablish natural conditions *but* such reestablishment will hardly ever be complete. Some material may be and usually is lost anyway, particularly at tidal inlets, and some lee-side erosion will almost always result. Therefore, beach and bottom profiles will still continue to show some of the updrift and downdrift characteristics.

During by-passing operations it is, however, never possible to by-pass exactly the quantity of material which is carried to the updrift side at any particular time. Sometimes overdredging takes place and sometimes less material is transported than accumulated. In the case of surplus transfer, an erosion form like Figure 7.51a develops which could have ill effects for updrift beaches. At the same time, an accumulation form develops downdrift. In cases where the opposite situation occurs, an accumulation form develops updrift and a lee-side erosion form downdrift (Figure 7.51b). If jetties are steep and non-energy absorbing, concen-

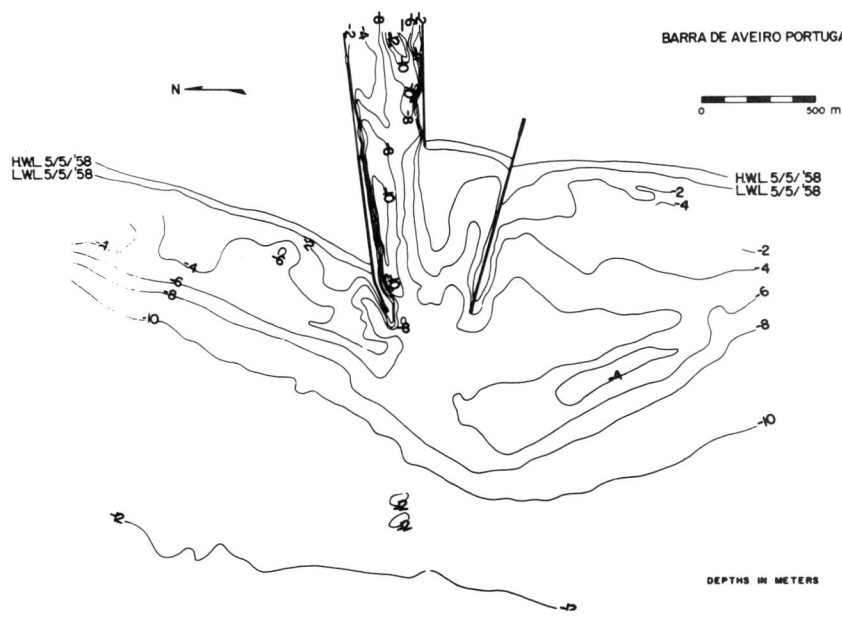

Figure 7.50. Practical example of the development of bottom configuration downdrift of littoral barrier Aveiro Inlet, Portugal (see also Figure 6.12).

tration of wave energy along the updrift jetty may take place, resulting in a setback in the updrift accumulation shoreline as depicted in Figure 7.40a. A rather strong current may then develop along the jetty; this situation is usually not desirable partly because material, mainly fine material, may wash out along the bottom to deeper waters, just as it happens in a normal rip current, and partly because the channel formation referred to may have adverse effects for the stability of the breakwater, e.g., if sheet piling is not carried down far enough. In order to stabilize the borrow pit from where transfer takes place, a spur jetty may be built (see Figure 8.8 on the Boca Raton Inlet, Florida—a model experiment carried out at the University of Florida). This will partly cause better accumulation of material during periods of insufficient by-passing giving rise to tombolo formation, and partly protect the updrift corner better during periods of excessive by-passing, because bottom profiles can remain steeper behind the spur jetty, which in turn causes less shoreline recession in the corner and thereby less shoreline recession in the corner and thereby less movement of the updrift shoreline.

The influence on bottom profiles by offshore dredging was investigated by experiments on "back-passing" (passing of material back to shore) at Jupiter Island, Florida (15) by using fluorescent tracers. The equipment used for the back-passing was a dragline with a 3-cubic yard bucket dragging in sand from 500 to 800 feet offshore at 8 to 13-foot water depth. Because the offshore bottom steepens by this operation, it is important that the borrow pit is far enough out to be filled by material from all sides and not mainly from the inside by transversal drift, which means erosion by outwash of material from the beach. The test results were that the summer seasons mainly demonstrated migration toward the shore from the bottom up to at least 17-foot depth, or possibly more, and that a similar movement apparently took place in the op-

314   Port Engineering

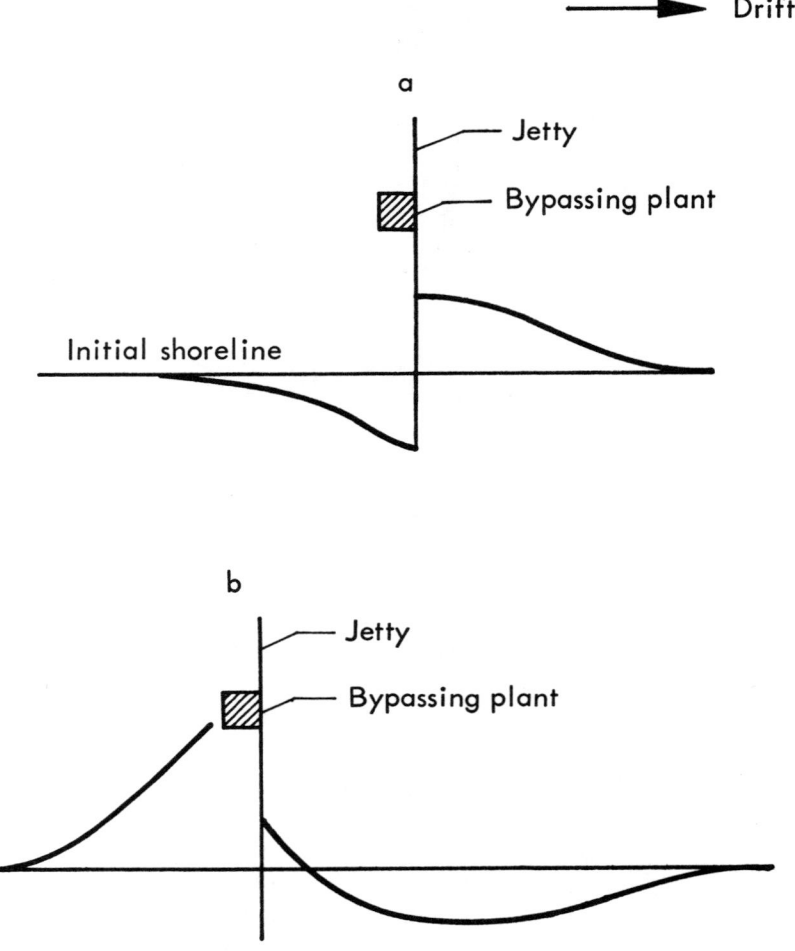

Figure 7.51. Shoreline configuration at littoral barriers with by-passing plants.

posite direction, although the material did not move perpendicular to shore but tended to move crosswise, in the general direction of the littoral drift. All borrow areas apparently were refilled by nearshore littoral drift material. It would undoubtedly have been advantageous to beach stability had it been possible to locate the borrow pits further offshore (assuming the same grain size). The beneficial effect on beach stability (on a short-range basis) of the scraper operation (about 250,000 cubic yards in 1963-66) were obvious to those who observed the development frequently.

The question may be raised as to what extent groins are able to influence the development of bottom profiles. The main influence of groins is that they slow down the longshore current. If the groins extend beyond the outermost breaker line, the longshore current, due to wave breaking, will be blocked and replaced by transversal currents between the groins. This will cause some local changes of shoreline and bottom configuration between the groins, but the bottom profile as a whole will not steepen unless there is an offshore (e.g., tidal) current which, together with the oscillating wave motion, is able to scour the bottom. In that case, bottom will steepen and gradually develop "maximum steepness." When this point in the development has been reached, shoreline recession may accelerate, but still erosion quantities have decreased when the situation without groins is compared to the situation with groins (11).

If the groins do not extend beyond the breaker line, longshore currents due to wave action may be very swift outside the groins. Combined with wave action, this may cause considerable scour. Often, the first result is that the offshore bar disappears; next, bottom develops maximum steepness which may result in rapid erosion during extreme storms, regardless of groin existence (11).

Ten Demands in Coastal Morphology
Versus Port Engineering

1. A port should not be placed downdrift of a large source of material like a river, an estuary or an eroding shore. It should be built on the updrift side.
2. The port should be built updrift of the area where erosion starts.
3. It is always best to place the port in a neutral area where drift goes to either side of the location selected for port installation.
4. On open littoral drift *coasts*, convex shores, which arch up against the resultant wave energy vector, thereby decreasing the quantity of littoral drift, are preferable for port location. On such shores a port should be built as far downdrift as possible.
5. On open littoral drift shores, concave shores which turn in the direction of the resultant wave energy vector by which the quantity of littoral drift increases should be avoided, unless the shoreline configuration passes the angle with the resultant wave energy vector which gives maximum drift (40° to 60°) and beyond which accumulation of material starts. On such shores the port should be placed either as far as possible updrift from the point of maximum drift where drift quantity is least or as far beyond the point of maximum drift as possible—that means beyond the point where accumulation starts.
6. On exposed shores, areas with relatively coarse material (coarse sand and gravel) are preferable for port installations.
7. Wherever an accumulation shoal is—in the ocean, in the lagoon, estuary or bay—the port should be placed downdrift of the shoal—that means in the direction where currents are leaving the shoal, but any interference with currents and wave pattern on the shoal and in its vicinity should be avoided.
8. If longshore currents carrying material are strong, breakwaters should be streamlined as much as possible in order to avoid formation of eddies and consequent accumulation of shoals by eddies.
9. The updrift side of a headland is usually steep, and it may be so steep that material leaves the nearshore drift area for accumulation in deeper waters offshore. Normally the shore is not steep enough, and if a port is built, material may have to be by-passed in its full quantity.
10. The downdrift side of a headland on shores with coarse material may offer good sites for harbor installations, but they must stay clear of accumulation areas. However, the offshore bottom may have developed to be relatively shallow so depths are inadequate for major navigation. If material is fine (e.g., silt and clay), downdrift side in general may be infested with large shoals making installation of harbors difficult and uneconomical because of the need for excessive dredging initially as well as for maintenance.

References

1. Bagnold, R.A. 1940. "Beach formation by waves; some model experiments in a wave tank." *Journal of the Institution of Civil Engineering* 1(5237):27-52.
2. ____. 1946. "Motion of waves in shallow water. Interaction between waves and sand bottom." *Proceedings of Royal Society* 187(series A).
3. Bascom, W.N. 1951. "The relationship between sand size and beach-face slope." *Transactions of American Geophysical Union* 32:866-74.
4. ____. 1954. "Characteristics of natural beaches." *Proceedings of the 4th Conference on Coastal Engineering.* New York. pp. 163-70.
5. Beach Erosion Board. 1950. *Beach Cycles in Southern California.* Tech Memo 20. U.S. Army Corps of Engineers.
6. ____. 1950. *Sand Movement in the Shallow Inter-Canyon Shelf at La Jolla.* Tech Memo 26. U.S. Army Corps of Engineers.
7. ____. 1950. *Longshore Bars and Longshore Troughs.* Tech Memo 15. U.S. Army Corps of Engineers.
8. ____. 1952. *The Source, Transportation and Deposition of Beach Sediment in Southern California.* Tech Memo 22. U.S. Army Corps of Engineers.
9. Bruun, P. 1953. *Forms of Equilibrium of Coasts with a Littoral Drift.* Tech Report 347. University of California, Berkeley: Institute of Engineering Research.
10. ____. 1953. "Measures against erosion at groins and jetties." *Proceedings of the 3rd Conference on Coastal Engineering.* New York. pp. 137-64.
11. ____. 1954. *Coastal Stability.* Copenhagen: Danish Technical Press.
12. ____. 1954. *Coast Erosion and Development of Beach Profiles.* Tech Memo 44. Beach Erosion Board, U.S. Army Corps of Engineers.
13. ____. 1954. "Migrating sand waves or sand humps." *Proceedings of the 5th Conference on Coastal Engineering.* Grenoble, France. pp. 269-95.
14. ____. 1962. "Sea level rise as a cause of beach erosion." *ASCE Journal of the Waterways and Harbors Division* 88(WW1):117-30.
15. ____. 1967. "By-passing and back-passing with reference to Florida." *ASCE Journal of the Waterways and Harbors Division* 93(WW2):101-28.
16. ____. 1967. *Tidal Inlets and Littoral Drift.* Oslo: University Book Company.
17. ____ and Manohar, M. 1963. "Coastal protection for Florida." *Engineering Progress at the University of Florida* 17(8), 56pp.
18. ____, et al. 1958. "Coastal engineering study at Fort Pierce Beach." *Engineering Progress at the University of Florida* 12(9).
19. Darling, John M. 1964. "Seasonal changes in beaches of the North Atlantic coast of the United States." *Proceedings of the 9th Conference of Coastal Engineering.* Lisbon.
20. Davis, W.M. 1912. *Die Beschreibende Erklärung der Landformen.* Berlin: Leipzig.
21. Dolan, A. 1965. "Seasonal variation in beach profiles along the outer banks of North Carolina." *Shore and Beach* 33(2):22-26.
22. Eagleson, P.S., Glenn, B., and Dracup, J.A. 1961. *Equilibrium Characteristics of Sand Beaches in the Offshore Zone.* Tech Report 41. MIT: Hydrodynamics Laboratory.
23. Edelman, T. 1963. "Littoral transport in the breaker zone, caused by oblique waves." *Proceedings of IAHR Congress.* London.
24. Fairbridge, R.W. 1961. "Eustatic changes in sea level." *Physics and Chemistry of the Earth,* vol. 4. New York: Pergamon Press, Inc. pp. 99-185.
25. Fenneman, N.M. 1902. "Development of the profile of equilibrium of the sub-aqueous shore terrace." *Journal of Geology* 10:1-32.
26. Grijm, W. 1960. "Theoretical forms of shorelines." *Proceedings of the 7th Conference on Coastal Engineering* 1:197-202. Holland.
27. ____. 1964. "Theoretical forms of shorelines." *Proceedings of the 9th Conference on Coastal Engineering.* Lisbon. pp. 219-35.

28. Harrison, W., and Krumbein, W.C. 1964. *Interactions of the Beach-Ocean-Atmosphere System, Virginia Beach, Virginia*. Tech Memo 7. Coastal Engineering Research Center.
29. Hartley, R.P. 1964. *Effects of Large Structures on the Ohio Shore of Lake Erie*. Department of Natural Resources, State of Ohio.
30. Homma, M., Horikawa, K., and Sonu, C. 1962. "Field investigation at Tokai, Japan, conducted by combined procedure of macroscopic and microscopic approaches." *Coastal Engineering in Japan* 5:93-110.
31. Inman, D. L. 1953. *Areal and Seasonal Variations in Beach and Nearshore Sediments at La Jolla*. Tech Memo 39. Beach Erosion Board, U.S. Army Corps of Engineers.
32. ____. 1957. *Wave-generated Ripples in Nearshore Sands*. Tech Memo 100. U.S. Army Corps of Engineers.
33. ____, and Rusnak, G.S. 1956. *Changes in Sand Level on the Beach and Shelf at La Jolla, California*. Tech Memo 82. Beach Erosion Board, U.S. Army Corps of Engineers.
34. Ippen, A., and Eagleson, P.S. 1955. *A Study of Sediment Sorting by Waves Shoaling on a Plane Beach*. Tech Report 18. MIT: Hydrodynamics Laboratory.
35. Johnson, D.W. 1919. *Shore Processes and Shoreline Development*, New York.
36. Johnson, J.W. 1949. "Scale effects in hydraulic models involving wave motion." *Transactions of American Geophysical Union* 30:517-25.
37. Kemp, P.H. 1958. "The relationship between wave action and beach profile characteristics." *Proceedings of the 7th Conference on Coastal Engineering*. Holland. pp. 262-77.
38. Keulegan, G.H., 1948. *An Experimental Study of Submarine Sand Bars*. Tech Report 3. Beach Erosion Board, U.S. Army Corps of Engineers.
39. ____, and Krumbein, W.C. 1949. "Stable configuration of bottom slope in shallow water and its bearing on geological process." *Transactions of American Geophysical Union* 30(6).
40. Lane and Eden. 1940. "Sand waves in the lower Mississippi River." *Journal of Western Society of Engineers* 44-45(6):281-91.
41. Larras, J. 1957. "Plages et cotés de sables." *Collection Du Laboratoire National D'Hydraulique*. Paris: Eyrolles Editeur.
42. Le Méhauté, B., and Brebner, A. 1960. *An Introduction to Coastal Morphology and Littoral Processes*. Civil Engineering Report 14. Ontario: Queens University at Kingston.
43. Richthofen, F. von. 1886. *Fuhrer fur Forschungreisende*. Berlin.
44. Schou, Axel. 1945. *Det Marine Forland*. Copenhagen: H. Hagerup.
45. Shepard, F.P. 1952. "Revised nomenclature for depositional coastal features." *The Bulletin of the American Association of Petroleum Geologists* 36(36).
46. ____, and Inman, D.L. 1951. *Sand Movement on the Shallow Inter-Canyon Shelf at La Jolla, California*. Tech Memo 29. Beach Erosion Board, U.S. Army Corps of Engineers.
47. Sonu, C.J. 1968. "Collective movement of sediment in littoral environment." *Proceedings of the 11th Conference on Coastal Engineering*. New York.
48. Steers, J.A. 1948. *A Picture Book of the Whole Coast of England and Wales*. Cambridge, England: Cambridge University Press.
49. ____. 1948. *The Coastline of England and Wales*. New York: Cambridge University Press.
50. Thierry and van der Burgt. 1949. *Proceedings of the 17th International Navigation Congress* s II - c 1:135-56.
51. Trask, Parker D. 1955. *Movement of Sand Around Southern California Promontories* Tech Memo 76. Beach Erosion Board, U.S. Army Corps of Engineers.
52. ____. 1956. *Changes in Configuration of Point Reyes Beach, Cal*. Series 14(43). University of California, Berkeley: Institute of Engineering Research.
53. Watts, George, and Dearduff, Robert. 1954. *Laboratory Study of Effect of Tidal Action on Wave-Formed Beach Profiles*. Tech Memo

54. Beach Erosion Board, U.S. Army Corps of Engineers.

54. Zenkowitch, V.P. 1962. *Coastal Morphology.* USSR: Academy of Sciences.

8 tidal inlets on alluvial shores

Tidal inlet technology includes a number of special topics, including tidal hydraulics, tidal inlets stability problems, density and pollution problems. This chapter briefly describes the tidal hydraulics aspects. It concentrates on stability problems as related to maintaining a tidal inlet on an alluvial shore in a fixed position with a cross-section which is stable against deposits of sediments.

Tidal Hydraulics

Tidal hydraulics is the field dealing with computation of tides and tidal currents in the sea, in estuaries, inlets, entrances, bays, lagoons and rivers. The basic equations for tidal hydraulic computations depend on given channel and tidal bay or lagoon area and on given conditions with respect to tides as determined by observation of actual conditions.

The following paragraph is an abstract of Reference 11 by Bruun and Gerritsen:

Tidal motion can be described as a long-wave phenomenon whereby the vertical velocities and vertical accelerations of the water particles are negligible, while the tidal currents and the corresponding differences in water-level elevation respect the basic hydraulic laws [11].

Tides are seldom of purely astronomical origin. They are often affected, sometimes considerably, by meteorological conditions. Important factors are the nature and propagation of storm tides from the sea into the coastal waters.

Mathematically, tidal motion can be described by two differential equations, the one expressing the conservation of mass *(equation of continuity)* the other the relation between the forces acting on the water particles and the resulting accelerations *(dynamical equation)*.

In clearly defined tidal channels where the direction of flow is determined by the bottom topography of the channels, the flow can be regarded as unidimensional. This means that the flow can be described by a set of equations in x direction, which is the direction of the flow. The transverse flow and Coriolis effects can be disregarded, the latter because of the restricted width of the inlet.

Assuming the bottom of the tidal area is horizontal, the differential equations are

1. *Equation of continuity:*

$$\delta h/\delta t + \delta q/\delta x = 0$$
$$(1) \quad (2)$$

in which q indicates the discharge per unit of width $q = Q/B$.

2. *Dynamical equation:*

$$\delta v/\delta t + v(\delta v/\delta x) = -g(\delta H/\delta x) - g(v|v|/C^2 R)$$
$$\quad (1) \qquad (2) \qquad\qquad (3) \qquad\quad (4)$$

in which v is the mean velocity in the direction of the channel; x is the distance along the channel; H is the elevation of water level; h is the water depth; g is the acceleration of gravity; R is the hydraulic radius; Q is the discharge; B is the width of channel; and q is the discharge per unit of width.

A solution of these equations that satisfies the boundary conditions of the particular channel of known tidal characteristics gives the actual water surface and flow velocities. To find the explicit solution of the equations for a given set of boundary conditions is time consuming, and iterative or numerical step-methods therefore have great advantage.

Another method is to introduce simplifying assumptions into the basic equations. The following assumptions are most commonly used:

1. Average elevation of water surface constant along horizontal canal or bay area
2. Simple harmonic tide
3. Friction term linearized
4. Constant rectangular channel cross-section
5. Nonlinear terms in differential equations neglected

Earl I. Brown (5) developed a method to further simplify the basic equations. Brown's method omits terms 1 and 2 from the dynamical equation and uses the equation of continuity in the integrated form. These simplifications involve eliminating the (tidal) wave characteristics of the solution.

The following are other assumptions in Brown's derivations.

1. The propagation of the tidal wave in the bay is neglected, so that high water and low water occur at the same time in all locations of the bay.
2. The inlet has a uniform cross-section and depth.
3. The tidal curves in the sea and in the bay basin are sinusoidal.
4. The basin is nearly circular, so that at any given instant the tidal plane is the same in the entire basin.
5. The length of the inlet channel is well defined.
6. The inlet channel under consideration is the only connection between the basin and the sea.
7. The fresh water draining into the basin from the upland area is inconsequential, so that the volumes of inflow and outflow during a mean tidal cycle are assumed to be equal.

The equation of continuity takes the form

$$\int_0^{T/2} Q \, dt = 2a\Delta$$

when $2a$ indicates the tidal range in the bay.

The dynamical equation is identical with the Chezy formula

$$v = C\sqrt{(RS)}$$

in which

$$S = (H_1 - H_2)/L$$

Brown derives a formula for the determination of the tidal mean range in the basin, the maximum current velocities and the mean tidal prism. Brown's approach is useful for preliminary estimates but not for detailed design.

Garbis H. Keulegan (24) gives a more precise approach to the problem. He omits term 1 of the dynamic equation but the term $[v \, (\delta v/\delta x)]$ is taken into consideration. With respect to schematization, his assumptions are similar to Brown's. By omitting one term with the time parameter t, the wave characteristics of the solution are eliminated also.

In combining the two fundamental equations, Keulegan arrives at

$$dH_1/d\theta = K\sqrt{(H)}\sqrt{(H_1 - H_2)}$$

for flood flow and

$$dH_1/d\theta = -K\sqrt{(H)}\sqrt{(H_1 - H_2)}$$

for ebb flow, which are the differential equations of the surface fluctuation in the basin. H_2 and H_1 represent the water level elevations in the sea and in the bay, $2H$ is tidal range in the ocean (sinus-curve), θ is phase angle, and K is the so-called "coefficient of repletion". In the results obtained, K plays a decisive role by summarizing the effects of the channels and the basin dimensions, the hydraulic roughness of the channel, and the period and range of the tidal fluctuations of the water level in the basin.

Keulegan's approach is quite rational for bay areas of relatively short length which can be considered as filling basins since the propagation of the tidal wave in the bay is to be neglected.

The Lorentz method (25) belongs to the harmonic methods because of the way the basic equation has been simplified.

1. Term 2 is omitted in the dynamical equation.
2. Friction term 4 is linearized.
3. Bay area and channel cross-section are introduced as constant values.
4. In the equation of continuity, term 2 is replaced by $h(\delta v/\delta x)$, in which h is considered constant.

The above assumptions result in the following equations:

$$\delta h/\delta t + h(\delta v/\delta x) = 0$$

and

$$\delta v/\delta t = -g(\delta h/\delta x) - kv$$

The linearization coefficient k is determined from energy considerations

$$k = (8/3\pi)(g/C^2)(V_m/h)$$

where V_m is an average maximum velocity along the channel section considered.

If one writes

$$k = \omega tg^2 \delta = (2\pi/T)tg^2 \delta$$

in which δ is a friction angle, expressions are found for the amplitude and phase of the tide and also for the flow conditions. Both tide and flow curves are harmonic functions because of the linearized assumptions.

The velocity of propagation of the tidal wave is:

$$c = \sqrt{[gh(1 - tg^2\delta)]}$$

Tidal characteristics are introduced as complex functions; the tidal motion must be analyzed into its principle harmonic components. Dronkers gives a solution of the harmonic method with real goniometric functions (14, 15).

In the prediction of tidal currents in important projects such as the damming up of tidal inlets, there is need for a method which considers typical local characteristics of the tidal motion. In Dronkers' exact method, the equations are subjected to a numerical integration process whereby all terms of both the equation of continuity and the dynamic equation are taken into consideration. An essential characteristic of this method is that the hydraulic friction is kept in its quadratic form.

The equations of continuity and momentum are solved numerically for successive sections of the tidal river or estuary; each section is generally not longer than 5 to 10 kilometers. Because continuity at the transitions between the sections exists for the flow, Q, and the total head, H, it is advantageous to replace h by $H = h + (v^2 / 2g)$.

The fundamental equations may then be written as follows:

$$\delta Q/\delta x = - B(\delta H/\delta t) + 2BUQ(\delta Q/\delta t)$$

and

$$\delta H/\delta x = - m(\delta Q/\delta t) + 2BUQ(\delta H/\delta t) \pm wQ^2$$

in which B is the width of channel; $w = 1 / C^2 A^2 h$; $U = (1 / 2gA^2)$, $UQ^2 = v^2 / 2g$, velocity head; $m = 1 / gA$.

The two differential equations are now solved by a method of iteration. A first approximation is found by substituting the approximation $Q = Q_0(t)$ and $H = H_0(t)$ in the right-hand members and then integrating from 0 to x. By substituting the first approximation into the right-hand member the second subsequent approximation is found.

$$Q_I = Q_0 - B(\delta H_0/\delta t)x + 2BUQ_0(\delta Q_0/\delta t)x$$

and

$$H_I = H_0 - m(\delta Q_0/\delta t)x + 2BUQ_0(\delta H_0/\delta t)x \pm wQ_0^2 x$$

The second subsequent approximations are found by substituting the expressions for Q_I and H_I and their derivatives to time into the differential equations and then integrating again.

$$Q_{II} = Q_I + \tfrac{1}{2}Bm(\delta^2 Q_0/\delta t^2)x^2 \pm BwQ_0(\delta Q_0/\delta t)x^2 + Q_s(t,x)$$

and

$$H_{II} = H_I + \tfrac{1}{2}Bm(\delta^2 H_0/\delta t^2)x^2 \pm BwQ_0(\delta H_0/\delta t)x^2 \pm \tfrac{1}{3}B^2 w(\delta H_0/\delta t)^2 x^3 + H_s(t,x)$$

Q_s and H_s denote sets of terms of lower order of magnitude. They can often be ignored. Continuation of the process yields Q_{III} and H_{III} but as a rule the approximation Q_{II} and H_{II}, are sufficient for practical computing.

Dronker's method has been applied on numerous tidal calculations in the Netherlands, such as predicting the tidal currents in the tidal gaps formed during the flood disaster in 1953.

Flow in entrances where cross-sectional areas change and fresh-water flow meets salt water presents special problems of current distribution and density phenomena which are mentioned in Chapter 6. Reference 19 is a classic work on velocity distribution in a jet issuing from a channel into an ocean. Reference 32 is the latest combined contribution on estuary and tidal channel hydraulics and sedimentaion. Practical aspects of the sedimentation problem are discussed in Chapter 6, and in References 6, 28 and 29.

Tidal Inlets on Alluvial Shores

Any tidal inlet on a littoral drift shore presents an integrated result of forces by flow, waves and sediment transport balancing each others in a state of "dynamic equilibrium." The history of an inlet generally demonstrates a continous change of its horizontal as well as its cross-sectional geometry. Normally, the inlet eventually closes because sand material cannot be deposited at the inlet in unlimited quantitieses. However, this closing may take a very long time. A study of old Roman maps of the Mediterranean or of old maps of the North Sea shows that several ancient inlets are still in

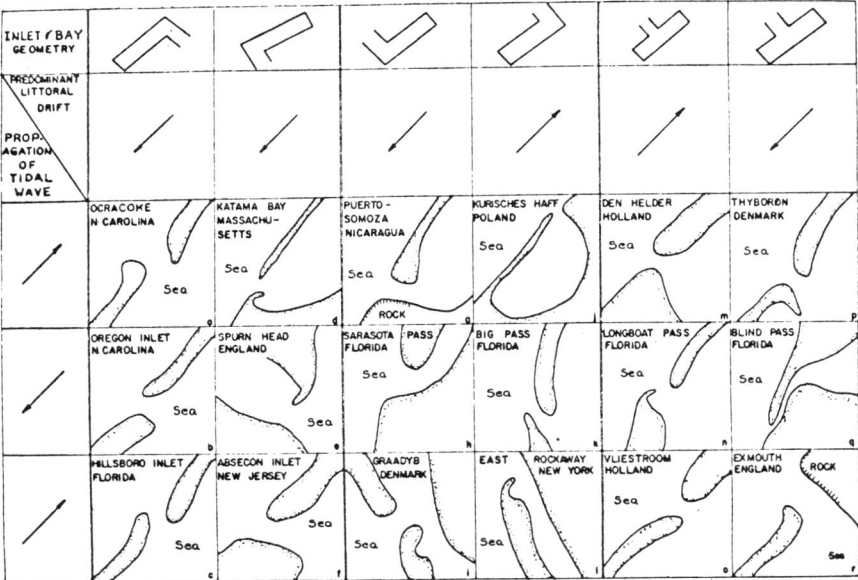

Figure 8.1. Inlet geometry (11).

existence, even though their location may have changed considerably. As explained in Reference 11, one may distinguish between location stability" and "cross-sectional stability."

Location Stability

Morphology

Most inlets on littoral drift shores migrate in the direction of the prevailing littoral drift. The migration rate of inlets on sandy coasts depends on the magnitude of littoral drift, the velocity of ocean tidal and other currents, and on the phase difference between any longshore tidal current and the tidal currents in the inlet. As a result of deposits on the updrift side, the inlet channel is usually forced to move in downdrift direction causing erosion downdrift (Figure 8.1a, b, and c). By this process the updrift barrier may extend seaward in front of the downdrift barrier or land area overlapping it (Figure 8.1q).

Such a situation is time-limited, however. Continued extension of the channel by deposits increases head losses, and the inlet may finally close. Closing often happens in connection with the breakthrough of a new inlet through the barrier making a shorter, and from the hydraulic standpoint, more "practical" ocean connection. Such a breakthrough may be a result of erosion or of a storm tide. In many cases, the breakthrough happens because the barrier was flooded by storage water in the bay or lagoon and could not escape fast enough through the "long" channel.

Some inlet channels migrate as a whole. Others keep the gorge (minimum cross-section for flow) at the same place while the channel through the outer bar or shoals migrates downdrift, often in certain cycles. Shifting from downdrift to a new updrift location, or to another position compared to the main body of the bay or lagoon, takes place at regular intervals, e.g., once every ten or thirty years. By this process large quantities of sand are transferred downdrift, influencing the erosion situation downdrift considerably.

It is interesting to note that as a result of nature's strategy of making things easy, inlets often place themselves where offshore conditions

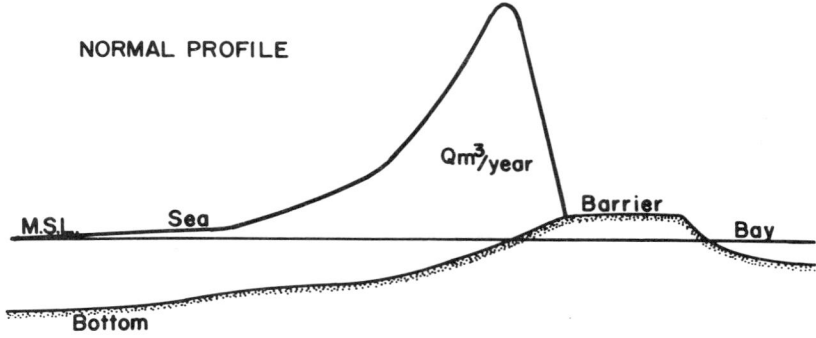

Figure 8.2. Relative distribution of littoral drift in a normal bottom profile (11).

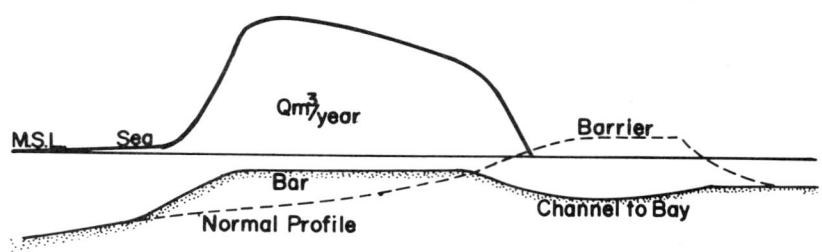

Figure 8.3. Change of littoral drift distribution caused by breakthrough (11).

are most practical for channel maintenance i.e., because of the wave refraction at reefs, islands or canyons which may cause a favorable distribution of sand drift. Examples of this are to be found at San Diego and at Coos River at the Pacific.

By-Passing by Nature

Many coastal inlets develop a natural transfer of sand from the updrift to the downdrift side. As explained in References 6, 7 and 12, most inlets transfer material partly by tidal flow action and partly by transferring sand from one side of the inlet to the other on a shoal or offshore bar. Figure 8.2 shows a normal bottom profile without an inlet channel. The profile carries a net quantity of M^3 material per year longshore. Figure 8.3 demonstrates the changes that occur in a bottom profile after a breakthrough. The drift then takes place mainly on a bar across the inlet entrance.

It is interesting to consider the sand drift budget at the inlet. If the total amount of material carried to the inlet from all sides is $M_t = M_{total}$, and p percent is transferred by inlet flow, $(1-p)M_t$ must be bypassed on a bar or shoal (Figure 8.4). The inlet currents carry bottom material forward and backward in the inlet. If an equilibrium condition develops, inlet currents are able to push the "surplus material" that entered the inlet from the sides out of the inlet channel for depositing offshore, in the bay, or for further migration on

Tidal Inlets 325

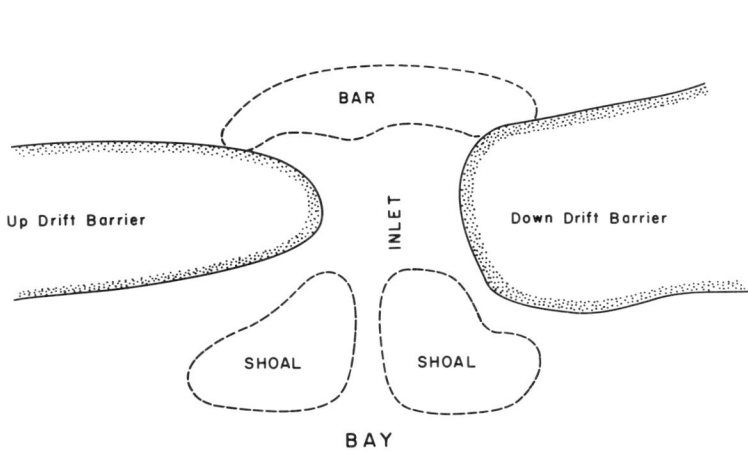

Figure 8.4. Coastal inlet with predominant bar by-passing (11).

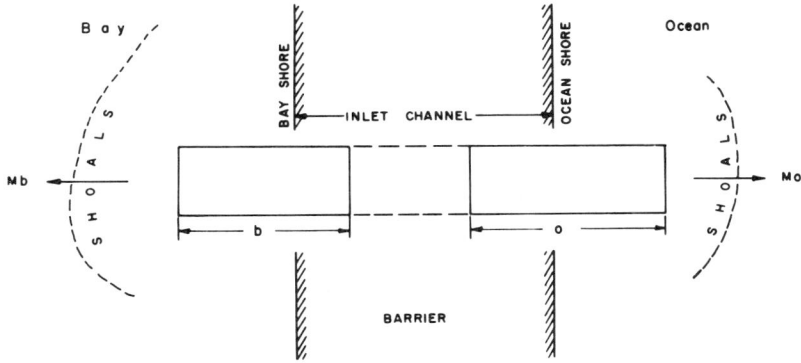

Figure 8.5. "Rolling carpet" of bottom material in inlet channel (11).

the ocean bottom. As explained by Bruun and Gerritsen (11), the dimensionless parameter $M_{net}/Q_{max} = r$ seems to be significant for the magnitude of by-passing. The value of this ratio indicates whether by-passing is predominantly a "bar" or a "tidal flow" transfer. By the latter method, material is flushed out of the inlet by ebb currents carrying the material away from the inlet entrance to the offshore area, possibly in downdrift direction.

From practical experience with by-passing, the following rule may be used as a guide: $r < 10 - 20$ indicates predominant tidal flow by-passing (little or no bar formation), and $r > 200 - 300$ indicates predominant bar by-passing with typical bar or shoal formation.

In the inlet channel bottom, material is moved in both directions by the flood and ebb currents, which in the event of no fresh-water flow and a large tidal prism may be symmetrical. In the initial stage of development, when the inlet channel may be short and the inlet cross-section is expanding, the situation is as depicted in Figure 8.5, showing a horizontal picture of the inlet.

The sheet-layer (bedload) motion may be compared to the motion of "rolling carpets," with lengths b (for bay) and o (for ocean). By the movement of these carpets, part of these is lost on sea shoals ($M_o = M_{ocean}$) and another part on bay shoals ($M_b = M_{bay}$). If no material at all is transferred to the inlet channel by littoral drift from both sides, the channel will gradually deepen and widen until it becomes nonscouring. If the material flushing ability of the inlet equals the amount of drift to the inlet from the sides ($M_b + M_o = V$), an equilibrium condition exists (but does not last because of the continuation of deposits at both ends of the channel). If the inlet channel grows very long, a situation may develop by which the inlet current gradually weakens and the cross-sectional area of the inlet gorge decreases simultaneously because of decreases in tidal prism; this may finally result in a lack of ability of the inlet channel to flush itself adequately for all the material brought to the inlet from the longshore drift. Considering the overall stability, there seem to be three separate cases:

1. Short channel: $V > pM_{total}$. This will cause an unstable condition. The inlet is widening and probably lengthening. A nonscouring channel may develop, as mentioned in the following paragraph on inlet stability.
2. Medium channel length: $V = pM_{total}$. This will result in a stable channel as long as $V = pM_{total}$ is valid.
3. Long channel: $V < pM_{total}$. This will result in an unstable condition. The inlet is shoaling because material is pouring into the inlet channel from both sides and inlet currents are not able to flush the material out. It may also happen that V increases to a maximum capacity, but if V still is less than pM_{total}, the channel will again start decreasing its flushing ability

at the same time as a bar or shoal may develop at the ocean entrance of the inlet. The ability to transfer material over the bar may then increase until a stationary condition develops by which $(1 - p)M_{total}$ is transferred over the bar, while pM_{total} is flushed out on both sides of the inlet channel for depositing on shoals. (Or, perhaps, it is mainly flushed out on one side, that is, on the ocean side if the ebb current is the strongest, which is often the case). If p is relatively small and the tidal prism is sufficiently large to meet temporary increases of p during extreme storms, an equilibrium condition may result that may preserve the inlet as a tidal channel for centuries.

The quantity of littoral material entering the inlet from the adjacent shores depends on many partly interrelated factors, including the longshore component of the wave energy, the geometrical shape of the beach and bottom profile, the shoreline geometry and material characteristics. There is, however, another important factor—the availability of material. It is known that coastal protection structures, whether groins or certain types of sea walls, slow down the amount of littoral drift. Inlets may sometimes severely decrease littoral drift for some miles downdrift. If the littoral drift is strong and the tidal prism is ample, more breakthroughs may then occur and the inlet may stay open for a longer period of time.

The East Coast of the United States includes an almost continuous barrier coast with numerous inlets, some of which have stayed open as long as they have been known. Others have opened and closed continuously. The tendency toward breakthrough usually increases in the downdrift direction, usually south, simply because the littoral drift decreases with the number of inlets accompanied by sea and bay shoals on which material deposits temporarily or permanently. At present, the North Carolina shore north of Cape Hatteras has only one inlet, the Oregon Inlet, but others have existed. The net south littoral drift is probably above 500,000 cubic yards per year. Occasionally new inlets have broken through and shortly closed again.

Oregon Inlet is depicted on English maps from the sixteenth century, but other historical sources indicate that the present inlet was opened by a seiche generated in the Pamlico Sound during the passage of a tropical storm in September, 1846. In the period from 1846 to 1952 this inlet migrated 1.5 to 2 miles southward.

Maintenance by dredging has been about 100,000 cubic yards per year. The ocean bar channel has project dimensions of 400-foot width and 14-foot depth, but shoals 8 to 9 feet deep occur. Another inlet was located 8 to 9 miles south of the present location of Oregon Inlet, possibly for centuries. However, it did close in January, 1922, and was reopened in 1924 as "New Inlet," but closed again in the 1930s. In 1962, the March 9 to 11 storm opened up a new inlet just north of Buxton (village of Cape Hatteras). This inlet was closed by a hydraulic dredge the following year.

West of Cape Hatteras the littoral drift is undoubtedly of much less magnitude. The first inlet is Hatteras Inlet, found open in 1585 and remaining open since then. The inlet migrated about 3,600 feet southwest between 1852 and 1905 and has been rather stable in location since then. With its 50,000-square foot gorge cross-sectional area, the Hatteras Inlet has swallowed huge quantities of sand. No wonder, then, that the next island, the Ocracokee Island, has suffered severe erosion which washed out all dunes in the northern part. The situation at the southern part of the Ocracokee Island is similar. Since 1830 the spit has extended about 8,000 feet in the southwesterly direction in the next inlet, the Ocracokee Inlet, and huge quantities of material have accumulated in shoals, thereby depriving downdrift beaches.

The shore from Ocracokee Inlet to Cape Lookout consists of washout barriers and inlets that cause continous drain of material from the shore for depositing in shoals. Many inlets, however, have not been able to stay open because of overwhelming littoral transport to the inlet entrance compared to the available tidal prism. The shore between Cape Henry and Cape Lookout (about 200 miles) today has only three open inlets but also 10 to 12 "fossil" inlets which have been open at various times.

Along the South Carolina and Georgia coast, many inlets are in a deteriorating state, surrounded by eroding shores and extensive ocean and bay shoals. Some important inlets, such as the entrance to Charleston Harbor and Port Royal Sound in South Carolina, the entrance to Savannah Harbor in Georgia and St. Mary's River, the border stream between Georgia and Florida, are maintained by dredging operations to satisfy urgent navigation needs.

The Florida Atlantic and Gulf Coast are particularly suitable for description of by-passing phenomena—by nature as well as by man. Information on Florida inlets is available from hydrographic serveys and dredging operations (6,7). Quantities of material by-passed by natural action and quantities of material that settled down in the inlet and its adjoining entrance areas are listed in Table 8-1. Most data are derived from reports of the U.S. Army Corps of Engineers, Jacksonville District. These data, needless to say, should still be considered approximate.

South of Cape Kennedy, "the big robber" of material for the lower East Coast, the number of inlets increases. The net quantity of drift increases from an order of magnitude of approximately 250,000 cubic yard per year predominantly south at the Fort Pierce Inlet, to perhaps 10,000 to 20,000 cubic yard per year at Government Cut (Miami Beach).

The number of the inlets and rivers on the upper East Coast of Florida, with its heavier drift, is one per 40 miles. The number of inlets on the lower East Coast, with less drift, is one per 20 miles (including some inlets which were cut by man, replacing earlier breakthroughs or inlets cut by nature).

On the lower Gulf Coast, the precominant littoral drift (about 50,000 cubic yard per year) is limited because of low wave energy input. There is presently one inlet per 10 to 15 miles in four lower Gulf Coast counties (about 150 miles of shore).

Table 8.1.
Predominant Drift *A* **and By-Passed Drift** *B* **at Florida Atlantic Inlets, in Cubic Yards per year.***

Inlet or entrance	Predominant drift A	By-Passed drift B
St. Mary's River	500,000	unknown
St. John's River	500,000	unknown
St. Augustine Inlet	500,000	unknown
Matanzas Inlet	500,000	almost all
Ponce de Leon Inlet	500,000	350,000
Canaveral Harbor (no tidal flow)	350,000	very little
Sebastian Inlet	300,000	200,000
Ft. Pierce Inlet	250,000	150,000
St. Lucie Inlet	200,000–250,000	30,000
Jupiter Inlet	200,000–250,000	150,000
Palm Beach Inlet	200,000–225,000	very little
South Lake Worth Inlet	150,000–200,000	40,000
Hillsboro Inlet	100,000	perh. 30,000
Everglades Inlet	50,000	very little
Bakers Haulover Inlet	50,000	very little
Government Cut, Miami Beach	20,000	very little

*All figures are approximated and give order of magnitude only.

The upper West Coast of Florida has only a few inlets. The predominant drift is perhaps on the order of 150,000 cubic yard per year, and the tidal prisms vary strongly because of the diurnal tide. There may even be no predominant drift for a year or two. Such a situation permits a few larger inlets to stay open while all smaller breakthroughs must close.

Some specific examples of by-passing in Florida on bar or by tidal flow or by both are mentioned in Chapter 6. Nature's by-passing is, however, always characterized by the existence of ocean shoals, bars and shifting channels with irregular depths and therefore does not offer ideal conditions for navigation. When man tried to improve the situation, he interfered seriously with nature's procedure by creating littoral barriers for the natural drift with dredged channels often protected by jetties. Downdrift erosion was the inevitable result.

By-Passing by Man

Several methods of by-passing by mechanical means exist. Table 8.2 is a review of the January, 1968, status of by-passing arrangements in the United States (9).

Table 8.2 considers six different solutions, five of which are in operation. One (the movable plant on a trestle) was studied but not built. Of the twenty-four cases considered, fifteen are on

Table 8.2. Sand By-passing Status in the United States

Location	By-passing arrangement	Status, 1970-1971
Moriches Inlet, L.I., N.Y	Fixed plant proposed	By-pass of jetties to be extended authorized
Shinnecock, L.I., N.Y.	Undetermined or being studied	By-pass of jetties to be extended authorized
Fire Island, L.I., N.Y.	Transfer from bay shoal	Has been studied/model study on trap arrangement
Virginia Beach, Va. (Rudee Inlet)	Fixed Plant	Revision planned; being studied
Masonboro, N.C.	Depressed weir and trap	Operation 3 years*
Ponce DeLeon, Fla.	Depressed weir and trap	Almost completed
Ft. Pierce, Fla.	Transfer from bay shoals	Has been studied/suggested
Sebastian, Fla.	Bay shoals	Permanent transfer from bay shoal trap suggested
St Lucie, Fla	Depressed weir and trap	Under construction
Jupiter, Fla	Transfer from bay shoal	Depressed weir and trap/proposed
Palm Beach, Fla.	Fixed plant	Revision planned
S. Lake Worth Fla.	Fixed plant	New jetties and pump in 1968
Boca Raton, Fla.	Trap in entrance	Transfer from trap behind updrift jetty connected breakwater suggested
Hillsboro, Fla.	Depressed weir and trap	In operation since 1952
Port Everglades, Fla.	Ocean shoal dredging	Transfer from shoals in ocean and entrance suggested (model)
Bakers Haulover, Fla.	Bay shoal dredging	Permanent transfer from bay shoal trap suggested
New Pass, Fla.	Ocean shoal dredging	Occasional transfer from ocean shoals
East Pass, Fla.	Depressed weir and trap	Weir jetty completed
Houston, Corpus Christi, Tex.	Bay and ocean shoal dredging	Sidecasting in operation
Port Hueneme, Calif.	Trap behind updrift breakwater	Transfer from trap behind updrift breakwater
Newport, Calif.	Undetermined or being studied	Recirculation by trap at lower end of ½-mile reach being studied
Twin Lakes Harbor, Santa Cruz, Calif.	Fixed plant	Operational 1972
Santa Barbara, Calif	Transfer from shoal inside updrift breakwater	Extension of west jetty, construction of east jetty and detached breakwater authorized
Ocean Beach, Calif.	Trap inside updrift jetty	By-pass from trap inside updrift jetty in operation
Canaveral Harbor, Fla.	Dredging of channel	Fixed plant to be constructed
Perdido Pass, Ala.	Dredging of channel	Weir jetty completed
Channel Harbor Island, Cal.	Trap behind breakwater	Operational

*1970: certain difficulties experienced because of channel shifting.
+1970: completed; part of weir section has failed because of erosion, causing concrete wall to topple over.

**Table 8.3.
Status of Sand By-Passing Plants
and Arrangements in the United States, 1972.**

Type	Operating	Planned
Fixed plants	4	2*
Movable plants	0	?
Depressed weirs and trap	6	1
Bay or ocean shoal	8	2
Trap behind breakwater	4	1

*but doubtful

the Atlantic, three are on the Gulf of Mexico and six are on the Pacific. Eight of these projects are undetermined and still being examined.

Table 8.3 is a summary of Table 8.2 and gives the number of plants, in operation or planned, distributed within each category.

A fixed plant has been in operation at the Palm Beach Inlet in Florida since 1957 (6,7) (see Figure 8.6). Capacity is about 250,000 cubic yards per year. So far this operation has not been too successful because of an insufficient supply of material caused by a groin on the updrift side. Improvements were made recently.

Figure 8.7 is an aerial photograph (1965) of the Hillsboro Inlet in Florida which was improved based on the results of hydraulic model experiments and tracer tests in the field (6). This inlet is provided with a depressed weir (in updrift jetty) and trap arrangement for periodic transfer for downdrift. So far results are satisfactory. Quantity is about 80,000 cubic yards per year.

Figure 8.8 shows a model experiment on the tidal inlet at Boca Raton, Florida. Here the trap is arranged inside the spur jetty on the updrift side, with a gate in the updrift jetty for the dredge. Quantity is about 80,000 cubic yards per year. A detached breakwater was built on the updrift side at Ventura Harbor, California, forming a trap inside (complete littoral barrier). This arrangement has not yet been successful. A lack of proper coordination between trap filling to capacity and dredging, rather than the design, is responsible.

Tests have been completed at the University of Florida on the small Blind Pass (Florida Gulf Coast) on by-passing from the inlet channel itself using a jet pump and deep dredging.

From Table 8.3 it may be noted that although four fixed plants are in operation, only two new plant installations are being considered and both are doubtful. The reason lies in the rigidity of the fixed plants which proved to be a drawback to efficiency, although the South Lake Worth plant in this respect has proved successful (6,7). Movable plants have been studied, and two were built in India (Paradip and Nagapatam). Experience so far has been that capacities of these plants are insufficient. They are too rigid and tend to be expensive due to the heavy trestle needed to carry the pumping plant. Durban, South Africa has been rather satisfactory.

Depressed weir and trap installations were built in six cases. New plants are planned and more will follow (6, 7, 9). They undoubtedly present the most highly developed solution to the by-passing technique, had have proved efficient and relatively inexpensive. They do not rely on a permanent pump installation, but on hydraulic pipeline dredgers which are moved in at regular intervals to dredge the trap and transfer the material to downdrift side shores.

Transfer from bay shoals does not require any special type of installation if the material is sucked in by inlet currents and is deposited where it does not hamper navigation. Traps are then created by dredging.

Tidal Inlets 331

Figure 8.6. The Palm Beach Inlet, Florida Atlantic Coast with by-passing plant (6).

Figure 8.7. The Hillsboro Inlet, Florida Atlantic Coast, with depressed weir and trap arrangement for by-passing (6).

Figure 8.8. Breakwater and trap arrangement suggested for the Boca Raton Inlet (model study), University of Florida (9).

The most complete littoral barrier is the detached breakwater with a trap behind it. This gives maximum protection of the entrance and maximum material transfer. However a breakwater may be expensive. Figure 8.9 shows the proposed expansion of Santa Barbara Harbor, California (3).

Tidal Inlets 333

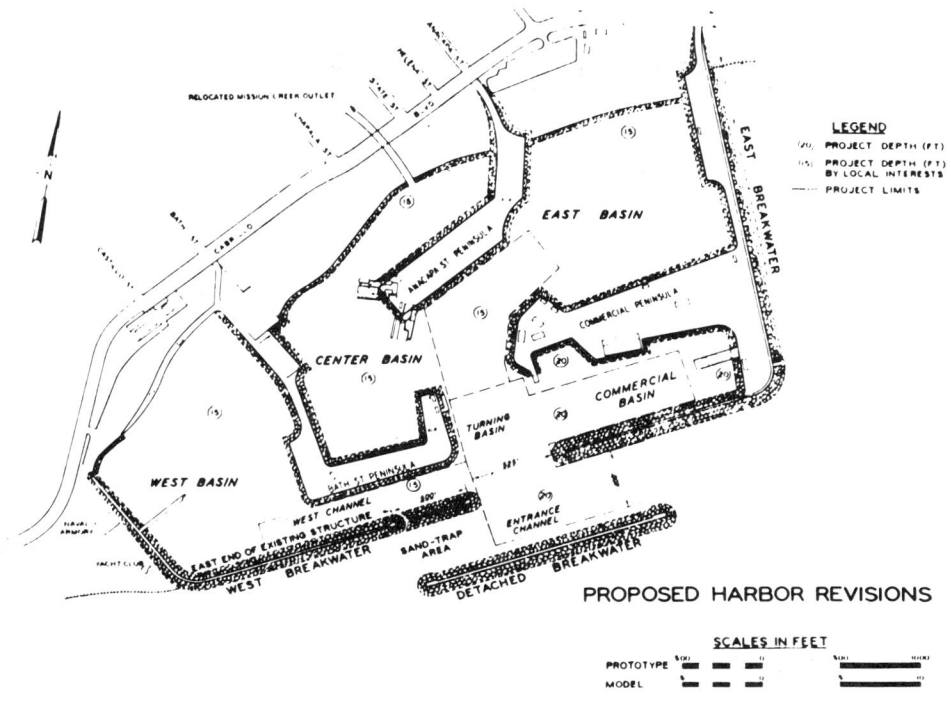

Figure 8.9. Detached breakwater and trap proposed at Santa Barbara, California (3).

Prices for material transfer seem to vary from about $0.40 to about $0.90 per cubic yard.

Cross-Sectional Stability

Studies by Bruun and Gerritsen (11, 12) and by Bruun (6,8) indicate the close relationship that exists between *horizontal stability,* which relies upon by-passing of material entering the channel from the channel sides and attempting to choke it, and *cross-sectional stability*. It is reasonable to assume that a tidal inlet arranges itself in the most practical way. To understand the interaction between sediment transport and tidal flow, it is necessary to recapitulate briefly some results on bottom geometry from river hydraulics (6, 8).

Figure 8.10 (23) demonstrates the relationship between slope, bed shear velocity, bed friction factor and depth (laboratory experiments, D_{ave} = 0.14 millimeter). In the velocity range where dunes are the characteristic bed form, slope is nearly constant and is less than the maximum slope for the ripple regimen. Bed shear velocity is also lower. The Darcy friction factor, $f = 8gdS_e/\overline{V}^2$, drops from 0.12 to 0.02 when the bottom configuration changes from rippled to flat. (Depth of flow in flume tests was about 0.3 feet and discharge about 0.5 cubic feet per second.)

The variation in resistance with bed form referring to the Manning n or the Darcy-Weisbach f for various sands and bed forms is mentioned by many authors, e.g., D. B. Simons and E. V. Richardson (30).

Changes in bed form observed in flume experiments also occur in natural streams (Figure 8.11). At one discharge, a duned bed may exist, and at a larger discharge the bed form appears as flatter dunes moving toward a plane bed. Later, with in-

334   Port Engineering

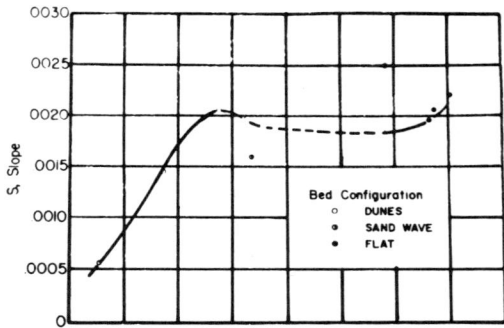

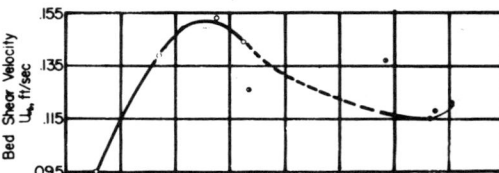

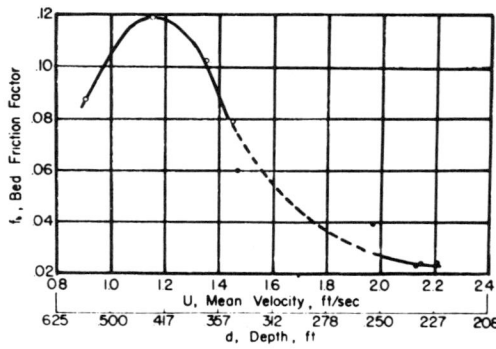

Figure 8.10. Variation of slope, bed shear velocity and bed friction factor with mean velocity and depth for constant discharge experiments (23).

creasing velocity, anti-dunes may develop. The resulting change in resistance to flow as bed form develops may cause a definite break or discontinuity in the stage-discharge relationship. The friction factors given by investigators for natural streams with similar bed material and bed forms as the flume experiments are approximately the same as those given for the flume experiments, whereas the actual location of the transition zone depends on a number of factors, including bottom material characteristics, relative roughness and Fourde number.

Reference is made to the considerable literature available on this topic, particularly by Garde and Ranga Ruja (20), by Engelund and Hansen (16, 17, 18) and by Simons, Richardson and Haushild (31).

Although it is difficult to compare flow in a tidal inlet channel with river flow because tidal ranges will usually be much smaller than the fluctuations related to river stages, it is certain that there must be a similarity between the development of bottom geometry in rivers and in tidal inlets. According to experience gained from flume tests, it takes a matter of minutes to develop a certain bottom geometry. What happens at tidal inlets is probably similar to what is described in Figures 8.10 and 8.11. Ripples develop at mean flow velocities of 1 to 2 feet per second and are replaced by dunes at 2 to 3 feet per second. With increasing velocity, dunes change character and offer a decreasing resistance to flow before finally approaching the plane bottom at mean maximum velocities of 3 to 5 feet per second.

When comparing tidal inlet and river geometry, it should be noted that tidal inlets usually have a clean sand bottom because they receive material from the littoral drift. Rivers are often loaded with fine sediments and may have clayish or silty bottoms, or a mixed sand, clay and silt bottom that may occasionally exhibit a hard surface layer. Most research mentioned above, however, refers to smaller, rather shallow rivers or creeks with sand bottoms. Depths may vary from 1 to 5 feet, whereas tidal inlets may have depths of 10 to 20 feet, or considerable more if they are improved by dredged channels, jetties or both.

The Froude number which exists in the case of tidal inlets is therefore smaller than that for the streams and rivers normally considered in unidirec-

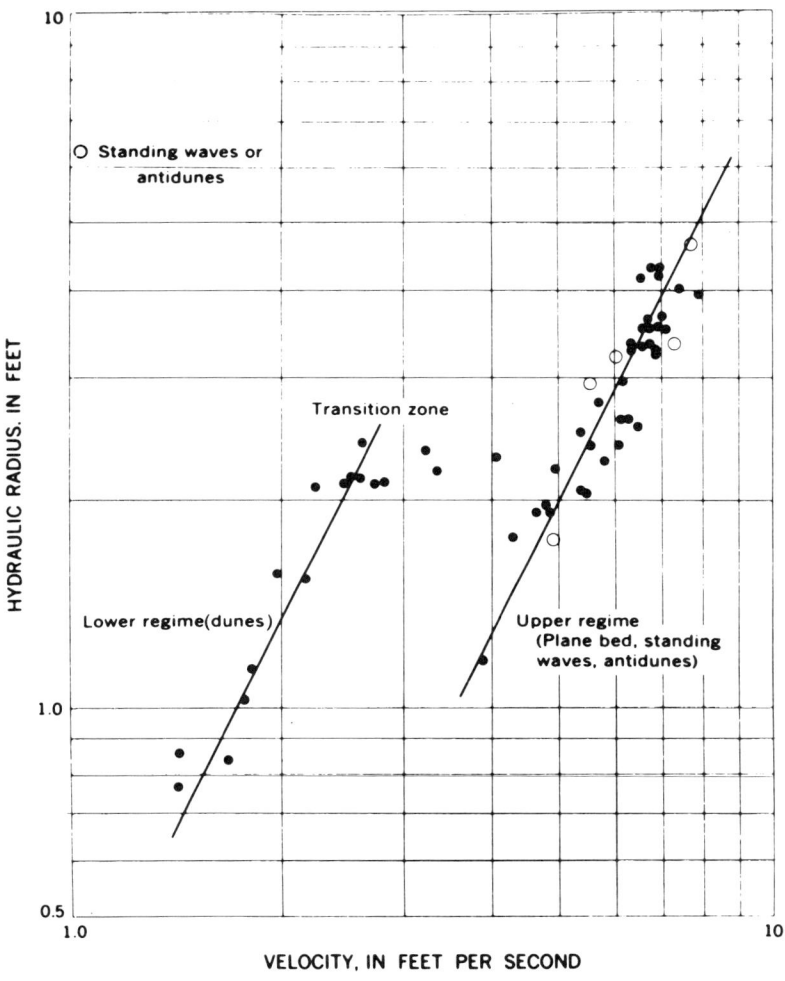

Figure 8.11. Relation of hydraulic radius to velocity for Rio Grande near Bernalillo (27).

tional flow studies — that is, about 0.2 at maximum current velocity compared to 0.4 to 0.6 for rivers at rising stages and even higher values for steep mountain streams, which may have Froude numbers above 1. In Reference 6, Bruun gives the ranges of determining shear stress for cross-sectional stability and its relation to bottom geometry in comparison with river data. Attempts to combine the effects of unidirectional and oscillating flow, referring to research on oscillating flow versus bottom geometry by Jonsson (22), are also mentioned.

Any stability consideration at tidal inlets must be related to the amount of drift transferred to the inlet from the sides. If this drift is small, no strong currents are needed to flush a normal tidal entrance (not estuary) not receiving any material from landward sources by stream flow.

Table 8.4 (6,11) gives some pertinent values for 11 tidal inlets, eight with semi-diurnal or

Table 8.4. Inlet Characteristics at Spring Tide, under Normal Conditions (6, 8).

Inlet	Ω (10^3 cu m)	$Q_m \times 10^3$ (cu m/sec)	$A \times 10^3$ (sq m)	R (m)	C (m ½/sec)	T^*_s (kg/sq m)	Remarks	$\bar{V} = 2\Omega/AT$ (m/sec)	$V_{\text{mean max}} = Q_m/A$ (m/sec)	$V = 2/\pi (V_{\text{max}})/C_1$ (m/sec)
Grays Harbor, Wash.	520	36.4	31.2	15.0	53	0.49	Two jetties—minor shifting of shoals	0.74	1.16	0.75
Mission Bay, Calif. (before dredg.)	12	0.87	0.79	6.0	45	0.60	Two jetties—well scoured channel	0.68	1.10	0.74
Old St. Augustine, Fla.	37	2.16	2.46	6.9	49	0.31	No jetties—changing bars, shifting channels	0.68	0.88	0.68
Ponce de Leon, Fla.	16	1.11	1.07	3.9	48	0.48	No jetties—shoals	0.67	1.04	0.69
Gasparilla Pass, Fla.	12	0.70	1.00	2.5	45	0.25	No jetties—shifting channel, unstable	0.54	0.70	0.55
Longboat Pass, Fla.	22	1.10	1.05	4.2	45	0.55	Refer to no jetties—minor shifting, one jetty built 1958	0.93	1.05	0.82

Big Pass, Fla.	9	0.55	0.56	1.7	42	0.55 0.55	No jetties—"hard-curving" channel	0.72	0.98	0.76
East Pass, Fla. (diurnal)	46	1.32	1.28	2.6	45	0.54	No jetties—changes considerably during storms	0.81	1.03	0.81
Port Aransas, Tex. (diurnal)	50	1.44	1.49	4.0	45	0.46	Two jetties—fairly well-scoured channel	0.75	0.97	0.77
Calcacieu Pass, La. (diurnal)	84	2.00	1.93	9.5	50	0.43 (0.47+)	Two jetties—fairly well-scoured channel	0.97	1.04	0.82
Thyboroen, Denmark	104	5.60	5.00	8.0	50	0.49	Two jetties—well scoured channel	0.93	1.08	0.84
Average								0.77	1.00	0.75

*$T_s = \rho g(Q_m/AC)^2$ where $\rho g = 1000$ kg (f) per cubic meter. +Average of four jetty improvet inlet including Grays Harbor.

Table 8.5.
$V_{mean\ max}$ and $\bar{V}$ for Inlets Presented in Table 8.4.

Velocities	All inlets	Semi-diurnal	Diurnal
$V_{mean\ max}$	1.00	0.99	1.03
$\bar{V}$ (Keulegan) (24)	0.75	0.71	0.81
$\bar{V}$ (mean)	0.77	0.70	0.87

mixed tides and three with diurnal tides. To evaluate the stability in various ways, the determining shear stress (24) was computed as well as the V_{max}, and $\bar{V} = (2/\pi)(V_{max}/C_1)$ and finally checked with $\bar{V} = 2\Omega/AT$. The Ω/M was computed from experience values of M.

Table 8.5 reviews the actual velocities for all inlets and for semi-diurnal and diurnal inlets separately. Most inlets are of the semi-diurnal type, and it may be seen from Table 8.5 that the $\bar{V}_{mean\ max}$ is about 0.99 meters per second and $\bar{V}_{mean}$ about 0.7 meters per second.

Some of the inlets considered are jetty-protected, or at least have some major groin protection as, for example, the Thyboroen Inlet in Denmark (Table 8-4 and Figure 44 in Reference 6). These jetties have an influence on the actual stability because they cut off part of the drift to the inlet. In this respect, it should be remembered that neither the length nor depth of the jetties is proportional to their effectiveness as cutoff walls for littoral drift. Tidal currents and wave action, as related to length and depth at the extreme end of the jetties, determine the extent that the jetties will be able to bar the littoral drift, which must then be transferred by man across the inlet if leeside erosion is to be avoided. Such evaluation may be made by the use of model experiments combined with field experience including tracing.

A preliminary attempt has been made to evaluate this matter in a different way. The determining shear stress for four protected single channel inlets was found to have an average value of 0.47 kilogram per square mile (see footnote, Table 8.4). The three nonprotected inlets, Long Boat Pass, Big Pass and East Pass in Florida (Table 8.4) are all relatively stable without jetties and have an average shear stress of 0.55 kilogram per square mile. The case of Mission Bay in California (before dredging) must be considered special. It is a small, narrow inlet channel with a high current that had to be improved by dredging and jetties to serve small craft navigation.

The result of the comparison is that the ratio between determining shear stress for jetty-protected inlets and nonprotected inlets is found to be 0.47/0.55 = 0.85. If bedload is the main transport (as is usually the case), the ratio between actual transport rates as bedload (8) is $(\tau)^{2.5}$. The ratio of material transport as bedload (per unit width of channel bottom) between protected and unprotected inlets is therefore $\alpha = (0.85)^{2.5} = 2/3$. If this philosophy is accepted, then the jetties in question seem to cut off on the average one-third of the drift to the inlet channel.

It is self-explanatory that this again must be considered a preliminary figure. Very few inlets exist, however, as almost complete barriers to littoral drift. Table 8.6 lists predominant drift and by-passed drift quantities for jetty-protected inlets in Florida (6,8).

By-passing takes place partly by combined wave action and tidal flow (Ft. Pierce Inlet) and partly on an offshore bar (Sebastian and Jupiter Inlets, where jetties are short). With respect to the Palm Beach Inlet, at present only about 50,000 to 100,000 cubic yard are passed by the by-passing plant and very little of the 175,000 cubic yard left

Table 8.6 Predominant Drift Quantity and By-Passed Drift for Jetty-Protected Inlets (6).

Inlet	Jetty Length	Drift, per year		By-passed, in %	
		Total	By-passed	Total maximum	By tidal flow
Jupiter	very short	225,000	150,000	60	about 20
Sebastian	short	300,000	200,000	60	30 to 50
S. Lake Worth	medium	180,000	about 90,000 flushed sea- and bayward	50	about 50
Palm Beach*	long	225,000	about 175,000 flushed sea- and bayward	(80)	(about 80)
Ft. Pierce	very long	250,000	200,000	80	about 80

*Condition 1964-65.

Table 8.7 Mean Maximum Velocities for Channels or Combinations of Channels (6)

Channel(s)	Velocity m/sec
Ebb channels, without flood channels	0.89
All	1.00
Ebb and Flood Channels	0.99
Ebb and Neutral Channels	0.98
Neutral channels only	1.08

seem to reach the beaches on the downdrift side. At least 175,000 cubic yards, perhaps more, seem to be flushed out into the sea, and a large accumulation has appeared on the southeast side of the entrance.

The situation is better at the South Lake Worth Inlet where about 80,000 cubic yards are by-passed by the plant. An average of 50,000 cubic yards per year are by-passed from bay shoals to which the material was flushed by flood currents; 50,000 cubic yards seem to be by-passed by natural action partly on an offshore bar. Disregarding the very shallow Jupiter Inlet (model study completed), the average by-passing or flushing by tidal currents is about 60%, or about two-third of the total drift for these four inlets, giving a qualitative confirmation to the two-thirds figure mentioned above for the flushing ability of jetty-protected versus nonprotected inlet shear stresses. Unfortunately by-passing quantities for all the inlets of Table 8.1 are not known.

Although the figures of Table 8.6 are of a very preliminary nature, it still seems obvious that jetty-protected inlet channels develop somewhat lower shear stresses because they do not need to flush out as much material as the nonprotected channels. The nonprotected channels, however, may by-pass considerable quantities in an offshore bar, as is the case for the Jupiter Inlet (6, 7, 12).

The results mentioned above (Table 8.6) were compared to results from observations in six tidal channels in Holland. Table 8.7 shows these results. From Chapter 6 on littoral drift, ebb channels carry predominantly ebb flow, flood channels mainly flood flow and neutral channel ebb as well as flood flow.

The figures in Table 8.7 show that the average velocity for neutral channels is 1.08 meters per second. The average maximum ebb velocity is 1.00 meters per second while channels carrying flood currents have an average velocity of only 0.75 meters per second.

The reason for the differences may be explained as a combined result of the flow pattern of ebb and flood currents and the littoral drift to the inlet, which takes place almost entirely from the ocean side in connection with a discharge excess during ebb compared to flow caused by freshwater discharge in addition to the normal tidal flow. The distribution of sediment transport in various combinations of ebb, flood and neutral channels is detailed in Reference 6.

With respect to ebb channels without flood channels, ebb channels do not occur without either flood or neutral channels. It is interesting to note that flushing by ebb channels apparently is the most effective and that flushing by neutral channels is the least effective because the material moves back and forth. Furthermore, if ebb and flood velocities from Table 8.7 are added, the average velocity is 0.99 meters per second, just the same velocity as for all ebb channels in Table 8.7. On the other hand, it is also seen that ebb channels in combination with neutral channels may have a slightly lower velocity (0.98) than when they are combined with flood channels (0.99). The small difference is probably incidental, although it could also be taken as an indication that the flood channels' flushing ability is relatively less important. Flood channels in the bay flush material to the bay, but flood channels on the ocean side bring in littoral drift material with which ebb and neutral channels must then cope. As mentioned above, ebb channels are undoubtedly the main cleaning agents when they flush on the ocean side, whereas they bring in little, if any, material on the bay side. This makes them more useful than flood channels.

The three sets of inlets (10 American, one Danish, six Dutch) mentioned earlier are subject to a considerable variety of meteorological conditions. The extremes are Grays Harbor, Washington, and Thyboroen, Denmark, which represent rough conditions, and the three passes on the Florida Gulf Coast, which present minimum activity of waves and currents.

From Tables 8.5 and 8.7, however, it is clear that there is a pronounced similarity between the behavior of these inlets. The easiest factor to consider for omparison is the mean maximum velocity. Together with experience values for the friction factor and known or computed hydraulic flow characteristics, mean maximum velocity gives the determining shear stress for channel stability, τ_s, and other factors pertinent to stability.

Table 8.8 lists the mean maximum velocity for the three groups of inlets. With respect to the American inlets, the Old St. Augustine Inlet, now closed, and the Gasparilla Pass (both in Florida) were left out because they represent unstable conditions with irregular or shoaling channel(s).

The conclusion, then is that the strong similarity demonstrated must be related to basic physical factors governing the interaction between flow and bottom and thereby the sediment transport balance budget for the inlet. These factors are related to bottom geometry as demonstrated by unidirectional (river) flow. The similarity may be extended to sediment transport.

Table 8.4 shows that the mean maximum velocity in the 11 tidal inlets considered changed only 10 to 20% in magnitude, compared with the great variation in hydraulic radii (mean depths) which ranged from 2.5 to 15 meters. This indicates that the actual flushing action of stable inlets is nearly proportional to the width.

It seems, therefore, that nature has managed itself in a practical and economical way. When a greater material transport capacity is needed, velocities increase to a value which decreases friction losses. At tidal inlets a shear stress corresponding

Table 8.8. Comparison between $V_{\text{mean max}}$ for Eight American, Six Dutch and One Danish Inlets (6)

Velocity	8 American	6 Dutch	1 Danish
$V_{\text{mean max}}$ m/sec	1.05 (computed)	1.00 for ebb 1.08 for neutral channels (measured)	1.08 (computed)

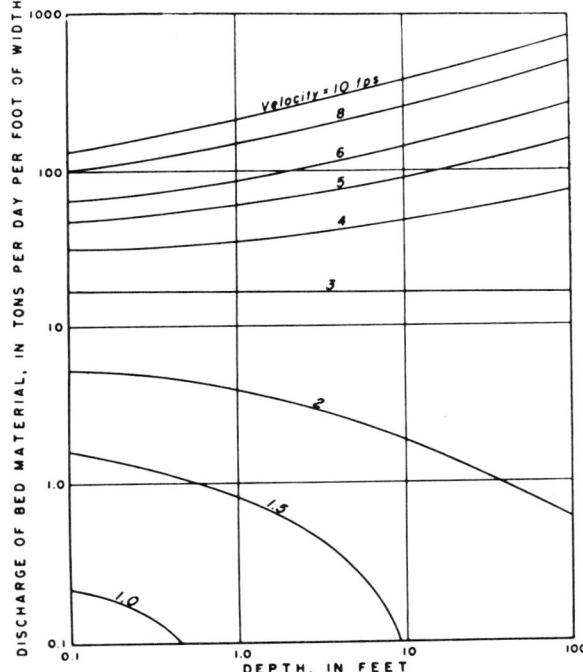

Figure 8.12. Effect of depth on the relationship between mean velocity and empirically determined discharges of bed material (13)

to a velocity of about 1 meter per second usually results because sand bottom having a 0.15- to 0.3-millimeter average diameter sand, with this velocity, changes its friction characteristics to flatter dunes. This causes less friction loss and develops toward a plane bed, thereby exerting the full power of shear stresses useful for sediment transport directly on the bottom material.

In reference to Tables 8.4 and 8.8, the following expressions for mean maximum velocities at spring tide in tidal inlets were developed.

$V_{\text{mean max}} = R^{1/8}$ meters per second $- 0.2$ meters per second for $R \geqslant 5$ meters, and $V_{\text{mean max}} = R^{1/8}$ meters per second $- 0.1$ meter per second for $R < 5$ meters.

The slightly higher reduction of the mean maximum velocity for the deeper inlets is undoubtedly related to the velocity distribution as a function of depth (26). The narrow range of mean maximum velocities is remarkable. It should be remembered that the mean maximum velocity is the top velocity occuring for about 2 hours in all on both sides of the theoretical mean maximum velocity.

Figure 8.12 from Colby (13), may explain this situation. Calculation of bottom roughness using Engelund and Hansen's results (16, 17, 18), for typical situations at maximum velocity for tidal inlets, and results by Garde and Ranga Ruja (20) reveal that we are moving into the transition zone where these mean maximum velocities occur in tidal inlets.

The above discussion should not leave the impression that tidal inlets always present simple cross-sectional geometry — on the contrary. Many tidal inlets have complex entrance areas, and the gorge itself may even be a composite of several ebb

Table 8.9 Ω/M Ratios for Various Inlets (6, 11).

Name of inlet (Kind of improvement)	Ω/M	Ω cu yds/half tidal cycle (10^6)	M cu yds/year (10^6)
Amelandse Gat, Holland (bank stabilization)	≅ 600	600	1
Aveiro, Portugal (jetties)	≅ 200	150	0.75
Big Pass, Florida (none)	≅ 100	12	0.1
Brielse Mass, Holland (before closing)	≅ 50	40	1
Brouwershaven Gat, Holland (closed)	≅ 450	430	1
Calcacieu Pass, Lousiana (jetties)	≅ 500	110 (diurnal)	0.1
East Pass, Florida (none)	≅ ,300	60 (diurnal)	0.1
Eyerlandse Gat, Holland (none)	≅ 300	270	1.0
Figueria da Foz, Portugal (before improvement by jetties)	≅ 50	20	0.5
Fort Pierce, Florida (jetties)	≅ 300	80	0.25
Gasparilla Pass, Florida (none)	≅ 150 (75)	15 (mixed diurnal semi)	0.1

Grays Harbor, Washington (jetties)	≈ 700	700	1.0
Haringvliet, Holland (closed)	≈ 350	350	1.0
Inlet of Texel, Holland (none)	≈ 1400	1400	1.0
Inlet of Vlie, Holland (none)	≈ 1400	1400	1.0
Longboat Pass, Florida (one jetty)	≈ 300	30 (mixed diurnal/semi)	0.1
	150		
Mission Bay, California Before dredging, no protection	≈ 150	12	0.07
Old St. Augustine Inlet, Florida (closed)	≈ 100	37	0.4
Oregon Inlet, North Carolina (none)	≈ 100	80	1.0
Ponce De Leon Inlet, Florida (none)	≈ 50	16	0.4
Port Aransas, Texas (jetties)	≈ 300	50 (diurnal)	0.08
Thyboroen, Denmark (jetties)	≈ 150	100	0.7

Note: Several of the inlets and entrances mentioned are subject to periodic dredging or to dredging on "as-needed" basis.

and flood channels if the gorge is not very long. This is the case at some of the Dutch inlets. Also, extreme tidal ranges in connection with heavy wave action may cause irregularities because of continued shifting of sand and subsequent shifting of channels. Extrances at Puerto Santa Cruz and Puerto Gallegos, Argentina, have a spring tidal range of about 30 feet. Puerto Santa Cruz has a complex entrance area with shifting shoals, but because of the geological structure, has a simpler gorge. The tidal prism varies considerably with the tidal range. At Puerto Gallegos, the situation at the entrance as well as at the gorge is very complex; it is a combined result of the strong wave action, a predominantly southward littoral transport and the strong variation of tidal prism.

Because the physical factors governing channel geometry vary continually, the entrance and gorge geometry seem to be seeking an equilibrium condition that is never reached, simply because the outside physical conditions are changing too fast and too frequently. Such cases, therefore, have to fulfill not one but several equilibrium boundary conditions and must operate within limits determined by the fluctuation and changes in the basic physical factors. Any improvement by man will be an attempt to limit the variance to a reasonable or practical size that man is able to handle. In the case of Bahia Blanca, Argentina, conditions are similar, but milder, and it will be somewhat easier to regulate the entrances by adequate channel design, probably including sand traps as buffers (6, 7, 9).

The numerous tidal inlets along the Indian shores in the Arabian Sea, and in the Bay of Bengal show similar features. Most of them are bar by-passers as demonstrated by large half-moon shaped ocean shoals and often by large bay shoals. Tidal ranges at spring tede reach 15 to 20 feet north of Bombay, and in such cases tidal flow may suffice to maintain a channel about 10 feet deep at mean sea level (examples at Versova and Sapati). In sufficient tidal prism resulting from the combination of a relatively limited tidal bay (or river) area and a modest tidal range, e.g., 3 to 5 feet, is normal down the west coast south of Bombay and on the greater part of the east coast of India. Another drawback is that the ocean bottom is often shallow and only able to absorb limited quantities of material jetted out by rivers and tidal channels.

Some good tidal flow by-passers, like the Bassein Creek north of Bombay, have gradually accumulated so much material on the ocean bottom that they are loosing characteristics of tidal flow by-passers, despite ample tidal flow. Others have a very long entrance channel. At Cochin on the Southeast coast, the entrance is about 15,000 feet long and passes through extensive shoals. Comprehensive dredging of some 1.5 million cubic yards per year is needed to maintain a 32-foot official depth through extensive ocean shoals.

On the Bay of Bengal a good many inlets close during the non-monsoon period but open up and develop as typical bar by-passes during the NE monsoon (states of Andhra Pradesh, Madras and Orissa).

Importance of the Ω/M or A/M Ratio

It is concluded that a tidal inlet flushes itself most adequately if it is able to develop mean maximum velocities of about 1 meter per second. Velocities of that magnitude, however, are not enough. The inlet channel, must carry enough flow volume (tidal prism) to cope with all the littoral drift material deposited in the channel during flood flow or under slack water.

Table 8.9 shows Ω/M ratios for a number of tidal inlets (6,11). It may be noted that those inlets having a Ω/M ratio in excess of 200, like Grays Harbor, Washington, Ft. Pierce, Florida, Port Aransas, Texas, and the Inlet of Texel, Holland, have the highest degree of overall stability. Inlets with Ω/M ratios < 100 like Big Pass, Florida, and Oregon Inlet, North Carolina, seem to belong to the group of inlets with predominant bar transfer on shallow bars or shoals across the ocean entrance, which is subjected to channel shifting at fairly regular and frequent intervals.

Inlets which have Ω/M ratios > 100 but $<$ 200 are the "in-betweens." They usually have a "fair" stability depending on the degree of regularity of the wave activity.

Using the expressions:

$$\Omega = (Q_m T) / (C_1 \pi)$$

and

$$Q_m = A V_{\text{mean max}}$$

where Q_m is the maximum discharge at spring tide, T is the tidal period, and C_1 is a dimensionless number (Reference 24) and accepting as a practical $V_{\text{mean}} \cong 2/3\ V_{\text{mean max}} \cong 0.67$ meters per second for *stable* inlet channels, then replacing Ω/M by A/M ($A = 2\Omega/T V_{\text{mean}}$), one may arrive at the figures of Table 8.10. The location of some practical characteristic examples is indicated by certain figure codes, and lines are drawn across the table indicating "poor," "fair" and "good" stability.

Since a practical case of inlet design would require as high degree of stability as possible, one is often faced with the fact that it is neccessary either to increase Ω or to decrease M, to obtain an agreeable Ω/M (A/M) ratio. The former is most difficult to achieve. Often consideration of a flood danger in the tidal bay or lagoon speaks against it. On the other hand, it is usually possible to decrease the material transfer to the entrance by means of sand traps which may be arranged as jetties, detached breakwaters, dredged sand traps, special sand transfer traps or arrangements, etc. A certain degree of natural transfer, depending on the flushing ability of inlet currents, may usually be accounted for. Table 8.1 gives such examples from Florida. The figures on littoral drift quantities are of approximate nature.

Use of the Ω/M ratio for evaluating the relative degree of stability of a tidal inlet assumes that Ω does not change very much from one season to another and that the tide is mainly semi-diurnal and not very skewed. Such ideal conditions do not exist at all tidal inlets, however.

Tidal ranges are often subject to seasonal changes, partly because of changes in the relative position of the moon to the earth. September and March tides have the highest ranges. Furthermore, meteorological conditions (barometric pressure and winds) may cause seasonal variations of Ω. This is particularly true for areas where trade winds and monsoons prevail for certain periods of the year. An example of this is the situation on the Indian shores where seasonal fluctuations of the mean sea level locally may reach 3 to 4 feet in parts of the Bay of Bengal.

In such cases the Ω may vary considerably, and to evaluate inlet stability each period of the year will have to be considered separately. This is not least true when M also varies greatly, as it may do in trade winds and monsoon areas. If Ω and M then vary in the same direction, e.g., in such a way that Ω gets a boost because ebb discharges are increased as a result of heavy rains at the same time as M increases because of more wave energy input (as in monsoon areas) the overall ratio Ω/M may still be descriptive for stability but most likely the ratio will drop because M increases relatively more than Ω. The result is that stability conditions deteriorate. In nature this may be demonstrated by the build-up of a major bar or shoal for predominant bar transfer of material, therefore less satisfactory depth conditions for navigation. After the period with relatively heavy drift, a period with less drift may follow resulting in increase of depths over the bar. If the inlet channel is to be improved, design should be based mainly on the period with the lowest Ω/M ratio. M then refers to the total drift during that period, which could be almost the total drift, M for one year.

The situation at the Udyavara Entrance (Malpe) north of Mangalore is typical in this respect. During the monsoon period, wave action is heavy and causes the build-up of a bar which scours out again to a navigable depth for the type of vessels used locally at most tides. At that time the littoral drift seems to be small because of little wave action.

346 Port Engineering

Table 8.10. $2/3 \cdot A/M$ and M in Relation to Inlet Stability.

$2/3\ AM$ (dimensionless); M = cubic meters per year

$A = RW$ m²	$2/3\ A$ m²	$M=$ 50,000	$M=$ 100,000	$M=$ 200,000	$M=$ 300,000	$M=$ 400,000	$M=$ 500,000	$M=$ 750,000
100	67	.0013	0.0007	0.0003	0.0002	0.0001	0.0001	0.00009
200	133	.0026	0.0013	0.0007	0.0004	0.0003	0.0003	0.00018
300	200	.0040	0.0020	0.0010	0.0007	0.0005	0.0004	0.00027
400	267	.0053	0.0027	0.0013	0.0009	0.0007	0.0005	0.00036
500	333	.0067*	0.0033	0.0016	0.0011	0.0008	0.0007	0.00044
600	400	.0080+	0.0040	0.0020	0.0013	0.0010	0.0008	0.00053
700	467	.0093	0.0047	0.0023	0.0016	0.0011	0.0009	0.00062
800	533	0.107	0.0053	0.0026	0.0018	0.0013	0.0011	0.00071
900	600	0.120	0.0060	0.0030	0.0020	0.0015	0.0012	0.00080
1,000	667	.0133	0.0067	0.0033	0.0022	0.0017	0.0013	0.00089
1,200	800	.0160	0.0080	0.0040	0.0027	0.0020	0.0016	0.0011
1,400	933	.0187	0.0093	0.0046	0.0031	0.0023	0.0018	0.0012
1,600	1,067	.0213	0.0107	0.0053	0.0036	0.0027	0.0021	0.0014
1,800	1,200	.0240	0.0120‡	0.0060	0.0040	0.0030	0.0024	0.0016
2,000	1,333	.0267	0.0133	0.0067	0.0044	0.0034	0.0027	0.0018
2,500	1,667	.0333	0.0167	0.0084	0.0056	0.0042 §	0.0033 §	0.0022
3,000	2,000	.0400	0.0200 ¶	0.0100	0.0067	0.0050	0.0040	0.0027
3,500	2,333	.0467	0.0233	0.0117	0.0078	0.0059	0.0047	0.0031
4,000	2,667	.0534	0.0267 ★	0.0134	0.0089	0.0062	0.0053	0.0036
4,500	3,000	.0600	0.0300	0.0150	0.0100	0.0075	0.0060	0.0040
5,000	3,333	.0667	0.0333	0.0167	0.0111	0.0083	0.0067	0.0044 ◆
6,000	4,000	.0800	0.0400	0.0200	0.0133	0.0100	0.0080	0.0053
7,000	4,667	.0933	0.0467	0.0234	0.0156	0.0117	0.0093	0.0062
8,000	5,333	.1067	0.0533	0.0267	0.0178	0.0134	0.0106	0.0071
9,000	6,000	.1200	0.0600	0.0300	0.0200	0.0150	0.0120	0.0080
10,000	6,667	.1333	0.0667	0.0333	0.0222	0.0167	0.0133	0.0089 ●
20,000	13,333	.2666	0.1333	0.0667	0.0444	0.0334	0.0266	0.0178
30,000	20,000	.4000	0.2000	0.1000	0.0667	0.0500	0.0400	0.0266 ⊕

Good   Fair   Poor

*Big Pass, Florida
+ Gasparilla Pass, Florida
‡ Mission Bay, California
§ Ponce De Leon, Florida
¶ Port Aransas, Texas
★ Calcasieu, Louisiana
◆ Oregon, North Carolina
● Thyboroen, Denmark
⊕ Grays Harbor, Washington

At open sea coast entrances the situation in most cases will be similar to the one mentioned above. Littoral drift depends upon wave height raised to second power. However, an increase in tidal prism of seasonal nature will usually not be sufficient to cope with the increase in drift.

The situation may develop differently if the increase in discharge by tide and fresh water is considerable and at the same time continuous wave breaking on an offshore bar stirs up material in major quantities so most material transfer takes place as suspension load. An increase in current velocities across the bar will then be able to increase depths. This situation may be advantageous, in particular if the tidal flow is skewed with predominant ebb flow. It the flow is unable to deepen the channel to such an extent that wave breaking does not occur in the channel section, this situation is of little advantage. For improvement, the flow may than be concentrated by training walls to provide more flushing power. For reasons of safe navigation, the flushing current should never exceed 5 feet per second. This would not result in wave breaking unless the wave height is almost equal to the water depth or approximately 0.8 to 1.0 times the depth under storm wave conditions.

The tidal inlet at Honavar, north of Malpe seems to belong to the group described above. The offshore bar is a result of the longshore current's collision with ebb flow. The material comes partly from the longshore drift, particularly on the downdrift (south) side, and partly from the ebb current's flushing of material. During the non-monsoon period, low swells also tend to push material from the offshore bottom up on to the bar.

With respect to design of cross-sectional geometry, one could make the boundary condition of an equal shear stress, including stresses by flow and by gravity over the entire cross-section. Reference is made to the theoretical approaches mentioned in References 4, 21 and 26. Practice usually calls for a navigation channel of a certain width and depth, which means a horizontal bottom in the middle and stable slopes along the sides. Perhaps the actually occurring side slope stability may be of the nature of deposits to certain slope angle then "slumping," then deposits, etc. Tidal inlets differ in this respect from rivers, because material is introduced everywhere from the sides too.

It should be emphasized that hydraulic model experiments may often be helpful in determining the most favorable horizontal as well as cross-sectional geometry (1, 2, 6, 10).

Design Procedures

Based on the discussion of tidal inlet stability, the following design procedures may be developed:

1. In the case of an inlet to be improved: get all necessary information on Ω (tidal prism), $Q_{\text{mean max}}$ (mean maximum discharge under spring tide conditions). Compare Ω, $Q_{\text{mean max}}$ and other Q's by computation and current velocity measurements in the gorge channel.
2. In the case of the design of a new entrance: evaluate bay (or lagoon) tidal range based on experience from cases of similar tidal range and similar geometry of bay (or lagoon).
3. Evaluate M_{mean} as closely as possible based on experience from neighboring shores. Check the Ω/M ratio (6).
4. Evaluate the most likely $V_{\text{mean max}}$ based on experience considering the local littoral drift capacity (6,11).

$V_{\text{mean max}}$ = 1 meter per second ± α meters per second

5. Introductorily use an overall relationship between tidal prism and cross-sectional area of gorge as $A = (\Omega C_2 \pi / T \cdot V_{\text{max}})$, when $C_2 \approx 0.9$. Compute $Q_{\text{max}} = A V_{\text{mean max}}$.
6. Design cross-section, horizontal bottom, slope 1 in 5 (sand bottom) or 1:X when X is the slope training wall or jetty.
7. Check velocity distribution introductorily (26).

8. Check $V_{\text{mean max}}$ again. Adjust gorge area to selected $V_{\text{mean max}}$ in greater detail with respect to velocity distribution.
9. Check Q_{max} and Ω by detailed computation (6, 15).
10. If Ω thereby decreases below acceptable value considering the Ω/M ratio (6), try to increase Ω by increasing A and repeat computations listed above. Observe the seasonal changes in Ω/M with special reference to low values.
11. If Ω cannot possibly be increased, try to decrease the active M by jetties, by traps or by an entrance geometry better suited for effective flushing, if possible. Model experiments may be advantageous or necessary to secure the most desirable velocity distribution in the inlet channel as a whole, as well as in the cross-section. See References 2 and 10 for model laws.
12. In the case of improvement of an existing inlet, use tracer experiments to clarify littoral drift pattern and, if necessary, also the littoral drift quantity, the latter being subject to long-time experiments. If possible, use experience values or energy flux considerations (see Chapter 6).
13. You may finally try to compute the bed-load transport in the gorge channel by using Einstein's (possibly modified), Bagnold's, Kalinske's or other procedures for bedload transport. Check available literature on sediment transport in rivers, estuaries and streams (Chapter 6 and references).

References

1. Barr, D.I.H., Huq, S.S., and Shaikh, A.H. 1969. "Vertical distortion in tidal model studies." *The Dock and Harbour Authority* 49(579):327-38.
2. Bijker, E.W. 1967. *Some Considerations about Scales for Coastal Models with Movable Bed.* Pub. 50. Delft Hydraulic Laboratory.
3. Brasfield, C.W., and Ball, J.W. 1967. *Expansion of Santa Barbara Harbor, Cal.* Tech Report 2-805. Waterways Experiment Station, U.S. Army Corps of Engineers.
4. Bretting, A.E. 1958. "Stable channels." *Acta Polytechnica Scandinavia* 245.
5. Brown, E.I. 1932. "Flow of water in tidal canals." *Proceedings of the American Society of Civil Engineers* 96:747-834.
6. Bruun, P. 1966. *Tidal Inlets and Littoral Drift.* Oslo: University Book Company.
7. ____. 1967. "By-passing and back-passing with reference to Florida." *ASCE Journal of the Waterways and Harbors Division* 93(WW2):101-28.
8. ____. 1967. "Tidal inlets housekeeping." *ASCE Journal of the Hydraulics Division* 93(HY5):167-84.
9. ____. 1968. "Shore protection in harbor construction." *Proceedings of the 5th International Harbor Congress.* Antwerp.
10. ____, and Battjes, J.A. 1963. "Tidal inlets and littoral drift." *Proceedings of the International Association of Hydraulic Research* 4(1.17):123-36.
11. ____, and Gerritsen, F. 1960. *Stability of Coastal Inlets.* Amsterdam: North Holland Publishing Co.
12. ____. 1961. "Natural bypassing of sand at coastal inlets." *ASCE Transactions* 126(4):823-54.
13. Colby, B.R. 1964. *Discharge of Sands and Mean Velocity Relationships in Sand-Bed Streams.* Prof. Paper 462-A. Washington, D.C.: U.S. Department of the Interior.
14. Dronkers, J.J. 1959. "Tidal computations on coastal areas." *ASCE Journal of the Waterways and Harbors Division* 85:13-24. *See also*, "Tidal computations for rivers, coastal areas and seas." *ASCE Journal of the Waterways and Harbors Division* 95:29-77.
15. ____. 1964. *Tidal Computations.* Amsterdam: North Holland Publishing Co.
16. Engelund, F. 1966. "Hydraulic resistance of alluvial streams." *ASCE Journal of the Hydraulics Division* 92(HY2):315-26.
17. ____, and Hansen, E. 1966. "Investigations of flow in alluvial streams." *Acta Polytechnica Scandinavia.* Danish Bulletin 9. Stockholm.

18. ___. 1967. *A Monograph on Sediment Transportation.* Copenhagen: Danish Technical Press.
19. French, J.L. 1951. *Second Progress Report on Tidal Flow in Entrances. The Velocity Distribution in the Jet Issuing from a Channel into an Ocean or Lagoon.* Report 1141. National Bureau of Standards.
20. Garde, R.J., and Ranga Ruja, K.G. 1963. "Regime criteria for alluvial streams." *ASCE Journal of the Hydraulics Division* 89(HY6):153-64.
21. Glover, E.G., and Florey, G.L. 1951. *Stable Channel Profiles.* Report Hyd-325. U.S. Department of the Interior: Hydraulics Laboratory.
22. Jonsson, I.G. 1965. *Friction Factor Diagrams for Oscillatory Boundary Layers.* Basic Res. Prog. Report 10. Technical University of Denmark: Coastal Engineering and Hydraulics Laboratory.
23. Kennedy, J.F., and Brooks, N.H. 1963. *Laboratory Study of an Alluvial Stream at Constant Discharge.* Misc. Pub. 970:320-30. Washington, D.C.: U.S. Department of Agriculture.
24. Keulegan, G.A. 1951. *Third Progress Report on Tidal Flow in Entrances.* Report 1146. National Bureau of Standards.
25. Lorenz, H.A. 1918-25. *Report on the State Commission Zuiderzee.* Denmark.
26. Lundgren, H.L., and Jonsson, I.G. 1964. "Shear and velocity distribution in shallow channels." *ASCE Journal of the Hydraulics Division* 90(HY1):1-21.
27. Nordin, C.F. 1964. *Aspects of Flow Resistance and Sediment Transport in Rio Grande near Bernalillo, New Mexico.* Geol. Sur. Water Supply Paper 1498-H. Washington, D.C.: U.S. Department of the Interior.
28. Permanent International Association of Navigation Congresses. 1957. "Siltation in coastal waters." *Proceedings of 19th Congress of PIANC* s II - c 3.
29. ___. 1961. "Orientation and layout of accesses to seaports." *Proceedings of 20th Congress of PIANC* s II - s 2.
30. Simons, D.B., and Richardson, E.V. 1965. *A Study of Variables Effecting Flow Characteristics and Sediment Transport in Alluvial Channels.* Misc. Pub. 970:193-207. Washington, D.C.: U.S. Department of Agriculture.
31. ___, and Haushild, W.L. 1962. "Depth-discharge relationship in alluvial channels." *ASCE Journal of the Hydraulics Division* 88(HY5):57-72.
32. Tidal Hydraulics Symposium. 1967. "Estuary hydraulics and sedimentation." *ASCE Journal of the Hydraulics Division* 95(HY1):1-160.

9 dredging technology

Dredging is moving material submerged in water from one place to another in water or out of water with equipment called dredges. Dredges today come in two classifications—mechanical and hydraulic. An excellent review is given by A.L. McKnight in Reference 15 which is abstracted in part below and supplemented with other information.

Mechanical types include the *clamshell* or *grapple dredges* (Figure 9.1). Larger dredges of that type are no longer favorites. The endless *chain bucket* (or bucket-ladder) dredge (Figure 9.2) was used widely earlier in Europe but not in the United States, although they were employed on a few projects like the Panama Canal.

The *mechanical dipper dredge* with its heavy bucket (Figure 9.3) moved by a very strong arm and boom is still used for dredging relatively loose (usually not solid) rock. The bucket may be provided with special cast iron teeth. "Big Boy" in Norway has a 2.6-cubic yard bucket.

The *hydraulic dredge* is the most important piece of dredging equipment. The *plain* section dredge (Figure 9.4) has no cutter but sucks material off the bottom and discharges it through a stern connected pipe leading to a spoil disposal area.

The *cutterhead pipeline dredge* (Figure 9.5) has a rotating cutter on the end of the ladder and excavates the material from *in situ* condition and discharges it through the stern to pontoon and shore pipe. The dredge is controlled on stern mounted spuds and is swung from one side of the channel to the other by means of a swing gear.

The *self-propelled hopper dredge* (Figure 9.6) has a large hopper in which the dredged material is loaded for later dumping through doors in the bottom. This type of dredge is normally employed where the water is too deep for a pipeline dredge or where spoil areas for such a dredge are not available within economic distances.

The development of the hydraulic dredge happened through random trial-and-error rather than by plan. The dredging pioneers were first of all interested in the practicable aspects of making money. Only those who work directly with the dredge have more than a passing knowledge of its operation or capabilities. Dredging is "a complicated and still empirical business and men spend their lives it it, learning almost wholly by experience" (15). A great improvement introduced in 1966 by the establishment of WODCON (World Organization of Dredging Contractors) which had its first international meeting in New York in 1967 and now issues its own periodical regularly and arranges world conferences every second year (23). Another organization, WODA (World Dredging and Marine Construction), publishes monthly magazines and also published the *1970 Directory of World's Dredges and Their Owners* (22).

Dredging 351

Figure 9.1. The clamshell or grapple dredge (15).

Figure 9.2. The bucket-ladder dredge (15).

Figure 9.3. The dipper dredge (15).

Figure 9.4. The plain section dredge (15).

Figure 9.5. The cutterhead pipeline dredge (15).

Figure 9.6. The self-propelled hopper dredge (15).

Table 9.1. Typical Specifications for Five Sizes of Dredges (9).

Specifications	Size of dredge, in inches				
	12	16	20	24	28
Length, in feet	100	120	140	160	175
Beam, in feet	35	40	45	50	50
Depth, in feet	8	9	10	12	15
Displacement, in tons	560	840	1,200	1,850	3,000
Pump power, in brake horsepower	570	1,000	1,500	2,700	5,000
Pump Speed, in revolutions per minute	500	400	350	325	300
Cutter power, in brake horsepower	150	200	400	750	1,000
Cutter speed, in revolutions per minute	5-30	5-30	5-30	3-30	5-30
Spud length, in feet	55	60	70	90	100
Ladder length, in feet	50	55	60	70	80
Maximum pipe line, in feet	2,500	4,000	5,000	7,000	9,000
Maximum width of cut, in feet	160	200	220	270	325
Minimum width of cut, in feet	50	60	70	90	90
Maximum digging depth, in feet	35	40	45	50	60
Minimum digging depth, in feet	4	5	6	8	12

The hydraulic dredge has, without any doubt, become the most important piece of equipment in the entire harbor engineering field. Without the dredge, commercial navigation of waterways and rivers would be ended. Water-borne industry would collapse. Ocean shipping as it is known would be nonexistent.

Hydraulic dredges dig canals, ports and harbors, do maintenance dredging in rivers, canals and waterways, and excavate for construction of piers, wharves, docks, dams and underwater foundations. They provide spoil for the reclamation of swamps and marshes; they construct dikes and levees, and dredge sand, gravel and shell, as well as coal, gold, diamonds and many other minerals for commercial purposes. The dredge's scope of operation is broad.

Small hydraulic dredges operate in water only a few feet deep. Larger dredges require more draft but can dig to greater depths. With the aid of booster pumps, the distances solids can be pumped are unlimited. Table 9.1 gives typical specifications for five dredges ranging in size from 12 to 28-inches discharge pipe.

Although the dredge's output is understandably greater in soft materials than in hard, it can excavate almost anything. It digs mud, silt, loam, clay, sand, hardpan, gravel, coral and even rock. Boulders weighing 1,000 pounds and more have been excavated and transported by dredges.

The self-propelled hopper dredge moves freely without any kind of mooring system. It can operate by pumping holes in the bottom side by side through a usually circular intake which is the reinforced end of the suction pipe, or it can trail along with its trailing suction head attached to the end of the suction pipe "vacuum cleaning" the bottom. This method is more practical and effective than the plain pipe sucking procedure where deep holes may become sediment traps for material which otherwise may have been flushed away. The Japanese Bureau of Port Construction has, however, built a "sea bottom grader," which was put in operation in 1968 at the port of Nagoya (10). The grader, which is 33 feet (10 meters) wide and 4 feet (1.3 meters) high, is hung from the gantry at the stern and can be operated by two winches controlled from the bridge. Depth indicators and incli-

Figure 9.7. Modern "27-inch" hydraulic pipeline dredge (9).

nometers are provided in the grader. A grader operation board is situated at the rear portion of the bridge where the gantry and the winches can be seen, and all kinds of adjustments can be made from the operation board which indicates depth, inclination of the grader and loads on winch and grader.

The cutterhead, pipeline, hydraulic dredge, with its supporting equipment, is essentially a floating power plant used to move material hydraulically to some other location without rehandling. It is always referred to by the size of its discharge; for example, a 24-inch dredge. Figure 9.7 shows a large and modern pipeline dredge. It has a total connected horsepower of 8,000, a 27-inch discharge pipe and a crew of 85 men.

Suction is provided by vacuum produced by a centrifugal pump. Assuming that V_m is the mean velocity in the suction pipe, the total vacuum pressure P_t may be written

$$P_t = \frac{V_m^2}{g}(1+\epsilon) + P_p + P_c$$

when ϵ is a dimensionless intake loss coefficient, P_p is the loss of pressure by friction in the suction pipe and P_c is the additional vacuum needed for mixture conveyance. V_m usually ranges from 15 to 20 feet. For maximum capacity, V_m should be high within limits and ϵ and P_p should be low. While it is difficult to vary P_p and V_m because they have to stay within certain practical limits set by hydraulic characteristics, it is possible to vary ϵ within wide ranges. Reference 7 mentions tests on intake geometry which demonstrates that the nozzle shape has the largest intake loss ($\epsilon = 5.5$) while the pear-shaped suction head, designed in accordance with theoretical considerations and used particularly in the USSR, has the smallest intake loss ($\epsilon = 0.022$). The concentration of solids, c, may be connected with the additional vacuum P_c by the following equations (7):

$$k_T = \beta_1(\beta_2)(\beta_3)P_c^{0.78}$$

where β_1 is a dimensionless coefficient, dependent solely on the bottom material β_2 is a dimensionless coefficient, dependent solely on the furrow depth and β_3 is a dimensionless coefficient, dependent solely on the intake form. β_1 decreases with decreasing grain diameter and pore volume; β_2 increases with increasing furrow depth because more material is conveyed if deep furrows are formed, causing more constant material supply to the suction head; β_3 depends upon intake design and geometry as mentioned later.

Figure 9.8 (9) is a schematic, showing dredge components. The dredge itself consists generally of a cutter, ladder, suction pipe, A- and H-frames, cutter motor, hull, house, lever room, hoisting machinery, main pump and prime mover, auxiliary pumps and enginer, spud frame and spuds. Figure

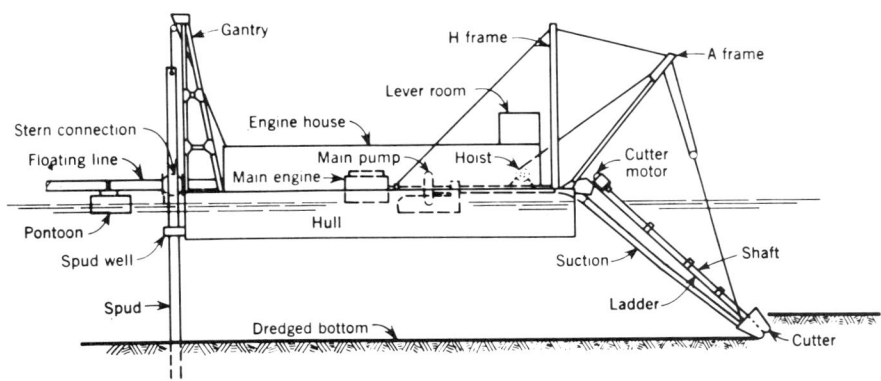

Figure 9.8. Dredge components (9).

9.8 shows these components and their locations on the dredge. During operation, the floating line and the shoreline are attached to the dredge. The supporting equipment is generally comprised of a derrick, one or more tugs to tend the dredge, fuel and pipe barges, surveying craft and other special equipment for the job at hand.

The cutter is attached to the forward end of the ladder, and it is connected by a shaft to a cutter motor which rotates it, the rotation agitating soft or loose material or cutting hard material so that it can be picked up by the suction. Cutters are usually classified as *basket* or *straight-arm*.

The basket cutter has a front hub, a back wearing ring and several spiral-shaped blades integral with the hub and ring. A closed-nose basket with spiral, integral blades is best suited for digging in soft materials or loose sands. An open-nose basket is suitable for clay or hard materials, because when dredging in stiff clay, the cutter with blades that are close together may become clogged. A closed-nose basket cutter with chisel-pointed teeth closely spaced on the blades is used for hard materials.

The straight-arm cutter with its blades extended beyond the hub and attached with bolts to a spider is used in hard clays. In exceptionally hard materials, serrated blades or blades with shovel-type teeth can increase the output. Pick-shaped teeth can be used to good advantage in coral and other brittle materials.

The ladder carries, in addition to the cutter, the suction pipe, lubrication lines and usually the cutter motor. The rear of the ladder is supported by heavy trunnions set in a well in the hull.

The suction pipe is supported beneath the ladder and is connected to the hull suction pipe by a ball joint, trunnion elbow or rubber sleeve located opposite the latter trunnions.

The cuttershaft is mounted on top of the ladder directly above the suction pipe. The cutter motor, usually located on the rear end of the ladder, is attached through a reduction gear or other mechanics to the shaft.

Sheaves are attached to both sides of the outer part of the ladder, and through these from the drums of the winding gear run cables attached to anchors. The anchors, when placed outward from them, allow the dredge to be pulled from side to side by the swing wires.

The dredge is held in position or moved ahead with the spuds (Figure 9.9). Spuds are usually round and generally made of cast steel or built-up plate, from 2 to 3 feet in diameter. They are located at the stern of the dredge.

The pipe on the dredge, from the pump discharge to the stern, is on the outside of the engine house and usually along the top of the hull. It is connected at the stern to the floating line by a flexible joint which is either a swivel elbow, one or more ball joints, or merely a rubber sleeve. Swivel

356 Port Engineering

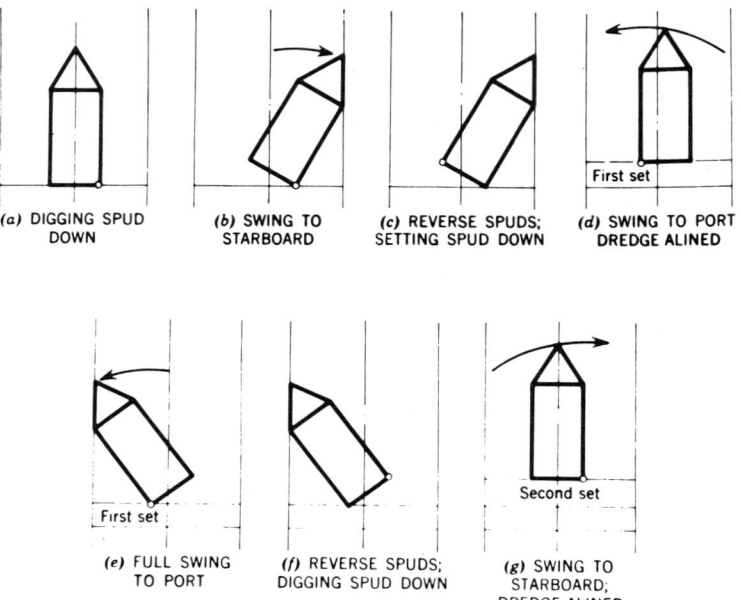

Figure 9.9. Process of stepping dredge ahead (9).

elbows are preferred because of their wide turning ability.

The floating line is made up of sections of pipe from 30 to 50 feet long and from ½ to 5/8 inch thick, each supported by one or more pontoons. These composite sections are generally referred to as pontoons. They are placed in the line and sucessively connected together either by flanges, ball joints or rubber sleeves. A typical floating line might be made up of two or more pontoons connected together by flanges, several of these assemblies connected by ball joints, a 90° elbow pontoon, additional pontoon assemblies and one special pontoon, often called a landing pontoon. The landing pontoon has an A-frame and hand-winch for elevating or lowering the pipe to compensate for differences in bank elevation. Small ½ to 5-ton anchor and winch assemblies are placed at strategic locations along the line to stablize it if required, and a walkway with a handrail is often installed atop the pipe.

The floating line is usually laid out in a wide arc from the dredge to the shore so that the dredge may advance or move about without frequent stops to add more pontoons, or with two elbows so that the line can remain along the shore to be out of way of traffic.

The shoreline consists of shorter and lighter sections of pipe than the floating line, usually being between 10 and 15 feet long and from 1/8 to ¼ inch thick. They are connected by ramming the tapered end of one into the straight, banded end of another—the tapered end always being pointed in the direction of the flow. Usually these connections are held together by wire which is wrapped around lugs welded to each side with the end of each located at the stern of the dredge, one on either side. Spud rigging includes a gantry for supporting the spuds, hoisting sheaves, wires from the hoisting drums and the spud wells. The wells carry any horizontal thrust created during dredging or bad weather and keep the spuds alined as well. When weather conditions are bad or the cut too deep, three-wire mooring is often used instead of spuds. Dredges have, however, worked on spuds in depths of over 100 feet.

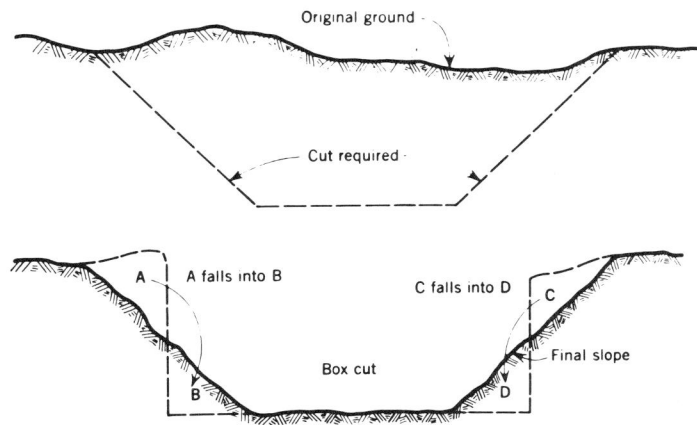

Figure 9.10. A dredging box-cut (9).

The discharge line is more easily described in three sections: (a) the pipe on the dredge, (b) the floating line and (c) the shoreline. Occasionally, when the line is under high pressure, they may be spot-welded together. The shoreline can have two discharges by placing a so-called *WYE* near to its end. One leg of the WYE can be closed by a valve and additional pipes are required as well as providing for better distribution of spoil over a wider area.

Figure 9.9 explains how a hydraulic dredge steps ahead on its spuds in large swings, and Figure 9.10 shows a dredging box cut which gradually sluffs down establishing stable side slopes (9).

During the last 10 years, a strong development of dredging technology has taken place, (4, 10, 13, 15, 23). As mentioned in Chapter 1, increasing the draft on ocean-going vessesl calls for deeper water in ports and estuaries. Modern dredging equipment must now be capable of working to depths up to 100 feet, and mineral dredging takes place in still increasing depths (14, 16, 23). The most spectacular development has been achieved in the field of free-floating suction dredges adapted to work in moving waters. Not only has their size increased, but their pumping equipment has been greatly improved, along with suspension devices and techniques for better emulsification. Existing dredges can drag up 17,000 to 18,000 tons of material per hour from a depth of 100 feet and, in exceptional cases, 150 feet. Stationary suction dredges for mineral exploitation also have been adapted to greater depths, some of them exceeding 300 feet (90 meters). Mechanical dredges still have their use in port work, wherever suction is not applicable. They can also reach 100 feet, even in hard ground.

In Reference 15, McKnight gives a vivid impression of this development of which following should be mentioned. The *direct-to-shore pump method*, by which the dredge pumps material dredged offshore to shore through a submerged pipeline connected to a special type barge, has proved its value but needs further development. This system is very important because, without any question, future coastal protection will mainly concentrate on artificial nourishment, and sand for this nourishment will have to come from offshore sources. In order to accomplish such nourishment, new type dredging equipment is being developed which is able to operate in open seas without being interrupted too often by wave action making operations impossible. Presently, most hydraulic dredges will not be able to work in seas exceeding approximately 5 feet with wave periods of 5 to 10 seconds. If operation is to be economical, rehandling of material must be avoided to the extent possible, and mobilization and demobilization should not require excessive costs.

Figure 9.11. The sump-handling method (15).

In 1966 the U.S. Army Corps of Engineers carried out an experiment at Sea Girt, New Jersey, in which a hopper dredge, with a pumpout to shore capability, picked up sand from an offshore borrow area and transported it to a docking barge 2,000 feet from the beach from where the dredge discharged to shore through a 28-inch submerged pipeline. As described in References 6 and 20, the relative movement of the dredge and barge made docking difficult and frequently broke the flexible connection from the barge to the submerged line. Even if the overall efficiency of this operation was relatively low, it was a success, because it demonstrated that sand could be obtained from offshore deposits and spoiled on the beach for nourishment. As described in Reference 20, sand has been picked up by hopper dredge 20 kilometers from shore in Holland and brought to the harbor at Ymuiden, dumped in the front port and redredged for construction work.

With respect to future offshore nourishment schemes, two new methods have been proposed. One is the offshore dumping and rehandling system by which a hopper dredge dumps offshore sand to be pumped to shore by means of jet pumps operated from the shore, delivering a sand-water mixture through a submerged pipeline discharging onto the shore (6). The landing barge, which was used at the Sea Girt, proved to be a sore point and is therefore avoided in this experiment scheme. When the hopper dredge has completed its operation at one point, it proceeds to the next location, leaving the jet pump(s) behind for completing the nourishment operation. Some tests have been run successfully in Japan.

The other method is the submerged dredge system operating by means of crawler type tractors, including a pump unit and an operation unit. This system has been in actual and successful test operation at Ft. Pierce, on the Florida Atlantic Coast (1970). The simplest method is still the direct pumping to shore from an ocean-going dredge, capable of operating in wave action of 10 to 12 feet. Such a dredging project was undertaken in 1970 at Pompano Beach on the south Florida Atlantic Coast, using a 24-inch dredge to pump 1.1 million cubic yards of material to shore from offshore sources located 3,500 to 4,000 feet from shore. This test was also satisfactory.

The use of pneumatic breakwaters to protect dredges has been discussed and tests have been run. The conclusion so far has been that "a curtain of air bubbles from a submerged pipe will materially reduce heights of waves that are not longer than five times the depth. Tests of pneumatic breakwaters and models indicate their inability to protect dredges from long ocean swells off the New Jersey shore" (11).

Dredging 359

Figure 9.12. The giant sidecasting dredge, Zulia (15).

The *sump handling method* has also been utilized. One dredge discharges its material into the hopper of another (usually old) dredge for rehandling and pumping to shore (Figure 9.11), thereby reclaiming land.

The *sidecasting method*, particularly suitable for maintaining long navigation channels, was developed about 10 years ago in an effort to maintain the mouth of the Orinoco River in Venezuela and is now becoming more and more popular. In a Japanese shipyard, a T2 tanker was converted so that the boom extended 250 feet off the starboard side through which the dredge pumped material directly rather than going through hoppers. The dredge was successful in providing a usable channel into the mouth of the Orinoco, which no previous equipment had been able to do. In a little less than three years, this dredge removed over 104 million cubic yards of material from the Boca Grande entrance channel. The success of this dredge concept was so great that the same dredging company built the $15 million giant dredge *Zulia* for operation in the channels of Lake Maracaibo, Venezuela, mentioned in Chapter 6. The *Zulia* was not only provided with a conventional hopper dredge capability but was also fitted with a 415-foot boom capable of being rotated 180° so that it could discharge from either the port or starboard side. The boom extends 328 feet beyond the side of the vessel. The discharge pipe in the boom is 57 inches in inside diameter. The vessel itself is 548 feet long and has a beam of 95 feet and a draft of about 26½ feet, with 11,000 total horsepower on its four dredge pumps (Figure 9.12).

The *Zulia* made an outstanding record at Lake Maracaibo (13, 15) and has permitted the maintenance of a usable deep draft channel for the heavy volume of tanker trade into that port. Records of the Instituto Nationale de Canaliziones of the Venezuelan government show that during the period between February 17, 1960, and July, 17, 1962, the *Zulia* pumped through the boom a total of 104,663,000 cubic meters of material and by conventional hopper dredging 2,801,000 cubic meters or a total of 107,464,000 cubic meters. In-place surveys showed the removal of 70,462,000 cubic meters, indicating an average efficiency of 67.32%. With the enormous pumping rates achieved, over 7,000 cubic meters per hour, it can be seen that very effective and economical dredging with the *Zulia* has been possible. The dredging cost during the period cited was 23 cents or about 17 cents per cubic yard. Tests demonstrated that sand only returned to the channel at a relatively slow rate.

A very small slidecasting dredge was placed in service in 1964 by the U.S. Army Corps of Engineers. Figure 9.13 shows the dredge in operation. It is a small dredge—only 108 feet long. The vessel has two 10-inch drags and discharges through a 12-inch inside diameter boom 80 feet long. The

Figure 9.13. The small sidecaster, Merritt (15).

Figure 9.14. The McFarland *sidecaster and hopper dredge (15).*

Merritt serves a very useful purpose, particularly in the Carolina inlets which are too rough for the economical use of pipeline dredges. The Merritt helps this situation by dredging pilot cuts through the ocean bars to permit safe operation of larger conventional hopper dredges. It is also excellent for emergency operations and permits shallow inlet channels to be maintained at comparatively low cost (11). In 1966 the Merritt was followed by another, somewhat larger, sidecaster, the Schweitzer (2, 18), which is able to sidecast 100 feet through a 16-inch revolving boom supporting the discharges pipe. Both "mini-sidecasters" work in similar fashion. As pointed out in Reference 11, the

Figure 9.15. The Prince of Netherlands *hopper dredge (commercial brochure).*

ideal situation is for the dredge to be able to sidecast on the ebb tide, with the sand drift away from the channel side being discharged on.

The newest dredge of this type in the United States is the *McFarland* (Figure 9.14), which also has a hopper, making it even more flexible. It was put in commission in 1967 and assigned to maintenance of Gulf Coast inlets. This dredge is 300 feet long and 72 feet wide, with a loaded draft of about 22 feet to permit efficient operation in some relatively shallow areas of the Gulf at Galveston and Houston. The boom can rotate on a turntable and permits discharging about 160 feet from the side of the vessel. Piping arrangements permit connecting the pumps parallel or in series for use in pumping ashore through one or two 26-inch pipes or boom discharging. Hopper capacity is 3,100 cubic yards. During its first year of operation, the *McFarland* dredged more than 7 million cubic yards, 20% by sidecasting. Its success may be followed by a shallow draft hopper and boom dredge.

Stationary by-passing plants by hydraulic pipeline equipment is mentioned in Chapter 6. The world's largest dredge, *The Prince of Netherlands*, is shown in Figure 9.15. This dredge was built specifically for dredging Europort, Rotterdams' new large seaport. The overall length is 430 feet; beam width, 72 feet and draft, about 33 feet. Suction pipe diameter is 48-inches; hopper capacity, 11,700 cubic yards and dredging depth, about 100 feet (30 meters). Despite its size, the dredge is very maneuvrable and is also suitable for river dredging.

A proper design of the suction head is very important for the efficiency, particularly of the large-scale dredging operations in navigation channels. As mentioned earlier, pressure drop at the head provides the suction. When dredging at great depths, there remains only a relatively small pressure drop available for suction at the head itself. The rest is lost in the pipe. The criterion for the hydraulic dimensioning of suction heads is mainly the effective pressure drop at the head and not the available carrying capacity of the pipe. It is, in this respect, interesting to note that laboratory tests (7) have demonstrated that, for dredging at a given pressure drop, long narrow heads with suction areas of four to five times the suction pipe section are the most favorable. The best geometry for the suction head seems to be the pear-shaped. In order to reserve as wide a margin as possible for pressure drop at the suction head, the pump should be placed as low as possible in the dredge, or it should be entirely submerged. Head losses above the pump should therefore, be avoided to the extent possible. Extra vacuum (carrying capacity) may be provided by water jets discharging in the suction pipe near the suction head (see Reference 21), increasing suction and carrying capacity. The future deep-sea mining operations will probably use this principle, limited only by considering the costs of incorporating "exterior jets" for loosening material and "interior jets" for increasing pressure for carrying capacity (21). Many new devices, including meters for measuring concentrations using density difference and momentum principles or radioactive tracing, have been developed.

Dredging minerals in the sea is still a new field (12, 14, 16) but is undoubtedly going to increase considerably in the future due to shortage of certain minerals such as copper, cobalt, tin, zinc, phosphorus and sulfur from land sources. Offshore dredging for tin has taken place for a number of years in Malaysia. Huge commercial sea mining projects were announced recently (1970) by Deepsea Ventures, Inc., Newport. The federal government has taken considerable interest in these prospects (17, 19).

The most promising piece of equipment to bring minerals up from the deep-sea bottom seems to be the jet pump by which energy directed upward is transferred to the suction pipe by water jets. Using this principle, the "theoretical depth limitation" is "unlimited," but economical consideration so far limits the depth to 300 to 400 feet. So far, only about 1% of all minerals is dredged at sea.

Mentioning dredging procedures would not be complete without noting recent efforts by the Federal Water Pollution Control Administration to reduce or eliminate water pollution incidental to the maintenance of essential depths in harbors and channels by government and private interests. Under this program, plans for disposing polluted dredged material within diked areas has been implemented at many harbors and navigation channels in bays, waterways, estuaries, etc. An example is the discharge of materials behind diked areas at "Grassy Island" in the Detroit River. The situation has created many new and unpopular administrative and technical problems which are in the process of being solved.

Other materials like coal, grain, sulphur, phosphates, iron pellets, etc., are now transported in pipelines of still increasing capacity and length.

For further information on dredging and dredging equipment, the reader can consult *Proceedings of the 22th International Navigation Congress*, 1969 (18) and *Proceedings of the World Dredging Conferences*, 1967 and 1969 (23). A comprehensive bibliography on dredging is given by J.B. Herbich (8), and a *Directory of World's Dredges* (1970) has been published (22).

References

1. Bruun, P. 1967. "Bypassing and backpassing with reference to Florida." *ASCE Journal of the Waterways and Harbors Division* 93(WW2):101-28.
2. Cable, C.C. 1969. "Latest development in the design and operation of dredging equipment, in particular as regards suction dredging in very deep water." *Proceedings of 22nd Congress of PIANC* s II – s 1:115-32. Paris.
3. Deep Sea Venture, Inc. 1969. "Hugh commercial sea mining project announces." *World Dredging and Marine Construction* (March): 24-28.
4. Dixhoorn, J. Van, and Koning, J. de. 1969. "Latest development in the design and operation of dredging equipment, in particular as regards suction dredging in very deep water." *Proceedings of 22nd Congress of PIANC* s II – s 1:87-113. Paris.
5. Erickson, Ole P. 1963. "Latest dredging practice." *ASCE Transactions* 127(4):1-14.
6. Govatos, G., and Zandi, I. 1969. "Beach nourishment from offshore sources." *Shore and Beach* (Oct.):40-49.
7. Hensen, W., Kobus, H., and Saltzman, H. 1969. "Latest development in the design and

operation of dredging equipment, in particular as regards suction dredging in very deep water." *Proceedings of 22nd Congress of PIANC* s I – s 1:5-16. Paris.
8. Herbich, J.B., and Snider, R.H. 1969. *Bibliography on Dredging*. Report 112-CDS. Texas A and M University, College Station, Texas.
9. Huston, J. 1967. "Dredging fundamentals." *ASCE Journal of the Waterways and Harbors Division* 93 (WW3).
10. Ito, H., Matsuda, J., and Fuse, S. 1969. "Latest developments in the design and operation of dredging equipment, in particular as regards suction dredging in very deep water." *Proceedings of 22nd Congress of PIANC* s II–s 1:65-85. Paris.
11. Long, E.G. 1967. "Improvement of coastal inlets by sidecast dredging." *ASCE Journal of the Waterways and Harbors Division* 93(WW4):185-99.
12. Marine Technology Society. 1966. *Supplement to Transaction of the 2nd annual MTS Conference and Exhibit*.
13. Mauriello, Louis J., and Lewis, Caccese. 1963. "Hopper dredge disposal techniques and related development in design and operation." *Proceedings of U.S. Army Federal Interagency Sedimentation Conference.* pp. 598-613.
14. McKelvey, V.E., and Wang. F.H. 1970. *World Subsea Mineral Resources, World Dredging and Marine Construction, 1970 Directory* 6(2). Long Beach, California, World dredging Association.
15. McKnight, A.L. 1966. "Dredging–past–present and future." *Proceedings of Coastal Engineering Specialty Conference*. Santa Barbara, California. pp. 727-747.
16. Mero, John L. 1965. "The Mineral Resources of the Sea. *Amsterdam: Elsevier Publishing Co.*
17. National Academy of Sciences. 1967. *Oceanography, Achievements and Opportunities*. Printing and Publishing Office NAC.
18. Permanent International Association of Navigation Congresses. 1969. "Latest development in the design and operation of dredging equipment, in particular as regards suction dredging in very deep water." *Proceedings of 22nd Congress of PIANC* s II – s 1. Paris.
19. President of the United States. 1967. *Marine Science Affairs First Report of the President to the Congress on Marine Resource, and the Engineering Development*. Washington, D.C.: U.S. Printing Office.
20. U.S. Army Corps of Engineers. 1967. "Hopper dredge improvement program–study in the use of hopper dredges for beach nourishment." *Shore and Beach* (May).
21 Witt, W. 1968. "Druckwasseraktivierung vom sandköpfen." *Proceedings of the 5th International Harbor Congress* (5-W1-1). Antwerp.
22. World Dredging Association. 1970. "1970 directory of world's dredges and their owners." *World Dredging and Marine Construction, WODA*. Long Beach, California.
23. World Dredging Conference. 1967. *WODCON Proceedings of World Dredging Conference*. New York. WODA, Long Beach, California.

10 fishing ports small craft harbors

The world catch of fish is about 50 million tons per year. Japan, China, Peru and the USSR are the four leading nations, providing about half the total catch. Fisheries in the United States have suffered a decline during recent years, mainly because of the low catch of the Pacific sardine and the general depletion of West Coast fishing grounds. On the other hand, Alaskan fishing is increasing after it suffered a severe setback in 1963 from an earthquake and damage to port installations by the quake and by the accompanying tsunami.

The world's most important fishing waters include the North Sea, the North Atlantic, the Barents Sea, the North Pacific and the Pacific off South America. Very rich fishing waters, still in only limited use, are found off the Brazilean and Argentine coasts, in the Caribbean off Venezuela and in the Indian Ocean. The approximately 50 million ton annual catch amounts to only 2% of the assumed annual production of fish and other ocean animals. About 25 million tons of the very important animal proteins are needed each year for a population of 3 billion people, the approximate world population predicted for the next decade. By year 2000, world population will have doubled. However, the sea is able to produce 400 million tons of animal proteins per year.

Establishment of Fisheries

There are many different ways in which fisheries may be established, ranging from the most primitive to the most advanced procedures. Table 10.1 is a general outline of main features, distinguishing what may be classified as primitive to advanced fishing establishments, listing developed establishments as a medium situation. The corresponding boat, harbor, processing and transport facilities are also listed.

With respect to this grouping, it should be noted that the method of catch in itself may represent advanced technology, even if the catch is not processed, treated or improved in any way on the vessel. An example is the herring fisheries on the North Atlantic which produces large quantities of fish for processing into oil and fertilizer. The vessels are modern and equipped with acoustic fish finding facilities, and all kinds of navigation aids as well as unloading facilities. The Peruvian fisheries now produce tremendous quantities of fish mainly for industrial purposes. It is favored by the confluence off the northwest corner of Peru of the cold Humboldt Current and the warm current from the north.

The most advanced fishing establishment may be the factory vessel, which processes its own

Table 10.1. Fishing Establishments

Facility	Primitive	Developed	Advanced
Vessels approximate size in dwt.	Small boats 2-15 ts for nearshore fishing of one day duration. No treatment of catch on vessel. No navigation aids.	Larger vessels 15-150 ts for fishing of several days or a few weeks duration. Possible treatment of catch by icing. Navigation aids.	Vessels 150-2,000 ts or more incl. factory vessels. May stay at high seas for weeks. Possible treatment by icing and refrigeration plants. Navigation and fish finding aids. Factory vessel may be mother ship for smaller vessels.
Kind of catch and processing.	Shallow water fish for immediate consumption upon landing.	Fish suitable for industry, incl. canning and other processing plants.	Fish occurring in schools suitable for mass-processing preferred.
Harbor facilities needed.	Landing facility possible incl. jetties providing protection against waves and currents. Fuel and minor equipment facilities.	Landing facility providing protection against waves and currents. Loading and unloading facilities, piers, wharves, supply, repair and some processing facilities. Ship building. Transport facilities.	Landing facility providing protection against waves and currents. Loading and unloading facilities, piers, wharves, supply, repair and some processing facilities. Ship building. Factories for processing inc. cold stores, deep freezing, canning, curing, oil and fertilizer facilities. Major transport facilities. Special meteorological forecasting facilities for fishing.

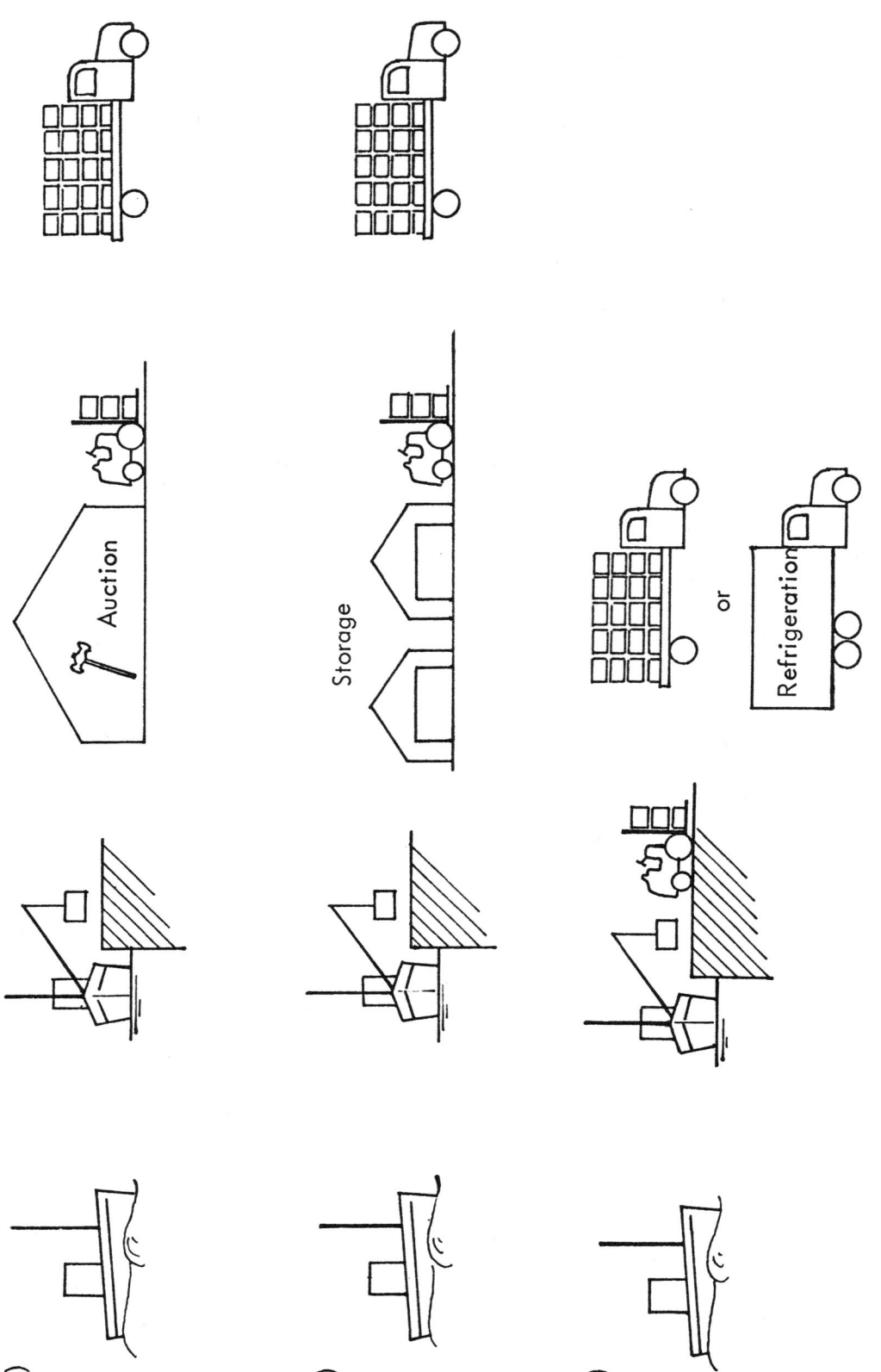

Figure 10.1. Steps in the transfer of the catch from the fishing vessel to wholesaler and/or consumer.

Figure 10.2. Small fishing boats: (a) Pacific Gilnetter (5) and (b) Norwegian shark.

catch mainly by freezing in blocks or through the land-based distributing agency after filleting directly for use by the consumer. Such factory vessels are mainly operated by Japan, the USSR and West Germany.

The schematic, Figure 10.1, indicates three main systems of fish transfer from fishing ground to consumer, each system representing an actual operating system as of 1969.

It is obvious that the landing (harbor) facilities needed for the three different kinds of operation are not identical. They must deviate considerably from each other in order to serve the needs in each particular case. Figures 10.2, 10.3 and 10.4 give examples of fishing vessels of various sizes corresponding to the distribution of Table 10.1.

Requirements of Harbor Facilities

Many requirements have to be fulfilled to create ideal conditions. One major requirement is that a clear separation should be established between facilities for unloading, parking, industry, repairs and supply. Other requirements include a number of the following factors.

Hydraulic

The harbor should provide safe mooring and/or berthing with only minor wave and current action. Short wind waves of periods up to 6 seconds should not exceed about 1/2 foot for smaller vessels and 1 foot for larger vessels at any berthing place in a fishing port. For periods above 6 seconds, wave heights should not exceed about 1/2 foot. Irregularities in the wave spectrum may cause harbor seiches, but as long as resonance does not occur, these seiches have very limited height (see Chapter 2). For resonance to exist, the basin(s) geometry must be rather regular, e.g., rectangular in shape, and elongated to maintain a seiche (3, 9, 10, 11). Waves of longer periods, i.e., 12 to 20 seconds (wave length $L = 5.12\ T^2$ in feet), may give rise to resonance seiches in basins of regular geometry and lengths which are equal to $n(L/4)$ with $n = 1, 3, 5$, if basins are wide open at one end, on $n = 2, 4, 6, \ldots$, if basins are closed or almost closed (Chapter 2).

Most fishing ports have an irregular shape because they are divided into many separate basins. Long period seiches of about 2 or 4 minutes occur in many natural harbors, e.g., in short fjords of

Figure 10.3. Medium size fishing boats: (a) Alaskan salmon purse seiner (5) and (b) Scandinavian North Sea trawler.

simple geometry, and may be of considerable magnitude, causing severe seiches. Some larger artificial (jetty-protected) harbors suffer from such surges, e.g., the harbor at Cape Town, South Africa (10), and the Port of Madras, India (3).

The basin entered first by the incoming vessel is located just inside the entrance. Fishing ports on the open shore almost always have a front port which is supposed to function as a stilling basin for wave action. An example is shown in Figure 10.5.

Figure 10.4. Large size fishing boats: (a) Californian tuna seiner (5) and (b) Scandinavian stern trawler.

If the harbor is located in a protected bay or fjord, the front port is less necessary and may be omitted. In the United States, because of the barrier and laguna shores, the general practice is usually to run two parallel jetties out into the ocean to simply absorb the wave energy by energy flux perpendicular to the direction of propagation of the wave action.

Figure 10.6 shows a model study on wave absorption, demonstrating the high efficiency of the parallel jetty entrance. Model studies at the University of Florida (2) have proven the great

Figure 10.5. Front ports at Skagen (The Skaw), Denmark.

Figure 10.6. Model study on energy absorption with parallel jetties at Horseneck Beach Inlet, Massachusetts.

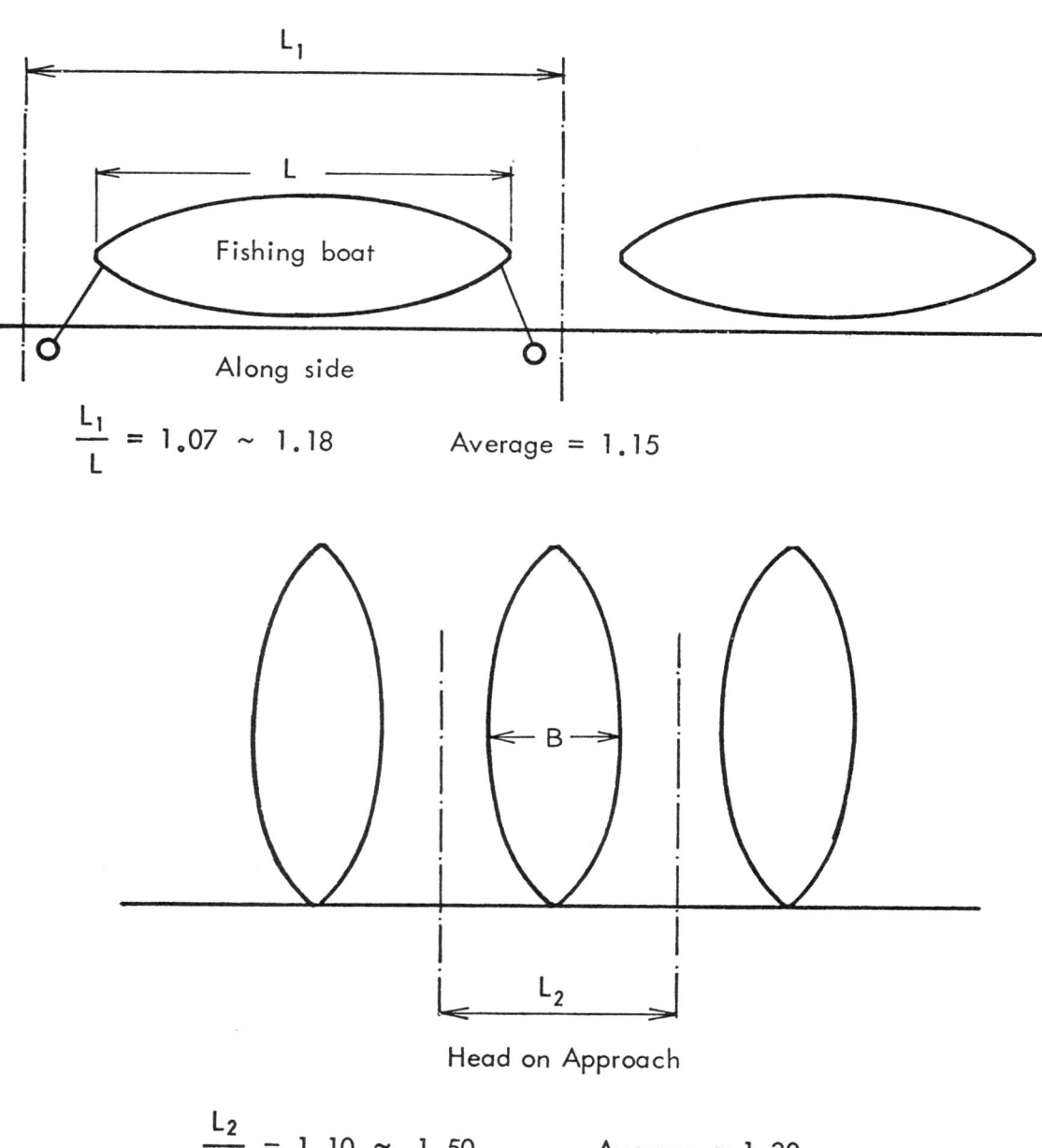

Figure 10.7. Berthing length for vessels (6).

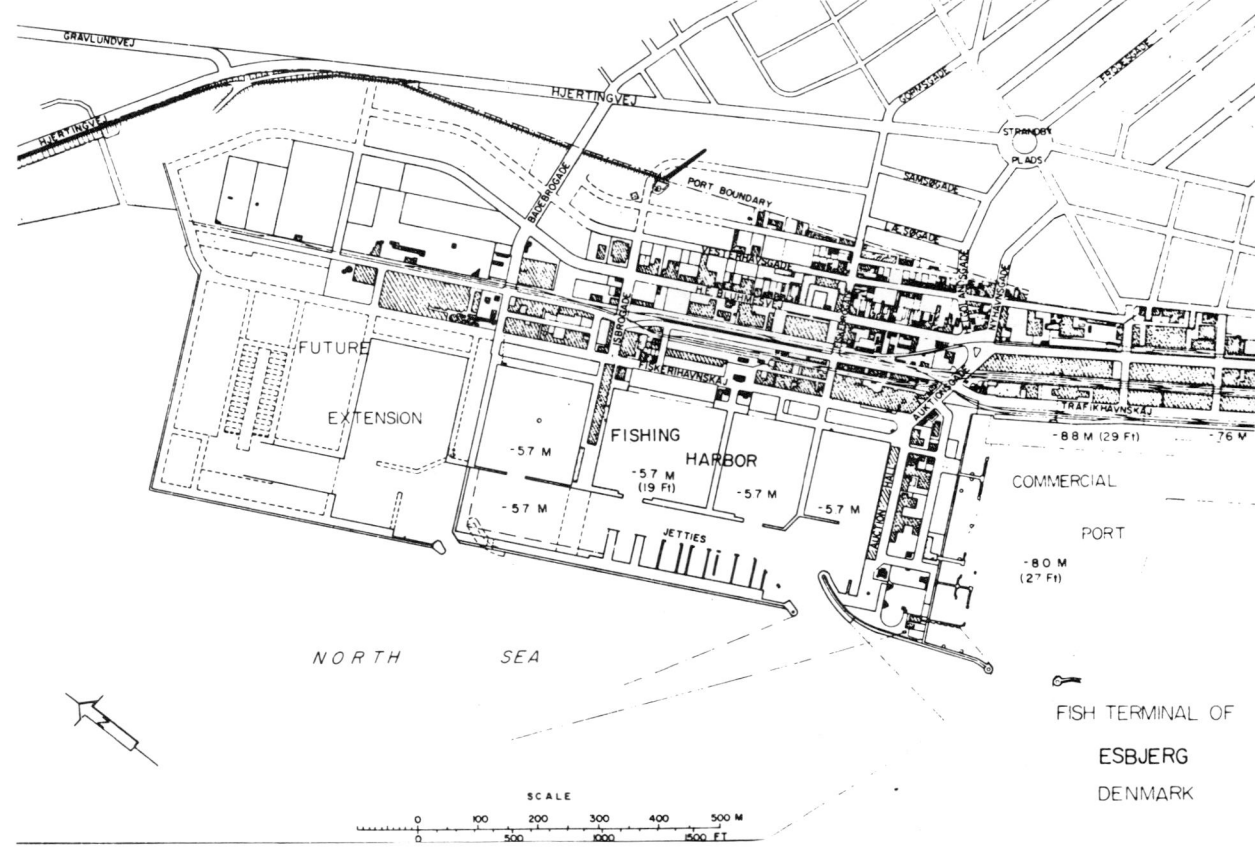

Figure 10.8. Fishing port at Esbjerg, Denmark (6).

efficiency of friction elements as baffles on parellel jetties. As already mentioned, wave heights exceeding 1 foot should never be allowed at any berthing place in any fishing port, but the allowable height depends upon the wave period. As soon as periods exceed about 5 seconds, wave heights must be still smaller.

Vessel size plays an important role, and mooring and berthing must be arranged so that a vessel's major movements caused by incidental seiches or surges are avoided in order to hinder collisions. Figure 10.7 (8) shows berthing length for vessels for perpendicular as well as parallel mooring. The short distances between the vessels call for very limited wave action. Higher wave action is permitted in basins which serve mainly as anchorage, but such basins usually have some piers or quay walls for berthing which do not permit excessive wave action. Entrance widths may vary from 20 to 30 meters for small fishing ports and from 60 to 120 meters for larger ports.

Size and Geometry of Basins

No rules exist for basin sizes in fishing ports, but a width of about 100 to 150 meters and a length of about 200 to 400 meters are common. Figure 10.8 shows the layout of the terminal at Esbjerg, Denmark and Figure 10.9, the terminal at Ymuiden, Holland. Figure 10.10 is a photograph

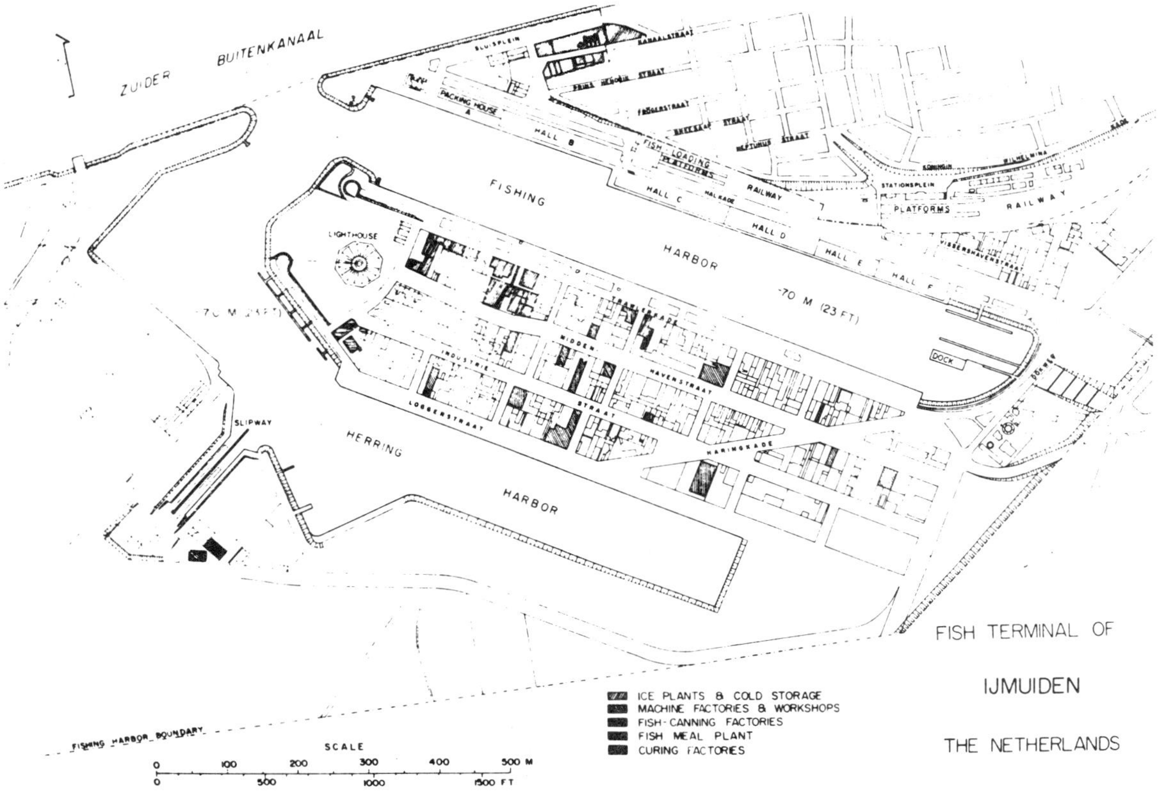

Small Craft Harbors 373

Figure 10.9. Fishing port at Ymuiden, Holland (6).

Figure 10.10. Fishing port at Boston, Massachusetts (6).

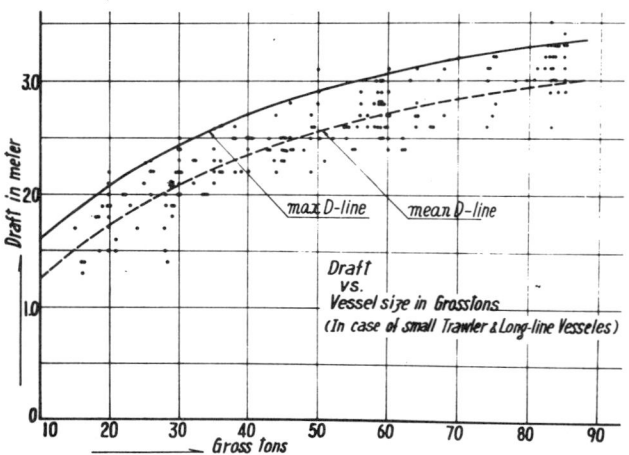

Figure 10.11. Average draft of vessels 10 to 90 BRT, brutto register tons (6).

of the fishing park in Boston, Massachusetts. For safety reasons, it is usually not desirable to have more than three to four vessels berthing side by side at a length corresponding to about 5 to 15 vessel lengths, depending upon the use of port facilities by the fishing vessels.

Depths correspond to the expected maximum vessel draft plus adjustments for maximum tides and their frequency and safety factor. Figure 10.11 shows the average draft of a vessel of 10 to 90 gross tons.

Quays, Wharves and Piers

In harbors where wave action is no problem, quay walls and wharves are of solid (impermeable) design, while piers may be of solid or open trestle design.

With respect to long waves, whether swells or 2 to 4-minute surges, it is of little or no importance whether quay walls are vertical or sloping, permeable or impermeable. However, sloping walls are desirable where short wind waves, such as those generated in a fjord, in the front port or in the harbor basin itself, can be reflected from a vertical or steep sloping wall. These waves would

Figure 10.12. Light wooden pier for smaller fishing vessels (Denmark).

break on a slope (about 1:2), and reflection would be small.

Figure 10.12 shows a light wooden trestle pier for smaller fishing vessels. Figure 10.13 is a pile deisgn for larger fishing vessels.

Necessary Handling Facilities

Table 10.2 is an outline of facilities provided in a base and supply port to accomodate fishing vessels and all their needs in a modern fishing port.

Small Craft Harbors 375

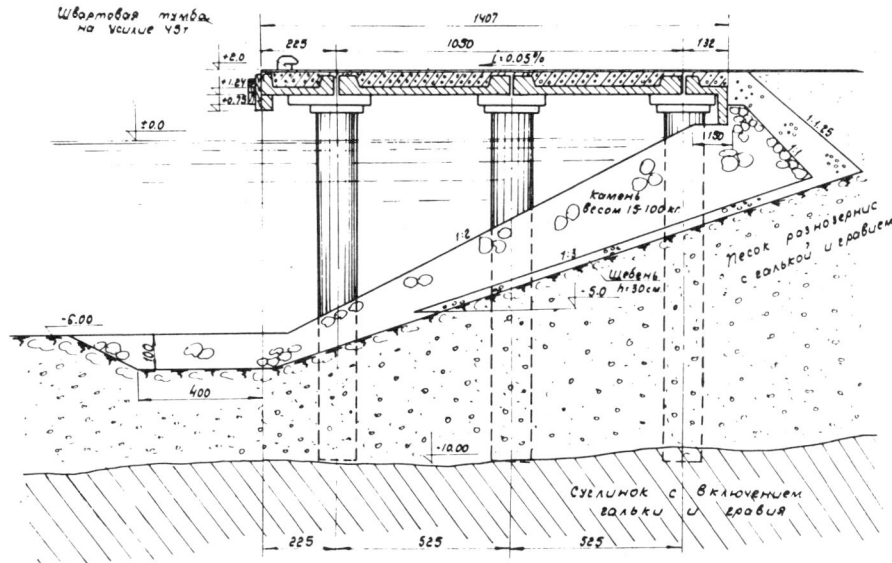

Figure 10.13. Quay wall for larger vessels, Russian and Norwegian design (7).

Table 10.2. Handling Facilities in Fishing Ports.

Vessel	Supplies	Repairs
Quay for unloading Quay for parking Unloading facilities Sheds for protection of catch	Fuel Oil Water Ice Fishing gear Engines Navigation aids	Hull Engine Radio Navigation aids Refrigeration

Main requirements for a landing port are that it be able to receive the necessary quantities of catch in a limited time period and that adequate transport facilities exist to move the landed quantities to the consumer and/or processing plants. Before the catch is transported away from the landing area, it has usually been sold through public auction, a cooperative fish market or individual agreements. It often happens that large quantities of fish are already sold before the fishing vessel reaches the landing port. Special conditions exist in the USSR when the catch is sold before it is caught.

Figure 10.1 showed various steps involved in passing a catch from the fishing vessel to the vehicle that carries the catch to the wholesale agency, factory, processing plant, etc.

The ultra-modern landing and auction terminal at Esbjerg, Denmark, has 18 separate berths arranged in a sawtooth geometry. Figures 10.14

376 Port Engineering

Figure 10.14. Landing and auction facility at Esbjerg, Denmark.

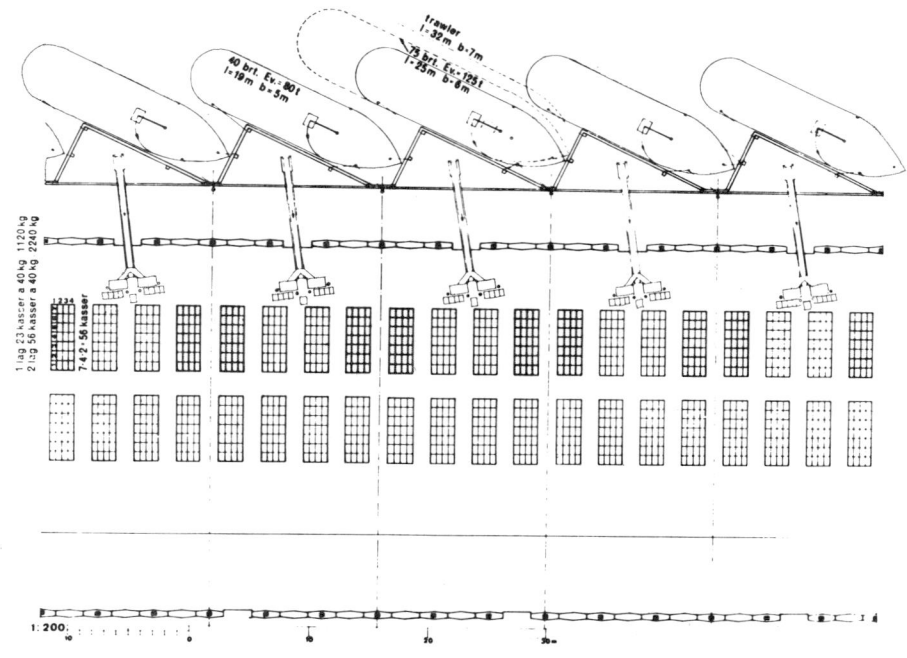

Figure 10.15. Layout of terminal at Esbjerg, Denmark.

and 10.15 show the landing and auction facility at Esbjerg, Denmark.

Processing Facilities for Fish and Fish Products

A great number of processing procedures and facilities exist, ranging from no handling other than icing before the fish is distributed to involved chemical processes for manufacturing oil, fish meal, medical products or to various curing, canning or deep-freezing processes. Figure 10.16 is a general outline of various procedures of handling the catch from the vessel to the wholesaler or the consumer. This figure gives only preliminary information on the great variety of processes associated with the fishing industry today.

The most remarkable development during the last decade was the rapid increase in the general consumption of canned shrimp and oysters and deep-frozen fillets of flounder, cod and haddock. The production of dried fish is still high in countries like Norway, Iceland and Canada, but a great deal of the production is for consumption in under-developed countries, where there is often a severe problem of financing the export. Therefore, it can be expected that industry in the future will concentrate mainly on canned and frozen products and in fertilizer and fish meal products. It is characteristic of this development that the FAO (Food and Agricultural Organization of the United Nations) is encouraging the establishment of fisheries mainly when the entire problem of catching, processing, transportation and consuming can be solved at the same time. If one link is missing, the chance of success is less or very questionable.

For detailed information on fishing ports, the reader is directed to References 6 and 7.

Marinas

The need for small craft marinas may be seen as a result of increasing prosperity in developed countries and the accompanying increasing need for recreational facilities. According to Falkner and Palmer (5), there are about 7 million small craft in the United States, including about a half million in California alone (1965). Even if a considerable part of these are very small and are stationed on rivers and inland lakes, in relatively well-protected waters, the demands for facilities on the seashore are already enormous and still increasing. It is no wonder that the American Society of Civil Engineers found it necessary to establish a Task Committee on Small Craft Harbor Development. A report by this committee (1) gives a considerable amount of guidance on a great number of aspects pertaining to the design of small craft harbors; so does the report on Coastal Harbors of Refuge prepared for the Division of Small Craft Harbors, California Department of Parks and Recreation (4).

Marinas in California (4) at Ventura (Figure 10.17) and Dana Point were built with federal assistance. Their size represents the importance of this new coastal and harbor engineering field.

Generally, the layout and design of such marinas follow the same main principles as those valid for larger ports, but some must be emphasized and some new requirements must be added.

Inasmuch as these are small vessels, it is important to keep wave action down to a minimum level. This can be done by narrow entrances and by front ports or front basins. However, local waves in the basins may arise. To keep them small, basins must be modest in size, and long, uninterrupted basins must be avoided. Wave problems can be solved by model experiments or simply by computation (see Chapter 2). Most small craft harbors have shallow depths, about 8 to 12 feet, and the requirement for full pollution control is therefore mandatory.

Most small craft harbors built at earlier dates had fixed, usually wooden, piers, which often had to be built of full creosoted timber to withstand attacks by marine borers and other animals. Many smaller piers are still built of creosoted wood. Covered berthing, quite common in Florida, is especially adaptable to fixed-pier construction.

Steel and aluminum structures suffer from corrosion in salt water regardless of coatings. Heavy steel sheet piling has been used occasionally for marinas with satisfactory results. The importance of the tidal variation for small boats and the

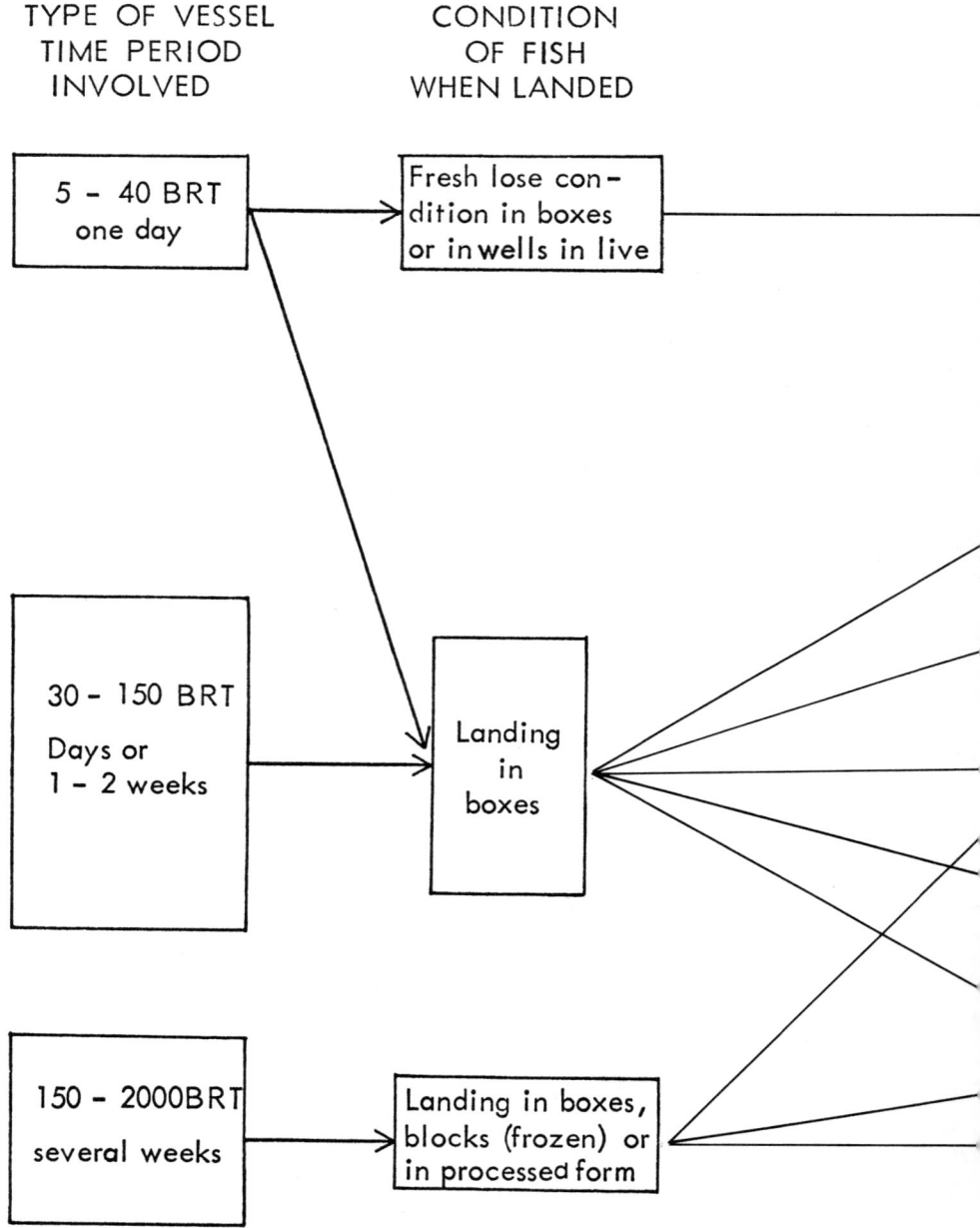

Small Craft Harbors 379

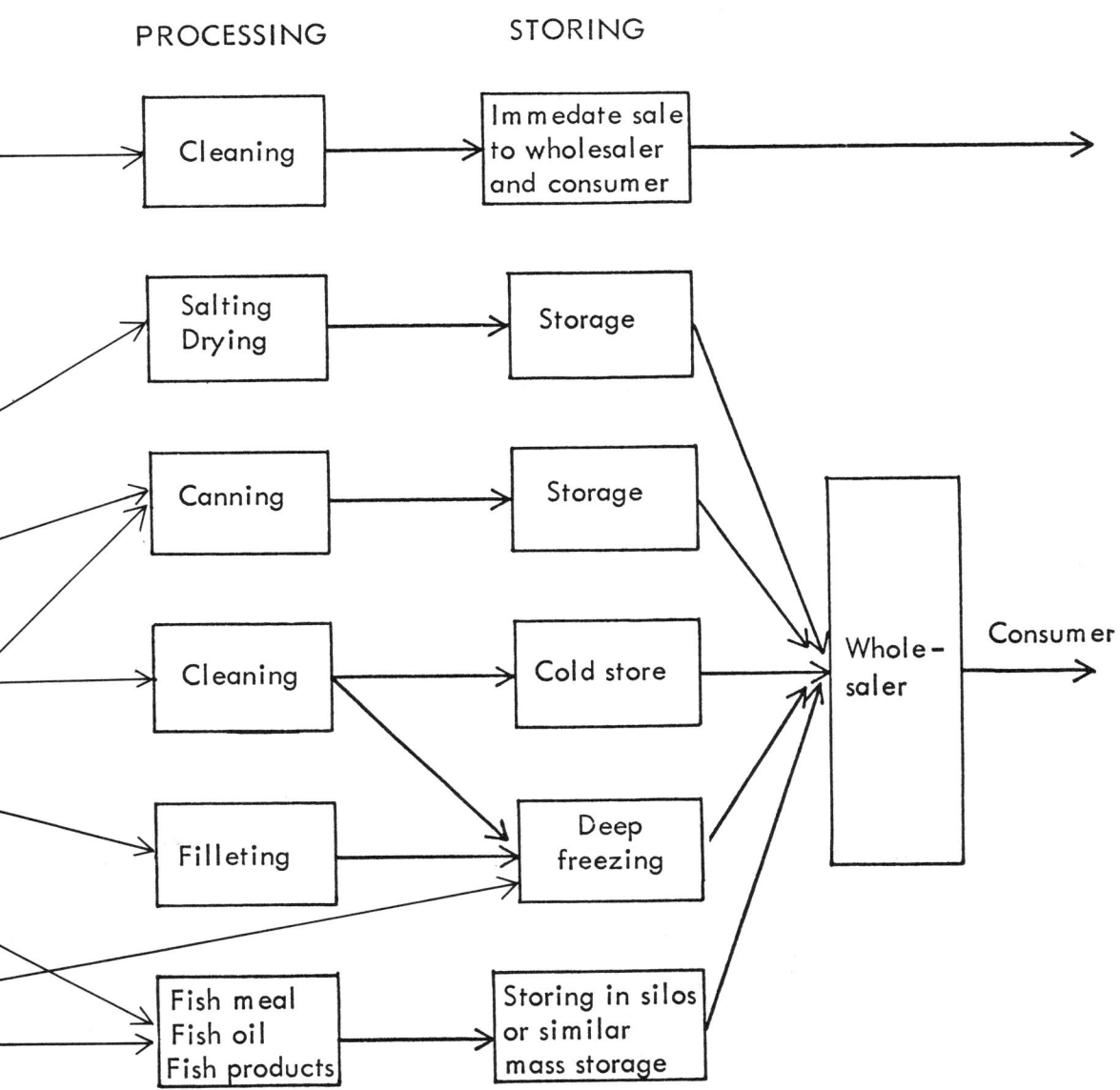

Figure 10.16. Various methods of handling fish from fishing ground to consumer.

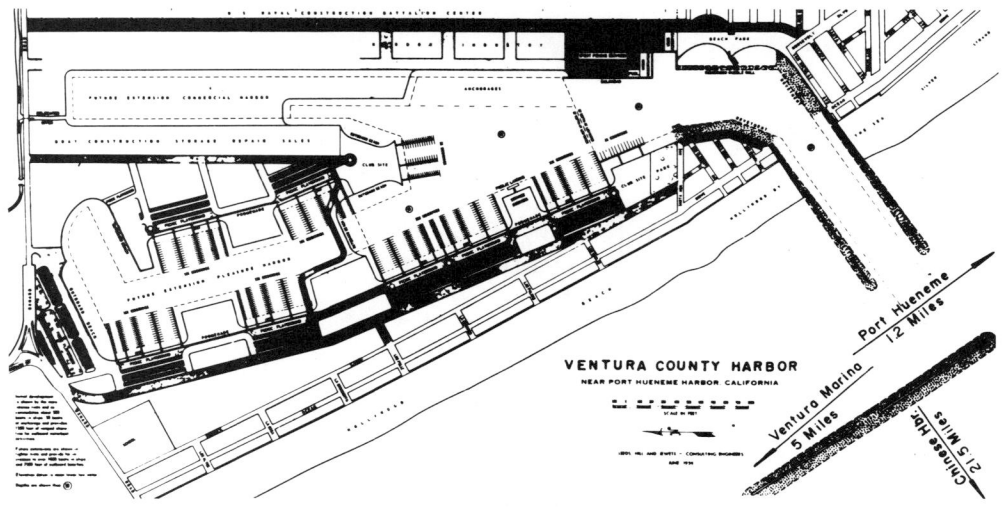

Figure 10.17. Ventura small craft harbor, California (11).

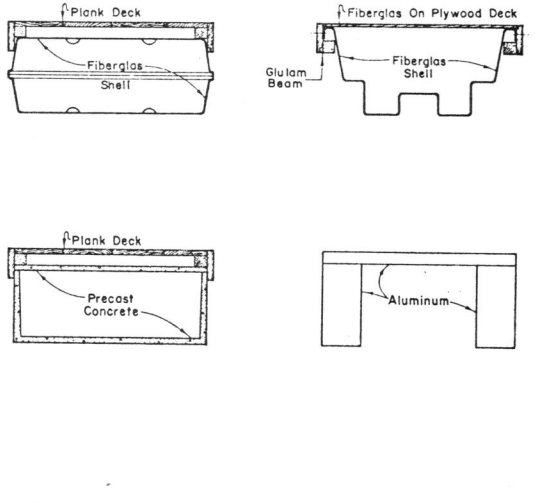

Figure 10.18. Various types of floats (1).

need for keeping the interior arrangement of basins flexible caused the development of floating berths, which have become more and more popular. A brief description of various types of floating berths is given in Chapter 4. Figure 10.18 shows various types of floating piers. For further information, see References 1 and 5.

References

1. American Society of Civil Engineers. 1969. "Report on small craft harbors." *ASCE Manuals and Reports on Engineering* 90(WW3):11-18.
2. Battjes, J.A. 1965. "Wave attenuation in a channel with roughened sides." *Engineering Progress at the University of Florida* 19(9).
3. Deacon, G.E.R., and Russell, R.C.H. 1957. "Origin and effects of long period waves in ports." *Proceedings of 19th International Navigation Congress* s II - c 1. London.
4. Division of Small Craft Harbors. 1963. *Interim Report on Coastal Harbors of Refuge*. Department of Parks and Recreation, State of California.

5. Falkner, F.H., and Palmer, R.Q. 1965. "Paper on planning of fishing ports." *Proceedings of 21st Congress of PIANC* s II - s 4:173-96. Stockholm.

6. Food and Agricultural Organization of the United Nations. 1966. *Landing and Marketing Facilities at Selected Sea Fishing Ports*.

7. Permanent International Association of Navigation Congresses. 1965. "Papers on fishing harbors and their installations." *Proceedings of 21st Congress of PIANC* s II - s 4. Stockholm.

8. Seo Goichi. 1965. "Paper on planning of fishing ports." *Proceedings of 21st Congress of PIANC* s II - s 4:101-24. Stockholm.

9. Wemelsfelder, P.J. 1957. "Origin and effects of long period waves in ports." *Proceedings of 19th International Navigation Congress* s II - c 1:167-76. London.

10. Wilson, B.W. 1953. "Table Bay as an oscillation basin." *Proceedings of Minnesota International Hydraulic Convention*. pp. 201-12.

11. _____, Hendrickson, J.A., and Kilmer, R.E. 1965. *Feasibility Study for a Surge-Action Model of Monterey Harbor, Cal*. Vicksburg: U.S. Army Corps of Engineers, Waterways Experiment Station.

appendix 1
pile foundations

By N. Janbu, L. Bjerrum and B. Kjaernsli.

Translated by Erik I. Hjeldnes, Technical University of Norway from *"Veiledning ved Losning av Fundamenteringsoppgaver" (Guide to the Solution of Some Foundation Engineering Problems)*. Publication 16, 1956, Norwegian Geotechnical Institute.

Usually the primary purpose of foundation piles is to transmit the loads down to underlying strata. When designing a pile foundation, care must be taken that (a) the loads on the single piles do not exceed the allowable loads; (b) the total load on a group of piles, considered as a unit, does not exceed the allowable load for the group; (c) the total and differential settlements of the pile group are harmless to the superstructure.

In principle the ultimate bearing capacity of a pile is equal to the sum of point resistance and skin friction or cohesion.

For piles in clay, the point resistance is small compared to the cohesive resistance. For piles in homogeneous sand, the contribution of the point resistance to the bearing capacity is rapidly decreasing with increasing pile lengths. For piles through compressible layers down to dense frictional materials, the point resistance will be the major part of the bearing capacity. This is also the case for piles to rock (see section on piles to rock).

In the following some methods are proposed for determining the ultimate bearing capacity and the allowable load on piles. A method is also given for estimating the settlement of pile groups. Only axially loaded piles are considered.

Piles in Clay

Ultimate Bearing Capacity

The static ultimate bearing capacity Q_u for a single cohesion pile in clay can be calculated from the undrained shear strength of the clay, provided the shear strength is known for a representative area and for a sufficient depth. (1).

$$Q_u = A_o s_o + 9 A_1 s_1 \qquad (A1.1)$$

where s_o = average undrained shear strength of the clay along the pile, s_1 = undrained shear strength of the clay at the pile point, A_o = pile surface in clay, A_1 = area of pile point.

Usually the first term of the formula is predominant. In cases where the pile is conical and the shear strength is varying with depth, the cohesive resistance ($A_o s_o$) should be calculated by dividing the pile into segments and summarizing the resistances from all segments. Concerning spliced wooden piles, with considerable change in cross-section at the splice, one should be aware of the fact that the cohesive resistance can be smaller than calculated. For the piles above the bottom pile, it is therefore recommended that the theoretical cohesion is reduced by 50%.

The method above is valid only for normally consolidated or slightly overconsolidated clays. In heavily overconsolidated clays, the actual cohesion along the pile will be considerably smaller than the undrained shear strength of the clay.

For a group of piles in clay, it is also necessary to calculate the bearing capacity of the group as a whole. This can be done by regarding the pile group as an ordinary foundation, and by taking into account the cohesion along the perimeter of the group.

Allowable Load and Factor of Safety

The allowable load, Q_a, for a single pile or a group of piles is determined by dividing the ultimate bearing capacity by a factor of safety, F, hence,

$$Q_a = \frac{Q_u}{F} \qquad (A1.2)$$

If the unit weights of the clay and the pile differ considerably, the difference between the weight of the displaced soil and the weight of the pile can be added to Q_u/F. In cases with uniform soil and well-investigated shear strength, a factor of safety of at least 2.0 should be used. One should apply a higher factor of safety, i.e., 2.5 to 3.0, if the soil is inhomogeneous and piles of different dimensions are used. When, in addition to soil explorations, reliable load tests are performed, one is allowed to use $F = 1.75$ in Norwegian marine clays.

The allowable load on each pile should not be greater than the load corresponding to the allowable stresses in the pile material. From an economical point of view, it will usually be correct to choose the pile length so that the allowable stresses in the pile material can be fully utilized.

Settlements

The settlements of single piles can be determined from load tests (see section on load tests on piles).

For pile groups in clay, the most important factors contributing to the settlement will be the compressibility and thickness of the layers below the pile points. The settlement calculations are performed in the same way as for deep foundations, assuming the net (additional) load to be uniformly distributed over the area limited by the outer pile points.

Piles in Sand

Ultimate Bearing Capacity

The ultimate bearing capacity, Q_u, for a single pile in sand or gravel can be calculated by using a pile driving formula, when knowing the permanent set of the pile at the end of driving, the dimensions of the pile and the applied driving energy (4).

$$Q_u = \frac{WH}{k_u \Delta s} \qquad (A1.3)$$

where WH = weight of hammer times height of fall of the hammer = applied driving energy; Δs = average permanent set per blow at the end of driving; k_u = dimensionless number (see Figure A1.1).

The guidelines for the detailed calculation are given directly in Figure A1.1 by means of an example. Practice has shown that the errors associated with this formula can be both positive and negative, and it is therefore advisable to measure the set per blow on several representative piles, so

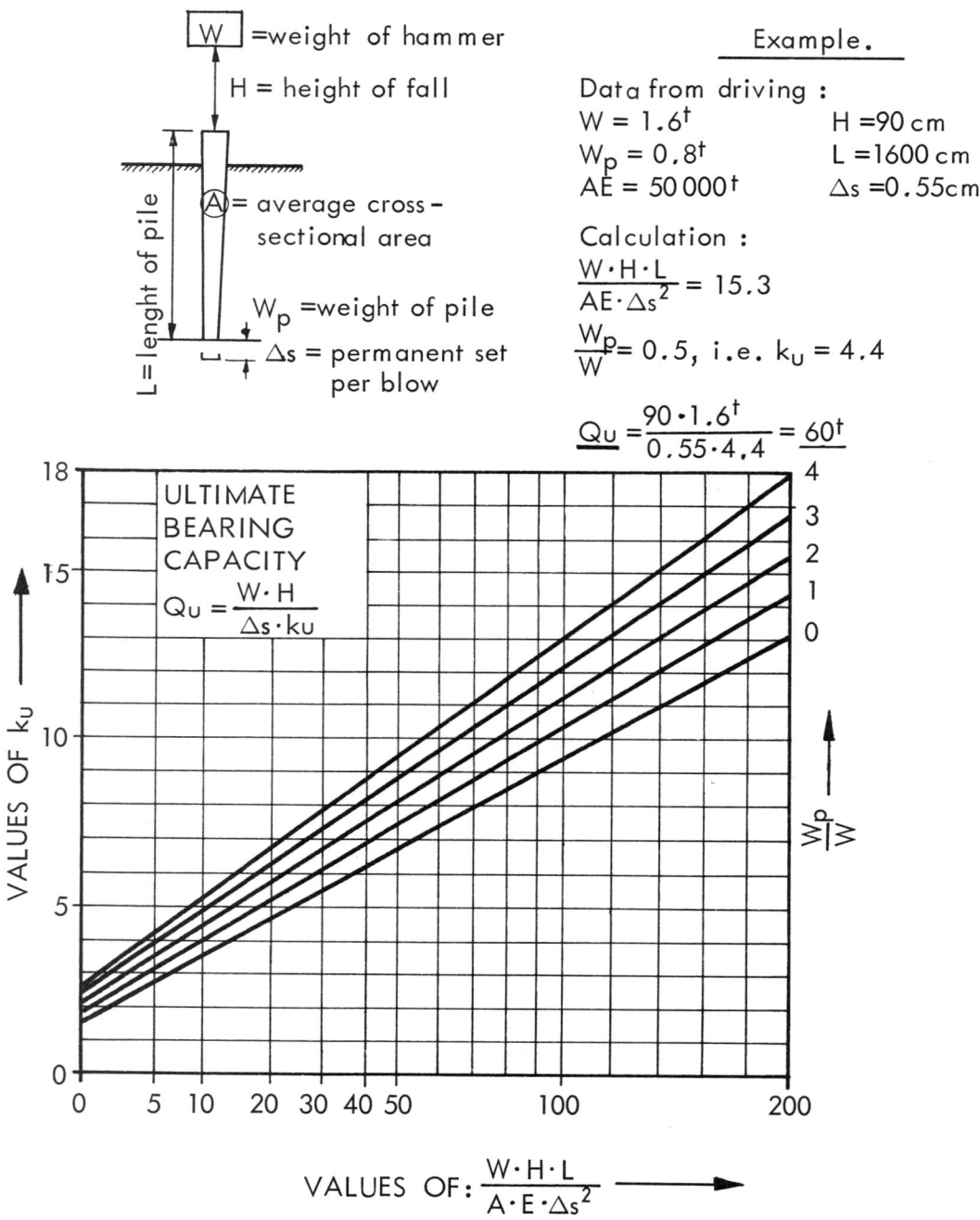

Figure A1.1. Calculation of the ultimate bearing capacity of piles in sand on basis of data from driving.

that the most reliable average value for the ultimate bearing capacity can be determined. Load tests (see section on load tests on piles) should be performed whenever possible as a control.

When driving concrete piles, it is of vital importance to prevent crushing of the piles by overdriving. Applied driving energy WH should not exceed a critical value given by the formula

$$(WH)_c = (\frac{L}{2500} + 2\Delta s)\sigma_o A \qquad (A1.4)$$

where σ_o = 100 to 150 kp/cm² for medium to good concrete. The remaining symbols are defined above and in Figure A1.1.

If a pile, acted upon by a driving energy $WH \leqslant (WH)_c$, shows a permanent set $\Delta s = O$ at the end of driving, the bearing capacity is at least equal to

$$Q_u = A_o s_o + 9A_1 s_1 \qquad (A1.5)$$

For a pile in homogeneous sand, an approximate forecast of the bearing capacity can be carried out, providing the angle of friction (ϕ) of the sand is known. For a given depth, the skin friction per unit area of the pile shaft can be calculated as the product of the vertical effective stress and ½ sin 2ϕ. The total frictional resistance is found by summarizing the skin friction over the whole pile surface. The point resistance is equal to the bearing capacity of the sand at the pile point times the point area. The calculation is carried out in the same way as for deep foundations, using a factor of safety F = 1.0.

In cases where Dutch sounding is performed, it is possible to determine both the point resistance and the frictional resistance for the applied equipment. On the basis of the results from such borings, an approximate estimate of the bearing capacity of a single pile can be carried out. When interpreting the results, one should be aware of the fact that the frictional resistance of the sound may be different from that of the pile (3).

Piles through compressible layers down to bearing strata of dense sand or gravel may be exposed to a downward drag (negative friction), if the weak layers consolidate and adhere to the pile surface. The force, thus created, acts in addition to the load on the pile top, and it must therefore be taken into account.

As an approximation, the ultimate bearing capacity of a pile group in sand can be calculated as the sum of the ultimate bearing capacities of the single piles. From a theoretical point of view, the bearing capacity of the group will be greater than this value, thus the approximation will be on the safe side.

Allowable Load and Factor of Safety

The allowable load, Q_a, for a single pile or a group of piles is determined by dividing the ultimate bearing capacity, Q_u, by a factor of safety, F:

$$Q_a = \frac{Q_u}{F} \qquad (A1.6)$$

If the ultimate bearing capacity is determined from Dutch soundings or calculated on the basis of the angle of friction of the sand or observations during driving, the factor of safety should not be less than 2.5. When load tests are performed on an representative number of piles, one may apply a factor of safety F = 2.0.

For piles in sand it will usually be economically correct to choose the pile lengths with a view to attain full utilization of the allowable stresses in the pile material.

Settlements

The settlements of single piles can be determined from load tests. When the average settlement for the single piles (δ_1) is known, the settlement of the pile group (δ) for the same load per pile can be determined from the diagram in Figure A1.2. The diagram, showing the relation between δ/δ_1 and the minimum width B of the group, is based upon observations from practice.

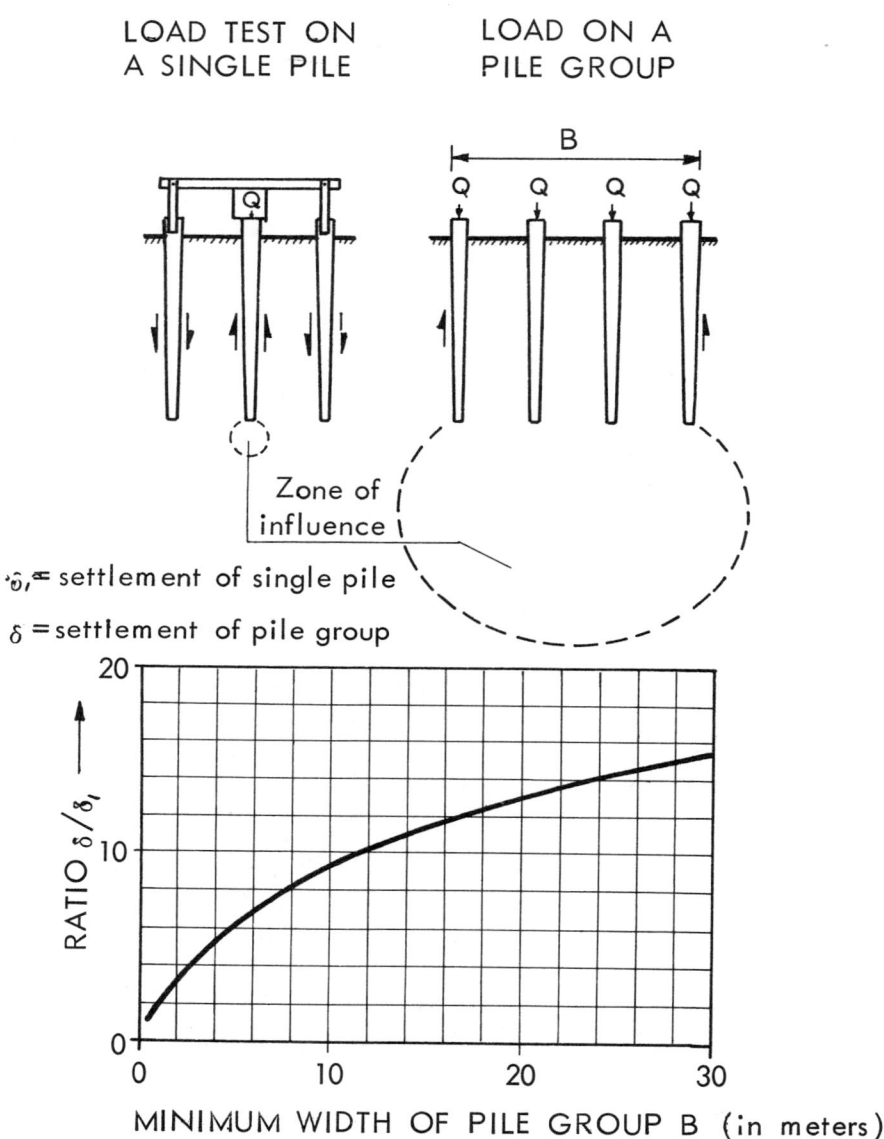

Figure A1.2. Settlement of pile groups in sand determined empirically from load tests on single piles.

Piles to Rock

The vital parameters for the working load on piles to rock will be the allowable stresses in either the pile material or the rock. The danger of buckling should be investigated by load tests when slender piles are driven through very soft clay ($s_u \leqslant 1$ t/m^2) down to rock or very firm layers (2).

During the last stage of driving, when the pile point is penetrating into the rock, overdriving must be avoided (4). In those cases where the main aim is to satisfy certain settlement criteria and to ascertain that the pile point is sufficiently fixed in rock for utilization of the allowable stresses in the pile material, it will be advantageous to perform dynamic load tests (5).

When steel piles are to be driven through marine sediments, one has to investigate the danger of corrosion. The choice of possible protective means against corrosion should be handled by specialists within this field.

Load Tests on Piles

Whenever a piled foundation is of great importance, the bearing capacity of the piles should be determined by load tests. Piles in sand can be tested a few days after driving. Piles in clay, however, should, at the earliest, be tested for bearing one month after driving. For structures where it is important that the piles are fully utilized, it may be necessary to carry out load tests at different time intervals after driving.

A load test is performed by stepwise loading; the load increments are chosen so that they represent say 10% of the estimated ultimate bearing capacity. At each load step, the load is held constant for say 10 to 15 minutes. When the pile load has reached about 60% of the estimated ultimate value, the load should be held constant for a longer period of time, say 1 to 2 hours. Thereafter, the pile is unloaded and reloaded, using the same load increments as for the first loading. The test is then continued by increasing the load stepwise up to failure. This ultimate load is kept constant long enough to ensure that the pile shows continued settlement. The settlements of the pile should be measured by dial gauges attached to a beam which is supported in such a way that it is not influenced by the movements of the test pile or the anchor piles.

References

1. Bjerrum, L. 1953. "Les pieux de fondation en Norvége." *Annales de l'Institute Technique du Batiment et des Traux Publics* 1953 (63/64): 375-76.
2. _____ *Erfaringer med Stalpeler (Experience with Steel Piles)* Norges geotekniske institutt. Publ. 23.
3. Eide, O. 1956. *Baereevne av Peler i Sand (Bearing Capacity of Piles in Sand).* Norges geotekniske institutt. Publ. 18.
4. Janbu, N. 1951. *Beregning av Frittstaende Pelers Bruddlast og Tillatt Belastning (*Calculation of Ultimate and Allowable Loads for Single Piles) Teknik Ukeblad, 1951, No. 26 pp. 507-15.
5. Vold, R. C. 1956. *Ramforsøk på Stalpeler (Tests on Driving of Steel Piles).* Norges geotekniske institutt. Publ. 17.

appendix 2
anchored bulkheads

By N. Janbu, L. Bjerrum and B. Kjaernsli

Translated by Erik I. Hjeldnes, Technical University of Norway from *Veiledning ved Losning av Fundamenteringsoppgaver"(Guide to the Solution of Some Foundation Engineering Problems)*. Publication 16, 1956, Norwegian Geotechnical Institute.

The bulkheads dealt with in the following are assumed to be anchored in such a way that they can rotate about the axis of anchorage. Bulkheads which are fixed at the top (so that certain restraining moments can be mobilized at this point) are not included.

Usually a distinction is made between dredged and backfilled bulkheads. Dredged bulkheads are here defined as bulkheads driven for their whole length in natural ground, whereafter the anchorages are installed and the earth masses on one side of the bulkhead are removed. Bulkheads, which are partly embedded in natural ground and on one side are supporting an earth fill, are defined as backfilled bulkheads. In practice the bulkheads very often will consist of combinations of these two types.

Basis for Design

The design of anchored bulkheads is here performed according to a method suggested during the last years. The method is partly based on the results of model tests and partly on previous design methods (2, 3, 4).

The following static quantities (see Figure A2.1) form the basis for design:

1. Necessary depth of embedment, D_n—to achieve a sufficient safety against failure and pressing-out of the embedded part of the bulkhead.
2. Maximum anchor pull, A_p—necessary for designing the anchorage.
3. Maximum bending moment, M_m—necessary for determining the cross-sectional area of the sheet piling.

The earth pressures acting on the bulkhead and the anchor (wall or plate) are determined in the same way and with the same factors of safety as for other earth-retaining structures (see Figures A2.2, A2.3 and A2.4).

Necessary Depth of Embedment, D_n

The key sketch in Figure A2.1a shows a profile through an anchored bulkhead. The earth pressure diagrams for a $c\phi$-analysis are also shown. Below the dredgeline, the resulting earth pressure is calculated as the difference between passive and

(a) Key sketch

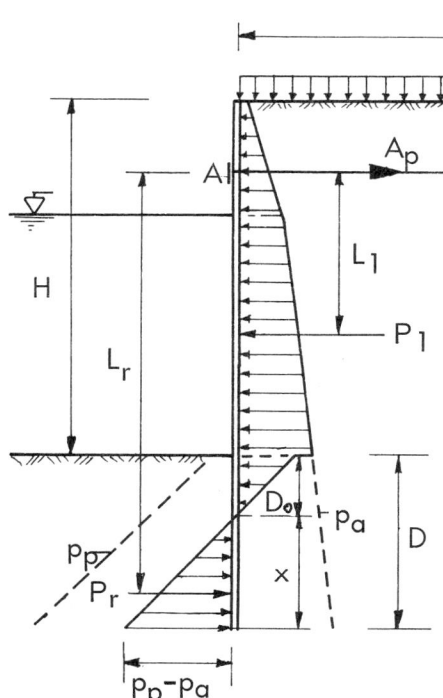

(a) Moment equilibrium around point A : $P_l L_l = P_r L_r$

Solved as regard to x gives x_n and hence

$D_n = D_0 + x_n$

(b) Horizontal equilibrium : $A_p = P_1 - P_{rn}$

where P_{rn} = reaction force corresponding to x_n.

(c) When x_n is known the maximum bending moment M_m in the wall is determined from the customary procedure of structural mechanics (M_m is acting at the depth where the shearing force equals zero). By all c_φ - analyses the final design moment M_d is calculated from the formula :

$M_d = \mu_d M_m$ where μ_d is taken from the diagram below.

(b) Bending moment reduction.

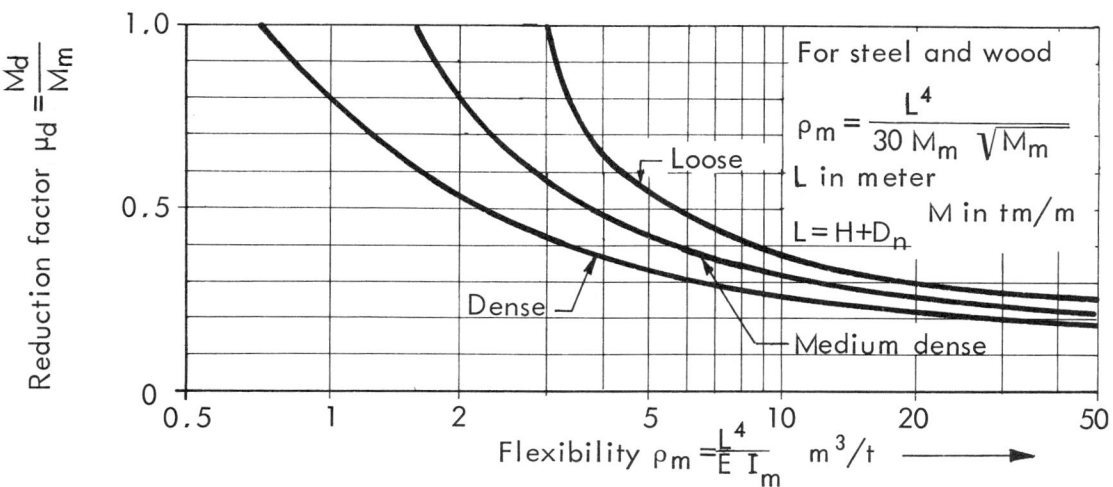

Figure A2.1. Anchored bulkhead: (a) key sketch and (b) diagram showing the moment reduction factor M_d.

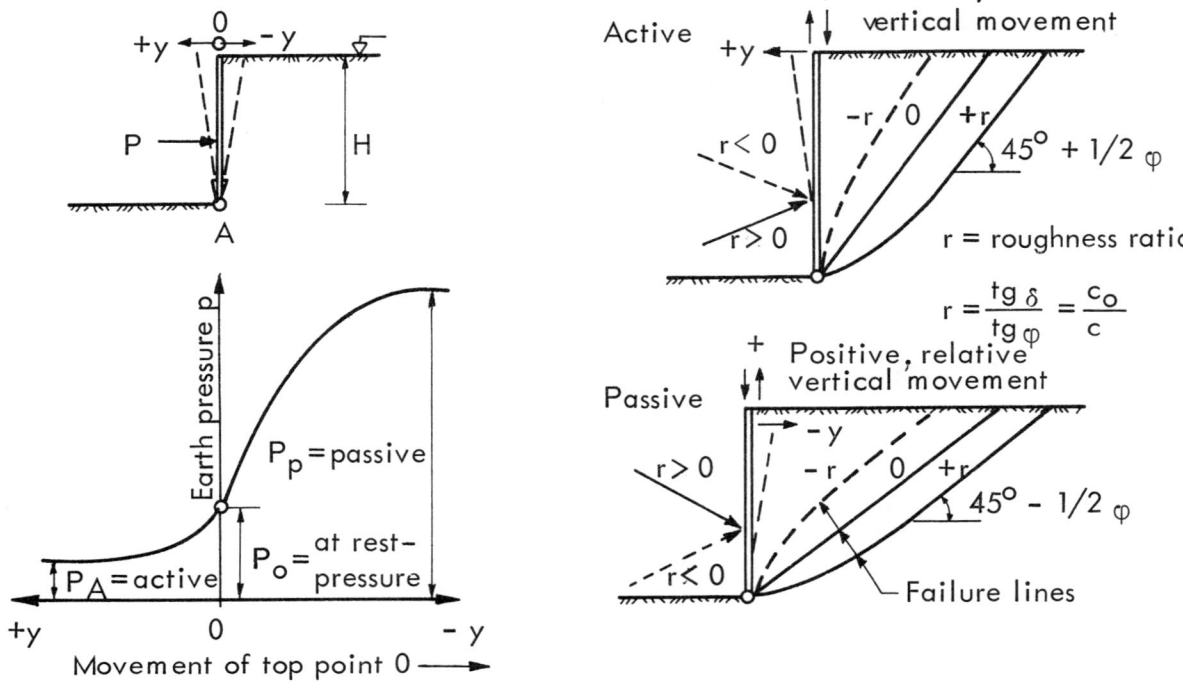

Figure A2.2. Key sketch illustrating active and passive pressure and the influence of the roughness ratio on the shape of the failure lines.

active pressure. Moment equilibrium around the anchor point A gives

$$P_1 L_1 = P_r L_r \quad \text{(A2.1)}$$

In this equation, both P_r, the area of the resulting earth pressure diagram on the front side of the bulkhead, and its distance, L_r, from the anchor point are functions of the depth, x, below the point of zero resulting pressure. By solving this equation with respect to x, one achieves the necessary value x_n and thereby the necessary depth of embedment, D_n:

$$D_n = D_o + x_n \quad \text{(A2.1a)}$$

In all cases where p_A and p_r increases linearly with depth, Equation A2.1 is a cubic equation in x, which can be solved in a simple way, say by substitution of trial values. For homogeneous sand and gravel and for all $c\phi$-analyses where $c = 0$, the equation has been solved once and for all, and the result is given in Figure A2.5a.

The calculation of the active and passive earth pressures is based upon a reduced shear strength, i.e., the shear strength of the soil divided by a factor of safety F. Hence, one automatically obtains a sufficient safety both against local pressing-out of the embedded part of the sheet piling and against total failure, provided there are no weaker layers below the lower end of the bulkhead.

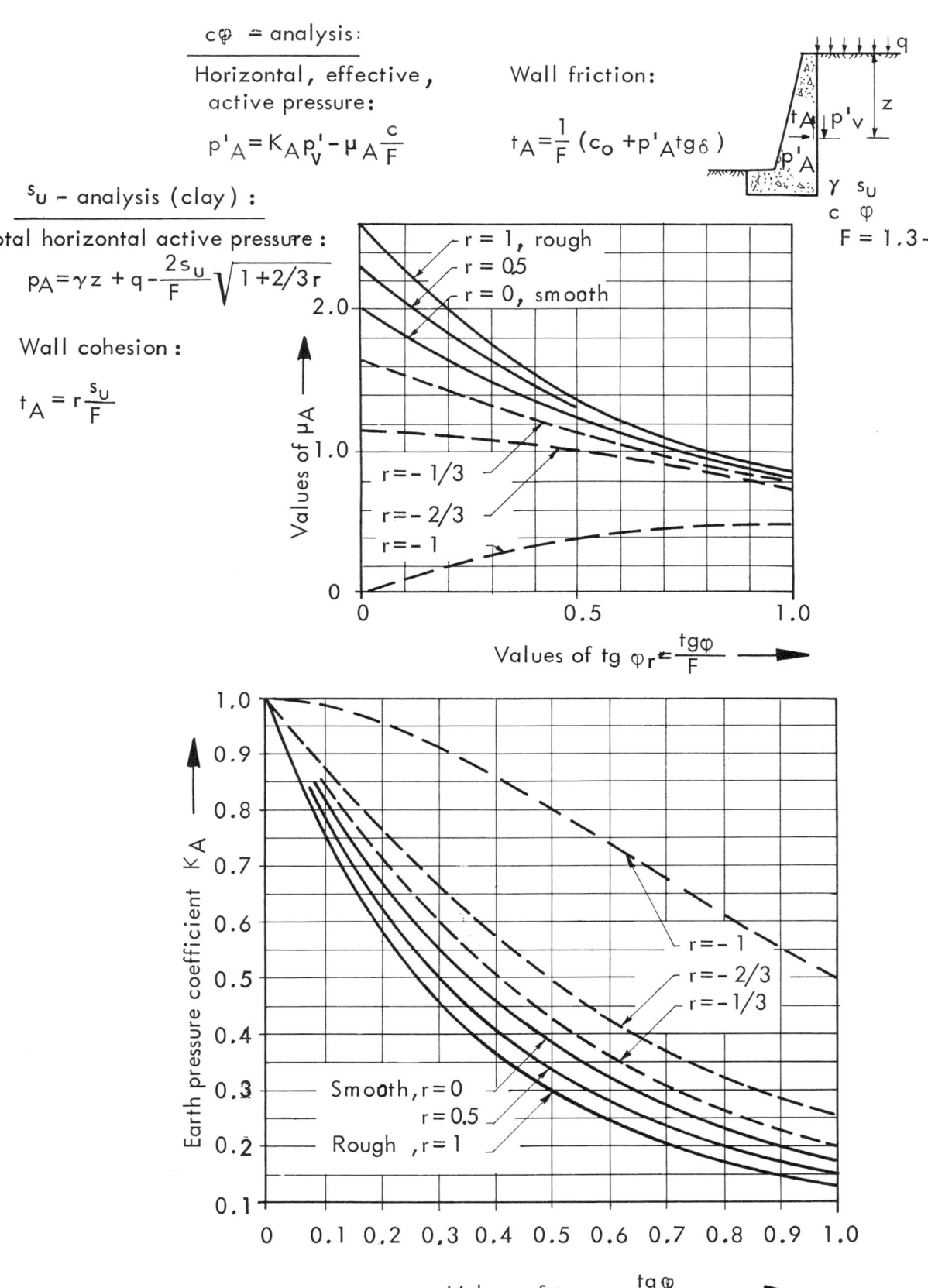

Figure A2.3. Analytical calculation of active earth pressure: vertical wall, horizontal soil surface.

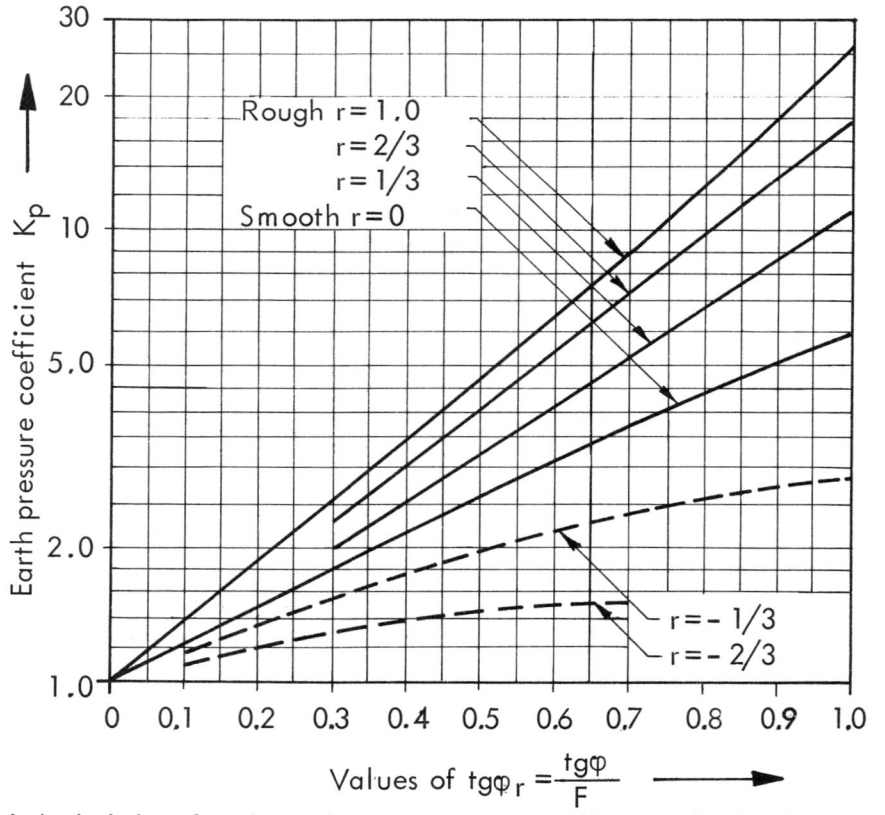

Figure A2.4. Analytical calculation of passive earth pressure: vertical wall, horizontal soil surface.

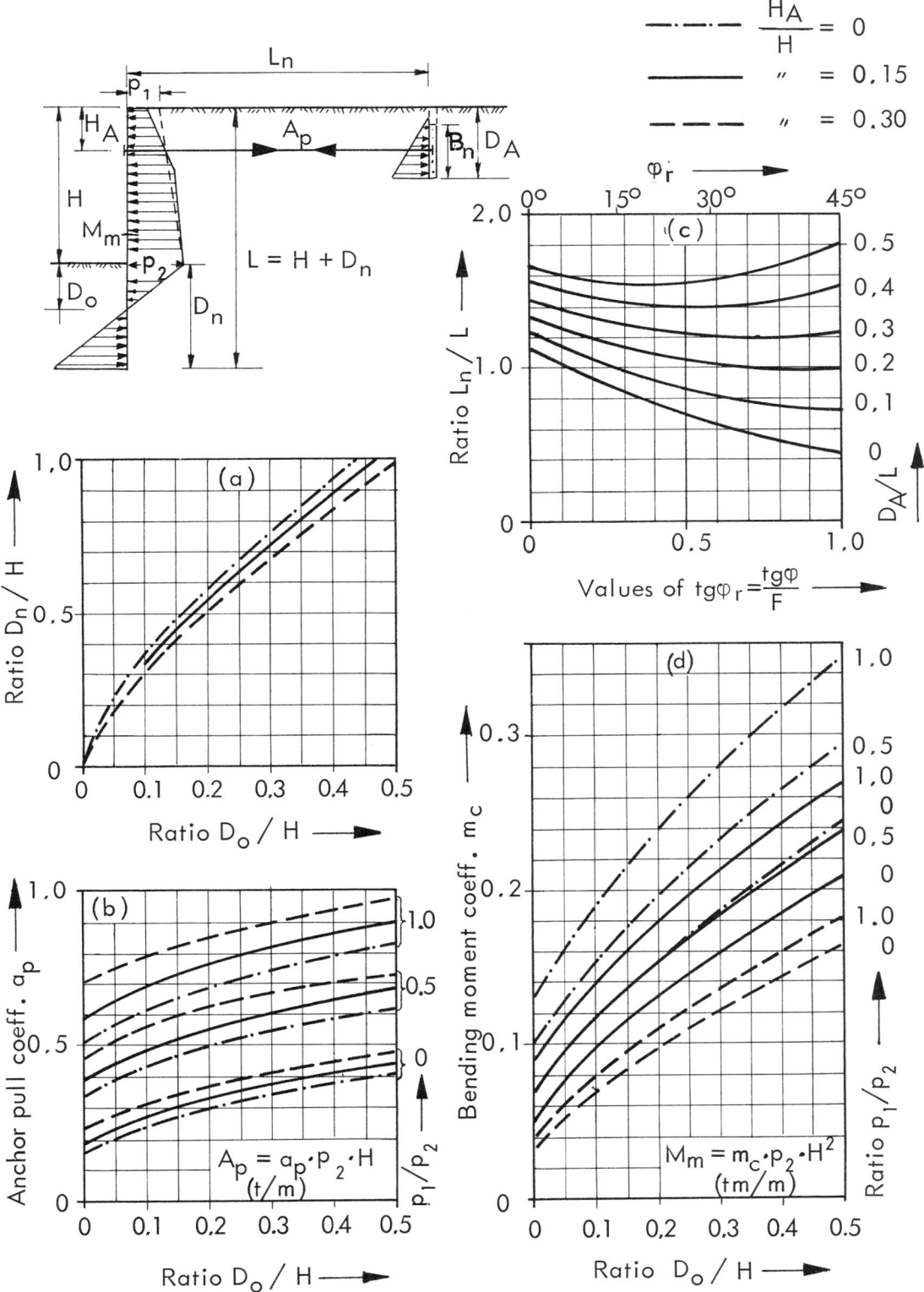

Figure A2.5. Diagrams for determining (a) necessary depth of embedment, (b) anchor pull, (c) necessary length of anchor rod and (d) theoretical maximum bending moment for bulkheads in homogeneous soils.

Anchorage

Once the depth of embedment is known, the anchor pull, A_p, giving the dimensions of the anchorage, can be determined from the condition that the sum of the horizontal forces is equal to zero:

$$A_p = P_1 - P_{rn} \qquad (A2.2)$$

Here, P_{rn} is the reaction force corresponding to the calculated x_n. The anchor pull has the dimension force per unit length of bulkhead.

For homogenous soils where $c = o$, A_p can be determined directly from the formula,

$$A_p = a_p p_2 H \qquad (A2.2a)$$

where a_p is a dimensonless parameter, given by the diagram in Figure A2.5b.

If the distance between the anchor rods is designated by 1, then each rod has to transfer a force $1 A_p$. Practical experience has indicated that failure or large deformations are mainly due to insufficient anchorages. It is therefore recommended that the cross-section of the rods is determined on the basis of the ordinary allowable stresses for the rod material. In addition, the fastening of the rod on to the sheet pile and to the anchor should be made slightly stronger than the rod itself. One should also see that the rods are protected against destruction by corrosion.

The dimensions of the anchor walls or slabs ("deadmen") are governed by the anchor pull which they have to resist. Consequently, the depth, D_A, of the anchor wall is determined from the condition that the area of the resulting earth pressure diagram ($p_p - p_A$) should be equal to the anchor pull. Usually it is considered allowable in these calculations to use the full height of the resulting pressure diagram when $B_n \geqslant 2/3\, D_A$ (see Figure A2.1a). The roughness ratio ($r = tg\delta/tg\phi$) used in calculating the earth pressures on both sides of the anchor wall must not be greater than what is consistent with the conditions of vertical equilibrium of the wall or the slab.

When the anchor rods are horizontal, the maximum roughness ratio for the anchor wall is given by

$$r \leqslant (W_A/A_p)(F/tg\phi) \qquad (A2.3)$$

where W_A = weight of anchor wall and the overlying soil and F is the factor of safety.

Usually the length, L_n, of the anchor rods has been determined from the condition that the active zone behind the bulkhead and the passive zone in front of the anchor wall should not overlap each other. In most cases, the different available methods lead to nearly the same values of L_n. For uniform soil and for $r = 0.3$ to 0.7, an approximate value of the length, L_n, of the anchor rod can be found from Figure A2.5c, when first the depth of embedment, D_n, and the depth of the anchor wall, D_A, are determined.

Design of the Sheet Pile

The first step in determining the necessary cross-section of the sheet piles is calculating the maximum bending moment M_m. This calculation (free-earth-support method) is based upon the customary procedure of structural mechanics, considering the sheet pile as a beam acted upon by the active and passive earth pressures and the anchor pull (M_m is acting at the depth where the shearing force equals zero).

In the cases where the soil behind the bulkhead consists of homogeneous sand, it is possible to determine M_m directly by using the diagram in Figure A2.5d and the formula:

$$M_m = m_c p_2 H^2 \qquad (A2.4)$$

The symbols used are shown in the figure.

For a long time it has been a well-known fact that the maximum bending moment determined in this way is usually greater than the maximum moment really acting in the sheet pile wall. Theoretical investigations (1) and model tests (2, 4), especially those conducted during the last years, have contributed to a better understanding of this problem. The results from model tests in sand have shown that the ratio between real and theoretical bending moment decreases with increasing flexibility of the sheet pile, ρ:

$$\rho = L^4/EI \quad (A2.5)$$

where E = modulus of elasticity of the sheet pile material; I = moment of inertia (per unit length of sheet pile); $L = H + D_n$ = total length of sheet pile.

If the calculation is based directly on the test results (2), the dimensions of the sheet pile has to be determined by a method of successive approximations. First, one calculates the theoretical maximum bending moment and determines the corresponding sheet pile dimensions. Then the flexibility of this sheet pile can be determined, whereafter a reduced bending moment can be obtained from the experimental curves. This reduced moment leads to a new sheet pile dimension, a new flexibility and another reduction factor, etc.

The above mentioned iteration procedure leads to a convergent value of the bending moment, and this value has *here been approximately determined once and for all*. The necessary calculations of this convergency are based upon an estimated ratio between allowable stress and modulus of elasticity for the sheet pile material.

The procedure for determining the sheet pile dimensions starts with calculating the theoretical maximum bending moment, M_m, obtained by the free-earth-support method, as described before. The final design moment is then obtained *directly* by the formula,

$$M_d = \mu_d \cdot M_m \quad (A2.6)$$

where the reduction factor, μ_d, depends on the flexibility of the sheet pile,

$$\rho_m = L^4/n\, M_m \sqrt{M_m} \quad (A2.7)$$

Here the sheet pile length, L, should be given the dimension meter and M_m, the dimension metric ton-meters per meter. The dimensionless number, n, is found to have a value around 30 for steel or wooden sheet piles and about 120 for concrete sheet piles. Figure A2.1b gives the reduction factor, μ_d, as a function of ρ_m and the relative soil density.

Usually the axial stresses in the sheet pile are ignored; thus, the necessary section modulus, W can be determined from the classical formula,

$$W \geqslant M_d/\sigma_a \quad (A2.8)$$

where σ_a = allowable stress in the sheet pile material.

Normally it is correct, from an economical point of view, to utilize the bending strength of the sheet pile material to the same degree as the shear strength of the soil. Hence for steel, the allowable stress can be chosen as high as 2/3 of the yield stress.

For steel sheet piles where the interlocks are located in the neutral axis, one should be aware of the fact that the effective section modulus is smaller than the value corresponding to rough interlocking but greater than the value corresponding to smooth interlocking. It is very difficult to calculate the effective section modulus exactly, and for very flexible sheet piles (great ρ_m), it is therefore suggested that, in Equation A2.8 giving the necessary section modulus, the allowable steel stress is taken as ½ of the yield stress. If so, and when using standard tables to obtain a suitable sheet pile dimension, the interlocks can be considered as rough.

In cases where a possible corrosion might cause a reduction in the cross-sectional area, this should be taken into consideration during design.

Bulkheads in Sand

The earth pressures on both sides of the sheet pile are calculated according to classical earth pressure theory with the necessary factors of safety (see Figures A2.3 and A2.4).

For bulkheads with free water on the front side, the calculations must be based upon the stage where the water level is at its lowest (LWL). If in this stage there is a difference (tidal lag), H_u, between the groundwater level (GWL) inside the wall

396 Port Engineering

Figure A2.6, Example A2.1: computation procedure for an anchored bulkhead in sand.

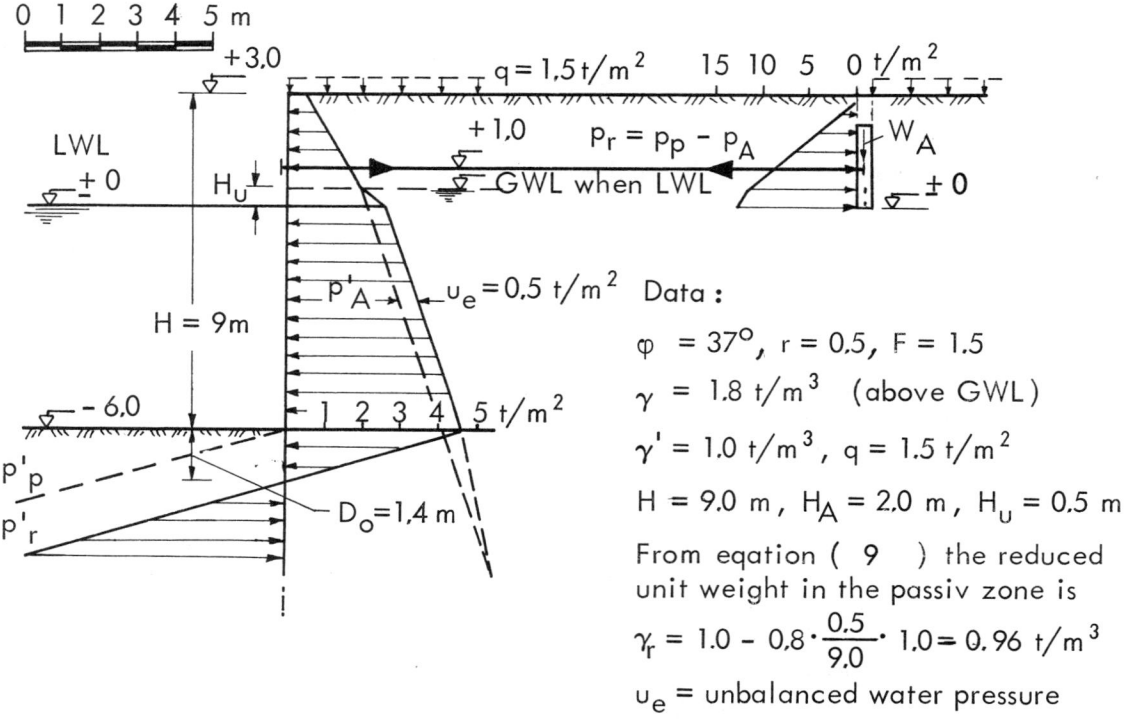

Data:

$\varphi = 37°$, $r = 0.5$, $F = 1.5$
$\gamma = 1.8 \text{ t/m}^3$ (above GWL)
$\gamma' = 1.0 \text{ t/m}^3$, $q = 1.5 \text{ t/m}^2$
$H = 9.0 \text{ m}$, $H_A = 2.0 \text{ m}$, $H_u = 0.5 \text{ m}$

From eqation (9) the reduced unit weight in the passiv zone is

$$\gamma_r = 1.0 - 0.8 \cdot \frac{0.5}{9.0} \cdot 1.0 = 0.96 \text{ t/m}^3$$

u_e = unbalanced water pressure

Earth pressure calculations for sheet pile wall (pressure in t/m²)							
	Active zone			Passive Zone		Resulting pressure	Remarks
Elevation	p'_v	p'_A	u_e	p'_v	p'_p	$p'_A + u_e - p'_p$	
+ 3.0	1.5	0.50					$tg\phi/F = 0.75/1.5 = 0.5$
+ 0.5	6.0	1.98	0				when $r = 0.5$. then
± 0.0	6.5	2.14	0.5				$K_A = 0.33$. $K_p = 3.7$
− 6.0	12.5	4.12	0.5	0	0	+ 4.62	(Figures A2.3 and A2.4)
− 9.0	15.5	5.11	≈0	2.88	10.65	− 5.54	

Estimated $W_A = 2.0$ t/m. Roughness ratio for anchor wall, equation (3)

$$r \leq \frac{2.0 \cdot 1.5}{17.6 \cdot 0.75} = 0.23 \text{ chosen } r = 0.2$$

Anchored Bulkheads

Earth pressure calculations for anchor wall (pressure in t/m²)						
	Active		Passive		Resulting pressure	Remarks
Elevation	p'_v	p'_A	p'_v	p'_p	$p'_p - p'_A$	
+ 3.0	1.5	0.60	0	0	− 0.60	When tgϕ/F = 0.5 and
+ 0.5	6.0	2.15	4.5	13.95	11.80	r = 0.2 then
− 0.5	7.0	2.50	5.5	17.05	14.55	K_a = 0.36. K_p = 3.1
						(Figures A2.3 and A2.4)

Necessary depth of embedment
Since $D_0/H = 0.155$ and H_A/H - 0.22, the necessary depth of embedment is determined from Figure A2.5a as: $D_n = 0.44 \cdot H \approx 4.0$ m $\supset$:L = 13.0 m

The anchorage
The anchor pull: $A_p = P_1 - P_{rn} = (29.1-11.5)$t/m = 17.6 t/m (From Figure A2.5b one gets: A_p = 0.43 · 4.62 · 9 t/m = 17.8 t/m). Necessary rod cross section: (17600/1400) cm²/m = 12.6 cm²/m. The resulting pressure for the anchor wall is calculated in the table above, whereof D_A = 3.0 m if the resulting force shall equalize A_p (full height of pressure diagram). Since D_A/L = 0.23 and tgϕ/F = 0.5 the necessary length of anchor rod, Figure A2.5c, is: $L_n = 1.10 \cdot L \approx 14.3$ m

Bending moment and necessary section modulus
Since $D_0/H = 0.155$, $H_A/H = 0.22$ and $p_1/p_2 \approx 0.26$, Figure A2.5d gives m_c = 0.105. Maximum theoretical bending moment: $M_m = 0.105 \cdot 4.62 \cdot 9^2$ tm/m = 39.3 tm/m
With flexibility: $\rho_m = 13^4/30 \cdot 39.3 \sqrt{39.3} = 3.85$ (m³/t) Figure A2.1b gives for "medium dense" μ_d = 0.50
Design bending moment: $M_d = 0.50 \cdot 39.3$ tm/m = 19.65 tm/m
Necessary effective section modulus: W = (1965000/1800) cm³/m = 1090 cm³/m

Figure A2.6, Example A2.1 continued.

and the outer water level (LWL), the unbalanced water pressure must be added to the effective earth pressure in the active zone, as shown in Example A2.1. Due to the seepage caused by the tidal lag, H_u, the seepage force will increase the unit weight of the soil in the active zone and reduce it in the passive zone. The change in unit weight is just equal to the seepage force = $i\gamma_w$, where i is the hydraulic gradient and γ_w, the unit weight of water. The gradient i can be determined from a flow net. However, the influence of the seepage froce can in many cases be taken into account approximately by using a reduced unit weight, γ_r, in the passive zone, where γ_r is given by the equation,

$$\gamma_r = \gamma' - 0.8(H_u/H)\gamma_w \qquad (A2.9)$$

Here γ' = the buoyant unit weight of the soil.
For backfilled bulkheads, where the backfill is placed by pouring in a mixture of sand and water, the earth pressure can be considerably greater dur-

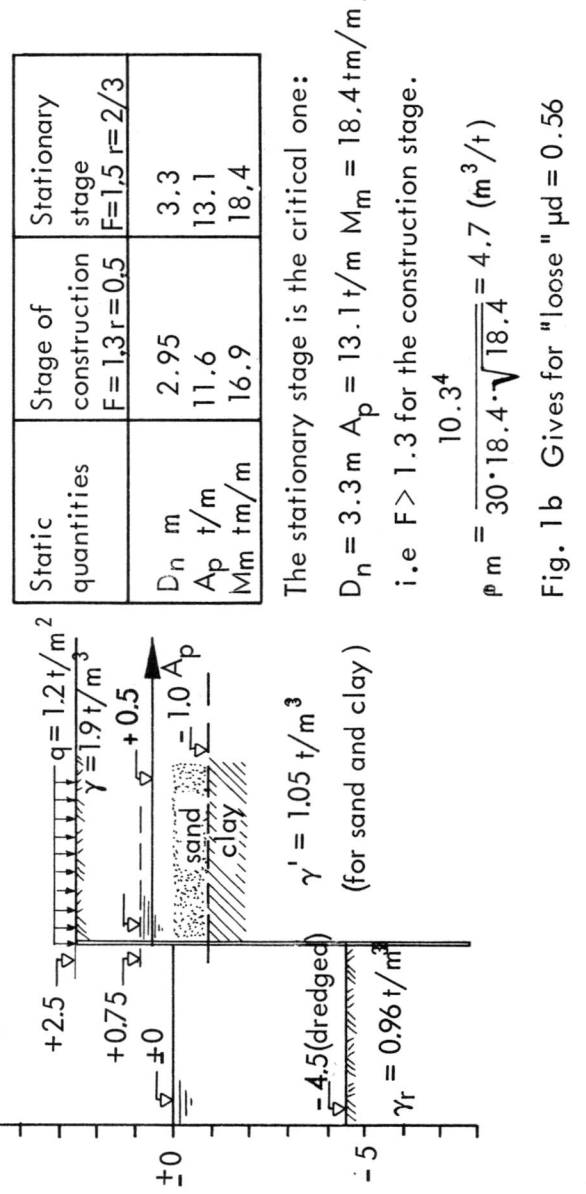

Figure A2.7, Example A2.2: computation procedure for an anchored bulkhead in clay, the earth pressures determined both from s_u-analysis and $c\phi$-analysis.

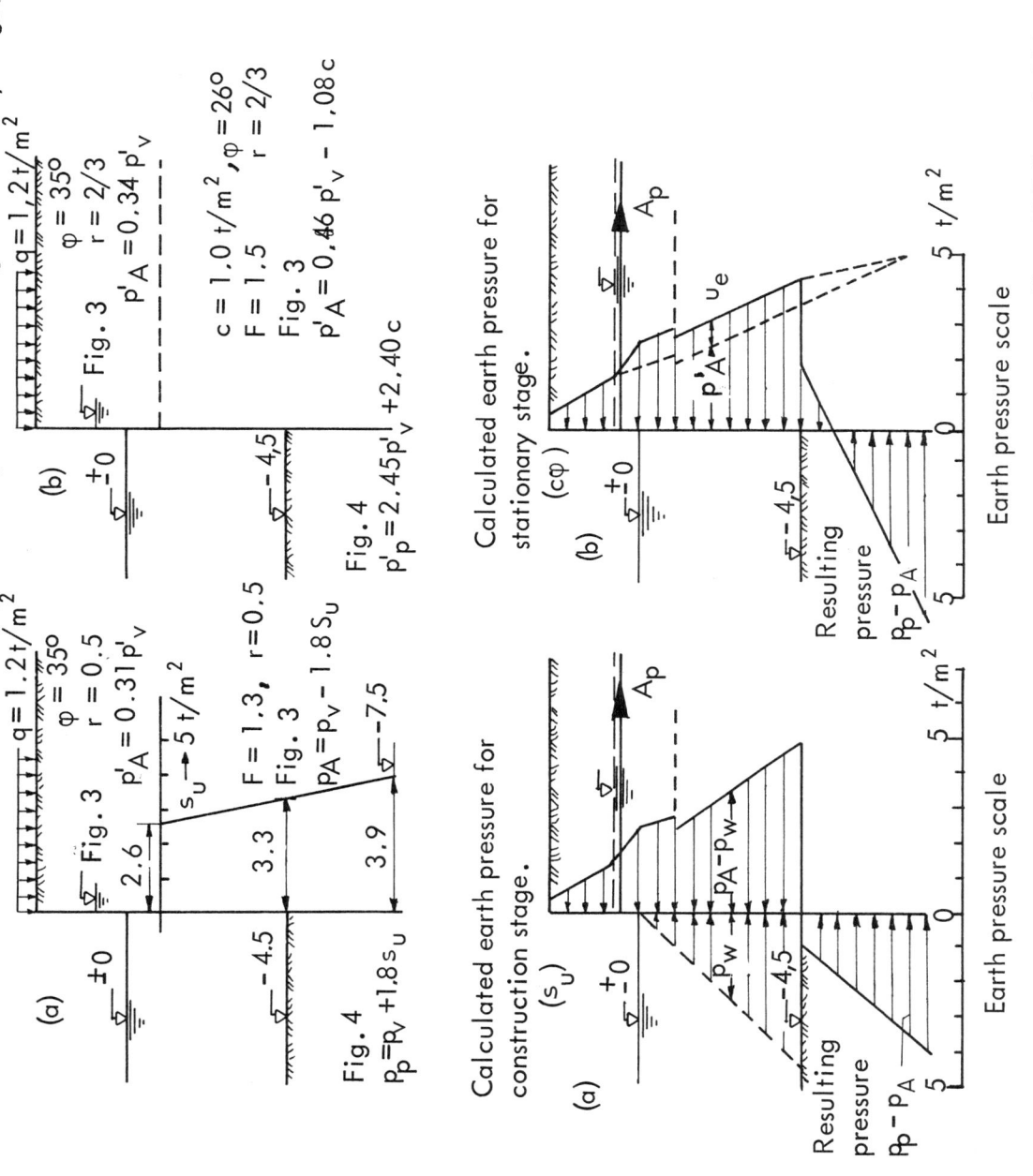

Figure A2.7, Example A2.2 continued.

ing the construction period than afterwards. In certain cases the "earth pressure" should be calculated as a fluid pressure, based upon the unit weight of the sand-water mixture and using a reduced factor of safety.

Knowing the earth pressures, the static quantities—D_n, A_p, L_n and M_m— can be calculated according to the guidelines given above. When using Equation A2.6 to determine the acting bending moment, M_d, one is permitted to employ fully the moment reduction given in Figure A2.1b.

The detailed calculations for an anchored bulkhead in sand are shown in Figure A2.6, Example A2.1.

Bulkheads in Clay

There are some particular distinctions between bulkheads in clay or fine silt and bulkheads in sand. First, the earth pressures for the construction stage can be determined on the basis of the undrained shear strength (s_u) of the clay. Next, any reduction of the theoretical bending moment for the construction stage cannot at present be taken into account, because experimental or practical experience is not available to the same extent as for sand.

When designing the stationary (long-term) stage, the earth pressures must be determined by a $c\phi$-analysis, and the theoretical bending moment can be reduced according to Equation A2.6. The reduction factor, μ_d, should be taken from the curve designated "loose" in Figure A2.1b.

The computation procedure for an anchored bulkhead in clay, both for the construction stage (s_u-analysis) and the stationary (long-term) stage ($c\phi$-analysis) are shown in Figure A2.7, Example A2.2. Details of the calculations are given directly in the figures.

REFERENCES

1. Hansen, J. Brinch. 1953. *Earth pressure calculation.* Copenhagen: Danish Technical Press.
2. Rowe, P.W. 1952. "Anchored sheet-pile walls." *Proceedings of Institution of Civil Engineers* 1 (1): 27-70.
3. Terzaghi, K. 1953. "Anchored bulkheads." *ASCE Proceedings* 262.
4. Tschebotarioff, G.P. 1949. *Large Scale Earth Pressure Tests with Model Flexible Bulkheads.* Princeton, N.J.: Princeton University.

appendix 3
berthing maneuvers of large ships

By Prof. F. Vasco Costa
Instituto Superior Técnico, Lisboa, Portugal

The maneuver of bringing a ship to a berth is so difficult and hazardous that the frequency of accidents during such maneuvers is about one accident a year per ship.

The increase in the size of ships has contributed toward rendering berthing maneuvers even more difficult—not only because of the difficulties inherent to the larger dimensions of the ships, but especially because the power of tugboats and the strength of mooring ropes have not increased in proportion to the mass of the ship. Besides, certain large ships, not being able to enter some harbors, now have to be berthed in exposed locations, under the action of waves and currents.

In this appendix some recommendations, based on simplified analytical treatments (see References 2 and 3), are advanced on how to maneuver a ship and so reduce her impact with the berthing structure. Some of these recommendations seem to correspond to practices already adopted in some harbors. It is hoped that the justification of such practices by well-known principles of dynamics will contribute to reducing the frequency of accidents.

Motion of a Ship

The motion of a ship on the water surface can be specified at any instant by the velocity of translation, u, of her center of gravity and by her angular velocity, w. In case $w = o$, all the points of the ship will move with the same velocity, and the motion is a simple translation (Figure A3.1). In case $u = o$, the velocity of each point of the ship is proportional to the distance to her center of gravity and the motion is a simple rotation (Figure A3.2).

The motion of a ship on the water surface can alternatively be specified at any instant as a rotation around a point, not necessarily on the ship, the so-called "instantaneous center of rotation." The position of the instantaneous center is usually changing from instant to instant. In the simple translation, the instantaneous center of the ship can be considered to be at infinity; in the simple rotation, to be coincident with her center of gravity.

For the purpose of studying the motion of a ship on the water surface under the action of forces applied to her due to the action of tugboats, ropes, wind or currents, it is necessary to consider the mass, m, of the ship concentrated in two points at a distance, k, from her center of gravity.

402   Port Engineering

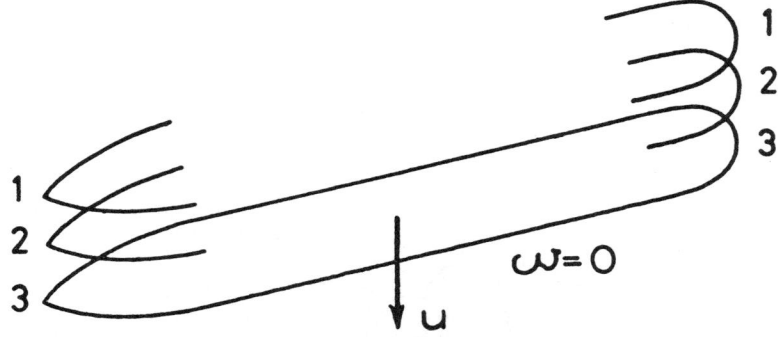

Figure A3.1. Simple translation of a ship.

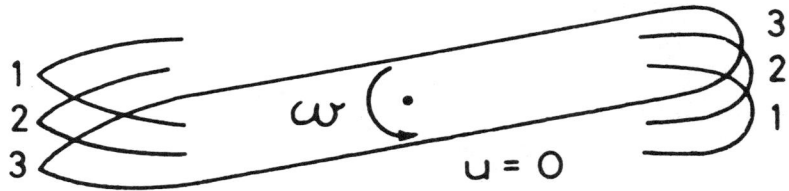

Figure A3.2. Simple rotation of a ship.

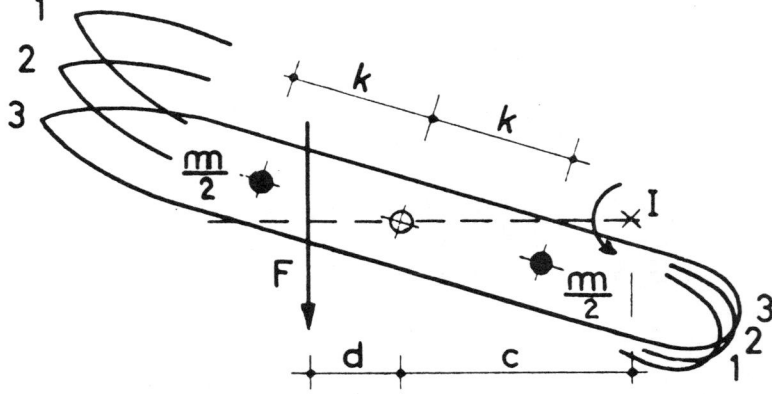

Figure A3.3. Rotation around the instantaneous center.

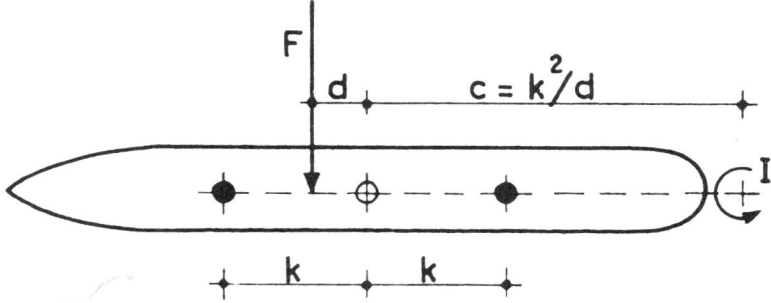

Figure A3.4. Rotation under a force applied near the center of gravity.

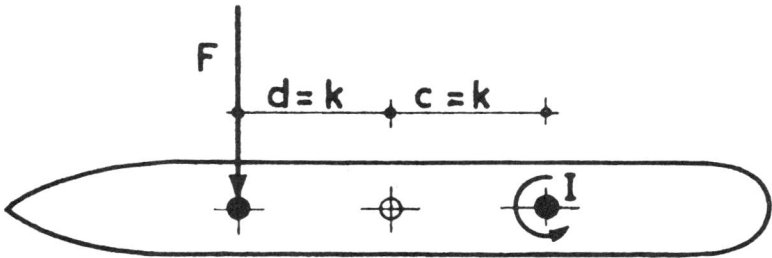

Figure A3.5. Rotation under a force applied at a distance k from the center of gravity.

The distance, k is called the radius of gyration and the product, $mk^2 = J$, the moment of inertia of the ship (Figure A3.3).

If a force or a system of forces whose resultant does not pass through her center of gravity is applied to a ship, her instantaneous center, I will be in a line perpendicular to the force and passing through the center of gravity at a distance on the far side of the center of gravity to such center,

$$c = \frac{k^2}{d} \qquad (A3.1)$$

where d is the distance from the resultant of the system of forces to the center of gravity (Figure A3.3). The position of the instantaneous center does not depend on the intensity of the force, but only on its position.

If the resultant of the forces acting on the ship is normal to the center line of the ship, the instantaneous center, I, will also be on the center line (Figure A3.4). If the resultant, besides being normal to the center line, is applied at one of the points in which we considered half of the mass of the ship to be concentrated, the instantaneous center will be coincident with the other such point, because in this case c becomes equal to d (Figure A3.5). Equation A3.1 shows that wherever d is smaller than k, c becomes larger than k (Figure A3.4), and vice versa (Figure A3.6). These considerations can be of use when choosing the position of forces to be applied to a ship to make her approach a berthing structure in the most convenient way.

Let us now consider what happens when a ship hits a fender. Let u_o be the velocity of the translation of a ship and w_o, her angular velocity at

$$W = \frac{1}{2} m u_o^2 \left(1 - \frac{a^2}{k^2 + r^2}\right) + m u_o \omega_o$$

$$\frac{k^2 a}{k^2 + r^2} + \frac{1}{2} m \omega_o^2 \frac{k^2 r^2}{k^2 r^2} \qquad (A3.2)$$

The berthing maneuver has to be oriented so as to reduce this amount of energy and thus render the berthing as smooth as possible. How this can be achieved will be discussed in the following sections.

Choice between Translation and Rotation

If, when entering into contact with the fender, a ship is moving in a simple translation normal to the quay wall (Figure A3.8), the amount of energy to be absorbed by the deflection of the fender and structure will be

$$W = \frac{1}{2} m u_o^2 \left(1 - \frac{a^2}{k^2 + k^2}\right) \qquad (A3.3)$$

If, when entering into contact with the fender, the ship is moving with a simple rotation (Figure A3.9), the energy to be absorbed will be

$$W = \frac{1}{2} m \omega_o^2 \frac{k^2 r^2}{k^2 + r^2} \qquad (A3.4)$$

In this case the velocity of the point of the hull that hits the fender can be evaluated by

$$v_o = \omega_o r \qquad (A3.5)$$

By substituting this value in Equation A3.4 one obtains

$$W = \frac{1}{2} m v_o^2 \left(1 - \frac{r^2}{k^2 + r^2}\right) \qquad (A3.6)$$

Comparing Equation A3.3 with Equation A3.6 and comparing a with r in Figure A3.7a, one verifies that for equal velocities of the point of the ship which enters into contact with the fender the quantity of energy to be absorbed is smaller when the ship's motion consists of a simple rotation. Only when the velocity of translation is normal to the straight line connecting the point of contact to the mass center does a become equal to r and the amount of energy to be absorbed in an impact due to rotation is the same as that to be absorbed in an impact due to translation.

It can, therefore, be concluded that, for equal velocities of the point of the hull which hits the fender, berthings made through a rotating motion are to be preferred to berthings made through simple translation motion.

Combined Translation and Rotation

The determining factor of the violence of the impact of the ship with the fender is the velocity of the point of the hull which first enters into contact with the fender. In order to reduce to a minimum the velocity of this point, the rotating and translating motion can be combined so as to oppose their effects. If rotation prevails over translation, as represented in Figure A3.10, the instantaneous center of rotation will remain near the center of gravity. If translation prevails over rotation, as represnoted in Figure A3.11, the instantaneous center of rotation will be in a point far away from the center of gravity.

It should be noted that a maneuver, such as that represented in Figure A3.11, in which the translation prevails over rotation, may later give occasion to an impact at the other extremity of the ship at a greater velocity than that observed during the first impact. The conditions in which this may happen have already been analytically determined (Figure A3.2).

Due to the fact that between the first and the second impact a great amount of energy is always dissipated in the water, the second impact is, in general, less violent than the first. Measurements made at Wilhelmshafen show that when the second impact is harder than the first the energy to be absorbed by the fender is never as great as when the first impact is the hardest (1). A berthing ma-

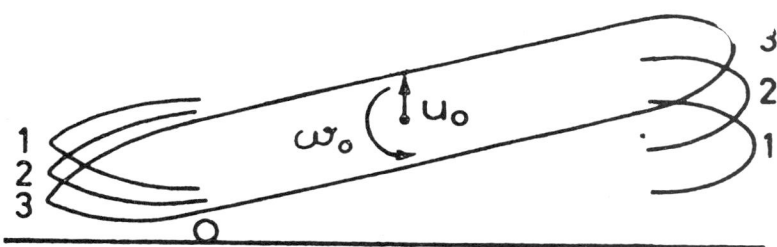

Figure A3.10. Impact with rotation prevailing over translation (recommended procedure).

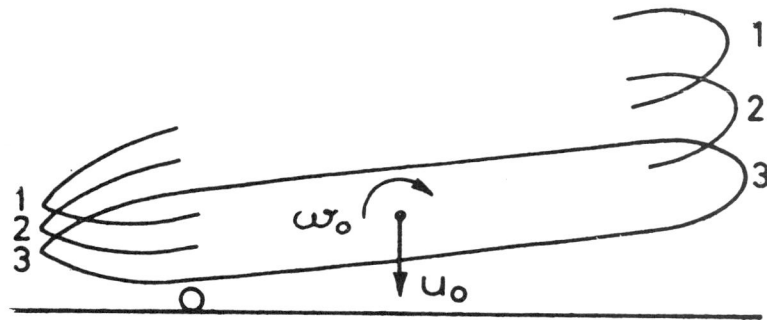

Figure A3.11. Impact with translation prevailing over rotation.

neuver in which the center of gravity of the ship approaches the structure at the same time that the ship rotates so as to reduce the velocity of the point of the hull which is going to hit the fender seems therefore to be an acceptable practice (Figure A3.11). However, the maneuver in which the center of the masses of the ship remains still or withdraws from the berthing structure, rotation prevailing over the translation, is to be preferred, because it eliminates the danger of a more violent second impact (Figure A3.10).

Impact on Berthing Structure

Equations A3.3 and A3.6 show that for equal velocities of the point of the hull that hits the fender the amount of energy to be absorbed decreases when the distance from the mass center of the ship to the point of contact increases. To have a gentle berthing it is, therefore, desirable to orient the maneuver so that the point which first makes contact with the structure is as far as possible from the center of gravity of the ship.

As the fenders only adapt themselves well to the hull when contact is established in the parallel middle body, it is recommended that the first contact of the ship with the fender be made right at the end of the parallel body.

It must be pointed out that, in case of a simple rotation, although for a given velocity v_o of the point that hits the fender, the further the point is from the center of gravity the smoother the impact (see Equation A3.6), the fact remains that for a given angular velocity, ω_o of the ship the farther such point is from the center of gravity the harder will be the impact (see Equation A3.4). However, as it is easier to think in terms of distances covered and velocities of the points of the

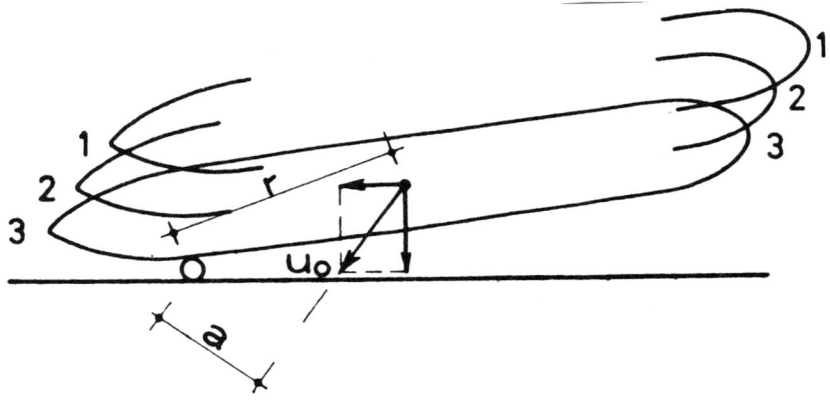

Figure A3.12. Velocity of translation with parallel component oriented toward the fender.

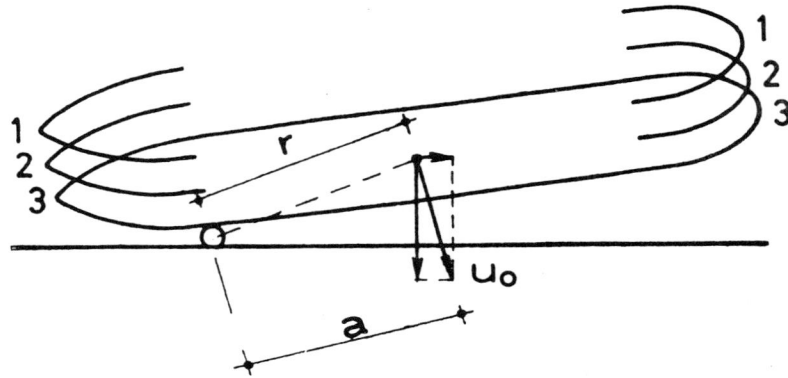

Figure A3.13. Velocity of translation with parallel component oriented away from the fender (recommended procedure).

hull than in terms of angular velocity of the ship and, furthermore, as a berthing operation always involves some translation, it seems advisable to choose the position of the point of contact as far as possible from the center of gravity.

Impact on Quay Wall

If, when entering into contact with the fender, the ship is moving in a simple translation, without rotation, the energy to be absorbed through the deflection of the fender and the structure can be evaluated, as already stated, by Equation A3.3.

In order that the quantity of energy be a minimum, it is convenient that the value of a be a maximum. This is obtained if the velocity of a ship has a small component parallel to the berthing structure in a direction opposite to that of the point where contact is established (Figure A3.13).

If the component of the ship's velocity parallel to the quay is directed to the point of contact (Figure A3.12), the energy to be absorbed at the

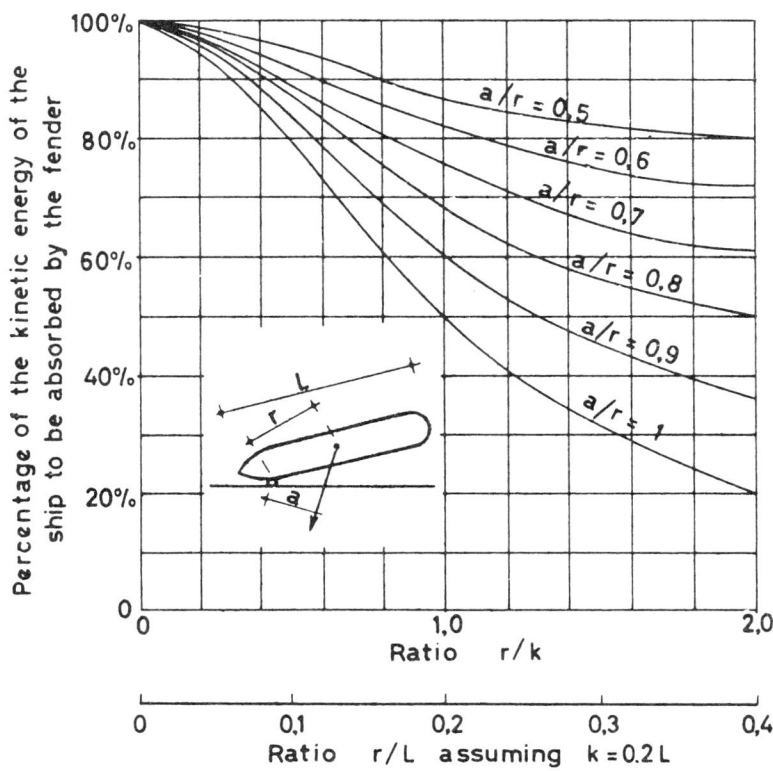

Figure A3.14. Influence of the direction of the velocity in the amount of energy to be absorbed by the fender.

first impact will increase, and the impact will be unnecessarily violent.

The graph in Figure A3.14 was prepared to show how much the amount of energy to be absorbed is reduced when the velocity of the translation of the ship is oriented in such a way as to render maximum the value of a. This graph gives the percentage of the ship's kinetic energy to be absorbed by the fender as a function of the ratios, r/k and a/r, and was prepared assuming that there would be no sliding between hull and fender. If there is sliding, and some energy absorbed in the process, the fender will only have to absorb the remaining energy.

The value of r/k depends only on the ship's position in relation to the fender and on the distribution of masses on the ship. The value of a/r depends on the position of the ship and on the direction of her velocity of translation.

Some authors, with the intention of simplifying Equation A3.3, admit $a = r$, which permits them to write

$$W = \frac{mu^2}{2} \left(\frac{k^2}{a^2 + k^2} \right) \quad (A3.7)$$

As a equals r only when the velocity of the translation of the ship is normal to the straight line connecting the center of gravity with the point of contact, the values given by this equation are always smaller than they should be.

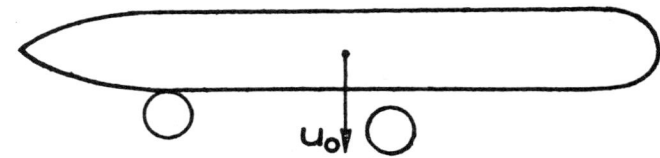

Figure A3.15. Berthing to a pair of dolphins with the ship in an off center position (recommended procedure for large ships).

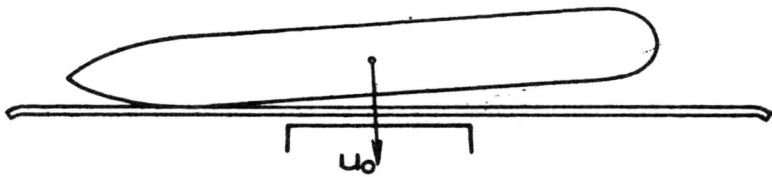

Figure A3.16. Impact of a ship to a berthing beam.

In Figure A3.14 the curve $a/r = 1$ corresponds to Equation A3.7. The comparison of this curve with the remaining ones permits the evaluation of the error committed when, in order to simplify the evaluation of the evergy absorbed, it is assumed that $a = r$. This error can attain particularly large values in the case of impacts made by points far away from the center of gravity of the ship, as is here recommended.

Berthing to Dolphins

The berthing of a ship to dolphins requires great care with the positioning of the ship in relation to the dolphins.

It has been shown that it is convenient to orientate the berthing maneuver in such a way that the first contact be established near the end of the parallel middle body. This implies that the berthing be achieved with the ship off-center to a pair of dolphins whenever the parallel middle body of the ship is of a length not precisely equal to that of the distance between the two dolphins (Figure A3.15).

It should be noted that the off-center berthing of a ship to a pair of dolphins, as recommended herein, may later give occasion to a particularly violent second impact on the other dolphin.

It should also be noted that if the ship is too off-center the impact will take place outside the parallel middle body of the ship, which may give occasion for the contact of the hull with the dolphins to be made under poor conditions.

The off-center positioning of the ship can be dispensed with, even in the case of a pair of dolphins being much closer than the length of the parallel middle body if, in the absence of currents and wind, one can be sure of berthing in a simple rotating motion. This is because, as already explained, the amount of energy to be absorbed decreases, for a given angular velocity, when the distance from the point of contact to the center of gravity decreases.

From the considerations stated above, it can be concluded that, when conditions for approaching a pair of dolphins are difficult it is convenient to make an off-center berthing in such a way that the first contact be established at the end of the

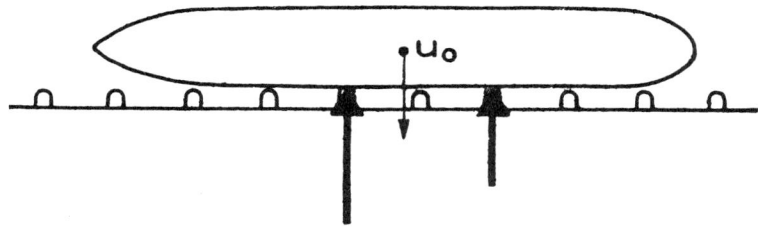

Figure A3.17. Berthing with the ship parallel to the wharf.

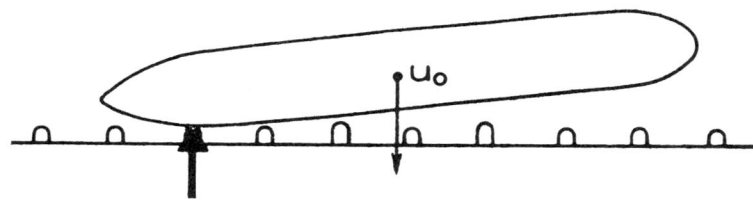

Figure A3.18. Berthing with the ship at a small angle to the wharf (recommended procedure).

parallel middle body. If the approach conditions are easy, and one can be sure of bringing the ship close to the dolphins and then berth it in a simple rotation motion, there is no need for an off-center berthing.

Berthing to Berthing Beams

Berthing beams, composed of rigid horizontal beams supported by flexible piles, are being built in several ports for the berthing of large oil tankers.

One of the advantages berthing beams present over dolphins is that the first contact of the ship always takes place at the end of the parallel middle body, no matter what the position of the ship is in relation to the beam (Figure A3.16). The risk of the contact being established in a point too close to the center of gravity of the ship, or outside her parallel middle body, is therefore eliminated.

For this reason it may be said that berthings to beams are less risky than berthings to dolphins.

Therefore, berthing beams are to be recommended for berthing large ships in exposed locations.

Berthing to Wharves and Piers

It is often stated that in a well-performed berthing, the ship enters simultaneously into contact with several fenders.

As the surface of the fenders in a pier are never in perfect alignment, it is not likely that contact will be simultaneously established with more than two fenders. In case these two fenders are at an equal distance from the center of gravity of the ship, each one of them will absorb half of the kinetic energy of the ship. But if the center of gravity is not at an equal distance from both fenders, the nearest fender will have to absorb a larger amount of energy, this giving occasion to a quite large reaction on the ship's hull (Figure A3.17).

If the berthing is done with the ship at a small angle to the pier, and if the first fender to recieve the impact is at a distance, r, from the center of

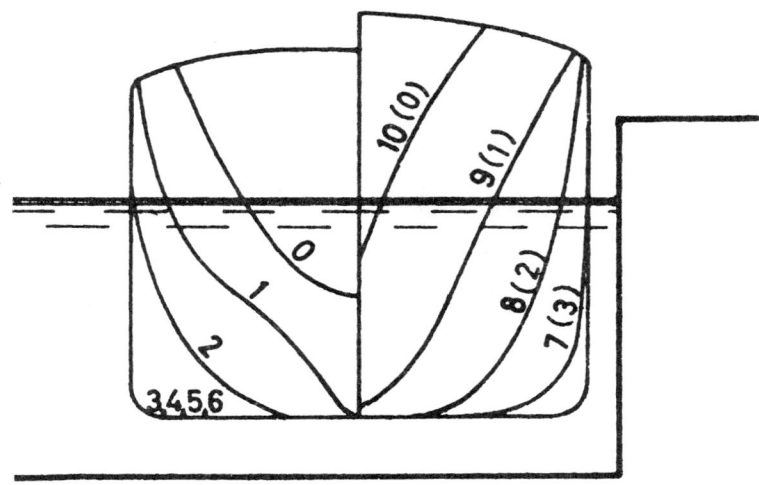

Figure A3.19. The hull of a ship at water level is more salient near the stern than near the bow.

gravity larger than the radius of gyration, k, of the ship, and if the translation velocity is oriented so that the value of a be close to that of r (see Figure A3.13), in Equation A3.3, it will be

$$1 - \frac{a^2}{k^2 + r^2} \leq \frac{1}{2} \qquad (A3.8)$$

As a consequence, a berthing to only one fender becomes gentler and safer than a berthing made simultaneously to two fenders, even if these are at equal distances from the center of gravity of the ship.

As it is difficult to make a ship touch two fenders that are at precisely equal distances from the mass center, but it is easy to make her have the first point of contact with the fender at a distance from the center of gravity superior to her gyration radius (circa 0, 2 of the length of the ship), it can be affirmed that a berthing with the ship at a small angle to the wharf and touching only one fender (Figure A3.18) is to be preferred to a berthing with the ship placed so as to enter into contact simultaneously with two fenders.

Moreover, the berthing of a ship parallel to a pier involves the risk of the first impact being established by a point too close to the center of gravity of the ship, if one of the fenders near it happens to be more prominent. With the ship at an angle, this risk is eliminated, the contact always being established at a point close to the end of the parallel middle body (Figure A3.18).

Choice of First Impact

Where the berthing is done with the ship head on to the current and governed by her own means, it is usual to berth bow first because it permits a somewhat better control of the motion of the ship.

If the motion of the ship during the berthing operation is mainly governed by tugboats, as is always the case with large ships, the control conditions of the motion of the ship are the same, whether the bow or the stern is first to touch the berthing structure. In this case the choice between berthing bow or stern first has to depend on other factors.

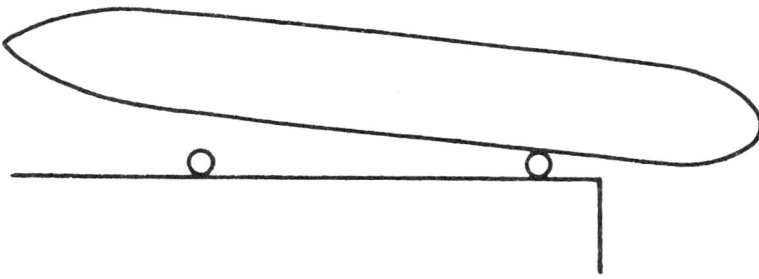

Figure A3.20. Berthing stern first when the stern stays clear of the quay wall (recommended procedure).

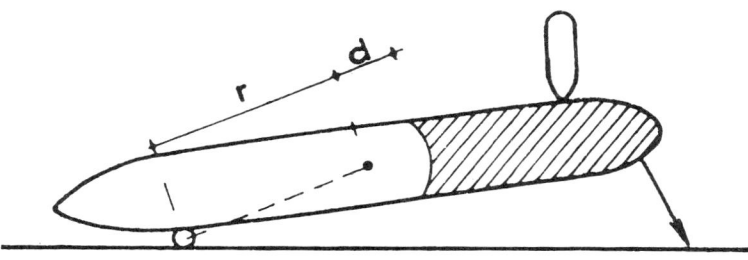

Figure A3.21. Forces toward the wharf applied on the traced zone will contribute to reduce the pressure on the fender.

In the majority of ships the water line is more prominent nearer to the stern than to the bow (Figure A3.19). Therefore berthing stern first, because it permits contact with the fenders at a greater distance from the center of gravity, is to be preferred to berthing bow first. However, it must be pointed out that berthing stern first implies the risk of the propellers bumping the berthing structure. Such a risk is minimum in the case of berthing to dolphins, to beams and to quay walls when the stern remains free of the quay wall (Figure A3.20).

Most large ships and tankers when loaded have their center of gravity nearer to the bow than to the stern. This contributes toward increasing the distance from the point of contact to the center of gravity and therefore, is one reason more for giving preferences to berthing stern first.

It must be pointed out that empty tankers, especially the ones with machinery on the stern, can have their center of gravity nearer to the stern than to the bow. In such cases berthing bow first seems to be preferred.

Improvement of Impact Conditions

In the analytical treatment that permitted Equation A3.2, it was necessary to ignore several forces that act on the ship while she rotates around the point of contact (Figure A3.7b), namely the forces due to wind, currents, mooring ropes, tugboats and to water pressure. All such forces can contribute to increasing or decreasing the reaction of the fender on the ship, depending on their location and their direction.

Table A3.1

Length of the ship (meters)	Distance r from center of gravity to point of contact (in meters)					
	20	30	40	50	70	100
100	20	13	10	8	—	—
150	45	30	22	18	13	—
200	80	53	40	32	23	16
250	125	83	62	50	36	25
300	—	120	90	72	51	36
350	—	163	122	98	70	49
400	—	—	160	128	91	64

It could be expected that the forces acting toward the berthing structure would contribute to increasing the reaction of the fender, and that the forces acting away from it would contribute to decreasing it. But that is not necessarily so.

In the study of impact on bodies that rotate around a fixed point, the point to which forces can be applied without affecting the reaction on the point about which the body is rotating is usually denoted as "center of percussion". The distance, d, from the center of percussion to the center of the body is given by

$$d = \frac{k^2}{r} \quad (A3.9)$$

where, as before, k is the radio of gyration and r is the distance from the center of gravity to the point around which the body rotates.

If we consider the ship as a body rotating around the point of contact with the fender, it can be stated that forces directed toward the berthing structure applied at a distance larger than d will contribute to the decrease of the reaction on the hull and that forces applied nearer it will contribute to its increase.

The region of the ship where forces applied to the ship and directed to the berthing structure will contribute to reducing the reaction of the fender and, eventually, give occasion to cease the ship's contact with the fender is represented in Figure A3.21 by a hatched zone. Forces applied outside the hatched zone and directed away from the berthing structure will have the same effect on the reaction.

Table A3.1 gives the distance, d of the center of percussion to the center of gravity as a function of the length of the ship and of the distance from the center of gravity as a function of the length of the ship and of the distance from the center of masses to the point of contact. The table was prepared assuming that

$$k = 0, 2 L$$

The farther the contact with the fender is made from the center of gravity of the ship, the larger will be the zone where forces applied toward the berthing structure will contribute to reduce the reaction of the fender on the ship.

Forces applied at a distance, d, from the center of gravity will not affect the reaction of the fender because for such forces the instantaneous center coincides with the point of contact of the hull with the fender, but on the condition that the forces are perpendicular to the line connecting the center of masses to the point of contact. If the forces are not perpendicular to such a line, they will have a component along such line. As most of the forces applied to the ship are perpendicular to

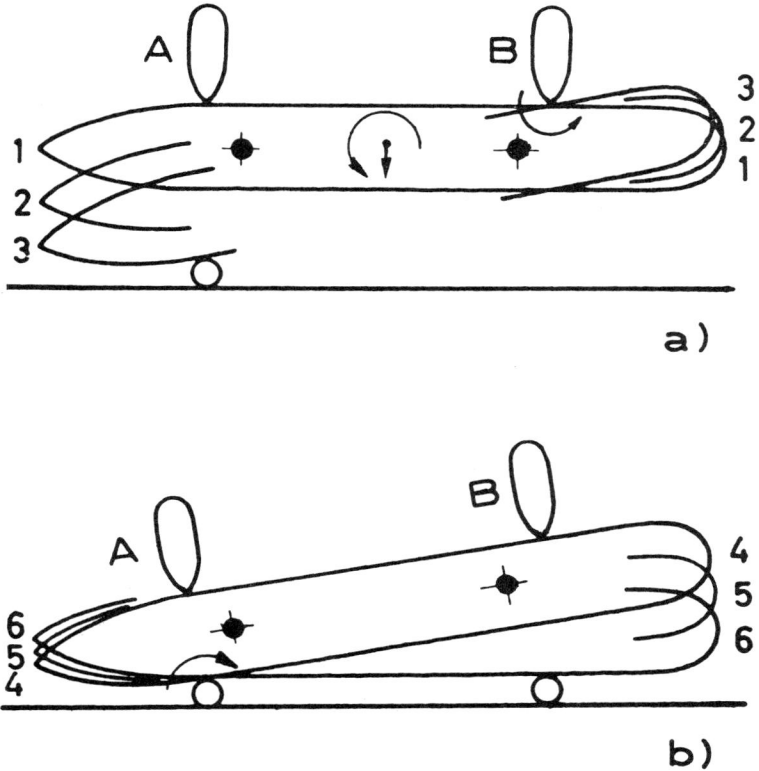

Figure A3.22. Use of two tugs to control the motion of the ship before and after contact with the fender is established.

the hull, and therefore almost perpendicular to the mentioned line, it seems reasonable to ignore the component along the line connecting the center of gravity with the point of contact.

It must also be pointed out that forces applied farther from the center of gravity than the center of percussion and directed toward the berthing structure will contribute to increase the violence of the second impact. Although the second impact is usually not so hard as the first one can be (1), this has to be kept in mind when berthings are made with translation over rotation, as represented in Figure A3.11.

Use of Tugboats

As ropes can easily break when pulling a large ship, there seems to be a marked tendency to berth large ships by using tugboats pushing directly upon the ship's hull. A way of using two tugboats or two groups of tugboats, pulling at the ends of the parallel middle body to control the motion of the ship before and after she hits the fender, is suggested in Figure A3.22.

The ship is first brought in front of her berth and placed parallel to and as near to it as local conditions permit. From such position the ship, under the action of the tugboat near the bow (A in Figure A3.22a) is made to rotate around a point near the bow of the other tug (B in Figure A3.22a).

Once contact is made with the fender, tug B will then be used to make the ship rotate around the point of contact (Figure 22b).

If the distance of each tugboat to the center of gravity of the ship is about the same as the radius of gyration of the ship, k, it can be expected that the action of one tugboat will make the ship rotate about a point near the bow of the other tugboat, this rendering the action of each tug almost independent on action of the other. But it seems advisable to make both tugboats act a little farther from the center of gravity than the radius of gyration.

If the hull is approaching the fender under the action of tug A at too high velocity, tug B can be used to reduce a little such velocity just by pushing the hull on a point farther from the center of gravity than the radius of gyration, k.

If there is a tendency for contact with the fender to be lost, tug A can be used to maintain it. If there is a tendency for the reaction to become too great, tug B can be used to reduce it, just by increasing the force applied on the hull at a distance from the center of gravity larger than the radius of gyration.

For the sake of clarity, it was assumed that neither wind nor currents would affect the motion of the ship. If they do, tugboats or mooring ropes will have to resist their action.

Summing Up

In the analytical treatment described earlier (motion of a ship), it was assumed that there would be no sliding and no change of the angular momentum of the ship while she rotates around the point of contact with the fender. Forces acting on the ship due to proximity of solid quay walls, to revolution of propellers, to seabottom form and to winds and currents were ignored. These were drastic simplifications, only valid in case the ship approaches the fender moving in a direction near the normal to the surface of contact, and the mentioned forces have either a resultant zero or a resultant that passes through the point of contact of the ship with the fender.

Based on the mentioned simplified analytical treatment, some recommendations can be drawn up, which are submitted to those who, because more familiar than the author with berthing maneuvers, are in a better position to judge their utility.

1. As the main factor which determines the violence of the ship's impact is the velocity of the point of the hull which first contacts the berthing structure, it is convenient that the translation velocity of the ship be combined with her rotation velocity so as to oppose their effects (Figures A3.10 and A3.11).

2. As for equal velocities of the point of the ship which enters into contact with the fender, the berthing is gentler if the ship's motion consists of a rotation. Berthings in which the rotation prevails over translation (Figure A3.10) are to be preferred to those in which the translation prevails over rotation (Figure A3.11).

3. As other conditions being the same, the farther the point of contact is from the center of the masses of the ship, the less violent is the impact. On the other hand, contacts established with warped areas of the hull do not permit the fenders to adapt themselves to the hull, the berthing maneuver should be conducted so that the first contact of the ship with the berthing structure be established at the end of her parallel middle body.

4. In order that the impact be as gentle as possible, the translation velocity of the ship should not have a component parallel to the quay directed towards the fender to be touched (Figure A3.12); it is convenient that such component be oriented in the opposite direction (Figure A3.13).

5. When approach conditions to dolphins are difficult, it is convenient to place the ship so that the first impact be established at the end of the parallel middle body of the ship, even if this involves berthing the ship off-center (Figure A3.15).

6. In comparison with dolphins, berthing beams present the advantage of guaran-

teeing that the first contact be established at the end of the parallel middle body of the ship (Figure A3.16).

7. When berthing to a wharf, in order to avoid that the first contact be established at a point too close to the center of the masses of the ship (Figure A3.11), it is convenient to berth with the ship at a small angle, and not parallel to the wharf (Figure A3.18).
8. When the ship's own means are used in moving her during the berthing operation, and whenever there is danger of its propellers colliding with the berthing structure, bow berthings are to be preferred.
9. When a loaded ship moves under the action of tugboats and mooring cables and there is no danger to the propellers colliding with the structure, stern berthings are to be preferred (Figure A3.20).
10. Empty tankers, specially ones with machinery on the stern, are to be berthed bow first.
11. When the point of the ship that is going to contact a fender is moving at an exaggerated speed, such velocity can be reduced by applying on the ship forces directed toward the shore beyond the center of percussion (Figure A3.21).
12. After contact is established and while the ship is rotating around the point of contract, forces directed toward the shore are to be applied nearer than the center of percussion if there is a tendency for the ship to lose contact with the fender, and farther than that center if there is a tendency for the pressure upon the fender to become too large.

Acknowledgments

The author is indebted to Commander José Cabido de Ataide, Chief of the Hydrographic Mission of the Continent and Adjacent Islands, to Commander Barbosa Henriques, of Soponata, to Commander António Araújo of the Port of Lisbon Authority, and to Engineer José Fiúza Perestrelo, of the Instituto Superior Técnico, for the valuable suggestions and criticisms which they contributed in the editing of this article.

P.W. Turner, Department of Engineering, University of Cambridge, revised the English version and contributed very valuable comments.

References

1. Jamm, Professor, and Rüssmann, W. 1966. *Measurement of Tankers Berthing Manoeuvers*. Report submitted to the International Oil Tankers Commission, Hamburg.
2. Pagés M. 1960. "Etude Mechanique du choc se produisant lors de l'accostage D.un navire a un quai." *Anngles des Ponts et Chaussées* (March/April).
3. Vasco Costa, F. 1964. *The Berthing Ship*. London: Foxlow Publications.
4. ———. 1967. "Floating berthing beam." *The Dock and Harbour Authority* (August).

appendix 4
use of tracers in harbor, coastal and ocean engineering

*Bruun, P. 1970. "Use of tracers in harbor, coastal and ocean engineering." *Engineering Geology*. Amsterdam: Elsevier Publishing Company.

Summary

This appendix describes the use of tracers in various engineering fields including ocean, harbor, coastal and river engineering and some special applications of tracers, e.g., in pollution control. Certain pertinent aspects of tracer technology and methods of analyses to determine drift pattern aspects of tracer technology and methods of analyses to determine drift pattern and quantity are mentioned. A list of references and a special bibliography are included, the latter giving examples of literature on actual tracer projects in various fields of science and technology.

Introduction

For many years methods of tracing sediments have been sought. In the past it was not unusual for scientists to investigate the mineralogic components of the sediments in order to determine the presence of a unique component or ratio of several components. If such a mineral were present, it could be utilized as a natural tracer. As an example several forms of the minerals, hornblende and augite, have been identified and utilized along the Mexican and Californian gulf coasts, respectively. Along the Gulf of Mexico coast, horblende is present in the sedimentary assemblage from both the Mississippi and the Rio Grande rivers. However, the type of hornblende derived from each of these sources is quite distinctive and can be separated readily by microscopic studies. Therefore, possibilities exist for identifying the source of the sediments for the area between the mouths of the two major river systems. In California the presence of augite in the bottom sediments at Santa Barbara indicates a source from rivers north of Point Conception, because the sediments from the rivers east of Point Conception do not contain augite (Trask, 1952). Kamel (1962) uses natural (radioactive) thorium as a tracer.

The study of natural tracer minerals has proven useful in fully deriving a concept of the processes functioning in a given area; however, the results may be misleading. It can be stated unequivocally that the tracer minerals mentioned above are not representative of the total sediments. Usually of all the heavy minerals, hornblende and augite are among these, representing from 1 to 5% of total sediments. The heavy minerals have densities greater than 2.80 grams per cubic centimeter, or greater than that of quartz (2.65 grams per cubic centimeter) and the feldspars ($\cong 2.7$ grams per cubic centimeter) which, in most cases, makes up the bulk part of the remaining 95% of the sediments. Because of the greater density, the fall velocity is greater and, therefore, the heavy mineral particles act as a larger particle of quartz or feldspar. The difference in fall velocity illustrates the cardinal rule of sediment tracing: the labeled tracer particle and the natural sediment must possess the same physical and hydraulic characteristics when exposed to wave or current forces. For this primary reason, the heavy minerals are not satisfactory tracers.

Dying of sediments had been tried in the past, but during the middle 1950s, two new methods of tracing sediment transport appeared involving labeling sediments with fluorescent or radioactive material. Both techniques involve the measurement of radiation—one in the visible spectrum and the other in the very short wave lengths. The former requires excitation by ultraviolet light energy of appropriate wave length, while the latter is self-energized, i.e., radioactive. Many different tracers are available for each technology. Reference is made to *Proceedings of the 20th International Navigation Congress,* Baltimore, 1961, Section II, Subject 5, "Methods of determining sand and silt movement along the coast, in estuaries and in maritime rivers. Use of modern techniques such as radioactive isotopes, luminophores, etc."

For the first method, a glue or resin containing a fluorescent material is painted onto the indigenous sediments, (see Newman, 1960). The sediments are injected into the environment, and samples obtained subsequently undergo laboratory analysis to determine the concentration of the labeled particles. Labeling for the latter method requires irradiation of the natural sediments if a proper purity exists (Inman and Goldberg, 1955), painting the sediments with a glue or resin containing an irradiated (excited or energized) isotope (Gilbert 1954), irradiation of a simulated (glass, plastic or concrete) sediment containing a tracer isotope (Putnam et al., 1954) or absorption of a radioactive isotope into the surface and interior of a natural sediment (Krone, 1957). Other special methods, such as forcing of radioactive gases in a carrier, exist. The sediments are injected into the environment, and the concentration of their presence is made in the field by Geiger counters or scintillators. While much has been said and written concerning the hazards of radioactive material, a well-conceived and carefully performed radioactive tracer experiment will not be detrimental to any of the living organisms using, e.g., irradiated Sc_2O_3 (common), Rb_2CO_3 Au 198, Ag 110, Co 60, Cr 51, etc. Table A4.1 is a comparison between flouescent and radioactive tracers, outlining advantages as well as disadvantages related to the practical application of the two different tracer techniques. No actual cost figures are given, mainly because the cost of radioactive tracers varies greatly with the type of tracer to be employed and the character of the specific task to be undertaken.

From Table A4.1 it is noted that the main difficulty involved in radioactive tracing lies in the production and transportation of these tracers which, in turn, are responsible for relatively high costs. Often government regulations make it almost impossible to use radioactive tracers. Detection by bottom instrument and analysis is relatively easy but may involve coring. Samples have to be analyzed soon after they are secured because of the fading out of activity.

The main advantage with fluorescent tracing is that it is harmless. Furthermore, it is usually less expensive because it does not require complicated safety measures and development of tracers. Labeling materials are commercially available at reasonable prices (e.g., $0.20 to $0.30 per pound) instead of having to be acquired from radiation laboratories, and no safeguards are required in transporting materials. This method has, however, one main disadvantage—namely that at this stage of the

Table A4.1 Comparison between Fluorescent and Radioactive Tracing.

	Fluorescent	Radioactive
Production of tracers	may be produced any place where it is needed; no health hazard	irradiation process at special installation (atomic station); a number of safety measures needed; health requirements by government
Type of tracers	a great variety of colors; a few main colors	γ-emitters preferred; a great variety in half lifetime available
Costs	relatively low, e.g., $0.25/lb.	relatively high because of cost of isotopes and all kinds of safety measures which are strictly enforced by government agencies
Transport and storage	no problems	numerous safeguards; special containers and storage requirements.
Injection	by seeding; no problems	difficult because of safety precautions
Tracing time	tracers are very durable when a resin-like ureaformaldehyde is used but may contaminate areas of injection for years; some glue tracers have limited lifetime depending upon exposure	a number of tracers exist with half lifetime for γ-ray emission ranging from a few days to half a year or more; it is usually possible to select a tracer with a half lifetime suitable for each particular purpose
Sampling or tracing	surface or core samples have to be picked up, dried and analyzed in laboratory	tracing must be done by a bottom instrument, e.g., geiger counter or scintillator, which is moved over the bottom on a sledge or similar device
Analyses	counting of particles by visual observation using ultraviolet energy-source or by a scanning machine with photoelectric cells; this may be laborious and time-consuming, therefore, a costly procedure	the reading on the geiger counter or scintillator recording instrument gives the result directly; calibration based on probings may be necessary; no further cost on analyses
Accuracy	accuracy depends upon number of samples and length of cores, and upon the accuracy of the scanning procedure itself; it is difficult for the human eye to count more than 3–4 tracers in one sample; samples must be very dry before scanning	accuracy depends upon the depth of disturbance or rearrangements of bottom material; in order to get more reliable data beyond surface readings cores may have to be taken and made subject to laboratory analyses; calibration based on probings possible under simplified conditions.
Scales	best on small scale problems	best on large scale problems

development, it is based on sampling to be followed by laboratory analysis of dry samples inasmuch as scanning of wet samples is not possible. This is time consuming and lacks flexibility because it is difficult to change a sampling program until the results of the sampling(s) already carried out are known. The technique, however, may be improved by preliminary scanning (e.g., on the survey vessel itself), using ovens to dry the samples whether secured as cores, by clamshell or scraper or bound in parafin plates pressed towards the surface of the bottom or by entirely new approaches, such as underwater tracing using TV cameras, or other photo techniques which, however, apply to the surface of the bottom sediments only.

Fluorescent tracings' great advantage lies in the fact that it can be put in operation with short notice and with little preparation in advance. By varying the color of the tracer label, it is possible to conduct successive tests in the same area, when conditions change quickly, without the waiting period required for radioactive tracers. Also, it is now possible to produce long-lived as well as short-lived tracers of all practical sizes needed for gravel, sand, silt and clay tracing.

Various Methods of Tracing

Tracing of Pattern

Tracing of pattern simply means that the movement of the sediment is followed by dumping and sampling in some grid system allowing a concentration versus time diagram to be drawn indicating the direction and relative distance traveled by the tracer grains. This method suffices for many practical purposes where knowledge of relative magnitudes is of primary importance. Publications on this topic are numerous. The papers published in the *Proceedings of the 20th International Navigation Congress* are typical. Examples of publications of similar nature are Hydraulic Research Station (1956); Zenkovitch, (1958); Russell (1960); Griesseier and Voigt (1965).

Use of Tracers as Velocity Indicators

This method utilizes tracers as velocity indicators only (Bruun, 1967, 1969). The quantity of migrating material is measured in traps installed on the bottom and the average velocity of the migrating grains is measured over a certain time period, which covers the time until maximum concentrations have been passed. The total amount of material is then concentrated in an "imaginary" surface layer with thickness corresponding to the average velocities found. This method can only be operated from permanent sampling stations using special sampling equipment. Using various colors of tracers dumped at different distances and distributing the layer thickness in the ratio between concentrations, one gets a clear picture of the multimotions which take place. This method is in principle similar to the method of "spatial integration" mentioned later.

Quantitative Tracing

Methods have been proposed to arrive at quantitative interpretation of tracer-measurements. The simplest method is the *steady dilution method* which utilizes a constant tracer supply over and assumes that an equilibrium concentration is obtained downstream of the injection point. The technical drawback of this method is that the supply must be given for a long time. This can be overcome by time integration (see Crickmore and Lean, 1962), but both methods are very time consuming.

The *spatial integration method* is based on separate evaluation of the mean particle speed and the depth of movement. The disadvantage of this method lies in the small concentration which may occur resulting in questionable accuracy. Determining the depth of travel may require meticulous surveys and/or corings. Reference is made to Lean and Crickmore (1962) and Hubbell and Sayre (1964).

The most practical and, undoubtedly, most versatile methods are those which apply theoretical dispersion models by which a connection is

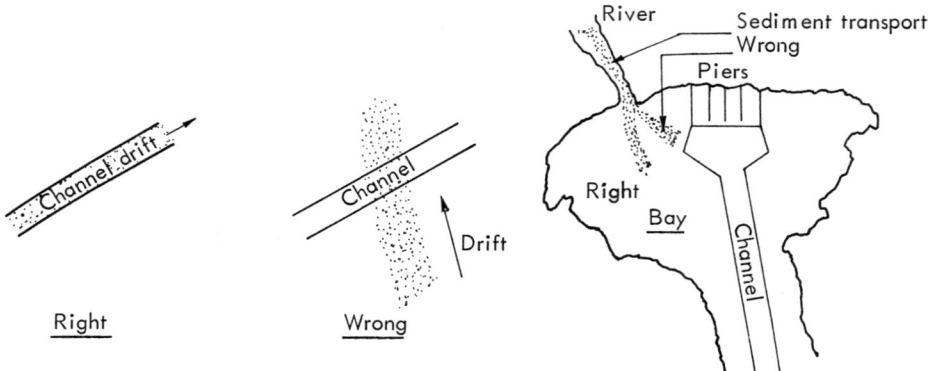

Figure A4.1. Tracing pattern of drift at navigation channel; planning navigation channel; investigation of sedimentation at navigation channel.

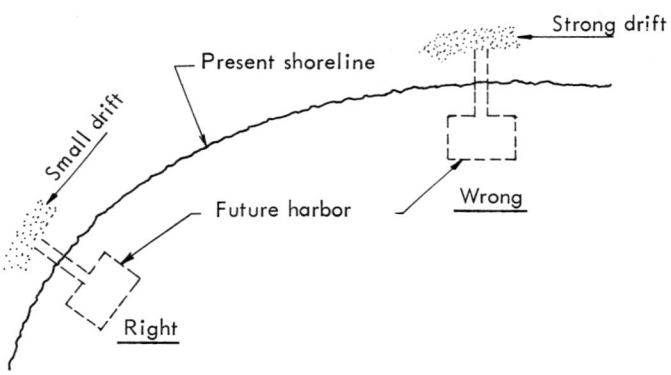

Figure A4.2. Tracing of relative magnitude of drift on an open shore; planning location of port on littoral drift coast.

found between the transport phenomenon and the development of concentration distribution. This mathematical modeling has given promising results. For details the reader is referred to the comprehensive thesis by De Vries (1966).

Practical Use of Tracers

Tracers, radioactive as well as fluorescent, have now been in use for more than 10 years, and usage is still being expanded by improvements in already existing fields as well as new applications. Utilization now covers a wide range of fields, including harbor, ocean, coastal and river engineering, littoral drift and dredging technology, pollution control, etc.

A number of examples of tracer applications in experiments already carried out or suggested applications are given in Figures A4.1 to A4.19. In the examples of projects already carried out, R indicates radio-active tracing and F, florescent tracing. Because some of the examples given are only described in commercial reports, the list of references includes a special section which gives a

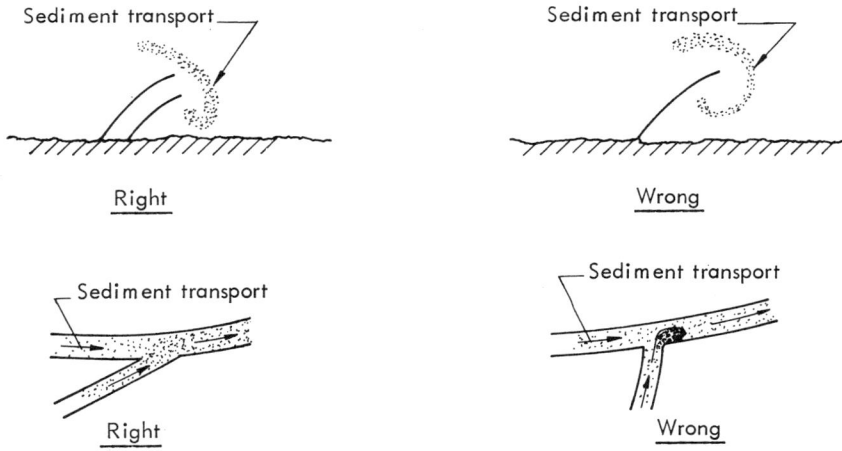

Figure A4.3. Tracing pattern of drift at navigation and other channels.

number of examples on practical tracing projects.

Tracing of Pattern(s) and Direction(s) of Sediment Transport

This application is of great importance for determining the location of a navigation channel, harbor entrance, pier or dock. Application of tracing technique may result in better planning of future maintenance of navigation channels.

Example: F-tracing on longshore drift in the Black Sea (USSR); R-tracing of bottom drift at Norfolk (England); F-tracing of longshore drift at several places in California and Florida. Special tracing of sediment transport pattern at inlets was carried out by R-tracing on the North Sea coast in Denmark at Thyboroen, by R-tracing in Portugal, e.g., at Figueira da Foz, by R-tracing in India of silt transport (at Bombay), by R-tracing in San Francisco Bay and by F-tracing at several inlets in Florida, e.g., at Palm Beach Inlet, South Lake, Worth Inlet and Hillsborough Inlet. F-tracing at Kingston, Jamaica, was undertaken to determine which rivers discharge sediment in navigation channels and harbor basins.

Figure A4.1 explains that a navigation channel, if possible, should not be built crosswise on a sediment transport lane (unless it is protected). It is also dangerous to build a navigation channel too close to rivers which discharge much sediment.

Figure A4.2 shows how tracers may be used to determine the location of a port on a littoral drift shore with minimum costs to maintenance dredging.

Figure A4.3 explains how jetties or breakwaters for a harbor may be built to protect against a known littoral drift pattern and how a confluence of sediment carrying rivers may be arranged to avoid deposition of sediments.

Evaluation of the Relative Magnitude of Drift in Two Opposite Directions

When a harbor on a littoral drift shore, a dredging operation or a coastal protection shall be planned, engineers are often faced with the problem of determining the direction of "predominant drift" as well as the relative magnitude of drift in two directions. This may be done by hindcasting of wave action and by computation of longshore wave energy based on meteorological data if wave action is the only responsible factor for material transport. Tidal and other currents, however, often play an important role, and even if the direction of predominant drift may be determined by observa-

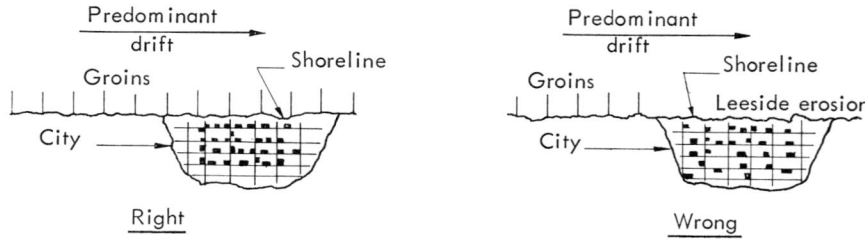

Figure A4.4. How far shall a group of groins extend along a shore?

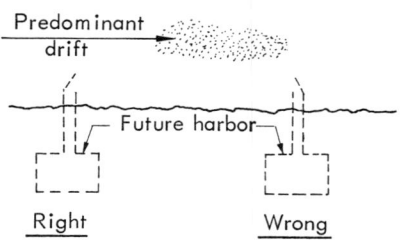

Figure A4.6. On which side of an inlet should the by-passing sand plant be installed?

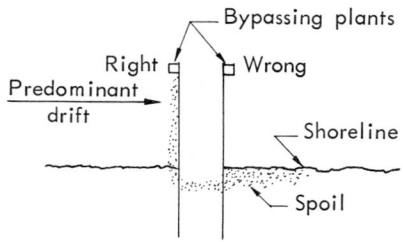

Figure A4.5. Which breakwater should have the greatest length?

tion of accumulation at structures extending into the sea, it is still very difficult to evaluate the relative magnitude of drift in two directions. Knowledge hereof is of great importance with respect to determining the location and extension of groin protection, the direction and relative length and shapes of jetties for protection of an inlet entrance, the location of sand traps for a navigation channel, planning of by-passing operations for beach nourishment and planning of artificial nourishment and other field operations.

Examples. F-tracing on the Florida Atlantic in the Palm Beach and Broward Counties. Figure A4.4 shows how the extension of a groin protection may be planned by tracer tests, Figure A4.5 how the configuration of an inlet entrance may be determined (by tracing and by hydraulic model experiments) and Figure A4.6 and A4.7 how tracing may be helpful in planning a by-passing or trap arrangement.

Determination of the Depth up to Which Sediment Transport Takes Place

This is important with respect to evaluating the depth up to which a navigation channel will be disturbed by sediment transport, evaluating possibilities for erosion and of the amount of overdredging which should be undertaken in critical areas, evaluating the possibilities for movement of material dumped offshore, evaluating the possibilities for deposit on the beach of material dumped offshore for beach nourishment or for bottom stabilizing purposes, as at Long Branch, New Jersey, evaluating origin of offshore deposits of sediments and minerals, etc.

Examples. F-tracing at Jupiter Island, Florida, to determine the success of offshore scraping for beach nourishment, F-tracing at Duluth, Lake Superior, for bottom stabilizing purposes, R-tracing at Japanese ports to determine the limiting depth of material movement, R-tracing at Cape

Tracers   425

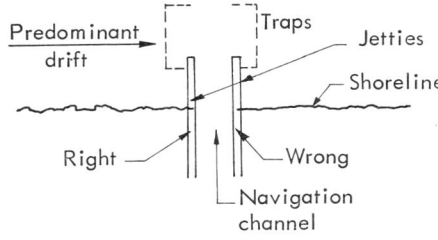

Figure A4.7. Shall sand traps be placed symmetrical or asymmetrical at an entrance?

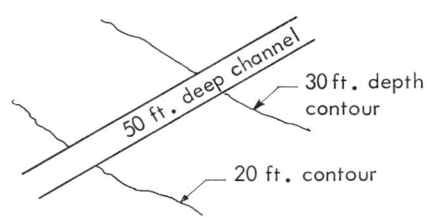

Figure A4.8. Is overdepth and maintenance required beyond the 20-foot contour?

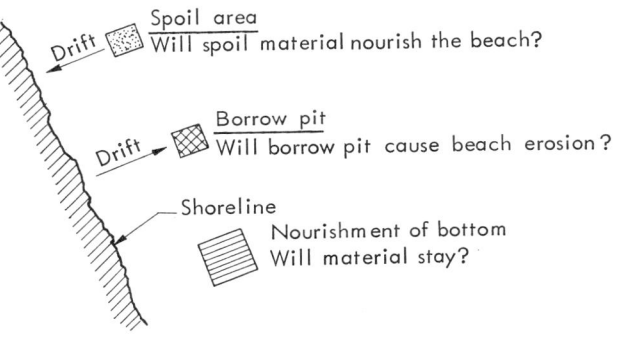

Figure A4.9. Beach or bottom nourishment problems.

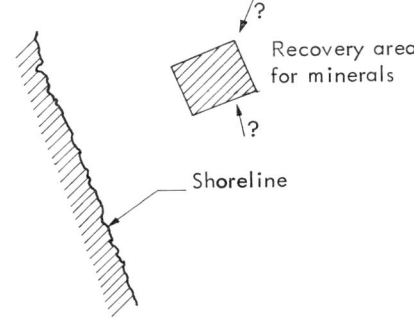

Figure A4.10. Where did minerals come from and where are they going?

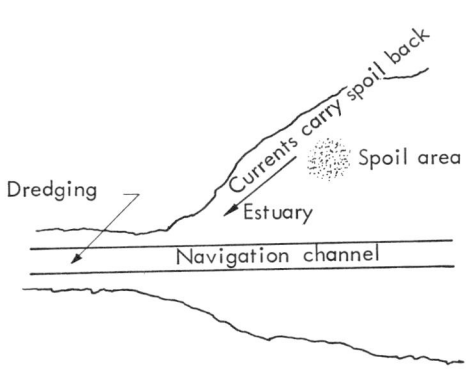

Figure A4.11. Will spoil from dredging of navigation channel return to the channel?

Fear River, North Carolina, to determine source of shoal materials. Figure A4.8 explains how tracers may be helpful in planning a navigation channel and the possible extent of maintenance dredging, Figure A4.9 how nourishment of beaches from offshore sources may be planned. Figure A4.10 refers to drift by currents at deeper waters where some minerals (placers) may tend to concentrate in certain areas carried by current concentrations.

Evaluation of the Possibilities of Effectiveness of a Dredging Operation

This and the performance of a dredging operation, including quantities of redredged material, the efficiency of agitation dredging, the deposit of material from overflow at a hopper dredge, the

Figure A4.12. Are currents able to move material on the bottom? Which way does it go?

Figure A4.14. Will material dredged at A by agitation or other dredging operations deposit at B?

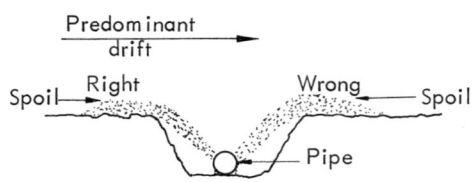

Figure A4.13. Will a trench dredged for a pipeline fill in again? Where should spoil be placed?

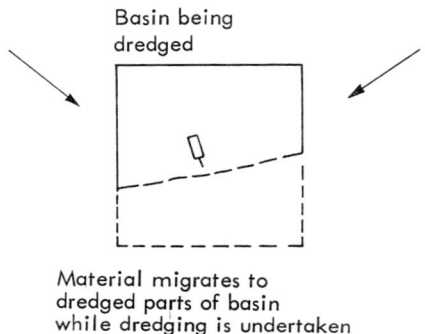

Figure A4.15. Problem of siltation during dredging operation.

possibility of sediment deposits by sand, gravel or shell dredges should be evaluated.

Examples. Figure A4.11 demonstrates schematically R-tracing in the Thames Estuary when some material dumped by flood current rapidly was carried back to the area when it was dredged. Such situation may be avoided by application of tracers in the spoil area before spoiling starts (Figure A4.12). On the other hand natural filling of a dredged area (e.g., a pipeline trench may be desired and the possibility for that may be looked into by tracing as shown in Figure A4.13. Figure A4.14 shows how dredging in a certain area may adversely affect dredging in another area. If dredging of these two areas is done on the same dredging contract, the contractor may face a loss because he redredges too much material. This has particular interest for agitation dredging where possibilities for deposits should be evaluated before dredging starts.

Figure A4.15 shows how material from distant areas may be carried down in an area to be dredged. The dredging contractor may face a considerable loss if he must keep dredging material which invades his dredging area from elsewhere.

Figure A4.16 demonstrates a sidecasting operation. Sidecasting, as undertaken at the Lake Maracaibo Bar, the Orinoco River Bar, at the Port Everglades (Ft. Lauderdale, Florida), the Oregon Inlet, North Carolina on a minor scale, as a forerunner for hopper dredging, and as undertaken at Gulf Coast inlets by the U.S. Army Corps of Engineers new multipurpose dredge "McFarland," has proven to be very useful if only a minor part of the material migrates back to the dredged channel. The possibility exists that the material dumped by sidecasting may form submerged "jetties" which decrease material transfer to the channel at the same time as it may be helpful in concentrating tidal flow through the dredged channel, thereby improving flushing of material.

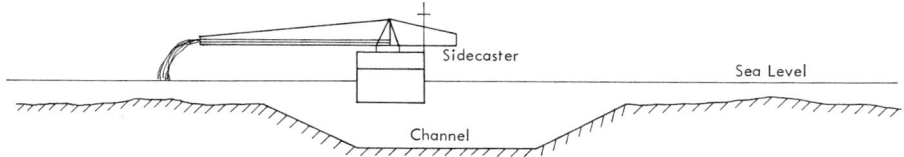

Figure A4.16. Sidecasting. Will material return to channel?

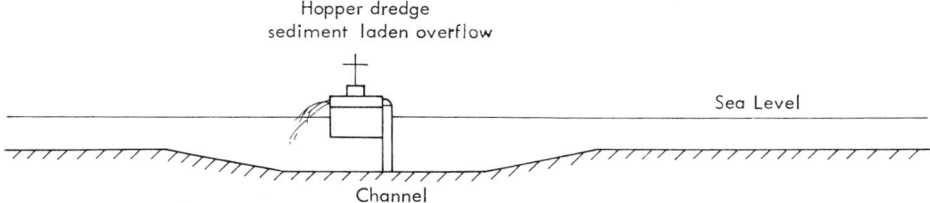

Figure A4.17. Overflow of silt laden water from hopper dredge.

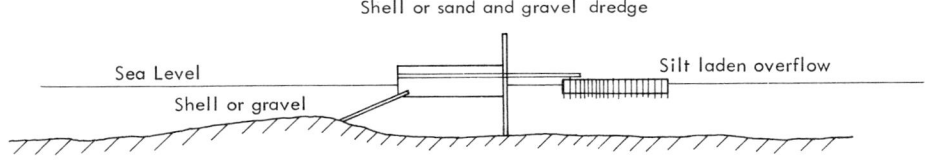

Figure A4.18. Overflow of silt laden water from sand and gravel dredge or shell dredge.

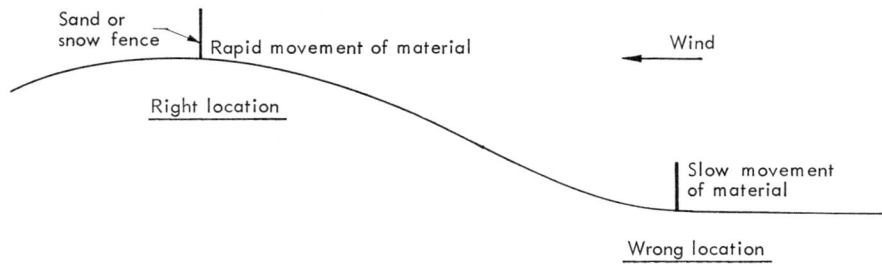

Figure A4.19. Where should a sand fence be located to assure highest efficiency? Where does the material come from?

Figure A4.17 shows overflow from a hopper dredge, and Figure A4.18 overlfows from a sand and gravel or shell dredge which may cause deposits in surrounding areas of the bottom, and perhaps adversely affect fish and wildlife. Tracers may help engineering planners and dredge contractors to demonstrate the possible extent of the incident sediment load.

Checking of the Most Effective Location of a Sand Drift Fence

A sand drift fence should be located where it causes maximum accumulation. Tracers may be helpful in determining the best location as well as in determining the most effective area on the beach for protection of drift sand.

Example. F-tracing on the Outer Banks (Cape Hatteras National Seashore, National Park Service, U.S. Dept. of the Interior). Figure A4.19 explains the application.

Application of Tracers in Pollution Control: Thermal, Biological, Chemical and Nuclear

Tracers in liquid form which could be fluorescent dyes like Fluorescin, Uranium (green) or Rhodamine B may be used for determining the best location of intakes and outlets for cooling water systems and determining the pattern and magnitude of pollution caused by outfalls containing sewage and/or chemical impurities. This problem is becoming increasingly more important because of the still increasing concentration of population and the vast increase in industrial, chemical and nuclear wastes. Examples of this are so numerous that no particular case should be mentioned specifically. The reader is referred to the special list of literature references.

It is unlikely that all applications have been mentioned. When a new technique is introduced, it takes some time before it penetrates all branches of a particular field. So much may be said that there is still much to learn. Radioactive tracers must be made easier to handle and have undoubtedly expanded future application, particularly as tracers in offshore waters and estuaries for pollution control. Fluorescent tracers must be made more flexible. Special and stable dyes with narrow emission bands must be introduced and correlated with the proper resins, glues and hardeners. Some coating should be hard, thereby securing a long lifetime. Others must be soft so that they wear off in days or weeks, thereby avoiding contamination of lasting character.

Various kinds of sampling equipment exist ranging from paraffin plates (used by the University of Southern California, Los Angeles) to scrapers and cores (used in Florida). As mentioned below, a combination of sampling, recording and analysis technique is desirable.

The method of analysis is probably the technique which, more than anything else, calls for improvement. The human eye is, from an optical point of view, not very satisfactory. Most people are able to count two to three different colors by visual counting. But it gets difficult with four, particularly if red/yellow/orange or blue/green are involved. And it takes much time to count visually. Photoelectric scanning machines developed are helpful but several difficulties have to be overcome including difficulties in correlating exitations and dye-emmission and the corresponding need for filters which often "get tired" and change character after a while. Although much progress has been recorded, we are still in the debugging stage with respect to scanning and the ultimate solution may not be solely optical insofar as direct counting is concerned. Solution and then optical scanning may be a "solution." Much has been tested and much remains to be tested. The development of underwater TV may be very useful for field tracing, particularly if the problem of underwater exitation of fluorescent tracers is solved.

References

Abulatov, N.; Griesseier, H.; and Sadrin, I. 1963-64. "Über den Sedimenttransport langs einer unregelmässig geslierderten Meereskuste." *Acta Hydrophyics* 8:5-21.

Arlman, J.J.; Santema, P.; and Svasek, J.N. 1958. *Movement of Bottom Sediment in Coastal Waters by Currents and Waves; Measurement with the Help of Radioactive Tracers in The Netherlands.* Tech Memo, U.S. Army Corps Engineers, 105.

Bruun, P. 1969. Quantitative field research on littoral drift using tracers. *Proceedings of the 22nd International Navigational Congress, Paris,* Section II, Subject 4.

De Vries M. 1966. *Application of Luminophores in Sand Transport Studies.* Meinema, Delft.

Gibert, A. 1954. Essai sur la possibilité d'employer Ag 110 dans l'étude du transport du sable par la mer. *Lab. Nacl. Engenharia Civil, Lisbon, Publ.*, 63.

Hubbell, D.W., and Sayre, W.W. 1964. "Sand transport studies with radioactive tracers." *ASCE Journal of the Hydraulics Division* 90(HY3):39-68.

Inman, D.L., and Goldberg, E.D. 1955. *Neutron Irradiated Quartz as a Tracer of Sand Movement.* Bulletin 66:611-13. Geological Society of America.

Kamel, A.M. 1962. "Transportation of coastal sediments." *I.E.R. Series* 185(1). University of California at Berkeley.

Krone, R.B. 1957. *Silt Transport Studies Utilizing Radio-Isotopes.* University of California, Berkeley, Calif.: Hydrological Engineering and Sanitary Engineering Research Laboratory.

Newman, D.E. 1960. *The Production of Fluorescent Tracers for Detecting the Movement of Sand and Shingle.* Wallingford, Berks.: Hydraulic Research Station.

Purpura, J., and Stuiver, M. 1969. Littoral drift by wave and current action. *Proceedings of the 11th Conference on Coastal Engineering,* ASCE, New York.

Putnam, J.L., Smith, D.D.; Welles, R.M. Allen, F.; and Rowan, G. 1954. *Thames Siltation Investigations-Preliminary Experiments on the Use of Radioactive Tracers for Indicating Mud Movement.* Wallingford, Berks.: Hydraulic Experiment Station.

Selleck, R.E.; and Pearson, E.A. 1960. *Tracer Studies and Pollutional Analyses of Estuaries.* University of California, Berkeley, Calif.: Sanitary Engineering Research Laboratory, College of Engineering.

Trask, P.D. 1952. *Source of Beach Sand at Santa Barbara, Calif., as Indicated by Mineral Grain Studies.* Tech Memo 28. U.S. Army Corps of Engineers, Beach Erosion Board.

Von Brauckhoff, K. and Griesseier, H. 1967. "Sandtransportuntersuchungen mit lumineszenten Sanden im Küstengebiet der Halbinsel Zingst." *Acta Hydrophysics* 11(3):137-69.

Examples of Pertinent Literature on Practical Applications of Tracers

All Papers in *Proceedings of the 20th International Navigation Congress.* 1961 (Section II, Subject 5). General Secretariat Permanent International Association of Navigation Congresses, Brussels, Belgium. Including papers on R- and F-tracing in the oceans and in harbors, estuaries and rivers in Denmark, India, Japan, The Netherlands, Poland, U.S.A. and the U.S.S.R.

Bruun, P. 1967. "Bypassing and backpassing with reference to Florida." *ASCE Journal of the Waterways and Harbors Division* 93(WW2):101-28.

____. 1966. *Stability of Coastal Inlets.* Oslo, University Book Co.

____, and Taney, N. 1967. "Use of tracers in coastal engineering." *Proceedings of 1st World Dredging Conference, New York* pp. 436-52.

Crickmore, M.J., and Lean, G.H. 1962. "The measuring of sand transport by the time-integration method with radioactive tracers." *Proceedings of the Royal Society of London.* Series A(270):27-47.

Gibert, A.; Abecasis, F.; Concaves Ferreira, M.; Reis Carvalho, J.; and Coroeiro, S. 1960. "Tracing undersea sand movement with radioactive silver." *Lab. Nacl. Engenharia Civil, Lisbon.* Tech Paper 150.

Griesseier, H.; and Voigt, G. 1965. "Lumineszenten Sand und sein Nachweis in Bodenproben." *Acta Hydrophysics* 9(3):151-67.

Hydraulic Research Station, Department of Scientific and Industrial Research. 1956. *Radioactive Tracing in the Thames Estuary.* Berks: Wallingford.

Ingle, J.C. 1966. *The Movement of Beach Sand.* Amsterdam: Elsevier.

Krone, R.B. 1960. *An Underwater Scintillation Detector for Gamma Emitters.* University of California, Berkeley: Sanitary Engineering Research Laboratory.

Lean, G.H., and Crickmore, M.J. 1962. "Methods of measuring sand-transport using radioactive tracers." *Proceedings of the Royal Society of London* Series A(266):402-21.

Pollard, D.D. and Timme, R.C. 1965. "Long term fluorescent studies." *Ocean Science Ocean Engineering* 2:1162-64.

Permanent International Association of Navigation Congresses. 1961. "Ocean navigation: methods of determining sand and silt movement along the coast, in estuaries and in maritime rivers. Use of modern techniques such as radioactive isotopes, luminophores, etc." *Proceedings of 20th International Navigation Congress.* Baltimore.

Russell, R.C.H. 1960. "The use of fluorescent tracers for measurement of littoral drift." *Proceedings of 7th Conference on Coastal Engineering.* pp. 418-44, ASCE, New York.

Sanitary Engineering Research Laboratory. 1960. *Third Annual Progress Report on the Silt Transport Studies Utilizing Radioisotopes.* University of California, Berkeley.

Smith, D.B.; Parsons, T.V., and Cloet, R.L. 1965. *An Investigation Using Radioactive Tracers into the Silt Movement in an Ebb Channel, Firth of Forth.* Wantage, Berks.: Wantage Research Laboratory.

Smith, D.B.; and Parsons, T.V. 1965. *Silt Movement in the Oxcans Spoil Ground, Firth of Forth, Using Radioactive Tracers.* Wantage, Berks.: Wantage Research Laboratory.

Zenkovitch, V.P. 1958. "Emploi de luminophores pour l'étude du mouvement des alluvions sablonneuses." *Bull. Inform. Com. Central Oceanog. Etude Cotes.* 10(5) Moscow.

index

Abidjan, Ivory Coast, 10, 222
abrasion platforms, 256
Absecon Inlet, 255
Adachi's formula, 203
agitation dredging, 6
air pocket, 54
akmon block, 66, 84
Algier Harbor, 50
amplification factor, 44
anchored bulkheads, 388, 394
anchor piles, 112, 146
angular foreland, 293
angular velocity, berthing, 401, 403
Antwerp, 6, 163
Antwerp, Port, 107, 170
approach of vessels, 5, 90
armor layers, 66
artificial nourishment, 262, 277, 305
Arviksand Harbor, 63
Atlantic Container Lines, 104
Aveiro Inlet, Portugal, 214, 312
Azobe wood, 115

Bahia Blanca, 344
Bakers Haulover, Florida, 224, 233, 329
Bandar Shahpour, Iran, 115
Bangkok, Port of, 196
Bantry Bay, Ireland, 86
bar, 257, 275
bar by-passing, 212, 223, 325

Barcelona, 163
barrier, 259, 270, 293, 299
basin, size and geometry, 372
basket cutter, 355
Basralocus piles, 115
Bay of Fundy, Canada, 117
beach profiles, 259, 273, 286, 289
beach ridge, 293
Beaver Harbor, New Brunswick, Canada, 117
bearing capacity, 382, 385
bedding layer, 74
bed load, 205, 229, 236, 326, 338
Benoto grabs, 113
Berlevåg Harbor, 64
berthing, 22, 25; force, 120, 122, 128; to berthing beams, 411; to dolphins, 411; to wharves and piers, 411
berth service time, 190, 194
Big Pass, 338
Boca Raton, 330
Boca Raton Inlet, Florida, 313
bollards, 141, 143
boom dredging, 6
Boston fishing port, Massachuetts, 374
Bovbjaerg, Denmark, 285
breaker distance, 286
breakwaters, 49, 57, 62, 69, 270, 301
breasting dolphins, 89, 90, 134, 135
Brooklyn Port Authority Terminals, New York, 103

bucket dredge, 350
bulk cargo, 156
bulk carriers, 1, 4
bulkheads: in clay, 400; in sand, 395,
buoys, 49
Burns Harbor, Indiana, 10
Burtoning, 147
by passing, 200, 212, 224, 325; at harbors, 222; by nature, 210, 324; plant, 224, 338

caisson, 57, 60
Calumet Harbor, Michigan, 60
Cambridge torque fenders, 134
Cape Kennedy, 327
Cape Town Harbor, 368
Catania, 50
Catania Harbor, 50
cathodic protection, 113, 117
cellular steel sheet pile bulkheads, 125
channel alignment, 17, 20
Channel Harbor, California, 210, 329
Charleston Harbor, 231, 243, 327
Chezy formula, 320
Churchhill Dock, 170
clamshell dredge, 350
coastal geomorphology, 255, 258, 315
coastal harbors, of refuge, 377
Cochin Port, India, 241
Columbia River, 249
Comeau Bay Harbor, Canada, 60
composite designs, 62
compression shocks, 52, 55
concrete crib construction, 125
Conneaut Harbor, Ohio, 305
container, 1
container cranes, 104, 170
container system, 7
container vessel, 8
Cook Inlet, 87, 297
Copenhagen, 163
Copenhagen Port, Denmark, 150
cordkapp fenders, 130
core, 64, 67, 73
core fill, 66
Coquille River entrance, 82
cranes, 158
crest elevation, 67, 70, 92
crest width, 67, 70, 73
crib, 50
cross-sectional stability, 322, 333
current forces, 129

current and navigation, 23
cuspate foreland, 293, 299
cutterhead pipeline dredge, 350

Danish rubble breakwaters, 63
Darcy friction factor, 333
David Taylor Model Basin, 13, 14
Deerfield Beach, Florida, 207
Den Helder, 255, 296
densimetric Froude number, 227
densimetric velocity, 225
density change, 12, 13
depressed weir, 330
depth of embedment, 397
design procedure, tidal inlet, 347
design wave height, 69, 75, 77
detached breakwater, 207, 330, 332
dipper dredge, 350
Directory of World Dredges, 350
discharged pipe, 359
diurnal tides, 338
dolosse, 66, 84
dolphins, 25, 49, 87
door-to-door system, 159, 160, 170
Douglas fir piles, 122
downrush, 285, 296
drag coefficient, 86, 91, 92
drain of littoral drift, 299
drain of materials, 210
dredging, 350
Dublin, 255
Dungeness, 268
Dunkirk, 163
Durban, South Africa, 330
dynamical equation, 319
Dyrholaey, Iceland, 300

East Pass, Florida, 329, 338
ebb channel, 218, 232, 340
economic feasibility, 85
Elbe estuary, 297
Elbe River, Germany, 206, 249
Elizabeth-Port Marine Terminal, New Jersey, 104, 124
Erlangian distribution, 192
Erlangian function, 189, 196
erosion, 255, 259, 305
Esbjerg, 163
Esbjerg Fishing Port, Denmark, 372
estuary, 200, 212, 218, 225, 231
Europe-Port, Holland, 76

equation of continuity, 319
equilibrium form: cross-section, 275; shoreline, 263

Fairport, Ohio, 306
feasibility studies, 198
Felixtowe, England, 162
fender, 49, 113, 115, 128, 130
fenders, impact, 130
fenders, protective, 130
Figueira da Foz Inlet, Portugal, 215
filter layer, 66, 68
fishing ports, 9
flats, 187
floating dock, 146
floating line, 356
flocculation, 226, 229, 230, 232, 240
flood channel, 218, 232, 340
Florida, 259
fork trucks, 157
Freemantle, 163
freight liner, 159
Froude number, 334
Ft. Pierce, Florida, 310
Ft. Pierce Inlet, 215, 327, 329

Gary Harbor, Indiana, 60
Gasparilla Pass, 340
Gdynia, 163
Gdynia Port, Poland, 109
general cargo, 156, 158
Genoa, 163
Genoa Harbor, Italy, 62
gifle, 58
Golden Gate, 256
Goliath crane, 171, 174
Gothenburg Harbor, Sweden, 187
Gothenburg, Sweden, 115, 163
Graadyb, Denmark, 221
grains, 288, 291
grain size distribution, 274, 280
grapple dredge, 350
gravity fenders, 132
Grays Harbor, Washington, 340
Greenland, 257
Grimsby, England, 163, 174
groins, 207, 264, 270, 305, 326
Gulf Coast, 259

half-portal cranes, 151
Hamburg, Germany, 163

hammer shock, 56
handling facilities in fishing ports, 375
Hanstholm Harbor, Denmark, 60
harbor: basins, 106; entrances, 10, 21; seiche, 27
Harwich, England, 162
headlands, 268, 288, 299
high level platforms, 125
highly stratified estuary, 240
Hillsboro Inlet, Florida, 233, 330
Honolulu, Hawaii, 164
hopper dredge, 350, 360
horizontal geometry, 258
horizontal stability, 333
Howth, Ireland, 255
Hudson formula, 68, 75, 82
Hudson River, 240, 248
hydraulic pipeline dredge, 354

Ilo pier, Peru, 117
impact on quay wall, 409
incipient motion, 291
inertial coefficients, 93
Inland Sea, Japan, 49, 86
Inlet of Vlie, Holland, 220
intake loss coefficient, 354
ISO, 184

jetties, 49, 63, 66, 82
Jupiter Island, Florida, 277, 313

Kalundborg terminal, Denmark, 136
K_Δ-factor, 68, 75, 82
Kobe, Japan, 163
Korsør, Denmark, 39

Lagos, Harbor, Gold Coast, 238
La Guaira Harbor, Venezuela, 65, 217
La Jolla, California, 274
Lake Maricaibo Channel, Venezuela, 6
Lake Worth Inlet, Florida, 339
LASH-system, 179, 180
Le Havre, 163
level-luffing cranes, 150
Liffey River, 255
lift off-lift on, 160, 171, 189
Lime Fjord, 274
littoral drift, 200, 210, 340; barriers, 259; Bijker formula, 203; Bonnefille-Pernecker formula, 202; formulas, 259, 301; Los Angeles formula, 200
Liverpool, England, 163

Liverpool Bay, 233
loaded draft, 12
loading facilities: open sea, 49; ore, 5
London, 6
Long Beach, 9
long boat pass, 338
Long Island, 257
long-period fluctuations, 279
long-period waves, 36, 43
longshore currents, 205, 206, 212
Los Angeles, 9

Mach-type reflection, 40
Madras Port, India, 208
Maricaibo, Venezuela, 359
marinas, 9
Marsa el Brega, Libya, 1
Marseille, 163
marshaling yard, 104
Masonboro Inlet, North Carolina, 337
mass coefficient, 91, 92
McFarland, dredge, 361
Melbourne, Australia, 163
Meritt, dredge, 360
Mersey River, England, 231, 233
Miami, 261
Migrating sand waves, 285
Mission Bay, California, 274, 280
Mississippi River, 231, 257
mobile cranes, 151
Monterey Harbor, California, 36
Mooring, 24, 102, 106, 128, 136; buoy, 2; cable, 141; dolphins, 135; facilities, wires, ropes, 141
morphology, 323
motion of ship in berthing, 415
multistory cells, 177
Møller Steamship Company Pier, Brooklyn, 104

Nagapatam, India, 330
navigation channels, 3, 6
New Orleans, 23
New York, 162
New York Harbor, 162, 248
North Sea, 285, 297
North Sea Coast, 275
North Sea trawler, 368
Norwegian rubble breakwaters, 63

Oakland Harbor, 162, 164
oil piers, 49
oil transport, 49, 86
Ooster Schelde, Holland, 219
open sea and pier facilities, 49, 86
optimum design, 85
Oregon Inlet, North Carolina, 327
Orinoco, Venezuela, 359
Orinoco River, 6
Osaka, 163
Oslo Harbor, 163
Oslo Port, Norway, 107
Ostia, Italy, 255
overnourished profiles, 275

Pacific Gilnetter, 367
pallet, 1
pallet elevators, 182
palletizing, 157
pallet system, 7
Palm Beach Inlet, 311
Paradip, India, 330
parallel quays, 102
partly mixed estuary, 226, 229, 243
Perdito Pass, Alabama, 329
perforated breakwaters, 50
piers, 25, 49, 102, 107, 115; fishing ports, 374
pile foundation, 382
piles: allowable load and factor of safety, 383, 385; groups, 383, 385; in clay, 382; in sand, 383; load tests, 385, 387; settlements, 383, 385; to rock, 382, 387
pillar quay, Norway, 113
pitching, 12
placed blocks, 66, 82
platform, 1
platforms, floating, 49
pneumatic fenders, 134
Point Reyes, 280
Poisson distribution, 189
Poisson function, 189
Pompano Beach, Florida, 358
pontoons, 356; of steel or synthetic materials, 144, 146; wharves, 144
Port de Muccuripo, Brazil, 217
Port Elizabeth, New York, 163, 164
Port Huneme, California, 310, 329
Port Latta, Australia, 5, 87
Port Royal, Jamaica, 255
Port Talbot, England, 5
Port-to-port, 160
port transportation studies, 196
Potomac River, Maryland, 231

Prestressed wharf, 117, 122
primary cover layer, 67, 73
Prince of Netherlands, dredging, 361
promontories, 299, 300
Puerto Gallegos, Argentina, 344
Puerto Santa Cruz, Argentina, 344
pumping capacity, 357
purse seiner, 368

Queuing (model), 189
Quays, 102, 106, 109, 115; fishing ports, 374

radius of curvature, 20
Ravenna Harbor, Italy, 251
Raykin fenders, 132
Rayleigh distribution, 91
recurved spit, 299
reflection, 33, 36, 40
regional transport planning, 197, 198
relieving platforms, 108, 123, 128
resonance, 33, 36
Reynolds number, 69, 86, 97
rise of sea level, 258, 261, 283
rolling, 12, 17
roll-on, roll-off, 1, 7, 160, 170, 174
Rota Harbor, Spain, 11
rotation, berthing, 406, 416
Rotterdam, 164
Rotterdam Harbor, 163
Rotterdam Waterway, 239
rubble-mound, 50, 63, 66, 74; breakwaters, 63, 67
rudder angle, 18, 20

Sainflou wave force diagram, 51
San Fransisco, California, 164
Santa Barbara, California, 217, 332
Santa Monica, California, 310
Savannah River, 231
Scandia Harbor, Gothenburg, Sweden, 115
Scheveningen fishing port, Holland, 217
Sea Girt, New Jersey, 358
sea-land service, 104, 125
secondary cover layer, 73
Seibu fenders, 132
seiches, 27, 36, 44
shed, 158, 171
sheet pile: cells, 59, 60; design, 394; walls, 58, 59
Sheibah Port, Kuwait, 109
shelves, 257
ships maneuvers, 25
shoaling of estuaries, 227

shock pressure, 53, 57
shore geometry, 262
shoreline geometry, 262, 299
short-period fluctuation, 278
sidecaster, 360
sidecasting method, 359
side-loaders, 172
side ports, 157
Sidon, Lebanon, 1
Skagen (Shaw) fishing port, Denmark, 370
Skaw Harbor, Denmark, 305
South Lake Worth Inlet, Florida, 329, 339
spatial integration method, 421
spit, 268, 299
spuds, 350, 354
squat, 12, 13
stabit (block), 66, 84
St. Augustin, Florida, 256
steady dilution method, 421
steel sheet profiles, 108, 113
stern trawler, 369
stevedoring pallet, 157
St. Lucie Inlet, Florida, 329
storage areas, 104, 152
storage of cargo, 155
straight arm cutter, 355
straight-wall sheet pile bulkheads, 125
stratified estuary, 225, 226, 229
Strouhal number, 97
suction pipe, 353, 354, 361
sufficiently nourished profiles, 275
summer profile, 274, 278, 293
sumphandling method, 359
supertankers, 86
surf beat, 283
surge, 36, 43
suspension load, 231
sway, 136
Sydney, Australia, 163

Taconite Harbor, Lake Superior, 60
terminal, 156, 158, 160, 170, 178
tetrapodes (blocks), 64, 66, 84
Thames River, 231
Thyborøen Inlet, Denmark, 255
tidal flow by-passing, 219, 223
tidal hydraulics computation, 319
Tilbury, England, 162
Tilbury Docks, London, 231
Tokai, Japan, 285
tombolo, 293, 300, 313

Tracers, 203, 225, 231, 248; types, 419, 420; use of, 418, 422; methods, 421
trailers, 171, 174
transfer function, 90, 98
transfer of cargo, 155, 156
transit area, 156, 158
transition condition, 287
transit sheds, 106, 147, 151
translation, berthing, 406, 416
transmission coefficient, 37
transportable breakwaters, 46
trap, 207, 224, 231, 233, 238, 330
tribar (block), 66, 84
Trieste, Italy, 163
trim, 12, 17
tsunami, 27, 43
tugboats, use of, 415
tuna boat, 369
turnaround time, 159, 179, 189
tween deck, 181, 182
Tyre Harbor, Lebanon, 50

Udyavara Entrance, India, 345
underlayers, 67, 73
undernourished profiles, 275
uprush, 278, 285, 296
U.S. McFarland, 361
U.S. Meritt, 360
U.S. Schweitzer, 360

Vancouver, British Columbia, Canada, 122
ventilated shocks, 52, 54
Ventura, California, 207, 208, 310, 330
Vertical breakwater, 50, 62

Wadden Sea, Holland, 220
warehouses, 102, 151
Washington D.C., 10
wave action in ports, 26
wave attenuation, 40
wave energy spectrum, 67
wave forces, 50, 74, 91, 122, 129
wave resonators, 43
wave run-up, 70, 80
wave run-up or uprush, 80
wave traps, 39
well-mixed estuary, 226, 229, 248
Wester Schelde, Holland, 219
widths: of channels, 17; of entrances, 17, 18, 21
wind forces, 129
winter profile, 274, 279, 293
wharves, 49, 102, 107, 109; fishing ports, 374

Ymuiden, Holland, 358
Ymuiden Harbor, Holland, 84, 238
Yokohama, Japan, 8, 160
yaw, 18

Zeebrugge Harbor, Belgium, 62, 222
Zulia, dredge, 359